A Comme

For the Day

As roofing tiles fit one to another,
God's words fit one to another
makes for a person's life a covering.

RLD

by
Robert L Doudna

A Comment For the Day

ISBN: 979-8-9893100-0-5

Cover photo and design by Robert L Doudna

Introduction

These comments are fit to the reading schedule. Even if you do not follow the reading schedule you will still gain from the comment. Not every comment will speak to all, but all comments will speak to someone. Each of these daily comments will take about five minutes to read. They are intended for a morning reading even if you do the Bible reading the night before. They are meant to be a comment you take into your day with you. Some of these comments will seem the same, or even open with the same question. Some of the comments will open with a statement as being spoken by God. Many will seem to begin the same but will come at a different angle bringing out things the other did not. I believe what the Holy Spirit is doing here, as I have sought Him in what to write each day, that He is doing a fine shaping a little at a time. This is not an intellectual presentation, if that is what you are looking for you should find another book. You may not even think the way I present some writings here are done well. I intend to affect, and maybe touch places in you not touched before, therefore I present things a different way, a way that makes a person to consider and to think. Sometimes I use words that are not even in the dictionary, but you will know what they mean. I don't consider myself the author, I only am the penman writing what I hear the Holy Spirit speaking within me.

RLD Bible Reading Schedule

Several years ago I wanted to be able to get God's word into my mind and heart more than I had been able to up to that point so I designed this schedule. My wife and I have used it now for many years. It will take the reader though the Gospels four times in a year keeping the words of Jesus fresh. It will cover the rest of the New Testament twice in a year. The Old Testament is divided into two parts for reading over two years, or in one year by reading both parts. The assignments will take on the average about forty-five minutes to read.

RLD Bible Reading Schedule

For our lives today which is under the new covenant given through Jesus Christ the most important thing for us to hear from the Bible are His words. Next important would be the words recorded by His followers in Acts, the epistles, & Revelation. And the third most important would be the Old Testament. All of the words in the Bible are important for our Christian walk and we should put them in the right priority. This schedule is arranged to take the reader through the New Testament gospels (the words of Jesus) four times a year and the Acts, the epistles, & Revelation two times a year. The Old Testament is divided into two parts so it can be read in two years by reading one part each year or in one year by reading both parts. The New Testament assignments are by full chapters and the Old Testament is adjusted to round out an average amount of reading. The Old Testament assignment is where to read to from the previous day.

	Old Testament		New Testament			Old Testament		New Testament	
Jan	Year I	Year II	Gosp.	A,Ep,R	Feb	Year I	Year II	Gosp.	A,Ep,R
1	Gen 1:31	Neh 2:20	Mt 1	Acts 1	6	Gen 35:29	Job 34:37	Mk 9	Rom 9
2	Gen 2:25	Neh 3:32	Mt 2	Acts 2	7	Gen 36:43	Job 36:33	Mk 10	Rom 10
3	Gen 3:24	Neh 5:19	Mt 3	Acts 3	8	Gen 37:36	Job 38:41	Mk 11	Rom 11
4	Gen 4:26	Neh 6:19	Mt 4	Acts 4	9	Gen 38:30	Job 40:24	Mk 12	Rom 12
5	Gen 5:32	Neh 7:38	Mt 5	Acts 5	10	Gen 40:23	Job 42:17	Mk 13	Rom 13
6	Gen 7:24	Neh 7:73	Mt 6	Acts 6	11	Gen 41:24	Ps 3:8	Mk 14	Rom 14
7	Gen 8:22	Neh 8:18	Mt 7	Acts 7	12	Gen 41:57	Ps 6:10	Mk 15	Rom 15
8	Gen 9:29	Neh 9:15	Mt 8	Acts 8	13	Gen 42:38	Ps 9:20	Mk 16	Rom 16
9	Gen 10:32	Neh 9:38	Mt 9	Acts 9	14	Gen 43:34	Ps 10:18	Lk 1	1Cor 1
10	Gen 11:32	Neh 10:39	Mt 10	Acts 10	15	Gen 44:34	Ps 14:7	Lk 2	1Cor 2
11	Gen 13:18	Neh 11:36	Mt 11	Acts 11	16	Gen 45:28	Ps 17:15	Lk 3	1Cor 3
12	Gen 14:24	Neh 12:47	Mt 12	Acts 12	17	Gen 46:34	Ps 18:50	Lk 4	1Cor 4
13	None	None	Mt 13	Acts 13	18	Gen 47:31	Ps 21:13	Lk 5	1Cor 5
14	Gen 16:16	Neh 13:31	Mt 14	Acts 14	19	Gen 48:22	Ps 22:31	Lk 6	1Cor 6
15	Gen 17:27	Est 1:22	Mt 15	Acts 15	20	Gen 49:33	Ps 24:10	Lk 7	1Cor 7
16	Gen 18:33	Est 2:23	Mt 16	Acts 16	21	Gen 50:26	Ps 26:12	Lk 8	1Cor 8
17	Gen 19:26	Est 4:17	Mt 17	Acts 17	22	Ex 1:22	Ps 27:14	Lk 9	1Cor 9
18	Gen 19:38	Est 6:14	Mt 18	Acts 18	23	Ex 2:25	Ps 30:12	Lk10	1Cor 10
19	Gen 20:18	Est 8:17	Mt 19	Acts 19	24	Ex 3:22	Ps 31:24	Lk 11	1Cor 11
20	Gen 21:34	Est 10:3	Mt 20	Acts 20	25	Ex 4:31	Ps 33:22	Lk 12	1Cor 12
21	Gen 22:24	Job 1:22	Mt 21	Acts 21	26	Ex 6:30	Ps 35:28	Lk 13	1Cor 13
22	Gen 23:20	Job 3:26	Mt 22	Acts 22	27	Ex 7:25	Ps 37:40	Lk 14	1Cor 14
23	Gen 24:28	Job 5:27	Mt 23	Acts 23	28	Ex 8:32	Ps 38:22	Lk 15	1Cor 15
24	Gen 24:67	Job 7:21	Mt 24	Acts 24	Mar 1	Ex 9:35	Ps 41:13	Lk 16	1Cor 16
25	Gen 25:34	Job 9:35	Mt 25	Acts 25	2	Ex 11:10	Ps 44:26	Lk 17	2Cor 1
26	Gen 26:35	Job 11:20	Mt 26	Acts 26	3	Ex 12:51	Ps 47:9	Lk 18	2Cor 2
27	Gen 27:17	Job 12:25	Mt 27	Acts 27	4	Ex 13:22	Ps 49:20	Lk 19	2Cor 3
28	Gen 27:46	Job 15:35	Mt 28	Acts 28	5	Ex 14:31	Ps 51:19	Lk 20	2Cor 4
29	Gen 28:22	Job 17:16	Mk 1	Rom 1	6	Ex 16:36	Ps 55:23	Lk 21	2Cor 5
30	Gen 29:35	Job 19:29	Mk 2	Rom 2	7	Ex 18:27	Ps 57:11	Lk 22	2Cor 6
31	Gen 30:43	Job 21:34	Mk 3	Rom 3	8	Ex 19:25	Ps 59:17	Lk 23	2Cor 7
Feb 1	Gen 31:35	Job 23:17	Mk 4	Rom 4	9	Ex 20:26	Ps 62:12	Lk 24	2Cor 8
2	Gen 31:55	Job 27:23	Mk 5	Rom 5	10	Ex 21:36	Ps 65:13	Jn 1	2Cor 9
3	Gen 32:32	Job29:25	Mk 6	Rom 6	11	Ex 23:33	Ps 68:35	Jn 2	2Cor 10
4	Gen 33:20	Job 31:40	Mk 7	Rom 7	12	Ex 25:40	Ps 69:36	Jn 3	2Cor 11
5	Gen 34:31	Job 33:33	Mk 8	Rom 8	13	Ex 26:37	Ps 71:24	Jn 4	2Cor 12

	Old Testament		New Testament			Old Testament		New Testament	
Mar	Year I	Year II	Gosp.	A,Ep,R	May	Year I	Year II	Gosp.	A,Ep,R
14	Ex 28:21	Ps 72:20	Jn 5	2Cor 13	3	Num 21:35	Pro 25:28	Mk 6	Heb 8
15	Ex 28:43	Ps 73:28	Jn 6	Gal 1	4	Num 22:41	Pro 26:28	Mk 7	Heb 9
16	Ex 29:46	Ps 75:10	Jn 7	Gal 2	5	Num 23:30	Pro 27:27	Mk 8	Heb 10
17	Ex 30:38	Ps 77:20	Jn 8	Gal 3	6	Num 24:25	Pro 28:12	Mk 9	Heb 11
18	Ex 31:18	Ps 78:31	Jn 9	Gal 4	7	Num 25:18	Pro28:28	Mk 10	Heb 12
19	Ex 32:35	Ps 78:72	Jn 10	Gal 5	8	Num 26:41	Pro 29:27	Mk 11	Heb 13
20	Ex 33:23	Ps 80:19	Jn 11	Gal 6	9	Num 26:65	Pro 30:33	Mk 12	James 1
21	Ex 34:35	Ps 83:18	Jn 12	Eph 1	10	Num 27:23	Pro 31:31	Mk 13	James 2
22	Ex 36:19	Ps 85:13	Jn 13	Eph 2	11	Num 28:31	Ecl 2:26	Mk 14	James 3
23	Ex 38:23	Ps 88:18	Jn 14	Eph 3	12	Num 29:40	Ecl 4:16	Mk 15	James 4
24	Ex 39:43	Ps 89:52	Jn 15	Eph 4	13	Num 31:54	Ecl 7:29	Mk 16	James 5
25	Ex 40:38	Ps 92:15	Jn 16	Eph 5	14	Num 32:19	Ecl 8:17	Lk 1	1Peter 1
26	Lev 3:17	Ps 96:13	Jn 17	Eph 6	15	Num 32:41	Ecl 9:18	Lk 2	1Peter 2
27	Lev 4:35	Ps 99:9	Jn 18	Philp 1	16	Num 33:56	Ecl 10:20	Lk 3	1Peter 3
28	Lev 5:19	Ps 102:28	Jn 19	Philp 2	17	Num34:29	Ecl 12:14	Lk 4	1Peter 4
29	Lev 7:21	Ps104:35	Jn 20	Philp 3	18	Num 36:13	Sol 3:11	Lk 5	1Peter 5
30	Lev 8:36	Ps105:45	Jn 21	Philp 4	19	Deu 1:46	Sol 5:16	Lk 6	2Peter 1
31	Lev 10:20	Ps106:48	Mt 1	Col 1	20	Deu 2:37	Sol 6:13	Lk 7	2Peter 2
Apr 1	Lev 12:8	Ps108:13	Mt 2	Col 2	21	Deu 3:29	Sol 8:14	Lk 8	2Peter 3
2	Lev 13:59	Ps111:10	Mt 3	Col 3	22	Deu 4:24	Isa 1:31	Lk 9	1John 1
3	Lev 14:57	Ps115:18	Mt 4	Col 4	23	Deu 4:49	Isa 2:22	Lk 10	1John 2
4	Lev 15:33	Ps118:29	Mt 5	1Thes 1	24	Deu 5:33	Isa 4:6	Lk 11	1John 3
5	Lev 16:34	Ps 119:56	Mt 6	1Thes 2	25	Deu 6:25	Isa 5:30	Lk 12	1John 4
6	Lev 18:30	Ps119:120	Mt 7	1Thes 3	26	Deu 8:20	Isa 7:25	Lk 13	1John 5
7	Lev 19:37	Ps119:176	Mt 8	1Thes 4	27	Deu 10:22	Isa 9:21	Lk 14	2John
8	Lev 21:24	Ps 125:5	Mt 9	1Thes 5	28	Deu 11:32	Isa 11:16	Lk 15	3John
9	Lev 22:33	Ps 131:3	Mt 10	2Thes 1	29	Deu 12:32	Isa 13:22	Lk 16	Jude
10	Lev 23:44	Ps135:21	Mt 11	2Thes 2	30	Deu14:29	Isa 15:9	Lk 17	Rev 1
11	Lev 25:22	Ps 138:8	Mt 12	2Thes 3	31	Deu 16:12	Isa 17:14	Lk 18	Rev 2
12	Lev 25:55	Ps140:13	Mt 13	1Tim 1	Jun 1	Deu 17:20	Isa 19:25	Lk 19	Rev 3
13	Lev 26:46	Ps144:15	Mt 14	1Tim 2	2	Deu 19:21	Isa 21:17	Lk 20	Rev 4
14	Lev 27:34	Ps146:10	Mt 15	1Tim 3	3	Deu 21:23	Isa 23:18	Lk 21	Rev 5
15	Num 1:54	Ps 150:6	Mt 16	1Tim 4	4	Deu 22:30	Isa 24:23	Lk 22	Rev 6
16	Num 3:13	Pro 2:22	Mt 17	1Tim 5	5	Deu23:25	Isa 25:12	Lk 23	Rev 7
17	Num 3:51	Pro 3:35	Mt 18	1Tim 6	6	Deu 24:22	Isa 26:21	Lk 24	Rev 8
18	Num 4:49	Pro 5:23	Mt 19	2Tim 1	7	Deu 26:19	Isa 27:13	Jn 1	Rev 9
19	Num 5:31	Pro 6:35	Mt 20	2Tim 2	8	Deu 28:46	Isa 28:29	Jn 2	Rev 10
20	Num 6:27	Pro 7:27	Mt 21	2Tim 3	9	Deu 28:68	Isa 29:24	Jn 3	Rev 11
21	Num 7:47	Pro 8:36	Mt 22	2Tim 4	10	Deu 30:20	Isa 30:33	Jn 4	Rev 12
22	Num 7:89	Pro 10:32	Mt 23	Titus 1	11	Deu 31:30	Isa 32:20	Jn 5	Rev 13
23	Num 9:23	Pro 11:31	Mt 24	Titus 2	12	Deu 32:14	Isa 33:24	Jn 6	Rev 14
24	Num 10:36	Pro 13:25	Mt 25	Titus 3	13	Deu 32:52	Isa 35:10	Jn 7	Rev 15
25	Num 11:35	Pro 14:35	Mt 26	Philem	14	Deu 34:12	Isa 36:22	Jn 8	Rev 16
26	Num 13:33	Pro 15:33	Mt 27	Heb 1	15	Jos 2:24	Isa 37:38	Jn 9	Rev 17
27	Num 14:45	Pro 17:28	Mt 28	Heb 2	16	Jos 4:24	Isa 39:8	Jn 10	Rev 18
28	Num 15:41	Pro 18:24	Mk 1	Heb 3	17	Jos 5:15	Isa 40:17	Jn 11	Rev 19
29	Num 16:50	Pro 20:30	Mk 2	Heb 4	18	Jos 6:27	Isa 40:31	Jn 12	Rev 20
30	Num 18:32	Pro 22:29	Mk 3	Heb 5	19	Jos 7:26	Isa 41:29	Jn 13	Rev 21
May 1	Num 19:22	Pro 23:35	Mk 4	Heb 6	20	Jos 8:35	Isa 42:25	Jn 14	Rev 22
2	Num 20:29	Pro 24:34	Mk 5	Heb 7	21	Jos 10:43	Isa 44:20	Jn 15	None

Genesis is a deep book with many things in it. It shows the creation and the first many generations of mankind. This first chapter is all about creation, from start to finish with chapter 2 giving us more detail. The first thing to notice is God's miraculous power: He spoke and it was. The very first thing God created may be more related to physics than what we normally think: He said, "Let there be light," and there was light. We think of light as we know it; sunlight, moonlight, starlight, light from a flame, light from electric light bulbs of some fashion.

But if we read on to v. 13 – 18 we see that the sun, moon, and stars were not created until three days later on the fourth day – so what was it God created on day one? It seems to be the physical existence of light. We are not able to separate the thought of light from the source of that light which we know. But we could not even know it as we do if God had not created the physical existence of light.

This is a short entry today, but the thought of what it brings up may fill your whole day.

In the land of Galilee is where God began to reveal to the people His Son, Jesus the Messiah. All of the apostles and probably most of the disciples who followed Jesus were from there. It may have been that Galilee was far enough from Jerusalem that the Pharisees, priests, and scribes of the Temple did not hold such a strong influence. There were gatherings of the Jews in Synagogues with rabbis but the hold the priest of Jerusalem had on the people may not have carried all the way to the rabbis in Galilee. It may have been there was more tolerances in Galilee than Jerusalem.

After the ministry of Jesus and His resurrection, God brought the main activity right into the heart of Jerusalem. On the day of Pentecost, the promised power of the Holy Spirit came to all who were gathered together, possibly 120 (see Acts 1:14 & 15 and tie it to 2:1; **they were _all_ assembled together**). When a crowd of Jews gathered by the strangeness of what was happening to the disciples, Peter, who had been hiding in fear before, stepped forward confronting the Jews of their part in the crucifixion, convincing them of their sin and the need of Jesus in their lives. This Peter (and we), a coward in and of himself, who spoke out wrongly at times before (rebuking Jesus, etc.), who denied knowing Jesus three times at the trial, who ran away and hid (with the rest of Jesus' followers), now with the power of the Holy Spirit, speaks out preaching such a powerful sermon that 3,000 Jews confess their sins and accept Jesus as their Messiah.

We must, as Peter did, have and allow to work through us the power and working of the Holy Spirit. The Holy Spirit will only work in and through us if we allow Him to. How many people in the body of Christ, the Church, are taught that they should allow the Holy Spirit to use them, to work through them? There needs to be a conscious allowing, a seeking to God to bring to us the empowering of the Holy Spirit to continue the work of the Kingdom of God.

	Old Testament	New Testament				Old Testament	New Testament		
Jun	Year I	Year II	Gosp.	A,Ep,R	Aug	Year I	Year II	Gosp.	A,Ep,R
22	Jos 13:23	Isa 45:25	Jn 16	None	11	1Sam18:30	Jer 34:22	Lk 1	1Cor 1
23	Jos 16:10	Isa 48:22	Jn 17	None	12	1Sam19:24	Jer 35:19	Lk 2	1Cor 2
24	Jos 18:28	Isa 49:26	Jn 18	None	13	1Sam20:42	Jer 36:32	Lk 3	1Cor 3
25	Jos 20:9	Isa 51:23	Jn 19	None	14	1Sam22:23	Jer 38:13	Lk 4	1Cor 4
26	Jos 21:45	Isa 54:17	Jn 20	None	15	1Sam23:29	Jer 39:18	Lk 5	1Cor 5
27	Jos 23:16	Isa 57:21	Jn 21	None	16	1Sam24:22	Jer 40:16	Lk 6	1Cor 6
28	Jos 24:33	Isa 58:14	Mt 1	Acts 1	17	1Sam25:19	Jer 41:18	Lk 7	1Cor 7
29	Jdg 1:36	Isa 59:21	Mt 2	Acts 2	18	1Sam25:44	Jer 42:22	Lk 8	1Cor 8
30	Jdg 2:23	Isa 60:22	Mt 3	Acts 3	19	1Sam26:25	Jer 43:13	Lk 9	1Cor 9
Jul 1	Jdg 3:31	Isa 62:12	Mt 4	Acts 4	20	1Sam28:25	Jer 44:30	Lk 10	1Cor 10
2	Jdg 4:24	Isa 63:19	Mt 5	Acts 5	21	1Sam29:11	Jer 46:12	Lk 11	1Cor 11
3	Jdg 5:31	Isa 65:25	Mt 6	Acts 6	22	1Sam30:20	Jer 46:28	Lk 12	1Cor 12
4	Jdg 6:24	Isa 66:24	Mt 7	Acts 7	23	1Sam31:13	Jer 48:33	Lk 13	1Cor 13
5	Jdg 6:40	Jer 1:19	Mt 8	Acts 8	24	2Sam 1:27	Jer 48:47	Lk 14	1Cor 14
6	Jdg 7:25	Jer 2:19	Mt 9	Acts 9	25	2Sam 2:32	Jer 49:22	Lk 15	1Cor 15
7	Jdg 8:35	Jer 2:37	Mt 10	Acts 10	26	2Sam 4:12	Jer 49:39	Lk 16	1Cor 16
8	Jdg 9:29	Jer 3:25	Mt 11	Acts 11	27	2Sam 6:16	Jer 50:20	LK 17	2Cor 1
9	Jdg 9:57	Jer 4:31	Mt 12	Acts 12	28	2Sam 7:29	Jer 50:46	Lk 18	2Cor 2
10	None	None	Mt 13	Acts 13	29	2Sam 9:13	Jer 51:32	Lk 19	2Cor 3
11	Jdg 11:28	Jer 5:31	Mt 14	Acts 14	30	2Sam11:27	Jer 51:64	Lk 20	2Cor 4
12	Jdg 12:7	Jer 6:15	Mt 15	Acts 15	31	2Sam12:31	Jer 52:34	Lk 21	2Cor 5
13	Jdg 13:25	Jer 6:30	Mt 16	Acts 16	Sep 1	2Sam13:39	Lam 1:22	Lk 22	2Cor 6
14	Jdg 14:20	Jer 7:34	Mt 17	Acts 17	2	2Sam14:33	Lam 2:22	Lk 23	2Cor 7
15	Jdg 15:20	Jer 8:22	Mt 18	Acts 18	3	2Sam15:37	Lam 3:66	Lk 24	2Cor 8
16	Jdg 16:31	Jer 9:26	Mt 19	Acts 19	4	2Sam16:23	Lam 5:22	Jn 1	2Cor 9
17	Jdg 18:10	Jer 10:25	Mt 20	Acts 20	5	2Sam17:29	Ezk 2:10	Jn 2	2Cor 10
18	Jdg 18:31	Jer 11:13	Mt 21	Acts 21	6	2Sam18:33	Ezk 3:27	Jn 3	2Cor 11
19	Jdg 19:30	Jer 12:17	Mt 22	Acts 22	7	2Sam19:30	Ezk 4:17	Jn 4	2Cor 12
20	Jdg 20:17	Jer 13:27	Mt 23	Acts 23	8	2Sam20:26	Ezk 6:14	Jn 5	2Cor 13
21	Jdg 20:48	Jer 14:22	Mt 24	Acts 24	9	2Sam21:22	Ezk 7:27	Jn 6	Gal 1
22	Jdg 21:25	Jer 15:21	Mt 25	Acts 25	10	2Sam22:51	Ezk 8:18	Jn 7	Gal 2
23	Ruth 1:22	Jer 16:21	Mt 26	Acts 26	11	2Sam23:39	Ezk 9:11	Jn 8	Gal 3
24	Ruth 2:23	Jer 17:10	Mt 27	Acts 27	12	2Sam24:25	Ezk 10:22	Jn 9	Gal 4
25	Ruth 3:18	Jer 17:27	Mt 28	Acts 28	13	1Kgs 1:53	Ezk 12:28	Jn 10	Gal 5
26	Ruth 4:22	Jer 18:23	Mk 1	Rom 1	14	1Kgs 2:35	Ezk 13:23	Jn 11	Gal 6
27	1Sam 1:28	Jer 20:18	Mk 2	Rom 2	15	1Kgs 3:28	Ezk 15:8	Jn 12	Eph 1
28	1Sam 2:36	Jer 22:9	Mk 3	Rom 3	16	1Kgs 5:18	Ezk 16:34	Jn 13	Eph 2
29	1Sam 3:21	Jer 22:30	Mk 4	Rom 4	17	1Kgs 6:38	Ezk 16:63	Jn 14	Eph 3
30	1Sam 5:12	Jer 23:22	Mk 5	Rom 5	18	1Kgs 7:51	Ezk 17:24	Jn 15	Eph 4
31	1Sam 6:21	Jer 24:10	Mk 6	Rom 6	19	1Kgs 8:30	Ezk 19:14	Jn 16	Eph 5
Aug 1	1Sam 8:22	Jer 25:38	Mk 7	Rom 7	20	1Kgs 8:66	Ezk 20:49	Jn 17	Eph 6
2	1Sam 9:27	Jer 26:24	Mk 8	Rom 8	21	1Kgs 9:28	Ezk 21:32	Jn 18	Philp 1
3	1Sam10:27	Jer 27:22	Mk 9	Rom 9	22	1Kgs 10:29	Ezk 22:31	Jn 19	Philp 2
4	1Sam11:15	Jer 28:17	Mk 10	Rom 10	23	1Kgs 11:43	Ezk 23:49	Jn 20	Philp 3
5	1Sam12:25	Jer 29:32	Mk 11	Rom 11	24	1Kgs 12:33	Ezk 25:17	Jn 21	Philp 4
6	1Sam13:23	Jer 30:24	Mk 12	Rom 12	25	1Kgs 13:34	Ezk 26:21	Mt 1	Col 1
7	1Sam14:52	Jer 31:40	Mk 13	Rom 13	26	1Kgs 14:31	Ezk 27:36	Mt 2	Col 2
8	1Sam15:35	Jer 32:25	Mk 14	Rom 14	27	1Kgs 15:34	Ezk 28:26	Mt 3	Col 3
9	1Sam16:23	Jer 32:44	Mk 15	Rom 15	28	1Kgs 16:34	Ezk 30:19	Mt 4	Col 4
10	1Sam17:58	Jer 33:26	Mk 16	Rom 16	29	1Kgs 17:24	Ezk 31:18	Mt 5	1Thes 1

	Old Testament		New Testament			Old Testament		New Testament	
Sep	Year I	Year II	Gosp.	A,Ep,R	Nov	Year I	Year II	Gosp.	A,Ep,R
30	1Kgs 18:46	Ezk 32:32	Mt 6	1Thes 2	16	1Chr 28:21	Amos4:13	Lk 9	1John 1
Oct 1	1Kgs 20:22	Ezk 33:33	Mt 7	1Thes 3	17	1Chr 29:30	Amos5:27	Lk 10	1John 2
2	1Kgs 20:43	Ezk 35:15	Mt 8	1Thes 4	18	2Chr 2:18	Amos6:14	Lk 11	1John 3
3	1Kgs 21:29	Ezk 36:38	Mt 9	1Thes 5	19	2Chr 4:22	Amos7:17	Lk 12	1John 4
4	1Kgs 22:53	Ezk 37:28	Mt 10	2Thes 1	20	2Chr 6:11	Amos8:14	Lk 13	1John 5
5	2Kgs 2:25	Ezk 39:10	Mt 11	2Thes 2	21	2Chr 6:42	Amos9:15	Lk 14	2John
6	2Kgs 3:27	Ezk 39:29	Mt 12	2Thes 3	22	2Chr 8:18	Obadiah	Lk 15	3John
7	2Kgs 4:37	Ezk 40:16	Mt 13	1Tim 1	23	2Chr 9:31	Jon 2:10	Lk 16	Jude
8	2Kgs 5:27	Ezk 40:49	Mt 14	1Tim 2	24	2Chr 11:23	Jon 4:11	Lk 17	Rev 1
9	2Kgs 6:33	Ezk 41:26	Mt 15	1Tim 3	25	2Chr 13:22	Mic 1:16	Lk 18	Rev 2
10	2Kgs 8:29	Ezk 43:27	Mt 16	1Tim 4	26	2Chr 15:19	Mic 2:13	Lk 19	Rev 3
11	2Kgs 9:37	Ezk 44:31	Mt 17	1Tim 5	27	2Chr 17:19	Mic 4:13	Lk 20	Rev 4
12	2Kgs 10:36	Ezk 45:25	Mt 18	1Tim 6	28	2Chr 19:11	Mic 6:16	Lk 21	Rev 5
13	2Kgs 12:21	Ezk 47:12	Mt 19	2Tim 1	29	2Chr 20:37	Mic 7:20	Lk 22	Rev 6
14	2Kgs 13:25	Ezk 48:14	Mt 20	2Tim 2	30	2Chr 21:20	Nah 1:15	Lk 23	Rev 7
15	2Kgs 14:29	Ezk 48:35	Mt 21	2Tim 3	Dec 1	2Chr 22:12	Nah 2:13	Lk 24	Rev 8
16	2Kgs 15:38	Dan 2:13	Mt 22	2Tim 4	2	2Chr 23:21	Nah 3:19	Jn 1	Rev 9
17	2Kgs 16:20	Dan 2:49	Mt 23	Titus 1	3	2Chr 24:27	Hab 2:20	Jn 2	Rev 10
18	2Kgs 17:41	Dan 3:30	Mt 24	Titus 2	4	2Chr 25:28	Hab 3:19	Jn 3	Rev 11
19	2Kgs 18:37	Dan 4:18	Mt 25	Titus 3	5	2Chr 26:23	Zeph 1:18	Jn 4	Rev 12
20	2Kgs 19:37	Dan 4:37	Mt 26	Philem	6	2Chr 28:27	Zeph 2:15	Jn 5	Rev 13
21	2Kgs 20:21	Dan 5:31	Mt 27	Heb 1	7	2Chr 29:36	Zeph 3:20	Jn 6	Rev 14
22	2Kgs 22:20	Dan 6:28	Mt 28	Heb 2	8	2Chr 30:27	Hag 2:23	Jn 7	Rev 15
23	2Kgs 23:20	Dan7:28	Mk 1	Heb 3	9	2Chr 31:21	Zec 1:21	Jn 8	Rev 16
24	2Kgs 24:20	Dan 8:27	Mk 2	Heb 4	10	2Chr 32:33	Zec 3:10	Jn 9	Rev 17
25	2Kgs 25:30	Dan 9:27	Mk 3	Heb 5	11	2Chr 33:25	Zec 5:11	Jn 10	Rev 18
26	1Chr 1:54	Dan 10:21	Mk 4	Heb 6	12	2Chr 34:13	Zec 6:15	Jn 11	Rev 19
27	1Chr 2:55	Dan 11:19	Mk 5	Heb 7	13	2Chr 34:33	Zec 7:14	Jn 12	Rev 20
28	1Chr 3:24	Dan 11:45	Mk 6	Heb 8	14	2Chr 35:27	Zec 8:23	Jn 13	Rev 21
29	1Chr 4:43	Dan 12:13	Mk 7	Heb 9	15	2Chr 36:23	Zec 9:17	Jn 14	Rev 22
30	1Chr 5:26	Hos 1:11	Mk 8	Heb 10	16	Ezra 2:70	Zec 11:17	Jn 15	None
31	1Chr 6:30	Hos 2:8	Mk 9	Heb 11	17	Ezra 4:24	Zec 13:9	Jn 16	None
Nov 1	1Chr 6:65	Hos 2:23	Mk 10	Heb 12	18	Ezra 6:22	Zec 14:20	Jn 17	None
2	1Chr 7:40	Hos 4:19	Mk 11	Heb 13	19	Ezra 8:36	Mal 2:17	Jn 18	None
3	1Chr 8:40	Hos 5:15	Mk 12	James 1	20	Ezra 10:44	Mal 4:6	Jn 19	None
4	1Chr 9:44	Hos 7:16	Mk 13	James 2	21			Jn 20&21	
5	1Chr 11:25	Hos 8:14	Mk 14	James 3	22	Isa. 42:1-9		Lk 1	
6	1Chr 12:40	Hos 9:17	Mk 15	James 4	23	Isa 9:6-7 & Isa 61:1-3		Heb1:6-13 Lk 2	
7	1Chr 15:29	Hos 11:12	Mk 16	James 5	24	Isa 7:14 & Mic 5:2	Mt 1&2	Gal 4:1-7	
8	1Chr 16:43	Hos 13:8	Lk 1	1Peter 1	25	Isa 53:1-12 & Isa 9:2		Jn 1 Heb1:1-5	
9	1Chr 18:17	Hos 14:9	Lk 2	1Peter 2	26	Psalm 8 & 23		Mt 5 & 6	
10	1Chr 20:8	Joel 1:20	Lk 3	1Peter 3	27	Psalm 33, 34, & 145		Mt 10	
11	1Chr 22:19	Joel 2:32	Lk 4	1Peter 4	28	Psalm 66, 67, & 68		Lk 15	
12	1Chr 24:31	Joel 3:21	Lk 5	1Peter 5	29	Psalm 138 & 139		Jn 14 & 15	
13	1Chr 25:31	Amos1:15	Lk 6	2Peter 1	30	Psalm 103, 104, & 105		Jn 17	
14	1Chr 26:32	Amos2:16	Lk 7	2Peter 2	31	Isaiah 55:8 & 9			
15	1Chr 27:34	Amos3:15	Lk 8	2Peter 3					

Since Peter was filled with the Holy Spirit and the power of the Holy Spirit was working in and through him, he was a changed man. Not only was he born again,* but now he walked in the power of the Holy Spirit, and with boldness commands a cripple to walk (healing him as Jesus had done to many others). With the crowd that gathers he again preaches that they should repent and accept their Messiah, repeating Old Testament scriptures to them like one of the learned scholars which he was not; he had only been a fisherman, but he had been with Jesus for about three years. That day, as many more believed from what Peter had said to them, the number of believers grew to about 5,000.

*When Peter was born again, it was receiving a new life in himself that was not there before. From my reading it seemed to happen in Jn. 20:22 when Jesus breathed on them and they received the Holy Spirit. Two other times in scripture God's breath gives life: in the Garden of Eden when God breathed into the nostrils of man (Adam) and he became a living being. (Gen. 2:7) The other time was when God commanded Ezekiel to prophesy to the dry bones (Eze. 37:4), and sinews and flesh and skin came on them. (v. 8) In two literal translations I have, the Spirit is the one giving the breath.

In The **Complete Word Study Dictionary** it says the Hebrew word here means: *spirit, wind, or breath* - it says this word was used by the Jews to refer to the Spirit of God. *"Thus said the Lord Jehovah: From the four winds come in, O Spirit, and breathe on these slain, and they do live"*(v. 9 YLT). As Ezekiel prophesied the breath of the Spirit came into the dry bones which now were bodies that came to life and stood on their feet. I believe when Jesus breathed on the disciples, they at that point received new life, the new birth. Salvation (the new life) by the blood of Christ was not available until Jesus died on the cross for all our sins.

Before the cross, as the disciples walked with Jesus there seems to be some special covering, anointing, or such that God had given them, but the new birth Jesus spoke to Nicodemus about was not available until after Jesus' death on the cross. What we read at Jn. 20:22 is the first time Jesus is with the disciples since He had rose from the dead, and the first time the new birth for them by His blood was available to them.

Jesus said, *"Man shall not live by bread alone, but by every word that proceeds from the mouth of God"* (Mat. 4:4 & Deut. 8:3 RSV). In the wilderness the Jews were given food from heaven, a type of bread which was their nourishment. Our diet today is much more than bread, we have many more things added, many that are delicious to our taste, and many that are very good for our health. In this scripture, the representation of all that good food is the word **bread**. The very important word in this verse is '**alone**'. Jesus is saying that man who exists alone by what food he provides himself is not really living at all. Man is in a state of living without being alive. Jesus said without Him in our lives we are dead, *"Truly, truly, I say to you, he who hears my word and believes him who sent me, has eternal life; he does not come into judgment, but has passed from death to life. Truly, truly, I say to you, the hour is coming, and now is, when the dead will hear the voice of the Son of God, and those who hear will live."* (Jn. 5:24 & 25 RSV)

Our diet of bread alone does not give us life. The fullness of life only comes when we accept Jesus Christ into our lives by that word of God. We know that the better we feed ourselves with good food the better our bodies are; physically fit, healthy, strong, having endurance to complete our work, etc. If this be true, we know then surely it is also true, according to what Jesus said, that a good diet of God's word will complete our lives to the fullest intended for us by the Father. That daily input of God's word will give us what we need for spiritual life; spiritual fitness, spiritual health, spiritual strength, spiritual endurance, spiritual knowledge, power from the Holy Spirit.

A daily intake of God's word will give us spiritual strength in word to convince the unsaved of their need of salvation, it will help us to strengthen the brethren, and most of all, to have a close relationship with our God personally. Jesus wants the best for us and a daily diet of God's word is just as important for us as a daily diet of healthy food.

<u>A quick note from Acts</u>: When we people hear the truth of our condition (who we are, how we are, and who God is, how God is) we are cut to the heart and have two choices; One is to respond as those Peter preached to on the day of Pentecost with 3,000 replying, 'what shall we do?' being told to repent and accept Christ as the will of God. (Acts 2:37 & 38) The second choice is to respond as those of the High Priest, the Pharisees, the Sadducees, and the Senate of Israel, when they heard the word of Peter becoming angry, infuriated, and wanted to kill those speaking the truth. (Acts 5:28 – 33)

Jesus speaking in the **Sermon on the Mount** said, "*Therefore, whoever nullifies one of the least of these commandments, and teaches others to do the same, shall be called least in the kingdom of heaven; but whoever keeps and teaches them, he shall be called great in the Kingdom of Heaven*" (Mt. 5:19 NASB). Hearing this verse only, it seems we must follow all the Law to have any hope of success in the Kingdom of Heaven. First we must see who Jesus is saying this to: it is the Jews primarily (and also extending in the course of time to us). The Jew saw his own right standing with God by his own works of following the Law. Even though none followed it completely, they thought highly of themselves by the majority of the Law they did follow (accomplish).

An example of this is the high priest during Jesus' trial before taking Him to Pilate. When Jesus said in Mat. 26: 63 – 65 that He was the Son of God the high priest tore his robe. It was said in the Law that the high priest was never to tear his robe. (Lev. 10:6 & 21:10) In the Sermon on the Mount as we read on we see in Mt. 5:19 – 28 that Jesus is making the case that none will make it by following the Law, that all have failed, and then goes on in the next verses to show the depths of the Law – that it is even more strict than what the Jews thought it was.

After hearing all this going back to v. 19 where Jesus says, "*but whoever keeps and teaches them, he shall be called great in the kingdom of heaven*" (NASB), we see that this could only be Jesus Himself Who follows the Law perfectly and teaches others. Jesus shows us how much we are in need. He shows us how much we need the gospel He offers, to be saved by grace through faith, for we cannot receive it by the Law.

How far do we reach to find what we already have? Do we each day continue to try to measure up? How many times do we end the day feeling defeated because of what we see as a failure to be holy in our actions? What is it we are not seeing, what is it we are not yet knowing, what yet is the love of the Father that we have not yet seen? Do we have His salvation that He has given us? If it is given, can it be earned? If we try to acquire it by our works, then is it a gift?

Often men tried to measure up, generations of the Jews tried to measure up, but as we read in the sermon on the mound Jesus showed how none had measured up, even when they thought they had Jesus showed them the depth of only two sins spoke of in the Law which many of them were failing at keeping them. [1] Do we not see clearly what Christ has done and brought us by His work on the cross? Do we not know the value of what He did by dying in our place on the cross. Have we not yet placed that precious blood of His on ourselves? We must allow, and know, what that blood has brought us. [2] It is the end of trying to measure up, it is the end of us working hard to be holy – we cannot by our own efforts, only by the gift given. [3]

Noah was given a gift of surviving the flood that God brought upon the whole earth. One might say this was not so for Noah built a great ark to save him from the flood. I would ask you, how did he know he should build it, how did he know there was a flood coming? Even of how he was to build the ark of it size and shape was given to him by God. Noah responded to what was said to him. Have we responded to what has been said to us, that we should accept Christ and His forgiveness, that we can be saved from our sins? If so will we not be carried above the flood of sin as Noah was carried by the ark above the flood waters? Do we not realize Christ is our ark as we are said by Paul that we are in Him? [4] *"Then the LORD said to Noah, "Enter the ark, you and all your household, for you alone I have seen to be righteous before Me in this generation"* (Gen. 7:1 NASB).

We gain righteousness as it is given us by Christ, [5] by what He did on the cross, and are able to enter into Him and to be carried above the flood of sin in the world. At our salvation we are totally cleansed of all our previous sins, and any sin that comes into our lives afterwards we have the blood of the cross to cleanse us. If we go in repentance seeking forgiveness it is immediately given that we will not drowned. We are carried by Christ in Himself to survive into eternity.

---

1   Mt.5:21-30
2   Rom.5:9, Eph.1:7, Col.1:14, Tit.3:4-6, 1Pet.1:2
3   Ps.143:1&2, Rom.3:20
4   Rom.6:11, 8:1, 1Cor.1:30, 2Cor.5:17, 1Pet.5:14
5   Rom.5:19, 2Cor.5:21

The Jews had been taken away to Babylon because of their wickedness as Nebuchadnezzar was instructed by God. They were in Babylon for seventy years and God began to bring back the remnant of Jews to Jerusalem. Ezra the priest was in the first group to return and Nehemiah the governor was in the second group to return. On a day set aside from their work rebuilding Jerusalem all the people were gathered and Ezra read from the Law given them through Moses. When the people heard the reading of the Law they wept, *"And Nehemiah...Ezra...and the Levites that taught the people, said unto all the people, This day is holy unto Jehovah your God; mourn not, nor weep. For all the people wept, when they heard the words of the law"* (Neh. 8:9 ASV).

The scriptures in the book of Nehemiah does not say why they wept but we can conclude it was not in joy because the people were told not to mourn or weep. Sometimes when we read God's word, read those things Jesus said, those things the apostles said, we tend to become remorseful and sad as we truly see what kind of people we are. It is good and spiritually healthy to see this, for until we do we don't know how full the grace of God is which was provided fully to us freely by the sacrifice of Jesus on the cross. The Jews were told not to mourn or weep, Ezra the priest told the people to go their way, eat the fat, drink the sweet drink, and give gifts to those who were without. Ezra said to them that it was a holy day to the Lord, not to grieve, not to be depressed, and that the joy in God was their strength and stronghold. After hearing this and being encouraged by the Levites the people went their way and rejoiced.

Today when we seriously take time to consider God in our lives and are confronted by our sinful ways as we hear what God has to say, then we get stuck there as the Jews did when they heard the Law as Ezra read it. The Jews were told by Ezra not to get stuck there, to get lose of it, and to rejoice in their God. We today have been freely given the grace which provides us salvation, the eternal life with God. In hearing this we have so much more to rejoice in than the people Ezra spoke to that day. I see this as a two-sided coin of much value with the greatest value on the second side: the first side of the coin is the truly seeing our sinful nature and always keeping that in mind, but the second side of the coin is the greater because it is there I see God has worked His work of grace fully, not partly, but completely paid for all of my sin which I could not do.

The rejoicing comes as I see the second side of the coin in what God has done for me, knowing about myself on the first side of the coin. We are called to rejoice in the Lord[1] and we cannot truly rejoice if we don't see and know what is on the first side of the coin, it is then as we look at what is on the second side of the coin that we can truly rejoice celebrating joyfully the God of our salvation for the great things He has done for us. This is the true rejoicing where it is said we will find our true strength and our stronghold which is in God. (Neh. 8:10)

---

1   Philp. 4:4

God gives promises, sometimes they are conditional on our part and sometimes God swears by Himself something that is a promise regardless of what man may or may not do. Sometimes the promises of God in scripture are called covenants, and sometimes called pledges, etc. It is a joy to man to hear promises which God makes to man, even when the promises are conditional on man's part. It shows God's desire of well being towards man.

In Genesis 9:9, God makes one of these promises which is not conditional of what man does or does not do, "*As for me—I am herewith establishing my covenant with you, with your descendants after you.*" (CJB) It is an everlasting promise God makes to man that will last until the end of time."*I will establish my covenant with you that never again will all living beings be destroyed by the waters of a flood, and there will never again be a flood to destroy the earth*" (v. 11 CJB). This promise was to never again destroy all of mankind and animals on earth with a flood. God put a mark on His promise so He would be reminded of the promise He made (no matter how wicked man again may become) which is the rainbow in the sky that comes at times that the rain again falls. (v. 16&17)

In Neh. 9:6, Ezra the priest gives praise to God for creation and the preserving of the earth and all that is upon it (man and animal). God preserved man and animal through the flood by way of the ark and then promised to never destroy all life on earth again with a flood. God keeps His promises. God promised through the prophets to send a savior and we see that happening as we are reading through the book of Matthew. God promised to send us power from high. [1]

This was not power common to man, it was not power found on earth, this was not an expanded power already in man, it was a power foreign to man until God gave it to man to perform and accomplish things that man of himself did not have the ability or power to make happen. We see this power at work in God's followers in the book of Acts. Some have said this power was specially given to the apostles alone to establish the church yet there were deacons (Stephen and Philip) who worked signs and wonders among the people. [2] These were not apostles, just disciples who were chosen by the people [3] and presented to the apostles who prayed and laid their hands on them for the assigned work. [4]

We then today as disciples of God should expect and seek this power promised to us to do the work of the Kingdom of God. If we think that we can accomplish God's work with our abilities alone we are deceiving ourselves and the enemy is having his way. It is only in this promised power that we in our daily walk and ministry can defeat our enemy and bring the blessings of God to man on earth that man can enjoy salvation and eternal life with God.

---

1   Lk. 24:49
2   Acts 6:8 & 8:6
3   Acts 6:3
4   Acts 6:6

Paul was a very serious and devoted Jew, taught by one of the greatest of Jews in Jerusalem, one named Gamaliel. [1] Paul, who at that time was called Saul, lived strictly by the Law, being far ahead of all his counterparts. [2] Paul makes this argument to defend himself as equal with any Jew, "*If any other man thinks he has reason for confidence in the flesh, I have more: circumcised on the eighth day, of the people of Israel, of the tribe of Benjamin, a Hebrew born of Hebrews; as to the law a Pharisee, as to zeal a persecutor of the church, as to righteousness under the law blameless*" (Philp. 3:4-6 RSV).

There was no fault to be found in him in his religiously following of the Jewish religion. Yet in spite of his devotion to God he missed the greatest thing of God, he missed the Messiah sent to Paul's own people – to bring them salvation by faith and not by deed. Paul even found himself fighting against God. Paul on his way to Damascus to do more harm to the followers of the Messiah had to be confronted by Messiah Jesus Himself, "*a light from heaven shone around him. And falling to the ground, he heard a voice saying to him, "Saul, Saul, why are you persecuting me?*" (Acts 9:3&4 ESV). Paul was very strictly devoted to God in the Jewish religion, yet missing the truth, the very thing that God was doing. Today we can accept Jesus' salvation for our lives and then in our religious fervor for God, as Paul had, be mistaken in what we believe to be God's truth.

It is easy to be mistaken, Paul was being the best Jew he thought he could be. We may think we are being the best Christian we can be and find ourselves fighting against the very ways of God. We need to be open to, and seeking, the Holy Spirit to reveal the truth to us as Jesus said, "*But the Helper, the Holy Spirit, whom the Father will send in my name, he will teach you all things and bring to your remembrance all that I have said to you*" (Jn. 14:26 ESV). If we are serious about following God in His ways we will be willing even to pray that Jesus would confront us as He did Paul, to get our attention, to show us we are going the wrong way, and to change our direction to go His way.

---

[1]   Acts 5:34 & 22:3
[2]   Gal.1:13&14

We need to be careful of what kind of box we put God in, because as a Christian brother of mine says, we can't keep Him in there. There are many who say that a person must believe and be baptized to receive salvation and eternal life. In today's reading in Acts chapter 10, we read that Peter was sent by God to a gentile's house to speak to them. Peter was trying his best to follow God. Peter had preached in Jerusalem a couple of times we know about where thousands came to Christ. He had prayed for the sick and lame who were restored to health. He had prayed for a dead woman who came back to life. From all that we see Peter is trying to do it God's way. Then this thing came up to be sent to the house of a gentile.

For some reason, the Jews thought they knew that they were not to enter the house of a non-Jew. Sometimes the thing that we think we know is the very thing we don't know. It implies in the scripture here that by Peter's action and his thought that he would not have gone to Cornelius' house if he had not heard, and seen, the directive that came from heaven, *he said to them, "You yourselves know how unlawful it is for a Jew to associate with or to visit any one of another nation; but God has shown me that I should not call any man common or unclean"* (10:28 RSV). We can see by Peter's obedience, without trying to argue the Law, that these Gentiles (Cornelius' household and friends) received salvation even before Peter had finished his presentation. Not only this, but they even received spiritual (supernatural) gifts the same as those received by the Jewish followers of Jesus on the day of Pentecost. It was most definite that they received salvation and eternal life which they received without yet being baptized for Peter says this after, *"Then Peter declared, 'Can any one forbid water for baptizing these people who have received the Holy Spirit just as we have?' And he commanded them to be baptized in the name of Jesus Christ"* (v. 46-48 RSV).

Sometimes we can think we are so sure of something and then God shows us we are wrong. Following God is an ever learning journey being enlighten more and more over every hill and around every corner. *"For this reason...I do not cease to give thanks for you, remembering you in my prayers, that the God of our Lord Jesus Christ, the Father of glory, may give you a spirit of wisdom and of revelation in the knowledge of him, having the eyes of your hearts enlightened, that you may know what is the hope to which he has called you, what are the riches of his glorious inheritance in the saints, and what is the immeasurable greatness of his power in us who believe, according to the working of his great might"* (Eph. 1:15-19 RSV). The fullness of God and all that He is to us and all that He has for us we will never know until we arrive in heaven. Allow God to move you past what you thought you knew.

To Antioch we go. We read of Antioch in Acts, what would we find arriving at Antioch in those days? We would find devoted people of Jews and Gentiles getting along together seeking after God and Christ such that they became known as Christ-likens (Christians). They were known of the populaces of Antioch as those who followed Christ. Are there those around you who know by your character you are one who follows Christ? We are in this world but not of this world.[1] We should not have the appearance of those of this world. It may not be how we purposely act, it is Who we are of, and of Who we associate with, that is to have a relationship with God. If we do it shows even if we don't know it, others notice. What a great reflection on us, to know the very presence of God in our life shows.

The more time we spend with God the more it shows on us. His very word builds character in us. The same as the food we eat shapes us, the word we read shapes us. It is not always by us trying to live rightly by it, even though we do, it is it grows in us a crop of which we know not that it happens, yet it does. Children who grow because of what they eat do not know how they grow, they only know they grow. For us sometimes we don't know we grow, yet those around us see that we do. Jesus said to do the will of His Father was food indeed, *"But He said to them, "I have food to eat that you don't know about...My food is to do what the one who sent me wants and to bring his work to completion"* (Jn. 4:32&34 CJB). To read the word of God is certainly one of the things that is His will for us. We are to continue to grow in Christ, to become more as His character. We are changed more and more into His likeness.[2]

To those around us, they see a certain likeness of Christ in us even if we don't realize it and they may not know what it is, yet they notice something. Who can know the effect we have on others? They are either drawn towards us or driven away. The scriptures tell us we have a spiritual odor: *"But thanks be to God, who in Christ always leads us in triumph, and through us spreads the fragrance of the knowledge of him everywhere. For we are the aroma of Christ to God among those who are being saved and among those who are perishing, to one a fragrance from death to death, to the other a fragrance from life to life"* (2Cor. 2:14-16 RSV). We are told, those of us who are saved are a light to the world. *"You are the light of the world. A city that is set on a hill cannot be hidden"* (Mt. 5:14 NKJV).

The effect you have on those around you you may never know of for we do not all harvest, some plant (even though we may not know we are planting), and some water. It may be that others have told someone about Christ and they see you which impresses more of the truth of Christ taking them ever closer to the day they accept Christ.

---

1   Philp.3:20
2   Rom.8:29, 2Cor.3:18

Don't be surprised when unbelievers accuse you of evil doings, even sometimes believers who do not believe all that God says and does will also accuse you. The Pharisees, and Sadducees, and other religious leaders said that Jesus was evil, even that He was Beelzebub and casting out demons by that power, or of being the prince of demons.[1] Jesus healed many, many sick people who were being held sick by demons. Jesus cast out the demon and the people were well again. This was a good thing that Jesus was doing, but yet the religious leaders found fault in it because He did not do it by their manner and their way.

Jesus implies in the parable of the Good Samaritan that the Pharisees and other leaders were not doing it at all. Jesus tells them God desires that they practice mercy, not sacrifice without mercy. He tells them they have more mercy on their animals. He may imply they are willing to break the Law to care for their animal having mercy on it for the animal's need, or worse it is their greed that they do it because the animal has a value of money, part of their wealth. Either way they are willing to break what they believed to be the Law to save or help the animal but not a man who is sick or in need. We need to be careful we do not accuse someone who may be doing God's very will. Jesus was falsely accused even though He was doing the will of God. There will be those who accuse, we should be careful we are not the one accusing.

Our level of maturity may be short, we may be unaware of what God has spoken to the other person. If we are the one accused we need to practice kindness with longsuffering. We all need time to mature, we are all at different stages of maturity, and no matter what stage we are at there is still more maturing and learning for each of us. No matter which end of the accusing we are on it is damaging to both. No one is hard shelled enough to not be affected by the accusation, and no one doing the accusing finds it easy later when they find they were wrong.

When we observe another claiming to be doing God's work but we disagree with it our first action should be prayer, not stones. Even though it was not spoke to us we need to hear the words of Gamaliel, "But a Pharisee named Gamaliel, a teacher of the Law, respected by all the people, stood up...And he said to them, "Men of Israel, be careful as to what you are about to do with these men...if the source is God...you may even be found fighting against God" (Acts 5:34,35,39 NASB).

---

[1]   Mt.12:24

In our reading in Matthew today we read of a very small parable, only two verses, *"the kingdom of heaven is like a merchant in search of fine pearls, who, on finding one pearl of great value, went and sold all that he had and bought it"* (13:45&46 ESV). In the parable Jesus tells that the man found something, a pearl, worth more than all he had, so he sold all he had, gave up all he had, to purchase this great pearl. Jesus said in the beginning of this parable *"the kingdom of heaven is like."* Have we found the Kingdom of God? Is this not what we are born into in our salvation? The Kingdom of God is also called Heaven. Paul says this, *"For our citizenship is in heaven, from which we also eagerly wait for a Savior, the Lord Jesus Christ"* (Philp. 3:20 NASB).

It is a great thing to realize we are citizens of heaven, that we have found that pearl of great price and gave all we had to purchase it. Ah, we received that pearl of great price and have received salvation, but did we give all we have? Jesus gives this salvation freely, He has already paid the true price of what it cost, His life on the cross. When we accept salvation from Jesus we are turning over to Him our whole life, that is what we pay to one who pays our debt. Jesus is kind and gentle, He doesn't force the issue, He asks and He waits. Let's look at something from the children of Israel as they go into the wilderness after being led out of Egypt by Moses.

They have been rescued by the great move of the hand of God on the Egyptians, they have come through the Red Sea on dry ground, God has destroyed their enemy of the army of Egypt by drowning them in the Red Sea, they have been to the mountain of God, even hearing His voice, Moses receives the Ten Commandments written in stone by the finger of God, and then they are lead into the wilderness. Stephen tells us something interesting about this in Acts 7:43, after all the amazing and powerful things God had done for them they still carried the tent of Moloch (a foreign god) and the star of Remphan (a foreign god) with them. God had just done all these great things for them, and they are still holding on to something else.

You have received a great deliverance from God, being delivered from your sins and given the great gift of salvation, but have you given up everything to Jesus? All you are and all you have are His, is there anything you are still carrying with you that you know He wants you to give up? Certainly, our salvation is a pearl of great price, the merchant gave up all he had to have this very precious procession. Have you gave up all you have for this very precious gift?

'The Hem of Jesus' Garment' When Jesus was on the way to the Synagogue ruler's house a woman who had a health issue, an ailment for twelve years, believed if she could only touch the hem of Jesus' garment, not even touching Jesus Himself, that she would be healed.[1] She received the healing as the power of Jesus went out to her and Jesus said, "Somebody touched me." We read today of Jesus walking on the water, and when He and the disciples arrived at the shore in the boat and the people brought to Him the sick so they might only touch the hem of His garment. *"brought to Him all who were sick, and begged Him that they might only touch the hem of His garment. And as many as touched it were made perfectly well"* (Mt. 14:35&36 NKJV). We see as we read through Acts that Paul and Barnabas takes the gospel to many lands.

We think Paul must have been a powerful speaker to preach the gospel to foreign peoples who did not know of the God of Israel, and yet many believed becoming Christians. We assume that if we just had men (preachers, missionaries, and evangelists) today that spoke like Paul that so many people could be saved. There is one important point in the scriptures that we miss and are not taught to see, for we all fall short in this area. It is recorded in Acts that many who were presented the word of the gospel believed because of the confirming signs and wonders that were done.

Many will say right away in argument that it was the 12 apostles only who worked the signs and wonders. In Acts chapter 14, where we read today this happens twice, *"Therefore they spent a long time there speaking boldly with reliance upon the Lord, who was testifying to the word of His grace, granting that signs and wonders be performed by their hands."* (v. 3 NASB) and *"And at Lystra there sat a certain man, impotent in his feet, a cripple from his mother's womb, who never had walked. The same heard Paul speaking, who, fastening eyes upon him, and seeing that he had faith to be made whole, said with a loud voice, Stand upright on thy feet. And he leaped up and walked"* (v. 8-10 ASV). Paul was not one of the twelve who walked with Jesus, Barnabas was not one of the twelve, the deacon Stephen was not one of the twelve, the deacon Philip was not one of the twelve. Search the scriptures in the book of Acts and you will find that all these did signs and wonders as they preached the gospel as confirmation to the truth of the gospel they preached.

The closeness of ourselves to Jesus is where the power comes from. These who I mention that we read of in Acts walked closely with Jesus. Paul even says that what he knows of the gospel he preaches is not what he was taught by the apostles and other leaders, it was by what he was taught by direct revelation from the risen Lord Jesus.[2] Many at the time Jesus walked among men believed if they got close enough to Jesus to only touch the hem of His garment that they would receive the power to be healed. Are we so far away from Jesus today? Do we not see signs and wonders in confirmation of the gospel today because we are too far away from Jesus? To walk closely to Jesus does not take great performances of holy living, Paul says we all fall short in that area.[3]

Our society in America (and much of the world) say if you want to get ahead you must perform, you must make it happen. This attitude has gotten into the Church and many think they must perform for God to approve of them and use them. This is not true, if it was the grace and mercy of God would be greatly devalued. The only thing that can gain us that closeness to Jesus is surrender. Surrender is what gained us our salvation, not performance. Why would God's way change after our salvation? When we totally surrender to God then His power can work through us and we can perform great things because the strength and power to perform comes from Him doing His works He wants done His way. No performance by ourselves of our own effort in the Kingdom of God will produce any lasting results. Jesus says to take His yoke upon us, to walk His way, to pick up our cross, and follow Him, going the way He is going. This is the same as He said He was only doing what He saw the Father in heaven doing. Now we are to follow and see what Jesus is doing.

---

1   Mt. 9:21
2   Gal.1:12, Eph.3:3 1Cor.11:23
3   Rom.7:18

In Matthew 15:22-28 a Canaanite (Syro-Phoenician) woman came to Jesus who had a daughter possessed by a demon. The focus I want to bring from this is the condition of the Canaanite woman. Here is a mother who loves her daughter and is willing to do all she can to help her daughter. When a child is in trouble, mothers are desperate to do all they can for their child, even at the cost of their own life. She, being a Syro-Phoenician woman, knows the treatment she may receive if she approaches a Jewish man.

She has obviously heard about Jesus and is convinced having faith that He can help her. She goes to Jesus and is turned down at first, totally ignored by Jesus, but persists to gain the help for her desperate need. She continues to seek Jesus' help and Jesus replies saying she is a little dog and the children of Israel come first. She came to gain help for her daughter even knowing this is how she may be treated. She had faith that Jesus could help her and persisted even after being called a little dog, which dogs had very little value in Israel.

Even after the insult she continues to seek help from Jesus where many of us would give up having no hope further. This reminds me of the parable Jesus told the people about the widow who kept going back to the judge to get justice in her case and because the widow did not give up the judge gave her justice.[1] Here, this mother is a foreign woman seemingly disqualified even before she began yet she was convinced and had the faith that Jesus would hear her request and help her.

Finally Jesus said He would not take the bread of the children (of Israel) and give it to the little (nearly worthless) dogs yet the woman in her faith replies that even the little dogs (humbling herself to be considered nearly worthless) eat the crumbs that fall from the master's table. Again, this mother, in her statement, she shows she has much faith because she says to Jesus even a crumb is enough for her need to heal her daughter. Because of this statement, Jesus grants her petition, her daughter is cured of the demon, and Jesus declares how great her faith is. We have much to learn from this woman, at the minimum there is this: humbleness, faith, and persistence (not giving up). There may even be more here and as we read this, we, each of us, should go to the Holy Spirit[2] and ask what it is He wants to teach us from the actions and belief of the Canaanite woman.

---

1   Lk.18:2-5
2   Jn.14:26

When we read scripture we must depend upon God to give us spiritual eyes to see. In the account of the three heavenly visitors who come to Abraham on their way to destroy Sodom and Gomorrah, there is more information than just the visit to Abraham announcing the birth to come and the plea of Abraham for the sparing of the cities for the few righteous that might be there. These words of the Lord are found in Genesis 18:19 and we should linger here a moment. The Lord said Abraham would teach and command his children and the sons of his house to keep the way of the Lord. This is an interesting statement, we in the New Testament times see what Jesus says and are drawn to the law given to the Jews, for what reason I do not know. When we hear the things said in the Old Testament subconsciously we relate them to the law. Here where the Lord says what He does in Genesis 18:18 it is before the law was given through Moses.

The Lord doesn't say it is a postponed thing that will be given through Moses, it is an immediate thing that Abraham will give Isaac and those men that are with him, those that were circumcised with him. We don't read of any law given to Abraham other than circumcision, that on the eighth day after birth all males are to be circumcised. Other than this we see only two other things in Abraham's life; the first is when God says to go to another land God would show him and Abraham went. The second thing is that Abraham made sacrifices to God. There is no long list of behavior laws that God gives him, only circumcision.

The Lord said in v. 19 that Abraham would teach the way of the Lord. This sounds much like what Jesus summarized the law to be: To love the Lord our God with all our hearts, soul, strength, and mind – and to love our neighbor like our self.[1] This sounds much like the way Abraham acted. He was commanded to be circumcised in his foreskin, we are to be circumcised in the heart. I would choose to live in relationship with God as Abraham had. I care not to put myself under a long list of do's and don'ts from the law, but to rather be in relationship with God by only the two laws Jesus gave us. And to follow and teach the way of the Lord that Abraham taught: to have a circumcised heart, to go when God says go, and to offer living sacrifices of my life to God. Another thing we see in Genesis chapter 18 is in v. 27, Abraham describes himself as only dust and ashes. Abraham here shows his state of humbleness.

He shows himself as having no value, declaring no great claim to accomplishment. Do we do the same, or when we go to God do we want Him to recognize some of the good things we have done? Do we go wanting to be recognized for accomplishing some good Christian character? Abraham in pleading with the Lord could have used his obedience of leaving his country to follow the Lord as some value in his plea, but he does not. Instead, Abraham humbles himself in the reality that is, that he (and we) is just dust and ashes. Another thing I see is the mercy of the Lord. In v. 32 the Lord says He will not destroy the city for the sake of only ten righteous people if they are found there. Today I hear much said that if God does not deal with America because of its sin that He would have to apologize to Sodom and Gomorrah.

First of all, where do we come off with such arrogance that we would say God would have to do anything? God calls us to have mercy and act justly.[2] Here we see Abraham doing just that in pleading for the well-being of only ten. I don't know the population of Sodom but I am sure ten is a very small percentage. I would dare to say that there is a larger percentage of Christians in America today and God is willing (it is His heart) to spare America. So rather than condemning America because of the sin we see, we should be like Abraham, pleading for God's mercy on America. These three things together show us some of the character of Abraham: he taught the ways of the Lord, not a regimented list of laws, but a close relationship with a God who is the giver and sustainer of life.

---

1   Mt.23:37, Mk.12:30, Lk.10:27
2   Mt.23:23

'I am the truth, the way, and the life, all who come to me shall have eternal life.'[1] These are the words of Jesus, do we believe them? Do we live our lives as if these were true? We go into our day with great expectations, or with doubt and despair not knowing how the day will end. If we believe the words of Jesus we will know the day, our day we enter, is in His hand. All of life is through Him for us who believe and have given our lives to Him. Yet we enter our day with our perspective of what it will be, or what we intend for it to be. Yet Jesus says through Him, and in Him is all for us, the way, the truth, the life. It seems Abraham knew this in his relationship with God, that it is as Paul told those of Athens, *"in Him we live and move and have our being"* (Acts 17:28 NKJV).

As we start our day, we need to place this in our hearts, that all is by God. Jesus has done a great thing for us coming from heaven and dying on the cross for our sins so that we have a way into God through Him. Abraham had a great relationship with God, but not the relationship we have with our sins forgiven, totally dependent on what Jesus has done for us. If we enter our day with this primary in our thoughts will it not change our expectations for the day? That we will have victory over our despair, victory in our intentions, all being brought into place by Christ who is in our lives giving victory to our day. Sometimes we lose sight of who controls the day.

As much as we take it on ourselves, which is not wrong to consider in which way we should go, but to know it has to be by Christ who is the way, our way, the truth, the truth for us, and the life, our life. Such a heavy burden at times we carry when Jesus says it can be light if we enter into the yoke with Him.[2] If we are in the yoke with Him He carries the greater load of the day. Do we trust Him, do we depend on Him? Or do we launch into our day on our own power to accomplish, even to accomplish for the cause of God? It is not we who do great works for God, for He needs nothing from us. Remember, He said let there be light, and there was light. What help would He need of us? Yet Jesus calls us into the work with Him, He who certainly does not need our help, yet calls us into the work with Him as He says, "**follow Me.**" If we begin our day knowing all must be through Him, and by Him, we would ask, OK Lord, what is up for today? I have my plans which you can alter at any time, how can what I plan for today bring you glory? It is not that we would do some great spiritual act, it is quite the opposite. It is how can I get out of Your way yielding all of myself to You so that You might do some great thing using me.

Sometimes what will be done for a heavenly cause through our life we may not even know about, but the person, or persons, affected know, and God in heaven knows. Ours is to yield ourselves over to Him, have faith He will use a yielded vessel, and bring glory to Himself by how He moves through us.

---

1   Jn.14:6
2   Mt.11:30

Jesus says if your hand or foot causes you to sin cut it off – if your eye causes you to sin pluck it out.[1] This then would be for a habit, a way of life, or a customary practice we have. If doing this habit, this way of life, or this practice causes us to sin, leads to us sinning each (or nearly each) time we do it, it is better for us to cut it off. Some of these things are things we do that we don't want to give up, at that point, it comes to a choice – are we going to do it God's way, or do we still want (demanding to have) our own way? This thing we do may not be sin itself but every time we involve our self with it we end up in sin.

An easy example would be to drink an alcoholic drink. Nowhere in scripture does it say we cannot drink an alcoholic drink – but if every time we drink some we want more and become drunk then we have sinned for the scripture says do not be drunk.[2] It is something we have a choice in, will we give it up, cut it off, or choose to continue is sin. There are many things in life which draw us, the question is what will our choice be. To sin is easy, to abstain is not. If we do nothing our flesh will draw us right into sin. There has to be a determined way we follow to move away from sin. Before we were saved we had no ability to move away from sin, we were a captive of it.[3]

Now in our saved lives, Jesus by dying on the cross has given us the freedom to move away from sin, the question is will we choose to? Sin is vicious, it has been brought into the world by a vicious predator. He even tried to over-through God on His throne in heaven and was cast out. Now he is after us, to cause us to yield to sin.[4] Before we were saved we were under his sway, but now his hold on us is cut off by the cross of Christ. We can choose, we should choose, but do we? The power is in the choosing, it is surprising of how fast the temptation goes away when we stop trying to fight it in our own strength and make a defiant choice, not the strength to push it away, but a choice to not sin. Even at times it is necessary that we speak it out loud to the Lord that we choose to not sin. That choice as we make it brings into play the victory of the cross, not the victory of our strength, but the power of the cross that broke the hold the devil had. Sometimes the temptation is instantly gone.

There are many temptations within ourselves as our flesh wants to take us that way. But there are other times it is a demon, and some, as we choose to not sin by the power of the victory of the cross, the demon is powerless and has to flee. We do not know the power we have in choice, not that of a strength of our own, but a power that upset all that exists the moment Jesus died on the cross. The great and powerful perfect sacrifice that affected all of time, from the Garden of Eden to the Day of Judgment, and even beyond. We have a choice, what will we choose?

---

1   Mt.5:29&30, 18:8&9
2   Eph.5:15-18
3   Rom.6:16-23
4   Rev.12:14-17

When we read of an account in scripture, especially in the Old Testament, we don't see the elapse of time. In Genesis chapter 20 Abraham goes to Gerar and tells people Sarah is his sister. Abimelech the king sees Sarah is a beautiful woman and takes her into his harem. God told Abimelech that he was a dead man if he did not give her back to Abraham. This all seems to take place in a manner of a few days but it did not. It may have been up to six months or more because Abimelech had seen the effect of what God had done to him in that his wife and none of his female slaves had been able to become pregnant and give birth. God had closed all the wombs of Abimelech's women – this is not something that is noticed in a few days. (v. 17&18) John at the end of his gospels, tells us if all the things Jesus did were written down the world would probably not hold all the books that would be written. If the Old Testament gave us all the details, how many volumes would it have taken to record it? Sometimes from one page to the other it may cover years. The time Moses was in Egypt sent there by God to deliver the people out of Pharaoh's hand surely is much longer than we think.

One time all the livestock is killed and the next thing we know they have livestock again. How long did it take for them to accumulate more livestock, months, years? So many times we read right over something in scripture and we don't really see it. This may have been part of the problem with the rich young ruler we read about in our New Testament reading today, he only saw part of it, maybe only what he wanted to see, not seeing all. The rich man asked what good thing it was he could do to receive eternal life. Jesus tells him of commandments he must follow to receive eternal life (Jesus is speaking in current time before the cross when the only way to receive eternal life was to do and follow all the Law given through Moses). The rich man said he had done all those commandments, then Jesus told him to sell all he had and give it to the poor. It may have been at this point Jesus was showing the rich man he had not followed all the commandments mentioned; Jesus said, "**love your neighbor as yourself.**" It may have been that the rich man had only loved the neighbor he chose like himself, but not all.*

When Jesus spoke of the poor these may have been the ones the rich man had not loved as himself. How many times may it be that we (maybe because of how we have been taught or what we understood scripture to say) think that we are doing what the scripture says but we are not. We need to continually ask the Holy Spirit to help us know the full and true meaning of scripture – this is why Jesus in John 14:26 said the Father would send the Holy Spirit, to teach us.

---

* I do not say sell all you own and give to the poor. But I do say do consider how you want others to treat you, then go treat them that way.

Jesus tells the parable of the land owner who hires workers for his vineyard. The owner obviously is God and the vineyard is the world and we who are saved and are taken into the Kingdom of God are the workers. One who works gladly wanting to see the harvest increase has a heart (if he becomes more and more like Jesus) that is glad to see more workers, more Christians, saved people come in, even at the last minute. Are we to expect a greater reward for our longer hard work than those who just recently entered when it was not we who paid the price for us to be permitted to enter the Kingdom of God? We are all granted more than we deserve. The work that we do is not the work to gain credit, for we can add nothing to the work Jesus Christ did on the cross. The work that we do is joining Jesus in His work of presenting the love of God to all people bringing as many as will come into the Kingdom of God.

When Jesus says pick up your cross and follow me He doesn't speak of any payment. Instead of to receive payment, before we are told to pick up our cross we are told to let go of what we have, to deny even our self putting no value in who we are any longer. It becomes all about Jesus who we are following. He and what He is doing becomes the focus. If He truly becomes the focus then we are glad to bring others in to know Him, even at the last moment. We find ourselves being glad these at the last moment have made it in, to be in eternity with all of us as we are with our God. We are all given more than we deserve, we could not gain this salvation we have with no amount of work we would do.

There was no amount of work to pay off our debt of sin other than giving our lives. Once we would have given our life, dying for our sins, we would no longer be living to receive the salvation. God is the One that calls, God is the One who paid the price we owed, God is the One who gives us freely salvation when we repent and ask Him.

Is our life a fruitless tree? There are many lessons I see in what Jesus says about the fig tree along the road that He goes to, this opening question is one of those. We can look to others as if being a healthy well standing Christian, standing tall, rooted well, dressed with all the right character that a believer should have and yet produce no fruit. This is crucial, looking right, seemingly doing right – even the very thing leaders/teachers maybe says to do and appear, yet produces no fruit that extends the Kingdom of God is a failure that is costly.

Jesus tells the parable of God as the vine dresser and the branches with no fruit He cuts off and throws into the fire.[1] There is only one way we can produce fruit – that is to receive from the vine which is Jesus. To behave rightly as a Christian, to practice all the right things as seen by others: go to church, be in Sunday School, go to Bible Studies, join in Prayer Meetings, etc – all seeming right things to do, but without producing fruit gets us nowhere except into the fire. The only way we can truly produce fruit is when we truly give up trying (producing from our own power) and totally trust in the vine (Jesus) to produce fruit in us. We can seemingly look right to others and to ourselves but unless we totally depend on receiving the sap (power) from the vine we will only look leafy with no fruit. It is only when we totally surrender to Jesus, totally yielding every effort on our part, that Jesus can, and will, produce fruit in us which we never thought possible.

Sometimes we try so hard at being good Christians that we get in the way of Christ to work in us. Have your children ever tried to help you do something? It is surely good that they want to help, but first they do not have the ability even though they want to help, and as long as they are trying, and trying very hard, the thing is not getting done and they are truly just in the way for us to do it right. As long as we in our own effort, even though thinking it is right, in our own force of work to produce the fruit, we are so busy at it Christ cannot get near in us to the work so fruit is produced. It is like the person who talks so fast and so much we cannot get a word in edgewise. When we try so hard this is the problem Jesus has in producing fruit in us.

Many things in God's word seems illogical, this is one of them. To allow Christ to produce fruit in us we have to try less, to get out of the way of thinking we know what we should do. Paul tells us God puts His will into our being[2] and if we stop trying so hard on our own thinking we know what to do, and instead look inside ourselves we will find an urging God has put there that He wants us doing. Remember you are in the yoke with Jesus,[3] better to find out where He is going than to pull on the yoke trying to go someplace else. Many times the urging inside us may be something we are uncomfortable with and we shy away from it, but it is the very thing God will give us victory in with Him getting all the credit, remember Gideon had to get rid of all the soldiers except for 300.[4]

God wants the victory and the glory in what fruit grows in us, it is the sap that comes from the vine, it is Jesus at work in us. I want to produce all the fruit I can to see the Kingdom of God move forward in this world – the only way I can do this is totally, 100%, no corner hidden, surrender to Jesus all that I am, all that I think, all that I do, even all that seems right to me. I must become less that Jesus can become more in me.[5]

1	Jn.15:1-6
2	Philp.2:13
3	Mt.11:29&30
4	Jdg. 7:2-7
5	Jn.3:29&30

The king asked, "How did you get in here without the appropriate wedding garment?" This was in the parable Jesus taught about the king who gave a wedding banquet for his son. (Mt. 22:2-13) It doesn't take much insight to know the Son is Jesus and the king is our Father in heaven. The scriptures in other places tell us there will be a wedding and a banquet. Is says we the church are the bride and we will be married to Jesus.[1] We are not even permitted to dress ourselves. It is someone else who dresses us appropriately.* The one who the king asked how he got in not being dress right is apprehended, tied hand and foot, and cast down into the darkness (of what the scripture refers to other places as the lake of fire). Again we see that if what we are dressed with as Christians is only that of which we have done ourselves without yielding ourselves (surrender) to another it will not be sufficient to remain at the wedding feast even if we think we have a right to be there. That appropriate garment that we must have seems to be the blood of Christ and His righteousness. We receive it freely when we accept Jesus Christ as Lord and Master.

There is nothing we can build on the blood to qualify us any more, not our behavior, not our obedience, not our sufferings. These things will benefit our lives in this world in blessings and God's favor, but none of them will help us get into the wedding banquet. It is only the blood of Christ that will get us into heaven – anyone without it will be cast down. It is hard for us in a culture where there are no blood sacrifices given to know the value, even though if there were they would do us no good. Yet it is difficult to relate to the value of the blood of the sacrifice. We must go into the Old Testament to find this value. In the course of Genesis 31:44-55 Laban and Jacob make a covenant between them. There is a heap of rocks made and they eat upon the heap. It doesn't make it clear of the timing of when they ate for later in the verses it tells us Jacob made a sacrifice which they ate on the mountain then saying that Laban left. It seems the sacrifice had something to do with the agreement between them, possibly a sealing of it.

There is a comment by the commentator of The Complete Jewish Study Bible about 1Sammuel 11:1 where he comments, *"Literally, to 'cut a treaty' is a reference to the animal sacrifice that was a seal of the covenant between two parties."* This may have been what Jacob and Laban did. In Genesis 15:8-18 God makes a covenant with Abram where five animals are sacrificed. In Exodus 24:5-8 we see the value of the blood as the blood was sprinkled on the altar consecrating it and on the people with Moses saying this to them, *"This is the blood of the covenant which the LORD has made with you according to all these words"* (v. 8 NKJV). There is a value God puts on the blood that is not understood in our day, yet we must believe because we are told of the value of it. In a spiritual way we must all be covered with the blood of the Perfect Sacrifice which is Christ to enter the wedding banquet.

To take note, when Jesus appeared with the apostles one of the first times after His resurrection He said to them, **"see I have flesh and bone."**[2] Do you notice what is missing? He says nothing of blood, he no longer has any, it was all given on the cross for all of us.

*Here there is something in the translation that trips us up. Many translations in Revelation 19:8 implies our fine linen is our righteous acts. This is wrong according to **The Complete Word Study Dictionary**, here is what they say the word means, *"The rights or claims which one has before God when he becomes His child by faith through Christ. In Rev_19:8, dikaiõmata is translated "the righteousness" of saints, and in Heb_9:1 "ordinances" of divine service, which word actually means legal rights of the saints"* It is the rights we have as adopted children. Scripture can not contradict itself and we are told there is none righteous, *'"There is none righteous, no, not one;...There is none who does good, no, not one."* (Rom. 3:10&12 NKJV). It is the righteousness of Christ that clothes us.

---

1   Rev.19:7-9
2   Lk.24:39

The book of Job has to be taken in the right sense. It is about a man who stood before God in integrity. Then the devil challenges that integrity with bringing calamity upon his life but Job retains his integrity through the whole ordeal. The truth that we can see of God is only in the first two chapters and the last five chapters for in 42:7 the scripture tells us that Eliphas, Bildad, and Zophar did not speak the things of God that were right. Even what Job says in the chapters between 2 and 38 cannot be given value because he speaks out of distress. God in 38:2 speaks directly to Job and asks *"Who is this--darkening counsel, By words without knowledge?"* (YLT) In the 36 chapters between 2 and 38 what there is for us to see is the foolish statements of men when they think they know more than they do. The main thing to see in these chapters is that Job never gives up his integrity even though he is without knowledge. Any teaching that uses any scripture in the chapters between 2 and 38 to show anything except the foolishness of man should not be given heed – the words found there are only the foolishness of men, not the truth of God.

There are always those who want to think they are more than what they are. These were the friends of Job wanting to give him council. We see the same in the time of Jesus. All of Matthew chapter 23 is about a rebuke of those who claim to be religious but are only on the outside with nothing changed of the evilness of the heart. This is a warning to us to be sure. We should make every effort to see that it is our heart that is changed. Jesus said that out of the heart man speaks. I think we can also see that many of our actions (natural responses) also originate from the heart. An angry response, a statement out of pride, an arrogant placing of ourselves above another, all are responses out of the heart that are wrong. Sometimes people speak without having all of the information, again they don't know what they think they know. This is what happens to Paul as he moves toward Jerusalem where he knows he must go. As we see what Paul does in Acts 21-23 we learn that sometimes those around us do not see what God has called us to do.

In Acts 21:4 the people shown what will happen to Paul by the Holy Spirit try their best to convince Paul not to go to Jerusalem. In Acts 21:10-12 again the people by the Holy Spirit are told what will happen to Paul if he goes to Jerusalem. Paul is determined to go seemingly knowing this is what the Lord wants him to do. It is evident this is what the Lord wanted because of what He says to Paul in Acts 23:11. Not all around us, even as sincere and faithful as they may be, can always see, or discern, what God is aligning us to do. Sometimes we have to resist their counsel permitting them, with grace towards them, to think we are not right – we must adhere to what it is that God has called us to.

Jesus, in Matthew chapter 24, speaks of His return and the end of the age (v. 3). This is a bit of a mystery, the apostles speak in their writings that they expected Jesus to return soon and now two millennia have passed and we are still waiting. We can be sure Jesus will return, the end of the age to come, the new heaven and new earth to be established, and God will be present with us and we with Him. Jesus tells us here to be watching, expecting His return. He tells us the signs that will take place so we will know. But that which we can know is only of the season that He will return, He says as you see the young shoots on the fig tree you know that summer is near.

There has been many who have predicted the day of Jesus' return (with their calibration and supposed insight) and have been wrong. Jesus tells us to watch, He also says, speaking to the disciples (and to us), that we will not know the day. Even more, Jesus says that it will be when we do not expect Him. Jesus tells us that no one knows, even the angels don't know what day or hour He will return. It is only the Father that knows. Jesus tells us in Acts, *"It is not for you to know times or seasons which the Father has fixed by his own authority"* (1:7 RSV). Our part is to be ready, He tells us, *"Watch therefore, for you do not know what hour your Lord is coming"* (Mt. 24:42 NKJV).

We want to think we will know the time and then we can hurry and prepare. Jesus tells a parable in chapter 25 about ten virgins who were waiting for the bridegroom's coming. These virgins are us waiting for our Lord's coming. We don't know when it will be, at noon, evening, or midnight. We must be ready. What is it to be ready? There were five virgins who did not make sure they had enough oil, but the other five made sure they had enough. We are to have enough oil in our lives when Jesus comes. In the scriptures, many times the oil represents the Holy Spirit. This is what we need to be sure of, that we have the Holy Spirit in our lives. The other five virgins let the Spirit slip in their lives. Are you in such a relationship with God that the Holy Spirit is active in your life? *"But the one who endures to the end will be saved"* (Mt. 24:13 ESV).

Those in the early days of the church thought that Jesus was coming soon.[1] He is still on His way waiting for the Father to tell Him when. We are the virgins, the bride waiting for His coming. We need to be ready, we need to be about His business, we need that river of life flowing through us in whatever it is that Jesus has for each of us to be doing.[2] Make sure your lamp is full with its light burning for others to see. *"Watch therefore, for you do not know what hour your Lord is coming."*

---

1   Philp.4:5
2   Jn.7:38

Yesterday, we read Jesus' answer to the disciples' question in Mt. 24:3. We spoke some of the ten virgins. Today we pick up where Jesus goes on to give examples by parables: 'The talents' and 'The sheep and the goats'. In the parable of the ten virgins one of the things He teaches is a continuation of what He spoke in Mt. 24:40-42 which is to be watching. The Amplified Bible in Mt. 24:42 and Mt. 25:13 give the meaning of watch therefore as: *'give strict attention and be cautious and active'*. In The Complete Word Study Dictionary some of the words in its definition are: *'attitude of alertness'* and *'in view of tests of spiritual life'*. These two definitions from the Amplified Bible and the dictionary are very much alike. Jesus speaks of being watchful (knowing He is coming and being about His business) for as the flood came with surprise on the people in the time of Noah Jesus' coming will be a surprise to many but we are not to be surprised.[1] Jesus re-emphasis this by telling the parable of the ten virgins ending with the same caution (or maybe even a warning) to be watchful (Mt. 25:13).

Jesus does not want us to be slothful about His business. The very next thing Jesus speaks about is that He has made an investment in us by dying on the cross paying a high price[2] and He wants to see that investment prosper. Those who have invested well He rewards and invites to share the joy which He enjoys. The last parable in chapter 25 Jesus speaks about those who pretend to do His will and those who really do His will.

The interesting thing is the ones who have really done the Lord's will are surprised to find out that they had. 'The servants the Master put in charge' (Mt.24:45-47), 'The ten virgins' (Mt. 25:1-12), 'The entrusted talents' (Mt. 25:14-30), 'The sheep and the goats' (Mt. 25;31-46) - all speak of how we are to live. We are to be aware He has given a work into our hands, to live our daily lives with our lamps full being a light to the world. We are to remember the investment He has made in us doing all we can to multiply our number. We are to allowing our light to shine[3] and the river flow from our innermost being,[4] allowing His Spirit to flow through us. If we let that light shine and the river flow we will be doing much of His work without even knowing it.

---

1   Gen.7:4,11,23
2   Acts 20:28 & 1Cor.6;20
3   Mt.5:16
4   Jn.7:37-39

Jesus knew that the end of His mission on this earth among men as one of them was soon to come. Jesus knew this was to come saying the scriptures had to be fulfilled. (Mt. 26:24, 31, Acts 26:22&23) He was telling His disciples He would be delivered over to men and crucified, that He had been prepared with perfume (by the woman) for His burial. Jesus knew this was to happen but even for Jesus, this was not easy. Jesus was distressed and went off to pray in the garden of Gethsemane, a place of agony, great sorrow, and a place of coming within one's self to the yielding to the purpose of God.

Jesus in leaving that place of prayer, where He had been alone, for even the close three that He took with Him and asked to pray were asleep. In His leaving that prayer, yielding to the will of the Father, He was immediately assaulted with the betrayal of a kiss as by one calling himself a follower, yet a leader to those who had come with sword and club to arrest Him. If those who came to arrest Him knew who Jesus was – even if they did not listen to Him – would have known that swords and clubs would not be enough if He were not willing to go with them.

Jesus knew there was a battle taking place, but not an earthly one. This battle was taking place in the spiritual realm and satan unknowingly was about to lose. Peter drew his sword and attacked in Jesus' defense but Jesus told him to put his sword away. Peter did not understand how the battle would be waged. It often seems to us as we try to follow Jesus and begin to do the work in our own thought of how we should do it, that Jesus would say **'Stop, put away your method, that He will tell us how it should go.'** To help know this better let us look at the following, *"For My thoughts are not your thoughts, Nor are your ways My ways," says the LORD. "For as the heavens are higher than the earth, So are My ways higher than your ways, And My thoughts than your thoughts"* (Isa. 55:8&9 NKJV).

As we follow Jesus, as we take up the work He gives us, as we pray about entering that work we need to keep these verses in mind. The other that helps is to know this, *"Not by might, nor by power, but by my Spirit, saith Jehovah of hosts"* (Zech. 4:6 ASV). Peter tried by his own might and power but Jesus got the job done by the Spirit.

ACTS – some say 'The Acts of the Apostles' yet the book of Acts is more than that. Acts is the record of the actions and happenings in the early Church of more than the apostles. If we take the attitude that it is only the apostles to be seen it is easy to assume it is only a record of history to see what happened then. When we see Acts as the actions and happenings of many in the early beginning of the Church we find there are examples there for us to follow. Not all of the preaching which was accompanied by signs and wonders were done by the apostles only. They were done by other disciples also and we as disciples of Christ should be doing some of these same things. It may be that the same phrase satan used on Eve in the garden is still used on us in the Church today to try to decrease the effect of the Church in the world.

The main emphasis of what satan said to Eve was 'Did God really say' which planted doubt in Eve's mind and today satan says the same thing to many in the Church. Because of the doubt satan plants in the hearts of many today in the Church, there is little belief that the things which we read in Acts should still be happening in the Church today. Many say that all the great moves of God through those believers were only for a short time in order to establish the Church. They listen to satan saying 'Did God really say' and come to the conclusion that the signs and wonders, and the hearing of angels, and the casting out of demons, and the raising the dead, etc. were only for the early Church, not believing, not praying about it, not trying. So therefore they have become a weak Church today trying to preach the gospel with no verification of any signs or wonders.

Acts is the name of the book that Luke wrote of a record of the happenings and actions of the early Church. Surely the name is of the acts or actions of the early Church, but to help see the broader fuller view of how it relates to us today we can remember ACTS as this: 'The Account Concerning the Truth of the Saints'. We all who believe are saints according to what the scriptures tells us.[1] We should see amongst ourselves the same accounts concerning us today as truth living in the Church as we see was living in the Church then in the book of Acts. God tells us to seek and search. This is one of those things we need to be seeking and searching to find the truth.

---

[1]   1Cor.1:2, 14:33, Jude 1:3

The greatest work that any Christian can do is 'Die to self'. We can see this is what Job ended up doing at the end of his complaint. In Job 40:3-5 after being confronted by God he dies to self saying he is of small account and vile and that he will close his mouth and even cover it with his hand. Job realizes he had spoken in arrogance and ignorance knowing nothing before God. Dying to self is the greatest work that we can accomplish but it may be the most difficult to accomplish. In our reading in the last chapter of Matthew today there is one verse that may skip our attention which has so much truth. Verse 15 speaks of a lie that was told to the Jewish people and was still believed by many in the day Matthew wrote his gospel record. When we people today do not want to hear the truth or don't want to believe it we latch onto a lie and give the lie power in our lives and we are deceived.

Paul at the end of his ministry speaks with the Jews in Rome fearing that the lies spoken in Jerusalem had reached and affected the Jews there in Rome.[1] Surely to Paul's delight they had not heard of any of the lies about Paul (Acts 28:21). But about the faith in Jesus Christ, the lie that began in Jerusalem (Mt. 28:15) and all the rest that had been said by the chief priest and elders (Mt. 28:11-13), had spread so far that even in Rome the Jews had heard that this sect was everywhere denounced (Acts 28:22). It seems that we, being people, are quick and willing to believe a lie rather than the truth. God says in Isa. 55:8&9 His ways and His thoughts are far high above ours. It takes a faith of believing and dying to self (a giving up of our opinion and the conclusion of our minds) to accept and put trust in what God speaks to us and teaches us in His word. It is only when we give up trying (when we die to self) that we can finally move ahead with God. Many times I think of Moses leading the Israelites out of Egypt at God's command. In our minds of strategy to escape the Pharaoh and his army we would have surely done something different. We would never have led the people up against a sea where there was no route of escape.

God's way is so much higher than ours. The people only feared, but Moses knew this was where God wanted them even if he may have not known when he led them there what God was going to do. Not only did God provide a great escape (His way) but also lured Pharaoh and his army into a trap destroying the enemy of Israel (His way). God's way is always the best and we must believe all that He says rather than the lie. Dying to self is the hardest work we will ever do but it will produce the greatest outcome as God begins to work through us (His way).

---

1   Acts 28:17-21

'**Prayer**' is the subject the Holy Spirit has spoken to me today. In Romans chapter 1 the first place we see Paul indicate his prayer is v. 8; he thanks God for the believers in Rome and for their faith. This is a form of prayer. Prayer seems to be more than a petition for our needs, it is a conversation with God. The high and greatest point of prayer is when God is replying to what we speak and His presence is experienced by our spirit. Most time spent in prayer is not this high point and many times we are the only one speaking – but we know God is listening to our every word. Paul has a confidence that God always hears him. Therefore thanksgiving should always be part of our prayer. The next verse (v. 9) Paul says he incessantly always mentions them (the believers in Rome) in his prayers. By the way Paul begins v. 9 we can see that it is probable that when he prays for them it is about the gospel spreading among the spiritual growth of that body of believers as indicated in v. 11&12. We should in our prayers pray for the spreading of the gospel – Jesus said that the harvest is ready, that we should pray for harvesters. [1]

There are those of us who have the courage to share with those around us what Jesus has done in our lives. You may note that I said each who has courage, there are a few who have courage on their own to share the gospel, but we are all called to speak to others. This is why we must pray for the spreading of the gospel – that we ask God to give all of us His children courage and boldness to speak about Him and of Him. In Acts 4:29, the apostles and believers in Jerusalem prayed for boldness to speak God's word. If the apostles needed the blessing of boldness from God, how much more do most of us need God's blessing of boldness today, even now. We must pray for one another to receive from God the courage to speak of His greatness. There is a prayer of Paul's which we need to see and hear. Paul speaks about what he prays for in v. 13-15. In the prayer in v. 10 he pleads that somehow he can go to those in Rome. When we ask for something in prayer, are we willing to accept how God works it out and brings it about? Paul was determined in his heart to go to Rome, "*Paul purposed in the spirit, when he had passed through Macedonia and Achaia, to go to Jerusalem, saying, After I have been there, I must also see Rome*" (Acts 19:21 ASV).

Then God revealed to Paul that if he goes to Jerusalem he would be arrested and imprisoned, [2] Paul responded, 'not only was he willing to be arrested, bound, and imprisoned – but even to die for the name of the Lord.' [3] Then Paul hears this from the Lord, "*But the following night the Lord stood by him and said, "Take courage, for as you have testified about me at Jerusalem, so you must bear witness also at Rome*" (Acts 23:11 RSV). Paul's prayer that he speaks of in Romans 1:10 is answered and the remainder of the book of Acts from chapter 21 speaks of all Paul went through as God answered his prayer to get him to Rome. Are we willing to go through what God has in mind to give us in the answer to our prayer? It is important that we pray, and we must be willing for God to answer our prayer in His way, our way may not bring the Kingdom results that God's way does.

---

1   Lk. 10:2
2   Acts 21:11
3   Acts 21:13

Today the Holy Spirit speaks to me the word 'Longsuffering'. As we read in Genesis chapter 29 today Jacob practices longsuffering with Laban. We will see in chapters to come how Laban keeps changing the arrangements made with Jacob constantly making the requirement more. Even the daughter Laban promises to Jacob for his seven years of work is substituted with her sister, the one Jacob was not interested in. I do not say Jacob was any angel, but I do see him practicing longsuffering with Laban. Jacob has a right to raise a great complaint but never pushed the issue to justice. Jacob continued putting up with Laban even though Laban did not do rightly. Jacob continued on with Laban another seven years for the daughter of Laban He really wanted. Even after that Laban kept changing the arrangements. In chapter 2 of Mark, today we can see that Jesus continues God's longsuffering as He speaks with the Pharisees, scribes, and the Jewish people as they complained about what He was doing and what He was saying.

The Jewish leaders for years had not seen the Law correctly, not allowed the effects of the Law to bring about good behavior in their lives. Jesus through His ministry speaks about what the Law was and how the Jews had misconstrued it, or misunderstood it. The Jews were like Laban with Jacob, they did not follow through on their part of the agreement of the covenant. In Romans chapter 2 Paul opens his argument with how the Jews promotes the Law to others, declaring the Jew's right to declare the Law by his belonging to God by his inheritance and circumcision. Paul more than likely uses this same argument he presented here at the beginning of entering any town when he went into the synagogue to preach first to the Jews.

Paul presents this to the Jews trying to show them by the way they live, by the things they do, and how they present the Law, are making their circumcision uncircumcision. The longsuffering of God is what has brought us all who believe to salvation. It was the longsuffering of God because if we are honest we will all admit we are guilty before God (Jew and Gentile) and should have been done away with long ago as those in the flood. God's longsuffering treats us as we do not deserve. We have received mercy and grace from a longsuffering God who did not only put up with our wrong doing, He pitied us, and made a sacrifice Himself, God the Father who offered God the Son on the cross as a sacrifice for sin. God did this in His longsuffering towards us to make a way we could be forgiven for our sins. We as mankind keep wanting to change the arrangement, but God never does. He calls out to us, *"Come to Me, all you who labor and are heavy laden, and I will give you rest"* (Mt. 11:28 NKJV).

Today we will look at 'Faith'. We see that Jacob had faith that God (the God of his father Isaac and Abraham) would bless him in spite of the way Laban threatened and cheated him. Jacob followed God even with all the obstacles before him. Following God, he finally comes back to the place of his father. Jacob is the father of the twelve patriarchs. Jacob ends up with all of his sons safe in Egypt, and you know the rest of the story. In our reading in Romans chapter 3 today Paul declares it is by faith, and by faith only, that we are accepted by God. Paul says the Law was there to do its job in guiding us to see we are imperfect. By the Law Paul later says it was how he came to realize that he coveted and coveting was seen by God as sin. Paul tells us (v. 5) that as we recognize our sinfulness it declares to us the righteousness of God.

Paul says (v. 1&2) that the Jews had a special place before God, not by their accomplishments or obedience – but because of Abraham and they were his children. Paul says that the declarations and knowledge of God was given through them over the ages since Abraham, and that the Messiah came from that bloodline. But Paul goes on to say that Jews and Gentiles alike are sinful people (v. 9) short of the acceptance of God by our accomplishment of good behavior (v. 20). Therefore Paul brings us to see that it is only by the faith as Abraham had before doing anything good or bad according to the law, that Abraham was seen with right standing before God. Paul tells us it is by that faith in the works God did in Jesus Christ on the cross that we have, and only by it (v. 26-28), right standing before God.

We are to remember, even though we are called to live rightly before God, that it is not by how we live, how we behave before God, it is by the faith, and only by the faith, that we are accepted by God and have eternal life. We only receive salvation by Jesus Christ and the work He did on the cross. It is a free gift, Jesus said, **'he who believes in Me has everlasting life'** [1] Many in the past walked with God by faith. What kind of faith did Abraham have to have to leave family and a place he knew to follow God to a place he did not know and had no idea of only because God said come? What about Paul, he followed a mistaken thought as he arrested followers of Christ until he had an encounter with the risen Lord receiving salvation. He then preached Christ being considered a traitor by the Jews. How was his faith to do such? Faith is something we must walk in with God.

---

1   Jn.6:47

The subject today is 'Peace'. It is interesting how the Holy Spirit has been putting together the subjects of the last five days. It started with 'Dying to self', then 'Prayer', then 'Longsuffering', then 'Faith', and today it is 'Peace'. I remember the words of Jesus, 'peace I give to you, not as the world gives, but as I give'. These all seem to be important elements in our Christian lives.

Dying to self is crucial, without dying to our own thoughts and judgments we are not able to accept what Jesus has to say. Not only did Jesus die for us giving us salvation, He also, if we will listen, tells us of a better way to live, this begins to grow in us from the new birth if we allow it. If we die to self then we need prayer to help us develop and find our new life by establishing a relationship with God. God's ways are not our ways[1] and longsuffering has to be part of our lives. Longsuffering seems to be that of patient endurance. The next thing the Holy Spirit spoke of was faith. Dying to self allows us to begin to develop faith. Without faith, longsuffering would be unbearable. We see these first four things practiced, even though not perfect, by Abraham. The thing that is brought to us today is peace. There is a peace when it is realized that God's blessing is fully ours. Paul in Romans chapter 4 today tells us our salvation and relationship are given to us by God through His grace. "For this reason it is by faith, in order that it may be in accordance with grace" (v. 16 NASB).

Paul tells us Abraham's righteousness (right standing with God) was given to him by God because of his faith. There were not works on Abraham's part that gained him this righteousness – the Law had not been given yet. The Law was given through Moses over 400 years later. Faith is how we gain salvation and righteousness today by believing in and receiving Jesus Christ into our lives. We no longer receive by the Law, but by grace given to us by God. When we come to the place that we know our right standing with God is complete because of our believing and accepting what Jesus did on the cross for us without works, any at all on our part, we find an eternal peace that is not like the peace the world gives (false peace), but the peace God gives.

When the burden of performing to receive is lifted from us we find we are able to much easier begin living the way Jesus calls us to live. Because of God's grace, the stress of getting it right is removed. "peace I give to you; not as the world gives do I give to you" (Jn. 14:27 NKJV). We could not have peace with the Law, but with grace we have it fully as Christ gives it. Receive it, know it, and believe it.

---

1   Isa.55:8&9

Liberty is what comes when we meet Jesus Christ. In Mark chapter 5 we see three that meet Jesus. The first was the man possessed by demons, Jesus orders the demons to leave him. The demon-possessed man is liberated, freed, given peace, and tells to all of his experience as Jesus instructs him. The second we see is the woman who had suffered for twelve years with an ailment which none of the doctors had been able to free her from. She met Jesus and by one touch of His clothes, even just the hem of His clothes, she was liberated from her ailment. Jesus told her that her faith (in Him and in the Father) restored her (liberated her to her former health) and to go in peace. The third one to meet Jesus was the (dead) daughter of Jairus. Jesus said to her, '**I say to you arise**' (from your death). At those words of Jesus the girl was liberated from death coming back to life, the fullness of life. The parents were told to give her some food to eat. Paul begins his 5th chapter of Romans with, *"Being therefore justified by faith, we have peace with God through our Lord Jesus Christ"* (ASV).

Paul is saying (and continues the argument for) that we are granted liberty when we accept (meet) Jesus into our lives. Paul's convincing evidence that he brings in this chapter is that even though sin has come upon all men because of the sin of Adam the greater power of grace has come upon (liberating) all men by (those who accept and receive) Jesus Christ which is the greater power. How blind the devil tries to keep mankind by putting in the heart of man the desire to accomplish in pride of self accomplishment and self worth by what one himself accomplishes. This is self pride at its height. Pride is the very thing that is in opposition of what God wants to do in our lives. Pride is what keeps us away from what God has to give us.[1] Pride is what moved the devil to rebel against God.[2]

Pride is what caused Adam and Eve to sin. Pride is even what keeps people trying to please God by following the Law. Pride only gets us into trouble, it prevents us from receiving all the good things God offers us. Even our salvation cannot be received if we remain fully in pride, if we do we will end up at the end of time in the same place as the devil.[3]

We may not give up all pride when we are saved, but we have faced our sinfulness knowing we need help. Dying to self is that dealing with our pride, even sometimes on a daily basis. If we go to God in a humble manner knowing our need God will help us, even on a daily basis, to liberate us from more and more of our pride – pride must die that we may live. Meeting up with Jesus, whether it was in the days He walked this earth, or as we meet Him spiritually today, brings liberty to each one who trusts in Him.

---

1   1Jn.2:16
2   1Tim.3:6
3   Rev.20:10

For Christ we live, to sin we have died, to eternity in heaven we go forward. Paul tells us (when we have accepted Jesus into our lives and received salvation) that our old self (sinful man) was nailed to the cross with Jesus and died with Jesus so that the power of sin no longer has authority over us. (Rom. 6:6) Before salvation we yielded to sin knowing no other way of life, even to what sometimes seemed to be good to ourselves and to society around us, and yet was sin when compared and measured up against God's holiness. Paul speaks of a confusing thing in Romans 6:14, he says we are no longer under the dominion of sin since we are no longer under the Law, but that we are free to choose since we are now under grace. There is this tendency of mankind to find self-worth (sometimes resulting in or abiding in pride) by wanting to accomplish so that before God we have earned a place, a position. We gravitate back to the Law to somehow try to show ourselves approved by our effort to receive from God.

We are not able to receive as wages the full place of perfect forgiveness because we are not able to perform the fullness of perfect work which is required. Paul tells us in Romans 5:12 that all men have sinned. Peter in Acts 15:10 tells his fellow Jews that they have not been able to (completely) bear the yoke of the Law. When we try to accomplish, to make ourselves approved, by the Law we again put ourselves (as slaves) under the Law that Jesus has freed us from. Some may say, 'Yeal, but the Ten Commandments, are we not to follow them?' What does Paul say in Romans 6:16 – that anything (which we strive) we continually surrender to we become its slave. We are to be obedient to grace, no longer attaching ourselves to the Law, even the Ten Commandments (v. 14).

The obedience which leads to righteousness is the obedience Paul speaks of. From where does this righteousness come from – it comes from believing in Christ, surrendering to Christ, choosing to live a life under grace rather than the bondage of sin. Jesus said, **'come to Me, believe in Me, follow Me'**. This is what we are to be in obedience to, His call. All that we need is in Him, the Author and Finisher of our faith.[1] He came, He offers, what will we choose, it is a liberty to choose now that we have been set free.

---

1   Heb. 12:1&2

It is hard to know the will of God, it is dangerous to go forward in our lives without it. To Know God's will, His immediate will, for our lives is important. He knows what He wants of us – how can we know? Life is not easy, even more difficult is finding the will of God. This is what drives us to written regulations (the obsolete Law given to Moses {Rom. 7:6} or the traditions of the elders {men before us}) where we can feel we are accomplishing yet it is like going by a place of business and continue to leave our payment even though the business no longer is operating and the payments are gaining us nothing. Jesus speaks about those who make an effort (and tries to get others to do so also) to follow the traditions of the elders. Paul speaks about the effort of following a Law that no longer gains us anything. [1] Paul tells us we are now to follow the Spirit and live by the Spirit. [2]

This is not an easy thing to do yet this is what God is calling us to do. Many denominations which have started with a man who learned how to follow the Spirit now after a couple of generations have developed rules and regulations. They have reverted to this because it is not easy to follow the Spirit as the founding leader had learnt to do. We are drawn to the easy way of doing things, even though being obedient to rules and regulations takes a diligence, it is easier than seeking and hearing and learning of the Spirit. God calls us to a difficult walk and a strong faith to expect the Holy Spirit to work in us and through us. Are we truly dead to self, [3] are we truly seeking to do it His way? Or are we in our own effort trying to please Him by following rules and regulations rather than following His Spirit who is willing and wanting to guide us? Have we really heard what Jesus said to the woman at the well?

He is telling her truth, a truth that goes into the future, the future of the Church which we now are part of. Jesus didn't tell her it would be that way for just a while, He didn't say it would be that way for the first one hundred years, not the first five hundred years, not even a thousand, He said this is how it will be. So what He said is for now as well, what was it He said: *"the true worshipers will worship the Father in spirit and truth, for the Father is seeking such people to worship him"* (Jn. 4:23 ESV). It is by Spirit we are to worship, it is by Spirit we are to follow, it is by the Spirit we will know of how and where to go. It takes a dying to self to find the leading of the Spirit. He wants our full attention so that He can tell us what Jesus is doing and what Jesus wants of us. Jesus wants us to follow Him, He knows what the Father's plans are, we are His servant-slaves to help accomplish the work of the Father.

Dying to self sometimes even means stopping what we are doing to wait on the Spirit. I heard one teaching that said God is a gentleman, He won't interrupt or enter where He is not invited. The Holy Spirit is God also and if He is not invited in He won't interfere, you have to invite Him. Will you stop, and wait, and invite Him in?

---

1   Gal.3:21,23-25, Heb.8:13
2   Gal.5:16,18,25
3   Lk.9:23, Lk.14:43

What are we doing? What is our being? All that we have as mankind is a failure. We, with our intelligence, our hard work, our accomplishments – anything we do of our own strength, efforts, intelligence, etc. has no value. We fail the test of God. He sets the standard and as much as we try we are always short. It started in the Garden of Eden, the only thing we had to do was not eat from one particular tree. All the rest of the trees in the garden were ours to eat from and do what we wanted. Just that one requirement from God – not to eat from that one tree, and we failed. You may say that was Adam and Eve, not us. Don't you realize they started off in life even better than we, they were the direct creation of God and they failed.

We have less to start with than they, so our thought that we can do better than they only comes out of our arrogance and pride which disqualifies us from the standard God set – we have failed. Paul tells us in so many words that God wanted us to know the truth about ourselves so He gave man (the Jews) the Law which Paul tells us shows us our sinfulness. There is an interesting thing about the Law that many may not see. The scriptures tells us the Law was given because the Jews (and us as mankind) were a stiff-necked people. Abraham followed no Law – he followed God without needing a Law. Abraham's children however, being delivered from Egypt seeing many of God's miracle, yet grumbled shortly after leaving Egypt. God delivered them from Pharaoh by luring Pharaoh and his army into the Red Sea destroying the whole Egyptian army. [1] Not so long after that while Moses was on the mountain again they showed their character – they were not like Abraham.

Paul and Peter and maybe James saw that man could not be justified or righteous by the Law. It has taken something greater than the Law to save us - it has taken God in His mercy giving us grace through Jesus Christ to do what we could not do. So as Paul is telling us in Romans chapter 8, that if in our flesh we failed the requirements of the Law, why would we believe we can meet the requirements of life with that same flesh? We are saved by the grace of God as we accept Jesus Christ as Lord, and it is only by the working of the Holy Spirit (again from God) in our lives that we can fully meet the requirements of life. We must not live by our flesh, we must search out, seek, find, listen, learn, and walk by the Holy Spirit if we want the best God has for us and for the Church, His people on earth.

---

1   Ex.14:23-28

The **peace of adoption**, the **blessing of belonging**, the **assurance of acceptance**. These are great things for the believer in Jesus to be aware of. None of us deserve what God has given us. Even God's chosen people, a people He took for Himself from among all the nations because of the faith of Abraham according to what Paul says in Romans 9:31&32 never accomplished under the Law to receive the blessing. They knew of God, heard of His ways, were given His Laws, shown (and made the keepers of) a copy of His temple which is in heaven, and yet were unable to be found righteous by their own merit. Paul says they walked in their own human effort trying to claim righteousness rather than obtaining the way their ancestor Abraham did by faith. Therefore Paul tells us that those who have become children of Israel, of Abraham, are children by faith, not by bloodline.

All that we receive as Christians from God is because of our faith, not from our works for God. This frees us to do the works of God by having a freedom and assurance of spirit being able to focus on the work and not on if we have done enough, or rightly, to please God. When we are preoccupied with meeting the requirement it takes up a place in our mind that constantly is drawing our attention. When we are freed from this preoccupation it permits us to listen and sense deep inside to what God has placed there, and what God has for us to do. I will remind you again what is missed by so many of what God will do in each of us: *"for it is God who is working in you both to will and to work for the sake of His good pleasure."* (Philp. 2:13 NKJV).

God works putting in you His will, that is where you will find His guidance in you, it is planted within. God works putting His desire in you to do the works He has for you, that is where you will find what He has for you as an individual to do, it is registered within you. We many times are looking outside of ourselves to find what God has for us, what He wants of us to do. We look to lists made up from scripture of what we should do, we listen to others who we suppose know what we should do. Sometimes we look far and wide to find what God would have us do when all the time it is within us where God has planted it.

When we know from that place what it is that God has arranged for us to do there is a confidence that we will succeed because God has arranged it, the only thing we have to do is give ourselves to it. How great are the things God wants to accomplish through each of us.[1] The peace, the blessings, and the assurance are ours by faith alone without any struggle on our part to accomplish. With this knowledge we can go happily into the work Jesus has given us to tell others of the gospel message, to teach and disciple those who are saved, and to expand the Kingdom of God on earth as it is in heaven.

---

[1]   Eph.2:4-10

There is an interesting progression in Mark chapter 10. The apostles become bewildered and perplexed. (v. 24&32) It starts out with the Pharisees questioning Jesus about a point of the Law that Moses had given them. Here are the disciples, chosen by Jesus, trying to be good Jews, walking with the first true prophet that has been in Israel in four centuries, even though He is much more than they believe. Now the Pharisees come speaking what all Jews knew was the words of Moses and Jesus says it is not quite so. Jesus says if a man divorces his wife and marries another he is guilty of adultery. Then people began bringing their children to Jesus and the disciples thinking they are a bother to Jesus try to keep them away. Jesus tells the disciples to let the children alone for to such belongs the Kingdom of God.

Not only this but Jesus tells the apostles that if they do not receive and accept the Kingdom of God like a child they will not enter it. Now this is way far away from the Law which is what all in Israel seen as the way to God. Then a rich man who has followed comes to Jesus asking what he must do to gain eternal life. Jesus tells him only of six commandments and the rich man says he has followed them all his life. Jesus checks the heart and not the Law, the rich man was told that if he wants to inherit eternal life he must sell all he has and give it to the poor, and then come follow Jesus. Now things for the apostles are getting difficult in their understanding. Jesus tells them it is easier for a camel to go through a needle than for a rich man to be saved. Then Jesus goes on.

When the apostles ask what they will get since they have given up all, Jesus tells them they will receive a hundred times more back along with persecutions. This has the apostles totally confused now. Jesus goes on to say that the first will be last, the last will be first, and to lead one must be slave of all. We many times read scripture and are confused, bewildered, and perplexed – we are not in bad company. Even the apostles many times didn't get it, their whole understanding of what they thought it was to be a follower of God was being turned inside out. The Holy Spirit is what helped the apostles to know as we see in the book of Acts and it is the Holy Spirit who will help us now who follow also to know. Read what Jesus said in Jn. 14:26.

As men (mankind before God) we can find ourselves thinking more of ourselves than we should. This is the place Job finds himself in, in the agony of his misery. It is not until the greatness of God is declared by Elihu that Job may have considered his right standing before God. At a point of right time God speaks out to Job (Job 38:1 & 40:1) questioning Job of really how great is he (Job). After God questions Job with many questions and Job realizes his place, he answers to God that he has no answer (no knowledge) and that he will say no more. Humility comes easy if we would but take our right place before God, but many of us have to be confronted with our shortcomings, being humiliated by God, to find this place of humility.

God is looking for a humble people (not wimps) to follow after Him, believing what He says, and do what/going where He tells us. Surrender is a great thing when we give up all we have and then are given by the Lord (in that state of humility) more than we ever had before. In the last week before Jesus was arrested and crucified He and His apostles/disciples were on their way to Jerusalem and Jesus cursed the fig tree. The disciples had seen Jesus do many strange things during their three years together, here is one of them. Jesus goes to the fig tree to find fruit and finds nothing but leaves. Mark tells us it was not the season for figs. Many things that Jesus did seemed odd, the very first one we read of is when He was with his parents at the age of twelve and He stayed behind in Jerusalem. Joseph and Mary finding He was not with the family traveling home returned to Jerusalem.

It may be they thought, what is this child, why would He do such a thing. By His answer when Joseph and Mary found Him He thought nothing wrong of it, He was in the Temple with those who spoke of God. Surely for Joseph and Mary this was odd behavior. If we truly humble ourselves before God doing things His way others will say we have odd behavior. Once we find out who we really are before God as Job did, we begin to act more and more like Jesus. This is how we look to a world that desires nothing to do with finding God, or following Him. Their condition is shaped by their own desires which are defective as compared to God. God calls us to come, to follow Him, to become more and more like Christ. This behavior does seem odd to the world.

What is sin? What do we see sin to be? Is it only those things in a list in the scriptures that are sins? What about anything that is opposite of God's way? Sin is what we constantly wrestle with, once we are saved there is a constant forgiveness available for those times we are not strong enough to stand against it,[1] yet we must stand against sin with all the power we have. To love our God is to shun sin, therefore it is in our heart, our soul, our mind, and our strength (Mk. 12:30) that we must make all effort to stand against sin. Sin may be much broader than we think. We are told if we think something is sin (which really is not) and we go on and do it then it is counted as sin to us. The sin here is our yielding to what we believe to be sin. It is our attitude many times that is the sin, not the action. Sin is what plagues the world. Paul tells us not to do what the world does, to go the other way not allowing ourselves to be overcome by evil (Rom. 12:2&21).

Even in the effort or disguise of being religious, if it is only our determined course, we are not doing it God's way and it may be sin. Jesus was time after time confronted and tested by the religious leaders in Israel as He thought and taught God's way. It seems many were in leadership by the sin of their heart. One time Jesus is confronted by the religious leaders and asked, **by what authority He did these things**[2] and He answered them by telling a parable which He shows the truth about them (Mk. 12:1-8). In v. 7 the vinedressers say to themselves **'let us kill the heir and inheritance will be ours'**. Jesus does not say that they say to themselves the vineyard will be ours, they say the inheritance will be ours. The inheritance is much more than just the vineyard, it is all of the man's wealth, it is about money. Some of the religious leaders may have maneuvered themselves into the position because of the wealth it would gain them.

In what Jesus was doing it would damage their path to that wealth so they are determined to stop Him. We have to be careful about what we do, we have to examining our motives (there are many others than wealth). We should look to see if our zeal to put forth religion is founded in an area where God does not want us. Even in living the Christian life following the easy path may not be God's way and a dangerous place for us to be.

---

1   1Jn.2:1&2
2   Mk. 11:28

What day is it? What time is it? Are we watching? Are we serving our Master rightly? Are we expecting His return at any time? Are we busy about His business? Are we doing what Jesus said? Are we living Jesus' way? Are we loving one another? This last question was Jesus' new (and last) commandment to us. It was not the world that He told us to love, it was one another, those of us in the body of Christ. We are found in Him, we are to be dead to self and alive in Him, we are to look like Him. Many times in the gospels it states, **'He loved'**. Paul reminds us that the sum of the Old Testament commandments is found in the second commandment Jesus gave us, to love our neighbor like our self. (Rom. 13:9)

Paul goes on to say that in practicing loving our neighbor we meet all the requirements of the Law. (Rom. 13:10) It is this which we are to be doing, to love one another. It is by this the world will know we are Christians, this is to be part of our witness to them. First of all, there should be a joy in those of us who are the Church (Church are the believing people, not a building). Is there a joy? This is not something you can put on and wear, if it is false the world will see it in a moment. The joy has to come from Christ being in us assuring us of the future, that our sins are forgiven, and that we have a place in heaven with God.

Sometimes this joy cannot come forth because we are holding on to something of this world. As many times I remind you we must die to self. This is when the joy comes, it is when we allow the life of Christ to come forth in us, His life in us, not ours any longer. The next thing is how they see us treat each other, do they see a sincerity in the joy we have together. Do we take care of each other, even like a family? This is what we have become, we are told we are children of the same Father, we are children of God. We should be looking forward to that time to come when we are all gathered together in heaven.

Jesus says to watch and be ready for His return at any time. (Mk. 13:32&33) Jesus tells us to be busy with the work He has given each of us to do. (Mk. 13:34) Then Jesus tells us to watch. (Mk. 13:35-37) So then we are to be busy with the work of the Kingdom of God: some planting the seed of the gospel, some watering the seed, and some harvesting. We are to be about producing fruit in ourselves and helping others to produce their fruit. We are to be busy about the business of the Kingdom of God, loving one another (not backbiting or gossiping), and watching (looking for Jesus' return and being alert spiritually). There is one thing Jesus says in the gospels that bothers me. Jesus asks the question **'When He comes will He find faith on earth?'** [1] What do you think? What will He find in you?

---

1 Lk.18:8

What is the opposite of peace? We may say confusion, chaos, war, etc. What Paul is telling us in Romans chapter 14, even though he speaks much of the Law, the Law is what he makes opposite of peace. Jesus said, **'Peace I give to you, not as the world gives, give I to you.'** [1] Jesus freed us from the Law by fulfilling it for us – it no longer has authority over us, we are under grace. This type of grace is what Paul is talking about. He is saying not to make new laws to govern believers, laws about what to eat and what not to eat. Not to make laws about what days to honor and what days not to honor. Paul's point: no matter how we live before God, when we are brought to that judgment seat of God we are all the same, all unqualified in and of ourselves. All, yes All of us have to have the blood of Christ that by grace our sins are forgiven.

The point Paul seems to be making is that if we, each of us our self, cannot meet the standard of God, how can we demand that others do what we see as right when we ourselves are not able to make ourselves right before God? We must understand grace, as it is what covers the entire body of Christ. Not to be confusing here, what brings the grace of God upon us is the blood of Christ that is upon us. We are spiritually covered in His blood, it is what keeps death away from us as the blood of the sacrificed lambs in Egypt on the doorposts and lintel keep death from entering the dwellings of the Jews that God was giving freedom. [2] We have been given freedom from the curse of death that came on us because of our sin. Our sins have been forgiven because of what Jesus did on the cross for us.

The grace of God is always sufficient for all who turn to it for the deepest of sin. [3] We must know this peace, we must have it by faith. The struggle of always trying to accomplish for God will always fail, there is never enough to pay for our sin. Jesus is the only one that could accomplish the task that would pay for our sin. God Himself died for us that we could be forgiven. Who could know, who could imagine, who can understand, that God would do this for us – yet He has.

---

1   Jn.14:27
2   Ex.12:23
3   Jn.1:16, 2Cor.9:8

The subject the Holy Spirit has spoken to me for today is 'love'. This is the God type love that He has for us. It is the fully giving type of love. It is the sacrificing for another type of love. It is the type of love that is a strange type of love in our American culture where getting ahead personally, individually, is the main force of our culture. It has come into our churches and is evident in our prayers which are more about our well-being and our needs and our pleasures. The God type of prayer in His type of love would mainly be others focused.

This is God's type of love. If we look with truth-seeking eyes we will see this type of love when we look at the cross. And we will hear of this kind of love when we are at the communion table hearing Jesus' words 'Remember Me'. This kind of love comes through clearly if we are willing to see and willing to hear in Paul's words of Rom. 15:1 *"We who are strong (mature spiritually) ought to bear with the failings and the frailties and the tender scruples of the weak: and not to please ourselves"* (AMPC).

In the last half of Mark chapter 14 and all of chapter 15 Jesus is acting in this type of love. He is falsely accused and arrested, He yields Himself to be taken by those who have come to arrest Him even though the power of His words is enough to push them back.[1] He is taken before the Jewish council to be judged by them not seeking His own pleasure to please Himself. Jesus could have taken the seat of the High Priest right then and there having twelve legions of angels from the Father to back Him up.[2] But that was not the will of the Father, that was not the God type of love. Self sacrificing for the benefit of others is the God type of love. In those last days before Jesus' arrest He gives the disciples His last commandment, 'to love one another' (believers).[3] He was speaking about the self sacrificing type of love. We can see this type of love in Jesus whom we are to become in His likeness.

Paul, after his confrontation by Jesus on the road to Damascus and the three days that followed was confronted by this type of love.[4] From that moment on Paul demonstrates and acts in this type of love and tries in his epistles to teach us of this type of love. Yes, it is a very foreign type of love in our culture, but if we allow and seek the Holy Spirit to help us know[5] we can be of this type of love. This is the type of love that Jesus acted in to bring us salvation. Paul demonstrated, even being will to be eternally condemned for the whole Jewish people to receive salvation.[6] God calls us to something that many of us know not. But if we truly seek it, and yield ourselves fully to God, He will work it in our lives to know and practice this type of love, the type of love we can see from Genesis to Revelation.

1	Jn.18:6
2	Mt.26:53
3	Jn.13:34, 15:12, 15:17
4	Acts 9:3-18
5	Jn.14:26
6	Rom.9:3

We are not so much different from those who followed Jesus for the three years, hearing His words, seeing His signs and wonders, and feeling the impression of His presence. Those were the ones who experienced Jesus in a special way. And we today have the benefit of following Jesus by their writings which we have in the New Testament, possibly a greater general knowledge of life. Yet in spite of all of this, they had and we have, both we and they, failings and difficulties in believing. Jesus said many times to those who were His disciples of how it would be yet they seemed surprised when Jesus was arrested, tried, and crucified. How many times has Jesus in our lives told us how it was going to be and we are surprised when it happens? Then there is that which makes us all equal, that which disqualifies us all, if nothing else does. That which regardless of rank, higher or lower, is a failure found in us all which is unbelief.

Mary Magdalene went to the tomb early in the morning, didn't find Jesus' body there, was spoken to by an angel, and was appeared to by the risen Jesus. Oh man, what a testimony to have! With this, she went with the great news to those who had been with Jesus and they refused to believe her (Mk.16:11). There were two of Jesus' followers who left Jerusalem after Jesus' crucifixion and were traveling to Emmaus when Jesus, who they thought was a stranger, walked with them speaking to them of how the scripture said this would happen to Jesus the Messiah. The two ask Jesus, who they thought was a stranger, to lodge with them that night. When they began their meal they recognized the stranger was Jesus in the way He blessed the food. Wow, what a testimony, they had walked for miles with the risen Lord, had set to eat with the Lord, and when He was recognized by them He vanished from their sight.

What great news, what an extraordinary experience. They hurried those many miles back to Jerusalem to share the great news that Jesus was alive, that Jesus had risen, with those who had followed Jesus and the other followers refused to believe them (Mk.16:13). The next thing that happens is Jesus appears to the eleven and He reprimands them reproving and reproaching them for their unbelief. We, like they, are found many times with unbelief. Sometimes it is what is written in scripture, or testimonies that others have, and because in our minds, as it was in the minds of those who were with Jesus, it seems impossible by our finite reasoning and thinking. If Jesus would appear to you right now, is there unbelief you have that He would speak to you about as He spoke to the eleven apostles?

The word the Holy Spirit brings to me today is **'Redemption'**. The definition which **Webster**(a Godly man) gives in his first two definitions are: *'1. Repurchase of captured goods or prisoners, the act of procuring the deliverance of persons or things from the possession and power of captors by the payment of an equivalent; ransom; release; as the redemption of prisoners taken in war; the redemption of a ship and cargo. 2. Deliverance from bondage, distress, or from liability to any evil or forfeiture, either by money, labor, or other means.'*

From what we see Webster saying it is a person or a thing that can do nothing to relieve themselves/itself from that by which it is bound being freed by the actions of another. In the scriptures we see God redeeming Joseph many times from the bondage he finds himself in, finally placing him as ruler in Egypt with none higher except for Pharaoh himself. Then, in a sense, we see Joseph redeeming his father, his brothers, and all that is theirs from the death a famine was bringing on the land. In the first chapter of Luke today we see the very first act of redeeming by God freeing Zachariah and Elizabeth from the bondage of barrenness. At the time of the dedication, purification, and circumcision of the child (John the Baptist) Zachariah, filled with the Holy Spirit, thanked and praised God because God had brought deliverance and redemption to His people (Lk.1:68). Because Zachariah was filled with the Holy Spirit he was speaking truth.

The redemption was being brought by Jesus which he knew well of because his relative Mary had stayed with him and his wife for three months (v.56). With the experience (and knowledge) Elizabeth had and by the praise Mary gives God (v.41-55) and surely many conversations they had (mostly Mary and Elizabeth, Zachariah only listened, not being able to speak) (v.20). Zachariah was speaking in v. 68 of Jesus. When Mary first arrived to visit with Elizabeth the child within (John the Baptist) leaped in her womb at Mary's voice of greeting. It may be that John the Baptist, even yet in the womb, rejoiced at the presence of his Lord Jesus Christ, even yet in the womb of Mary. Once Jesus was born and taken to be dedicated a man named Simeon praised God because he had been permitted before his death to see God's salvation for the people (the act of redemption) (Lk. 2:30).

There was also a prophetess named Anna there who also praised God talking of the child (Jesus) to all who were looking for the redemption of Jerusalem (Lk.2:38). Paul's writing in 1Corinthians1:4-9 with special attention to v.8 we see all that Paul is saying is about redemption and Paul ends the chapter at v.30 saying Jesus Christ has been made (by God) our wisdom, our righteousness, our sanctification, and our redemption. These things that we are made in Christ are made by the redeeming act of God through and by Jesus Christ. We are those who by our own effort were unable to free ourselves from the bondage we were held by and have been redeemed by God. There should be a speech of thanksgiving in our mouth and a gratitude in our heart for the redemption God has paid for us (Jesus on the cross) even if God never gave us another blessing in all our life.

Humbleness, sooner or later we are all faced with it. We can slip it on ourselves as a garment and wear it benefiting from the things God is able to use us for as long as we have it on. But it seems there are many of us who God has to strip and break down before we are willing to clothe ourselves in humbleness. We have an ego and pride that is constantly fighting the putting on of this garment. We read today of the sons of Jacob who's egos and pride sold Joseph off into slavery, lived a lie before their father, and come face to face with their guilt. God has provided a wonderful thing for them in making Joseph, the one they had cast out, governor of Egypt. But before receiving this blessing God has to strip them down and break them because they were unwilling to put the garment of humbleness on themselves. We read today in 1Corinthians chapter 2 how Paul said he came to the Corinthians in a humble state (v.1-5).

Paul did not put on the garment of humbleness easily. He was in Jerusalem full of the pride and arrogance of being a self-made Jew unwilling to accept Jesus was the Messiah.   Before Paul became a follower of Christ he called himself Saul. Saul, as along with many of the other Jews, said Jesus could not be the Messiah because Jesus did not come to them in the prescribed manner that they had determined He would come. Saul was so full of himself he went to the high priest to receive authority to arrest and bring followers of the way from Damascus.[1] We read of two men in the New Testament who came to wear the garment of humbleness by a very hard breaking by God. Both were full of pride. Peter nearly swore he would not deny Jesus and would even die with Jesus if need be.[2] Then in less than 24 hours he denies knowing Jesus or even knowing anything about Him. Paul gets confronted by the risen Lord on the road to Damascus and affects him so much that he refuses to eat or drink anything for three days.[3]

How much do we need God to do with us before we are willing to wear the garment of humbleness? We can see that Peter and Paul were used of God greatly once they were willing to put on that garment of humbleness. How much do we want God to use us? And how much will God have to do to get us there? Will it be the easy way or the hard way? Or maybe a little bit of both. It seems it is up to us to how much we will do – then whatever is left GOD WILL DO.

---

1   Acts 9:1&2
2   Lk.22:31, 22:54-62
3   Acts 9:9

God is God, there is no other. He is the alpha and the omega, the beginning and the end. All are His. Paul tells us in 1 Corinthians 3:22&23 that (those of us who are saved) whether it be Paul or Apollos or Peter, or the universe or life or death, or the immediate and threatening present of the future – all are ours, and we are Christ's and Christ is God's. We do have everything because we are in Christ and Christ is in God. The family of Jacob thought they would end up with nothing because of the famine.[1] But God made the promise to Abraham that his children would possess the land.

They would not possess the land if they perished in the famine. The same as all things are ours because we are in Christ and He is in God, all things were Jacob's family's because they were in/of Abraham and Abraham was of God. Just when the sons of Jacob thought all was lost, their life because of the famine, or their freedom because of what this high authority of the governor of Egypt was going to do to them,[2] God comes through and Joseph announces the unbelievable, that he, the governor of all Egypt,[3] with all provisions, is their brother Joseph, and Joseph would take care of them putting them in the best of the land. Jacob's sons were sons of Abraham and what was Abraham's was God's. God takes care of what is His. God, even when we cannot possibly see how, when all seems at loss, provides for us in a way we could never imagine, and even when it happens we can scarcely believe it to be true.

This is where we must have faith. As long as we are viewing our situation from our own perspective we will see things as the sons of Jacob did, all is lost. We must give up our perspectives allowing them also to die in dying to self. Our perspective of all things has to become that of God, of how He views them, of how are His ways and His thoughts.[4] Surely they will go far beyond ours. His ways and His thoughts towards us are that which sustains us – even into eternity. His word tells us of Him, we are to believe what He says, this is our faith, this is our future. We will find God will work the unbelievable, that which we could never think or imagine, this is the specialty of God – He does the impossible.[5]

As Paul says, for us who are saved, all is ours and we belong to Christ and Christ belongs to God and God takes care of what is His.

---

1   Gen.42:2
2   Gen.42:6-20, 43:8, 44:4-13
3   Gen.45:3
4   Isa.55:8&9
5   Lk.1:37, 18:27

Life, what is it? Without God, we have nothing, not even real life. Jacob and his family, because of the famine had a questionable future, would they survive or die? Life, without God, Jacob may have not had life. But God working in him and for him provided in a way he could never have dreamed. Life was given to him in the fullest from his very birth. Now Jacob was in the land of Egypt with more than he ever could have dreamed because God had been working at this, possibly, from the time Joseph had been born and even before. If Joseph had been well accepted by his brothers he would have never ended up in Egypt.

In Egypt is where God raises Joseph up to the place of none higher except Pharaoh himself. God had been providing for Jacob (and his family) even before Jacob knew he had a need, far before the famine began.   How many times do we think God does not know our need, we ask and ask and nothing! Yet it is God knows our need even before we do.[1] He arranges things for those who come to Him in a way we see not, yet it arrives exactly at the moment we need it. Part of our problem is we want to know we have it right in our hand way before we need it, God does not work this way.

Faith is not getting it when I want it, it is getting it when I need it. God is always watching over us, He sees every need we have, we are never alone. How much do you trust Him, it comes to that question? Do you know God has you in His hand as David knew? David in Psalm 18 gave praise and thanksgiving to God because he knew his life was rescued and subsisted because of God's infusion of power and work into his life. Jesus replied to the devil when tempted by him, *'Man shall not live and be sustained by bread alone but by ever word and expression of God'* (Lk. 4:4 AMPC).

If all we have is bread (food) Jesus says we do not have life. Jesus replied to the man who said he would follow Him, but only after he buried his father, **'Let the dead bury the dead'** implying those who are without God do not have life. Our life is from God and we should go to Him daily for our necessary portion to have life.

---

1   Mt.6:8, Ps.139:4, Isa.46:9&10

New wineskins – Old wineskins. God is still trying to get those of the church to accept all of the New wine and the new wine skin. Jesus says any who have had the old says the old is better and does not immediately desire the new. (Lk. 5:37-39) The main difference I see between the new and old is that the righteousness of man in the old is attributed to him by what he accomplishes, and in the new, righteousness is attributed to him by what God has accomplished for man's behalf. We continue to want some credit for something we can do right. The teaching of Christ tells us the only way we can receive righteousness and eternal life is by accepting Him and what He has done for us already. On the cross, Jesus said, **"It is finished."** [1] It wasn't His life on earth that was finished, it was that the work in His life on earth that He was sent to do was finished. That work was to pay for the sins of all of mankind. There will be many who will not accept the work Jesus did on the cross for them to receive redemption. [2]

There will be the few as Jesus says that will go through the narrow gate, who will accept what Jesus did for them. In trying to still practice some of the old, making accomplishments of our own, we insult Jesus and say that He did not accomplish all on the cross, we are saying He is wrong. We say that it is not finished and that we have to add some to finish it in each of us.

Does Jesus call us to live a life His way? Yes. Did He finish the work on the cross? Yes. That work is finished, but His call to us is to live His way as we all from day to day are changed into His likeness more and more. The work on the cross of paying for all our sins, beginning to end of our lives, is complete. There is nothing we can do to pay for our sins other than to apply the payment already made by asking for forgiveness which comes to us by His grace. The New Wine goes against pride in our flesh which will always cause difficulty. Paul comes to the conclusion that it is not he who sins, it is his flesh. [3] We have to try to put down our pride and pray for God to help us, to enable ourselves to take in more and more of the New Wine and less and less of the Old Wine.

John the Baptist said he must become less and less with Jesus becoming more and more. [4] In our lives as Christians we are to become more like Christ. In our life we should strive and pray to become less and less of self with Jesus becoming more and more in us. Could it be, would it be, that the world would see Christ living in us!?

---

1   Jn.19:30
2   Mt.7:13
3   Rom.7:20&25
4   Jn.3:30

The blessing, God gave the blessing in the beginning at creation.[1] We read today of Jacob blessing the sons of Joseph (Gen. 48:20). In our reading of Luke chapter 6 today Jesus gives the same teaching here as He did in the **Sermon on the Mount** in Matthew, here He is on a level place. We could call it **The Blessed Be Sermon**, at least for the first part of it because Jesus starts out saying **Blessed Be**. In Luke it is recorded four of the **blessed bes** (Lk. 6:20-22) and in Matthew there is recorded nine **blessed bes**.[2] At the end of the **blessed bes** in both Luke and Mathew Jesus says, 'Rejoice'.

In Luke 6:23, *"Rejoice in that day"* (NKJV) and in Matthew 5:12, *"Rejoice and be exceedingly glad"* (NKJV). The last **blessed be** in both Luke and Matthew is where we see that blessings do not always mean **good times**, it only means there are good things coming to us from God. If it were not Jesus saying it, but a man, we would question him about how he figured it was a good thing, a blessing. *"How blessed you are whenever people hate you and ostracize you and insult you and denounce you as a criminal"* (Lk. 6:22 CJB),   *"How blessed you are when people insult you and persecute you and tell all kinds of vicious lies about you"* (Mt. 5:11 CJB). Yet it is Jesus who says it, therefore we know it to be truth. Jesus goes on after this and says rejoice for your reward in heaven is great. The blessing is to us from God, but not always does it come in a manner we desire and expect. I am sure there are many amongst us believers who at one time or another have prayed God would bless them bringing them closer to Him and then enter immediately into a difficult trying time of life.

They did find after the struggle they were closer to God but didn't know when they prayed what road they would have to go down to get there. Maybe even Paul in his fervent desire to serve God as a Pharisee prayed this type of prayer. Then found himself driven to the ground, confronted by the resin Lord on the road to Damascus, and afterwards be blind for three days. The larger the error in what we believe the larger the struggle to get close to that place with God. Does the difficulty make it not a blessing?

A blessing is not always a **feel good thing now**, but it is God's way to get us to a better place of relation to Him, and many times a more content place in this life we live on earth. The blessing is not always about today, but about eternity. God told Abraham and Isaac and Jacob He would bless them (and their children) making a great nation of them and bless the world by them.[3] A few generations later they find themselves enslaved to Egypt and treated harshly. The blessing spoken to Abraham, Isaac, and Jacob of becoming a great nation came later, probably mostly during the reign of David and Solomon. And the blessing to the world came as Jesus, born of the Jewish people, died on the cross paying for the sins of all the world.

If we are in a relationship with God by receiving Jesus as Lord then God's favor towards us (because of what Jesus has done for us) puts us in a place we are continually receiving God's blessings even though many times we don't recognize them. We need to be thankful constantly for God's blessings for we are receiving them each and every day.

---

1   Gen.1:3-31
2   ·   Mt.5:3-11
3   Gen.12:2, 46:3, 18:18, 22:18

Far be it from me to think I have great knowledge. It is He who guides us all who has the great knowledge. It is He who guides us on our path. It is He who gives to us (to each of us) the knowledge needed to accomplish the portion and position He has given each of us in the body of Christ. His knowledge is greater than our knowledge and thought. Many times as we see things and think how they should be we are wrong and it is His ways that are set in place. Joseph, as great a man close to God as he became in Egypt, yet did not know what it was that God was doing. Joseph took his two sons, Manasseh the oldest and Ephraim the younger to his father Jacob for them to be blessed by him. Joseph set the oldest at Jacob's right hand and the youngest at his left hand.

The custom was that the oldest would carry through the greater blessing which was of and at the right hand. Joseph should have seen (the same as we should see) from his own past and his father's past; it is not always the older that carries the greater blessing. Jacob was twins with his brother who was the oldest of Isaac's sons, and Jacob was the younger of the twins. And of the sons of Jacob Joseph was next to the youngest and yet the greater blessing is brought through him. We know and we don't know the ways of God. It takes a constant seeking, yielding, and a desire to have the knowledge God has for each of us. Jacob had the knowledge God allotted to him and when Joseph put Manasseh at his father's right, Jacob knowing what God had given him crossed his arms giving the greater blessing to Ephraim. [1]

Jacob goes on shortly after this in chapter 49 to bless and speak of the place each of his sons will have who would become the twelve tribes of Israel. It is God's knowledge that surpasses ours. It is He who knows all things. It is we who have to put down (cast out) what knowledge we think we have in dying to self and pray that God will plant in us His knowledge He has for us to have.

At this point we can begin to move forward making progress in the Kingdom of God. One of the very first scriptures God planted in my heart as a revelation directed by Him at the time is Isa. 55:8&9, *"For my thoughts are not your thoughts, neither are your ways my ways,"* says the LORD. *"For as the heavens are higher than the earth, so are my ways higher than your ways and my thoughts than your thoughts"* (NKJV).

---

1   Gen. 48:13-19

Who is God? Is Jehovah the only god in your life? Are there other things in your life that gets more attention from you than Jehovah God does? In today's culture in America, we don't have many idols as we think of as in biblical times. Are there religions that speak of a different god than Jehovah? Yes, but as Christians, we recognize these and stay away from them. There are those who say they follow the god of creation, calling him Ala, or Jehovah without Jesus. As Christians, if we don't have a firm relationship with God we could be drawn into one of these that may seem right but is not. The gods of this world which we know are nothing like our God, and those who seem similar, are not those in our lives in competition with Jehovah that I am asking about. Is Jehovah the only god in your life?

Things can become gods, or idols, to us. Is there something in your life you give more allegiance to by how much time, money, or heartfelt devotion you give it to where in your life it is in competition with your allegiance to Jehovah?   Anything that we are more anxious about, even if it is subconscious, to give a place in our lives than Jehovah, it is an idol to us. This can be a career, an accomplishment, a car, sports, a spouse, a house, our children, etc. Sometimes we are blinded to what is robbing our allegiance to God and wonder why it is so hard to have a relationship with God. Sometimes we can even place our accomplishments in being religious higher than our relationship with God.

Paul tells us today in 1Corinthians 8:9&12 that being too religious in the liberty we know we have can damage a weaker brother. Being hard core in our liberty which has nothing to do with our close walk with God, we must be willing to sacrifice (give up) for the well-being and growth of another. Jesus gave us His last commandment, to love one another. [1] In this we must succeed. We must place God Jehovah in the highest place, above all else. And we must place our fellow believer right under that. This is the greatest of all, that we **Love the Lord our God, with all our heart, soul, mind, and strength. And love our neighbor as our self.**

---

[1]   Jn.13:34&35, 15:12&17

Peace and assurance is what many seek for, but few find. Everything about it takes our attention, even if it is subconsciously. The world around us is constantly seeking for peace and assurance. They are looking for it in wrong places. Some seek it by higher education, some seek it by a successful career, some seek it by popularity as an entertainer, some by political position, some as a sports figure, etc.

Mankind has been blinded by the great deceiver from the beginning. King David speaks in Psalm 27 of his peace and assurance he has in Jehovah (LORD). v. 3,5,10 & 11 record David's trust in Jehovah, finding his peace and assurance in his God. David, as one of God's prophets, tells us where to find peace and assurance in v. 14, "Wait for the LORD; be strong, and let your heart take courage; yea, wait for the LORD!" (RSV).

The world looks for, and seeks, peace and assurance looking for it in the wrong place. The minds of men are deceived by the devil in their search of where to find that great peace and assurance. The very way that God provides for us seems wrong to mankind. Even those of us who have received salvation have difficulty with finding that peace and assurance. The very way which seems the right way to us to peace and assurance is the opposite of how Jesus tells us we can find it. In Lk. 9:24 Jesus says he who would preserve his life will lose it and he who loses it for Jesus' sake would preserve his life.

The Jews were looking for the Messiah to come taking authority (the throne in Jerusalem), and to rule the world removing the Romans from authority in Judah. God's way was for Jesus to come, be overtaken by the Jewish and Roman authorities, and give up His life, dying Himself on the cross to accomplish the goal. Peace and assurance is found in Jesus – in God's way. Jesus says in Lk.9:23, "If any man would come after me, let him deny himself, and take up his cross daily, and follow me" (ASV). Promoting self, the great deception of the devil, is how the world thinks it will find peace and assurance, but Jesus tells us only by dying to self and following Him will we find that sought after peace and assurance.

We speak about having blind faith, that which believes even though we do not see it yet, the faith to follow even though we cannot physically or mentally see. We are called to believe what we do not see. It takes blind faith to see what we don't see. Jesus told Thomas that blessed are those who have not seen Him and yet believe. [1] It is difficult to follow in what God wants us to do. We are of the earth, we are of this world, and we tend to depend on earthly abilities in order to follow God. In our effort by earthly means and strength we are so deficient in producing the spiritual fruit.

Spiritual fruit must be produced by spiritual strength by spiritual ways. It is by the Spirit that we follow God. For many of us who have lived much of our earthly life before being saved, it is difficult to learn how to live by the Spirit. This is where we find blind faith, the faith that comes by the Spirit as our need. Jesus sent out the seventy, no doubt empowering them with some special anointing, for the power from on high had not yet been given to heal the sick, cast out demons, etc.

The apostle John tells us the Spirit had not yet been given. [2] When the seventy returned they had been able to deal with demons, taking authority over them in the Lord's name. They were sent out by Jesus' words to them, in some way they walked in blind faith able to heal the sick (not just giving first aid), able to speak of the Kingdom of God, and able to cast out demons in Jesus' name. Blind faith does not come by more and more learning. Jesus said He thanked the Father that He had concealed these things from the wise and understanding and learned, and had revealed them to babes.

Blind faith comes by more and more believing. It comes by being willing to believe more and more of what God says in His word. That which He says to our hearts rather than what the world tells us and what we think ourselves. It comes by expecting God to do what He said He would do. It is those of us who are willing to believe even though we don't understand, to stand on God's words in faith, believing and doing only because He says so, regardless if we can reason why or how. God is looking for brave people who are willing to look foolish to the world, believing what seems foolish and unreasonable. Walking in blind faith is difficult but it is a blessing when we are there.

---

1 Jn.20:29
2 Jn.7:39

Asking of God. By our asking of God, we declare our belief that he is able to give. In our not asking of God we declare we have doubts that He can give us what we need. I realize that many times we don't ask because of feeling unworthy and undeserving. Did we deserve salvation, yet God gave – and Oh how He gave! If there was nothing we could do to deserve salvation, how can we do anything to deserve our request of God of what we are asking after our salvation?

When Jesus was asked by His disciples to teach them to pray He didn't say anything about accomplishing, performing, having great obedience, etc., He just said pray like this. Jesus gives the parable of a man going to his friend for his need of bread for a guest and shows us we are to keep asking and asking until we receive. Jesus doesn't say anything about, 'after you have done this or that – then you can come and ask'. In another place Jesus gave a parable about a widow who keeps coming to a judge until the judge gives her justice. [1]

Jesus is teaching about asking of God, to keep coming with confidence He will hear us and respond to us. How much do we believe God will hear us – this is the question we must answer to ourselves. The only thing we are required to do in prayer asking of God is to believe. Jesus gives the example of a child coming asking his father for bread or a fish – the child has a confidence his father will hear his request and act on it with what his father has in his possession. Jesus says in another place we must come to God like little children believing like little children. [2]

Little children always believe their father can, and will, give them what they ask for – they never question it, they just ask. Jesus tells us it takes very little faith (belief) on our part for God to do marvelous acts on our behalf. Asking of God declares we believe He is able to give us good things with Him working on our behalf. Asking of God declares we believe He is willing to hear our request, not because of what we have done to deserve it, but He will hear our request because of what Jesus has done to give us the right to ask it.

---

1   Lk.18:1-8
2   Mk.10:15

Why try preparing that which is not for you to prepare? How many times do we take on things which are not ours to do? Once we give ourselves to God in salvation we are to serve Him. His responsibility then is to provide for us. He does the managing, He is who gives out the assignment to each servant, He is the one to make sure all the servants are taken care of. Take time to find out what the Lord has for you to do, don't take on something that He has assigned to someone else. It may be that God assigns several to the same task, but be sure that is where you are assigned.

God wants to run a smooth shift. If the people are not listening, only doing what they thought they should do, some work is being done double and other work is not getting done at all. We get so tied up in making our own list of all that we should do for God that sometimes we don't even hear Him when He is speaking to us. When we get saved we are to deny ourselves.[1] We do humble ourselves when we get saved, confessing we are sinners repenting of those sins, and ask Jesus to be Lord of our life. How quickly we are back at running things in our life again instead of Him.

What is denying self, is it denying 20% of our life, is it denying maybe even 50% of our life? No, it is denying 100% of ourselves in control of our life. Yet as it is 100% we have to let go of, we are the ones who have to give it up, Jesus won't just reach in and take it. Another term used here is we die to self. This means all that has to do with our life we give up fully to the Lord, we have no control any more, we have zilch, we retain no control any longer. So much trouble we cause ourselves because we push ourselves into things the Lord has no intention for us to be doing. Serving does mean out there working hard at accomplishing something, it means listen so we know what it is the Lord wants us to accomplish.

In our reading today in 1 Corinthians chapter 12, verses 14-21 Paul talks about the Church (us) being like a body with all its parts. He says if the foot wants to be a hand it don't work, if an ear wants to be an eye it don't work. Same is if each part thinks it has to be doing the work of all the other parts also, this will not work either. When God calls Moses in Exodus we see in chapter 3 and 4 God directing Moses, saying this, *"I Myself will be with your mouth and his mouth, and I will instruct you in what you are to do"* (4:15 NASB). God is the one who decides and gives orders, we are the ones who follow. Don't weigh yourself down with a load of work God may have not called you to do. Take that special time with Him allowing Him to guide you, speak to you of what He has for you to do.

---

1   Mt.16:24, 2Cor.5:15

Longsuffering is an attribute of God that we are called to take on, that we must take on. If each of us is truthful we will confess that it took much longsuffering on God's part for us to receive the salvation which we now possess. It seems that longsuffering is that which emanates out from great love. Jesus speaks in our reading today about the owner who had a fig tree in his vineyard that produced no fruit – the owner said to cut it down.(Lk. 13:6&7) The vinedresser, the one with love for it said, 'let me stir it up and add nutrients to it and maybe it will produce fruit'.

This is our loving God who gives us another chance, practices longsuffering, stirs us up and puts the nutrients of His word in us with great hope we will produce. Even with all the opposition of the Pharisees and Jewish leaders Jesus continued to speak truth to those of them who would hear. At the end of Luke chapter 13 we read of Jesus' heart, His love, His longsuffering; He says that Jerusalem continued to kill and stone those sent to them with the truth of God, and yet He says of how He had desired to gather them like a hen gathers her young under her wings. Within a few days after this Jesus performs the greatest action of love, He dies on a cross for undeserving people – you and I. Today we read Paul's great chapter on love. (1Cor. 13) In all that Paul says about love we see longsuffering to be patient and kind, to never be envious or jealous, to not be boastful or haughty before others. It takes longsuffering to not be conceded and to not be rude. In longsuffering we do not insist on our own rights, and are not insulted easily.

It takes longsuffering to account nothing to those who do evil to us, and for our suffering when we have done no wrong. It takes longsuffering in standing our ground not rejoicing in injustice, but waits for truth to prevail. It takes longsuffering to bear up under whatever comes and being ready to believe the best of every person. In longsuffering we continue to hope when all seems hopeless.

God's longsuffering emitting out from His love is what has brought us salvation. Jesus came to earth, lived as man - yet being God, put up with all the resistance of those who would not believe, and finally suffered the cross that we, the unworthy, could be saved. This is the height of longsuffering perfectly, and He asks us to do our best to practice it in our lives with those around us. We are to be like Christ.

Really, what is life? How do you see it? What the world sees it to be is not life. Jesus in His ministering over the three years constantly says if we want life we must believe in Him. It is not just eternal life He speaks of, He says that those who do not have Him in their lives are already dead walking around in death.   Life is an existence knowing God, interacting with God, having the influence of God in our lives, of God giving us spiritual breath in our lives. Without God in our lives, there is not an eternity of life, only an eternity of death. There is an eternity that plays out after this life on this earth. Even we as Christians have a hard time knowing what real life is.

We continue to fall back into what the world says it is, we are emerged into how the world lives and it takes a diligence not to be affected by it. It is a pursuit following after, and living, God's way. His way brings fullness to existence that is the thing that fills us with joy and assurance. We are those who are to follow, He is the One leading. The fullness of life is found as we are led by God into something we didn't even know existed before we welcomed Jesus into our lives. Each day is in His hand to bring us what we need. He is the One who knows the way that we are to go, each one of us individually. God led Moses in ways he never dreamed of, even to walk in the midst of a sea.

David speaks of how God leads us in his Psalms. Psalm 36:5-9 David speaks of how it is when we follow God ending it with the last part of v. 9,"In Your light we see light" (NASB). In Psalm 37 David says in v.5 to commit your way to the Lord and goes on to the first half of v.7 of what that will be for you. In leading up to v.39&40 in v. 34 David says, 'Wait for and expect the Lord and keep and heed His ways.' God's way is true life which lasts into eternity. God's way is what Jesus tells us about in Luke 14:33 that His way is for us to give up all claim to what is ours, to forsake all that we have in order to be His disciple. Do we qualify to be His disciples?

ACQUISITION – that of acquiring. We have acquired a life that was purchased by another – the only requirement of us was surrender. The price required of us seems such a small part and yet it is huge. To accept such a great thing as salvation (eternal life) from another who purchased it for us means we admit we are not able ourselves, that someone else has to do it for us. At salvation, we repent and ask Jesus into our lives but very few fully surrender – that takes time, even years. We in America are shaped to be a proud people – all around us implies we must accomplish, we must become somebody, we must be successful. It takes pride and a selfishness to pursue and arrive at the place all that is around us tells us we need to be. These very things are what are at odds with what Jesus has taught us and calls us to do. Surrender is not an easy thing to do. It usually takes a brokenness of ourselves for that to happen. This seems to be the place David found himself in Psalm 38. David recognizes in v. 3 he is in this condition because of his sin.

He feels the full weight of his iniquities. (v. 4) He comes to the place he sees his own foolishness. (v.5) In his brokenness he finds humbleness which allows him to put all his trust in the Lord. (v. 9) In knowing his answer is only in the Lord (v.15) he confesses his condition in v.18 and tries his best to be close to and depend on the Lord. (v. 21) David confesses his salvation is in the Lord. (v. 22) Surrender can come easy or it can come hard. If we totally yield, even though it seems hard, but fully yield ourselves to the Lord it is so much easier than if the Lord has to break us. It seems many of us the Lord has to do the latter.

It is painful, almost more than what we feel we can bear, but I would not go back to where I was before God broke me for anything in this world. Brokenness is a blessed place to be. God begins to become more to us than we ever thought He could be. **Acquisition** – I have acquired and am in the process of acquiring, more than I ever dreamed, more than I ever deserved. The acquisition was made by another, by Jesus Christ, and given to me freely as a possession that is all mine, truly mine – lock, stock, and barrel mine. We are the wayward son (child) who has come to the Father and have been given all that we have received, freely, fully, lovingly. [1]

---

1   Lk.14:11-23

We are to be steadfast people. How are we to be steadfast? We are to cling to, and to hold tight to God. David begins Psalm 40 in our reading today this way: *"I waited patiently for the LORD; he inclined to me and heard my cry. He drew me up from the pit of destruction, out of the miry bog, and set my feet upon a rock, making my steps secure. He put a new song in my mouth, a song of praise to our God"* (ESV). This is how it is to be in our Christian life. We cannot be holding on to God tightly if we are holding on to something else also for our security.

All of our grip must be on God. We are to be always holding on to the Lord, every minute of the day. If we practice steadfastness it will keep us out of many troubles. Paul struggled with his flesh and out of his struggle comes good advice to us. He gives us a list of good things and says think on these things.[1] This is part of steadfastness. It keeps us out of troubles by not allowing our minds to wander to places we should not go. God wants us thinking on the good things He speaks to us about and to keep our minds set on Him. Just trusting in God, depending on God to supply our needs. We are not to hoard possessions, but to know God will take care of us for God is in control of our tomorrow and all the tomorrows after that. He wants us to know He will take care of us. Jesus says, 'where your treasure is, there will your heart also be'. Putting our confidence and our trust in God shows our treasure is in Him.

This is clinging. In another place Jesus speaks of us clinging to the vine which He is.[2] This is steadfastness. Can you imagine a branch producing fruit if many times a day or many days at a time it detaches itself from the vine, this is surely a foolish thought? How can we produce not being attached? This type of behavior only brings weakness and sometimes even death. Clinging and trusting is very important. Clinging is the act of being very close, we stay close by being in a relationship. Part of how we do this is to hear what God has/is saying to us.

To be in His word much is part of the clinging, it is that of garbing a hold, and holding on. At first it may seem difficult to be steadfast. But after practicing it for a time it becomes a thing we feel we cannot live without. When we find the truly rich things that we are fed by the Vine Jesus we wonder how we ever lived without them before.

---

1   Philp.4:8
2   Jn.15:4

In all that we are, we are under Him who created all things.[1] Those of us who have given over our lives to Him have received salvation from the punishment that was laid out against us for our sins. We have been redeemed with a most valuable price, that of who God paid even from Himself to Himself that He might draw some of mankind back to Him.

In all His goodness He has redeemed us by His own work to bring us close to Him. Our lives are in His hands, that we should have gratitude to Him for what He has done. It is a mighty wonder of the greatness of His actions that permits us to come close who in our own sin had went far off. The Psalm writer of Psalm 42 makes it clear his hope is only in God. He looks to God for that help. Even then they knew help had to come from God. We have now received that help that has been coming to man as spoken by Moses as the seed of Abraham was promised[2].

God has reached out to a creation that most had turned away from Him. We in our foolishness, we in our thought of our own knowledge, had went our own way reaping nothing but sorrow and hardship not even knowing we had done so, for with nothing to measure against what we have seems right. God reveals Himself so we will have something to measure ourselves against, and we find we come up short, our performance is so short.[3] For us who realize this, repent of our wrong going, and wrong doing, yielding to our Lord who we have found and He by what He has done gives us life, life in this world as we never had it before, and life eternal in which we will be with Him forever.

There is a great day coming for those who love the Lord: *"For just like the lightning, when it flashes out of one part of the sky, shines to the other part of the sky, so will the Son of Man be in His day"* (Lk. 17:24 NASB). So great will be the day that Christ comes again that none will not know. We have found the greatest thing that any person anywhere could ever find. Jesus tells the story of the man who found the greatest of pearls and gave up everything he owned to have that great pearl.[4] This is the great salvation God offers, it is for any who seek Him out, to find a God that has the richest treasure we will ever know. The Psalm writer yearns for the Lord, even as a deer with great thirst yearns for the water. For those of us who have found this salvation we have to realize it is the greatest thing we will ever find, and that it is worth giving up all else we have that we might have it.

---

1 Gen.1:1, Eph.3:9
2 Acts 3:22&25
3 Rom.3:23
4 Mt.13:45&46

Do I (we) know where I (we) am going? Yes we are going to heaven because of what Jesus did for us on the cross and we have accepted Him. But what about right now in our lives, do we know where we are going? We may think we know the way to where we are going but if we are not getting there through and by Jesus, we are not getting to where we are supposed to. Jesus said He is the way, the truth, and the life.[1] Who makes the plans for your next year and your next decade?

Some say, 'Well you can't wait sitting on a stump until you hear a voice from the sky.' My question is, Have you asked God what He wants to do in or through your life in the next year? Some may say, 'Well I asked God yesterday and He hasn't said anything so I guess I better get at it with the information I have.' The information we have in the Bible is important, but how God wants to apply it in our individual lives may be different than what we have figured.[2] We also must be patient with the time we give for God to reply. Jeremiah was asked by the people to go to God for them to ask a particular thing and God did not answer for ten days (remember this is Jeremiah that had ask).[3]

What is waiting on God for ten days, Jesus went to the wilderness for forty days before starting His ministry – He had a lot to do in the next three years, should He have used up forty days? The apostles had a lot to do – those things Jesus told them to do just before He was taken into heaven for the last time.

Yet Jesus instructed them to **wait** in the city until they were endued with power from on high.[4] Are we willing to wait when God says **wait** (if we are listing)? Are we willing to go if He says go? Are we willing to stand if God says stand? Too much of the time we govern if God is directing us by what seems to make sense to us. But things of God many times do not make sense to us, only to Him, they are His way. We only can know where God is going if we ask Him. Jesus said, **'pick up your cross and follow Me.'**

To plan for our next year is up to God, if we yield our lives to Him, for His work. God might give us privilege telling us about the year ahead or He might only reveal it day by day. The whole secret in knowing where we are going is putting ourselves totally in His hands and we will arrive right on time and exactly at the right place. When we think we ourselves know we get in our own way of really knowing. In Luke 18, Jesus says we must come like little children. Seeking like little children, believing like little children, following like little children.

---

1   Jn.14:6
2   Jer. 9:11 RSV, ESV, or NASB
3   Jer. 42:2&7
4   Lk.24:49

Life, it is a continual struggle. We at times say, **'life is good.'** But if it is not handed to us on a platter it takes work on our part to get there, and after we get there (the good life) it is work to keep it. Of course, I speak of earthly life that is lived without Jesus in it. Life is good when we finally hand it all over to Jesus. Accepting salvation and finally handing our life over to Jesus do not always happen at the same time. Many of us live for years having salvation given to us by Jesus before we give all of our lives to Him for His work, in us and in the world. Jesus is patient, kindly waiting, always beckoning, wanting what is better for us.

Paul speaks of the glory that was seen on Moses' face after being with God and how it faded away in time. Paul tells us Jesus' glory on us increases after time, it does not fade. The thing is, we have to be exposed to Jesus, day after day, for this to happen. Is Jesus' glory in you still stuck where it was at your salvation or is it increasing? There are all kinds of treatments that man gives from beauty treatments to chemo for cancer which we submit ourselves to for them to have their effect. The greatest treatment we can submit ourselves to for the greatest effect is a daily dose of Jesus.

We can get a dose of Jesus by being in the word, by being in meditation on His greatness and who He is, by being in prayer, by being in worship, by being in a study, etc. The main thing is we have to be in, handing ourselves over to Him daily for Him to work His effect in us, and that glory of His on us can increase more and more as time passes. [1] His working in us as we yield and present ourselves to him is what brings the good life. The world around us has no idea what this kind of good life is, but if we submit ourselves daily to the treatment of Jesus the world around us will begin to see His glory on us and begin to wonder what we got. We got Jesus, and we need more and more of Him every day. Thank God for His goodness that He sheds on us as we yield to Him.

---

1   Jn.3:30

Home, this is where we dwell. Spiritually what can we say of home? Some would say home is where the heart is. So, where is your heart, where is my heart? Paul speaks of home in a way we may not normally think of, *"it is my eager expectation and hope that I shall not be at all ashamed, but that with full courage now as always Christ will be honored in my body, whether by life or by death. For to me to live is Christ, and to die is gain. If it is to be life in the flesh, that means fruitful labor for me. Yet which I shall choose I cannot tell. I am hard pressed between the two. My desire is to depart and be with Christ, for that is far better. But to remain in the flesh is more necessary on your account"* (Philp. 1:20-24 RSV).

To Paul being with Christ in heaven would be great, He would be home. But he also seems to feel an attachment to this life on earth since here he is able to minister to the body of Christ. In Paul's letters to the churches, he speaks of always praying for them and many times longing to be with them. Being with the Church (God's people) to Paul was also being home. He was hard-pressed to choose and finally decided to stay on earth as much as possible was the best for it was the best for the Church. [1]

He put aside that which would have given him great delight of being in heaven to be able to instill the gospel into one more person. Do we feel the most at home when we are with the brethren? And if not, why so? Maybe some soul searching needs to take place. Someday all of us who follow Christ will be with Him in heaven for eternity, but what about now? Paul seemed to always be content where he was looking forward with eager anticipation to when we all would be in heaven. *"knowing that he who raised the Lord Jesus will raise us also with Jesus and bring us with you into his presence"* (2 Cor. 4:14 RSV).

We can see a joy in Paul's life no matter how difficult it was at the time and in that he finds home, *"So we do not lose heart. Though our outer nature is wasting away, our inner nature is being renewed every day"* (2Cor. 4:16 RSV). Home, it is the place God has us at the moment. Finding that contentment that Paul had seems to be where we find home, here for now – heaven for eternity.

---

1   Philp.1:26 & 2 Cor.4:15

Hearing, are we listening? We ask God for guidance but are we listening? We want to know what way to go but are we listening? We ask for God's favor, His blessings, but are we listening? For those people around us who are soft quiet speakers, we have to pay attention and listen to hear what they say. God speaks in a still small voice, [1] do we take time to pay attention and listen to hear what He says?

The experts in communication tell us one of the biggest problems we have in communication is we don't know how to listen. Something we do is to condition what the other is saying by what we want to hear therefore not really hearing what the other is saying. Sometimes our whole thought is on what we want to say and we don't even hear anything the other says. If we do this with those around us, who are easy to hear if we listen, then how much more do we do this with God who is difficult to hear? God tells us and we hear, but do we hear? What He says may not be what is in our reasoning so we take what He says and condition it to our reasoning and follow that. Jesus was upset with the religious leaders of the day because they did this.

We have to accept God's word as God's word even if it does not make sense to us. If He is so much greater than us it is logical that what He speaks of will not always make sense to us. When God gave Manna to the Israelites (Ex. 16:14) He gave them instructions about it. They were to gather it each morning and keep none to the next day. (Ex. 16:16 & 19) Some of the people heard only what they wanted to and tried keeping some until the next day. (Ex. 16:20)

Then they were told to gather twice as much on the sixth day to keep half over until the next day for there would be none to gather. (v.22 & 23) Some may have reasoned in their minds that they had kept it overnight before and it rotted with worms so they didn't keep any over and went out on the seventh day to gather their manna for that day but there was none. (v. 27) Has so much changed with us people since then, are we not yet much the same? I fear we are the same, and many times hear what we want to hear or we reason it could not be so. We must listen with an open mind, we must listen with confidence in the Lord that He knows what He is talking about, we must listen not thinking of what we want to do or what we want to say. God Loves His children (us) and He wants to instruct us but are we listening?

---

1   1Kg.19:12

The offering. What do we think of when we think of offering? First, it is that which one offers to or for another. Typically in the church, we may think of our financial support of the ministry. That is something which we need to keep in mind. God asks of us to support His work. Paul tells us the laborer is worthy of his pay, that the ox that treads out the grain is not to be muzzled.[1] Paul also says the one from which we receive spiritual blessings should share in our financial blessings.[2]

We also are to support the work in the church taking care of those within who are in need. We are to support God's word going forth in evangelism and missionary work. We are to support orphans and widows.[3] It is to be a giving from the heart for these things and not thought of as paying dues to be in the club, the Church is not a club, it is a body of Christ functioning for Christ. But even with all of this there should be a much greater impact of thought attached to offering.

Paul tells us in the last verse of 2Corinthians chapter 5 that God offered Jesus Christ to be sin who knew no sin (to stand in our place to receive our punishment) so that in Jesus and through Jesus we could become the righteousness of God. Do you realize how gigantic that is, that we become the righteous from no effort on our part, none. Paul goes on to call us to not treat the (great) grace of God in vain. (2Cor. 6:1) Paul speaks in v. 2 about the great deliverance and salvation we have received. Is this not the greatest awesome offering that anyone could possibly give?

It was sufficient to save you and me and the multitudes that have been rescued from sin over all the course of time. This is the offering which should be foremost in our minds, hearts, and spirits. By it we are motivated to do many of the things God has called of us. Today in Luke chapter 22 we read of the arrest of Jesus, the main episode of God's offering for our salvation and so much more. I encourage you to see with your heart in the remaining chapters of Luke the great offering God has made for you.

---

1   1Cor.9:9 & 1Tim.5:18
2   Gal.6:6
3   Jas.1:27

Life, Scripture, Righteousness. It is strange to me that the Holy Spirit would bring these three together to me. Yet there seems to be a rightness to them. Life we live, life eternal we seek, true life before God is our goal. So what does it take to find this life that is fulfilled, eternal, and pleasing to God? We could conclude on our own in what we think, in what we reason in our minds as good, that good would accomplish this. That would not get us very far because Paul said the wisdom of the world did not find Him (us trying to figure it out on our own), that by foolishness to men we are saved. [1] So it leaves us to find out what God has to say and that is found in the scriptures. We need to read God's word believing Him, totally disregarding our own thought, reasoning, and logic. If we could acquire what we are seeking (fulfillment, eternity, and to please God) by our own Jesus would have not had to come. The scriptures will lead us into finding true fulfillment, eternal life, and the way to please God. We must believe what we read in God's Word, what He says to us.

We believed the word of God, as strange a thing as it is to any thinker who considers and reasons things out, His word said if we repented and ask Jesus into our lives we would experience the new birth. When we do this something happens and takes place in our lives that we have a hard time explaining to a nonbeliever. Yet it happened, something supernatural took place, there was a spirit born in us that was not there before which changed the way we thought, the things we thought were important before now seem unimportant. We found our likes and dislikes changed yet we could not explain why, it was not a decision we had made to change – we were just different after receiving salvation. The greatest thing that could ever happen in our lives, that of receiving eternal life, happened because we believed at that moment what the scripture said. We must continue to believe the scriptures now as we did at salvation.

Believing the scriptures is what brings us to righteousness. Righteousness does not come to us by our accomplishments, it comes to us by faith. The Jews tried for years to accomplish it by the Law but Paul said they failed. Paul tells us we receive true righteousness by faith the same as Abraham did. [2] We must believe by faith that Jesus is the Son of God, the Messiah sent from heaven to redeem mankind. We must believe the offering that God gave on our behalf and not be like so many who were not willing to believe Jesus was the Messiah when He preached to them in the country, in the houses, and in the Temple.

We must not believe that Jesus was killed by unruly men who fought against God's will putting the Messiah on the cross. Even this was God's work to save a lost people, which we were. It is easy to read the account of the arrest, trial, and crucifixion of Jesus and blame all those evil men who did it. In Acts in Peter's prayer to God he tells why all this happened to Jesus, he says it was predetermined by God that it should happen this way. [3] How could we be saved if there was no offering for our sins, no blood to wash us clean, and no resurrection to show we too will be resurrected. Life, Scripture, Righteousness: they do all fit together. We could not have righteousness if there was not the scriptures, God's word to have faith in. And the scripture is what has shown us how to be saved and have true life in God. We are to follow, we are to believe, and we are to live.

---

1   1Cor. 1:21
2   Rom.4:1-9
3   Acts 4:28

Today the subject is 'security'. In this world around us with all its calamity and unrest, even if those of the world say they are secure, it is a perverted sense of security. Most will say, 'If I just had X, I would be happy and secure.' When they finally receive/acquire/possess X they find they are not truly happy and secure. Many phrase it that God has put a voided place in our being that can only be filled with Him. Those of you who have accepted Jesus Christ into your life now have that void filled. Yet, even though we are in this world but not of this world,[1] because of the calamity and unrest around us, our faith becomes weak and our security begins to shake. The truth is we have Christ in us,[2] we have God filling that void, we have the Holy Spirit to teach us and guide us.[3]

Our faith becomes shaky because the devil is lying to us trying to convince us God is not as great as He says He is. The devil started this in the garden with Eve and has continued the lie to all of mankind.

The question is, are we going to believe God, or are we going to believe the devil? I paraphrase what the devil said to Eve a bit with, **'Did God really say**?' This I believe is the main thing the devil is still saying to us today trying to cause us to doubt. The devil tries to get us to engage our brain to try to figure it out and conclude a slightly distorted thought of what we think the truth is. The truth is we are fallible people and anything we come up with is in error. God gives us truth, plain and simple, but because we don't like some of the things He says we try to manipulate it. Our pride, our ego, our desires, (what Paul calls the flesh) does not want to align with what the truth is that God gives us. David's writing of Psalm 61 is all about security. What David writes here surpasses life, it carries into eternity. There were many times in David's life which we see in his Psalms that he was fearful, the same as many times in our lives we are fearful, but that didn't change where David's foundation of security was at. It was to that very security (his God) that he was crying out to. In Luke 24 today we read of fearful disciples. They had just lost their leader who they thought was the promised Messiah who would take authority on earth and set everything right. (Lk. 24:21)

Instead of setting things right the Jewish leaders had turned Jesus over to the Romans, the very ones they thought Jesus was going to conquer, and they had Him executed. The women went to the tomb to tend to the body of Jesus and were told by an angel Jesus had risen from the dead and was not there. They in fear and amazement told the eleven apostles which to them seemed like an idle woman's tale. (Lk. 24:11)

The apostles had heard the truth from the very lips of Jesus many times, He told them He would be arrested, delivered to the gentiles (Romans), be executed, and on the third day rise from the dead. We find ourselves in this place many times, we hear, and we hear, but we don't hear. Every time Jesus said He would rise on the third day the disciples would ask each other what it meant, and obviously because they could not understand it they did not believe. We are called to believe even if we don't understand or if it makes no sense to us. This is where security is found, believing the truth no matter how improbable it may seem. Our faith is what keeps us in the truth, our yielding to God is what allows us to have faith, our total surrender to Him is what gives us security.

---

1   Jn.17:14
2   2Cor.13:5
3   Jn.14:26, 16:13&14

To Love? Shakespeare said, "**To be or not to be, that is the question.**" From Paul's emphasis threw-out his writings I can hear him say, 'To love or not to love, that is the question.' Paul makes a great point about love in 1Corinthians chapter 13. Paul accomplished much for the Kingdom of God with much hardship which encourages all of us to do more, yet he said that all which he accomplished was for nothing if he did not love. God's kind of love is a kind which is almost absent in our American culture of today. The first love that God calls us to is to love Him. God shows His love to mankind from the very beginning in the Garden of Eden by first creating man in His very own image. God gave man every good thing in the wonderfully blessed garden for his needs. We take a stroll and sit in a beautiful garden today and enjoy its beauty, a garden that man has made, can you imagine what the garden that God had made and gave to man. In loving man God allowed him to name all the animals that God had created, which was God's right to name but He gave that privilege to man. In loving man God gave mankind a free will that they could choose but warned them not to eat of a certain tree, which they did and it has brought sorrow and hardship ever since.

God seemingly desired companionship coming in the garden walking in the cool of the day seeking Adam and Eve calling out to them, "**where are you?**"[1] As God had loved Adam and Eve providing everything they would ever need and warning them about dangers which He knew would bring them heartache and despair, He called, wanting them to love Him. We have been reading in Exodus chapters 20 & 21 of the things God began to speak to the Israelites through Moses. They have just been out of Egypt three months[2] where God had worked miracle after miracle to prove to all who He was and we would think this would cause the Israelites to love Him. God says that on the fathers who practice wrong things He will visit their iniquity to the third and fourth generation of their children (20:5). (God did resend this later[3]).

But, Oh so much more did God have a positive effect on those who loved Him, not just to the third and fourth generation, but to a thousand generations (20:6). Later in Deuteronomy 6:5 the Israelites were commanded to love the Lord their God with all they are. Jesus brings this again carrying it through into the new convent. And Jesus pulls a piece out of Leviticus 19:18 and says to love their neighbor as themselves. In essence Jesus says love is the fullness of all things that God says to us by saying, *"On these two commandments hang all the Law and the Prophets"* (Mt.22:40 NKJV).

In the first half, and even into the rest of John chapter 1 we can see the great statement John makes in 3:16, *"For God so loved the world"* (ASV). Jesus was the lamb, the Lamb of God.[4] This may not say much to us other than to think of a beautiful lamb all fuzzy and white that wouldn't hurt anyone, until we put it in the context of the Passover practice where each man (we will call one Abijah) was to take a lamb to be with him for four days. The lamb of Abijah was with him, close to him, always there, for four days and then Abijah killed and sacrificed his lamb. Now do you get the picture of The Lamb of God? This is how much God loves us, can we help but return such a love for what He did for us even while we were still in sin deserving only wrath.[5] In this Jesus also calls us to love our brethren with this same type of love, *"love one another; even as I have loved you"* (Jn. 13:34 ASV).

---

1   Gen.3:9
2   Gen.19:1
3   Eze. 18:17&20
4   Jn.1:29&36
5   Rom.5:8

Fathers, there is a great responsibility that fathers have. Fathers are to be a foundation for their children, to be a guide, a protector, a provider. Being a father is no light task. Oh, there are many who are a biological father only. There are others who are fatherly to children who are biologically not theirs. Then there are within the church spiritual fathers. Paul refers to himself many times as the spiritual father of the churches he writes to.

All through the history of the Jews from in Exodus where we are reading as Israel is brought out of Egypt and given the Law through Moses on to David and the other Psalm writers we can see the handprints of a loving Father looking out for, guiding, directing, and chastising His children. Jesus, in John 2:14-17 says, *'What have you done to my Father's house!'* (my paraphrase). Jesus speaks of God as His Father. Jesus tells us that He has made the way and we can go to God the Father with confidence as children seeking guidance, protection, and provision.

God the Father is our foundation, everything we are, everything that we are doing, and even where we are going all stands on the foundation of who He is. We were created by Him, every breath we take is by Him, we are guided by His word, and by our response to that word we have our security into eternity. A father is important, whether it be God the Father, or a spiritual father such as Paul, or even us who are fathers for our children. As we see of our heavenly Father, all of us fathers are to be a foundation to our children giving them guidance and direction, teaching them what it is we have to offer, helping them as they grow physically and spiritually in life. Why the Holy Spirit chose to speak of fathers today I don't know but some of you fathers reading this may. I want to end this with some of the scriptures we have about fathers.

"Fathers, do not provoke your children to anger, but bring them up in the discipline and instruction of the Lord" (Eph. 6:4 ESV).

"Fathers, do not provoke your children, lest they become discouraged" (Col. 3:21 ESV).

"as you know how we were exhorting and encouraging and imploring each one of you as a father would his own children" (1Thes. 2:11 NASB – Paul compares his care as a father does/should).

This one from the Old Testament does not say fathers but could certainly be added to the list; *"Train up a child in the way he should go, And even when he is old he will not depart from it"* (Pro. 22:6 ASV).

In times that were before there have been many who of their faith have followed God in hardship, in sorrow, in gladness, in joy, and in thanksgiving. All who followed God knew that all was in God's hands and no matter what condition they were in they knew God held it. The one confidence Paul always had was that he would one day see God as he would stand before Him in heaven to be with Him for all time with no end. His was always Paul's joy and life. He says in one place that to be absent from this world would be to be present with Christ his Lord.[1] This would be joy to him. Do we find joy in the same place that Paul did? Or are we still finding as much, or even more here in this world of this world? How do we conduct ourselves?

Are we glad when we come close to God, or is it somewhat yet as a duty rather than privilege? There are those who find joy in God as did Paul the apostle, but many times they are looked upon strangely, even by some of those in the Church. What is the cost to walk with God? The devil takes his punches. The world laughs and sneers, we are excluded from various things. Many of the things of the world we no longer find any value in, much of it only having value in evil. This is the world Paul was in, this is the world we are in, it will always be this way in some sort. Sin has come in and affected all of creation on this earth.

A day is coming when all will be made right again, but until then we must walk in the strength Paul did, in the strength he got from his Lord, from his relationship with Christ. Paul even said he lived in Christ,[2] this was how he survived and existed. Have you reached the place where you realize you are only able to live (in these troubled times) because you are in Christ where you receive life that cannot be taken from you. Are you so tied into Christ that you are somewhat in your eternity even now? In a sense Paul was for he says to depart from here was to be with Christ, and yet to live on in the world was Christ. He saw himself in Christ always[3] and that one day all would be made right again.

Paul in his life had responded kind of in a retroactive way to what Peter said on the day of Pentecost when the first sermon of salvation was preached to the Jews. *"that times of refreshing may come from the presence of the Lord, and that he may send the Christ appointed for you, Jesus, whom heaven must receive until the time for restoring all the things about which God spoke by the mouth of his holy prophets long ago"* (Acts 3:20&21 ESV). Paul looked forward to that time of restoration and until it came his life was Christ. Can you say your life is Christ?

---

1   2Cor.5:6&8, Philp.1:20-26
2   Gal.2:20
3   Rom.14:7-9

Fasting as a lifestyle, this is what we will look at today. Fasting is typically thought of as doing without food, but this could not be a lifestyle. Some who practice fasting on a regular routine, such as on a certain day of the week each week may refer to it as lifestyle. But what I want to speak of today is a lifestyle that affects every day of our life, every moment we live. A fasting of food is usually the denying ourselves of certain foods or all foods we desire. To broaden the meaning of fasting to that of a lifestyle means in following God we live a life of denying many things we desire, those things God has spoken to us and shown us are not good for a mature spiritual life. At salvation (and in the first weeks that follow) we find that many things we desired before we no longer desire.

This is a lifestyle that changes within us automatically, it is part of the new birth. After that there are conscious choices we have to make as part of Kingdom living. In the Lord's Prayer, the one He taught His disciples, it starts out with, 'Our Father who art in heaven, hallowed be thy name, **Thy Kingdom come...on earth as it is in heaven.**' The Kingdom of God coming on earth as it is in heaven is us living His way: valuing what He values, doing what He is doing, going where He is going, blessing as He is blessing, etc. Part of that Kingdom living is not doing the things He tells us are not good for us or that should not be in our lives. Choices, we have to make them every day. We turn away from those things we desire because God tells us we should. This is a type of fasting.

Jesus tells the woman at the well that the way the Samaritans worship, and even the way the Jews worship in Jerusalem is going to change, that true worship is going to be worshiping the Father in spirit and in truth. Jesus is telling her that the ways the Samaritans desire to worship God and the way the Jews desire to worship God is going to have to change, for by spirit and truth is the way the Father desires those who follow Him to worship Him. (Jn. 4:20 – 24) We can get so stuck in our ritual of religion that we are no longer following God in spirit and truth. Denial of those things we desire, even of many of those things we think we should do or have, is what the Father is looking for in us. Jesus said, '**Pick up you cross, and follow Me.**' [1]

Jesus didn't say, 'find a cross you like, pick it up and go where seems right to you.' He said pick up your cross, the one God has designated for you, and then come and go where I am going, doing what I am doing. Jesus as He taught for some three years before going to the cross said that He only did what He saw the Father doing. [2] Are we only doing what we see Jesus doing, or are we doing what we want to be doing not willing to give up what we desire as our way of living the Christian life? God decides what part He wants us to be in the Body of Christ: foot, noise, hand, etc. (1Cor. 12:14-18) We need to deny what we desire seeking God to find out what He wants us to be, and to do. Denying food we desire is a fasting in the way we eat, denying the things/the ways we desire to live is a fasting as a lifestyle.

---

1   Mt.16:24, Mk.8:34, Lk.9:23
2   Jn.5:19

Dependency, is that not faith. The question is do we really depend on God, or do we take the reins in our teeth and go for it making it happen by our sheer determination? By our sheer determination we can make ourselves look like Christian people should. I once heard of a prayer a man had made to the Lord, it went something like this, 'Lord I pray that you make me like a sponge and fill me with Yourself so when I get squeezed you are the only thing that comes out.' We can by sheer determination behave (on the outside) like we should but what happens when we get squeezed? I want to be such that my natural reactions to situations are how a Christian should behave even if I'm not looking quite right (according to how others judge me) the rest of the time, than to just wear a costume that looks good.

Asking God to help us remove the facade and take of the mask, and then go take a good long look in a spiritual mirror can help accomplish this. Dying to self is never an easy thing to do, we have to face our failures, our pride, and our ego. Dependency, where are we putting it? God wants us to put it fully on Him. But our ego and pride want us to put it on ourselves. This is why so many want to, still in some way, follow a bit of the Law. Pride and ego want to be able to say 'I' did do some myself. The truth is the only thing we have done ourselves is come up short when it comes to qualifying by the Law. All has been done for us by Jesus on the cross.

He paid for our sins,[1] it is His blood that covers us,[2] it is by His sacrifice[3] that we have eternal life. Today we read in Psalms, *"Blessed be Jehovah God, the God of Israel, Who only doeth wondrous things"* (Ps. 72:18 ASV). It is He alone who does wondrous things, and we are the recipients of many of them. Sometimes the receiving of the many great wondrous things God wants to give us are prevented because we are in the way trying to do it ourselves. We have all seen this in children, we want to do something for them and they say, '**I want to do it myself.**' We wait while they try, we can't do anything many times while they are trying, and when they finally give up we are able to do it for them. Today in John chapter 5 we read of the Jews who were questioning Jesus about what He was doing.

They, in their minds, had concluded how a Jewish religious person should behave. Jesus was not behaving this way and they persecuted Him for it. (v. 16) There are always going to be those who by sheer determination are going to behave on the outside like Christians should but not have what needs to be on the inside. They will many times persecute others who don't always look right in their eyes on the outside but when those others get squeezed more of Jesus comes out than of self. A sponge only soaks up much water because of all the empty places inside. We need to empty ourselves of self so we can soak up much more of Jesus.

---

1   1Cor.15:3, Gal.1:4, 1Pet.2:24, 1Jn.2:2
2   Rom.3:25, 5:9, Eph.1:7, Col.1:14, Heb.9:22, 13:12&20, 1Pet.1:2&19
3   Heb.9:26

The bread of life, Man can live on bread (that made from a grain of some sort) and water alone. It is the stable substance that will sustain us in life. It is interesting that all of our body can be sustained by one source even though most of us have much more in our diets. We desire many other things than bread but bread by itself could do it. Man's appetite is wide, yearning for many different things to eat. In the same way in our spiritual lives man yearns for much more than that one thing that will sustain his spiritual life. The Jews had this problem. In the Law they were told to have no other god before them than Jehovah.

Yet the yearning of man caused the Jews, even though they had seen all the great works, the great signs, the great wonders, done by God, after time they began to seek the gods of the nations around them and put a difficulty between themselves and Jehovah. In our world today there are many gods from many nations and man with his yearnings tends to want a diet of more than one. In our culture in America for many the god seems to be **Self**. Even in the Church there are many who cannot serve the one God Jehovah, they also serve the god **Self**. Because of man's yearning it takes a constant effort to keep ourselves to one God. Even within the Church there is the constant danger of another gospel creeping in.

The gospel that Jesus presented us with is straight forward, to repent of our sins, accept Him into our lives, pick up our cross, and follow Him. Paul was the great apostle to the gentiles, which most of us are. He presented the gospel as it was presented to him by Jesus. Yet as simple as it is Paul has to write to the Galatians about not accepting another gospel. Jesus tells us He is the bread of life which has come down from heaven. In Him is all we need. He is the sable diet that will sustain us in life, we need no more. We need no other gospel, no other god, Jesus is sufficient. (Jn. 6:32 - 35)

Jesus told the woman at the well to ask Him for the living water so that she would thirst no more. [1] In our spiritual diet we will be supplied all we need of The Bread and The Water which comes from, and is Jesus. He will sustain us and we will live.

---

[1]   Jn.4:10

'Breakfast of Champions.' We have all heard the phrase. This is certainly speaking of one's physical strength. But what would it be if it was applied to spiritual champions? A daily diet of God will strengthen us and cause us to develop spiritually. Spiritual champions are fighting battles much greater than those fought in the physical. In the Name of Christ, we do not know what power we possess. Even demons must obey us. The problem seems to be that most of the Church is still walking, trying to do God's work in their own power assuming God's power is of course working in them behind the scenes. It is our place as followers of Jesus to know, not assume.

God called us to a work, to a faith in Him, and to take up the weapons and tools He has told us to use. If I am a carpenter I don't go to work assuming I have a hammer and saw, I make sure I have a hammer and saw. We are to know for sure we have the weapons and tools God intends for us to use. The same as we go to the tool shed to get the hammer and saw, we go to God, request, and knowingly receive the things He intends for us to use. God's weapons and tools are powerful and awesome for tearing down strongholds. If strongholds are spiritual can we fight against them in our own power? We cannot even control the behavior in our own lives to live how God wants us to, so how would we have any success in pulling down strongholds in our power?

There is too much assumption in the Church today. We think we know but we do not. We are like those supposed mature spiritual leaders who we read of in John chapter 7 today, who knew (in their own power), and told the rest of the people, that Jesus could not be the Messiah. They said they knew where Jesus was from and of the Messiah none would know. (v.27) The problem was they didn't know as much as they thought they knew because of the Holy Spirit being the father of Jesus' earthly birth they really didn't know where He was from. The leaders also in thinking they knew where Jesus came from said He could not be from the line of David which the Messiah would be. Again in assuming they knew, they were not aware of David in Psalms referring to Jesus as his Lord therefore proving the Messiah could not be a son of David. In the assumption of the leaders they did not know that Jesus was born in Bethlehem, the town of David.

Even when they are questioned by Nicodemus to consider who Jesus is, they replied in their assured assumption, to search and see if any prophet ever came out of Galilee. We need to be careful about making assured assumptions. To assume we are the spiritual champions without having the right breakfast is a foolish and dangerous thing for us to do. We need to know, not assume, that we have the weapons and tools needed to do the job God has for us. *"For though we walk in the flesh, we do not war according to the flesh (for the weapons of our warfare are not of the flesh, but mighty before God to the casting down of strongholds)"* (2 Cor. 10:3 & 4 ASV).

'The obstinateness of a people.'   Webster's definition of <u>Obstinateness</u> is: *'Stubbornness; pertinacity in opinion or purpose; fixed determination.'* And of Obstinateis: *'Stubborn; pertinaciously adhering to an opinion or purpose; fixed firmly in resolution; not yielding to reason, arguments or other means.'* This word can be used as a good thing; In one's obstinateness to the Lord, he was not overcome easily with evil. But most of the time it is our resistance to the Lord and His ways that obstinateness represents: *"I have declared the former things from the beginning; They went forth from My mouth, and I caused them to hear it. Suddenly I did them, and they came to pass. Because I knew that you were* **obstinate**, *and your neck was an iron sinew, and your brow bronze, even from the beginning I have declared it to you"* (Isa. 48:3, 4, & 5 NKJV).

Obstinateness seems to be a thing that we, given a free will by God, have taken on ourselves and causes us much trouble. We think we know and in our obstinateness refusing to see the truth, but truth will prevail. We have a merciful and loving God, but sometimes because of how we pray, wanting the fullness of who God is in our lives, He hits us with a hard blow to break our obstinateness so we can receive that fullness we are asking for. This happened to our brother Paul on the road to Damascus. Paul, as a Jew following Judaism with all of his heart[1] (even though it was misguided), was fighting against the very purpose of God.[2] His heart was toward God, it was just not accepting the full truth of God. God seeing the desire of Paul's heart, and of him seeking God with all his heart, maybe even in Paul's prayers that we know nothing about, yet with obstinateness, God struck him with a hard blow.

We can be an obstinate people. Today we continue reading in John chapter 8 of Jesus' dialog with the Jewish religious leaders and in their obstinateness are not hearing or accepting what Jesus is saying. They were the leaders of what would be the Church today. Are there still leaders in the Church today who even though they are saved by the blood of Christ are obstinate like those Jewish leaders at that time when Jesus was speaking to them.   Do we, as Paul did at first, fight against the very purpose of God. Is God speaking to us but we are not hearing or accepting what God is saying. Jesus said in John 14:26, *"But the Helper, the Holy Spirit, whom the Father will send in my name, He will teach you all things, and bring to your remembrance all that I said to you"* (NKJV).

Jesus said the Holy Spirit would be our Helper, our <u>Paraclete</u>. **Webster's** definition of <u>Paraclete</u> is: *'Properly, an advocate; one called to aid or support; hence, the consoler, comforter or intercessor, a term applied to the Holy Spirit'.* In **The Complete Word Study Dictionary** part of the definition of the Greek word <u>parakletos</u> says: *"...the Holy Spirit is designated by Jesus Christ as equal with Himself..."*   If we were one of the disciples of Jesus at that time we read of in the gospel of John, would not each of us go to Jesus and ask Him what was the very will of God for us in our life. Then today, according to the definitions given above, each of us should go to the Holy Spirit and ask what is the very will of God for us in our life today? Are you going to the Holy Spirit and asking Him?

---

1   Acts 22:3, 23:6, Philp.3:4-6
2   Acts 9:3-6

Authenticity, are we authentic people? Is what we do and how we act really who we are? Are we being real? Jesus calls us to live in truth. Are we living in truth, or is most all we do a facade? How will the world ever see who Christ is if He is hidden by us? We are to let our light shine, we are to sing His praise, we are to show His love, we are to allow Him to live through us to a starving world. One of the last things Jesus commanded His disciples (and us) was to love one another. [1] Now this is talking about the Body of Christ, the Church. Many would try to make this more, that we are to love the world. This is true but here Jesus is speaking of the brethren. We, the Church, are to love one another but I'm not sure we are doing a good job of it. If the world cannot see a lovingness in the Body of Christ how can they believe we love them as Christ loved a lost world when we tell them we do and want to help them. They see right through it and know if we are not loving one another we ain't gon'a love them.

We are supposed to have Christ living in us, they are supposed to see Christ in us – what are they seeing, is it Christ, or us in our bickering, backbiting manner? Before we can ever invite, and attract the lost world into the family of Christianity we need to have our house clean and attractive. God is a great God but if we are not behaving the world will wonder how good of a God He could be. God wants to save the world and He wants to use us, but if we leave a bad taste in the mouth of the world they may not want us, and they may even spit us out as fast as they can. What kind of a favor are we doing God if we are this way? In the time of Jesus in the gospels the Pharisees were the representation of God to the Jewish world. In our reading today Jesus heals a blind man who is taken to the Pharisees by others.

In being questioned by the Pharisees he was authentic and said, *"Whether he's a sinner or not I don't know. One thing I do know: I was blind, now I see...What a strange thing,"* the man answered, *"that you don't know where he's from—considering that he opened my eyes! We know that God doesn't listen to sinners; but if anyone fears God and does his will, God does listen to him"* (Jn. 9:25, 30 & 31 CJB). The Pharisees who questioned him were not being authentic, they were play acting before the people wanting the people to think they (the Pharisees) were being holy. Jesus spoke of the Pharisees and to the Pharisees many times telling them that what was inside of them was not holy, some He even said were sons of the devil.

Paul had taught the Galatians to be authentic, to be who they were in Christ. Jews had come along after Paul had left them in his first visit of teaching about Jesus. The Jews wanted them to begin putting on garments of Judaism by taking on certain Jewish rituals, the following of the Law. Paul is pleading with them, coaxing them not to listen to these false teachers, not to put something on that false teachers themselves were not. The act may look great but the heart is still defiled. God calls us to be authentic, God calls us to love one another, God calls us to let our light shine that those in a dark world can see. What does the world see in you?

---

1   Jn.13:34, 15:12&17

Are we wise people? Sometimes we get wisdom and education mixed up. It is how our society has programmed us. We have been told that education is what we need. Even in the gospels the intelligent/educated of the time thought of themselves as wise people. God said He would confound the wisdom of the wise bringing it to naught.[1] All scripture has to agree together and God said if any of us are without wisdom to ask Him for it and He would give it to us. Once we receive the wisdom from God are we included in those who God will confound? It must be that this was said of the intelligent/educated so they would know for sure it was them He was talking about since they considered themselves wise and Him (and His disciples) foolish. How many of us today need to ask God for wisdom but are blinded to our need because we have education considering ourselves intelligent assuming that equates wisdom?

If that was wisdom and true knowledge then the universities and colleges of America would be full of people following God knowing that by Jesus Christ is the only way. Most are so deceived that they don't believe there is an eternity to life. Eternity will be in one place or the other - heaven or hell (the lake of fire where the devil is cast). Wisdom comes to man difficultly. Not even when God performs miracle after miracle do we get it, that He is God and we should follow Him. We are reading in the book of Exodus of miracle after miracle in Egypt and in the wilderness and yet they refuse to follow God. Asaph, the writer of Psalm 78 recounts the history of Israel and how time after time they provoked God's anger (v. 58). In John chapter 10 Jesus' dialog goes on with the Jewish leaders, trying to convince them to hear Him, to know He is the Messiah, and that He and the Father are one. He tells them their wisdom is not wise or they would recognize Him. Their wisdom is not wise, all they see is their own standing as righteous. Paul in Galatians continues his argument of why would they give up the freedom they had received by the gospel to become ensnared again by the Law. The whole trouble in Galatia is because some Jews came in declaring to be wise telling the people they are not complete in what they have, a salvation given freely by Christ.

These outsiders tell them that there yet needs to be a work on their part. We as people like to think of ourselves as wise, it bolsters our ego, even if we don't consciously admit it. A wisdom before the Lord is a brokenness, a believing all He says, accepting all He says, and expecting what He says. In that place of brokenness many of us find we have no wisdom and must ask God for it. Solomon asked for it, *"asked wisdom and knowledge for yourself"* (2Chr. 1:11 RSV).

We are told in James1:5, *"If any of you lacks wisdom, let him ask God"* (ESV).Paul prays for those in Colosse that they would receive wisdom, *"we have not stopped praying for you, asking God to fill you with the knowledge of his will in all the wisdom and understanding which the Spirit gives"* (Col. 1:9 CJB).It is not a wisdom recognized by the world, but it is recognized by God.

---

1   Isa.29:14, 1Cor.1:19, 3:19

A stiff-necked people, this is what God called those who Moses brought out of Egypt. It is speculated that part of what God had for Moses to learn during his forty years outside of Egypt was how to herd sheep for he would have to, under God's guidance, herd the people out of Egypt to where God wanted to take them. I, myself, grew up as a child on a farm with farm animals. We had very few sheep but in being acquainted with farm people I heard about sheep. They are one of the most stupidest, stubborn animals there is. Moses was called by God to bring His people Israel out of Egypt because of the promise He made to Abraham, Isaac, and Jacob. God called them a stiff-necked people. [1] They were a stiff-necked people and stubborn, they were like trying to work with stubborn sheep. It is interesting that Jesus refers to us as sheep. He does say some good things about sheep, such as; My sheep will know My voice. Yet as people I think we are still sometimes a stubborn people. We do not yield easily to His call of salvation, we many times refuse to believe what He says, we balk many times of what He has told us to go do. He says to go through this place and we go through another.

Yes, it seems there is still a little stiff-neckedness left in us. God's grace is marvelous, His mercy is grand, His longsuffering is huge. Jesus dealt with stiff-necked people during His three years of ministry before He gave Himself on the cross for us. Many of them refused to believe He was the Messiah. In John chapter 11 today we see Jesus called Lazarus forth from the dead. (v. 43) [side track: in a sense this is what Jesus has done for all of us who are now saved, He has called us from the dead. For before we accepted Him into our life we were all dead.] Jesus knew that Lazarus would not remain dead so when He wept it was not because Lazarus was dead as the others wept and assumed He was weeping. He came to raise Lazarus from the dead in order to establish to many His authority on earth as the Messiah.

It seemed to sorrow Him that (v. 33) some of these who were dear to him had to suffer in order that His Messiahship could be shown. Verse 37 is most certainly true, that if Jesus had been there Lazarus would not have died, but then He would not have been able to demonstrate to all that He was sent from heaven from the Father and that He had power over death. (v. 42) Jesus and the Father certainly set this up from what we read in v. 4 & 6. Jesus after hearing Lazarus was sick had waited two more days. Jesus knew even before He left where He was to go to Bethany that Lazarus was already dead. (v. 11 & 14) It sorrowed Jesus that Jerusalem was so stiff-necked, He spoke over it, *"Jerusalem, Jerusalem, who kills the prophets and stones those who have been sent to her! How often I wanted to gather your children together, the way a hen gathers her chicks under her wings, and you were unwilling"* (Mt. 23:37 NASB).

It sorrowed Jesus that Mary and Martha, and those with them had to sorrow over Lazarus' death that His own glory could be shown. How much does Jesus sorrow over us when He wishes to gather us closely but we would not have it. Many times it is our stubbornness that keeps us away from Jesus, won't you yield and come close?

---

1 Ex.9:10

'Peace' is the subject that comes up again today. A divine peace is what we really all are searching for. A peace that settles all the unrest that we all sense inside of us. The world talks much of a peace but the only one they know or think of or imagine is that all people on the earth would be at peace with each other. This is not a divine peace, it is a false peace and if the world were able to have it, no more war, no more arguments with others, no more hatred, they would find still that unrest within themselves that is still searching for peace. The counterfeit has been spoke of ever since the Garden of Eden when the devil spoke to Eve.

It is only when we accept Jesus into our lives that this type of peace, a divine peace, takes its place in that part of our inner self that has been searching for peace. Even then we continue to struggle with having peace inside of us, but it is not because this divine peace is not full enough. We are not of this world but we are still in this world. [1] I am not sure that any of us will experience the fullness that this divine peace is until we arrive in heaven. We still have uncertainties in us, we still have fears in us, even though we have the fullness of the divine One living within us. More and more peace comes as we allow more and more of Christ to live in us. Yes, we receive the fullness of Christ at salvation, but it is still up to us of how much we yield ourselves to how much of Christ can live in us and through us. As we read today of Moses being on the mountain in the presence of God and when he returned to camp his face shone (with the glory of God) with a special light.

At this moment I believe Moses knew the greatest amount of divine peace that anyone still on this earth can have. It is after being in God's special presence that we experience that divine peace, but as that light upon Moses' face faded with time our peace will fade also unless we continue on a regular basis to expose ourselves being in the presence of God. As we do this there will be that light in our lives and that peace that others in this camp called earth will see as we walk through it. Are you getting your daily dose of God's special presence by spending time with Him each day?

---

1   Jn.15:19, 17:14, Philp.3:20

Where are you? What have you become? How do you imagine yourself to be? How do you see your value in life? These are important questions to answer. If you answer them in your own wisdom and intelligence your answer may be in error. The true answers to these questions are what God says about you in His word, in the Bible. Have you seen what God gives as answers to these questions about us? We may not feel what God says about us applies to us. We may conclude that what God says does not apply to us because we are unworthy to receive such blessings. We may even look at our sinfulness and conclude that God's blessings would be unwisely spent if given to us. Our conscience does have a right to show us our sinfulness but it does not have a right to determine what God can give us or not give us. It is the giver who has that right, it is God who decides what we are worthy or unworthy to receive. We in our own standing have no right to receive anything, yet we do not receive by what is our worthiness or unworthiness, it is by the worthiness of Jesus and He is certainly worthy.

This is why we receive, the only part of the formula that we have to play is to believe this. When we believe that we receive because of Jesus' worthiness, it is then that we receive. We have to believe we have a right to receive, a right given to us by Jesus Christ dying on that cross in our place, in the place of every one of us who will believe it. The right is ours, given freely by God, to a needy people in His love, to redeem all who are lost. Before we are saved it is our pride which keeps us away from receiving God's loving gift of eternal life. After salvation, if we truly see ourselves as we are, our shame and feeling of unworthiness, we hesitate to go to God. It keeps us from all the other great things that God has for us in His Kingdom here on earth. When it comes to us receiving or not receiving it is not by our worthiness, it is by Christ's worthiness. Paul tells us that even while we were dead (Eph. 2:1) by our trespasses (sins), under the influence of the prince of the power of the air (Eph. 2:2), conducting ourselves by the passions of our flesh and the thoughts of our own mind, deserving the wrath of God and were heirs of indignation (Eph. 2:3), that in that death being totally unworthy, God in His great love (Eph. 2:4) made us alive in Christ (Eph. 2:5).

If God did all this while we were unsaved why would He hold any blessings of the Kingdom from us now? God wants to give us so much but the same as with salvation which we could not receive until we believed, it is the same with all the rest He wants to give us. Paul tells us, even though we are still living our lives here on this earth that also we are seated in the heavenlies in Christ. We are there in Christ because of His worthiness having nothing to do with our worthiness or unworthiness. (Eph. 2:6) Read again what Paul says in Ephesians 2:7 – 10 absorbing what he says. In v. 7 it says that God did this (our salvation and seating us in the heavenlies) that He would demonstrate the immeasurable riches of His grace in kindness of heart towards us in Christ Jesus. Can you tell me how many are the immeasurable riches? Now go back to the questions I asked in the beginning and answer them according to what God says about you.

Time for all things. All things have their time and there is a time for all things. *"He has made everything beautiful in its time. Also He has put eternity in their hearts, except that no one can find out the work that God does from beginning to end"*(Ecc. 3:11 NKJV). And *"Because for every matter there is a time and judgment, Though the misery of man increases greatly. For he does not know what will happen; So who can tell him when it will occur?"* (Ecc. 8:6&7 NKJV). The time of man, the time of God, the time of judgment, all these are important times. The time of man only God knows exactly. The time of God of the work He does from beginning to end no one knows exactly. The time of judgment we know is coming, but exactly when we do not know. Jesus speaks to the disciples the night before His crucifixion telling them that when He leaves going back to heaven He will prepare a place for them and that He will come back for them (Jn.14:2).

When the time will be we are given hints, but the exact time we do not know. The important thing to know is that God has designated a time for it to take place. [1] It is not just a may be, it is an exact. God does all things in exactness. We are not able to understand God so the way He does things we cannot understand either.

At times what we read in scripture seems God is a little confused or surprised, but God knows all things. There is something going on at these times in God that we cannot comprehend. There is a time for all to be revealed. Jesus said that when the judgment comes all will be known. We are told there is a time when we will know as we are known. [2] There is a time coming when we will see God as He truly is. There is a time coming when this earth will be folded up and put aside and a new earth will come. [3] Before Jesus came, taught, and died on the cross, it was a mystery of God's plan for mankind.

Paul spends most of Ephesians chapter 3 speaking of this mystery. The confidence we have to have (faith), is that God has set a time for everything, and everything will happen right on time. It won't be made different by what we do or don't do. It won't be made different by what satan will do. It will be right on time. God has a schedule from beginning to end of what He is doing. If we are willing to have Him as Lord the times are set even for all things in our lives. We must believe all things are in God's control and they will happen like clockwork. He is God.

---

1   Acts 1:7
2   2Cor.13:12
3   Isa.65:17, 66:22, 2Pet.3:13, Rev.21:1

On this day what are we to be? The world is all around us having an influence on each other and can have an influence on us if we are not careful and guarding against it. We are to be in this world but not of this world. Jesus said He was not of this world and if we are in Him then neither are we of this world. [1] We must guard against the influence of the world and know who it is that influences all of them. [2] We are called to be a peculiar people. [3] Certainly, if we follow after Christ, become as much like Him as we can, to the world we will seem to be a peculiar people, odd and different. It is easy, as a Christian, to begin to look like the world in many ways. We are bombarded by those things the world runs after every day. When there are enough contaminants in the air that settles on a plant it will reduce its production of fruit. We are to keep guard of the contaminants that can settle on us from the world around us.

We are to get our substance, our spiritual nourishment, our strength for living, and the input that comes into us to bear fruit from Christ. Jesus tells us, 'Abide in me, and I in you. As the branch cannot bear fruit by itself, unless it abides in the vine, neither can you, unless you abide in me.' *"I am the vine, you are the branches. He who abides in me, and I in him, he it is that bears much fruit, for apart from me you can do nothing"* (Jn. 15:4&5 RSV). Paul appeals to and begs the Ephesians (and us) to live worthy of their calling by which they had been called. (Eph. 4:1) We are called to be different than the world, living in a way that honors God.

Paul says we must strive earnestly to keep the harmony of oneness. (Eph. 4:3) Paul goes on in Ephesians chapter 4 to speak of how we should be in contrast to how the world is. Much of this boils down to something Jesus said, He commanded us three times to love one another. [4] Jesus said by this all would know we are His disciples. [5] Paul speaks of this in our reading today; *"walk worthy of the calling to which you have been called with complete lowliness of mind and meekness, with patience, bearing with one another and making allowances because you love one another"* (Eph. 4:1&2 AMPC).[Here are other related scriptures: 1Cor. 1:20&21, Col. 2:8, Jas. 2:5.]

We are called by Jesus to be different, we are instructed and encouraged by the apostles to be a Godly people living in God's way. We are to be attached to the Vine, we are to be producing fruit, we are to be a peculiar people, we are to have the light of Christ. This is what we are to be on this day and every day. *"walk worthy of the calling"*

---

1   Jn.17:15&16
2   Jn.14:30, 2Cor.4:3&4, Eph.2:2
3   Tit. 2:14, 1Pet.2:9
4   Jn.13:34, 15:12, 15:17
5   Jn.13:35

My God is God. This is a statement that we should all become familiar with. We must state it, we must believe it, we must live by it. It is God that is everything to us. He is our creator. He is our guide. He is our savior. He is the one who calls to us from afar. He is the Mighty King. He is the Lord of all. He is the beginning of all things. He is the end of all that we know. He is the Alpha, and the Omega. He is everything, and all we need. He is our need. He is our supply. He is the one who causes us to know. He is everything to us. Without Him we would not live. Without Him we would not know. Without Him we would not be aware of our need. Without Him we could not be fulfilled. Without Him we would have no future. Without Him we would have no reason to live. He is our all in all. How great it is to know Him. How great it is that we have been redeemed by Him. How kind and merciful is He to us. All we are and all we can ever be is in Him. Sometimes it has been said people are too full of themselves. Many Christians would apply this thought to the world around us but not to themselves.

The world is lost, and those who will never allow Christ in their lives are going down that wide path to destruction. So whether they are full of themselves or not will make no difference in their outcome as they travel that wide path. The ones who are affected by being too full of themselves is us who travel down the narrow path. When we are too full of ourselves it gives very little room for God to work in our lives. As we see more and more all that God is we are able to value less and less of who we are. God works in the yielded vessel, the more room we give Him the more He works in us. That which comes off the potter's wheel is a container of a sort, to fill with something. God is the potter and we are the clay[1]. In creation He made us into a vessel, with what we are filled of depends largely on us.

Although God has made us He gives us a free will to determine what we are filled with. If we relate our hearts, our soul, our who we are to harden rocks, then we start out our lives as vessels full of nothing but rocks. When we accept Jesus into our lives we are reborn and the Spirit is born in us. Many times in scripture the Spirit is referred to as living water. Now our vessel is filled with rocks from our former state, but now in salvation living water has filled the gaps between the rocks. The rocks represent the hard places in our lives that the living water cannot fill. It is by our free will that we remove more and more of the rocks (hard places) from our vessel and as we do God continues to give us more and more living water to fill those voids. Paul tells us, *"Therefore, pay careful attention to how you conduct your life—live wisely, not unwisely. Use your time well, for these are evil days"* (Eph. 5:15&16 CJB). In the former chapter and in this chapter Paul describes what may still be rocks in our vessels that we should remove and the things that should take their place is more and more of the living water that comes into us. Paul tells us, *"Don't get drunk with wine, because it makes you lose control. Instead, keep on being filled with the Spirit"* (Eph. 5:18 CJB).

As we allow ourselves to be filled more and more with the spirit (living water) and less and less with ourselves (the rocks) we will find there will be more and more of God in our life. Hearing the truth and believing more of it is how we become more and more willing to cast out the rocks from our vessels. In some of Jesus' last words to His disciples before His arrest He told them the truth was that even though they were sad because He said He was leaving them, that what was coming for them was even better.

We would think that to walk with Jesus would be the greatest thing that could be for us, but Jesus says there is something greater. *"Nevertheless, I tell you the truth: it is to your advantage that I go away, for if I do not go away, the Helper will not come to you. But if I go, I will send him to you...When the Spirit of truth comes, he will guide you into all the truth, for he will not speak on his own authority, but whatever he hears he will speak, and he will declare to you the things that are to come. He will glorify me, for he will take what is mine and declare it to you"* (Jn. 16:7,13,14 ESV).Remove the rocks that something greater you might have in you as Jesus has promised.

---

1   Isa.64:8

How do we stand before God today? We do stand before Him by grace, covered by the blood of Christ that cleanses us from our sins. To fully apply this we need to have a good consciousness of the fear of the Lord. Fear requires respect because of knowing what the one we fear can do. The wrath of God is dreadful and awesome. God's wrath is what we deserve because of our sin. Some sweet young innocent woman may think, 'who me, I've never done a mean thing in my life.' There may be men who think they have never done anything that bad as to deserve the wrath of God.

The scriptures tell us there is none good, no not one.[1] Compared to God we are a wicked people. When we are able to admit we are a wicked and evil people the grace of God becomes soooooooooooo..... much more valuable. When we know the grace we have been given, the depth of such grace, it causes our respect for God to broaden extremely. Do we stand before God in fear and trembling? No, because we know His grace. If we understand that such greatness is the grace we have been given by God in salvation, why would we doubt anything else He wants to do in our lives?

If we can realize the great hump we have been taken over in salvation by that grace the rest should be an easy climb. God asks us to believe, so after having faith (believing) to be saved (such a huge event) why should believing what God has to say after that be so difficult? I suppose we struggle with believing because we try to get our brain engaged in it. Faith is more in the heart, soul, spirit, than in the brain. If the brain could accomplish such great things then we could have followed the Law to receive salvation. We couldn't, none of us could. We must have faith to please God to receive much of what He has for us. Jesus states that the disciples had this faith, they believed. (Jn. 17:7&8)

Even though we see that all abandoned Jesus at his arrest and trial it was by their faith in God's grace that they returned. (see what Jesus says to Peter in Luke 22:32) In John chapter 17 Jesus was praying for us also. (Jn. 17:20) Jesus' prayer is also for us who have believed (had faith) in what the disciples have spoken and taught. It is by us that the world (those who will) may come to faith (believe) and be convinced that the Father had sent Jesus to save a lost world. (Jn. 17:21) Paul encourages us to stand in our faith with these words in Ephesians 6:10&13 *"Finally, my brothers, let your hearts be strengthened in the Lord, and in the power of his might....take up all of the armor of God that you may be able to resist in the evil day, and having worked out all things, to stand"* (NKJV).

---

[1]   Rom.3:10&12

A dear friend, that is what we have in Christ. He is always close, caring about our well-being. He came from the Father to bring us freedom, to give us joy, and to show us a better life. This world has a distorted view of what makes a person truely joyful. The very first thing about true joy is it comes when we find a peaceful relationship with God. When Jesus was born (came into this world) the angels announced peace on earth, this was the peace that was later made as Jesus died for us on the cross. Jesus' death paid for our sins and removed the barrier between us and God.

Right after the last supper with His disciples, Jesus said He would send a comforter to them (and us) and then He said, *"Peace I leave to you; my peace I give to you, not according as the world doth give do I give to you; let not your heart be troubled, nor let it be afraid"* (Jn. 14:27 YLT). Who but a dear friend would do such a thing for us? Jesus also said we were His friends in this statement as He knew He was going to His death on the cross, *"Greater love hath no man than this, that a man lay down his life for his friends"* (Jn. 15:13 ASV). This is the song we sing **'What a Friend We Have in Jesus'**. He even tells us; *"Yes, indeed! I tell you that whatever you ask from the Father, he will give you in my name"* (Jn. 16:23 CJB). What a friend Jesus is to us, He gives us an entitlement to go to the Father and ask. [1]

This relationship Jesus has given us with God causes great peace. We need to allow what we read today in the second part of John chapter 18 and what we will read in the first part of chapter 19 tomorrow to penetrate our soul, it is all our dear friend Jesus did for us. Paul in all his letters right after the greeting says, 'peace from God our Father and the Lord Jesus Christ'. Paul always reaffirms that peace we have with God. Paul in his life of presenting the gospel went though much hardship because of the relationship and friendship he had with Jesus.

Paul also practiced the relationship and friendship with those he had led to Christ. This is the type of friendship Jesus is calling all of us to have with one another in the midst of the Body of Christ: *"I am among you as one who serves"* (Lk. 22:27 RSV). Jesus says we should serve one another just as He served us. And He says, *"keep on loving each other just as I have loved you"* (Jn. 15:12 CJB). Jesus says in this we will find peace; in relationship/friendship with God and relationship/friendship with our brethren.

---

1   Jn.16:26&27

Humility, how do we describe it? I guess Jesus would be the description of humility. Being humble doesn't mean allowing people to run over you, Jesus didn't. He had rights that no one knew about. In humility He put up with all the objections. He showed them miracles that never had been done before, and yet in their unbelief they condemned Him. Over and over Jesus' disciples didn't get it and He kept on teaching and teaching and teaching – never giving up. Only when His work was finished did He stop, and even then right up to his arrest was He teaching. Even His arrest was an act of humility. In John 18:6 when Judas and the crowd with him came looking, asking for Jesus of Nazareth, Jesus said, 'I AM,' and they drew back and fell to the ground.

This certainly was not to worship the one they came to arrest. The truth seems to be that they were overwhelmed (overpowered), the 'I AM' had the victory, and still He allowed Himself to be arrested and led away to trial. Peter, in his effort to show himself strong, after being told by Jesus he would deny Him, struck out with the sword at one who came with Judas. Jesus told Peter to put the sword away, that He could request from the Father twelve legions of angels to rescue Him.[1] This is the height of humility, to have the power to overthrow, and allow Himself to be taken away and crucified for the good of mankind.

We can see the humility of Jesus in the prophecy of Isaiah, *"In fact, it was our diseases he bore, our pains from which he suffered; yet we regarded him as punished, stricken and afflicted by God. But he was wounded because of our crimes, crushed because of our sins; the disciplining that makes us whole fell on him, and by his bruises we are healed. We all, like sheep, went astray; we turned, each one, to his own way; yet Adonai laid on him the guilt of all of us. Though mistreated, he was submissive—he did not open his mouth. Like a lamb led to be slaughtered, like a sheep silent before its shearers, he did not open his mouth"* (53:4-7 CJB). We see this played out in our reading today in John chapter 19.

Also in our reading today we hear what Paul says about humility, *"make my joy complete by being of the same mind, maintaining the same love, united in spirit, intent on one purpose. Do nothing from selfishness or empty conceit, but with humility consider one another as more important than yourselves; do not merely look out for your own personal interests, but also for the interests of others. Have this [humble] attitude in yourselves which was also in Christ Jesus"* (Philp. 2:2-5 NASB).Pride has no place in the Body of Christ. We all struggle with *"selfishness or empty conceit,* "it needs to be a constant effort on our part to put it down within our self and walk humbly before God.

---

1   Mt.26:53

How be it we are blessed? How is it we receive so many great things from God? How is it we have such beautiful surroundings of the earth, all the natural things that are so beautiful? The majestic mountains, the perfectness of the hummingbird in flight, each and every beautiful detail of each and every flower. How is it we are so blessed? It is because of the love of God our creator. Even though we have sinned: Adam and Eve as the bases of mankind, and each and every one of us individually, He has continued to love us in the ways He has created this earth we live on. At the initial sin in the garden of eating the forbidden fruit God could have not only forced mankind out of the garden to live by the sweat of his brow,[1] But God could have spoke the word and made this earth more like the terrain of Mars or the Moon. God didn't, He left it as beautiful as He had created it.

Through time God kept calling to man so He could bless him, and as we all have heard in the first part of time none heard His calling except one, the man Noah. God preserved the life of mankind through Noah and his family. Later God called the man Abram and made a nation of Abram's children by which God would bless all mankind. From that nation, the Jewish people, God in His love bless us all to the fullest. God sent us a savior from heaven to live amongst mankind as a man, yet still being of the heavenly divinity of God. Jesus who did no wrong suffered the consequences of sin in our place, that anyone who would accept Jesus as Lord would have their sins forgiven.

This is the greatest blessing God has given mankind. Much of the world benefits from the blessing of creation, experiencing the beauty of the earth, but the greatest blessing they miss out on, the forgiveness provided for their sins, instead they go through the wide gate to destruction. In our reading yesterday of John chapter 19 Jesus said, "It is finished."It could be taken that He meant it was over, that He had tried His best but so many would not listen, and that there was no hope for anyone past this point of His preaching. This was not the case. The disciples thought it was, they hid from the Jews, mourned the loss of Jesus.

They didn't know how they would carry on, they were devastated because they did not understand what Jesus had been telling them over and over. Jesus had said 'I will rise again and you will all be blessed.' Today, in John chapter 20, we read of Jesus' resurrection and His blessings on His followers. How is it we are blessed? This is how we are blessed, from the beginning of time to the end, it is by the love of God fully applied to mankind through Jesus. *"For God so loved the world that He gave His only begotten Son, that whoever believes in Him should not perish but have everlasting life"* (Jn. 3:16 NKJV).

---

[1]   Gen.3:19

How joyful it is to serve the Lord! The liberty that God has given us by His grace and mercy, the forgiveness He has given through the sacrifice of Christ, should give us extreme joy. Do we really know what we have been forgiven of, the bondage we have been freed from?[1] This is where joy comes from, knowing our God and what He has done.[2] Yes, we are to know our sin, but to not stay there, do we really know what Jesus has done for us on the cross. He is the one who took our sins upon Himself and suffered the penalty, we are no longer held guilty.[3] What a joy if we accept it. All has been done by Christ, the only thing left for us to do is as Jesus said, 'pick up your cross and follow me'.

Following Him should be a joy, even the carrying of our cross can be joyful if we know what we, each one of us, have been forgiven of and the privilege to work with Him. It was the motivation of love that Jesus was willing to carry His cross to help us who could not help ourselves. We should be willing to do the same thing and in doing it there is a joy in our love of helping others. When we only see our own needs and not the needs of others also, we are not being like Christ.

Jesus saw our need and was willing to come to this earth, put up with us (mankind) and die for us. This was His joy because of His love. *"Just as the Father has loved Me, I also have loved you; remain in My love. "If you keep My commandments, you will remain in My love; just as I have kept My Father's commandments and remain in His love. "These things I have spoken to you so that My joy may be in you, and that your joy may be made full. "This is My commandment, that you love one another, just as I have loved you"* (Jn. 15:9-12 NASB). From our vantage point, still being on earth, we need to see what it will be for us in the future as Jude says it will be, *"Now to Him who is able to keep you from stumbling, And to present you faultless Before the presence of His glory with exceeding joy"* (Jud. 1:24 NKJV).

This is where our joy comes from, it is based much deeper than happiness or satisfaction with life. I will assume in our reading of John chapter 21 today that when the disciples saw Jesus on the shore it brought them joy. Peter, knowing of his great sin of denying knowing Jesus three times, now also knew his forgiveness by the Lord, otherwise if I were in Peter's shoes I would be the last one to get out of the boat, if I got out at all.

This was the joy that Peter knew. Also, we can struggle through the night trying to do the work with no success, then find if we just listen to Jesus He will tell us how to apply the work and where to be successful. Following Jesus in the work is what brings us joy. Are you following Him today, or just trying to be the fisherman of men without the guidance of Jesus?

---

1   Jn.8:31-34
2   Eph.2:12,13,16,18, Acts 10:15, Rev.1:5
3   Acts 13:39, Rom.8:2

Get out, get out of the world. We are to live in this world but to not be part of it. How many of you are still being part of it, or allowing it to be part of you? We are not to leave this world but we are to make sure that it is not in us or we in it in the sense we live its way and value its values.[1] When the Israelites entered the promised land they were told not to take up the ways of those they were putting out and not to take up their gods. Are there ways of this world that you have taken up which are in opposition to God's ways? Have you adhered to some of their gods and are not totally given over to Jehovah God?

Jesus said you cannot serve God and mammon[2] (wealth) which implies that wealth can become a god. If there is something in your life you live for as much or even more than Jehovah God then this thing is a god to you. The world serves many gods that we do not recognize as gods. Is your career more important to you than Jehovah God, then it has become a god to you as many in the world have made it a god for themselves sacrificing spouses and children for the sake of their career. There are other things such as this that can become gods of the world which unnoticed by us we have taken up as our gods also. God says come out from among them, not practicing their ways and their values.

We are to be a holy people, which we gain from Christ, He is the one who makes us a holy people, but then we are called to live a Christ-like life. Are you doing that? When Jesus came around (in those few years He lived on earth) people noticed He was different, He wasn't like the rest. Is there anywhere you go that those around notice you are different? I don't mean a 'holier than thou' difference, I mean a genuine caring for people, a God type love for people, a desire that they could come to know the grace of God that saved you from your sins. Do people notice, or are you so camouflaged with spots of the world on you that others around you don't even notice. We are supposed to be noticed, there is to be a light in us, the light of Christ that they see, a love that they experience, a genuine concern. What are people around you seeing, what are they sensing? We pray for the world to be saved, even that God would bring a revival. Are they seeing anything in us that they would want, or maybe that which they see they want to shun?

In the Old Testament, the Jews suffered because they took up the ways of the nations around them and they took up their gods (idols). We see this in our reading today in Psalm 106:34-40. We are not to destroy the world around us as the Jews were to do but we are called to live the Christ-like life that will convince the world, in observing us, of their sinful ways. In our reading in Colossians today we read what Paul has written to them, *"We give thanks to God the Father of our Lord Jesus Christ, praying always for you, having heard of your faith in Christ Jesus, and of the love which ye have toward all the saints"* (Col. 1:3&4 ASV). Paul says because of the hope of heaven which they have it is bearing fruit and growing. (v.5&6)

We want our lives to bear fruit and that the world around us would be saved. If we live the Christ-like life, maybe others around us will think that they have never heard others speak like we speak (with love as Jesus did) and have true compassion for them that care about their eternal well being. I, and you, need to work on our lives so we reflect Christ, praying that He will work in us and through us that the world might see that there is a better way, an only way to eternal life.

---

1   Jn.15:19, 17:14-16
2   Mt.6:24

Have faith. This statement only has two words in it and yet how hard it is to do. We struggle and strive, we bolster up ourselves to believe and still we are weak. I, myself, many a time have had to confess to the Lord, as did the man with the epileptic son, Lord I believe but help me with my unbelief.[1] I many times look at Abraham seeing his faith and desire to have the same. Did Abraham ever doubt, it seems so a couple of times, yet God found Abraham's faith such that He accounted it to Abraham as righteousness.[2] Abraham was not given righteousness because he followed the Law, the Law did not come until later through Moses. Abraham was accounted righteousness because of his faith, he believed God. *"To Abraham his faith was reckoned for righteousness."* (Rom.4:9 RV) This is the kind of faith I strive for and want in my heart. It is difficult so I ask God for His help. Will I like every lesson that God uses to teach me? No, but I am willing to go through it to get a little closer to the type of faith Abraham had.

Abraham's faith was such that God establish a whole nation from Abraham, even though when God told Abraham He would do it Abraham's body was already very old to produce an offspring. This is great faith, it is believing the impossible can be done by God.[3] We say today that it is hard to have faith. We are barred from believing by our mind which is educated believing what we have been taught by man (remember yesterday of how we sometimes take up the gods of the world unknowingly, this is one of them) which is in our country today in opposition to having faith in God. Our faith has to come from someplace else other than our brain, it has to come from a person's heart. If it is established there, then the brain will align itself with what the heart believes and expect great things from God.

Many today will say that Abraham was just a sheep herder and in absence of intelligence it was easy for him to have faith. This may not be true, we make assumptions we should not. In the city where Abraham's family was from, the city of Ur, the archaeologists have found that at that time (when Abraham grew up there) they were advanced in mathematics with multiplication, division, square root, and cube root. We assume because a society is old and herds sheep they are uneducated people. God calls us to believe no matter at what place we find ourselves in life. In our reading today we read a great Psalm by David. If we have faith in what God will do in us and through us we will find ourselves giving such praise to God, it will not be because we are commanded to praise Him, it will be a heartfelt joy. Did David have troubles - Yes, continually. Did David sin – Yes, we know he did. So where did this praise come from, it came from his heart because he believed God.

In our reading today in Matthew chapter 2, if Mary and Joseph did not have faith our Lord may have not survived His first two years on the earth. If God had determined Jesus would live to His thirties and die on a cross none could change that, but I want you to see Mary and Joseph's faith as they did what God spoke without question, but only with action and belief. We all who are saved had a great faith to be reborn not understanding in any way how it happened in us. Yet each one of us can testify that something was different in us after accepting Jesus into our lives. Such faith we should continue to walk in through the rest of our Christian life. Paul admonishes us as we read today, *"Therefore, as you received Christ Jesus the Lord, so walk in him, rooted and built up in him and established in the faith, just as you were taught, abounding in thanksgiving"* (Col. 2:6&7 ESV).

---

1   Mk.9:24
2   Gen.15:6
3   Lk.1:37, 18:27

'**My friends.**' This is what Jesus said to us through the disciples. If Jesus calls us friends then surely we should call each other in the Church friends. It is amazing to me that the Church, that is all those in the world who believe in Christ and have accepted Him as Lord, should be so divided into so many parts. There is no division in Christ, Paul tells us this.[1] Paul says even though we are still in this world we are also spiritually in Christ in heaven.[2] How then is it that if we are all in Christ, having the same Lord, have so many divisions? Denominations are formed for one reason or another, but should not be for the dividing of the Church - the Church which is the Kingdom of God on earth as it is made up of all of us who have Christ as Lord. Jesus said the Kingdom of God would not be something we would see coming or a place on earth to go to, He said it would be in us.[3]

As we are together we are the Kingdom of God. But I have seen that denominations have become a dividing factor, even the building of walls within the Church of one not associating with another. As individuals many times, when away from home, we will only visit a Sunday service of the same denomination. We need to take down these walls, accepting our brothers and sisters who are saved from their sins by the same blood as we were from our own sins. We seem to divide ourselves, as though we did a better job of getting our sins forgiven and are living a more acceptable life before God than another denomination.

Paul says we all have sinned, therefore we are all equally disqualified.[4] If we are disqualified to enter, then how can we do anything more after being brought in only by Christ's blood, do anything to be more qualified? Nothing we do can gain any favor with God, it is only as we surrender accepting more and more of Christ to work in us becoming Christ-like that we can come closer to God. Jesus said that because we have loved Him and believe in Him we can now go directly to the Father with our request.[5]

It is not by something we have accomplished or a way we live that permits us to go to the Father, it is by what Christ has done and that we are in Him. We are doing damage to the Kingdom of God if we continue to build these walls, or reinforce those that are already in place. There can be no true peace among the Church that is to represent Christ to the world if we continue to separate ourselves. Christ called us to be one in Him, are we really hearing what He is saying, or only the things we like which are different from what someone else likes causing divisions. Today our reading of Paul's epistle to the Colossians in chapter 3, he speaks of what causes disunity and how it should not be. In v.3 Paul says our lives are hidden in Christ, all of our lives as one. In v. 11 Paul tells us there can be no division, so what have we done, and what must we fix?

In v. 13-15 Paul gives us the formula to make this oneness happen. We need to get this formula down in our hearts and minds applying it amongst us. It may be that with our divisions, and even sometimes bickering, that the world wants nothing to do with us. We are supposed to love one another, attracting the world to Christ because of what they see in us. What are they seeing in you?

---

1   1Cor. 1:13
2   Eph.2:6
3   Lk. 17:20
4   Rom. 3:23
5   Jn. 16:23,26,27

Here I am Lord, use me. How many of you have spoken these words to the Lord in prayer? We are here in the world living a life to be a witness to the world. We can try on our own strength in our own way, and many do, using the same method as they do in promoting things of the world, maybe methods from their career or from their education, etc. Maybe they are a salesman and try to promote God like they do the product they sell. Now I ask you a question, do you think God should be promoted in the same way we promote the things which He has made? Does it not seem we should promote God in a greater way than those things He has made? God is Spirit and maybe we should promote Him in Spirit. We are to testify the things He has done in our lives, have these things not been done in Spirit? We are to worship God in Spirit and truth,[1] should we not testify of Him and witness of Him in the same way.

You may ask how it is to testify in the Spirit. When you tell someone your testimony, do you trust in your own words and speak in a way to try to convince them that what you say is truth and that God loves them? Or do you pray beforehand or within yourself as you speak to people that God will do His work in that person's heart that is hearing so they will be convinced and convicted by the Spirit, by a supernatural effect on them that will cause them to hear as they have never heard it before.

Sometimes we depend too much on ourselves. When Isaiah knew the greatness of God[2] he said he was undone. Have you known the Lord such that you realize of your own self and of your own strength and of your own wisdom you are undone as Isaiah did? When Isaiah realized he was a man of unclean lips, those lips that were to speak God's word, it was God who cleansed and prepared Isaiah's lips to speak His words. Have you asked God to cleanse your lips and prepare them to speak His words (supernaturally)? Once Isaiah's lips had been cleansed and prepared he heard the Lord say, *"Whom shall I send, and who will go for us?"* (ASV) Upon hearing this Isaiah immediately replied, *"Here am I; send me"* (Isa. 6:8 ASV).As we read on in the book of Isaiah we can see what Isaiah speaks is what he hears God speak to him. He does not go thinking he can convince others by his own ways, his own words, and his own methods. We are not able to convince anyone of the things of God in our own ability, it is only when the supernatural takes place as we speak.[3]

Jesus puts out His call to those who will follow, He put out his call to the first four disciples, telling them they will become fishers of men.[4] Later we know after Jesus rose from the dead He sent these same men out to preach the gospel and teach the ways of God. Have you been called to speak of the Lord, have we not all been called to witness of His great love to mankind? Have you followed the procedure that Isaiah did: to find truly who you are in your own ability, then ask God for that supernatural preparation that only He can do? In Colossians chapter 4 today we can see in what we read that even the great apostle to the Gentiles, Paul, asks for prayer for the supernatural ability to accomplish what God has commissioned him to do; *"praying at the same time for us as well, that God will open up to us a door for the word, so that we may proclaim the mystery of Christ,...that I may make it clear in the way that I ought to proclaim it"* (v. 3&4 NASB).

Paul did not try to witness on his own strength, he knew where his strength came from. We also must know and trust in that supernatural strength God gives and have faith that the words of our lips go forth in spiritual power to affect those we speak to. Pray that you may be such powered in all that you do by the Spirit of God.

---

1   Jn. 4:23&24
2   Isa. 6:1-4
3   Heb. 4:12
4   Mt.4:19&21

My life is in You Lord, all that I am is in You Lord, Amen. Is this your prayer, is this your belief? Do you know how blessed you are? Do you know how good the intent of God is toward you? God will not overpower you, He has given us a free will. It is up to us to actively receive all of the good intent that God has for us, all the great blessings. We don't have to wait until we leave this earth arriving in heaven to benefit from the great blessings of God. We do have to allow Him to decide what are the good things for us rather than we ourselves. Our children when small (and not so small) want things we know are not good for them so we decide what is good and not good for them. If we, being carnal beings, know what is and is not good for our children, how much more does our heavenly Father know what is and is not good for us? If we conclude that God is or is not blessing us from what we think we should receive but don't, then God will always be a disappointment to us.

We need to desire and seek to receive, allowing God the Father to give us what He says is good for us. Many times we want carnal and earthly things[1] not realizing it is most important that we receive those spiritual things that work and bring in us spiritual maturity. Those unspiritual things will pass with this old earth as it is put away,[2] but the spiritual will past on into eternity.[3] We need to listen as we read God's word searching for God's intent for us in what we are reading. It is good to be reading God's word, but if we do not allow some of the things in our reading to grab our attention, and take time to meditate on it, to ask the Holy Spirit for clarification,[4] and allow that part of God's word to sink deep into our soul – the reading does us little good except that we can quote it.

God is good all the time, we need to open ourselves to Him so we can gain all the good God has for each one of us. Today in our reading we read the shortest of the Psalms, 117, yet it is fuller in spiritual everlasting eternal truth than many of the rest: *"O praise Jehovah, all ye nations; Laud him, all ye peoples. For his lovingkindness is great toward us; And the truth of Jehovah endureth for ever. Praise ye Jehovah"* (ASV). Once we allow this to soak into our hearts our lives become easier as we realize all that is required of us in works for righteousness has all been done by Jesus on the cross. All that is left which we have to do now is believe it and actively receive all the good God has for us. It seems from what we read of Paul's epistle today that the Thessalonians must have got it. Paul in remembering them knows *"your* [their] *work energized by faith"* (1Thes. 1:3 AMPC). He does not say they were energized by the righteousness they gained, it was by the faith of what Christ has done for us.

Paul goes on to speak of their *"service motivated by love"* (1:3 AMPC), it was because of the love God had planted in their hearts, it was not about the reward they would receive. Paul goes on to say *"and* [their] *unwavering hope in our Lord Jesus Christ"* (1:3 AMPC). Their hope was in the finished work of Jesus Christ on the cross. Jesus said Himself, *"it is finished."* When something is finished there is nothing else anyone can do to finish it more, it is done. The Thessalonians had such a reputation of the working of God among them that Paul heard of it at places he went, *"For from you the word of the Lord has sounded forth, not only in Macedonia and Achaia, but also in every place. Your faith toward God has gone out, so that we do not need to say anything"* (1Thes. 1:8 NKJV). I pray for myself and for you that our walk with God is such that a reputation has gone out from us to others of how good God is.

---

1   Jas.4:3
2   Mt.24:35, Rev.21:1
3   Heb.12:27&28, 2Pet.3:12&13
4   Jn. 14:26

Are You there? This is sometimes our prayer to God in those times of uncertainty. The only stable we have in this life is our faith, and as we have faith we experience God. My wife at one time in public was sitting reading her Bible quietly and a man asked her, 'Do you believe that crap?' I have realized lately that I not only believe it, but also I experience it.

As we have faith God verifies Himself to us. As we begin to grow inwardly from the new birth, our perspective, our thought, our motivations take a change that we can attribute to nothing else other than God working in us. We experience His care and His safety as He watches out for us as we go through life. God speaks to us in our inner being, He guides us in ways we cannot comprehend, He gets us through the hard places in life. Each of us may come to that place in our lives (maybe more than once) when we ask the question, 'Are You there?' If we look back at what God did on that day that we received our salvation we can know He is there. If we think about our lives since that day we can remember many times when we experienced God working in and through our lives.

When hard times come it is easy to forget our encounters with God in the past. When we stay conscious of what God has done in the past it gives us faith when we are in the hard times. I believe God does take us through hard times to learn. Do I believe all hard times are from God, some are there to shape us as the potter pushes in on the clay to give it a better shape, but many of hard times are not from God, yet He may use them. There are hard times we bring on ourselves, we will reap what we sow. *"whatever one sows, that will he also reap. For the one who sows to his own flesh will from the flesh reap corruption, but the one who sows to the Spirit will from the Spirit reap eternal life"* (Gal. 6:7&8 ESV). It does not say here if we are saved we won't reap the bad things if after we are saved we still sow that which is not good.

The devil can also put us in hard times, making things difficult. We read in the book of Job what the devil did to Job. And Paul tells us today in our reading in 1Thessalonians *"because we wanted to come to you—I, Paul, again and again—but Satan hindered us"* (2:18 ESV). The question of 'Are You there' will become less and less if we are doing what Jesus tells us in Matthew chapter 6 today, *"when you pray, go into your room, and when you have shut your door, pray to your Father who is in the secret place; and your Father who sees in secret will reward you openly"* (v. 6 NKJV). This is the best thing I know that will give you an awareness of God's presence and a faith to walk in His ways.

What is our withal? Withal is a unity of us believers being tied together in Christ. Therefore our withal is Christ. None of us are anything without Christ. Therefore we are only anything in Christ. This takes away our individuality, our own accomplishments. Our withal is Christ as we are all in Him. [1] Until I looked up the definition of 'withal' I thought that it meant something different. Webster says it means: *'With the rest; together with; likewise; at the same time.'* I had thought from the way I had heard it used it meant our ability to do something, that by which we accomplished.

As I looked deeper I found I had it confused with the word 'wherewithal' which is a related word. 'Wherewithal' is the force or power by which we accomplish something. In Jesus' prayer [2] the translators of the KJV use it this way: *"And I have declared unto them thy name, and will declare it: that the love wherewith [wherewithal] thou hast loved me may be in them, and I in them."* 'Withal' is our unity in the body of Christ, one body with many parts under the head of Christ. And its related word 'wherewithal' is the force by which we in the church accomplish. In the body of Christ, there are no loners, there are no superstars, there are none in a higher position (by their own efforts) before God.

We are all made holy, we are all made righteous, we are all made worthy by Christ, therefore we all have right-standing before God by the act of another, that of Jesus Christ. As we surrender to this God does put those He chooses in different positions of authority in the body. [3] If we truly work together (our withal) using our wherewithal we can accomplish great things for the Kingdom of God. But before our wherewithal (the force by which we accomplish) can be used our withal (unity) has to be in place. We greatly disturb the work of God, throwing monkey wrenches into the gears, when we cause division in the body of Christ. The devil would so delight in us doing so he may be our encouragement to do so. He cares to thwart the works of God in any way he can.

I believe the devil is very active in the body of Christ (the Church) and we are not even aware of it. We need to get our 'withal' together and move to be without the influence of the devil in our midst. Don't get me wrong, I'm not saying that all the problem in the Church is the fault of the devil, most of the time it is our own flesh that causes much of it, but we have to remove the devil and his demons from being the cheerleaders when our flesh makes a touchdown. Our own pride and ego also cheer when our flesh makes a touchdown. Jesus starts out in our reading today speaking about some of those things of our flesh that cause problems. (Mt. 7:1-5) Part of what our 'withal' should be Jesus speaks of in v.12: *"So whatever you wish that others would do to you, do also to them, for this is the Law and the Prophets"* (ESV). This is the second greatest commandment. *"You shall love the Lord your God with all your heart and with all your soul and with all your mind. This is the great and first commandment. And a second is like it: You shall love your neighbor as yourself. On these two commandments depend all the Law and the Prophets"* (Mt. 22;37-40 ESV).

One of the last commandments Jesus gave His disciples before His crucifixion was to love one another [4]. This Paul well knows and in our reading today he prays such for the Thessalonians: *"may the Lord cause you to increase and overflow in love for one another, and for all people, just as we also do for you"* (1Thess. 3:12 NASB). This should be in our daily prayers; that God would help us love one another, putting down divisions that start in ourselves and are working in others which are permeating the Church (*"a little leaven leavens the whole lump"* 1Cor. 5:6&7 NKJV), and that He would help us be aware of the works the devil and his demons, that they are trying to thwart the work of God amongst us. We must remember that, as Christians, our withal is Christ, He is the head which unites the body.

---

1   Rom. 12:5, Gal. 3:28
2   Jn.17:26
3   1 Cor. 12:28
4   Jn.13:34. 15:12&17

Be aware, lest you be deceived. It all started in the Garden of Eden, and deception has continued unto today. We can be deceived by the devil, we can be deceived by the world, we can be deceived by our own flesh, we can even be deceived by other Christians who are mistaken in their understanding. God presents truth to the world, the inanimate objects that do not think have no problems with what God says is truth. Jesus said even the stones would cry out His praise if man did not. It is we who have the ability to think and have a free will which refuse to believe God's truths. Being deceived can only happen if we are willing to listen to the deception. If we don't know the truth in God's word then what is deception may seem as truth to us.

In polls taken by the Barner Group of what scripture that Christians know the most, it was found that most would quote; 'God helps those who help themselves.' This is a deception the majority of those Christians polled have, it is not in the Bible, it is not God's word. When we don't know God's word, deception comes in easily. That is the part that comes because of our unawareness. There is also the deception of our own flesh as we refuse to believe God's word. This is what happened in the garden, the devil basically said to Eve, 'Did God really say?' and Eve, not believing she would really die, took of the fruit. Then Adam, not really believing he would die as God had said, was willing to take the fruit when offered to him by his wife Eve.[1] They did not believe and suffered the consequence. How many times do we suffer the consequences because we do not believe, whether it be the good not received or the bad we had to suffer.

We do need to be aware of other Christians who are mistaken. We do need to be aware of the world who does not live God's way. We do need to be aware that the devil and his demons are trying to deceive us every chance they get. Maybe the most aware we have to be is of how our own flesh continues striving against the Spirit[2] in us convincing us to not believe because it can't confirm it to be true by its thinking. Believing when it does not seem possible is what is called faith.[3] Many in the Church have another meaning of what faith is but this is it, to believe God when it seems most impossible. In our reading today in Matthew chapter 8 a centurion came to Jesus with this kind of faith. He asks Jesus to heal his servant even from the great distance that Jesus stood from the centurion's house. He believed Jesus didn't have to touch the servant physically. He believed Jesus didn't have to be in his house. He believed Jesus didn't have to work some great ceremony.

The centurion believed that Jesus only needed to speak a word and his servant would be healed. (v. 5-8) Jesus comments about the centurion's faith to the crowd, that He has not even found such faith in Israel (where it should have been). Jesus tells the centurion to go his way, that as he had believed it had been done for him. (v. 13) The centurion found his servant not well in a day or two, he found the servant was well from the moment Jesus spoke the word. So where do we find ourselves today? How is our faith, do we believe? Be aware, lest you be deceived.

---

1   Gen. 3:1-6
2   Gal. 5:17
3   Rom. 4:18-20

Just suppose – suppose Jesus was to return tomorrow. Suppose you were to hear the trumpet blast, suppose you were to hear the shout of the archangel, suppose you were to hear the mighty call of the great warrior upon His white horse to the resurrection, are you ready? Will we know exactly when He is to come? No, we are to know the season but His coming He says we will not know.[1] That day and hour has been assigned by the Father and none other knows.[2] Jesus told His followers that He would return at a time they do not expect Him. Many think this is said about the world, which it is, but this He said to His disciples.

Let's all be very honest here, we know how we are and how we behave. If we knew it would be five years yet before Jesus came back we would not be behaving our best until nearly before He returned. Jesus tells the parable about the evil servant, his bad behavior thinking it would be some time before the master would return.[3] Jesus tells us not to be that way, to be at His business, the business of the Kingdom of God. We should look up and see that the season for His return is at hand, we are to read the times as men read the sky to know if rain is coming.[4] Do we know if He is coming tomorrow? No, but we should be about His business as if He were.

One of these days, even though we know not which, it will be He will come tomorrow. Every time there is one in the body of Christ that begins sounding the alarm of Jesus' soon arrival there is a stir in the camp of His people, a scurry of busyness – what were all those people doing before? We should be very busy about His business of the gospel and the strengthening of His body, the Church. Are we walking in His ways? Have you looked in His word to see what it is we have been called to?

Are you allowing His ways to sink into your heart desiring to be busy at the things He wants you doing? Or are you determining in your mind to force yourself to do what He says but grumbling under your breath that you have to do them? Don't be like the scribes and Pharisees who grumbled when Jesus didn't do things the way they thought He should. (Mt. 9:3,11,34) We should not be like the crowd that belittled the things Jesus said He would do in their midst. (Mt. 9:24) Our hearts and spirits should be aligning with what it is Jesus wants to do in our midst, praying to Him that He changes our hearts to desire to do what is in His heart. We do not know when His return will be, but Paul even speaks in his epistles that he expected it any day. We are still watching and should be expecting Jesus' return any day as Paul did.

In 1Thessalonians chapter 5 today in our reading Paul goes on to speak of the return of the Lord. In v. 4 Paul tells us Jesus' return should not take us by surprise and in v. 11 he tells us what we ought to be about. In v. 23 Paul prays that God will (continue to) do His work in us and that He who has called us is faithful (to us) to complete His work. Therefore pray that God will do His work in you that you might join Him wholeheartedly in the work He is doing in the world.

---

1   Mt. 24:32,33,36,42,44
2   Acts 1:7
3   Mt. 24:48-51
4   Mt. 16:2&3

How is life, how do you find it? Is it good, is it bad, is it hard, is it easy, how do you find it? We are born and we die, life is that which happens in between, or is it? It is too easy to get locked into only seeing life as what we live here on this earth. If you are born again, that spiritual birth, you are born into eternity. How does that thought affect what you think of life now? If we are truly born into the spiritual life that life goes on into eternity. We have not yet made it to heaven but the spiritual life we live there is the same spiritual life we are now living here since we have been born anew, [1] and old things past away. [2] Paul tells us we have died to the world as Christ died and we are now alive in Him. [3] Paul also tells us we are seated in heavenly places even now for we are spiritually seated there in Christ. [4]

Our eternity started on the day we accepted Christ into our lives and were reborn. Did you know that you are living in that spiritual realm even now? [5] We are living in this world but we are told we are not part of this world. So then of what world do we belong? We are citizens of heaven, [6] this is where our credentials are from, we are here as ambassadors. [7] Since we are citizens of that far land of heaven we also already have all the rights as citizens of that land. Sometimes it is hard having faith for certain things. Once we understand we are already citizens with all the rights as citizens, having rights to things which all citizens there have, faith comes easier.

In Matthew chapter 10 Jesus sends out the twelve. The first thing in the list of things they are to do is: *"As you go, proclaim, 'The Kingdom of Heaven is near"* (v. 7 CJB). They were to preach the same thing Jesus did in chapter 9: *"And Jesus went about ... teaching in their synagogues and proclaiming the good news of the kingdom"* (v. 35 AMPC). In Luke Jesus says: *"The kingdom of God does not come with observation......For indeed, the kingdom of God is within you"* (17:20&21 NKJV). The Kingdom of God is already in you and you in it, it has been thus since you received salvation. You are part of the Kingdom and it is part of you. Your life of eternity has already started. Claim the rights that you have, have faith in what God says about you in His word, walk in faith and believe.

---

1   1Pet. 1:3&23 (RSV)
2   2Cor. 5:17
3   Gal. 2:20, Rom. 6:8-11
4   Eph. 2:6
5   Gal. 5:25,
6   Philp. 3:20
7   2Cor. 5:20

"What did I say?" Many times this is what God asks us. Many times what we are asking is what God has already spoken to us about. Is it because we are stupid or is it because we didn't like what it was God said before. For me I guess it is a little of both. Sometimes, as with a little child who does not like the answer we gave them will come back later asking the same question hoping the answer will be different, this is what we do with God. And sometimes, we just don't get it the first time around. That does not put us in bad company for even the disciples of Jesus didn't get some of the things He said until after His resurrection.[1] God is so different from us that some of what He says takes a while, even seeming nearly a lifetime, to sink in so that we know. It all takes faith, from new birth in salvation to resurrection at end of life, and from our beginning of walking with the Lord until we leave this earth, our faith continues to grow.

The rate at which our faith grows depends on the level of yielding we offer and the amount of feeding of our faith we give it by being in God's word (which gives life[2]). Every time we are in God's word our faith is fed. We may think we have read His word enough we know it yet we find that every time we read it again He shows us something we never saw before, something new, a little bit more of Him. God is marvelous but are we really listening when He speaks? If we were, He would never ask, "what did I say." It is interesting as over the last few weeks we have been reading in Exodus and Leviticus of how clearly God spoke to the Israelites and yet they were not hearing.

God begins to speak to them giving them His ways and His laws in Exodus chapter 19 and in chapter 24 Moses, Aaron, Nadab, Abihu, and seventy elders of the people saw the presence of God on the mountain and the pavement at His feet as sapphire stone.[3] Then Moses was called up upon the mountain to meet with God and receive the tables of stone. Then after all this, of all the miracles, after seeing the presence of God on the mountain, they go in a contrary way and giving up on God - not being willing to wait, they ask Aaron to fashion them a god to go before them.[4] Aaron who had been called by God, who had seen the presence of God replied, 'give me your gold' and with it he molded a gold calf idol.[5] God had been speaking but Aaron had not been listening. And what about the seventy elders?? Are we so much different than they?

I would dare not to say anything bad about John the Baptist yet here it is in what we read today in Matthew chapter 11, that even John wonder after a time if Jesus was the one they were awaiting: *"Are you the one who is to come, or shall we look for another?" And Jesus answered them, "Go and tell John what you hear and see"* (v. 3&4 ESV). Here we see even John the Baptist, with all the great things Jesus says about him, yet was a man like us who needs to hear it again. Some of us out of stubbornness are not willing to hear what God says. Jesus said that generation was like little children who pretend when they play.[6] He was speaking here about the unbelieving religious leaders of the day but I believe that is our case at times, for we are only saved by the mercy of God. Do we believe, are we listening?

In what Paul writes that we read in 2Thessalonians chapter 2 is mostly about how the returning of Christ will be, but he starts this chapter with, *"But in connection with the coming of our Lord Yeshua the Messiah and our gathering together to meet him, we ask you, brothers, not to be easily shaken in your thinking or anxious because of a spirit or a spoken message or a letter supposedly from us claiming that the Day of the Lord has already come"* (v. 1&2 CJB). This that Paul is writing to them about has to do with hearing God, listening to God, and believing (continually). How many times will we have to hear what it is that God has said? I pray for us all, that we can yield more and more of ourselves so we can hear more and more of what God is saying.

---

1   Mt. 20:19, Mk. 8:31, Lk. 18:33&34, Lk. 24:6-8, Jn. 20:6-9
2   Acts 20:32
3   Ex. 19:9-11
4   Ex. 32:1
5   Ex. 32:2-4
6   Mk. 11:16&17, Lk. 7:32

Be still (quiet) and hear the Lord. Does this mean we are too busy talking to hear the Lord? Stillness sometimes may mean non-business. Are we too active in getting the work done to hear God speaking to us? Paul tells us in our reading today that if we don't provide for ourselves (as he gave example) then we should not expect to eat from another's table. (2 Thess. 3:6-8) Yet Paul tells us that what he knew of the gospel was given to him by direct revelation from the Lord.[1] There must then be a time for working but also a time to stop to spend time in prayer, in relationship with God, and listening for His voice.[2] I do at times hear God's voice but for me to tell you how to, I'm not sure I can.

It seems to be the one wanting to hear God's voice has to be seeking Him. It is only when we empty ourselves of ourselves that we begin to find more of God. God wants to be found, but He also wants to be sincerely sought. Are we really seeking Him? Is He really more important to us than anything else in life? Is He our heart's desire? These are questions that have to be answered by all of us. We need to look deep into that spiritual mirror to see who and what we really are.

Our walking with God, our seeking God, and our listening to God cannot be something we do flippantly. Maybe for that first time to hear the voice of God you may have to spend hours in stillness before Him before He speaks. There is an interesting thing that I never seen in all the years I have read through the Bible; when Moses went up on the mountain to receive the stone tables he was there six days waiting before God spoke to him. (Ex. 24:15&16) If Moses had to wait on God then maybe we might have to wait also. We live in a world around us of everything being a quick response. We call anyone expecting them to answer because their phone now is in their pocket. If we want to know anything we just key it into the internet and boom – there's the answer. We buy instant zap'n food, we eat and run. We go to quick serve restaurants, eat and run.

There is little of the cooking all day with the house full of the great aroma of the food cooking. We take little time to actually go visit some, we just give them a quick call on the phone (unless there is something we want then we go to their house). We are a quick pace world wanting it right now with no investment on our part. With God it doesn't work that way. It is He (Jesus) who died for us, can't we wait on Him a little while? In our reading today in Matthew chapter 12 we see the scribes and Pharisees asking for a sign from Jesus to satisfy their own demands on Him. (v. 38) He basically tells them they will have to wait on His timing to see Him in the heart of the earth three days and three nights, and then rise from the dead. It is always God's timing, not ours.

---

1   Gal. 1:11&12
2   1Kg. 19:12

"My name is 'I AM'" This is what God said to Moses when he asked God at the burning bush, 'who shall I say sent me?'[1] Jehovah God is God, there is no other god before Him. There is none greater, there is none mightier, there is none wiser, there is none more powerful, and the list goes on. For God to say 'I AM' sums it up, He is all that there is. Can we ever hope to know who He is? Maybe on that day we arrive in heaven with our new heavenly being we will instantly know but to comprehend with the being we have now on earth is impossible. Can we know of Him? Yes. He reveals partially to us who He is, more and more as we seek Him. But if God, the 'I Am', was to reveal all there is of Himself to us we would go into overload and be destroyed.

What did He say to Moses when Moses asked to see all of His glory, 'you can't handle seeing all of me, I will put you in a crevice and cover you with My hand until I have passed and then remove it so you can see My backside.'[2] God basically said, '**My glory is too great for any person to see all of it.** "I AM', what a great statement God says about Himself. When the crowd with Judas came to arrest Jesus and Jesus replied 'I AM' the statement had such power they were driven back and knocked to the ground.[3] Any other sensible person would have at that point jumped up and ran away, yet this was not the will of the Father.[4] The 'I AM' is the Great One, from the beginning of time to the end of time, He is the one beyond time from before time and after time, He is eternal, always in the now. God is the constant that always is. How could we comprehend all of His glory when we can't even get our heads around this, that His is eternal, always being.

It is difficult enough for us to think on the fact that from our point of salvation forward we will be with God for eternity without considering He was eternal before the creation. Today in our reading of Psalms 139 David speaks of God's greatness. It would be good for us to meditate on what David says in Psalms 139. We read today of what those of Nazareth thought when they heard the teachings of Jesus and seen His miraculous powers, *"Where did this man acquire this wisdom and these miraculous powers?"* (Mt. 13:54 NASB). What they did afterwards does not go along with their momentary awareness of His greatness. They had been in the presence of 'I AM'. We, as they, many times are in the presence of 'I AM' hearing His teachings and see His miraculous powers and soon we forget acting sinfully. If we, like David, take time to be still before God we may begin to see more and more of 'I AM'.

---

1   Ex.3:14
2   Ex.33:18-23
3   Jn.18:4-6
4   Jn.18:3-6, Acts 4:27&28

'I AM...LIFE.' This is what Jesus says to us. Without Him what we have is not life. Without Jesus we are living in death. The judgment against how we live without Jesus is eternal death.[1] One of the things we need to see is the birth we experience first, the fleshly birth does not bring true life, only the re-birth that happens when we accept Jesus as Lord are we truly born.[2] Many in the world struggle in various things and in various ways to extend their life yet they don't even realize that they are not even yet truly alive. All that live in darkness are in death,[3] to say they live is not even accurate according to truth. We, those of us who have salvation, need to know that as we are now reborn and live in Christ, that the only thing of any good in us is Christ. If there had been any bit of a good thing in us before our re-birth then there would have been a bit of life in us but there was none.[4] Before we were reborn all we had was our flesh, now that we are reborn we also have the Spirit.

Paul tells us that the flesh and the Spirit are at war within us.[5] Paul finally concludes it is not us any longer that sins, it is the flesh within us.[6] This does not get us off the hook of the need to take the guilt of our sin to the Lord to receive forgiveness. It does show us though that before Christ came into our lives all we had was death. Any good thing that is in us, any good thing that we do, it is Christ in us empowering us to do it, without Him we could do nothing good.[7]

We can take good all the way to miraculous since for us to do anything good, being evil as we are (our flesh), it is a miracle worked by Christ, our reborn life now is a miracle. We often speak of the Man who walked on water referring to Jesus, although another man did walk on water. In our reading today in Matthew chapter 14 we read of Peter walking on the water until he became fearful (without faith) he began the sink. (v. 29) By Peter's words, 'if You command me' shows he knew without Jesus he could not do it, but with Jesus, he could. Jesus in our life and working through our life is how we do anything good. We think too much of the time thinking of what we can be doing for the Kingdom of God, yet it is then limited by what we have to offer. We are limited by our faith of what we see. We gather all we can, from all the sources we can find, from the generosity of all those who give, to feed the hungry and we limit ourselves by that amount which we see we have gathered. Are we to feed the hungry? Yes. But do we ever go having faith that with the amount that we were able to bring God would multiply it to feed the masses?

Jesus ask the disciples to bring all that they had and then He multiplied it to feed the masses, 5,000 men plus women and children. Do we do all we can and then expect Jesus to multiply it or is our faith limited by only what we see? This is an example, but it applies to all areas in our life, in our faith. It is Christ who enables us to do anything good, why should we not expect Him to multiply it also? Our faith is limited by how much we believe, do we expect Him to do the impossible[8], or are we only believing what appears possible to us?

When I am doing anything for God, sing a solo in church or bringing a teaching, I do my part bringing as much as I can by practice or study, but I expect God to supplement my effort to deliver to the people what is needed. Many times I am astonished at the outcome. It is not I who am working the good thing in me, when I expect God to He multiplies what I bring. Once we know there is nothing good in us we can do, the effort to do good on our own dies. When we know that all good that is done in us, and by us, is by Christ in us, it allows us to believe in even great works by Him through us.

---

1 Rom. 7:5
2 Jn. 3:1-8
3 Lk. 1:79, Jn. 8:12, Acts 26:18, Col. 1:12-14, Eph. 2:1-5
4 Ps. 14:1, 53:1,3
5 Gal. 5:17
6 Rom 7:18,20,23,25
7 Rom. 3:9-12
8 Gen. 18:14, Mk. 10:27

'I AM in you.' Is this not a great thing to know, that God is in us? Jesus said He would never leave us or forsake us. Jesus said He and the Father are with us. Jesus said the Holy Spirit would come and be in us. Isn't this great! Now the question is, 'do you believe it?' By now in your walk with Jesus, you should know He is with you. [1] He said He came that none should be lost. [2] You, if you have received Jesus as Lord and are no longer lost, you have found the truth.

We are told over and over in the scriptures that we are in Christ and He is in us. [3] Since it is said over and over it must be a thing we all have difficulty with knowing/believing. Something happened in you when you accepted Jesus. In the weeks to follow you found yourself, your thinking, your actions, your responses, different because something in you changed. Was that change totally by your efforts to be different? You may have tried to live good before and it never totally worked. This time, at accepting Christ, life for you changed, why? There was that part of the image of God in Adam that died when he sinned and is dead in us until we are re-born.

At re-birth that part of man that was originally in man, dying because of sin, is re-born in us when Jesus pays the price of our sin. Now that part of the image of God is alive and growing in us again. What a great thing to know, that there is something of God alive and growing in us. Can you see the picture now, how it has been that thing of God growing in us making us different. That now behaving rightly is not all left up to us, but God is working in us. Does that not make us a peculiar people, that the very ever living God is working in us and through us. As we take this on, as we begin to wear it, as we begin to know who it is working inside of us does it not make it easier to take the good news to a dying world?

For what God is working in us we can join David as he gives praise to God in Ps. 145; *"I will exalt You, my God, the King, And I will bless Your name forever and ever. Every day I will bless You, And I will praise Your name forever and ever. Great is the LORD, and highly to be praised; And His greatness is unsearchable. One generation will praise Your works to another, And will declare Your mighty acts"* (v. 1-4 NASB). Can we not thank God for what He has worked in us by His love, as David says; *"Jehovah is gracious, and merciful; Slow to anger, and of great lovingkindness"* (v. 8 ASV). Also David says of God, *"The Lord is righteous in all His ways and gracious and merciful in all His works"* (v. 17 AMPC). David gives all this praise to God who at that time David says in v. 18 is near all who call upon Him. We now, because of what Jesus did on the cross, not only have a God who is near us, He is in us. By this how much more should we align with David's praise, and even surpass it, for the Holy Spirit is in us even helping us with our praise. [4] Since we know He is in us, how great should our thanksgiving now be?

---

1   Heb. 13:5
2   Jn. 5:24, Acts 2:21, 1Tim. 2:3&4, 2Pet. 3:9
3   Jn. 14:20, 1Jn. 3:24, 4:13
4   Philp. 3:3

Glory be to Thy Name. Do we live in a way that glorifies God? Do we fill our minds with things that glorifies God? Do we fill our hearts with things that glorifies God? We must remember that what we have without God is nothing and what we have with God is everything. Therefore I must make an effort to push aside and to cast out of my mind, my heart, and my life what there is left of me, of my flesh. At the same time those voids I make in my mind, my heart, and my life, I must fill with God. Emptying ourselves of ungodly things is not enough because we will just fill up those places with the wrong things again. We must fill ourselves with things of God, of his ways, of His truths. Paul tells us to think on these things and then list some things that are godly.[1]

Paul knows that we must fill ourselves with the good things of God or the wrong will seep back in again. We cannot fill ourselves with the good things of God if we are not in His word, reading what He has to say. We cannot fill ourselves with the good things of God if we are not spending time in prayer.[2]

From what we read of the Psalms that David wrote he seems to spend much time in prayer. We read Paul telling us to pray always.[3] Walking with God is not a flippant thing we do, it is a conscious thing we do. God says He will never leave us or forsake us.[4] Jesus said the Holy Spirit would be in us.[5] If we believe what He said we should be conscious of that presence of God. As we remove our attention from those things in our lives which are ungodly and consider the things of God instead, we will be surprised at what becomes planted in us.

Living Godly lives is not all by us striving to discipline ourselves to that way, it is by allowing those things God plants in us to grow. When a plant grows from a seed we don't hear it struggling, disciplining itself to grow, it just grows. When a baby is born we don't hear it struggling, disciplining itself to grow, it just grows. When all that is required for growth is provided, it is in the design of God given in creation for these things to grow. Why should we believe spiritual growth is any different? God has planted the seeds in us at our re-birth. All we have to do is provide those things needed for that natural growth to take place.

There are those in the body of Christ who think all Christian growth has to be by forcing ourselves to take the shape God orders. God wants to be involved in that growth, He wants good things to develop in our lives. He wants to touch and mold and shape us into something beautiful. With our own efforts alone we could never make anything as beautiful of ourselves as He can. Being in God's word is like the nourishment to the soil for a plant to grow, praying before God/to God is like the sun rays that the plants need to grow healthy and strong.

Our growth should be from a one on one relationship with God. Yes, that relationship is encouraged and reinforced by teachers and preachers but the focused relationship has to be by that one on one relationship with God by being in His word and by prayer. Jesus warned the disciples in our reading today to beware of the leaven of the Pharisees. (Mt. 16:6) If we are not in God's word and in prayer how will we know if what we hear from teachers and preachers is truth or leaven? In our reading today Paul gives warning of what will happen when people listen to the leaven of men. (1 Tim. 4:1-8) 'Glory be to Thy Name'. As we provide the things needed for that natural spiritual growth, which God is involved in causing it to happen in us, we will find the praise of God comes more natural to our lips and to our hearts. May God be praised!

---

1   Philp. 4:8
2   Mt. 6:6, Lk. 18:1, 1Tim. 2:8
3   1Thes. 5:17
4   Heb. 13:5, Jn. 14:18
5   Jn. 14:17

Peace, everyone wants peace. On the bumper sticker of a car that I had seen in front of me I saw the words, 'Image World Peace'. All people want peace, Jesus said, *"Peace I leave with you; my peace I give to you. Not as the world gives do I give to you"* (Jn.14:27 ESV). The world's peace is a false peace, a perverted peace, it is like the type of peace Eve thought she was getting when the serpent convinced her to eat the fruit of the tree of the knowledge of good and evil. Jesus said, *"I am the way, and the truth, and the life"* (Jn.14:6 ASV)- this is where true peace is found, The world does not know this peace because the world does not know Jesus. The words of God which came from the cloud tell us how to find peace: *"This is my Son, whom I love, with whom I am well pleased. Listen to him!"* (Mt.17:5 CJB)Jesus came to give us peace.

The angels, in announcing His arrival, said, *"on earth peace, goodwill toward men"* (Lk. 2:14 NKJV). The true peace that man finds is peace with God, a peace that because of man's sin he could not have with God until Jesus took the penalty of sin for all of us on the cross. Jesus speaks something very drastic to His disciple in our reading today, yet it is the very thing that truly brings us peace: *"The Son of Man is about to be delivered into the hands of men, and they will kill him, and he will be raised on the third day"* (Mt.17:22&23 ESV). This that they heard was so drastic that they nearly didn't hear it, yet after Jesus rose from the dead they remembered. So it is by Jesus that we find peace, true peace – not a false peace that the world seeks after but will never find until they find Jesus.

There was a man among the Pharisees, a ruler among the Jews who had to know who was searching for peace. Many times when Christians are dying they are looking for peace, wanting the assurance that they truly have salvation and eternal life. Nicodemus came to Jesus when he would not be noticed by others, coming to Jesus at night. Nicodemus says something to Jesus not even asking a question but Jesus knowing the question that is in his heart, his searching for assurance of peace with God, answers him, *"Yes, indeed," Yeshua answered him, "I tell you that unless a person is born again from above, he cannot see the Kingdom of God "* (Jn. 3:3 CJB). This is the peace Jesus brought by dying on the cross and rising from the dead. This is the peace every person is searching for even though many search in the wrong place. There never will be world peace, Jesus said there would be wars and rumors of wars. [1]

The true peace does not come to nations of people, it comes to the heart of the individual person, it comes as that person accepts Jesus into their life, it is a peace that will take that person into eternity because of what Jesus did for him on the cross. Jesus is our peace and eternal sanctuary.

---

[1]   Mt.24:6

Why should we follow God? Once we have salvation isn't that enough for eternity? Yes, it will gain you eternal life, but possibly having your rob scorched as you enter.[1] Accepting Jesus Christ by; confessing you are a sinner, asking Him to be your Lord, and having Him cleanse your life by His blood, is the salvation that God calls all mankind to. Having salvation does gain you the joy you will experience for eternity in heaven, but what about the rest of your life here on this earth?

Salvation is not something we receive and then go on living our lives as we think and want until that day we depart from this earth for heaven. In the prayer Jesus taught His disciples (and us through them) Jesus said pray this way, *"Our Father, who is in heaven, Hallowed be Your name. Your kingdom come. Your will be done, On earth as it is in heaven"* (Mat. 6:9&10 NASB). There is an establishing of God's Kingdom on earth even now. Jesus told the people the Kingdom of God would not come with observance (be seen), He said the Kingdom of God would be within the person.[2] If you are saved by the blood of Christ the Kingdom of God is in you, you are part of that Kingdom of God on earth. How can you be part of a Kingdom and not live by its ways?

You have a great privilege, that of being counted as a citizen of the Kingdom of God without having to pay a great price.[3] That great price was paid, marked **'Paid in full'** by Jesus on the cross. If you live in a Kingdom not choosing and desiring to live by its ways then you are considered a rebel. Are you a rebel against the great gift of eternal life Jesus has given you? None of us who are saved want to think of ourselves as a rebel, yet if we are not following God, choosing to live by His ways, are we not a rebel? Many say they don't want to be forced into living a certain way. God is not forcing, otherwise Jesus would not have came and died for the lost.

God is wanting us to choose and desire to live His way in His Kingdom. The great thing about this is as we choose to live God's way in our life there is a peace from striving that comes which cannot be described, it is by heavenly powers from God.[4] That joy, that peace, comes in a very particular way, it comes in surrendering all you have and all you are to the Lord God, giving Him yourself, choosing to live His way, desiring to follow Him wherever He leads.[5] In our reading today we hear these words; *"Trust in the LORD with all your heart, And lean not on your own understanding; In all your ways acknowledge Him, And He shall direct your paths...Happy is the man who finds wisdom, And the man who gains understanding...She is more precious than rubies, And all the things you may desire cannot compare with her"* (Pro. 3:5,6,13,15 NKJV).

In 1Timothy chapter 6 we hear Paul calling Timothy (and us) to live God's way. This he says in v. 6,7,17: *"But godliness with contentment is great gain: for we brought nothing into the world, for neither can we carry anything out...Charge them that are rich in this present world, that they be not highminded, nor have their hope set on the uncertainty of riches, but on God, who giveth us richly all things to enjoy"* (ASV). So we see the scriptures tell us that to surrender to God's ways brings us great gain, great contentment, and great enjoyment. Should we follow God, yes, if we want these great things in our lives.

---

1   1Cor. 3:11-15
2   Lk. 17:20&21
3   Philp 3:20, Rom. 5:18
4   Jn. 14:27
5   Lk. 9:23

How am I to live? Do each of us ask ourselves this question every morning as we rise for the day? In our sleep we get into very little trouble but what about those hours of awakeness? Do we awake with the awareness of God in our lives? Do we go through our day considering His ways? Are the dos and don'ts becoming more and more our natural responses as we allow more and more of God to change us, in the renewing of our being by the growth that takes place from the new birth? I believe the awareness of God's goodness, His blessings, His Love, His mercy, and His grace is the things we are to be most conscious of as we go through our day. By this we shall find praise well up from a thankful heart.

As we become aware of God's love and the good things He has done in our lives the dos and don'ts become a constant desire rather than a disciplined obedience. We need to remember the disciplined obedience was what was required of the Israelites, and according to Paul, Peter, and James they failed. It is by grace and grace alone of what Jesus did for us on the cross that we receive the blessings we have. When we truly see that, then the things we are called to be obedient to become desires of our heart as we know what has been done for us. In my early years of being a Christian after accepting Jesus and being saved by Jesus, I had the immature idea and desire to pay back Jesus for what He had done for me.

I wanted to give back, I wanted to serve Him in some way which would return the favor He gave me. I have found that there is no way I could pay Him back even a little, it would be as a pebble on the seashore, of His favor toward me. I am left with a gratitude for what I have been given free and clear. This gives me a freedom to serve knowing there is no high mark I have to accomplish, only to do the best I can and know His blood covers me.

This seems to be the conclusion Paul came to from trying to live by the rigid Law as a Jew under the Law to one who knew it was all by the grace of God. He states that what he wills to do he does not and what he wills not to do is the very thing he does.[1] We join him in his struggle for we experience the same. He found it was all grace and nothing but grace. In our reading today in Matthew chapter 19 we hear of a man asking Jesus what excellent and perfect good deed did he need to do to possess eternal life. Jesus replied with some of the Law of how he was to live of which he replied he had followed all.

Then Jesus showed him how he could not measure up by the Law and the man went away sad. (v. 16-22) This is the case in each of our lives, no matter how much we do it will never be enough to measure up, there will always be something lacking. We should go through our day living with a heart full of gratitude knowing the great thing that Jesus has done for us.

---

1   Rom.7:15

Why are you afraid? I suppose we all from time to time are afraid for some reason. We are afraid because life is not going so well for us at the moment. We are afraid because there are those who are seeking to harm us in some way. We are afraid because it is ourselves that causes us to fear, we are not acting as we believe we should act as Christians. I suppose in our imperfectness there will be times that we fear. If we were able to believe knowing what God has said, what He has proclaimed, we would have no fear. The longer we walk with God, the more we grow in Him, the less we fear.

The devil wants us to fear, the people of the world (who the devil controls) wants us to fear, even sometimes those Christians around us who are not being very Godly want us to fear. What combats fear? It is faith. The more we come to believe, and to know what God gives us to know, the less fear we have. Faith is a matter of believing, believing like a little child. The child does not make a strong effort, applying all his internal strength, saying I will believe. A child believes just because a child believes. They accept what is told to them to be truth, not running it through the filter of their brain and intelligence. Our brains and intelligence is what keeps us from believing many times. Do you realize that if you don't believe because of your thinking, you are challenging God saying by your intelligence it cannot be so.

You may have great accomplishments among men in your initial pursuit, but compared to God you have accomplished nearly nothing. God tells us; *"For my thoughts are not your thoughts, neither are your ways my ways, saith Jehovah. For as the heavens are higher than the earth, so are my ways higher than your ways, and my thoughts than your thoughts"* (Isa. 55:8&9 ASV). I ask you, how high above the earth are the heavens? God doesn't say this only to the foolish, the stupid, the uneducated, He says this to all mankind. If God had the wisdom and the knowledge to make us from dust[1] and at the end of time to collect us from the dust[2] who are we to suppose we can come close to any of His knowledge?

Some of the world, even some in the Church, would say we would be as foolish as a child to believe such things. Let it be, let me be as a child! Only in my pride and arrogance would I refuse to believe because of my intellect. Oh, to draw close to God, to hear His great words, such a pleasure it is.[3] We must believe all of God's word, not just the part that gets us saved. We all are equal before God, none of us can accomplish to where we deserve more than another. In our reading today in Matthew chapter 20 Jesus tells the parable of the land owner and the workers.

All receive the same from the master, it was not the accomplishments of the workers that they received, it was the generosity of the master that they received. Faith comes from believing, believing what God has said. We don't believe that we receive because of what we are able to accomplish for God, we believe because of His generosity to freely give to all who will receive.

---

1   Gen.2:7
2   Dan.12:2
3   Lk.10:39-42

World in chaos. What comes next? This is what many were saying to each other as Jesus enters Jerusalem with great fanfare. This was not the kind of thing they were used to, except for another Roman big wheel coming to town. But this was not a Roman, who is it? The question was astir in all of the town. The whispers and talk were going from corner to corner. What was all these shouts and the celebration all about? Hundreds of people are involved, they're waving palm branches and crying out in great joy, what is happening? Who is all this commotion all about? This was the question being asked in Jerusalem by many. And this was during a busy time for Jerusalem, there were people coming from all parts of the country, even from some foreign lands. It was a week before the Passover and Jews came from all over to celebrate – and to do according to the Law. The population multiplied many times over when Passover time came. And even now a week before the festival and already the city was starting to swell. And now this commotion, how far off the timing for such a thing, it is surely not right, not with all who are coming to the city now. How much they did not know.

How much the timing was perfect. How much they did not know this happening had all to do with Passover, a Passover that had never been before, or would ever be again. The commotion was that the Perfect Lamb was coming to town in Triumphant Entrance of Victory. How little did most know what was going to happen. It was Jesus the Messiah entering town, many thought He would take the throne of His ancestor King David. There were a few who had heard what was going to happen, the disciples had heard Jesus tell them what was going to happen, yet they didn't know because they missed it when Jesus said it.[1] How many times do we have in mind what we expect to happen, then when we are told the truth we totally miss it.

This is what happened to the disciples. It seems a few of them began to get the picture as the next week unfolded, but most would not get it until about ten days later.[2] The greatest thing ever to happen was taking place right before their eyes and nothing turned out the way they expected it to. Jesus was being given a Victor's welcome, they were honoring Him as He came into the city. How all this would change in a week's time. Some of those cheering now may even be some who will be calling for His crucifixion at the end of the week.

They thought He would take the Throne, rule the world from Jerusalem, their town, and kick out the Romans – He did none of this and they were upset with Him. He had failed them, He did not bring the victory they wanted. How many times does God not bring the victory we want? Do we have in mind the things of God, or just the things we have in mind? How many times is our intent right, but God does it totally different, so much so that at first we think it is all wrong, that even maybe the enemy is winning? When God speaks we need to be listening, not have something predetermined in our mind so much that what God says He is doing a different way we almost miss it.

God's ways are not our ways, His ways are far beyond ours.[3] The Jews of Jerusalem were looking for some relief at their time from their occupiers the Romans. What God had in mind was relief from sin that would last into eternity. The very way they thought God was losing was the very way God was winning. Is God winning in your life in ways you never saw coming. Are they ways you never had in mind, or considered? Are they eternal victories, and not just something for the current time you're in? We go to God with something in mind we need from God, we have it all laid out of what we need to happen – do we ever ask God if He has a better idea? Maybe better to present the problem to Him and find out how He may wants to handle it. In the midst of our problem we forget God said, **'Let there be light, and there was light'.**

1   Lk.18:33&34
2   Lk.24:1-8
3   Isa.55:8&9

Along our travels. As we travel through this life (for this is not our final destination) what is our experience along the way? Much of our experience is that of being in the culture we live in. For some of us in moving around this earth we are exposed to multiple cultures. Then there is the next closer thing we are exposed to which is the family we grow up in. Those experiences of the family around us are very close to us and have a great effect on us.

The closest thing that has an effect on us is ourselves, or make up, our notions, our emotions, our opinions, etc. These shape who we become, and who we develop to be, as we go along the travels of this life. That which can have the greatest effect on our lives is the farthest away and yet can be even closer than ourselves. For all of you who believe know that this is God, who until we believed in Him and accepted Him into our lives was far from us because of our unbelief. God is always close to all, but if we are in unbelief He might as well be on the far side of the galaxy. Once we have accepted Jesus Christ as savior, not only is He close, He changes our very being to something better than we could ever have been without Him. Things along our travels affect who we are, even after we become Christians those things can affect how we are.

The Israelites were God's very own chosen people because of their father Abraham, yet as we see reading about them in the Old Testament they were many times affected by those nations around them to the point they were doing the very thing God had told them not to do. We can be affected by those around us, those we keep company with.[1] God has forgiven us by what Jesus has done on the cross, it is finished, Jesus said so.[2] Now as we live this life in the Kingdom of God, fully forgiven, fully accepted by the Father, we are called to live a life of His lifestyle. We are not always successful. Paul says the things he wants to do he does not do, and the things he does not want to do are the very things he does.[3] Paul had trouble living God's lifestyle and we do too. But as we mature in our Christian life it should become more and more like God's lifestyle. The things along our travels of this life affect who we are.

If we are to live God's lifestyle we need to be around those who are trying to live God's lifestyle. Unless we are supernaturally blessed with protection to minister to a particular group which is evil in the way they live, then we should not venture there. We are to be in the world as a witness to the world of God's goodness, but we should stay away from certain groups unless we are specially gifted to minister to them. In and of ourselves we don't have the power to keep the influence of those who are especially evil, in one way or another, off of us for in some sort of way we were such ourselves before we were redeemed by Jesus Christ.

Be cautious in your travels in the world today, it is usually easy to recognize those who are especially evil, but some who seem to be followers of God are not so easy to recognize. There are those who are just playing the part. Jesus had to confront them much of the time, we see that in our reading today; *"Then the Pharisees went and consulted and plotted together how they might entangle Jesus in His talk. And they sent their disciples to Him along with the Herodians,...But Jesus, aware of their malicious plot, asked, Why do you put Me to the test and try to entrap Me, you pretenders?"* (Mt. 22:15,16,18 AMPC) See also Lk. 7:32.

For many years I did not know what Jesus was talking about here, now I know, there are those around us who are just pretenders wanting us to do like them. Paul speaks of those who may not be pretenders, but will have itching ears to hear only what their liking is, not willing to hear the truth and wandering away from it. (2 Tim. 4:3&4) At the end of this word to you today I want you to hear what Paul says about himself, and us: "henceforth **there is laid up** for me **the crown of righteousness, which the Lord, the righteous judge, shall give** to me at that day: and not only to me, but also to **all them that have loved his appearing"** (2Tim. 4:8 RV). Be careful in your travels along this life.

---

1   1Cor.15:33&34
2   Jn.19:30
3   Rom.7:15

'I am God.' He speaks this to us often, the question is , are we listening? When we hear this from God, do we fully encompass the understanding of its meaning? There is a profoundness about Him being God. There is nothing, no one, greater in any way. He is the supplier of all our needs. He is the answer to all our problems. He is the creator of our being. He is the director of the universe. He is the one who keeps the order of our solar system in which we live. He is the one who keeps our planet earth that we live on just in the right place spinning at just the right speed with gravitational forces balanced with centrifugal forces so that the gravity does not crush our bodies into the earth by its force or that the centrifugal forces do not fling us into outer space.

If He, in being God, is doing all of that, then He is certainly capable of controlling the small orbiting things in our everyday life. The greatness of this God we have is that even as He is ruling the universe, keeping all of it in order, He is also willing and desiring to help keep our lives in order. Jesus said to trust God and He would feed us as He feeds the birds. [1]

Jesus said to trust God and He would clothe us like He does the flowers. [2] You are to trust Him with everything in your life, He is willing and desiring to take care of all your needs. Are you trusting Him to do so? This is what He requires: that we believe in Him, trust Him fully, depending on Him with expectation to work in our lives, even supernaturally. All of this has to take place somewhere else than in our brain. Our brain cannot trust in this manner, it is our heart and spirit that trust in this manner. We are to walk in the Spirit, we are to worship in the Spirit, we are to abide in the Spirit. As mankind we like to feel we have accomplished something.

This accomplishment usually has to do with the brain, even an athlete who performs well with his body – it is the brain that is making all the split-second calculations and ordering muscles in the body to respond. Since the things of God are things our brains cannot calculate, it must be our spirit that responds to God. In spiritual life, the life of the Christian which is the reborn part, it is the Spirit that guides us in the way we should go. It is the Spirit that hears what God is speaking to us. It is our spirit who reacts to the Holy Spirit which teaches us all things. [3]

We so much of the time have trouble following God, learning from God, even doing for God, because we are engaging the wrong part of us. It is not by might (strength of our body) nor by power (the working of the brain), but by My Spirit, says the Lord. [4] Are we hearing what God is saying to us? Do we get the fullness of God's statement when He says to us, 'I am God'? The heart of God and all He wants to be for us is emphasized in Jesus' words we have read today, *"Jerusalem, Jerusalem, who kills the prophets and stones those who have been sent to her! How often I wanted to gather your children together, the way a hen gathers her chicks under her wings, and you were unwilling"* (Mt. 23:37 NASB).

This was God the Son wanting them to know how God wanted to bless them. There are those who do not want God to say to them that He is God. Paul speaks of these in our reading today of Titus chapter 1; *"To the pure all things are pure: but to them that are defiled and unbelieving nothing is pure; but both their mind and their conscience are defiled. They profess that they know God; but by their works they deny him, being abominable, and disobedient, and unto every good work reprobatek "* (v. 15&16 ASV). These are those who refuse to hear that God desires to cover them, protect them, provide for them, and be close to them. Are you hearing God when He says, 'I am God' ?

---

1   Mt.6:26, Lk.12:24
2   Mt.6:28, Lk.12:27
3   Rom.8:16, Jn.14:26
4   Zech.4:6

What am I? Do you ever ask yourself that question? It is an important question to have an answer to. When you know who you are, who you eternally are, there is a stability that can pass through many storms untouched. With many of us today we don't know who we are. Those in the world surely don't know who they are even if they think they know. Jesus said that if they don't have, even what they think they have will be taken away from them. [1]

There are many in the Church, the body of Christ, who don't know who they are. Many don't get into the word of God and read, they just listen to others who talk/teach/preach. If the person they listen to doesn't have it down knowing who they themselves are they cannot instill it in others either. Even when we are in the word of God, hearing what it has to say, we may not clearly understand what it is saying because of the wrong teaching we have received has deterred us from the truth.

The word of God can be colored in the wrong color if the teaching on it has been wrong. Many times we see things as we have been conditioned to see them. This applies to the word of God also. When we read God's word we should read it with an open mind and heart, even of asking God in prayer to clear away any deception of His word we have been taught. The Holy Spirit has been sent to each believer, not just the priest, pastors, or preacher/teacher. [2] Ask the Holy Spirit to help you to know what God's word is saying. Every time I write 'A Comment for the Day' I ask the Holy Spirit to guide me, to speak to me as I write. He knows better than I what it is you need to hear today.

Jesus' words today in our reading in Matthew chapter 24 says, *"And Jesus answered and said to them, "See to it that no one misleads you"* (v. 4 NASB). Jesus is speaking here about the end times, but it would seem to apply to all the word of God. Be careful, be a good Berean, check the scriptures for the truth as they checked all the things Paul was telling them. [3] I began this with the question, 'Who am I?' If you are a believer in Christ Matthew 24:22&31 is speaking of you, you are one of God's elect, do you see what it says about you? I find it interesting when the epistle reading assignment for the day in the New Testament speaks of something that was in the Gospels the same day.

Today is such, Jesus spoke of how it would be when He returned and Paul says; *"looking for the blessed hope and appearing of the glory of our great God and Saviour Jesus Christ"* (Tit. 2:13 RV). Who am I? - I am and you are those who Jesus is returning for. A last thing in this writing today for you to hear is what Paul tells us Jesus did for us: *"who gave himself for us, that he might redeem us from all iniquity, and purify unto himself a people for his own possession, zealous of good works"* (Tit. 2:14 RV). This is who we are.

---

1   Mt.13:12, 25:29, Lk.8:18
2   Jn.14:26, 16:13&14
3   Acts 17:10&11

How are you progressing in life today? Are you growing? Are you stalling? Are you being tossed by the wind? Are you well anchored? Are you a slip of foot? What is your condition today? An athlete getting ready for a competition checks over his condition working on those areas that are a bit weak to strengthen them for the event.

As Christians, our event is life lived for Christ in a lost world. So, what is your condition? Have you checked it over lately? Are you working at strengthening the weak areas of your life? God calls us to stay in shape, constantly seeking Him to work in us and through us. We can do nothing of ourselves. If that were possible then certainly someone would have been able to be perfect by the Law and Jesus would not have had to die for us to pay the price we owed.

It is only God working through us that we can do anything good. Jesus shows this to be true in what He says; *"Now behold, one came and said to Him, "Good Teacher, what good thing shall I do that I may have eternal life?" So He said to him, "Why do you call Me good? No one is good but One, that is, God. But if you want to enter into life, keep the commandments"* (Mt. 19:16&17 NKJV). There was nothing good this person could do as Jesus shows him in the further conversation, he went away sad because he could not do what was good. It is only God who is good and it is only Him working in us and through us that we can accomplish anything good. We are not good, BUT, in Him we can do all that is good. It is when we find there is nothing good in us that God can do much good through us and we can become a great asset to the Kingdom of God. It is amazing what God can do when we yield to Him.

There are examples after examples in God's word. When we give up on ourselves and take up on God in us is when we go forward in great victory. We can look at the battles in the Old Testament where God went first and the people followed seeing the great victories God brought. There are also the battles that the people thought they could surely handle and were terribly beaten back. It is God who wins the victory, it is God who won our salvation, it is God who wins the battle in the end putting the devil in his place, [1] and it is God who takes us as His prize into eternity. We can see in our reading today we need to be yielded with our lamps burning brightly and our containers full of oil (Spirit) when Jesus comes for His bride.

It will be by His victory that we are taken into heaven. (Mt.25:1-10) Also in the parable of the talents given, what was accomplished by the servants was by what the Master invested into them. (Mt. 25:14-23) Make all efforts that your progress in life is good, and that can only happen when the One and only One that is good is working in you and through you. Seek Him and abide in Him as much as you possibly can.

---

1   Rev.20:10

For what do we live? Many live for riches, even being willing to sell themselves to get riches. From what I see in scripture the Lord is telling us that the pursuit after riches only brings misery and disappointment. If we are created with a need for God then finding Him is the only thing that will bring satisfaction to our souls. A pursuit of riches goes on all around us and if we get caught up in it we will find nothing but misery. **'I am the way, the truth, and the life,' said Jesus.** He is the only thing that can bring fullness of life, He is the only one who brings us the truth, and by Him is the only way to God and heaven.

As I look around (read of things happening in the Church around the world) it seems the poor and miserable, by the world's standards, are many of those who have found through Jesus the greatest happiness and richness to be found on the earth. When a person has very little it is easy to live for and develop a relationship with God. Those of us who have, it seems the more we have the harder it is to fully give ourselves to God and seek a deep relationship with Him. We are pulled in a direction away from God by our wants and desires. Our desire has to be for God, no matter what the cost.

A rich man struggles with living for/with God - Jesus said it is easier for a camel to go through the eye of a needle than for a rich man to enter the Kingdom of God.[1] Yet even for the rich, it is possible, for Jesus follows saying all things are possible for God. Maybe this is why the Church in America struggles so much, compared to many in the world we are rich. Jesus is the way, the truth, and the life – this is where we must look. Our success lies in Him and our failure lies in what the world seeks after. Jesus said that the way to life is narrow and the way to destruction is wide.[2]

There will always be more in the world who have not found salvation through Jesus Christ and fewer of us who have. If we do not keep our eyes on Jesus and believe what He says, then at times, we may think the world's way of life might be better. What the world has is only temporary, their joy will not last long, weeping and gnashing of teeth will become their lot.[3] Go not their way, seek after God with all your strength, with all your heart, with all your soul, and with all your mind. This is where we find true joy, not just a declared joy that we are to believe we have, but one we can experience more and more as the closer and closer we get to God.

The scriptures tell us that God is reaching out to us but to get close to Him we have to move close first, and as we draw close to Him He will draw close to us.[4] What a great place to be, in the very arms of God! Today we read of a woman who came and poured a very costly perfume on Jesus' head. (Mt. 26:7) There are other times it is mentioned that a woman came anointing Jesus with costly perfume, on the feet, and on the head. One of those places is John 12:3-5 where the perfume is valued at 300 denarii. One reference Bible I have said that was about a man's yearly wage. Whether all these women are the same Mary (the sister of Martha and Lazarus) or different women I don't know, but what we need to see is the value the woman in each record is willing to yield finding Jesus of much more value. Jesus is the most valued, the most treasured thing she/they had found in her/their life. Is Jesus the most treasured thing you have in your life?

---

1   Mt.19:24
2   Mt.7:13&14
3   Mt.25:29&30
4   Jas.4:8, Heb.11:6

'My grace is sufficient for you.' Paul prayed to the Lord about troubles he had (thorn in the flesh) and the Lord replied to him, *"My grace is sufficient for you, for my power is made perfect in weakness"* (2Cor. 12:9 ESV).This is what God told Paul and for us it would be the same, in our weakness HIS power is perfected. I am reminded of the history of Gideon in the Old Testament when God was to answer the prayers of the people of Israel freeing them from their oppressor.

God called Gideon, not a fearless man, but one hiding from the oppressors while thrashing the wheat. Not only was he not a fearless man, but when he gathered the troops from Israel God gleaned them down to 300 men so the people could not in their hearts try to take credit for the victory, it would clearly be a work of God.[1] God is victorious working through us even in the midst of our troubles and weakness. The very thing which gives us eternal salvation is that which God did for us when we were in our weakest hour, confessing we are sinners needing forgiven, giving us salvation by His work, at a time we deserved nothing good. If God can work that great work which changes our course in eternity from total loss to total gain, then in our weakness as we continue to live before Him He can surely show His power working through us in ways we cannot in our hearts take credit for the victories. How many are there in the Church today who walk with pride in their hearts trying to take credit for something that God alone has done?

God is not pleased with those who make efforts to steal the glory that is God's alone. We can't even be sure (make it happen) we will get up in the morning let alone accomplish any great work that it is only God can do. Our God is sufficient. And if we are willing to humble ourselves He can and will work great things and great victories through us. Weakness is good, for then God can work mightily through us. In Matthew chapter 27 today, we see the end of the trial by the chief priest and the council, the delivery of Jesus to Pilate the Roman governor, and Jesus' crucifixion and burial.

In all of this Jesus remained humble, starting in the garden of Gethsemane until His death. Even with all the things the Roman governor said to Him He said very little. The greatest victory of all time, from the beginning of creation to the moment time will end, was won by the humbleness of Jesus on the day He allowed Himself to die on the cross. He could have fought a great battle with the Romans, as many of His followers thought He was going to do. He could have won the victory against Rome, the greatest nation in the world at that time, but what victory could that be for us today? The victory that Jesus won that day by being humble, allowing these things to be done to Him, has brought victory to all who will accept Him as Lord. Jesus died and offers this to any person who will accept Him, He died for ALL. (Tit. 2:11&12)

---

[1]   Jdg.6:11-7:22

'Have faith in Me and I will give you rest.' Well I don't know of any scripture that states it this way but Jesus does say, *"come unto me...and I will give you rest"* (Mt. 11:28 ASV). What is it to come to Jesus, is it not accepting, believing, following? Is this not having faith in Jesus? Why is it we struggle so much if Jesus has said He would give us rest? Are we still trying to do the work ourselves? Hasn't Jesus already done all the work, didn't He say it's finished? We are to come alongside of Him in His yoke with Him where He is the Master Ox who is pulling the load.[1]

We are to take up our cross, as Jesus took His, and follow him working in what He has already accomplished. We are to preach the gospel, to share our testimony of what Jesus has done in our life with the world. As we follow Jesus in sharing the gospel we are only inviting unsaved people into the work Jesus has already done. Why do we make it so difficult in our lives to live the Christian life? Are we still trying to accomplish a little of what we couldn't accomplish before when we accepted Jesus into our lives?

Everything God makes easy for us by the way of faith, we make it difficult in unbelief. God has blessed us, God has redeemed us, God has sanctified us, God has empowered us, God has renewed our being by giving us the new birth. With all He has given us, why do we try so hard? There is nothing we can add. All we can do is accept and follow in the work Jesus has already done. In a sense of applying an overview of all that Jesus says to us it can be said that he would say to us, 'have faith in Me and I will give you rest'. Are we experiencing that rest, are we having faith? Believing is not an easy thing, even the disciples had a problem with it. Jesus had said many times to the disciples that He had to be crucified and buried, and then He would rise from the dead. They did not all believe this.

In the last chapter of Mathew we read today of the women going to the tomb and finding Jesus was not there (in death). The women were told by an angel that Jesus was not there, He had risen, and to tell His disciples. (v. 5-7) Later in Galilee Jesus appears to them and some still doubted. (v. 16&17) Yes, we will doubt, it seems to be part of what we inherited from the fall in the garden of Eden by Adam and Eve. But the more we push doubt away and believe what Jesus has said the easier our Christian life will become and the more rest we will find.

---

1   Mt.11:29

'This is the day, this is the day, that the Lord has made, that the Lord has made.' I remember this first line of a song we sang when I was first saved, you may know it also. Do you believe it? Do you believe this is the day that the Lord has made? How can our lives be better? As we yield over more and more of our lives to Jesus by dying more and more to self we will begin to experience more and more the day, and each day, He has made. Our walk as a Christian is not easy, Jesus said if we follow after Him they (the world) will persecute us as they persecuted Him. [1]

Even though Jesus was persecuted He walked in each day with confidence in the Father. Even though many days for Jesus were difficult (in the sense of dealing with the people) He walked in a joy that came from His relationship with the Father and the confidence He had in the Father. If Jesus has made the day we should be able to find joy in it because of our relationship with Him and our confidence we have in Him. Paul must have found this joy for he said he had learned how to be content in all circumstances. [2] Paul is one of those who tell us to rejoice always. [3]

With all the troubles (I would dare to say none of us has the sum of troubles Paul had, even being stoned once) Paul said he had learned how to rejoice and know the day, his day, each one of them, was in the Lord's hands because the Lord had made the day. Our God is a busy God, even though it may be easy to Him, He has control of and has conditioned each day for each individual person who belongs to Him. Wow! I can't even take care of one and He is doing it constantly for every Christian on this earth today. What a mighty God we have! Do you believe you have a mighty God, a God that is by custom making the day you have just for you, conditioning your path, setting up protection for you from difficulties so that they go no further than He knows they should.

Not every day Jesus had was easy in our view, but the Father had set the limit of how far they could go. The devil couldn't get at Jesus enough to destroy the works He was doing. [4] The people couldn't get at Jesus, look how many times the religious leaders wanted to arrest Him before it was time. And how many times did they want to stone Him, and it says Jesus walked right out of their midst and they couldn't touch Him. With all the trials, shipwrecks, beatings, etc. Paul was unstoppable until God said Paul was done with his work. Do we have confidence that God is setting our day no matter what it seems to bring? Yesterday I spoke about faith. Here is one of those areas we need to have faith, to be confident that God has control of our day, that He has set the limits, and that it is custom made for us.

God knows what we need in our day, He does not allow us more difficulties than we can handle, and He puts in it the things we have to learn each day. God is a good God, God is a mighty God. Our part is to have faith that He is working in our day. The Israelites that came out of Egypt did not have this faith that God had control of their day or they would have marched into the promise land believing He would give them victory no matter what the obstacles were.

The writer of Hebrews is speaking of this in chapter 3 today in our reading. There is encouragement we can get from what we've read: *"For every house is builded by some one; but he that built all things is God...but Christ as a son, over his house; whose house are we, if we hold fast our boldness and the glorying of our hope firm unto the end...for we are become partakers of Christ, if we hold fast the beginning of our confidence firm unto the end"* (v. 4,6,14 ASV). The final verse of chapter 3 tells us why the Israelites who came out of Egypt were not able to find the rest God had prepared for them: *"And we see that they were not able to enter in because of unbelief"* (v. 19 ASV). So, I encourage you today: have faith, enter into the day God has made just for you, and remember to rejoice in it.

---

1   Jn.15:20
2   Philp.4:11-13
3   Philp.4:4, 1Thes.5:15b-18
4   Mk.1:13, Mt.4:1-11, Lk.4:1-13

'I am the way, the truth, and the life'. This is what Jesus tells us so why would we go looking anywhere else? There are those who say, 'Why look for more, we are what we got'. Who are we to judge, we can't even tell about tomorrow. You are the one who must believe. If you don't believe then what you got is all you got. I will ask you a question, how did you get here? Do you really know the answer, were you there when the human race started? How can you know anything if you do not ask God? You are unwilling to believe so you will never have anything more. Jesus is the way, the truth, and the life. Without Him what have you got? This is all an argument to get you to see your need for Christ.

Without Him you have nothing and with Him you have everything, not everything the world has to offer, but everything God has to offer. Now that I have your attention, think about what your life would be like without Christ in it. He is the truth, the way, and the life – without Him we have nothing. The eternal God has reached out to each one of us with eternal salvation which we have accepted by accepting Jesus as Lord into our lives. He has made that way that we could not. He has shown us truth about ourselves and about Him. He has given us what true life is. Yet in our nature we continue like Adam and Eve to reach out in the other direction. We look back as we read about Adam and Eve and condemn them because they had it made in the garden with God coming as company in the cool of the day – so why would they blow it by desiring of fruit from the tree they were to not to eat of.

Do we not do the same thing, are we not truly their children? It is hard to admit we are a mess. You know what you are, even if you don't what to look, it doesn't change who you are. We are all fallen, none of us measuring up. I would like to ask you another question, where does your help come from, is it not God? We struggle, and we struggle, and we struggle. Why don't we just give up, and allow Jesus to show us and give us the way? Why don't we just give up, and allow Jesus to show us and give us the truth? Why don't we just give up, and allow Jesus to show us and give us the life? These are questions we have to answer, the answers will show us what is keeping us from the great fullness God wants to give us.

In reading Mark chapter 2 today we see the questioning of Jesus over and over. (v. 7,16,18,24) Jesus was constantly being cross examined, with those asking the questions not willing to believe. Do we cross examine Jesus with our thoughts of how we think something He said cannot be, so we refuse to believe? There is much in Hebrews chapter 4 today: *"For we who have believed enter that rest...For the word of God is living and active, and sharper than any two-edged sword, even penetrating as far as the division of soul and spirit, of both joints and marrow, and able to judge the thoughts and intentions of the heart...And there is no creature hidden from His sight, but all things are open and laid bare to the eyes of Him to whom we must answer...Therefore let's approach the throne of grace with confidence, so that we may receive mercy and find grace for help at the time of our need"* (v. 3,12,13,16 NASB).

We who have accepted Jesus as Lord have believed, we have entered that rest. What keeps us from entering all of that rest, why do we struggle – God knows all there is to know about us. Surrender is all it takes to have everything He offers and yet we struggle. God wants to give us grace, all grace at the throne of grace. And He wants us to have mercy, all the mercy that He has for us. Why do we struggle, what we have to come to grips with is Jesus is the way, the truth, and the life. If we truly have entered God's rest all this is ours, we don't need to struggle any more, only believe.

'I am God and you are man.' Do we hear God saying this to us? Is He really God or just a figment of our imagination? He tells us to try Him and see if He is real. Have you tried Him, have you made your way His way to find if it is real or not? Maybe for many of us, He is not much more than the figment of our imagination in the sense that we accept Him as Lord to receive salvation and then afterward make Him out to be what we want Him to be instead of finding who He really is and what He wants to do in our lives. Jesus said pick up you cross and follow Me. Jesus did this in following the Father in what the Father want Him to do. Are we not to do the same thing?

There have been those who have said the Bible is God's letter to us. Are you reading His letter to find out about Him, or are you still in 'make believe land' trying to make God in your life to be what You want Him to be? Many times as we read the gospels (Matthew, Mark, Luke, John) we see Jesus going off to a solitary place spending time with the Father in prayer. Are you praying, are you having that daily conversation with God so that you are more involved in His life and He in yours? Where are you, what is your spiritual state? Why make excuses, He sees your day, He sees everything in it, He sees your struggle. Why try so hard when God wants to bless you. Have you ever had a grandparent, who when you as a child went to see them, they would just gather you up into their arms and just love you? God wants to do so much more than this but you stay at arm's length away from Him. He wants to provide for you, He wants to protect you, He wants to settle that place of unrest within you. Take the time, spend it reading His letter to you, then go to Him to talk to Him about what He had to say, and what more He wants to say to you.

In our reading today of Mark chapter 3 we see in the first half how the people flocked to Him, but only because they wanted healing from their sickness, and not to hear the eternal words He spoke. In one place in the gospels Jesus tells the crowd, 'you only follow me to get more bread to eat'. There were those who followed Him because He had the answers to life, eternal life, but most that followed were only after the immediate help of their situation. One time Jesus gave a very hard teaching to accept and many who had followed Him up to that point left Him then.

How much are you willing to follow? Are you one of those who the writer of Hebrews is speaking to; *"About this we have much to say, and it is hard to explain, since you have become dull of hearing. For though by this time you ought to be teachers, you need someone to teach you again the basic principles of the oracles of God. You need milk, not solid food"* (5:11&12 ESV). How much are you willing to follow, are you, or can you be, one of those who this is said about; *"solid food is for the mature, for those who have their powers of discernment trained by constant practice to distinguish good from evil."* (5:14 ESV)

How is your day going? If you are one who reads this early in the morning there may not be such the answer of how it is going as how do you expect it to go. The main point is how much are you expecting and how much are you allowing God to be involved in your day? Where are you going, do you know? If you don't know and it is in faith as when Abraham followed God, great!   But if it is without God then even if you think you know where you are going do you really know? You have to decide if you want God along or not, He will not intrude. How can you go without a guide, someone who has been there before? There is nowhere where God has not been, He does know the way. Are you willing to allow Him to lead? If not, and you say you know where you are going, are you not still wandering aimlessly? If you cannot know what tomorrow will bring, how can you know what is just around the corner in your travels? It is better to have a guide when traveling, who better to be the guide than God Himself?

I know that for some it is difficult to sense the voice of the Lord. When you plan a vacation not everyone is able to hire a personal guide so we find a book written by a well known guide. When you get ready to go on that vacation you get into that guide book reading about where you are going. While you are on that vacation you turn to the guide book many times to read about the place you are visiting. Ah, for our travels though life there is a travel guide written by the best guide possible, the Bible written by God. We need to read the guide book God has written about where we are going and about where we are at right now. God wants to help us as we travel through this life on earth with our final destination of heaven.

When we are on our travels during a vacation how great it would be when reading the guide book if we could call the guide who wrote it and ask questions and get clarifications. With God we can call in prayer, how much better can it be! If we have accepted Jesus as Lord in our life experiencing the new birth then we are now part of the Kingdom of God. The effects of being part of the Kingdom of God causes us to grow as the mustard seed Jesus speaks of today in our reading in Mark chapter 4.

Our act of seeking guidance on our travels through life may start out very small but with time will grow, but the seed will not grow until you plant it, until you begin to trust and seek God's guidance. We all have our weak times just like the disciples on the sea; *"A furious windstorm arose, and the waves broke over the boat, so that it was close to being swamped...They woke him and said to him, "Rabbi, doesn't it matter to you that we're about to be killed?"* (v. 37&38 CJB). The disciples knew Jesus was along but didn't really believe He had full control of the situation. When the storms come in our travels we may even wonder if Jesus is along. If we are His, He is along: *"So we can confidently say, "The Lord is my helper; I will not fear; what can man do to me?"* (Heb. 13:5&6 ESV).

Jesus is along with us in our travels, do we acknowledge Him and believe He has control of our situation, or does He say to us as He said to the disciples: *"Why are you afraid? Have you no trust even now?"* (Mk. 4:40 CJB). I don't think any of us want to hear Jesus say this to us, so believe He is with you, seeking Him to guide you, and trust He has control of the situation.

'Going my way?' This is a line from one of Bing Crosby's movies. This is what Jesus would ask each one of us, 'Going My way?' Jesus invites us all to go His way, He has even already paid the fare.[1] We don't even have to pack because He says He will provide if we come along and go His way.[2] Each of us have to make that decision, each of us have to accept Jesus as Lord to receive what He has already done for us. Most of you reading this have done this and this is why you are reading this today.

Now that you have your ticket to get to heaven are you going Jesus' way, or are you still going a little your own way? God gives us all the information we need to go Jesus' way, we find it all in the Bible. It comes to the question for many, are you reading the Bible man's way or God's way? You may ask the question, what is the difference? If you are reading it like you would a textbook in school, only to get information from it, its help will be very limited to you. God says His word is alive.[3] It has the ability to bring us to repentance, it has the ability to bring us great joy, it has the ability to give us strength, it has the ability to take us close to God. The difference is that reading the Bible God's way we would read it with prayer expecting God to work in us by it. There is no other book that gives us what this book gives us.

There is no other book that the words in it are alive like this book. These are the accumulated recorded words God has spoken and as God is alive forever His words are alive forever, never losing the power they were spoken with. From the creation to Revelation they are alive having eternal effect on those who read them expecting God to work in their lives. There are some of you who take a vitamin every day to keep your body healthy. What do you suppose you need every day to keep your Spirit and soul spiritually healthy? If we begin our day with that spiritual dose of God's word, even if it is only one verse, it will make a difference in how our day goes, in how healthy our Spirit and soul is. There are those of you who eat right, exercise right, live right, sleep right, for a healthy life. What about reading right, receiving from God each day? 'Going My way?'

In our reading today in Mark chapter 5 we see something interesting about the disciples. They had been with Jesus now some time, they had seen Him heal many and cast demons out of many. Yet when Jesus said who touched me, they basically tell Jesus he doesn't know what He is asking, all the crowd is touching Him, what kind of a question is this? (v. 30&31) They were questioning what Jesus said thinking He couldn't know what He was talking about. When we read the word of God we must believe He knows what He is talking about. Also in Mark we read about the ruler of the synagogue, Jairus. Some people come from Jairus' house telling him his daughter is dead, don't bother the Teacher any more. We need to hear what Jesus told Jairus; *"Do not be seized with alarm and struck with fear, only keep on believing."* (v. 36 AMPC). It seems Jairus did keep on believing, we read no indication he did not. In what we hear today in these scriptures we are told to believe what we read in God's word and to keep on believing. **'Are you going My way?', God asks.**

---

1   1Cor.6:20
2   Lk.12:37
3   Heb.4:12

Why is life so difficult? We make it harder than it needs to be, we don't really listen to all God says and because of it life for us is more difficult than it needs to be. We still do today what was done in the beginning, we don't listen, we don't follow what God says. In the beginning, God said do not eat from the tree in the center of the garden, everything will be well for you with all the other trees of the garden, but this one of the knowledge of good and evil do not eat from.[1] Mankind (Adam & Eve), being convinced by the lying serpent did not listen to God, ate from the tree they were not to eat, and life became difficult.[2]

In the Old Testament, many times God says the Israelites were a stubborn people. I'm not so sure we today are any different, Jew or Gentile. Humanity has a stubborn streak, an unwillfulness to follow all that God says to us. We are as the infant in the crib trying to tell their adult parent how life should be lived. That is ridiculous for an infant to assume it knows more than the adult parent yet this is what we do with God all the time. An infant who can't even wipe its noise, or the other end, surely can't know better than the adult parent. We are that infant compared to God who is the parent of us all. One of the greatest things for any of us to learn is that God knows what He is talking about and as improbable as it seems to be, if we will follow it, life will be better. We struggle and we strain, muchly because we don't listen.

In our reading today in Mark chapter 6 it is interesting the progression that takes place in the people of Jesus' hometown of Nazareth; *"And on the Sabbath he began to teach in the synagogue, and many who heard him were astonished, saying...What is the wisdom given to him? How are such mighty works done by his hands"* (v. 2 ESV). When Jesus begins to teach they are amazed at what He has to say and how impressive are His words. At first when we in our lives today are saved we are very impressed with God's words and teaching. The next thing that happens with those of Jesus' town is this; *"Is not this the carpenter, the son of Mary and brother of James and Joses and Judas and Simon? And are not his sisters here with us?" And they took offense at him"* (v. 3 ESV). They began to consider who they themselves were and that He was just one of them, so they were offended by what He said and what He did, rejecting His authority and making their own more valuable. In the same account of this in Luke, or possible a later time Luke speaks of, when Jesus went to Nazareth this is what the people did; *"On hearing this, everyone in the synagogue was filled with fury. They rose up, drove him out of town and dragged him to the edge of the cliff on which their town was built, intending to throw him off"* (Lk. 4:28&29 CJB).

So what happened to what they thought earlier; *"And all the people were speaking well of Him, and admiring the gracious words which were coming from His lips"* (Lk. 4:22 NASB). Sometimes, as it is said, we get a little too full of ourselves. We begin to think a little too highly of ourselves and in our hearts reject something God has said. Dying to self is believing God knows all and we know nothing. When we totally give up on what we think we know, and take up what God says to be as all that we know, life will not be so difficult.

---

1   Gen.2:16&17
2   Gen.3:1-5, 3:6&7, 3:17b-19,24

Life seems unfair at times. The interesting thing is to whom it seems unfair, is that not us? Are we, in making that statement, saying we are the ones with the right to judge? God judges all things, God decides all things. God judged in the Garden of Eden that we of mankind should have a free will, which we did have, and then we chose wrongly. God always gives us a choice, we do have a free will, but God does tell us that in the end of time what that choice will bring us.

Mankind is given the choice, the question is does he believe God speaks truth or not. Whether we are willing to accept what God says is truth or not, God will have the final judgment. He is eternal and His ways are eternal. Man will always do according to his own will for we are given a free will, anything less is not free. It is those of us who have received salvation who have, by our free will, chose to believe God, to believe His grace and His mercy, confessed to Him we are sinners, and accepted Jesus Christ as our Lord and Savior, who will have eternal life. This is not as other religions, who mandate a way of life before they can receive - even though there is nothing for them to receive. This salvation is a receiving with no mandated way of life and when we have received Jesus as Lord, He helps us to change.

The outcome of the free choice given to mankind has nothing to do with the performance of man, it has to do with the performance of God, and if we are willing to believe in God's work done on our behalf. God's love reaches from the beginning of time, over the years, to us today with the greatest gift He could ever give. Salvation, an eternity with God, given with no works on our part is the greatest gift ever given. Have you thanked Him for it today? Those we read of today in Mark chapter 7 had a free choice. The Pharisees and scribes chose not to believe God so much so that they had made up their own rules rather than continuing in God's rules. (v. 5-7,13)

Mankind likes to make up their own rules and standards to live by. They are willing to give up all the blessings of God for their own self pride. Mankind likes to accomplish by his own rules so he can take pride in it, God calls for surrender and there is no pride in surrender. Jesus said it is what comes out of our heart, that which we speak, which shows if we are unclean before God. Pride is that which causes all the things listed to come from our hearts; *"For from within, out of a person's heart, come forth wicked thoughts, sexual immorality, theft, murder, adultery, greed, malice, deceit, indecency, envy, slander, arrogance, foolishness.... All these wicked things come from within, and they make a person unclean"* (Mk. 7:21-23 CJB)

What do we believe? Do we believe God or do we believe what man has to say? Most of you reading this have chosen to believe God. We have been reading in Hebrews of what a great, truly, eternal High Priest we have in Jesus. Today we read: *"But Christ came as High Priest of the good things to come, with the greater and more perfect tabernacle not made with hands, that is, not of this creation. Not with the blood of goats and calves, but with His own blood He entered the Most Holy Place once for all, having obtained eternal redemption...And for this reason He is the Mediator of the new covenant, by means of death, for the redemption of the transgressions under the first covenant, that those who are called may receive the promise of the eternal inheritance...For Christ has not entered the holy places made with hands, which are copies of the true, but into heaven itself, now to appear in the presence of God for us...so Christ was offered once to bear the sins of many. To those who eagerly wait for Him He will appear a second time, apart from sin, for salvation"* (9:11,12,15,24,28 NKJV). What a great gift we have been given, what a great choice to make, what a kind God to offer it!

Make up your mind today. Be willing to follow. Jesus does call us to pick up our crosses and follow Him. The world knows nothing about Jesus' ways. It is only us who have been reborn that know the ways of God. The world can read His word, the Bible, but not get much from it because they are not born into the family. We have a great inheritance, eternity with the King of kings and Lord of lords who calls us friends.[1] **'Take up your cross and follow Me'** is what Jesus says to us all. We are to be His people to the world.[2]

How was Jesus to the world? He wanted them to understand what had been done for them by the Father, that they no longer had to labor. He healed most who were sick, restored those who were lame, freed those who were held captive by demons. He tried to help people understand the ways of God. The only one He had a problem with, confronting them in their actions, was those who thought they were religious already. He didn't mind being with the tax collectors (seen as traitors by their own nation of Jews), prostitutes, and outright sinners.[3] These were willing to hear His good news, that they could be forgiven for their sins, which none of them declined that they were sinners – they knew they were. It was those who thought they were not sinners who needed Jesus' forgiveness the most, but only a few of them finally came to Jesus. So where are you at today? Do you side with the tax collectors, prostitutes, etc., or do you feel you are more on the side of those who didn't believe they were sinners?

Any of us who cannot in our own actions come up to the glory of God fall short of His righteousness, which classifies us with sinners. The New Testament tells us we are the righteous but don't get confused, it is Jesus' righteousness that we have, He is who we get our righteousness from.[4] It is His and He shares it with us. Glory be to God for He has allowed a way for us to get to heaven.[5] If we had to gain entrance by our own accomplishments none of us would make it in. We can't say yes to the Lord today to receive salvation and then go on our merry way, when we make up our minds it has to be for a lifetime. In our society today when we are in debt and can't pay we file bankruptcy.

To a certain extent that is what God has done for every one of us who are saved. In the Old Testament times it wasn't that you were forgive your debt, it was that someone else paid your debit and you became their property, their slave. When we accept Jesus, He pays the debt we owed for our sins that we could not pay, so now we have become His property.[6] But He is good to us, calling us friends and providing our needs. In our reading today in Mark chapter 8 Jesus asks; *"Who do men say that I am?"*(v. 27 ASV). Have you made up your mind? Who do you say Jesus is? Do you answer as Peter did, that He is the Christ, the Messiah, the Anointed One of God? For those of you who do in v. 31 Jesus speaks of what He will do (has done for us) to pay the price we owe and free us from debit: *"the Son of man must suffer many things, and be rejected by the elders, and the chief priests, and the scribes, and be killed, and after three days rise again"*(ASV). Can we ask for anything more when we deserve so little?

---

1   Lk.12:4, Jn.15:13-15, 17:20&21
2   Jn.17:18,23
3   Mt.21:31, Mk.2:16
4   1Cor.1:30
5   Jn.3:15
6   1Cor.6:20, 7:23, 2Pet.2:1

What shall we do today? We plan, and we make arrangements, but only God brings about the things of the day. Are we ready for what He brings? Are we willing to follow if He says come? What about our life, are we willing to set aside what we have planned for it to follow God when He asks us to deviate from it? If we are not, are we then saying we know better of what we should do in our life than God? If we choose to do what it is we think is best in our life and not what God is speaking to us at the moment is this not rebellion? I think most all of us have this happen some in our lives.

The thing is to recognize it and ask forgiveness for it. The more we recognize it the less and less we will do it. Not recognizing it, or being hard headed about it is what takes us a distance from God. If we continue in this manner soon we will be so far from God that we will no longer hear His voice at all. Even in the distance when a person recognizes he has left God behind, humbles himself and asks forgiveness God will bring him back, God did it over and over with the Israelites. [1] Repentance has to be a way of life for the Christian. I am not saying that sin and sin and sin has to be the way of life for the Christian, but I am saying that we all fall short of the glory of God and it is a repentant heart which allows us to come close to Him.

A consciousness of repentance will even keep us from sinning at times because we are conscious of our shortness before God. The awareness of our sinfulness will push us away from sinning at times knowing that it is what got us into this mess in the first place. None of us will ever totally be without sin, even the apostle Paul after his salvation in Damascus and in his ministry to the Gentiles struggled with his sin saying the things he wanted to do (the things of God) he didn't do and the things he did not want to do (sin) is what he found himself doing. [2] Paul even goes on to say: *"Wretched man that I am! Who will deliver me from this body of death* [the flesh]*?"* (Rom.7:24 ESV). Do not allow these words of Paul's to get you down and defeat you, listen to what Paul says just a few verses later; *"There is therefore now no condemnation to those who are in Christ Jesus, who do not walk according to the flesh, but according to the Spirit. For the law of the Spirit of life in Christ Jesus has made me free from the law of sin and death"* (Rom.8:1&2 NKJV).

It is our awareness of sin that takes us farther and farther away from sin and closer and closer to God. God's ways are always better than our ways, even when the situation makes no sense to us. I could not do what Abraham did in being willing to sacrifice his son Isaac to God. Even though God stopped Abraham at the last moment, Abraham believing God knew better than what he could understand, he did what God spoke to him. It is by faith and faith alone that we walk with God – sometimes we see and understand, and sometimes we don't. The emphasis in Hebrews chapter 11 today is that of faith. In the very first verse it says: *"Now faith is the substance of things hoped for, the evidence of things not seen"* (v. 1 NKJV). The writer goes on to speak of those who walked in faith before God, he even says there is not time to speak of them all. (v. 32) It would be good for you to read chapter 11 again, maybe at lunch, maybe this evening, maybe as you walk along. The answer to the question, 'What shall we do today?' is to have faith.

---

1   See the book of Judges
2   Rom.7:19

God is supreme. Can you accept that? Can you believe that? If it sticks sideways in your brain what is it you have a problem with? Maybe you don't believe God created everything just as it is stated in Genesis. Maybe you don't believe God works in the ways the Bible says He works. Maybe you find a conflict in what God says and what you have been educated to believe that man says. In the days of the world flood when only Noah and his family survived, the people of the earth were satisfied to believe what they told each other. Some will say it can't be as the Bible says it was because we have proven otherwise. How can that which operates solely in the physical realm disprove what happens in the supernatural realm? The supernatural realm always overrides and trumps what happens in the physical realm. No matter what is proven to be the limits in the physical, that is only the limits of the physical realm, not the limits of the supernatural realm. Those things which man says cannot be are the very things at times that God does. He is able to go even beyond our greatest dreams and imaginations. [1]

If God could do nothing more than man or what man figures, should He, and could He still be God. And if He couldn't then He would be no God and man himself would claim to be god in a sense. How can a supernatural God claim to be God if He is held back by the same limits that Man is held by? We either believe or do not believe. There is nothing that man can accomplish which will prove or disprove there is a God. Anyone who believes there is a way to prove there is will never find God because God is high and above all that man says or thinks. Man looks in all the wrong places for God. Man looks to the places of all those things that have been created. Man schemes and thinks and contrives the ways he thinks we got here, how life began, of itself without any working of an intelligence in the process. Yet with all man wants the rest of us to believe he tells us that by his intelligence he can explain it to us.

There is something inconsistent here. There cannot be the need for us to be intelligent to understand that there was no intelligence in us getting here. For those who think they think this does not compute. The only way we can have true intelligence is to go to the one who has supernatural intelligence and learn from Him. We are not able to think, to comprehend, to calculate, to control, to prove, to plan, to design, to create, as He is able. If we are not able to do these things that God is able to do, then much of what He does and what He says we have to take by faith and believe it, even if we are not able to comprehend. The more we believe God is able the more He enlightens our mind with things that come from Him which we could not know by any other way.

God wants to work more and more in all our lives but He requires us to believe in Him and believe in what He says. God calls for us to have faith in Him. The more faith we have in Him the more He works in our lives and the more we believe He is God and is supreme. This is the way it works, and we have to start somewhere for this process to begin. That place is when we finally realize we need God in our lives, that we are sinners, and that we need the salvation He offers us. This is the starting place, it is not the finishing place to be able to say it is done and nothing more to do. Once we have received salvation it is the beginning place because now we have entered the Kingdom of God. In our reading today in Mark chapter 10, Jesus speaks of the ways it is in the Kingdom of God and how it is in the world the way man wants to make it. The discussion comes up about a man divorcing his wife.

The Pharisees say that Moses allowed men to divorce their wives, but Jesus speaking truth, says they were only allowed this because of the hardness of their hearts. It is God who joins together a man and his wife and what God has joined together no man is to separate. (v. 2-9) Life would be so much easier if we would just believe all that God says. Today let us finish with the first words of Hebrews chapter 12: *"Therefore, since we also have such a great cloud of witnesses surrounding us, let's rid ourselves of every obstacle and the sin which so easily entangles us, and let's run with endurance the race that is set before us, looking only at Jesus, the originator and perfecter of the faith, who for the joy set before Him endured the cross, despising the shame, and has sat down at the right hand of the throne of God"* (v. 1&2 NASB).

---

1   Eph. 3:20

How are you doing today? That question can bring different answers from many people or many answers from one person. We may think we know how we are doing but do we really know, is not our knowledge limited, even of knowledge about ourselves? God says He knows how many hairs are on your head,[1] do you know? If we can't know such a thing as how many hairs are on our heads how can we know much other about ourselves? If God knows about the hairs on our heads He knows about the rest of us as well. His word tells us about ourselves. His word tells us what He wants to do in us. In the Garden of Eden Eve thought she knew better than God, eating the fruit He said not to eat of. Adam thought he knew better than God, listening to Eve, in his own ability not seeing any bad results in Eve from eating the fruit, so he took and he ate also.

We think we know better than God at times, we think we know what we are doing, and yet we don't. God tells us who we are, who we can be, and where we can be in eternity. Are you willing to hear who you are in yourself and your own efforts? Can you hear what God is saying you can be if you do it His way? His way for us is sometimes difficult, it takes waiting, watching, and listening. We in our nature as mankind do not like doing this. By not being willing to do this are we not in some way saying we know better than God? He wants to guide us, He wants to bless us, He wants to give us all good things.

Some things we are to do right away such as repent and accept Him as Lord and Master. Some things we have to wait, watch, and listen to, such as following Him, waiting for Him to tell us where and how He wants us following Him. If we are not willing to wait for His specific instructions for each of us for where He wants us working with Him how can we know? He is working in many places at the same time, something we cannot do, so we must listen for what place He wants us to follow Him working with Him there.

We can come to many conclusions of where we should be working, but we won't know if we are following in the exact place He wants us if we don't ask and seek His guidance. Can you imagine how great life would be for mankind if Adam and Eve, and none of the rest of mankind coming after them, would have ever eaten from the tree God said not to eat? We, so many times even after salvation, think we know when we don't because we don't ask and wait for God to answer. I am amazed at the waiting God requires us to do sometimes. There was a time when the people asked Jeremiah to pray to God for them and Jeremiah said he would and when to pray to God.[2] Jeremiah had to wait: *"And it came to pass after ten days, that the word of Jehovah came unto Jeremiah"* (Jer. 42:7 ASV). I am always amazed by this. Here is Jeremiah, one of the great prophets, who I would believe could have a conversation with God and receive an immediate answer, but Jeremiah even has to wait ten days for God to speak back to him with the answer. If this is how it is with Jeremiah how is it with us? Are we willing to wait?

In our reading today in Mark chapter 11, we see this account: *"And those who went before and those who followed were shouting, "Hosanna! Blessed is he who comes in the name of the Lord! Blessed is the coming kingdom of our father David! Hosanna in the highest!"* (v. 9&10 ESV). Even many of those who followed Jesus that day did not know what God was doing, as can be seen in many other places in the scriptures. They thought that Jesus was going to bring back the authority and rule of the world the same as king David had. Even some of the twelve may have not been hearing what Jesus had been saying.[3]

If they truly believed of what Jesus said was going to happen, that He was going to be treated horribly and be killed, would James and John have asked and been willing to receive what Jesus was going to receive? It was not going to be the honor and authority given to king David, it was going to be death. We can't always, in our own figuring, know where God is going and what He is doing, we have to ask, wait, watch, and listen.

---

1   Mt.10:30
2   Jer.42:1-4
3   Mk.10:34&35

Why are you doing what you're doing? Do you ever consider this question? Too many times we go through our day the same as we did yesterday and the day before that. If you are a believer in Christ then you are to be changing day by day into the likeness of Him. For this to happen we have to give ourselves over to Him. There is the parable of the four types of soil that the seed is planted in.[1]

The first has no chance since the devil snatches the seed away (I am convinced that for these we should pray the most – that God would keep the devil away so that they might hear and experience the good news). Second, are those of seemingly almost a party-spirited person who grabs onto the latest and greatest thing going around but when things get tough let go moving on to the next thing. Third are those who see value and truth in the good news – accepting it but allow their concerns for earthly things to completely occupy their lives so they are unproductive, these may be the ones who the Father cuts off the vine and cast aside because they produce no fruit.[2] Fourth is the seed that falls into good soil, sprouts and grows producing fruit.

If you are the fourth type of soil then the seed planted in you by God in the new birth should be growing, is it? If the soil becomes too hard it stifles the growth. Are you keeping the soil of your life lose so God can work in it, is it being nourished by God's word daily, are you submitting the soil of your heart to God daily by prayer in time alone with Him[3] that He can bring the rain and cultivate your soil? We can get so busy in this life with all that goes on and all that the world tells us we have to have that we never take time to ask ourselves why we are doing what we are doing. God is very patient or He would have given up on most of us long ago. I am here to say God is kind, loving, and generous. We have received what we did not deserve in salvation.[4] What we did deserve because of our behavior we have not received,[5] Jesus received it in our place on the cross.

The inheritance into God's family we have been given is that which we had no lawful right to. With all that has been done for us by God should we not at least stop long enough to figure out what it is we should be doing? Jesus said the farmer plants the seed and knows not how it grows.[6] The seed of the gospel has been planted in us, we received it gladly. But we, like the farmer, know not how it grows.[7] Yet, like the farmer, we need to see that the soil doesn't become hardened, we need to see that the soil is nourished, we need to do our best to keep the weeds out. These things cannot be done if we are doing things the same as yesterday and the day before that. We must be seeking, we must be searching, we must be desiring more and more of God in our lives.

In our reading today in Mark chapter 12 there are a couple things I see that relate to this. We have been told we live in this world but are not part of this world,[8] taking this with the reply Jesus gives to the Pharisees and Herodians to give to Caesar what is Caesar's and to God what is God's, I believe it shows us something of how we are to live in this world. (v. 17) Taking this beyond taxes I see that we in this world do have responsibilities to the world, to live in it in all that it involves; work, home, family, etc. But we have to not allow ourselves to get so caught up in these things that we don't give God what is God's (remember you have been purchased with a price and you belong to Him[9]).

The second thing I see in Mark is the widow who gives all she has. This widow trusts God to take care of her allowing Him to have all that is hers. (v. 42-44) We are in this world therefore we are involved to an extent in it, but we must not be so involved that we are not giving to God what is God's. Have you asked yourself why you are doing what you are doing today?

1	Lk.8:5-15
2	Jn.15:2
3	Mt.6:6
4	Rom.5:8
5	Isa.53:4&5
6	Mt.13:31&32
7	Mk.4:26&27
8	Jn.17;14&18
9	1Cor.6:20

'**I have come to you that you might have peace.**' This is a summation of what Jesus said. (Lk. 1:68,78,79 Jn. 14:27 & 16:33 Rom. 5:1 Col. 1:20 Jn. 10:10) This is a peace He has come with and does offer to each and every individual. Jesus did not come to establish peace in the world.[1] Jesus came to pay the price that each of us owed for our sins that we could have peace with the Father in heaven. What a wonderful peace, the only trouble is it goes against our pride and our pride goes against it.

It is not easy for man (mankind) to say he is unable. We pride ourselves in our accomplishments. To say we can't do something does not come easily. Repentance, if we are willing to see its completeness, states to God we are unable. It takes us from a place we thought we were able, to confessing to God we are not able, that we need His help. It goes against our pride to turn from where we have been trying hard in our own power to walk in God's way to confess we need His help. Pride and ego, the very things that brought down the devil, will bring us down also if we continue to determine to walk in them.

Pride and ego in us will be the opposite of peace because we will never be satisfied. Once we have accepted Jesus Christ as Lord, accepted the work He has done for us, we can have true peace because it no longer rests on what we do. Peace, eternal peace, is what all people desire but few gain. There is that uneasiness in us down deep, even though many ignore it, it can only be given rest by the work Jesus did on the cross. The things we accomplish in the Christian life are good but none can come close, or even help, that which we gain by the blood of Christ which He gave gladly on our account. Jesus said at the end of His suffering on the cross, '**It is finished**'. In other words, '**Price Paid in Full**'. There is nothing we can add, only gladly receive and serve. When we believe we still have part to pay by our works then we will have difficulty finding peace because we will never know when it is enough. What Jesus has done, what He has finished, is enough. There is no more needed.

Hearing the words of James in chapter 2 can be encouragement for our peace; *"did not God choose them that are poor as to the world to be rich in faith, and heirs of the kingdom which he promised to them that love him?"* (v. 5 ASV). We can become confused by what James says later about faith thinking we have to work to gain our way into heaven but I am convinced by joining it with the rest of scripture this is not what he is saying. We are to have faith like Abraham and Rahab had, they had faith, believing God and acted accordingly.

The action of faith in a believer is what brings about works showing that faith is alive and growing in that believer. (v. 22) We are born again by faith and that which is born in us begins to grow as a seed put into the earth sprouts showing the evidence that it is alive. If we have faith, it will sprout from our hearts and the product will be desired works from our hearts, but if we are doing works to gain approval the product will not be faith, but guilt. I will finish my comment today with this statement: Works of obedience will be a glad chore if by our faith we have established a relationship with God allowing His will to be in us.[2]

---

1   Mt.10:34, Lk.12:51
2   Philp.2:13

'Let God arise.' This is the beginning of one of the Psalms by David. Can you say this in your own life, do you say this? You should, you should know that God is the one who can in your life. Do you ask God to rise up in your life? David goes on to add to this what God's arising is to those who are his enemies, and to those who are His followers. What will happen if you ask, and allow God to rise up in you? Will He deal with those who are your (and His) enemies, I believe He will. But as He rises up in us He also deals with us to bring us to that place He wants us to be.

It is good that our heart's desire is that God will rise up in us, but know that means He is going to work in us straightening out what is not right in us. This is a good desire to have, don't be afraid of it. 'Let God arise.' As he rises up in us and around us the Palmist goes on to what we should do; *"But let the righteous rejoice and be glad in God's presence; yes, let them exult and rejoice. Sing to God, sing praises to his name; extol him who rides on the clouds by his name, Yah; and be glad in his presence"* (68:3&4 CJB). Are you a sports fan or a fan of other activities? Do you cheer their accomplishments? What about God's accomplishments, do you cheer for His? We all may think God is the greatest in our lives until we realize we cheer and rejoice in the accomplishments of others more than we do His. I won't make a conclusion here, I will let you come to your own.

God is great, always great, He can't be anything else but great. Do you know how great He is? How great is He in your life? Did He give you salvation? Was that great? Did He stop there or did He continue to do great things in your life? Is He not greater than any other you cheer for, has He not been more involved in your life than any other? Once in a while we need to be shaken into reality, to look into the mirror to see some of the things we don't always look at. David tells us we should rejoice in the Lord and he goes on to tell us for some of the reasons we should; *"A father of the fatherless and a judge for the widows, Is God in His holy dwelling. God makes a home for the lonely; He leads out the prisoners into prosperity"* (v. 5&6 NASB). Do you see yourself in one of these two verses?

This is only a beginning of the good things God does. 'Let God arise.' Let God arise all around us. Let God arise even within us. 'Let God arise.' He is the Victorious One, the One who sets all things right. He has conquered our enemy destroying the devil's hold on us by His victory on the cross, we are no longer in the devil's bondage of us, we have been freed. In our reading today in Mark chapter 14 Jesus says; *"This is my blood of the covenant, which is poured out for many"* (v. 24 ASV).

His blood is what conquered our enemy, freeing us and it is this covenant that allows us to stand before the Father. 'Let God arise.' (see v. 28) Later the High Priest asked Jesus, 'Are you the Christ (Messiah), the Son of the Blessed?' Jesus answered: *"I am, and you will see the Son of Man seated at the right hand of Power"* (v. 62 ESV). 'At the right hand of Power,' see what Psalms says: *"Show thy marvellous lovingkindness, O thou that savest by thy right hand them that take refuge in thee"* (17:7 ASV). Many times in the Old Testament the term right hand meant power. Here, by what Jesus said in Mk.14:62, He is that power that saves us from our enemy. **'Let God arise.'**

'**Come unto me all you who are heavy laden.**' Are you heavy laden with more than you can carry? These words of Jesus are about salvation, of owing a price we cannot pay. Jesus does pay that price for us and we are accepted. But I ask you who have walked the road of Christian life with Jesus many years, are you heavy laden? While life goes on and we are following Jesus do we get weighted down again with a heavy load.

Jesus said, '**and I will give you rest.**'[1] Is that rest He gave over, is it exhausted to where He has no more to give you? What has happened to that rest? Jesus invites us into His yoke. Remember how a yoke is made, it is for two, not three, not four, not even for one. We are invited in as the lesser while Jesus is the Major One in the yoke. He is the heavyweight, He is the Master Ox, He is the One who is carrying the load, the One pulling the furthest forward of the two who are in the yoke. Even if we are only a few inches behind in the yoke we are following what it is that He is already doing. We are only joining Jesus in what He is already doing, the weight is already on Him, He is carrying it. We are only asked along to help complete the work He is doing. If we do not have rest could it be we are trying to pull forward in the yoke to where we are ahead of Jesus.

He never meant for us to carry the full load of the yoke, nor even equal with Him, we can't. Maybe it is that we are trying too hard on our own part rather than simply trusting in Jesus as we join in the work that He is carrying the load of. We are call to pick up our cross,[2] the one He assigns us, which is individual as the body is made up of many different individual parts,[3] and to follow Him where He is going. Sometimes in the body of Christ (we Christians) it is thought we are all to be following Jesus in that one place He is and that one thing He is doing. Let us broaden our thinking. Jesus is in a yoke with each one of us, that is one yoke for every individual Christian alive. Jesus is in that yoke with each individual person, He is omnipresent in many yokes at the same time. He is also omnipresent doing work in many different places at the same time. He is leading each one of us individually in the work we are doing while corporately building the Kingdom of God.

Each of us has to seek, and search, to find what the cross is that God has for each of us to carry. We need to seek, and search, where it is Jesus wants us following Him to do the work that is building the Kingdom of God on earth. As you begin to realize that Jesus is the Master Ox who is carrying the major load we can again come into that rest which He offered to us in the beginning of our walk with Him. How is your walk now, have you backed off a bit in the yoke walking along with Jesus at His side working with Him in His work? Have you allowed Him to carry the major load walking along with Him helping Him with the work He is doing? We sometimes in our eagerness to serve get ahead of Jesus and then wonder why the work is so hard. In the yoke with Jesus we can't sit down or drag our feet, we have to keep walking with Him, but we were never intended to carry the majority of the load. Sometimes, even many times, we don't know what God is doing, the only thing we can do is believe and follow.

In today's reading in Mark chapter 15, we can see this if we open our spiritual eyes to see. Put yourself in one of the disciple's place. This Jesus is one of the greatest teachers to ever have come to Israel. He works miracles, teaches with authority, calms the storm on the sea, and controls demons casting them out. Who could be like Him, yet here He is in the hands of the Romans. Many of Jesus' followers thought He was going to free them from the bondage of the Romans.

Now He is arrested and set to be crucified. The Roman governor offers to set one prisoner free but the chief priests stirred up the crowd to ask for Barabus. A little speculation on my part: 'the priests could have argued that this Jesus was doing nothing to relieve their bondage, at least Barabus was fighting against the Romans.' How little we know sometimes of the great thing God is doing. The best thing we can do is stay in that yoke with Jesus walking closely with Him in what He is doing. *"Draw near to God, and he will draw near to you"* (Jas. 4:8 ESV).

---

1   Mt.11:28-30
2   Lk.9:23, Jn.12:26
3   1Cor.12:18-27

We have all sinned and fallen short of the glory of God. How many times have we heard this? It says something about us, and it says something about God. Let's separate the two for discussion. In the first part it states we have all sinned. There are none who have been perfect, none able to declare themselves righteous by their own acts to God. Ever since the forbidden fruit was eaten in the garden of Eden there has been none able to measure up to that perfect mark. *"for all have sinned and fall short of the glory of God"* (Rom. 3:23 ESV)

We all, in one way or another, have sinned at least once. Most of us would be glad if it was only once. Most of us by our sin have proven to ourselves over and over of why we need a Savior who does forgive us. I am glad the apostle Paul wrote as he did, being honest as he was, that he also struggled with sin. By what he has written I am not left alone. The very first step to a good relationship with God is not good behavior, it is saying we are a sinner falling way short of the mark. As we are honest with God He comes alongside of us giving us salvation, the forgiveness through Jesus Christ that we could not get any other way, and then helps us to become good in behavior.

Now to the second part, God could be a little god and still we would fall short. But this part speaks of the glory of God. What is God's glory? It is God in all the fullness of who He is. Who is God? He is the One who spoke and it existed. The stars, the moon, the sun, all came into existence at His word. We, mankind, came into existence as God formed us from the dust.[1] With a God so Superior to us to be able to do all this, He is certainly no little god.[2] The glory of God, His fullness of all that He is, is important for us to attest to Him as we consider His involvement in our lives. We can't, He can.

It is that simple, we have to believe and put our faith in Him. *"even the righteousness of God through faith in Jesus Christ unto all them that believe; for there is no distinction; for all have sinned, and fall short of the glory of God; being justified freely by his grace through the redemption that is in Christ Jesus"* (Rom. 3:22-24 ASV). I will end this today bringing your focus on the fact that it is by this grace freely given that we are saved. In the last words that Jesus speaks in Mark chapter 16 today, He says this, *"Whoever believes and is baptized will be saved, but whoever does not believe will be condemned."* (v. 16 ESV). The glory of God is great, and He is willing to save all freely who are willing to believe.

---

1   Gen. 1:27, 2:7
2   Ps. chapter 104

Why grief and heavy bearing? Sometimes our grief is only because of our unbelief. It is not just that simple, we all have a certain amount of unbelief, hopefully becoming less and less the longer we walk with the Lord. We must pray as did the father who met Jesus when He came down from the mount of transfiguration saying, Lord, I believe but help me with my unbelief.[1] As we look to Jesus to help us our faith should become stronger and stronger. This is not just a nice cliché, it is true, but it takes a dying to self daily before the Lord being willing to believe ourselves less and less and believe Him more and more.

There is a god in this world greater than all the rest which opposes the Lord, that god is our pride. Even the devil does not have any power over us if we are dead to self, believing all that God has to say and all that He wants to do in us. But pride causes us to shut the door on much of what God says and wants to do in our lives, it also opens the back door of our lives for the devil to work on us moving us away from God. Pride is the god that must be sacrificed to the Lord. Jesus won't walk on us, coming into our lives taking our pride away by force, we have to give it up.

It is a hard thing to sacrifice our pride, it doesn't go easily and we don't send it away easily. Sometimes we don't even know who we are for many times it is our pride who dictates to us who we are, and pride is a liar. We see many people in the world who claim to be great. And the world around them also declares them to be great. A Nobel Prize Winner is considered great in the world but I tell you if they do not accept Jesus and are covered by His blood in salvation they will go to hell with the rest of those who are headed there. Sometimes we get caught up in the pursuit of the world and think, 'if I just had a little more money, a few more things necessary for my life, I would then be content'. We have all read the parable of the rich man who came to Jesus and went away sad.[2]

Possessions do not satisfy, we continue to have grief and heavy bearing of the difficulties of life. There is only one way to relieve ourselves of grief and bearing of heavy loads, that is to take them to Jesus, believing He is able to lift them from us giving us joy in their place. Hear the words again from our reading today; *"May grace and peace be given you in increasing abundance"* (1Pet. 1:2 AMPC). Peter goes on in that chapter with much encouragement. Here is more from chapter 1 to hear again; *"the genuineness of your faith, being much more precious than gold that perishes"* (v. 7 NKJV). This is where the value of life lies, not where the world makes it out to be. Don't be downcast because of your unbelief, but take courage to believe more and more.

Today in our reading Zachariah had some unbelief but there must have been enough belief, that is faith, that God was able to work in his and his wife's life to bring about God's purpose. God will build in your life the same faith that He built in Zachariah's life over that 9 month period to the time John the Baptist was born. As part of your time with God today go back and read the praise of Zachariah again. (v. 67-79) Allow it to sink in that if we apply the faith we have, God will help us with the faith we do not have (unbelief) and bring us to a place we are able to give Him praise from our hearts just as Zachariah did at John's birth.

---

1   Mk.9:23&24
2   Mk.10:21

Life is good, that is if you have God in it. There is a great thing He says to us about Himself: *"For My thoughts are not your thoughts, Nor are your ways My ways," says the LORD. For as the heavens are higher than the earth, So are My ways higher than your ways, And My thoughts than your thoughts"* (Isa. 55:8&9 NKJV). I learned this early in my Christian life and it has helped me ever since. When we know His ways are so different than ours it helps us to have confidence in Him even when in our own appraisal our life is coming all apart. Confidence in God is not an easy thing, it goes against our grain. It seems that this is partly why we have to die to self. If God's ways are so different from ours we have to go to Him constantly to learn of His ways.

Wow, what a difficult chore, to take everything we think we know (and are encouraged by those around us to know) and lay them all aside to gain what it is we should know to be children of God. Wow, another revelation to our minds (and hearts) that God considers us His children, what a great privilege. Does not every little child (for we are as little children compared to God) want to be like their parent? How be it we continue to question such a wise Father as we have in God. His ways should become our ways, and His thoughts should become our treasured thoughts.

The things He says in His word should become treasures in our minds. We must learn from Him, we must know from Him, our life even must be from Him. The apostle Paul says that he lives only in Christ, that his old self has died.[1] Has your old self died, or even in salvation is it still kicking around in there somewhere? There is a dying that takes place at our salvation of a significant part, that which says we can't and we ask God to take over. Did you know for God to take over, the things He wants to do for us, we have to continue in that act of dying?

It must be a continued act of dying daily. As we die daily looking to God to know of His ways, giving up our ways, He will show us many marvelous things. A few days ago we spoke of Jesus calling all of us to Him who were heavy laden. We spoke of how Jesus wants this to continue through our lives giving us rest. Here we are at that place again learning more about that rest. As we give up our ways (dying to self) and take up God's ways life gets easier. I don't say that life in this world gets easier, Jesus said if they hated Him they would hate us also.[2] What it is that gets easier is our eternal security, we know who it is in. And as we begin to do things God's way it brings an assurance that we could not have in our own ways.

There is a peace that surpasses all understanding, one that we cannot understand, only know that we know – that is God's doing in us. We will not understand God's ways, we can only know them and live by them. It is God who brings us what is true life. In our reading today in Luke chapter 2 it is all about the birth of Jesus into this world. Amongst what is recorded by Luke we need to hear the words of the angel to us: *"Then the angel said to them, "Do not be afraid, for behold, I bring you good tidings of great joy which will be to all people. For there is born to you this day in the city of David a Savior, who is Christ the Lord..."Glory to God in the highest, And on earth peace, goodwill toward men!"* (v. 10,11,14 NKJV)

We need to know God has good will towards us in giving us a savior, He only wants the best for us as any good parent would want for their children. We conclude today with hearing Peter's words from chapter 2: *"if you have tasted the kindness of the Lord. And coming to Him as to a living stone which has been rejected by people, but is choice and precious in the sight of God, you also, as living stones, are being built up as a spiritual house for a holy priesthood, to offer spiritual sacrifices that are acceptable to God through Jesus Christ"* (v. 3-5 NASB).

---

1   Gal.2:20
2   Jn.15:18&19

This is my story, this is my song. These lines many of us know from a popular Hymn. How often do you think of your story, how often does it cause you to sing? To keep that vibrant relationship with God we need to keep that story fresh. Do you remember that day of your salvation? Do you remember the great event where God did something marvelous in your life, even if it was only an inward working in your heart or soul?

Some of the most greatest and marvelous workings of God is what He does within us changing us from what we were to what we are becoming. There are times we all can remember that God has done something marvelous. These are as anchors for our faith. We walk forward knowing we serve a living God because of the evidence of those things we have seen Him do. He moves in our lives in a way no other can.

There is no experience of this world that equals what God does in our lives in salvation. This is because with our salvation with God we are given a connection with something outside of this world, we are connected with heaven and He who dwells there. It is easy to get bogged down in desperation in our situation with our faith seeming to weaken in us. We have to keep the things God has done for us in the past fresh so that the events of the current time are supported by knowing what God has done in the past, and will do again. The most amazing thing God has done for any of us is our new life, our salvation, where everything of our life changed.

That event we must keep fresh in our memory and knowledge, it is what supports all other things God will do in our lives. It is what gives us the faith for tomorrow that God will continue to work in us, that we are not alone, even though at times it may seem so. Waiting is not easy, but faith must continue. One day completion of waiting will be over as each of us enters heaven with all made right. But until then we have to walk in faith knowing our God has all in control, even when we can't see it. He has known our life since the beginning of time and nothing passes His notice, He sees all that goes on in our lives.

How many times has God spoke to you and you have not listened? We are all guilty, we have all not obeyed as we should. If we could there would have been those who were able to follow the Law completely and Jesus would not have had to come. But none were able to follow the Law completely.[1] We are those who Jesus died for. We will never be perfect this side of heaven but we are to continue to try to become Christ-like. The more we depend on the Spirit the easier it will become because He is at work in us making us more and more into the image of Christ.[2]

We have an advocate who is with the Father praying for us,[3] He is praying we will succeed in becoming Christ-like more and more every day. Jesus did everything that the Father spoke to Him during His ministry here on earth. This is part of being Christ-like, doing what God says to us. We are surely lost if we don't have His guidance. Our main guidance from God is the Bible, His word that has been written for us to read. The other way He guides us is with that still small voice. Jesus, even as being man and still being God, took time to get away and spend time with the Father in prayer.[4]

Our prayer life is very important for being able to do what God speaks to us to do. It is during that time of prayer that we hear that still small voice of God much of the time. It is also during that time of prayer that we ask God to strengthen us to do the things He calls us to. *"whoever serves is to do so as one who is serving by the strength which God supplies"* (1Pet. 4:11 NASB). We will never be able to do what God calls us to do on our own power alone. It must be God working in us and through us that we are able to do what He says. We couldn't get saved without Him and we can do none of the rest of it without Him.

God constantly wants to speak to us to guide us. If you as a parent seen you small child going in a direction he was going to get hurt would you not want him to listen to you so he wouldn't be hurt? We go through a lot of troubles and a lot of pain we could avoid if we would just listen to what Papa is saying to us. God wants the best for us. He also wants us to grow. As we grow we become more Christ-like. Listening - everyone of us has a rebellious streak in us, it has to be that we die to self to hear the voice of God. The more and more we die to self the easier it is to hear God and do what He says. Today in our reading in Luke chapter 4, we need to hear what Jesus replied to the devil; *"man shall not live by bread alone, but by every word of God"* (v. 4 KJV). Jesus said man (us) needs God's word to live. We have His written word, we also need His word He speaks in that still small voice. What is He saying to you today?

---

1   Jn.7:19, Rom.3:20&23, 1Jn.1:8
2   Tit.3:5
3   Rom.8:26&27
4   Mt.14:23, Mk.1:35, Lk.4:42, 6:12

In the name of Jesus. Do you realize the power you have been given? We are told in His name even demons have to flee. Do you believe this, do you use His name? We have been given this power to ward off attacks of the enemy. We need to know the arsenal we have of weapons for the fight. We are told that the enemy will attack us until the day he is cast into the lake of fire for ever.[1] *"But the earth helped the woman, and the earth opened its mouth and drank up the river which the dragon had hurled out of his mouth. So the dragon was enraged with the woman, and went off to make war with the rest of her children, who keep the commandments of God and hold to the testimony of Jesus"* (Rev. 12:16&17 NASB).

Peter in our reading today tells us to resist the devil. (v. 8&9) Part of the way we resist the enemy is in using the arsenal of weapons we are given. Do you realize the power of the name of Jesus, it is a whole arsenal of weapons all in one.

There is nothing that can stand up against the name of Jesus and His blood He gave for us.[2]

Demons cannot stand hearing of the blood of Jesus brought against them for it is the very thing that defeated their master the devil.[3] Don't try to struggle in your own strength to push back against the devil and his demons, you can't do it. Remember, this is the one who tried to take on God, he was defeated and cast out of heaven.[4] But do you really think you are any match for him, it takes a higher power than yourself to ward off him and his demons. We have been given the power in the name of Jesus as our weaponry, who would be foolish enough to go out to battle leaving their weapons behind not using them.

James tell us the same as Peter: *"resist the devil, and he will flee from you."* (Jas. 4:7 ASV). Paul tells us the reality of our situation: *"For our wrestling is not against flesh and blood, but against the principalities, against the powers, against the world–rulers of this darkness, against the spiritual hosts of wickedness in the heavenly places"* (Eph. 6:12 RV). How could we consider to fight these in our own power. They are out with all the force they have to try to destroy God's Kingdom, to kill off God's children. They will not be successful, but we must stand our ground. Don't let the devil and his forces deprive you of the great things God (Papa) has for us. Stand your ground, use the name of Jesus against the demonic forces, don't let them take what is yours. Declare the blood of Jesus over your family, especially you fathers. Tell the demons that you are covered with the blood of Jesus and you belong to Jesus.

Declare who you are as children of God and that they, the demons, have no right to you. Don't let them get away with anything, they are just trying to fool you. The serpent in the Garden of Eden said to Eve, *"Did God actually say"* (Gen. 3:1 ESV). He continues to use the same ploy on us. He tries to fool us so we won't use the force of power we have against him. The demons cannot stand against the name and blood of Jesus. They want to pull the wool over our eyes so we won't think we have power to stand against them. They are defeated, they have been sentenced. They are just trying to ruin as much as they can before they are cast into the lake of fire. Don't let them get away with anything, stand against them with the arsenal Jesus has provided for you. Remember what Paul said, *"our wrestling is not against flesh and blood"* (Eph. 6:12 ASV). and *"the weapons of our warfare are not of the flesh, but mighty before God to the casting down of strongholds"* (2Cor. 10:4 ASV).

---

1   Rev. 20:10
2   Acts 16:18, Philp.2:10
3   Rev.12:10&11
4   Rev.12:7-9

Which way do we go? There are things in our lives that pull us in all different directions, which way do we go? There are those things which our flesh wants us to go after. There are the things the world wants us to want. There are even those things which the people close to us think we should go to or want. Which way do we go? As Christians, there is only one way we are to go, the way God tells us in His word.

All these other things pull and tug at us, even demons get into the act and will detract us if we allow them. It is not easy in this world to follow God, yet if we do it God's way it is not as difficult as it seems. The Apostle Paul said he had learned how to be content with plenty or in want.[1] Once we find our trust is truly in God all worry and concern vanish in the presence of His provision. Our need is not satisfied with a delicious piece of pie, but only with the very presence of God. There have only been a few times in my life that I have experienced God's presence in a great fullness and I would trade many a pie for His presence again. Paul knew that presence.

When God is with us, even when we don't experience His special presence, but just know that we know in our Spirit that He is with us very little else gets our attention. When we stop listening to the Spirit within us is when we drift away into the world and its ways finding ourselves in trouble. This is what happened to Israel over and over finally ending up in Babylon for 70 years. We need to be cautious, we need to stay close to Jesus. Do you realize Jesus is praying to the Father for you?[2] He has so many good things for us but we can't receive them if we are drawn away to the world and its ways. Devotion can be difficult but the rewards are so grand. King David was close to God, his devotion ran deep, he was drawn away only one time we know of. David's rewards were grand, greatest king Israel ever had, and his son Solomon was the wealthiest king Israel ever had.

David was promised by God that he would always have a son of his bloodline on the throne of Israel if they followed God's ways. Abraham was given an impossible son, God blessed them with Isaac. Abraham was told he would be the father of a great nation. Even Paul who started out as Saul seemed to have been close to God in what he knew, he was just confused in what God was doing. Ever been confused in what God was doing? Saul was confused in what God was doing, he was confused in how he should be serving God – he might have thought that he had it right but Jesus said, '**stop Saul**', confronting him on the road to Damascus.[3] After Jesus set Saul right he became Paul as recorded in scripture. Paul was close to Jesus, he was even taught by direct revelations from Jesus while he was in Tarsus.[4]

From what we read Paul never had a real need that God did not meet and he was protected from death many times in his ministry. Which way do we go, we go directly to God, staying close to Him as we go through this life. Being close to God is being in ways that are like God.

Today in our reading in Luke chapter 6 Jesus speaks much of how we should be, which many of are the ways God. There is advantages in being close to God, Peter speaks of some of these we read today; *"His divine power has granted to us all things that pertain to life and godliness, through the knowledge of him who called us to his own glory and excellence, by which he has granted to us his precious and very great promises, that through these you may escape from the corruption that is in the world because of passion, and become partakers of the divine nature"* (2Pet. 1:3&4 RSV). What great things God has for us. In one of the verses in 2Peter we may not see it at first but it is speaking about us staying close to God; *"Therefore, brothers, be all the more diligent to confirm your calling and election, for if you practice these qualities you will never fall"* (v. 10 ESV). With this that Peter has said, why would we want to go any other way? Which way will you go?

---

1   Philp.4:11-13
2   Rom.8:34
3   Acts 9:4-6
4   Gal.1:12, Eph.3:1-3

Now is the day, this is the time, are you ready? This is what the parable of the ten virgins is about, will you be ready when the call comes?[1] My opening question is not for today, not right now, but one day it will come. Will you be ready, full of oil in your lamp burning brightly? When the call does comes it will be too late to get oil in your lamp. It is now that we are to be living for God with Him in our lives every day, every hour, every moment. Jesus gave us the signs for the season, but the day He would come He told us we would not know.[2] We are to always be ready for His return, when the call goes out it will be too late to get ready. There is something Jesus said that always makes me a little uneasy, *"However, when the Son of Man comes, will He find faith on the earth?"* (Lk. 18:8 NASB).

I am not totally sure why Jesus said this but it causes me to be cautious and diligent about my following Him. I have no fear of being left behind because as long as I stay close to Him, it is in His control that I will get to heaven. There are many things said in scripture which should cause us to be cautious, not to be careless or sloppy with the grace we have been given. I don't say we have to earn it, but it must be valued much more than diamonds or gold. In all of eternity there has never been anything of greater value given. Where are you right now, how is the oil in your lamp? I don't mean to put you into a panic, but are you serious or not, are you surrendered or not. Is there more surrendering that needs to happen, so more oil can get in, so your lamp can burn brighter?

These are things you have to answer before the call comes, when it comes it will be too late. Are there still some hard spots in your heart - get some more oil in, it will soften them. More oil in by being in God's word, more oil in by praying more, more oil in by joining a home Bible Study/Fellowship Group. Find a way to get more oil in, and you will be amazed at what God can do. It is easy to wear Christianity like a new dress or a new suit but when the call comes they won't do you any good. When the call comes will you be ready? There will always be those who pretend, Jesus said this to the Pharisees comparing them to the children in the marketplace who in their play pretend to be something they are not. (Lk. 7:30-32) There will always be those who pretend with no intention of truly following God.

They do it for the fame (in whatever way they see that) or they are wolves in sheep's clothing. There are many more who have an intention to follow God but are careless or sloppy about how they do it. Half of the ten virgins were careless and sloppy with their lights going out because of not having enough oil. Half of the ten virgins were wise making sure they had their containers full. Which five are you? We don't earn our way into heaven but we are to treasure what we have been given, to be cautious with it not being careless and sloppy.

Be careful to check your oil from time to time, don't be like the Pharisee in today's reading in Luke chapter 7 who thought he was in good staining with God and scowled at the sinful woman who was washing and anointing Jesus' feet. We see the same point being made yesterday at the end of our reading in Luke chapter 6. Make sure, be careful, that you have built your house on a solid foundation. Are you ready – at any moment?

---

1   Mt.25:1-10
2   Mt.24:32-34,36

How is your life today? What do you really put your trust in? When you leave for work you jump in your car, hit the key, and away you go. Where is your faith, a subconscious faith, when all this happens? For some of you your faith is in the car manufacturer that the car will start and go. For some of you your faith is in the mechanisms involved that make the engine run. For how many of you is your faith in God that He will bless your day including the car starting so you can be on your way?

It is easy to take things for granted. Without the knowledge God gives man allowing him to think and develop the manufacturer could not have made that car. Without God creating the laws of physics the mechanics involved in making the engine run wouldn't work. Everything we touch, even the air we breathe, were all made by God. If you are one of those Christians who have a difficulty giving thanksgiving to God, maybe it is because you really haven't realized what He has given you. Salvation is our assurance that we will have an eternity with God, but there is so much more He has given us. He has given it to the unsaved as well as the saved, He causes it to rain on the unsaved as well as the saved.[1]

With difficulties in our lives a lot of times the problem is not that we don't satisfy God with what we do, it is we are not really seeing who He is. With some of us our life is so busy we don't even have time to stop long enough to look into the sky at night to see all the wonderful stars God put in space. On a very clear night the longer you look at the stars the more you see. They become beautiful and mysterious, luring you to be amazed by them wondering more and more about them. God put them in place.[2] God calls them by name.[3] Once you've been amazed with outer space, begin looking at interspace, all the things around us on this earth that we are in contact with every day.

Until a couple centuries ago scientist considered what they would discover was to tell them more of their God and the way He made them, and what He was allowing them to do with it. It is only in the recent decades that scientist have been trying to disprove the existence of God. Take a look at what scientist have discovered about the atom, a planetary system by itself.

We get too busy, we have too much subconscious faith in things that are secondary, for without God's touch they would not work. Where are you going in such a hurry? When you arrive at the grave there is only one thing that is important; where has the focus of your life been? Has it been around God and all He does for us, and what He has asked us to do for Him? Or has it been so busy with life, all the things you think you got'a have, and all the things you think you got'a do? None of that stuff will go to the grave with you: *"the heavens shall pass away with a great noise, and the elements shall be dissolved with fervent heat, and the earth and the works that are therein shall be burned up"* (2Pet. 3:10 ASV). When you arrive in heaven that stuff won't be considered, what will be considered is; what did you do with what God gave you? Fruit or no fruit, what do you think about yourself? Thanksgiving is a sacrifice of praise. It is easily given when we realize all the great things God has done for us, and keeps doing. God wants family, not inherited children in a foreign land that He never sees.

He wants His children close, He wants to see what they are doing, He wants to have conversation with his children. God likes seeing His children active in His Kingdom, He likes to make suggestions on how to get some of the work done. Sometimes He walks us through the process, He has us working guiding us step by step. None of this can happen if we are too busy to see how God is involved in our life already, and how much more He wants to be. *Since all these things are thus to be dissolved, what sort of people ought you to be in lives of holiness and godliness,"* (2Pet. 3:11 ESV). So **how** is it your life is **going** on today? Is God involved in it even though you haven't noticed? Hear Peter's closing statement; *grow in the grace and knowledge of our Lord and Saviour Jesus Christ. To him be the glory both now and for ever. Amen"* (ASV).

---

1   Mt.5:45
2   Gen.1:16, Ps.8:3, 2Pet.3:5&7
3   Ps.147:4

It is time, are you ready? Where are we going, what do we know? Who is it we are to follow? It surely is not the world, the world will take us far away. The Israelites drifted away from God so far He had just about had it with them. Look at what God says in the beginning of Isaiah today in our reading of chapter one. *"I have nourished and brought up children, and they have rebelled against me...Ah sinful nation, a people laden with iniquity, a seed of evil-doers, children that deal corruptly! they have forsaken Jehovah, they have despised the Holy One of Israel, they are estranged and gone backward"* (Isa. 1:2&4 ASV).

Do we ever wander away from God to where He might say this about us? I hope I do not. God's mercy and grace are huge, but if we are not close they will do us very little good. There are those who God says will keep their salvation but have their tails singed as they enter heaven.[1] I want to be as close to God as I can be. This does not mean I have to work hard to be approved,[2] it means I must come close, spend time with God in that secret place, and to be in His word to know Him and know about Him.

Out of that relationship will come my works because they will not be my works but His works that sprout out of me. God does not say, 'work hard and I will come close to you', what does He say? *"God opposes the proud but gives grace to the humble." Submit yourselves therefore to God.... Draw near to God, and he will draw near to you"* (Jas. 4:6-8 ESV). First of all we have to approach in humility, not pride of work we have accomplished. We have to come close, not try to gain from God at a distance. What father wants his child always at a distance only receiving text messages from him, but never comes close? We are God's children, He is the Papa, He wants His children to come close, spend time with Him, etc. If He sees us coming He will draw close to us as we draw close to Him.

The amazing thing is if we take the time to come close to God the works will pour forth out of us in a way we never thought they could. This is what James tries to tell us about faith proven by works. How can we have faith if we are not close to God? And if we are close to God we will find His will He puts within us[3] sprouting out in works we never thought we could do.

This is where faith is proven by works, if faith is real they will sprout. God wants us close, He paid a heavy price to have us close, to be saved, and made holy so we could come close. With all the hard work God has done so we can come close, what kind of an offense is it if we resist? This is what Israel did and ended up in Babylon. Who wants to go to Babylon and beg to come back? Stay close to God and He will stay close to you, it is the desire of His heart.

---

1   1Cor.3:15
2   2Cor.10:18
3   Philp.2:13

'It is my way that I have for you to go.' Would this be what Jesus has said to us all? He has called us to go His way for those of us who follow, to go where He is, to do what He does. Today in our reading He sent out the seventy, He sent them to minister in the cities and places He was about to go. It was the places He was soon to come that they were sent. Again soon it is that He is to come. Are we to be as the seventy, are we to go out for Him? What were the seventy told they should do? This is what He said to them, *"The harvest truly is great, but the laborers are few; therefore pray the Lord of the harvest to send out laborers into His harvest. Go your way; behold, I send you out as lambs among wolves...heal the sick there, and say to them, 'The kingdom of God has come near to you.'...Then the seventy returned with joy, saying, "Lord, even the demons are subject to us in Your name"* (Lk. 10:2,3,9,17 NKJV).

Are we going and praying for the sick? Are we casting out demons? Are we doing the work He has called each of us to, do you know what He has called you to do? We are His Church, we are His Body, we are His representatives until He comes soon. From what the world sees in us do they know who Christ is? Would you want to follow someone who is as you are? Jesus will return one of these days we do not expect Him.[1] I fear the world will not be ready for Christ when He comes, I even wonder if the Church will be ready for Him when He comes. We need to be doing our part.

I don't mean putting on a show, but I do mean we should be living the Christian life in truth and how it is we should live. If we truly trust our God there should be joy in our lives, a true joy the world can see. When we are trying to live genuine lives in God, the world sees a joy in us we don't even know we have. It may not be that they see us laughing and happy all the time, but we have a peace they don't see in others, a peace that is not fake. It may leave them scratching their heads at times, finding us different than the others around them. Remember a few days ago we spoke of **'This is my story, this is my song.'** Have you been singing? Have you been remembering what God has done for you? This alone will give you more joy than those around you in the world have. Maybe one will ask you some day how you have this joy, maybe greater yet they will ask you where they can find it. Jesus will be coming soon, are you doing your part?

---

1   Mt.24:42

He who is born again sees what the world does not see. We have been given to know God, and to see Him with spiritual eyes.[1] Not that we will see His form, but we will see His ways. In those ways we will follow. First place we see His ways is in His written word. As we grow in these ways we will begin to hear His voice that directs us day by day; turn this way, don't go that way, etc. What a great thing to be given to know the great God of all eternity.

Do we ever realize how great He is? He asks us to pray to Him, He wants to hear of our needs. Have you ever thought how great He is by how many other people in the world are praying to Him at the same time you are, and He gets none confused, and hears every prayer responding to each one. We have a God, a Savior, that is far beyond anything we can think or imagine. Why would a God so grand even bother with such as us? How many times have we heard the answer to that. *"For God so loved the world"* (Jn. 3:16 ASV).

Only a God like we have would have that kind of love, that would love each one of us, even those in the world who will never come to Him, who will never accept His salvation He offers to all. Do you see the strength of that love? To see it we only need to look at all He accomplished in its full completeness to save a sinful world, a sinful people, you and me. What kind of love is this? One might say it is out of this world. Surely this is true. God calls us to also love as He loves. We are incapable to love as He loves, but if Christ is in us and we in Him (v. 24) then by Christ in us we can love as He loves, for it does not originate with us, it originates from Him and moves through us.

This truth might slip right past us and we not see it here because John has it in the form of a question: *"how does the love of God abide in him?"* (1Jn. 3:17 NKJV). Do you see of who the love is of that abides in us? What a grand God we have! This is the verse that our reading in 1John starts with today: *"See how great a love the Father has given us, that we would be called children of God"* (1Jn. 3:1 NASB). John goes on in the last half of this chapter (v. 11-23) speaking about love and what it is and what it is not. As His children we will love as He loves, and as children this will be something we grow in just as children grow. At first we love a little, then we grow more and more, loving more and more. Are you not glad that God has such great enormous love that He loves you and me?

---

1   2Cor.3:16

Why are we here? **Why** are we on this earth? **Why** are we in the location that we are on this earth? **Why** are we right at this point of time as we are? **Big questions – one answer: Because of God.** Are you willing to believe that? Are you able to believe that God created the universe, put the earth where He did, and put you on it where you are at this time? God is able, the question is: are you willing to believe it? I could go back to Genesis and start their filling in all the details that are in the Bible, but that might not meet you where you are at. It may be possible for you to believe the creation account in Genesis, but have doubts about where you are right now. Have you given your life to God accepting Jesus into it as Lord and Savior? If you have done this and have not determinedly told God to get out of your life, get away from your life, to leave you alone, then you are His, you gave yourself to Him.

There is a principle that was used in the nation of Israel: if you owed a debt you could not pay you could sell yourself to another person. In selling yourself what happened was that person would pay your debt and you would become theirs as a servant or slave for a period of time. We had a debt we could not pay (the debt of the penalties for our sins) and in asking Jesus to save us He paid the debt and we became His. If we are truly given over to Him, fully surrendered, then our life is not ours to live anymore, it is His. The apostle Paul puts it this way: He says he died with Christ when he surrendered to Jesus asking Jesus to become Lord of his life he gave up claim to any and all of it and now he lives in Christ. Paul believed all that was alive in him, all that moved in him, all that was accomplished by him, all that was spoke by him, was Christ involved in it.

When we come to that place, that we know what we are not any longer, and what it is we have become, confidence of why and where we are becomes solid. Jesus is Lord, Jesus decides where we should be, Jesus decides what we should be doing, Jesus decides how we should do it, He decides all. However we are not just robots being programmed with no action on our part. The action on our part is surrender, asking the Lord to guide us into what He is doing today that He wants us involved in. He has a great plan for all of our lives, independently and united as the body of Christ. Our confidence has to be in Jesus, not in ourselves.

Let me ask a question: have you ever failed at anything? Jesus never has. If we trust Him doing it His way we will have many more successes than we have failures. We may be doing exactly what it says in the Bible to do with all the effort we have, but if we were to find out from Jesus what part He wants us to be involved with we will find we accomplish so much more for the Kingdom of God by doing it His way. We have an obligation to ourselves to be the best we can be in this life. And the best we can be is being it His way. Are you surrendered, are you given over totally, are you allowing Jesus to take full possession of what is His, of what He has paid for with His own blood? How much greater the world could be if we all were doing what God has decided is the right thing for us to be doing. Can you imagine the effect on the world if we were doing exactly what Jesus decided His servants should be doing instead of themselves deciding? One very basic thing God tries to get us to do, like He does, is to love. Not the world's kind of love, but God's kind of love. [1]

Jesus said the summation of the law was in two commandments; Love the Lord your God with all you got, and to love those around you like you want to be loved. [2] How far we could all get if we could just love the way God loves. He even said to love our enemies, do you get that? That is a hard one but they are lost needing a savior the same as we did. In our reading today the apostle John talks about loving one another; *"Beloved friends, let us love one another; because love is from God; and everyone who loves has God as his Father and knows God"* (1Jn. 4:7 CJB). John goes on speaking of this to the end of the chapter. If we surrender, yielding to God to decide how we should be, what we should be, and where we should be doing it, life will become a blessing. Paul was confronted on the road to Damascus by the love of God which would not allow him to continue the way he was going. Paul seems to have decided shortly after that to allow God to do the deciding for his life, day in and day out. Paul tells us he finally came to a place in his life where he was content in all situations. Now the **whys** are not so important since we know the **Who** it is we belong to.

---

1   Jn,15:13
2   Mk.12:30&31

Where are the children? Where are the children of God? What makes them God's children? We could answer it very simple minded saying that all the little children (young offspring of mankind) are all around us. Are we not God's children, even as adults?[1] He takes care of us as a good parent does. He watches over us. He protects us. He makes sure we have food and shelter. He teaches us. He even chastens us as a good parent does to train a child.[2] Most definitely we are God's children. If we are His children doesn't the way we act reflect on His character, even if He is good and we do not act so good, will people that don't know Him think He is not as good as they are told He is? Are we helping His reputation in the world or damaging it with our behavior? Do you think the world is misguided in who God is and how He is by what they see in us? Oh my, I'm stepping on toes, even my own, but these are things we must consider.

By the way you act, would anyone want to know the person who taught you to be that way? When we look at scripture and what it says about how we are to be it hurts a little sometimes because we have let Daddy down. The world thinks bad of Him when they shouldn't. What does scripture say we should be: we are to be a light shining in a dark world so they can see who and how they are.[3] We are to be salt which gives things flavor and disinfects what is infected.[4] We are to have living waters flowing out of us to a thirsty world who don't even know they are thirsty until they get a taste of the water we have.[5] We are to have a peace that goes past all their understanding.[6] We are to have a confidence of where we are going to spend eternity and that there is an eternity.[7] We are to know where we have come from and where we are going. We have found a value to life that they can't know as an unbeliever, that value of our relationship with the Father in heaven.

Do I need to bring up more? Do we need to go back to God our Father for more instruction as His children. The Israelite fathers were told to speak the things their children were to learn as they sat in the house and as they walked along the path. Why should we think that our heavenly Father would not do the same thing with us? Our learning should not only be in church or in a Bible School. We can learn setting in our house if we ask the Father to sit with us and teach us. We can learn as we walk along the path if we are willing to believe the Father is walking there with us willing to teach us if we expect it and are willing to listen. I do what I call walking talking prayers. As I go through my day I talk to God a lot as I go along. Sometimes it is out loud speaking of how great He is or praising and worshiping Him or discussing a problem I'm having, or even sometimes of how to do the work I'm doing when I get stumped. Most of the time these are silent prayers which are in my mind and heart only which I know He hears. Walking talking prayers are great. He helps me find my hammer I have mislaid. He helps me get the screw started that is being contrary. He gives me strength at times when I need just a nudge with something – I sometimes wonder if it is the angels that gives me a hand.

God is always with us whether we acknowledge it or not. If He is there why not have a conversation, He wants to talk with you, do you want to talk with Him. Sometimes God can be quiet for some time, but Oh those times that He does speak. Our relationship with the Father and the Lord Jesus should be such that the world wants what we've got. According to what the apostle John said in our reading today we are children of God. (1Jn. 5:1) As children of God we should draw close to Him to learn. Shouldn't all children grow up to learn and be like their parents? If we get close to God He will help us grow.

In Luke chapter 13 Jesus says the Kingdom of God is like a mustard seed a man planted in his garden and it grew very large. (v. 18&19) The same as that mustard seed was caused to grow by God He will cause us to grow if we spend time with Him, walk along the path with Him, desiring Him to teach us. He is the one who does most of the work, we just have to get close.

---

1 Jn.1:12, 1Jn.3:1
2 Duet.8:5, Heb.12:6
3 Acts 26:17&18, Eph.5:8&11
4 Mk.9:5
5 Jn.4:10, 7:37&38
6 Philp.4:7
7 Jn.3:15, Rom.6:23, 2Cor.5:1

How are things going? Do you feel good about your life, and the things going on around you? Do you have a complete confidence in God? If your answer is a little fuzzy then you are like most of us who do our best to follow Jesus. Jesus is the only one who is never fuzzy about His confidence, after all you would say He is God. Yes, that is true but for those thirty-some years He was with us here on this earth He was fully God and at the same time He was fully man (of mankind).

He had all the same temptations as we have.[1] He had all the involvement of life that we have such as eating, sleeping, getting the cast offs of the foods He ate out of His body the same as we do. He was uncomfortable in the heat of summer and He got cold in the winter. He was as much of mankind as anyone can be except for the yielding to the temptation of sin. For the rest of us we struggle with sin, and when we slip Jesus' blood is there to provide forgiveness when we ask for it.[2] Yes, our confidence in God is a little fuzzy for if we didn't have a difficulty with it Jesus would not have had to come to die on the cross for us. What a kind and loving and great God we have, that He would provide a way that we could come to Him even though we in ourselves were disqualified. Yes, God does deserve praise and worship and thanksgiving.

It may go against our grain, but we need to realize really who and what we were before Jesus came into our lives and how desperate we needed Him. Our pride does not like to think that we could not do it ourselves, but if Jesus did not do in us what He has done we would be worthless and lost with no course but ruin. Pride has to leave our lives, we must cast it out if we are to survive. Pride will take many who follow the wide path to the eternity of hell.[3] Jesus said in our reading today; *"For everyone who exalts himself will be humbled"* (Lk. 14:11 ESV). I don't want to end up there, I do the best I can to cast my pride out of me, how about you? The interesting thing is: the less of self, the less of our pride, the less of our ego, the less fuzzy we are in our confidence in God.

The more I say **I can't** the more God can- for the **I can** in myself has gotten out of the way. God is marvelous in all His ways but He will not intrude into a life where He has not been invited to be involved. Fuzzy, we will all be fuzzy a bit until the day we leave this earth, but it can become less and less. Jesus tells us something very important for our lives, we may not want to hear it but it is what He said; *"If anyone comes to Me and does not hate ..... his own life also, he cannot be My disciple"* (Lk. 14: 26 NKJV).

This is hard stuff, this is why we must stir up as much strength as possible and cast out of ourselves as much pride as we can. There are many who speak of doing great things for God. Casting out our pride is one of the greatest things we can do for God, it allows Him to get to work in us (and through us). After you have cast out the pride read Lk. 14: 27 and ask God (not figure yourself) what your cross is He has for you, and while you're asking you might ask Him to help you learn how to carry it, it won't be easy.

---

1   Heb.4:15
2   1Jn.1:7, 2:1
3   Mt.7:13, 25:46

Is it well with your soul? Horatio G Spafford, writer of a great song wrote, 'It is Well With My Soul'. As we read the lyrics of the song he declares that whatever it be, blessings or trials, buffeting by the devil or total victory, it is well with his soul. He says that God had taught him this, that no matter what, it was well with his soul. How is your soul today, where is your confidence? As we look around the world today, or any day, it leaves us a little shaky if we don't have that confidence that God has authority over what we see around us. The world likes to brag and brag as though they know what they are talking about, and some even claim great power. How do you go through your day, in fear or in confidence? The devil causes a lot of troubles in the world, every person is under his control until they accept Christ as savior. [1]

We, I assume most of you reading this have accepted Christ as savior, are exempt from the devil's power because we belong to the one with the ultimate power over all things. The devil may buffet us but he can't take us, we are someone else's merchandise. [2] Now if you do not believe Christ or the gospel message, that which the apostle Paul called the mystery, then there is no authority that will do you any good. God has the ultimate authority, it makes no difference of the power of this or the power of that, God's power is greater. There is no power that exists that is greater than God's power.

In the gospels (Matthew, Mark, Luke, and John) we read time after time of the demons being cast out by Jesus, none had any power against Him, not even enough to stand their ground for a moment more. Even the legion of the demoniac that came from the tombs could not stand off Jesus begging to be allowed to go into the pigs. They knew what Jesus ordered them to do they had to do. If a God with that kind of power is who we belong to (He bought us by paying the price) then we surely should not have to fear, He will protect what is His. Jesus once said of Jerusalem that He would have gathered her children under His wing as a hen gathers her chicks under her wings. [3]

When Jesus had not yet paid the price with His own blood, He said this about the children of Abraham – how much more will He gather and protect us who He has bought with His own blood? Is it well with your soul, do you have the confidence and the faith to say so? How much further in your Christian life do you have to go before you know God loves you? After the investment God has made in each one of us who have accepted Jesus, do you think He would allow us to be lost to the wolves? God cares about each one of us. He watches each one of us to protect us. Jesus said He went to heaven to prepare a place for us. [4]

Does it sound like He has any intentions to allow anything to happen to us. Take courage, God cares for you. This is what Horatio G Spafford says the Lord had taught him, that it was well with his soul no matter what his state in this world, God has control over it all. Look at the parables Jesus taught in Luke chapter 15 today. Do you see the emphasis put on the lost sheep (v. 4), the lost coin (v. 8), the wayward son (v. 11-22). Look at the great effort to find the lost sheep and the lost coin. Look at the father with the wayward son that must have not ever given up looking for his son's return for he saw the boy before the boy saw him. With all these there is rejoicing at the finding. We are the lost sheep found, the lost coin found, the wayward son who returned home. If we know God cares this much for us how could we ever believe He would let anything happen to us. I know where my confidence and my faith lies - It is well with my soul.

---

1   Acts 26:18, Heb.2:14&15
2   1Cor.7:22&23
3   Lk.13:34
4   Jn.14:2

How is your day going? This is a question that has to be asked many times. It helps us to focus on where the things in our day come from. If they come from the world, the world has much to offer, but what they offer isn't much when it comes to eternal things. Some of us in this society today are going so fast we don't slow down long enough to ask this question – let alone answer it. At that kind of pace, you are going to crash right into judgment day unprepared. Ask the question, answer the question, and do it honestly, no one is looking but God. Where do the things in your day come from? Who supplies you with what you need to keep going? Who takes care of where you are going to land in eternity? Very basic stuff but very important for you to consider. How do you know what you're doing is what God wants you doing? Have you been into God's word lately?

These daily comments have a daily reading schedule included, are you using it, even just part of it. We need to know what God has told us about where we're going, how we get there, and who provides the way. Reading God's word will tell us this. I would hope that most of you reading this are using the reading schedule to get God's word into yourselves. No matter how many times I read through the Bible, each time I read it the Holy Spirit shows me something new that I never noticed before, or something I really never understood before. The more we read the Bible the more we know of God.

This is crucial to how our day is going. Without God in our day who knows what is coming? But with God in our lives for each day what we face God has already been there before we arrive. If we are praying about it and are in God's word on a regular basis God has set up each day for us. The day may not always seem on the positive side – it may be a teaching God has prepared for us, it may be a chastisement for God says He chastens those He loves, it may be we are reaping something we have sown. [1] Not all days seem negative, there are more positive ones than negative, but have you ever noticed how good days just glide by without us even noticing sometimes? When you are physically well do you ever notice how many days it has been? When you have been physically sick do you know how many days it has been? Yes, we are all guilty of not noticing how much good God puts into our lives.

When we begin to notice all the good it is easy to do what the Apostle Paul advises, **Rejoice in the Lord always.** [2] Now that you have begun to notice, how is your day going? Hear again the last part of what Jude writes; *"keep yourselves in the love of God, looking for the mercy of our Lord Jesus Christ unto eternal life...Now to Him who is able to keep you from stumbling, And to present you faultless Before the presence of His glory with exceeding joy, To God our Savior, Who alone is wise, Be glory and majesty, Dominion and power, Both now and forever. Amen"* (v. 21,24,25 NKJV). Ask yourself often, 'how is my day going' and answer it.

---

1   Gal.6:7&8
2   Philp.4:4 1Thes.5:16   Paul speaks to rejoice more than 16 times in his epistles.

I sit and consider all the things of God. It is an undertaking that will never be complete for any of us until we arrive there with God where He dwells. Yet we are to strive to know as we can, as much as each of us can while still here on earth. He dwells in the hidden place, in the secret place. [1] God tells us much about Himself, yet knowing all that He is we will not know full of Him until we arrive in heaven and know all as we have been known. [2] We read the word of God pursuing a spiritual relationship with Him. God moves in mysterious ways, some by faith we come to know, some even with faith we cannot know. We have a tendency to think of eternity as something that goes forever with no end. We think of eternal life for us will go on forever. This is true of us but when it is the eternity of God it is that which goes on forever in both directions, where God has always existed and God will always exist with no limit of time.

This in itself limits us from knowing all there is to know of God. God tried to express and reveal Himself to the Hebrew people yet they did not know fully what He was showing them. In these times after the cross where we are under the New Covenant and receive the Holy Spirit at salvation to help, we are still limited from knowing all that there is of God. Even though we are told we belong to a three-in-one God who is one with three within Himself we cannot grasp how He is. The one thing we can know about God is that He is far beyond us in existence and He has sent His Son Jesus Christ that we can receive salvation because of the sacrifice of the Lamb of Heaven. [3] Even though we cannot fully know God, He fully knows us, and knows our needs. We must take on the forgiveness of God which He forgives us and forgives those around us also.

This only can truly be done with the faith of God that works in us, that of the renewing of the mind which the Spirit does within us. [4] And we see we have no right to hold any unforgiveness against anyone since being before God we are both seen as unworthy in our own doings. [5] God forgives one as well as another who comes to Him, so how do we have the right to not forgive? We must be cautious and make sure forgiveness is in our hearts. There will be that day when Christ comes again in His awesome appearance as He is described in the book of Revelation where all will be called and judged. I don't want to be one found with unforgiveness in my heart, I want to be found forgiving all as He forgives. We on this earth continue to say we have rights, but before God without Christ we have no rights, it is only by what Christ did on the cross that we have any rights, that right to be saved by His blood.

---

1   Ps.91:1
2   1Cor.13:12
3   Rev.5:12, 7:10, 21:27
4   Tit.3:5, Rom.12:2&3
5   Mt.6:15, 18:33-35, Lk.6:36&37

I thank God He does not reveal all truth to me for the immenseness of it would overwhelm me and I would die. He does not reveal Himself fully to us because He knows our frame of weakness.[1] He is a loving God who died Himself in order to get us to the place we could not get on our own. We all have been short since Adam and Eve sinned in the Garden of Eden. None has been able to be holy as God is holy since Adam and Eve ate from the tree they were forbidden. Until then I believe they were holy as God is holy, as God had created them in the beginning. But now we are all short of the glory of God and need forgiveness.[2] Yet God is a merciful God who provides a way since we are unable to make ourselves holy, or to behave in a holy way. How can we not love and devote ourselves to a God who makes a way for us to Himself by the works He Himself does? Scripture tells us, *"Herein is love, not that we loved God, but that he loved us, and sent his Son to be the propitiation for our sins"* (1Jn. 4:10 ASV). And *"Grace to you and peace from God the Father, and our Lord Jesus Christ, who gave himself for our sins, that he might deliver us out of this present evil world, according to the will of our God and Father"* (Gal. 1:3&4 ASV).

We are those who have received a great gift, the gift of salvation given to them who are willing to receive it. We have been blessed more than what we can know here on earth. When we get to heaven then we will fully know the fullness of what we have received from God for all of eternity. That gift which we receive of salvation is precious and we are to retain it as precious. Once we have received this gift God calls us to live a different life. The Holy Spirit works to change who we are. The Spirit regenerates us giving us spiritual birth and begins the process of renewing our minds.[3] As Adam and Eve were given a free will to choose what they would do, we also are given a free will to do what we choose.

Even though the Holy Spirit works in us to change us we can refuse to live by those changes within us, determining ourselves to go another way. We can sense inside ourselves the way the Spirit is leading to go, then become stiff-necked and go in another way we should not. This is clearly seen in what Jesus says to the seven churches. To three of them He says, **"But I have this against you,"** to one He says they are dead, to two of them He says they are to continue to follow Him and have faith, to the last of the churches he tells them they are neither hot nor cold in relationship to Him and He will vomit them out if they do not change in repentance. Salvation is not a done deal. We need to listen to the Holy Spirit as He works inside of us, no matter how still that voice may be in the beginning, the more we listen the clearer it will become.

Once we are saved Jesus calls us to deny ourselves making His way first in our lives, no longer our way being first. Then we need to pick up our cross which is service to others first, rather than to ourselves. Then Jesus calls us to follow Him doing what He does being guided by the voice inside us which is the Holy Spirit revealing to us what and where Jesus is calling us to follow. *"However, when the Spirit of Truth comes, he will guide you into all the truth; for he will not speak on his own initiative but will say only what he hears. He will also announce to you the events of the future. He will glorify me, because he will receive from what is mine and announce it to you. Everything the Father has is mine; this is why I said that he receives from what is mine and will announce it to you"* (Jn. 16:13-15 CJB).

---

1   Ps.103:14
2   Rom.3:23
3   Tit.3:5

'I am the way, the truth, and the life'. These are the words Jesus said to us so we would know. He followed it with these words, 'No one gets to the Father (to heaven) except by Me.' [1] In this world today there are many who try to convince all the people, including us Christians, that there are other ways to God. The devil has tried to deceive since the beginning and continues in this manner of saying there are many ways to God. There is even the presentation which puts all the religions of the world together saying we can get to God by any of them. What Jesus has said is truth, that He is the only way to God, that there is no other way. People have trouble with truth, Pilate asks Jesus what is truth as if to imply there is no absolute truth. [2]

Many would say truth is what seems right to them. Truth only comes from God, anything that does not agree with it is not truth. We will find God's truth in the Holy Bible. Anything we think we hear God say must align with what is printed in our Bibles, if not then it is not truth from God. The devil tried to take from the Bible the words of God to deceive Jesus. Jesus knew the action that the devil was using to get Jesus to take what was not the truth of those words. We find we are in a world of unrest. It is in this state of unrest because it does not have the truth fully working in it, it is deceived. We in our Christian life need to be on our guard, the deceiver is busy working, even to deceive us if he can.

The word of God tells us what is the truth, we need to be reading it to know the truth. I have heard many things said by Christians which are assumptions, not truth. Many things of God seems to us almost as unreasonable, yet they are truth because what God speaks is truth. God tries to help us to know this when He says, *"For My thoughts are not your thoughts, Nor are your ways My ways," says the LORD. "For as the heavens are higher than the earth, So are My ways higher than your ways, And My thoughts than your thoughts"* (Isa. 55:8&9 NKJV). If God's thoughts and ways are so far above us they at times may even seem wrong to us.

This is where faith comes in, believing what God says is truth, a knowledge He has that we do not have. The Jews were given truth through Moses from God. Yet they did not follow it and many times found themselves in difficulty. We cannot say any different of ourselves today. We have the gospel, that of the New Covenant, with salvation given as a gift to those who will receive it. Yet how many times do we question the word of God in our own hearts? We see that God tries to speak to us through the letters to the seven churches, seven conditions Christians are in. God is calling us to Himself, trying to show us truth. In this we must deny ourselves, our ways, and our thoughts, and adhere ourselves to Him and his truth.

---

1   Jn.14:6
2   Jn.18:38

'I can see the stars, I can hear the rolling thunder.' We are all familiar with these words, but are we familiar of the great awe of God they represent? God is gloriously great, greater than we can even imagine. Do we give Him the honor He deserves? Quite frankly I do not believe we have the ability to give Him that full honor He deserves. The four living creatures spoken of in our reading of Revelation today seem to be the only ones able to worship and give the full honor to God that He deserves (4:6-8).

Even the twenty-four elders are prompted to worship by the four living creatures (4:9&10). Yet are we giving the awe and honor to God that we can? This may vary with the spiritual maturity of each Christian, but do each of us have an awe of God and worship Him as we are able? Sometimes we get so tied up in all of life we forget, or don't take the time, or place too much value on the things of earth, and God gets short-changed of the awe and worship each of us can give. From time to time we need to get reminded of what we have received from God.

Our salvation alone is enough to give praise and thanksgiving to God for the rest of eternity. We know from where we have come deserving nothing of salvation, that of eternal life with God. We know the greatness of that salvation which makes us children of God giving us rights to the things of God which we have no right to by our own actions or accomplishments.

He is the one who takes the lead. *"We love, because he first loved us."* (1Jn. 4:19 ASV). and *"But God, who is rich in mercy, out of the great love with which he loved us, even when we were dead through our trespasses, made us alive together with Christ"* (Eph. 2:4&5 RSV).

Our awe and gratitude goes up as we consider who we are and what God has done for each of us. Sometimes in our fast pace of life we have to halt everything and see the great things God is doing for us each day, even each moment as our life moves forward in His great salvation He has given us. Sometimes we need to stop, step back, and see all God is doing as He blesses our lives. When you get to work making it OK do you say, 'shwoo, glad I got through all that traffic' – do you even consider of how it is you might have made it?

Even if it was not God would it be a good thing to thank God that you did make it OK? We are blessed by a great blessing to have salvation given to us freely. All else beyond that are just perks because we are children of God. There is a turn we all reach when we see all these great things God has done, is doing, and will continue to do. That turn is when our focus of the things God gives us changes to being concerned totally to how we can serve Him.

There is a bliss in this place where we are consumed with the greatness of God and all He is. We become dedicated to Him looking to Him for the opportunities we may have to serve Him. We do not serve a hard task master, He is kind and loving providing all we need and leads us into what He has for each of us individually to do. Serving God viewed from outside by those unsaved may seem as an endless list of do's and don'ts, but to us who have reached this place of servanthood it is a pleasure and a joy.

'My time is Your time , Oh Lord.' Can we all say this? It is how it should be but have we truly reached that point? I do hope I have reached that point, but have I? Our flesh wars against our spirit.[1] So is all our time given to the Lord, or does the desires of the flesh sometimes take us were we do not want to go with that time not being given to the Lord? I am not speaking of the flesh taking us into sin necessarily, even though at times it may. I am only speaking of times when we go the way of the flesh and not the way of the Spirit. This is the times the flesh leads the way which is not giving ourselves to God. Over time as we mature in our spiritual walk there will be more and more of our time led by the Spirit rather than the flesh. I believe the words of John the Baptist may speak for us all who have received salvation, *"He must increase, but I must decrease"* (Jn. 3:30 ASV). All that we have and are belongs to the Lord since we have been sold to Him as He has redeemed us by paying for our sins with His blood.[2]

Jesus could, by rights, demand all our time, yet He is a merciful and gracious God knowing our weakness. He calls to us and He waits, and continues to call us into a more spiritual life following Him. If it were not for the regenerating and renewing the Holy Spirit does in our lives we would have little hope of being able to change.[3] In Deuteronomy, the Law is given of the way the Jews were to live but they failed over and over. We today certainly would fail also if the Holy Spirit was not working in us by the New Covenant. We need to be thankful to God He has taken over the hard work of making us holy rather than us having to reach that mark ourselves. God is good to us, and the more we see this the more we decrease and the more He increases in our lives. Yet we can fight this change, resisting at every turn what the Spirit wants to do.

We must hear the Holy Spirit within us as He tries to help us in our way. That leading of the Spirit does not always come as a voice within us, sometimes it is an instant awareness about something that we don't know where it came from. Sometimes it is a desire to do something that we know did not come from ourselves. We must have, and make room for the Holy Spirit to lead us. There is a time coming which will be the end when Christ returns and we all come to the judgment.

In Luke today Jesus tells His disciples, and us, how things will be at the end of the age. So many times before us there were those who may have thought they were in those times. It may have been for many of the Jews, who had received salvation by their Messiah Jesus, being taken by Hitler thought it must be the end times Jesus spoke of.

There may have been other times we know nothing of where a society was treated in such a way by their rulers that they thought they were in those times Jesus speaks about in Luke chapter 21. We need the Holy Spirit within us to help us know when these times come for real. And we will need the Holy Spirit within us to get through these times, that inward witness to guide us through them. Jesus tells us about those times, *"Settle it therefore in your minds not to meditate beforehand how to answer, for I will give you a mouth and wisdom, which none of your adversaries will be able to withstand or contradict"* (Lk. 21:14&15 ESV). A companion scripture to this is, *"But when they arrest you and deliver you up, do not worry beforehand, or premeditate what you will speak. But whatever is given you in that hour, speak that; for it is not you who speak, but the Holy Spirit"* (Mk. 13:11 NKJV).

There are troubled times in the world today, Jesus said there would be wars and rumors of wars.[4] We need to be alert, we need to be listening to the Spirit, and we need to be ready when the Lord comes if it should be in our lifetime. We also need to be ready each day for each of us do not know what day and hour our lives on this earth will end, and then not be able to change anything. We need to try to live rightly before God each day, as it might be our last day.

---

1   Gal.5:17
2   Mt.26:28, Eph.1:7, Col.1:14, Rev.1:5
3   Tit.3:5
4   Mt.24:6

I am glad in this day because I know it is in God's hand. He watches over the earth with a watchful eye with nothing escaping His notice. We can have a confidence in this. He governs, and guides, and directs the affairs of those who love him. Sin has taken its course upon the earth, its infection has reached all the land. Even the rocks and the trees are infected because of the sin of mankind. It is only by the grace and mercy of God that any of us can escape it. What we could not do to heal ourselves from this infection God Himself took action to provide the healing for us. We are not the ones who struggle to bring a healing of ourselves from the infection of sin which entered the world through the actions of Adam and Eve in the Garden of Eden.

God Himself in His persons suffers to bring to us the healing from sin we could not accomplish on our own. Jesus, who was sent by the Father, took upon Himself the work and the sufferings, *"You are those who have continued with me in my trials;...For I tell you that this scripture must be fulfilled in me, 'And he was reckoned with transgressors'; for what is written about me has its fulfillment"* (Lk. 22:28&37 RSV). There were many things prophesied about Jesus Christ which would be fulfilled for our redemption. *"Yet it pleased the LORD to bruise him; he hath put him to grief: when thou shalt make his soul an offering for sin"* (Isa. 53:10 KJV). We are the guilty. We are those who went astray.

But the loving God we have never fully gave up on mankind making a way by which we are permitted to enter heaven and be with Him for eternity, *"While we were still weak, at the right time Christ died for the ungodly...But God shows his love for us in that while we were yet sinners Christ died for us. Since, therefore, we are now justified by his blood, much more shall we be saved by him from the wrath of God"* (Rom. 5:6,8,9 RSV). Even of all the treatment of being accused of being ungodly, and even evil, none would compare to the suffering Jesus went through in the Garden of Gethsemane. *"Father, if you are willing, take this cup away from me; still, let not my will but yours be done." There appeared to him an angel from heaven giving him strength, and in great anguish he prayed more intensely, so that his sweat became like drops of blood falling to the ground"* (Lk. 22:42-44 CJB).

If in our life at some point we truly grasp the struggle Jesus went through for us on that night there may be tears of our own we shed. God has loved us, greatly loved us, a love that only God could generate to such power to save us out of such an ungodly world. We must have thanksgiving running through the core of our being for what it is that God has done for us. Peter in his prayer after the death and resurrection of Jesus was aware of all that God, the three in one God, had done for us when he said, *"for truly in this city there were gathered together against your holy servant Jesus, whom you anointed, both Herod and Pontius Pilate, along with the Gentiles and the peoples of Israel, to do whatever your hand and your plan had predestined to take place"* (Acts 4:27&28 ESV).

We sometimes see Jesus as a victim of the Pharisees and Pilate, but the Father in Heaven is the One who put Jesus on the cross that we might have the opportunity of salvation, **'Your hand and Your purpose determined before to be done'**. The Father, the Son, and the Holy Spirit has provided for us what we could not provide ourselves. Our praise, our gratitude, and our worship should be given in remembering of what God has done for us. God wants us to remember and gave this to us in His word, *"I have earnestly desired to eat this passover with you before I suffer...And he took a cup, and when he had given thanks he said, "Take this, and divide it among yourselves... And he took bread, and when he had given thanks he broke it and gave it to them, saying, "This is my body which is given for you. Do this in remembrance of me"* (Lk. 22:15,17,19 RSV).

Life is all about survival. There are those who speak of the survival of the fittest, there are those who speak of the survival of the species, there are those who speak of the survival of the nation or the country, there are those who speak of survival of the learned, etc. All of these spoke of are that which happens on this earth, in this world. Is not true survival that of being with God in heaven for eternity? So if life is about survival and survival is eternity with God in heaven, then life should be all about ensuring we get to heaven. Many would say they have never really done anything really bad, that they have been good to all. Jesus said none is good except God,[1] so being good is out.

Not really doing anything really bad is also out because the scriptures tell us all have sinned falling short of the glory of God.[2] Now we are in a pickle, if all are bad and none can do good we will never make it to heaven - except by the work that Jesus has already done for each one of us who accept Him as Lord. True survival is dying to self and to this world. To live we must die.[3]The apostle Paul says he died with Christ and he now lives in Christ.[4]

To survive in the eternal we must die in the temporary. This life that we now live will end, it is not eternal, it is temporary. Dying to the desires of this world, dying to the ways of this world, dying to our worldly flesh and all that goes with it, is how we will survive. Leaning on Jesus, living in Jesus, depending on Jesus, is how God has provided for us to survive. The way of our survival has been planned from the beginning of time by God.[5] Anyone who is willing to accept Jesus as Lord and repent of their sins being re-born becomes a survivor. The salvation they receive makes them a survivor for eternity.

That's true survival. How can we get so wrapped up in so many things that have nothing to do with eternity? We Christians may have lost our focus, and we may have our priorities mixed up. It is easy in this world of busy life to forget what is most important. We must constantly remind ourselves – the world won't, they'll take us in the other direction. It is important that we see what is most important. Eternity is most important. Do you need to realign your priorities, do you need to change your focus? God is always willing to help us, just ask. Let Him know you realize you need to change your focus and your priorities, that you have come to Him for His help. He will answer, He will help you reshape your life. In our reading today in Luke chapter 23 there were two criminals also crucified that day with Jesus, one on one side and one on the other. The first criminal speaking had his focus and priorities wrong, he only cared about survival in this world.

Basically what the first criminal said was, 'If you are the Christ (God) get us all down from here and we can be on our way'. The second criminal was concerned about true survival, read what he says, "*But the other* [second criminal], *answering, rebuked him* [first criminal], *saying, "Do you not even fear God, seeing you are under the same condemnation? "And we indeed justly, for we receive the due reward of our deeds; but this Man has done nothing wrong." Then he said to Jesus, "Lord, remember me when You come into Your kingdom."* (v.40-42) I would hope and pray that none of us have to be at the gate of death before we get our focus and our priorities in order. If you need help, ask God today.

---

1   Lk.18:19
2   Rom.3:23
3   Lk.17:33
4   Rom.6:23, Gal.2:20
5   Jn.17:3-5

In this day we need to believe. Not what the world wants us to believe, but what God wants us to believe. He is able to raise us out of our deepest doubts. He is able to lead us into the truest of truths. He calls out to us calling us to Himself that we might receive from Him. Yet are we willing to believe? The Holy Spirit is constantly speaking His truths to our hearts. Are we listening, are we willing to believe? I will not say it is an easy thing to believe.

We are conditioned by the things around us and what we are exposed to. The world is what we are exposed to, and we grow and live in it. We have to come to a place of faith in God. In the past, I did studies to find out 'what is faith'. I have discovered in my latter years it is simple, it is being willing to believe what God says is truth, without an objectionable thought of my own.

In the very early years of my Christianity God burrowed a truth into my heart from His word and it has been with me ever since, *"For My thoughts are not your thoughts, Nor are your ways My ways,"* *says the LORD. "For as the heavens are higher than the earth, So are My ways higher than your* *ways, And My thoughts than your thoughts"* (Isa. 55:8&9 NKJV). By what God says here I realize much of what God does and says will make no sense to me, His ways and thoughts are too high above for me to understand or make sense of. The only thing I am left to do is to believe, believe what He says is true, and yield myself to it in faith. I might argue with God, but I will never outmaneuver Him. His ways and thoughts is always how it will be whether I am willing to accept it or believe it. God has final say about all things. One day even this earth will be folded up and put away[1] with a new earth taking its place for the New Jerusalem to come down[2] from heaven on it, and we shall be there with Him.

As mankind a lot of times we don't get it. God tells us, and tells us, and we don't get it. Many things can get in the way causing us to not get it, mostly it is our unbelief. If we keep seeking Him He will help us reach the place we can believe. The disciples were told many times by Jesus that He was going to go to Jerusalem, be arrested, killed, and then rise from the dead. Even with all those times He told them, they didn't get it. When the women who went to the tomb early who had seen two angels which told them Jesus was risen told this to the disciples, the disciples yet did not get it. *"But these words appeared to them as nonsense, and they would not believe the women"* (Lk. 24:11 NASB).

In time they all believed. Sometimes we know a truth in our heart right now, other times it takes time for the truth to settle in. As long as we keep coming back to God seeking truth He will help us to arrive there. There are many opponents to God's truth, the great deceiver most of all. We have to be willing to believe what God says is truth before we can know it is truth. Having faith is knowing what God says is truth. That truth is that which will carry us to the very end where we step into heaven to be with Him for eternity.

---

1   Mt.24:35, Rev.21:1
2   Rev.21:2

It is not good to only know of God and not hear Him and follow Him. Some would say they believe in God, but if that is all the further they go it will not help them. Jesus said He is the truth, He is the life, He is the way, the only way to the Father. [1] To believe in God is a good thing, but it is not enough, we must have Jesus in our lives, in our hearts as Lord and Savior if we are to make it to heaven where the Father is. We are told the demons believe in God, but it will not get them to heaven. [2]

Jesus is our way, He becomes our life, and we find the truth through Him. We are blessed, we have been given mercy and grace from God as he presents to us a way to Himself which is not our work of the Law, but His work in mercy and grace to us. We are benefactors of that which we do not deserve. The only requirement for us to receive redemption from God is to humble ourselves, confessing our condition of being sinners, and ask Jesus to become Ruler and King of our lives. The amazing thing is that with only these three small things that are required of us He does all the rest. We are called by Jesus to follow. [3] This does not mean we take the lead in getting things done for God, it means Jesus is the one getting things done for God, and He calls us to be involved with Him in getting the things of God done.

We take too much of a load on ourselves many times when all we are ask to do is follow. Each of us needs to be in a relationship with Jesus to be able to know where we are to follow. Whether you hear the guidance of Jesus directly as He speaks to you, or as you are reading in His word and He impress you strongly about something you read, or even by a situation of some sort which He speaks to you through, we all need to be guided by Him in what work He has for each of us individually to do.

Many times this guidance is delivered to us by the Holy Spirit, *"But when He, the Spirit of truth, comes, He will guide you into all the truth; for He will not speak on His own, but whatever He hears, He will speak; and He will disclose to you what is to come. "He will glorify Me, for He will take from Mine and will disclose it to you"* (Jn. 16:13-15 NASB). In the Godhead this is part of the responsibility of the Holy Spirit. He is also the One Jesus and the Father sent to us to tell us of truth and remind us what Jesus said. [4] We have much help from the Three-in-One God which each person in the Godhead is blessing us and helping us.

In the Old Testament we continue to read of all the Law God gave to them through Moses. We read in John chapter 1 that Jesus who is the Word came to us as the Light shining in a dark place that we might know of God, and know of His mercy and grace, and know of His gospel that bring us life, true life, eternal life. It is no more by our works of the Law, it is by the willingness on our part to receive what God offers to us. All of the Law given through Moses is fulfilled in Jesus and by Jesus. [5]

We are called to a new law, not that we gain salvation by it, it is the law we are to follow after receiving salvation, it is the law to love, to love God first and then to love all others as Jesus loved us, *"A new commandment I give to you, that you love one another; even as I have loved you, that you also love one another. By this all men will know that you are my disciples, if you have love for one another"* (Jn. 13:34&35 RSV). It is so important that Jesus repeats it, *"This is my commandment, that you love one another as I have loved you"* (Jn. 15:12 RSV). and *"These things I command you, so that you will love one another"* (Jn. 15:17 ESV). Love is to be at the center of our lives, and at the center of all we do.

---

1   Jn.14:6
2   Jas.2:19
3   Mt.16:24, Jn.12:26
4   Jn.14:26
5   Jn.19:28

'Who do you say I am?' Jesus asks this question to the apostles.[1] If He asks it of you, what would your answer be? Remember you have the advantage over the apostles at the time they were asked. Christ has died on the cross and rose from the dead since that moment. You have the advantage of the teachings of the apostles, of what they came to know after that moment. With all the information available to you in the Bible and the invited spiritual relationship with Jesus now how would you answer His question: 'Who do you say I am?' A great question, but how many of us can answer it as we should? Do you know who Jesus is really? The answer to the question Jesus put to the apostles was the answer in accordance to Jesus' mission that the Father had sent Him to earth for, Jesus was the Messiah, the very Son of God, who would become the savior of all who would receive Him as Lord. That is a bit more than what Peter stated at the moment Jesus gave the question, yet they do declare later that he is the savior of the world. But let us broaden the question to all that Jesus is, what can we say?

Well, the scriptures tell us all was created through Him and for Him. We are told He is the great 'I AM'. We are told He is the perfect Passover Lamb sacrificed for many. He is the great conqueror over our enemy the devil. We are told He is our friend, our elder brother. We have read resonantly in Revelation that He is the Lamb worthy to open the seven seals that no one else could open. He is the Alpha and the Omega, the first and the last. He is the great redeemer. He is the Lord of lords and King of kings. He is the Lion of Judah. If we truly search the scriptures the list goes on and on and on. It is a good thing to review who Jesus is. Sometimes our faith gets weak, or we find ourselves in fear.

These both are overcome when we remind ourselves of who Jesus is. He walks on water, He calms the storm, He orders demons away, He strengthens the weak, He cheers the broken hearted. Who is Jesus to you, how will you answer His question?

In Isaiah we read this today; *"Therefore thus says the Lord GOD: "Behold, I am laying a stone in Zion, a tested stone, A precious cornerstone for the foundation, firmly placed. The one who believes in it will not be disturbed"* (Isa. 28:16 NASB). John the apostle told us in our reading yesterday what John the Baptist said about Jesus; *"John bore witness about him, and cried out, "This was he of whom I said, 'He who comes after me ranks before me, because he was before me"* (Jn. 1:15 ESV). Then John the apostle goes on to say this; *"And from his fulness have we all received, grace upon grace. For the law was given through Moses; grace and truth came through Jesus Christ. No one has ever seen God; the only Son, who is in the bosom of the Father, he has made him known"* (Jn. 1:16-18 RSV).

Again John the apostle tells us more of what John the Baptist said; *"The next day John saw Jesus coming toward him, and said, "Behold! The Lamb of God who takes away the sin of the world! "This is He of whom I said, 'After me comes a Man who is preferred before me, for He was before me'...."I did not know Him, but He who sent me to baptize with water said to me, 'Upon whom you see the Spirit descending, and remaining on Him, this is He who baptizes with the Holy Spirit.' "And I have seen and testified that this is the Son of God"* (Jn. 1:29,30,33,34 NKJV). Jesus says this of Himself; *"Yes indeed! I tell you that you will see heaven opened and the angels of God going up and coming down on the Son of Man"* (Jn. 1:51 CJB). In today's reading in John we find this; *"In the Temple grounds he found those who were selling cattle, sheep and pigeons, and others who were sitting at tables exchanging money. He made a whip from cords and drove them all out of the Temple grounds, the sheep and cattle as well. He knocked over the money-changers' tables, scattering their coins; and to the pigeon-sellers he said, "Get these things out of here! How dare you turn my Father's house into a market?" (His talmidim [disciples] later recalled that the Tanakh [scriptures] says, "Zeal for your house will devour me"* (Jn. 2:14-17 CJB). Somewhere in our reading every day there is something about Jesus, are you noticing? Can you answer Jesus' question, **'Who do you say I am?'**

---

1   Mt.16:15, Lk.9:20

Who can take away our sins? Can one of the great prophets, can Moses, can Abraham, can Mary the mother of Jesus, can Peter, can Paul? Who is it that can take away my sin, to pay the price I owe, the giving of blood in death? Jesus is the only one, none other is perfect without spot or blemish which is required of all sacrifices by the Law. It also could not be an animal even though thousands upon thousands, even millions were sacrificed in Israel, they could not pay for sin.[1] Only the very Son of God was He who was perfect without spot or blemish and could be that sacrifice which could pay for our sins. Sin has been here since Adam and Eve was in the garden, being told by God to not eat of a certain tree with the choice to obey or disobey. Mankind has had the choice ever since and none of us down through time have obeyed.

Many have come close but close does not count, it has to be without spot or blemish that we obey God. Because we all have sinned, none of us obeyed, God in His love provided the perfect sacrifice in Jesus, that Jesus' blood would pay for what we could not. His blood is what cleanses us from sin, it is His blood that washes us whiter than snow.[2] There is a certain believing of receiving. If you do not believe that Jesus' blood has fully paid for your sins you will continue to believe you have to work at getting them paid for. The devil likes this line of thought because he will continue to try to convince you that you have to keep working at it, that the work Jesus did was not enough. Do you realize what that does to Jesus if you believe what He did was not enough, that you need to work at it too? It says Jesus is not perfect because the work He did on the cross was not perfect.

We must believe, we must receive, we must live knowing all our sins are paid for. This gives us the liberty from the work we think we need to do for our sins to be paid for, to a freedom to follow Jesus in whatever He wants us to do, whenever He sends us to do it. This does not give us a license to sin all the more, if anything knowing what Jesus went through to pay for the sins we have done, the love and respect we have for Him should help us to stay away from any more sin as much as possible. Knowing what caused Jesus to go through the suffering He did on the cross helps keep me from doing again what put Him there in the first place. Sometimes we have to practice an active receiving of the full price Jesus paid until it becomes such a part of us deep down inside that even the storms of life can't shake it. What I mean about active is telling yourself every day, even maybe every hour, for a while that Jesus said, 'It is finished', that He is the only perfect one who was qualified to pay the price, and it is 'Paid in full'.

Once we are free of feeling we have to pay a price we are able to tell others about the love of Jesus, how He has paid the price for sin, and if they are willing to accept Him as Lord He will forgive their sin as well. This is our great commission – to preach the gospel, to tell people God loves them and has made a way that their sins can be forgiven. It doesn't take a Preacher to preach the gospel, only someone who knows they are fully forgiven by the blood of Christ.

In our reading today in John chapter 3 we read this; *"so must the Son of Man be lifted up, so that everyone who believes will have eternal life in Him. "For God so loved the world, that He gave His only Son, so that everyone who believes in Him will not perish, but have eternal life. "For God did not send the Son into the world to judge the world, but so that the world might be saved through Him. "The one who believes in Him is not judged; the one who does not believe has been judged already, because he has not believed in the name of the only Son of God"* (v.14-18 NASB). Listen again to the words of the last verse, 'The one who believes in him is not judged.' If we still need to do some of the work to pay for our sins then we would be judged of if what we done was enough. These verses tell us anyone who believes has eternal life, the only thing for us to do is receive and believe 'It is finished' as Jesus said on the cross.

---

1   Heb.10:4, 9:12
2   Rev.1:5, Ps.51:2,3,7

'My life is yours, Lord'. How many of you have said this to the Lord with fullness of meaning? Yes, we have been purchased with the blood, we no longer belong to ourselves.[1] Yet the Lord does not force us to do anything. He could, but what would he have other than a programmed follower only doing and responding as they are programmed? God wants relationship, what sort of relationship can one have with a robot? To say 'My life is yours Lord' takes surrender, full surrender. This type of surrender will not be a one-time deal like one general of a war surrendering to another, this type of surrender will be an on-going surrender.

It will be a daily surrender, a hour by hour and a moment by moment surrender. The advantage of a surrender like this to a gracious King like Jesus is we will enjoy all the power and splendor, and involvement of His Kingdom. As we surrender He empowers us to do His work (not our own work). As we surrender we enjoy all the splendor of His Kingdom being well taken care of as one of His dear subjects that He takes a personal interest in.

As we surrender we are called into the work of His Kingdom on this earth with the rest of the people of this world. If we are willing by surrendering He will give us ways to get His work done on earth that are heavenly ways, Godly ways, that we can only receive from Him. For now we are His subjects in a Kingdom on this earth that is not of this world. If we were to practice Christianity the same as the other religions of the world then we would have nothing more than they do. If there is no supernatural realm then all religions, including Christianity, are just formalities and practices made up by mankind that accomplish nothing. If there is a supernatural realm and all these other religions are following gods who are demons[2] then we need God's supernatural powers and abilities to accomplish His work on this earth among the host of demonic powers which oppose the work of God. Sometimes we wonder why when we try to tell someone about Jesus (in our own power) that they seem as though they hear nothing we have said. The very first type of soil Jesus tells of the seed falls on, He says the devil comes and snatches away the seed.[3]

We need God's supernatural power to accomplish the work He left for us to do; *"Go therefore and make disciples of all nations, baptizing them in the name of the Father and of the Son and of the Holy Spirit, teaching them to observe all that I have commanded you"* (Mt. 28:19&20 RSV). and *"Go into all the world and proclaim the gospel to the whole creation"* (Mk. 16:15 ESV). and *"he said unto them, Thus it is written, that the Christ should suffer, and rise again from the dead the third day; and that repentance and remission of sins should be preached in his name unto all the nations, beginning from Jerusalem"* (Lk. 24:46&47 ASV). and *"you shall be my witnesses in Jerusalem and in all Judea and Samaria and to the end of the earth"* (Acts 1:8 RSV).

This work cannot be done with the natural power we possess, that which we have of ourselves, it takes that supernatural power that only God offers. There is a small glimpse of this in our reading today. In John chapter 4 the disciples have went into town to buy food leaving Jesus at Jacob's well to rest. Jesus has a conversation with a woman and then the disciples return with food. They try to convince Jesus to eat some of the food they have bought but He puts them off by saying He has food they know nothing about; *"I have food to eat that you don't know about"* (v. 32 CJB). Jesus goes on to explain what that food is. The food that gave Jesus the stamina to continue the work the Father had sent Him to do was supernatural, what the disciples had for Him to eat was only the natural. If Jesus needed the supernatural food to do the Father's work, then we also certainly need the supernatural food to do the work Jesus has sent us to do.

---

1   Acts 20:28, Rev.5:6&9
2   1Cor.10:19&20
3   Lk.8:12

Why waste time seeking something that is not there? We are always looking for something over the rainbow. God is a sure thing. If you know of a sure thing do you not bet everything on it? God is a sure thing, He is real, it is His Kingdom that is going to last forever. Jesus said not to invest in things that will corrode away, but to build our treasure in heaven.[1] This does not mean our money only, this means all there is of us. Our life isn't even ours if we are a Christian, it has been bought with a price.[2] Why should we complain if we don't get to use all our life on our own wants?

We get the best of the deal (in our eyes) when we yield to God and ask Jesus into our lives. Jesus pays our debt, He provides for our needs, He protects us from our enemy, He calms the storm that rages around us, He gives us guidance when we are at a loss, He gives us a joy that we could have no other way, He prays for us to the Father, He prepares a place for us in eternity in His Father's house, He conquers death that we can live. Would you put your all on a sure thing? Here is a sure thing: God the Father in heaven loves you, God the Son Jesus Christ came and died for you making a way into heaven for you, God the Holy Spirit has been sent to you to help you develop into what God wants you to be. If this all be true why should we not give our all? God wants blessings for us that we can't even imagine.[3] We spend a lot of time trying to get ahead in this world. What if we gave that time to God and allowed Him to get us ahead in this world? This is not a holy prosperity thing I'm speaking about, this is a yielding all to God allowing Him to manage it, allowing Him to provide for us as He said He would.[4] We will always have enough, just maybe not an abundance. Who would not invest in something with a long-term payback?

Eternity in heaven is a long-term payback – a very long term. God offers us something that we cannot buy, why would we ever resist? Many given this type of opportunity to invest in something in this world with a great pay back would jump at it with all they have.[5] So what is the problem, so many refuse to believe – the greatest deal offered in all of eternity, and so many refuse to believe. I have been reading the Bible through every year for more than twenty years now, some would ask why I read it over and over – mainly I need to be exposed to God's word daily.

Another reason is I continue to find, or God continues to reveal, new things every time. This time through I have seen something I don't remember ever noticing; *"therefore He lifts Himself up, that He may have mercy on you and show loving-kindness to you. For the Lord is a God of justice. Blessed are all those who wait for Him, who expect and look and long for Him"* (Isa. 30:18 AMPC). What a great deal, even if we surrender all to God look at what we get. In our reading today in John chapter 5 Jesus says this; *"I assure you, most solemnly I tell you, the person whose ears are open to My words and believes and trust in and clings to and relies on Him who sent Me has eternal life. And he does not come into judgment, but he has already passed over out of death into life"* (v. 24 AMPC).

This is His promise to us. Jesus goes on to say this: *"Don't be surprised at this; because the time is coming when all who are in the grave will hear his voice and come out—those who have done good to a resurrection of life, and those who have done evil to a resurrection of judgment"* (v. 27-29 CJB). We should seek what is eternally there, what is true. We can spend our whole life chasing after a rainbow and when we get to it the pot at its end is empty. The one thing that is sure in life is death, what then?

---

1   Mt.6:19&20
2   1Cor.6:20, 7:23
3   Ps. 139:4, Mt.6:8
4   Mt.6:25-34
5   Mt.13:46

Who do you think you are, and who does Jesus say you are? Well, I guess the answer would depend on if you are saved or unsaved. We can get very mixed up on who we are. Some think they are more than what they are and others think they are less than what they are. For the unsaved Jesus would say they are a sinner needing His gift of salvation. For those of us who are saved, we are the children of God adopted into the royal family who have the promise of eternal life.[1] We are conquerors, but sometimes we act like, and think like, we are the victims. Sometimes we think we are left out when our names are written in the Lamb's book of life. Many times in saying who we are we say we are trying very hard to gain our salvation and a place in heaven. Jesus would say, 'you are in, I've paid the price.' For us to say we are too short and not much value to God would not be the truth. We might think it is but it is not.

Do you believe the Father would have allowed His only begotten Son to be beaten and crucified on a cross for people who are too short with no value? Yes, it is true that in and of ourselves we do fall short of the glory of God, that in and of ourselves we have little value in who we are or what we do, but grace has brought us in. In Jesus, who the apostle Paul says we are now in, we are most valuable and with Jesus enabling us we are never short when we put our trust in Him. If we think too much of ourselves God has a way of dealing with that attitude. God says He will humble those who lift themselves up (in pride) and that He will lift up those who humble themselves. Jesus tells the parable about the Pharisee and the tax collector in the Temple, the tax collector would not even lift up his head in prayer confessing he was a sinner while the Pharisee was proud that he was not like other men, especially this tax collector.[2]

Jesus said the tax collector was the one who God justified. God puts value on the repentant heart, do you have a repentant heart? If you have a repentant heart, what does that say about who Jesus says you are? We are constantly being bombarded by those in the world and by our spiritual enemy the devil to think less of ourselves than what we are. If you are not hearing what God says in His word about who you are you may end up listening to the voices of the world you hear around you. God says a lot in His word about who we are. If we are not reading His word then we may begin to believe the lies of the world and the devil.

We are blessed, we are given much, we are made into something we could never have been without Jesus. We need to hear who Jesus says we are, we need to know we are special to Him, we are the beloved of Christ.[3] We need to stop listening to what the world says about us and what the devil whispers in our ear. God the Father says we are valuable, He sent His Son to die on the cross for us. As far as eternity goes, once we have accepted Jesus as Lord it makes little difference in eternity of who we say we are, it only matters about who Jesus says we are. But on this earth, it does matter about who we think we are. If we know who we are in Christ we will be able to weather the storm and to conquer opposition.

If we don't know who we are in Christ life will be difficult. Even though the disciples had been with Jesus for some time they still didn't know who they were. In our reading in John chapter 6 today Jesus had gotten done with teaching the crowd and had sent the disciples on ahead of Him across the lake while He went to pray. Later that night as the disciples were making their way to the other shore a great wind was against them. (v. 18) Jesus came walking on the water and when He got into the boat the wind ceased.[4] There is another time similar where Jesus is asleep in the back of the boat, the disciples wake Him because of the storm, Jesus rises and orders the storm to be still.[5] If Jesus is with us the storm will not overtake us. We have to know who Jesus says we are in this world to weather the storms and conduct His business.

---

1   Jn.1:12, Rom.8:16, 1Jn.3:1
2   Lk.18:10-14
3   2Thes.2:13&16
4   Mk.6:51
5   Mk.4:37-39

'I Am God.' Do we really need to hear this more if we have faith? Yet God declares Himself over and over throughout the whole Bible. He declares Himself to us in our own hearts if we are listening and seeing. God Himself chose a nation of people for Himself because of the relationship He had with their fathers. He has said of them they were a stiff-necked people.[1] Can we claim we are anything better? The scriptures tell us we deserve the wrath of God for our ways of life, for our sins. God gave a way by which we could enter into His blessings. That way is Jesus Christ who died on the cross with your sins, and my sins, and the sins of all the world upon Him.[2] It is by this we are forgiven and cleansed. Yet from time to time do we not find ourselves again with a bit of a stiff-neck towards God?

It is our flesh that fights against our Spirit trying to take us its way.[3] Paul, who knowing of his sins in the past, seemed to be searching for a way he could present himself holy to God. This may have been the Pharisee of Pharisees in him. He failed, he found he could not, and search for why. He said the things he wanted to do he did not, and that which he did not want to do was what at times he did.[4] It seems he discovered that the flesh is an opponent to the Spirit who is leading toward God and God's ways. Even with the blood of Christ in our lives bring forgiveness to us we still are taken off at times by our flesh to a place we do not what to be.

There is grace upon grace for us.[5] We do not get to heaven because we live a perfect life by our own efforts. We get to heaven by the efforts of Christ who died for our sin giving redemption to those who will receive it. One of the songs we sing says, 'My life is in You Lord'. If our life is in Jesus we should not struggle to be holy because it is God who makes us holy. We are told, 'be holy, for I am holy.'[6] The interesting thing here is if we take the Greek word here for 'be' and put it into a translator for modern day Greek it comes back in English as 'You are born.'

If we are truly born of God in the new birth and now are children of the Father then it is in our DNA being holy because we are born of Him and He is holy. Once we realize this it frees us up from trying in our own efforts to be holy allowing us to serve Him fully with no distraction of trying to make ourselves holy. In our reading today Jesus tells the Jews they have the Laws given through Moses yet none of them keeps the Law (Jn.7:19). To try to be holy by the Law, or our own efforts does not work. It is only by the work that Jesus has already finished that will make us holy prepared to go to heaven. Jesus said this, *"If anyone thirsts, let him come to me and drink. Whoever believes in me, as the Scripture has said, 'Out of his heart will flow rivers of living water"* (Jn. 7:37&38 ESV). Those rivers of living waters it tells us in the next verse is the Spirit which we receive, and that Spirit brings life, *"it is the Spirit who gives life"* (Jn. 6:63 CJB). For us to try to be holy by our efforts is useless because of what was said in Revelation today in our reading, *"Who will not fear You, Lord, and glorify Your name? For You alone are holy"* (Rev. 15:4 NASB). The only way to be holy is to have the DNA of God. We get that by becoming children of God by adoption through Christ by the work He did on the cross for us.

1	Ex.32:9, Duet.9:13
2	1Jn.2:2
3	Gal.5:17
4	Rom.7:15
5	Jn.1:16
6	1Pet.1:16

Love is to all, all who will come to God and receive from Him. Love was to Adam and Eve until they turn away from God listening to another: Eve listened to the serpent, Adam listened to Eve.[1] In our flesh we have that tendency to true away from God. For us who considered our state of being in sin and sought forgiveness of God He has redeemed us by Jesus Christ to Himself. We can say little of ourselves except by our flesh we were not wanting what God was wanting. We are redeemed, we are cleansed, we are brought close to God where love is found. What kind of love does it take to love those who do not return that love? This is the kind of love God loves us with, it is a never-ending love. This kind of love is always reaching out to us, calling and calling hoping we will respond.[2]

God called out and Abraham responded. Because of Abraham, his children were blessed. God called out and Moses responded. Because Moses responded the children of Abraham, Isaac, and Jacob were taken to the promise land. God because of His love was calling, but few responded. Finally, it seems God saw He needed to do something so those who heard Him calling had a way to come. We all now who hear God calling can come by the way of Jesus who paid for our sins so we are acceptable. God does love us with a love we cannot understand, when we arrive in heaven we may understand, but for now we cannot know it.

Many things of God are high and far away from us.[3] We, of us who are saved, have experienced that love as it changes our lives. Many hear of how they should live, even within wanting to live that way, but are unable. When we receive salvation it is God in His love toward us that changes us in a way we could not, then calls us to live by it. God calls, are we listening? He wants to guide our every moment. Whether that guidance is moment by moment as sometimes is the need, or guidance given for the day which covers every moment, or guidance which is for a season covering every moment in it. Today we have read John chapter 8 which never mentions the word love but yet is all though it. The first place we see it is as it is given to the one condemned, the woman caught in adultery.

Jesus says to her, 'go and sin no more'. Jesus knew the darkness they walked in and He said He was the Light who came into the world, that those who follow Him would have the light of life. Because of God's love the Father reaches out to us calling us. Jesus says, *"He who sent Me is true; and the things which I heard from Him, these I say to the world"* (v. 26 NASB). Jesus tries to tell us, He tries to get through to us, He wants us to know of the Father's love toward us. Jesus tells us, *"If you continue in my word, you are truly my disciples, and you will know the truth, and the truth will make you free"* (v. 31&32 RSV).

Free of the darkness of not knowing, free of the sin that would devour us, free of the inability to get to God on our own. Jesus is telling us of the Father's love and His own love towards us, a love to help us find our way to God, a loving God, who reaches out to us calling us to Himself. Death will overwhelm us if we do not find life, Jesus says, *"if anyone keeps my word, he will never see death"* (v. 52 ESV). God loves us, making a way that we can come to Him. *"For God so loved the world that He gave His only begotten Son, that whoever believes in Him should not perish but have everlasting life. For God did not send His Son into the world to condemn the world, but that the world through Him might be saved"* (Jn. 3:16&17 NKJV).

---

1   Gen.3:13,16,17
2   Rom.5:8
3   Isa.55:8&9

Does it make sense to be still before the Lord? Who can take the time, even people in full-time ministry have so much to do, who can take time to be still before the Lord? The greater question is: Who can afford not to be still before the Lord? Jesus says, *"Come to me, all of you who are struggling and burdened, and I will give you rest"* (Mt. 11:28 CJB). Is the coming to Jesus a one-time deal at salvation or is it a continual coming to Him daily from our salvation onward? For no one can carry the load by himself, every day we need Jesus' help. Every day we need to continue to seek Him.

We have a refuge in God, does it not make sense to seek the one who protects us.[1] He looks for us to come to Him, He wants us to know His word and to come spend time with Him for a relationship. If all that we have comes from the Lord, if all the work (ministry) is Him doing it through us, then should we be so concerned in what we need for our lives and the work we are doing that we don't have time for Him who provides our needs and empowers us for the work? All that we need, spiritual and physical, He provides. We are called to follow, Jesus said, 'follow Me.' If we observe the actions of Jesus we see that He often went off to a secluded place to pray, sometimes early in the morning before He started His day.[2] He prayed to the Father, He spent time with the Father, He listened to the Father, He said He did only what the Father was doing.[3]

If Jesus while He was living here on earth as man needed to do this, how much more do we need to do it? Have you ever been in a conversation where you were the one doing all the talking, the other person couldn't get a word in? If not, maybe you were the one who could not get a word in. If when we go to prayer and do all the talking does God have an opportunity to get a word in. Some will say, 'God never speaks to me', yet they may never give God an opportunity. God is not always quick to speak, it may be He wants to see how much we want to hear Him speak, how willing we are to wait. Being still for us is hard, we have a busy life and a busy mind, it is hard to stop our bodies or our heads for very long. Yet waiting seems to be something the Lord expects from us.

The first time Moses went up on the mountain to receive the tablets of stone he had to wait; *"Then Moses went up on the mountain, and the cloud covered the mountain. The glory of the LORD settled on Mount Sinai, and the cloud covered it six days; and on the seventh day he called to Moses out of the midst of the cloud...And Moses entered the cloud, and went up on the mountain. And Moses was on the mountain forty days and forty nights"* (Ex. 24:15,16,18 RSV). Moses had to wait six days before God spoke to him. We have difficulty waiting in stillness before the Lord six minutes.

Yet it may be that very offering of silence on our part is what God is waiting for. Are we willing to wait, willing to know all things are under His control. The things we think need to be done which prevent us from being still, maybe those things we are trying to take over control rather than allowing God to be in control. The question would be, 'who is running the show?' If God is running the show maybe the first work He has for us to do is to be still before Him. If that is what He wants of us then the rest which needs done, which is under His control, will get done on time. Being before God will also help us in our difficulties. In our reading today in Isaiah chapter 37 we read, *"As soon as King Hezekiah heard it, he tore his clothes and covered himself with sackcloth and went into the house of the LORD"* (v. 1 ESV).

King Hezekiah had just heard that an enemy was coming against Israel. His first action was not work on his part, to assemble the army, but it was to be before the Lord. In reading the rest of the chapter you have seen what a great victory God brought, Hezekiah and his army didn't even have to fight. Could you use some of those kinds of victories in your life? Are you willing to go before God as Hezekiah did as your first move? God wants to do good things for us but sometimes we are just not willing, instead of the way God wants we try doing it the way we want. Read Isa. 55:8&9 again.

---

1   Ps.9:9, 46:1, 48:3, 59:16, 62:7, 94:22, 142:5
2   Mk.1:5, 6:46, Lk.5:16, 6:12, 9:18, 9:29
3   Jn.5:19

It is time to seek the Lord and His goodness. Do we ever take leave from this, of not seeking His goodness? He is always seeking to bless us, are we seeking it? We need to come to a knowing that the Lord is with us always. He is not only with us when we are in church. He is not only with us when we study His word. He is not only with us when we are in prayer.

The Lord is with us always, at all times. It is He who reaches out to us in the beginning bring us to the place we find salvation in Him. If the Lord is reaching, and keeps on reaching to us, until we find that salvation, why would He discontinue to be with us even for a moment afterwards? He is always with us, we should always know He is with us. Our dependency should always be on Him with knowing He is there with us any time we have a need. He is there during our day to help us find something we cannot, call out to Him, He will help. He is there when we are having difficulty in accomplishing something, call out to Him, He will help. If we are in the night with things of the night that cause us trouble, call out to Him, He will help. [1] The scriptures are filled with verses telling us He is right there with us. Jesus is with us, *"The one who keeps His commandments remains in Him, and He in him. We know by this that He remains in us, by the Spirit whom He has given us"* (1Jn. 3:24 NASB).

The Father is with us, *"If anyone loves me, he will keep my word, and my Father will love him, and we will come to him and make our home with him"* (Jn. 14:23 ESV). The Holy Spirit is with us, and in us, *"and the fellowship of the Holy Spirit be with you all."* (2Cor. 13:14 RSV). and *"But you are not in the flesh, you are in the Spirit, if in fact the Spirit of God dwells in you. Anyone who does not have the Spirit of Christ does not belong to him"* (Rom. 8:9 RSV). We are even told that God, Yahweh, is in us and we in Him, *"Whoever confesses that Jesus is the Son of God, God abides in him, and he in God"* (1Jn. 4:15 RSV). and *"I do not ask for these only, but also for those who will believe in me through their word, that they may all be one, just as you, Father, are in me, and I in you, that they also may be in us"* (Jn.17:20&21 ESV). With such an abundance of scripture we should surely know God is with us, always with us.

---

1   Heb.4:16

In our reading today I began with Joshua chapter 5 as any of you reading by the schedule of year 1 and 2 of the Old Testament. When I came to verse 10 and read these words: 'and kept the Passover', there was an instance of excitement in my Spirit, that which is separate from my flesh and is birthed in me from God. It amazes me the amount of times that the reading assignments in the schedule all fit together, this is one of those days.

Here are just a few of the scriptures I see: *"While the people of Israel were encamped in Gilgal they kept the passover on the fourteenth day of the month at evening in the plains of Jericho"* (Jos. 5:10 RSV). Now remember the value of the Passover. *"Comfort, comfort my people, says your God"* (Isa. 40:1 RSV). Do you realize the comfort is brought to us as we associate this with the act of Passover? *"Behold, the Lord Jehovah will come as a mighty one, and his arm will rule for him: Behold, his reward is with him, and his recompense before him"* (Isa. 40:10 ASV). Do you realize who this speaks of? *"Have you not known? Have you not heard? Has it not been told you from the beginning? Have you not understood from the foundations of the earth?"* (Isa. 40:21 RSV). Do you realize all that we have received has been planned from the foundation of the earth, from the very beginning of time? *"To whom then will you compare me, that I should be like him? says the Holy One. Lift up your eyes on high and see: who created these? He who brings out their host by number, calling them all by name; by the greatness of his might, and because he is strong in power not one is missing"* (Isa. 40:25&26 RSV). The great plan of Passover, can we question the One who has planned it, and done it? *"Hast thou not known? hast thou not heard? The everlasting God, Jehovah, the Creator of the ends of the earth, fainteth not, neither is weary; there is no searching of his understanding"* (Isa. 40:28 ASV). With the One who is unsearchable here is the hope we receive: *"He gives power to the faint, and to him who has no might he increases strength...but they who wait for the LORD shall renew their strength, they shall mount up with wings like eagles, they shall run and not be weary, they shall walk and not faint"* (Isa. 40:29&31 RSV). Now to the next book in our reading: *"Did I not tell you that if you would believe you would see the glory of God?..."Father, I thank thee that thou hast heard me. I knew that thou hearest me always, but I have said this on account of the people standing by, that they may believe that thou didst send me"* (Jn. 11:40-42 RSV). Here is the Passover Lamb of Heaven showing who He is. **"Lazarus, come forth"**

These words, the very words of God, the One who all the earth was created through, cuts through all of creation, even taking authority over death, bring he who had died back from death. *"So the chief priests and the Pharisees gathered the council, and said, "What are we to do? For this man performs many signs. If we let him go on thus, every one will believe in him, and the Romans will come and destroy both our holy place and our nation." But one of them, Caiaphas, who was high priest that year, said to them, "You know nothing at all; you do not understand that it is expedient for you that one man should die for the people, and that the whole nation should not perish." He did not say this of his own accord, but being high priest that year he prophesied that Jesus should die for the nation"* (Jn. 11:47-51 RSV).

Here even the high priest does not know of what he speaks. This is the very One who would be the Perfect Passover Lamb who would bring us all who receive Him protection from eternal death. *"Hallelujah; Salvation, and glory, and power, belong to our God"* (Rev. 19:1 ASV). Can we not also speak these words after all we have seen in the scriptures about the great Passover that God worked on our behalf? *"Hallelujah! For the Lord our God the Almighty reigns"* (Rev. 19:6 RSV). Does not a shout come from our hearts saying the same? *"Then I saw heaven opened, and behold, a white horse! He who sat upon it is called Faithful and True, and in righteousness he judges and makes war. His eyes are like a flame of fire, and on his head are many diadems; and he has a name inscribed which no one knows but himself. He is clad in a robe dipped in blood, and the name by which he is called is The Word of God...From his mouth issues a sharp sword with which to smite the nations, and he will rule them with a rod of iron; he will tread the wine press of the fury of the wrath of God the Almighty. On his robe and on his thigh he has a name inscribed, King of kings and Lord of lords"* (Rev. 19:11,12,13,15,16 RSV). This is the Mighty One who brings us the great Passover by His own blood that we can be saved.

'For Thou are my God. You are the One who keeps me safe. You are the One who leads me down the path to eternity. You are my God and I will follow as you lead.'

Do you ever pray this way? Do you speak to God giving Him credit for who He is and what He is doing in your life? We many times come to God with our supplications for our needs as a priority in our prayer not thinking about the greatest need we have He has already supplied, our salvation, life into eternity with Him. [1] If we were to start all our prayers consciously and consider the salvation He has given us we would start our prayers with praise. When the Israelites were saved from Pharaoh and his army when God drowned them in the Red Sea, Miriam and the other women sang a praise to God for saving them from their enemy. [2]

Our sin was as an enemy to us because it was what would keep us out of heaven. Jesus dying on the cross paid the penalty of our sins and now by accepting Him as Lord we are freed to enter heaven because our Name has been written in the Book of Life. Knowing that we didn't have to perform, didn't have to sweat, didn't have to work hard at following a rigid format of religion to get our names written in that book, it should give us reason to do what Miriam and the other women did at the Red Sea. You are the one to decide who you are going to praise, God or yourself. When we do not want to praise God isn't it our pride that prevents it. Our pride doesn't want God worshiped, it wants 'self' worshiped.

You may have never thought about it that way before, but what else is it then? Our pride constantly fights against the will of God in our lives. We are told to come as little children, [3] we are to pray in humility, [4] we are to be concerned about the welfare (spiritual & physical) of others before ourselves, [5] etc. None of these things in truth can co-exist with our pride. God says if we lift ourselves up He will put us back down, and if we come in lowness of heart He will lift us up. [6] Once we get pride out of the way, or even partially out of the way, we will find thanksgiving and praise for God will come easy as we realize all the great things God has done for us already with a confidence of the future. You are going to have a struggle if you have not already dealt with your pride. Even if you have the courage and audacity to kick it out of your life the devil will get his kicks in to try to keep it there. Persistence in this will win, the devil has no power over your life, he will try to brow beat you but he can't do any more than that.

The devil has lost the battle and he wants you to lose with him and tries to take you down. [7] Aren't you glad about the cross, aren't you glad Jesus has paid for your price you owed, aren't you glad you are headed for heaven? Thinking of all this should bring praise to your lips and thanksgiving to your heart. We can be glad that our names are written in the Lamb's Book of Life preventing us from being cast into the lake of fire, and because our names are written there we will be ushered into heaven. Many times I like to try and see the back side of a statement, the reverse of it.

This may be what the back side of Rev. 20:15 might look like; 'And anyone found written in the Book of Life was not cast into the lake of fire.' We whose names are written in the Lamb's Book of Life should rejoice with praise and thanksgiving. Think of these things the next time you go to prayer.

---

1   Rev.21:3
2   Ex.15:20&21
3   Mt.18:3, Lk.18:17
4   Rom.12:16, Lk.18:10-14, Jas.4:10, 1Pet.5:6
5   Jas.2:15&16, Gal.5:14
6   Lk.14:11
7   Rev.12:16&17

'In my time I will call all mankind to Me.' This is what God has done. He has called and even made the way. The only response of mankind, the individual person, is to accept the work that has been done by Christ that we of mankind may enter into that New Jerusalem that we read of in Revelation today. The biggest problem here that interferes is man's pride. It is always in the way of the things God has for us. The Garden of Eden was a most perfect place to live. It is spoken of today on talk shows of where is the most perfect place to live in the world, this was it. The climate was always perfect, the beautiful landscaping for taking a stroll in mid-afternoon, the best of all foods, the selection endless, the company wonderful – what a place! Yet there was one problem – pride. This is what the serpent appealed to in humanity, humanity's pride.

To be like God was the ploy that moved mankind into doing what God had told them not to do. We read today in Joshua of one man who ruined it for the whole nation of Israel causing them to be defeated in what seemed to have been an easy take. Pride to have what this man saw before him, he reached out and took, and the nation of Israel suffered. Is this any different than what happened in the Garden, pride to have what mankind saw before him, he reached out and took, and all of mankind suffered. God is stating His case against mankind in the chapter 41 of Isaiah we read today, v. 21-29 (ASV translation suggested).

In our reading in the gospel of John today Jesus cuts to the quick, slams pride of mankind down, and says to be someone you must move to the lowest position. Many have made a religious ritual of washing feet. Even in this there is a bit of pride lurking. This is not about washing another's feet, it is about being will to be in, to serve in, the lowest position of all. In the culture of the day the servant placed at the door to wash the feet of the guest coming in was one of the lowest positions of the servants, if not the very lowest position. Humility is what God calls for in us which is in opposition to pride, pride will ruin it all.

We read today of how great it will be in the New Jerusalem where all will be perfect again. We will be with our God and He will be with us. *"nothing unclean, and no one who practices abomination and lying, shall ever come into it"* (Rev. 21:27 NASB). There will be no place in it for pride, it will be perfect like the Garden started out to be, and God will be with His people and His people will be with Him.

What if all that is was not? In the beginning was God. *"And the earth was a formless and desolate emptiness, and darkness was over the surface of the deep"* (Gen. 1:2 NASB). God shaped and ordered the earth, and added the sun, the moon, and the stars. Without God's word speaking all things into existence, what would we have – not much. We wouldn't even have us. Do we make ourselves aware of this? When we are driving down the road to work in the morning do we realize that all we see God made? Take all that you see and imagine life without it, what would that life be like? Is God good, are not all His works marvelous?[1] Will He receive the credit due Him on this side of heaven?

In heaven His praise is sung,[2] but what about on earth? **'Peace on earth and good will towards man'**, isn't that what the angels said when Jesus was born? Do we remember that? As we drive down the road going to work in the morning, do we remember we have peace with God because of what Jesus did for us? We are to do a good job at work, we are told to do all we do as though doing it for the Lord.[3] But if in that process the awareness of what the Lord is to us becomes secondary what value has the good job we are doing? We have to be careful of the effect the world's values are having on us, we may end up getting our priorities backwards. The devil surely wants that to happen, he wants to devalue God in our lives any way he can. We are to walk by faith, there can be very little of it if we are not thinking upon God's goodness and greatness as we go through our day. Take away something we depend on every day and we are missing it quick, either complaining about it or praying God will bring it back for us. What about when we always have it – because of God's blessing? My comments are not a 'sit down, listen, and I will teach you' – they are to get you thinking about spiritual things, the stuff that is really important.

If you were to figure a ratio, a percentage of time we spend on the earth compared to what we will spend in heaven (remember that is eternal) what would the percentage spent on earth be? I assume you have figured it would be very, very small. So why do we put so much importance on our daily activities of life in this world which sometimes pushes any thought of God and eternity right out of our minds? I question myself as I question you. We too easily forget where all that we have, all that is around us, all that we enjoy, where all of it has come from. What if all that is was not?

We read today in Isaiah chapter 42; *"Thus says God the LORD, Who created the heavens and stretched them out, Who spread forth the earth and that which comes from it, Who gives breath to the people on it, And spirit to those who walk on it: "I, the LORD, have called You [Jesus] in righteousness, And will hold Your [Jesus] hand; I will keep You [Jesus] and give You [Jesus] as a covenant to the people, As a light to the Gentiles, To open blind eyes, To bring out prisoners from the prison, those who sit in darkness from the prison house"* (v. 5-7 NKJV). We also read, *"Then he showed me the river whose waters give life, sparkling like crystal, flowing out from the throne of God and of the Lamb. Through the middle of the broadway of the city; also, on either side of the river was the tree of life with its twelve varieties of fruit, yielding each month its fresh crop; and the leaves of the tree were for the healing and the restoration of the nations"* (Rev. 22:1&2 AMPC). And from yesterday's reading: *"he will wipe away every tear from their eyes, and death shall be no more, neither shall there be mourning nor crying nor pain any more, for the former things have passed away"* (Rev. 21:4 RSV). This we should carry in our hearts every moment of our day, it will cause us to believe and act differently.

---

1   Rom.1:19&20
2   Rev.4:9-11, 5:9-14, 11:15-17, 14:3, 15:3&4, 16:5&7, 19:1-7
3   Eph.6:5-7   applies to any servant or worker

To you it has been given to know the Lord, how is that relationship going? Part of it is automatic, when we are re-born there is a new birth that takes place in us which is spiritual.[1] The same as any newborn, we begin to grow, the Spirit grows within us.[2] In those early days after receiving salvation, we notice something different inside of our being. It will grow to a certain point on its own, that is the blessing of God working inside of us.

We are legitimate, what grows in us is of the same as the heavenly Father. We are not the same as Him, that would make us another god as He is. But what His makeup is, we now have some growing inside us, it's like having the same blood in our vanes as our earthly father has. A newborn babe grows as the parent gives it what it needs, we grow as our heavenly Father gives us what we need. As the child gets older the parent requires more and more of the child's own effort. The child has to learn to feed itself, it has to learn to walk, it has to learn to dress itself. With the spiritual birth it is the same way.

After a period of time our Heavenly Father requires us to take a certain responsibility of our spiritual well being. We have to learn to feed ourselves by reading God's word and by prayer. We have to learn how to apply what we read and hear from God to our daily walk in this world. We have to learn how to clothe ourselves with spiritual clothing and no longer dress like the world does. With all honesty examine at what stage you are; new born (yet), toddler, adolescent, teenager, or matured adult. Where did you find yourself when you looked honestly?

This should help you in your spiritual journey, and what direction to go next. We will never arrive at fully mature Christians while here on this earth but we can get close, it will be a constant growing process until we enter heaven. As we go along the Father will help us grow but we have to ask for the help. So many times when we think of the scripture: **'you receive not because you ask not'** applies to many things in our life, but never thought it could apply to help with our spiritual growth. Jesus made it clear in saying the Holy Spirit would teach us all things and cause us to remember what He Himself said.[3] I do believe that would be classified as help, do you ask the Holy Spirit to help you learn and grow spiritually? Some of you may balk at this, not believing we should pray to the Holy Spirit. Do we not serve and belong to a three in one God? Is He not God the Father, God the Son, and God the Holy Spirit? Is it okay and are we supposed to pray to God? What about the Holy Spirit, is He not part of the Godhead, the three in one God?

According to what Jesus said we should pray to the Holy Spirit for help in our spiritual growth. Any child, no matter what age after infancy, that does not feed itself well does not grow well. The same is true spiritually, any Christian that does not feed himself well does not grow well. As long as the child feeds his body well it grows as it is programmed to do. The same is true of our spiritual self, as long as we feed our spiritual being as we should God will cause it to grow in ways we know nothing about, it's how we are programmed. In our reading today in John chapter 15 we read this in v. 5: *"I am the vine and you are the branches"* (CJB). It is that ever flowing life that flows from the vine to the branches that causes growth.

As long as we are doing our part God will cause us to grow in ways we know not how. In v. 22-25 Jesus talks about those who will not believe Him. To receive what God has for us we have to surrender to what He says, believe who He is, and accept Him as Lord. The surrendering does not end at salvation, it continues through our Christian life, and the more of ourselves we surrender to Him the more He works in us doing things in us and through us.

---

1   Jn.3:6
2   Tit.3:5
3   Jn.14:26

'I am the God who knows who you are.' Is there anything hidden from God? He sees all, knows all, controls all. He set the universe in place, He established the Earth and all that is in it. We are of His making, making us even from the dust. Can we believe God when He says He knows us? There are many who try to hide from Him, but they are not able. We who are saved even sometimes think we can hide something from Him. All of our life is laid out before Him like a scroll. God knows our life from one end to the other. He tells us He even knows of us before we are in the womb. [1]

There is nothing in our lives He does not know. [2] Man has taken a course which has brought sin into the world. That sin is as an infection which affects all of life. [3] Many of the things which happen are a result of that infection. God does not always interfere with that course. For those of us who are saved, He does interfere, some a bit, and some much. We cannot, even dare not, to think wrongly of what He decides to do. We were under the wrath of God before we were saved, so what right do we have to think wrongly about something He does or does not do?

We were saved by His great mercy which removed the sentence of wrath from us. God does decide, but we are given the opportunity to alter what God does as He has given us access by prayer. *"Let us therefore draw near with boldness unto the throne of grace, that we may receive mercy, and may find grace to help us in time of need"* (Heb. 4:16 ASV). Our very base of this mercy and grace given us is asking for salvation which is provided and given by the blood of Christ. [4] From that base of salvation then we are invited as Children of God to go to Him with our needs. Today in our reading Jesus tells us this: *"Truly, truly, I say to you, whatever you ask of the Father in my name, he will give it to you"* (Jn. 16:23 ESV). Scripture also tells us He knows what we need before we ask it: *"your Father knows what you need before you ask him"* (Mt. 6:8 RSV).

God does know all about us, He knows what our need is, He calls us to come to Him in prayer and ask for it. If God already knows what our need is, why should we hesitate to ask? What is it He tells us: *"You do not have, because you do not ask"* (Jas. 4:2 RSV). We need to go to God in prayer knowing He will accept us because of the blood which Jesus gave for us. There is a great encouragement at the end of what Jesus is telling us about prayer in our reading today, *"On that day you will ask in My name, and I am not saying to you that I will request of the Father on your behalf; for the Father Himself loves you, because you have loved Me and have believed that I came forth from the Father"* (Jn. 16:26&27 NASB). Because we believe Jesus and love Him, and believe He has come from the Father, the Father loves us and waits for us to come to Him with our prayers.

---

1   Ps.139:16
2   2Chr.16:9, Isa.46:9&10
3   Rom.8:21
4   Mt.26:28

Make your time to find God, He is always looking toward you. In general God looks out toward all mankind offering them salvation through His Son.[1] In those of us who now believe and have received salvation God is looking out towards us to do us good. We now have become part of His family, God wants family. His desire for you is greater than your desire for Him, no matter how great your desire for Him may be. We get saved, we find God makes a great change in our lives when we have ask Jesus Christ to be Lord in our lives. Our gratitude is great towards God for what He has done for us. The years pass by and our gratitude turns into something we take for granted and we find we are not seeking God as we did in the past. God has not changed, He still is looking out towards us for good, but we may not be looking to Him for it as we did in the past. There is a great warning in Revelation about those who become lukewarm.[2]

I am not saying you are there, but it is for each of us to always be cautious of it. Sometimes we drift away from closeness to God by an intellectual pursuit of becoming a better Christian. God is Spirit and He wants relationship in Spirit.[3] It is good to study the word of God but what good does it do us if we don't have that spiritual relationship with God that the word we study tells us about?

We read today of the great gift of the promise land God gave Israel as they came into it. Yet the Law God gave to them in time became a hard thing of the intellect only and the relationship with their great God diminished. We hear much of what is written in Isaiah about when they came to the point to where God sent them off to Babylon in affliction. In the days of Christ the Law had become hardness in the hearts of the religious leaders again. God wants people in relationship with Him in Spirit. To find that relationship it takes us spending time with Him, sometimes even in silence in our prayer closet as we sit with Him.

This is where we find that special closeness to God. In our busy life we have to make time for this, there is no time when all the other things are finished. We may even have to set a priority putting God in first place and some on the other end of the priority list has to fall off and be given up. God went to a lot of work on His part to make a way we could come to Him, should we not make a little effort to go to Him? God is constantly reaching out to us. Are we reaching out to Him?

Today we hear how Jesus prays for us, "*I pray for them. I do not pray for the world but for those whom You have given Me, for they are Yours...Holy Father, keep through Your name those whom You have given Me, that they may be one as We are...But now I come to You, and these things I speak in the world, that they may have My joy fulfilled in themselves...Sanctify them by Your truth. Your word is truth...And for their sakes I sanctify Myself, that they also may be sanctified by the truth...And I have declared to them Your name, and will declare it, that the love with which You loved Me may be in them, and I in them*" (Jn. 17:9,11,13,17,19,26 NKJV). You might have the thought this prayer was for the apostles only. Jesus said this in His prayer, "*I do not pray for these alone, but also for those who will believe in Me through their word*" (v. 20).

We all who have come to believe by what the apostles taught are those who Jesus prayed for. It might be good to take a couple more minutes to read John chapter 17 again, maybe with altered eyes to see, ears to hear, and heart to receive.

---

1   1Tim.2:3-6
2   Rev.3:15-17
3   Jn.4:23&24

Why do we need more and more and more of God in our lives? We give Jesus Christ the throne of our lives when we get saved, but have we permitted Him to totally rule? Jesus surely has the capacity to completely rule in our lives, but then we would only be spiritual robots. God wants us to want Him. He waits passionately for us to come more and more to Him. His desire is that we will of our own free will want more and more of Him. Part of this process is us giving up more and more of ourselves to Him. This is hard work, getting saved is easy, but to give ourselves over fully and completely is hard work. We have to fight against our own pride which is very powerful. We have to take up the fight against our flesh for the flesh wars against the Spirit and the Spirit against the flesh. [1]

We surely want the Spirit to be winning, yet it is a great struggle. We have to continue strengthening the Spirit for it to win the battles. This is one reason we need more and more of God in our lives. We know of those times the flesh wins and we are not pleased with it. The only way for this to happen less and less is to strengthen the Spirit more and more. I have taken up for myself something that John the Baptist said, *"He must increase, but I must decrease"* (Jn. 3:30 ASV). I need more and more of Jesus in my life, but that means there has to be less and less of me. Are you working at there being less and less of you, and more and more of Jesus? This is not done by more and more study, it is done by more and more dying. Jesus died for us that we could receive salvation, now it is us who have to die more and more to receive all the great things Jesus has for us in addition to that salvation.

Jesus went through quite a struggle to bring this salvation to us. We don't think of Jesus ever having a struggle with the flesh, yet what was it He struggled with in the garden of Gethsemane? [2] He took up the battle against the flesh finally yielding to the will of the Father. What Jesus suffered after that even brought Him much pain. The pain of being rejected by His own people, the pain in the body of all that was done to Him leading up to Him being hung on the cross, the pain of carrying all the sins of the world, and finally the pain of being forsaken by the Father for that moment. Should we not, after all Jesus did for us try to give more and more of ourselves to God allowing Him to be involved more and more in our lives?

In our reading today in John we see the religious leaders in their very holy manner ask for the death of Christ, *"They did not enter the headquarters building because they didn't want to become ritually defiled and thus unable to eat the Pesach [Passover] meal...Pilate said to them, "You take him and judge him according to your own law."The Judeans [Jews] replied, "We don't have the legal power to put anyone to death"* (Jn. 18:28&31 CJB). Jumping ahead we will hear tomorrow, *"Away with him, away with him, crucify him!"* (Jn. 19:15 ASV). How many times in our religious vigor do we treat Christ as we should not? How many times is our religious vigor really about us rather than about Christ? In our lives Jesus must increase and we must decrease.

---

1   Gal.5:17
2   Mt.26:36-39, Lk.22:39-44

'I am content in Christ.' Can we all say that? Have we reached that place where we have full contentment in regard to Christ in our life? Apostle Paul got to the place he could say, " I have learned in whatever state I am, to be content:...I can do all things through Christ who strengthens me" (Philp. 4:11&13 NKJV). Christ intends for us to find that contentment. This only comes with faith as we move closer to God believing all things He says. We have to believe our sins are forgiven, fully forgiven. The thing of penitence for our sins only brings guilt rather than relief.

God prescribes how we are to receive forgiveness of our sins, it is only by repentance, then asking, and then receiving that forgiveness. There is nothing else that will provide more forgiveness. When God forgives it is complete, there is nothing else that will bring more. Sometimes we want to do more because we want to think we can do something that will show we deserve forgiveness. With God, it does not work that way. What we deserve is wrath, but Jesus gave His blood so we have a way to escape wrath and receive full forgiveness.

The only requirement God has is we repent asking forgiveness. There is nothing less that we can do than repent and nothing more we can do than repent. God offers this great gift of salvation to us who come to Him because of His great love, and His great work. Even though the cross of Jesus came about later in history it has been His intent since the beginning. In Isaiah, we are many times told of the salvation that was to come through Jesus Christ. In Isa. 51:4-8 we see God is speaking of Christ in speaking of the Light, Jesus told us He was the light. [1]

Salvation through Jesus was planned for a long time by God. It was not an idea that just popped into God's head and He decided to do it. Nothing surprises God, He knows all things. [2] He knows all things about each of us. If man could perform well enough to become holy then Jesus would have not had to die on the cross. The thing is it only takes one sin for a person to become unholy. The wisest man of all time was King Solomon, who God had given wisdom, said, *"there is not a righteous person on earth who always does good and does not ever sin"* (Ecc. 7:20 NASB). This forgiveness God has given us is complete, there is nothing we can do to deserve it more. And once we ask it is complete, we need to believe this.

It is in this belief that God forgives us that contentment comes. In John chapter 19 we read of Jesus' trial and crucifixion. In v. 30 Jesus says, **"It is finished."** If it is finished is there anything more we can do? If we fully understand this we can find contentment in it. There may be those of you who would say, 'but you don't know what I have done.' Was this thing you did worse than those who condemned Jesus, an innocent man, to die? Was it worse than the Roman soldiers who drove the nails through His flesh pinning Him to the wood? Hear what Jesus says about them and then decide if you can be forgiven, *"Father, forgive them; for they do not know what they are doing"* (Lk. 23:34 NASB).

---

1   Jn.8:12, 9:5
2   Isa.46:9&10, Jer.23:24, 2Pet.2:3

'In Me you have life, life more abundantly.'[1]*"I am the way, and the truth, and the life"* (Jn. 14:6 ASV). Is there anything we can have that is greater than what Jesus has provided us with? He is all our source for all that is truly necessary. There are many great people in our history, even those who helped humanity greatly, but even those without Jesus have no hope. Those who have benefited from them where only benefited in this life on earth. Jesus is the only One of whom we receive benefits, that those benefits will go from this life into the next. Those other great people could not provide to you anything for the next life. Jesus said, *"In My Father's house are many rooms; if that were not so, I would have told you, because I am going there to prepare a place for you. And if I go and prepare a place for you, I am coming again and will take you to Myself, so that where I am, there you also will be"* (Jn. 14:2&3 NASB). Is this not a great promise? Is there anything that Jesus said that is not true?

This is the great promise to us that we will be with Him where He is, we will be with Him for all of eternity. What a great promise, what a great hope we have in Christ. His love extends to us now where we are, and will extend to us into all eternity. He is our hope, He is our joy, it is Him who has given us life, true life, spiritual life.[2] No matter how difficult life for us gets on earth we have this great promise of eternal life. We are told of Heaven, that God who will be with us will be all we need. In heaven there will even be no need of the sun, the moon, or the stars because the glory of our God will illuminate all things.[3] There will be a light coming from the throne of God so that there will not be any darkness. Can we ask for more? Everything we have need of He will provide. Even though we may have some difficulties during our lives here on earth, they are short compared to what we will receive in heaven. As we draw closer to God these difficulties will become less, either by diminishing or we will find they are not as difficult as we thought. The greatest thing we can receive from God is our salvation, everything else after that are just perks. God has planned to bless us from a long time before.

In Isaiah chapter 53 God talks about His plan to send a savior, a redeemer, to make a way to bring us to Himself. *"But he was wounded for our transgressions, he was bruised for our iniquities; the chastisement of our peace was upon him; and with his stripes we are healed...He shall see of the travail of his soul, and shall be satisfied: by the knowledge of himself shall my righteous servant justify many; and he shall bear their iniquities"* (v. 5&11 ASV) There was no way for us to get to God through the Law so God the Father put our iniquities on God the Son and He died in our place to pay for our sins so there was a way we could come to God. *"Jehovah hath made bare his holy arm in the eyes of all the nations; and all the ends of the earth have seen the salvation of our God"* (Isa. 52:10 ASV). We have received a great salvation.

There may have been many in the past before Christ who died for someone else, but Christ is the only one that said after He died for us He would rise again. In John chapter 20 today we read of that again. Jesus did not leave it in question to His followers of if He rose or not. *"Now when it was evening on that day, the first day of the week, and when the doors were shut where the disciples were together due to fear of the Jews, Jesus came and stood in their midst, and said to them, "Peace be to you"* (v. 19 NASB). Jesus came into their midst presenting Himself to them so they knew He rose from the dead. Then He gave to them that new life which was gained by His suffering on the cross. *"And when he had said this, he breathed on them, and said to them, "Receive the Holy Spirit"* (v. 22 RSV).

Here is where Christ first gave life to us, a redeemed life, an eternal life. 'he breathed on them', in the beginning during the creation God breathed into Adam giving him life. Jesus breaths into our lifeless body, which is dead without Him, and gave us a new spiritual life we did not have before. Our life is sustained, is upheld, is given eternity, by what God has provided for us in Christ.

---

1   Jn.10:10
2   Jn.3:6, 3:5, 3:15
3   Rev.21:23, 22:5

There is rest in God, a rest we can't find anywhere else. There is a rest that only God can give which will reach the depth of our soul. He is the one who gives peace that goes beyond our understanding.[1] God can speak into our lives in places no one else can reach. Sometimes there are others who want to try to help us but we shun them away.

It is the same way with God, He wants to help us but sometimes we shun Him away for one reason or another. Because of His love He never gives up, always trying to reach us. We could have so much peace if we would seek Him and allow Him to work in our lives. God wants to shape us into one like Himself. It is not a physical shape He wants to work, it is a spiritual shape He wants to give us. This spiritual shape is what will go on into eternity where we will be with God forever. I am not speaking of the shape we will receive when we enter heaven, I am speaking of that shape God is wanting to work in us right now. It is that spiritual shape God wants to give our inner person, that part of us which is not flesh, that part which lives forever.

This is the place in us where we communicate with God in our quiet moments.[2] If it is not audible that we hear with our ears then this inner place is usually where we hear the voice of God, that still small voice. In that part of us is where we were born again or born anew. That is that place where we had an awareness that something was amiss, that something was not as it should be. The absence of God was that something that was amiss. Once we have God in our life that peace comes in and settles into place. That peace remains as we continue in a relationship with God. It is something given to us that if it comes to us at salvation and then we allow our relationship with God to slip the peace will begin to diminish.

Our rest and hope is with God. Our peace is with God. If our rest and hope and peace are with God then it seems we need to stay close to Him to maintain them in our lives. In John chapter 20 yesterday we heard Jesus asking Mary, *"Woman, why are you weeping?"* (v. 15 RSV). Are there times we are weeping, maybe not on the outside, but we are weeping on the inside? What is it Jesus tells Mary? *"I ascend unto my Father and your Father, and my God and your God"* (v. 17 ASV). In this statement Jesus assures her of her heavenly Father and her heavenly God. Here they were, all the disciples traumatized by the death of the One who had become so precious to them. He was gone, the authorities had crucified Him. He was dead and laid in the tomb. Jesus had told them many times He would rise from the dead but it was not until after He was resurrected that many remembered. Here Jesus reassures Mary all is well, I go to your Father and my Father, your God and my God. We in our weeping need to know that God is our God and that Father is our Father.

This is where we find that rest and that peace, it is that we know we are His. The first time that Jesus appears to the disciples where they were assembled His first words to them is, *"Peace be to you"* (v. 19 NASB). Jesus does not want you to have trauma inside, He wants you to have peace, a peace that comes to us from the Father through Jesus to us. In Luke, we are told the Lord will guide our feet into the way of peace.[3] In chapter 2 of Luke the angel appears and says, *"And on earth peace, goodwill toward men"* (v. 14 NKJV). Here is that peace between God and man announced. God sent it to us through Jesus. Jesus comes and gives it to His followers which we are. Hear His words, **"Peace be with you."** and maintain a relationship with Him. In John chapter 21 today in our reading Jesus asks Peter three times if Peter loved Him. Is this also not His question to us? One of the last things Jesus says to Peter is, **"Follow Me."** This is also what Jesus would say to us. This is where that rest and peace are found, following Jesus and staying close to Him.

---

1   Philp.4:7
2   Mt.6:6
3   Lk.1:76&79

'God is Love.' Do we really believe this? Does it permeate our life? Are we settled in it, or at times are we adrift? It is important for us to face such questions. If we do not face them we cannot come to the answer which will bring us closer to God. He is our hope, He is our life, He is our eternal security. There is one in this earth who would want to deceive us, to keep us away from such questions and keep us adrift. We must anchor ourselves into Christ for He is the sure Rock which will never fail us. When a ship or barge is moored by an anchor, those in charge on a regular basis check the mooring to make sure it is secure. We in our spiritual lives should do the same thing. God in His love is always reaching out to us, are we reaching out to Him on a regular basis check the mooring, to make sure it is secure?

If we respond to God He will always respond to us.[1] The very first way God reached out to us was through the cross and Him who was put on it. God reached out to us through His Son whom He sacrificed in our place to pay for our sins which we could not do. I have a little saying, '**Jesus took me out of a place I could not get out of, and took me into a place I could not get into.**' In God's love God has provided for us what we could not provide for ourselves, what a great God. We will not find security anywhere else, we will not find this fullness of love anywhere else. At times this earth and the world we live in may seem very sure to us, but what is sure is eternity. All will go there, for us who have God in our lives will be able to spend that eternity with Him.

This life is but a brief blur passing by and then we are in eternity, in one place or the other, there is nothing between these two. It is important for us to stay anchored to God, there are always strong winds and storms that come at us.

We need to check our mooring, we need to know we are secured to Him. God will always be there when we reach out, at the moment we are in the storm it may not seem like it, but after the storm is over we can look back and see how He held us in place. In a very miraculous way we see how God reached out to help us in the first chapter of Matthew, *"Now the birth of Jesus Christ took place in this way. When his mother Mary had been betrothed to Joseph, before they came together she was found to be with child of the Holy Spirit"* (v. 18 RSV). In Luke it tells us what the angel said to Mary, *"And behold, you will conceive in your womb and bring forth a Son, and shall call His name JESUS...Then Mary said to the angel, "How can this be, since I do not know a man?" And the angel answered and said to her, "The Holy Spirit will come upon you, and the power of the Highest will overshadow you; therefore, also, that Holy One who is to be born will be called the Son of God"* (Lk. 1:31&35 NKJV).

The very first step in what God would do in His love to reach out to us to provide us with salvation is truly miraculous. The great thing about God is that in many years before He had told us He would do these things, *"behold, a virgin shall conceive, and bear a son, and shall call his name Immanuel"* (Isa. 7:14 ASV). God's reaching out to us was even many years before Jesus Christ died on the cross for us. He is a God with a depth of love that we find nowhere else. Look how long God has been reaching out to you, are you reaching out to Him?

---

1   Jas.4:8

Does God say, **"My ways are not your ways"**? We know that He does, so where does that put us? We know from Paul's writings the flesh is what takes us in ways which are not God's ways.[1] Jesus came to die for us, this was part of God's way. Part of God's ways are giving and loving, even if sometimes it causes pain. It was not easy for Jesus to go to the cross.[2] Sometimes we get it in our head that the Jewish authorities came after Him turning Him over to the Romans and Jesus had no choice. This is not true, what is it Jesus says to Pilate? *"You would have no authority over me at all unless it had been given you from above"* (Jn. 19:11 ESV). This was part of the Father's purpose.

Jesus said to Peter (and the rest), *"Do you think that I cannot appeal to my Father, and he will at once send me more than twelve legions of angels?"* (Mt. 26:53 RSV). This was right after Jesus had come from prayer in the garden of Gethsemane where He had yielded to the will of the Father.[3] Part of this will of the Father was that Jesus would become a sacrifice given for all mankind.[4] There is another thing which happened that shows us the great power that Jesus had, *"Now when He said to them, "I am He," they drew back and fell to the ground"* (Jn. 18:6 NKJV). In many of our English translations of this verse they make Jesus say, 'I am he'. The 'he' has been added, here is a more accurate translation, *"When he said, "I AM," they went backward from him and fell to the ground"* (CJB).

Did you ever wonder why they drew back and fell to the ground? Where those who came to arrest Jesus bowing to worship Him before arresting Him, I think not. There is something in the Old Testament which will give us a hint. *"It happened that when the priests came from the holy place, the cloud filled the house of the LORD, so that the priests could not stand to ministering because of the cloud; for the glory of the LORD filled the house of the LORD"* (1Kg. 8:10&11 NASB). In Chronicles it speaks of the same event, *"the house of the LORD, was filled with a cloud, so that the priests could not stand to ministering because of the cloud; for the glory of the LORD filled the house of God"* (2Chr. 5:13&14 NASB).

Because of the glory (the cloud) of God the priest could not stand. Could that mean the presence of God was so great they could not get off the ground? Is there possibly times when the presence of God is so strong that man has no power to stand and falls to the ground. Jesus asked those who came to arrest Him, **"who are you seeking."** They said they wanted Jesus of Nazareth. As soon as Jesus said **"I AM"** the force of that statement drove them back and knocked them to the ground. If one does a comparison study they will see this is the same statement which God at the burning bush said to Moses of who He is.

A great evidence that the Father was orchestrating the crucifixion and death of Jesus is that these did not get up from the ground and run away. They got up and arrested Jesus who had just knocked them to the ground by His power and they took Him away to be crucified. So many times before this there were those who wanted to do away with Christ, but as Jesus said at times, 'it is **not My time yet'**.

We read of this in Matthew chapter 2 today. Herod tried to kill the child Jesus who was said to become King, but it was not his time yet. He was swept away in the night as Joseph was instructed by an angel to take Him quickly to Egypt. God had Jesus' course laid out from birth to resurrection and nothing could interfere. This was God's way, our way would have not brought the Hero to die on a cross. So knowing God's ways is not our ways what should we do? Yield.

---

1   Rom.7:18, 8:1, 8:8, Gal.5:19
2   Lk.12:50, 22:28
3   Lk.22:42
4   Eph.5:2, Heb.9:26, 10:8-12

In today's reading we read of God's favor, of God's grace. Even though the Jews did not follow the covenant He gave through Moses disobeying His commandments (Jdg. 2:2) God still had mercy on them: *"Whenever the LORD raised up judges for them, the LORD was with the judge, and he saved them from the hand of their enemies all the days of the judge; for the LORD was moved to pity by their groaning because of those who afflicted and oppressed them"* (Jdg. 2:18 RSV).

Many times we do not deserve the blessings of the Lord, yet He gives them. Isaiah chapter 60 is full of promises of God showing His mercy, His grace, and His blessings. In Matthew chapter 3 God begins the ministry of Jesus on earth to bring salvation to men, not from their own works, but the works of the Father and the Son. God spoke to them (and us): *"This is my beloved Son, in whom I am well pleased"* (v. 17 ASV).

In Acts chapter 3 a man is healed by the mercy, grace, and blessings of God which came through the power of the name of Jesus and the faith of those who follow Him. God's mercy, and grace, and blessings are all around us, if we are willing to see them. Our salvation alone is the greatest mercy and grace to us that we will ever know. Then the years following our salvation there are blessings upon blessings and grace upon grace: *"And from his fulness have we all received, grace upon grace"* (Jn. 1:16 RSV). How many times can we even look back at the years before our salvation and see those things which God was doing to kept us safe.

His mercy, His grace, His blessings all flow out from His throne to give good to our lives. Sometimes they breeze right on by blessing us and we don't even notice them because we are not spiritually attentive to them. We are to be aware, we are to perceive by our Spirit the great things God is doing all around us every day. There is a story of a minister who needed to go to a very important meeting and on the way got a flat tire. He wondered where the blessing of God was since now he was going to be late for the meeting. Finally he was able to continue and as he went on he came to a fatal auto accident. As he considered this accident he realized that if he had been on time not having the flat tire he would have been right in the middle of this accident, maybe even losing his life.

Sometimes we don't see what is coming and wonder where God's blessings are. We need to reach out to God, seek a relationship with Him so we may receive His blessing and not miss noticing any of them. God has always reached out to mankind with mercy, grace, and blessings. He gives us salvation which we do not deserve by His own works of Jesus on the cross, the sacrifice made for us, that all who would receive Jesus Christ would be forgiven. This is the first of God's mercy to us, highly valuable, but certainly not the last. God blesses us in many ways, we just need the spiritual eyes to see them.

'Today is the first day of the rest of my life.' This is a phrase many times spoken. Of all the days that are remaining of my life, today is the first day of them. This then means when tomorrow arrives tomorrow it will be the first day of those days that remain in my life. It seems that the most important day in our lives is today and what we do in it. In the Book of Judges we see the people not choosing well in the day they had. They could have chosen each day they had to follow the commandments of God given to their fathers through Moses, but they did not.

Time after time they went another way, going after foreign gods, those idols of other nations. Because of this God turned them over to the foreign nations and at some point they realized what they had done crying out to God. God sent Judge after Judge to rescue them, yet time after time they went astray. We cannot say much better of ourselves. Most of the world does not even look for Jehovah God, some not even looking for any god. Many go after foreign gods, which the Bible calls idols, and we are told idols are only demons. [1]

The deceiver is still deceiving those who will listen to him. In our reading today in Matthew chapter 4 Jesus was taken by the Spirit into the wilderness for forty days and at the end the great deceiver came with lies to try to deceive Jesus. The words the deceiver said may have been scripture, but the meanings he gave them were lies. Jesus confronted every lie with truth. Jesus said the truth shall make us free. [2] The truth is what freed Jesus of the devil's deception, and truth is what will free us of the deception which is in the world. The deception today which is presented as truth from an idol who is a demon trying to change the meaning of what truth is, is the same as the devil tried to do with Jesus in the wilderness. We need to know the truth so that we may not be deceived. So much of the time what we hear from the world and foreign gods sounds so right, but we need to be in the word of God to know what truth is, therefore knowing what truth is not. The deceiver is always at work trying to deceive all he can. Even with Jesus we are told after the encounter in the wilderness the deceiver looked for another opportune time. [3]

The devil is always after us, trying to take us away from the truth. We saw in Acts today how those who did not have the truth, those leading the Jewish people at that time, were confronted with the truth by a great miracle healing of a man over 40 years old. Still, even seeming to know it was revealing the truth that Jesus is the Son of God, they would not yield to God and tried to keep others away from God by telling the apostles they were not to speak or teach in this name any more.

There are still many today who say not to speak or teach in this name any longer. But truth will stand into eternity with those who will hear it and follow it being taken into the eternity of heaven being with God forever. We need to hear truth, act according to truth allowing truth to work in us. We have something the Jews in Judges did not have, we the redeemed have the Spirit of truth working in us which provides the renewing of our minds to know the things of God. [4] We need to be in the truth of God which is His word, and the truth of God needs to get into us.

Exposure to the Word is the only thing that will cause this to happen, and as we expose ourselves to the word the Spirit plants the truth in us. If it was not for the work of the Father and Jesus on the cross which provides salvation for us by Christ's blood giving something we have not earned, yet freely given, we would be in the same condition of the Jews spoke of in Judges. No longer do we have to work for a relationship with God as the Jews did before the cross. Now the work has been done by God, we only need to humble ourselves to receive the free gift of salvation from God who offers it to us, taking advantage of all He offers. Yes, truly, truth will set us free. We need God's word, we need His truth, we need the freedom from the great deceiver and truth is the only thing that will free us from the deception.

---

1   Duet.32:16&17, 1Cor.10:19&20
2   Jn.8:32
3   Lk.4:13
4   Tit.3:5

'Wait' Is this something we are willing to do? Is it something easy for us to do? We live in a fast-paced society all in a hurry with smartphone that give instant access to what we are looking for. Yet when we are looking for God, even though He is always with us He does not respond to our request the same as our smartphone does. Many times God says **"wait**, or **search**, or **seek."** We find Him many times in the quiet place, the still place, where we are settled to hear His voice. God is in control of the universe, why do we act as though it depends on us? God is the One who is supposed to lead us, why do we sometimes act as though we are leading Him? He knows best for us, we really don't. We should look to Him to set the day and know that He has our tomorrow in His hand. Nothing will happen that He does not know about.

God is always watching out for us, it is just that what we see as important He may not and does not act in it. It is just that it takes a while for us to get our heads turned around to truly see what is important. God is always moving in what He knows is important for us and it takes a bit of time for us to learn this. One thing He may do quickly, instantly, for that is the true need at the moment. Other times of something we think is very important He seems to move very slowly on. To Him just yesterday He created the universe. The one thing Jesus called us to is to follow. But even before this we have to deny self completely. [1]

Have you accomplished this yet in your Life. Is Jesus really Lord of your life, or are you still running things? The next is we are told to pick up our cross. What does this mean? What was Jesus doing when He picked up His cross? He was serving others, helping others where they needed help. What did Jesus tell the disciples when He was with them? *"the Son of man came not to be served but to serve, and to give his life as a ransom for many"*(Mt. 20:28 RSV). These two things of denying self and picking up our cross we have to accomplish before we can even follow. To come close to God this is part of the process. We are saved, yes, but have we become the servant?

Jesus says an interesting thing about the servant: *"And which of you, having a servant plowing or tending sheep, will say to him when he has come in from the field, 'Come at once and sit down to eat'? But will he not rather say to him, 'Prepare something for my supper, and gird yourself and serve me till I have eaten and drunk, and afterward you will eat and drink'? Does he thank that servant because he did the things that were commanded him? I think not. So likewise you, when you have done all those things which you are commanded, say, 'We are unprofitable servants. We have done what was our duty to do"* (Lk. 17:7-10 NKJV). Do you ever feel God owes you anything? A true servant knows it is his duty to do as his Master calls him to do.

We should be willing to serve without expecting anything, it is our service to our Lord. Jesus begins in Matthew chapter 5 the sermon on the mound today in our reading. I'm not so sure His teaching here is about us learning how to behave. I think Jesus was trying to show the Jewish people they could not behave. By the way of the Law some of them might even have thought if they perform the Law then God was obligated to reward them. Jesus was trying to show them they could not accomplish.

This would have to be done for them to realize they did need the mercy and grace He was preparing to bring them by the way of the cross. The one advantage they had over us is they understood the service of what the sacrifice does for us. That heavenly Lamb became the sacrifice [2] of God that would provide forgiveness for any person who would come to receive it. We are an undeserving servant who has been saved by the blood of the Lamb of God. We have no right to think God should respond to us quickly. We have received so much already.

---

1   Mt.16:24
2   Eph.5:2, Heb.9:21-26

'I am coming soon.' What does that mean to us, what does it say to us? We are the ones waiting, looking forward to Christ's return. He gave us light, He showed us what was real, He gave us a way to live forever. Sometimes we don't like to wait. Jesus said He would return, *"I come again, and will receive you unto myself"* (Jn. 14:3 ASV). How many have given up hope? How many will not believe since it has been so many years they believe it is not true? Yet what is truth except the word of God?

Our faith must stand, we must believe what God has said to us. All of us who are saved have had at least one time they know God touched their life in a way that it could have been no one else. That time is a verification that God is real, His word is real, and His promises are true. Part of our faith is built on remembering those times God brought about great works in our life. Remembering the activity of God working in our past gives us a confidence of Him in our future. Those times in the past are anchor points which gives strength to our faith for the future. The very way our life changed after we received salvation verifies that God is real. If Jesus said He will return for us to take us to heaven to be with Him then we can know it is true. God exists in a place where there is not time so to speak of how many years it has been since Jesus left, it only has value to us, He doesn't notice. If we fully give ourselves to Him it doesn't matter how many years it has been, it is that it will be.

God spoke and the stars came into being, how could we think that he has lost awareness of His returning? His return will be exactly right, it will be on the right day and exactly the right hour. There is no mystery to God, He knows how all things will be. It is not God that we need to look at in this, it is us. Let's make our faith stronger. We make it stronger by spending more time with Him. You may say there is little time in your schedule for this, then maybe the priorities in your schedule have to change moving God up, to spend more time with Him even if something on the bottom has to be let go.

Another thing that will help your faith to grow is reading His word more, this is not an intellectual thing, it is a spiritual thing that happens. We are not exposing ourselves to dry printed words on the page, God's words are living, and moving, and active. They come into our lives, they move our heart, they nourish our Spirit. This builds faith and the interesting thing is that the more our faith is built up the more we want to do these things. How much will it increase our faith just by hearing this short phrase, *"greater is he that is in you than he that is in the world"* (1Jn. 4:4 ASV). But if you are not getting into the word of God you won't hear it.

I have had people tell me that they have read the Bible and remember what is there. They may be able to remember more than I can, but God knows more than they do. God reveals His truth to us in a manner that will strengthen our lives, He reveals more and more each time we read it. God has things hidden from us until He is ready to reveal it, He will always have more for us each time we go to His word. He is faithful and true, He will do what He says. Jesus will come and take us to be with Him. The books of the prophets are full of His words. As we read in the New Testament we begin to know what was being said by the prophets so many years ago. One part of God's word supports another, confirming the truth of the word. Jesus today in our reading in Matthew speaks about us having faith. He tells us to believe in saying this, *"Isn't life more than food and the body more than clothing?"* (6:25 CJB).

There is more to life than those things we see, there is spiritual life that is everlasting. Jesus is telling us here not to be so concerned about what is temporary. Food and clothing are only for our body which will one day die, but we will live on with God. Jesus is trying to get us to see that which has more value to us comes by faith. We have to have faith, and we must wait. Jesus speaks to this, *"Therefore do not be anxious about tomorrow, for tomorrow will be anxious for itself. Let the day's own trouble be sufficient for the day"* (6:34 RSV).

'He who is with Me is for Me.' Do you remember Jesus saying this? Some things we know by how Jesus declares the opposite, *"He that is not with me is against me"* (Mt. 12:30 & Lk. 11:23 ASV). If this is true then 'He who is with Me is for Me' is also true. There is so much more to God's word than just what is printed on the page. Here there is one thing printed on the page, but by it we know of two things that are true. As we read through the word of God and trust the Holy Spirit to help us learn[1] of these words He begins to show us things that are deeper than what we saw at first.[2]

God is so wise in His doings that some of what He has written has several different truths within it. The other thing about God's word is that it is alive and active.[3] What is printed on the page is just showing us what that living word which cannot be printed on a page is. If we are willing and wanting, God will show us something new every time we open His word, even if it is verses we have read before and thought we knew. God's word, how can we put a value on it? I am not speaking of the printed word, the Bible. I am speaking of the word in the beginning that launched forth from the mouth of God.

What great things have come about, what great truth we have heard from heaven, what great comfort and liberty has been brought to us by those words? These words are the very heart of God reaching to the hearts of His people. If you question how those words could be alive, have you ever been reading a verse and something great and deep touched your heart? Was it not those alive words of God that moved on you? Another thing about the word of God is that living it has authority throughout all creation, throughout the whole universe. *"by the word of God the heavens were of old,...the heavens and the earth which are now preserved by the same word"* (2Pet. 3:5&7 NKJV).

God's word, it is not what some men have written down on the page, these are God's very words put into the hearts of men who the best they could wrote them on the page.[4] Does God give word for word? Sometimes I believe He does, but also it is at times thought by thought given to man's heart. I have times when I hear the very words that God speaks to me about something. Then there are other times very strange, God gives a knowledge about something that I know fully what has been given me, yet I am the one who has to give words to it, for it came without words.

It will not override any of the recorded words of God with what I have heard within, if it disagrees in any way then it was not from the Spirit of God and I give it no value. God wants to communicate with us, He wants us to hear Him speak to us. Sometimes this is by His printed word, and sometimes directly to our heart. God has wanted to have fellowship with mankind since the beginning, *"they heard the sound of the LORD God walking in the garden in the cool of the day...the LORD God called to the man, and said to him, "Where are you?"* (Gen. 3:8&9 RSV). God wants us to come to Him, to talk to Him, to have conversation with Him.

In our reading in chapter 7 of Matthew today Jesus finishes up His sermon on the mount. *"Ask, and it will be given you; seek, and you will find; knock, and it will be opened to you. For every one who asks receives, and he who seeks finds, and to him who knocks it will be opened"* (v. 7&8 RSV). When your children come to you to ask you for something do you not want them to spend some time with you, more than what it takes to ask for what they want? Would God be different? We are to come, we are to ask, but we are also to visit, we are to have fellowship. Take some time with God, let Him speak His word to you that you might see something you have not seen before.

---

1 Jn.14:26
2 Dan.2:20-22
3 Heb.4:12
4 2Tim.3:16

'I am here, are you hearing Me?' I am sure God is saying this to me many times when I am not hearing Him. I wonder if we give as much attention to hearing God as we should. There is a busy world buzzing all around us taking our attention. It may even be that in the days of Christ it was the same. Maybe not the rush that we have today, but because it took much longer to do anything in those days there was always more to get done.

Busy, busy, busy, and God has trouble even getting a word in edgewise sometimes. We have to take time out to hear what God is saying, or maybe get to that place we can have one ear turned towards heaven all through our day. Hearing God is important, it is more important than anything else we are doing. In our busyness we forget how important it is. We are off to work to earn our livelihood, if we don't work we don't eat – or any of the rest that has to do with life. Yes these things have to happen for our life here to be. The question we have to ask ourselves is, 'where are we going to live the longest?' For me I am going to live the longest in heaven, the life I live here is short.

This does not mean I should not give it my attention, even if it is short compared to heaven I still have to give it my attention while I am here. The things here are important, but the words of God are eternal. How many times while you are working are you having a conversation with your coworker?

With God it is even easier because God can hear your inside thoughts and respond speaking to you inside in that still small voice. We are a creatures of habit, if we would practice speaking to God in our day it will eventually be our habit. What a great thing during our day to ask God's help in something, or thank Him for something that just happened, or to speak to Him about something on our heart. Over the years I have had a confidence that God was listening and when I lost my screwdriver, or didn't remember where I laid my hammer I asked God and many times the very next place my eyes went, there it was.

If your father and you were working together during the day would the day go by without talking to him or hearing what he said? With our heavenly Father it is the same way. He wants to have a conversation with us telling us about great things, both of the future, and even of the moment we are in. In Judges chapter 6 we read of Gideon. Gideon heard God's words and responded. There is an interesting thing in our reading in Matthew today. Jesus is speaking and teaching Israel, and a foreigner comes, seemingly having heard (or heard of) Jesus and was willing to believe what Jesus could do.

This man came believing Jesus could help him with his need. If we believe Jesus can help us with our need should we not be speaking to Him more, and listening for His response? God will not do anything outside of His will, but if it is within His will He hears you. God wants a relationship with us, that won't happen when we pray or listen only once in a while. A relationship happens when there is much time spent together. The same as you would listen and talk with your earthly father as you spent a day with him, listen and speak to Your heavenly Father as you go through your day today with Him.

Where is it you are going? Do you know? God calls all of us to Him, He has the help we need. Do you go to Him for it? We are busy in this world, do we have our eyes on that world that will be eternal? When we come to the realness of the world eternal and see it is our goal it changes us.[1] The eternal of heaven with God begins to become brighter in our sight and this world dimmer.

God wants us to come to Him, closer and closer. Jesus spent three years trying to get this across to us. Jesus sent those after Him who would write of Him and God. God is a loving God, He wants things for us that are even greater than we could imagine. Everything else after our salvation will be less than our salvation no matter how great they seem. Giving us salvation who are unworthy is the greatest act of all eternity. There are great things in eternity, but none compares to the actions God took within Himself to provide redemption for undeserving people. We have received a great gift, something none of us can pay for in any way. As the reality of the greatness of our salvation settles in on us we will move closer and closer to God.

Our gratitude and our worship will increase. We will desire to spend more time with Him and in His word. God is love, there is no greater definition of love. The world likes to think they know what love is, even trying to say that the worldly type of love they have, that it is good. How wrong they are. Love has been before the beginning and will go far beyond the end. Eternity is filled with love, it is filled with God, who is love.[2] We can think of God in all the greatness He is and we cannot separate any of it from His love.

It was in creation; even of God, once He created man, said it is not good for man to be alone giving him woman.[3] Love is what brings about the end and all who come to Him being taken into heaven to be with Him forever. We can see in our reading of Matthew chapter 6 of Jesus giving His love over, and over, and over. First, we read of Him giving in love healing a paralytic brought by four men who were convinced Jesus would heal him. Next we see Jesus call Matthew the tax collector who no Jew had anything good to say about such men, Jesus calls this tax collector to follow Him, Jesus was even willing to step into such a man's house and eat with him. Jesus says He has come to help those who are sick in sin.

Next, He tries to help them to step into the new He is bringing them saying the new He is bringing cannot be put into the old. Then in His love He blesses a woman who came to Him for healing, only touching the hem of His garment she is healed. Knowing that power went out from Him he asks who it was and then sends this woman on her way in peace. Just before the woman was healed a synagogue ruler asked Jesus to come to his daughter who had just died to bring her back to life.

Jesus goes to the man's house, and to his daughter. Jesus says to her, child arise, and her spirit returns and the girl gets up. The love of Jesus continues as next He heals two blind men. Next a demon possessed man who is mute is brought to Him, Jesus casts out the demon and the mute man speaks. Then His love continues on and we are told, *"And Jesus went about all the cities and the villages, teaching in their synagogues, and preaching the gospel of the kingdom, and healing all manner of disease and all manner of sickness. But when he saw the multitudes, he was moved with compassion for them, because they were distressed and scattered, as sheep not having a shepherd"* (Mt. 9:35&36 ASV). Jesus is that love of God, who was sent to us, to die for us that the greatest gift of all, that gift of salvation, that by it we may be with God for eternity.

---

1   Jn.3:15, 12:25
2   Jn.14:23, 15:9, 15:13, Rom.5:5-8, Eph.2:4, 3:19, 1Jn.3:1, 3:16, 4:9&10, 4:16, Jude1:21
3   Gen.2:18

You are kind, and lovely, and good. How many times do you speak this to the Lord? Even if it is only the thought that comes out from your heart He will hear it. Do we really comprehend what He has given us? I know I don't fully comprehend the blessings He has toward me. There is always more than that which I will know of. He never runs out, He is never found short. Do we ever know the greatness of what our God is to us? I am convinced when I get to heaven I will know, but as long as I am in this tent of flesh I will be short to understand. When we start to know how great God is, certain things in this life begin to become less important.

He is my all in all, He is my substance and need, He is my secure foundation, He is creator and the One who cares for me. He has all that I need and all that I have is His. Some have said He is even more important than the air we breathe. Is that how important He is to you? I think that one of the greatest things we need to grow in our spiritual life is desire, that desire deep in our hearts for more of Him. We must have it, and get to the place we say as John the Baptist, *"He must increase, but I must decrease"* (Jn. 3:30 ASV). The more that Christ is in our lives the greater the victories we will have. Can you imagine the great desire of Cornelius we read of in Acts chapter 10 today.

Here is a man who is an outsider. There is no indication he is a proselyte. Even more, he is one of the occupying Roman army. Yet his desire was great and his devotion to God was great. God sends an angel to speak to him, and instructs Peter to go to him with no prejudice. Can we say we have even one tenth of the desire Cornelius had? There may be some who do, but I am not sure I am there. Desire for God, desire to serve God, desire to worship God, these are great desires we need to stir within ourselves, within our hearts, and in our souls.

As we grow spiritually we find in our hearts that the things about us or for us become less in our relationship to God, and things about Him and for Him have become greater. He is our true parent, John the apostle tells us we have become children of God, *"But to all who did receive him, who believed in his name, he gave the right to become children of God, who were born, not of blood nor of the will of the flesh nor of the will of man, but of God"* (Jn. 1:12&13 ESV).

I think of the little girl who thinks her daddy is the greatest of all, and can do anything. We have to become like that little child, we must think that our heavenly Daddy is the greatest of all, and can do anything. Are you finding yourself closer to God? Can you say, **'You are kind, and lovely, and good?'**

"I am the way, and the truth, and the life; no one comes to the Father, but by me" (Jn. 14:6 RSV). The world does not want to hear this. They want to go another way. Some don't believe there is any god and they make themselves a god to themselves. Whether we believe or not believe it makes no difference, God does not just exist just because I believe He does. He exists and I am left to believe He does or does not. God has reached out to us and we have responded by believing Him and accepting Jesus Christ into our lives. We try our best to follow Jesus which He has called us to do. We read His word, and we pray. But there is a deeper place to be, that is to be of the Spirit.

The Spirit of God is born into us at salvation, this is the rebirth or the new birth. Jesus told Nicodemus this, *"Truly, truly, I say to you, unless one is born of water and the Spirit, he cannot enter the kingdom of God. That which is born of the flesh is flesh, and that which is born of the Spirit is spirit"* (Jn. 3:5&6 RSV). To live we need to be born of the flesh, all the world has life this way. But Jesus said if we want to get to the Kingdom of God we must also be born of the Spirit.

In the flesh, that of our own actions and intellect, we can in a certain way do the things amongst men which Jesus said to do. But we need to have working that new part we are given by God in addition to that what we already had, we need to have the Spirit which we now also have born in us working. It is easy to say to ourselves we are going to go do this for God and head out to accomplish it. We need to trust the Holy Spirit within us to be going with us, and to be guiding us in what we go to do. When you are ready to go, do you sense the Holy Spirit leading you that way?

If He is, do you continue to be attentive to the Holy Spirit as you go to possibly hear more detailed instructions? This is what makes us different than the world. We could have gotten salvation from God and at the end of a normal life God would snatch us off to heaven. But that is not how it is, we have something new in us we never had before.[1] That of God is now in us. We live different than the world around us. If we are listening within there is something new that guides us, and changes us.[2] God is a great planner of all things, look at the universe. He wants to plan the things that go on in His Kingdom here on earth,[3] are you listening to His guidance? Do you know what part of that Kingdom He wants you working in and want He wants you to be doing?

These are things we need to seek for, they don't just pop up. If Peter was not listening in what we read about him in Acts 10 yesterday do you think he would have heard God? Do you think God would have just pushed this vision onto Peter? We are told in Acts Peter went up to the roof to pray. Peter was taking time for God, to talk to Him, to listen to Him, to be in His presence. God was with him, God's Spirit was guiding him. He could have decided he would go do a certain thing for God that day, been off to it, and been busy in it instead of taking time with God to be guided and hear God.

But Peter, if he would have done this he would have missed the message God had for him, he would have missed the three men at the gate, and he would have missed being the one to bring into the fold other sheep. (Jn. 10:16) Today in Act 11 Peter is confronted by other Jews wanting to know what place he had of going into a Gentile's house. Do you think Peter would have had a strong defense if he had just decided that was what he ought to do that day? Peter had a great defense straight from God that convinced them so much they rejoiced. We need to give the Spirit of God a chance to guide and direct us.

---

1   Jn.3:8, 6:63, Rom.8:11, 2Cor.3:6
2   Tit.3:5
3   Col.1:13

Here is the truth, Jesus is the same yesterday, today, and tomorrow.[1] He is always loving, He is always saving those who come to Him, He is always protecting those who are His. Jesus has a great investment in us. We are His possession which He values very highly.[2] Jesus is the way, the truth, and the life. Kindness and loving are His ways. He wants to lead us into good things. We are the children of the Father and Jesus is our elder brother.[3]

Jesus in our reading today in Matthew chapter 12 is trying to help these to know. Jesus is trying to help them know the Sabbath of God is about loving, not about the hardness of Law. What we see Jesus always doing throughout His ministry during His three years is healing those who come to Him, *"Then He said to the man, "Stretch out your hand." And he stretched it out, and it was restored as whole as the other...And great multitudes followed Him, and He healed them all...Then one was brought to Him who was demon-possessed, blind and mute; and He healed him, so that the blind and mute man both spoke and saw"* (v. 13,15,22 NKJV).

We need to hear what Matthew reminds us Isaiah said, *"Behold, my servant whom I have chosen; My beloved in whom my soul is well pleased: I will put my Spirit upon him, And he shall declare judgment to the Gentiles. He shall not strive, nor cry aloud; Neither shall any one hear his voice in the streets. A bruised reed shall he not break, And smoking flax shall he not quench, Till he send forth judgment unto victory. And in his name shall the Gentiles hope"* (v. 18-21 & Isa. 42:1-4 ASV).

This was the prophecy about how Jesus would be and we can see here in Matthew how He is a loving Savior. We can see that the Father confirmed these words. In the middle of verse 18 we see, *'Beloved in whom My soul is well pleased.'* The Father from heaven speaks nearly the same words twice during Jesus' ministry, *"This is my beloved Son, with whom I am well pleased"* (Mt. 3:17, Mk. 1:11, Lk. 3:22 ESV), and *"This is My beloved Son, in whom I am well pleased. Hear Him!"* (Mt. 17:5, similar-Mk. 9:7, similar-Lk. 9:35 NKJV).

Jesus is One we can trust in, as He was on earth, and now as He is in heaven. He will always be doing good for us even if we don't see it. Sometimes we are not intended to see what He is doing in our life. Sometimes we can't see it because we are distracted by other things. But He is always doing good for us, *"In My Father's house are many rooms; if that were not so, I would have told you, because I am going there to prepare a place for you"* (Jn. 14:2 NASB).

Jesus is always watching out for us, working for our well-being. It began when Jesus gave up His position in heaven to come to earth,[4] it continued in His ministry to us here by dying on the cross for us, and now in heaven He is still caring for us His possession. We need to draw close to Jesus, the closer we are the better we will hear. We should be of a love for Him that we do like Mary Magdalene, *"Mary, who was seated at the Lord's feet, listening to His word"* (Lk. 10:39 NASB). Jesus is wanting us to come, He is calling us to come, He wants us close to Him. I hope you can take some time today to get close to Jesus.

---

1   Heb.13:8
2   1Cor.6:20, 7:23, Acts 20:28, Eph.1:11-14
3   Rom.8:29
4   Philp.2:5-8, 2Cor.8:9

'I have come to take you into a better life.' What is that better life? We immediately think of a good place to live, a good place to work, a good family to be in, a good group of people in the church we belong to. Yes, these are good things to want, but let's look at what Jesus told to His disciples, *"Truly, I say to you, there is no one who has left house or brothers or sisters or mother or father or children or lands, for my sake and for the gospel, who will not receive a hundredfold now in this time, houses and brothers and sisters and mothers and children and lands, with persecutions"* (Mk. 10:29&30 RSV).

This is a good promise, all the good things we want – Wait a minute, what is persecutions doing in this list! Jesus does bring us many good things in this life, but what is it He promises to us if we believe in Him? *"whoever lives and believes in me shall never die"* (Jn. 11:26 RSV). and *"that whoever believes in him may have eternal life"* (Jn. 3:15 RSV). This world we live in will have its troubles, some we will be exposed to, and some we will escape.

This does not mean God's blessings will not be in our lives on earth, it only means this world we live in is not perfect. We many times get drawn down in our thinking and emotions to this life not having that consciousness within of the true life we belong to that will take us into eternity. We have been born into a life that is eternal. In comparison to eternity this life breezes by and is gone. If this life breezes by so quickly where do we need to have our conscious connection? Jesus has brought us into a better life as we live it in this world, but really where is the better life?

In Acts chapter 13, where we read today, Paul starts in v. 16 to speak of the good things God did for the people, and then brings them to the greatest thing. He tells them that Jesus has brought them the greatest thing, that through Him forgiveness of sins is proclaimed to all, that which the Law could not provide. *"through Him everyone who believes is freed from all things, from which you could not be freed through the law of Moses"* (Acts 13:39 NASB).

Paul is talking here about the way to salvation, the truly better thing, eternal life which is a much higher and greater thing than what we live here in this world. As we are those who believe because of the words of the first disciples, the promises given to them are also given to us. [1]

Jesus says in our reading of Matthew 13:11 this, *"To you it has been granted to know the mysteries of the kingdom of heaven"* (NASB). All through chapter 13 Jesus is talking about the Kingdom of heaven, that place of eternal life. Eternal life is the better life by far, we are told this about heaven, *"God himself shall be with them, and be their God: and he shall wipe away every tear from their eyes; and death shall be no more; neither shall there be mourning, nor crying, nor pain, any more: the first things are passed away"* (Rev. 21:3&4 ASV).

This surely is the better life, but it is easy to get distracted to the things going on in this world we live in. We need to get a grounded place within ourselves that keeps us focused on the better life. Here is what we are told, *"But when these things begin to take place, straighten up and lift up your heads, because your redemption is drawing near"* (Lk. 21:28 NASB). These things may not be happening yet, but we do need to keep our sight upward to heaven for that is where our true life, our better life is.

---

1   Jn.17:20

Jesus is our supply and knows our need. He does provide for all we have need of. Once we receive our salvation He takes care of us. It may be in our opinion that at times He does not, but could it be at that moment we don't know what our real need is? And then we should consider what our need is that goes far into the future. There may be something we think Jesus should be providing, or doing in our life now, but we should be realizing this circumstance may have to do with providing what will be our need in heaven. As I have spoken before, our most important need has to do with eternity. Now let's get back to how Jesus takes care of us here on earth.

First Jesus is our Master, a Good Master and we are His servants. What really good master does not take care of His servants well? Let's go one step further, if we really see the truth of what the original scriptures tell us we were in debt and could not free ourselves from the penalty for sin, Jesus got us out of hock by paying for us with His blood. *"You are not your own; you were bought with a price"* (1Cor. 6:19&20 RSV). and *"Worthy are You [Jesus] to take the book and to break its seals; for You were slain, and purchased for God with Your blood men from every tribe and tongue and people and nation"* (Rev. 5:9 NASB).

What we have to get through to ourselves is that since we were not able to pay the price required for our sins, that in Jesus paying that price we became His property, we became His slaves with Him holding the deed to our lives. If we are His property, what good master would not see that His slaves are taken care of well. Most times when we speak of being slaves it brings a negative thought. Being slaves of Jesus should bring a positive thought because we are now His possession for him to take care of, seeing that we have all we have need of. In our reading today we read about the five thousand being feed.

Here were these people who had walked a long distance, even some ran, to come hear what Jesus had to say to them. He was the first one in a long time that had the words of God – that somehow touched their hearts.[1] Jesus taught them till evening. Here are these people, over five thousand who had come a long way on foot, stayed the whole day, and now they had a need. It is most unlikely that there was anything anyone could do to take care of the hunger these thousands had need of. How many times is it we think because of the greatness of our need Jesus cannot help us?

The disciples think like we do, *"This is a deserted place, and the hour is already late. Send the multitudes away, that they may go into the villages and buy themselves food"* (Mt. 14:15 NKJV). We see our need as great and look to conventional ways to take care of it. What did Jesus do? *"And he commanded the multitudes to sit down on the grass; and he took the five loaves, and the two fishes, and looking up to heaven, he blessed, and brake and gave the loaves to the disciples, and the disciples to the multitudes. And they all ate, and were filled: and they took up that which remained over of the broken pieces, twelve baskets full"* (Mt. 14:19&20 ASV). Seeing the need of this multitude and Jesus providing their need, do you think Jesus is not able to take care of your need? If you read v. 14 Jesus did not only feed them, he healed those who were sick. If you have a need and are going to come to Him who has what no one else has to help us, surely our need is much smaller than the five thousand.

---

[1]   Mk.6:32-24

'I am coming for you.' Are you really able to grasp this? We all know in our knowledge of scripture Jesus is coming back for us. There will be those who rise from the very place they stand when Jesus' return will be in their lifetime. [1] For most of us, Jesus comes at that moment when we breathe our last on this earth. No matter which way it is, does your heart, your inner person, know this is reality? This is what Jesus said to us, *"when I go and prepare a place for you, I will come again and will take you to myself"* (Jn. 14:3 RSV). As we move through our life here in this world it is easy to lose track of this very important thing that our Christian life is attached to. We get so busy in this life that the reality of heaven, that place where we will all go which is a permanent place, gets lost in the fog of our minds. We watch and count each moment, each hour, each day going by not realizing our whole life will be over before we know it. Our stability has to be in heaven and our God who is there.

When we make this adjustment we will not be so wound up about things going on here on this earth because we know in our heart where our permanent place is. It becomes easy to live each day for the Lord when we have our lives anchored into heaven. Even though we walk on the solid ground of this earth it is temporary. [2] We need to make sure of what our lives revolve around. It is easy to get tied up with those things around us here on earth and end up with our whole life revolving around something here instead of heaven where we all who are saved will go one day. Jesus tried to point us toward heaven and the Father who dwells there. We do need to be attentive to those things of our lives in this world, that is much of what Jesus and the apostles taught us. But these are the things we do while we are in this temporary life on earth.

As we do all these things following how Jesus taught us to live there has to be that constant awareness down in the depth of our being that we are of heaven. Paul tells us, *"For our citizenship is in heaven, from which we also eagerly wait for a Savior, the Lord Jesus Christ; who will transform the body of our humble state into conformity with the body of His glory"* (Philp. 3:20&21 NASB). See where your life is headed. It is a glorious place we are all headed for, far beyond anything we could think. God tries to tell us about heaven but I believe that with all He tries to reveal to us it will be far short of what each of us find when we arrive. We read today of the council of Jerusalem discussing the state of the Gentiles. There were the Jews who had a problem letting go of the Law completely, they said the Gentiles had to be circumcised.

It was a large discussion, but they lost sight of what the more important thing is, we are citizens of heaven. Are we going to get to heaven, are we seeing it as a major part of our lives. We can discuss all day long how it is we should be living as Christians, but if it is not about our tie to heaven what real value does what we discuss have? We can spend much time in seeing we live each day rightly, but if it is not with eyes looking forward to heaven being with God what value is it? James quotes a verse which seems to be more, *"After this I will return; and I will rebuild the tent of David that has fallen; I will rebuild its ruins, and I will restore it"* (Acts 15:16 ESV). Who is it we know that has rebuilt the tents of David? It is Jesus who has built a new Kingdom on earth and our future home will be heaven. All our discussion and arguments over how we should live has no value if our hearts are not tied to heaven.

---

1   1Thes.4:16&17
2   2Pet.3:10,12,13

How goes your day? Can you say it is blessed by God? Do you know in your heart that He desires to bless you? Are you confused in what it takes for you to receive blessings from God? Working harder trying to please God will not gain you His blessings. Sometimes we get confused because we see others who seem to be working hard for God receive many blessings. Maybe you need to find the place they started. It is not by trying harder, it is by trying less. In fact it has to come to the place we totally give up, this is where God wants us all to arrive. It is when we totally give up to God that the blessings come. When we are trying so hard God can't even do much work in our life because we are in His way. We have to come to the place we totally yield all over to Him so that it is totally His doing it and no part of us.

Let's look at a couple of examples: *"And the LORD said to Gideon, "The people who are with you are too many for Me to hand Midian over to them, otherwise Israel would become boastful, saying, 'My own power has saved me'"* (Jdg. 7:2 NASB). There is another time God wanted the people to go in and take the land with Him being with them. They refused to go, then later said they would go when God said not to go because He would not be with them: *"And they rose early in the morning and went up to the top of the mountain, saying, "Here we are, and we will go up to the place which the LORD has promised, for we have sinned!" And Moses said, "Now why do you transgress the command of the LORD? For this will not succeed...you have turned away from the LORD, the LORD will not be with you...Then the Amalekites and the Canaanites who dwelt in that mountain came down and attacked them, and drove them back as far as Hormah"* (Num. 14:40, 41, 43, 45 NKJV).

It must be God who is in charge, and God who is moving in us. In the beginning I mentioned those who seem to be working hard for God receiving many blessings. What it usually is these people have found that place of totally yielding to God allowing Him to be in charge and all that you see happening is not by these people, it is God working through a yielded vessel. God blesses them because they allow God to be fully in control.

Reading in Matthew chapter 16 today Jesus speaks of this, *"Then Jesus said to His disciples, "If anyone desires to come after Me, let him deny himself, and take up his cross, and follow Me."* (Mt. 16:24 NKJV). Denying self, what is that? Jesus tells us in the next verse, *"whoever loses his life for My sake will find it"* (NKJV). This tells us we must lose ourselves. What is it to lose something? If we have totally lost it is there anything left? No, there is nothing left, it is all gone. This is where we need to strive to get, where there is nothing of ourselves left. I don't know if this side of heaven being in this flesh we will ever completely succeed, but it should not stop us from trying. We should be as John the Baptist said, *"He must increase, but I must decrease"* (Jn. 3:30 ASV).

'Take My hand and walk with Me.' Have you ever heard, or felt, Jesus say this to you? We have a great concept of Jesus in the sky (Heaven), but do we have a concept of Him with us? Once we have a faith that Jesus is with us every moment we also will have an expectation that He will speak to us. He can speak to us even from heaven, but He is closer to us than that. He is right alongside of us, even more, He is in us.[1] Jesus does not rule our lives from heaven, He rules from within us. If we have to send a message a distance there is a hope we will get a reply. But if we have someone walking right along with us and we say something we do expect a reply. Can you see how the awareness of where Jesus is makes a difference in our expectation, in our faith that Jesus will speak to us. What is it to have this kind of awareness, this kind of faith? What it takes is the word of God, He tells us what is true, what it is we should believe. Are you willing to know the truth that God speaks to us?

At some point we all need to come to that place we say, 'Lord I sure do not understand this, but because You say it I will believe You'. We also come to the place we say, 'Lord my life is in Your hand'. Once we get these things anchored into our heart, our inner person, we will not so much think of prayer as a submitting of a request, but as a conversation with our Lord. One of the real difficulties here is we get confused, we tend to think of the temporary as the permanent, and the permanent as that of far off. The permanent is heaven and eternity. Where we are right now is the temporary, it will pass in a moment. The eternal and heaven are not far off. We are born of the Spirit into the spiritual realm.

As we are born of Spirit and of flesh then these two coexist.[2] If they, the physical and the spiritual, coexist in us why would it not be they coexist in this world around us? We see the physical around us, but I believe the spiritual realm is here also, most of us just don't have the eyes to see it. The physical realm and the spiritual realm coexist, with the spiritual realm having overriding power over the physical realm. This would help explain some things about miracles. God's spiritual realm is everywhere, the earth's realm, this world, is within that spiritual realm.

This world we live in is not just floating along in space, it is given orders from the spiritual realm of God where He gives orders for it to be just exactly where it is. Sometimes we as Christians give too much credit to science, and not enough to God. Until recent years science was never an opponent to God, it was the discovering the things of God and how He did some of them. It was even to prove the truth of God. Let us come close to God, know His touch, know His voice, know His workings. God wants us close to Him. Let us grow close to Him finding Him where He is, how He is.

The core of three: Peter, James, and John, got to see some of how Jesus really is as they were on the mountain top with Him. A spectacle sure greater than they might ever think they would ever see. We may not see how the real is, but it does not change that it is. Jesus is calling us to come walk close to Him knowing He is there: *"All who keep his commandments abide in him, and he in them. And by this we know that he abides in us, by the Spirit which he has given us"* (1Jn. 3:24 RSV). Jesus is always encouraging. He speaks in Matthew something encouraging, He speaks about our faith needed to move a mountain. This also would apply to all other applications of our faith.

Jesus tells us we only need a little, and then to let it grow from there, *"if you have faith as a grain of mustard seed"* (17:20 RSV). Jesus told His disciples just four chapters earlier what a mustard seed is like, *"like a mustard seed which a man takes and sows in his field. It is the smallest of all seeds, but when it grows up it is larger than any garden plant and becomes a tree, so that the birds flying about come and nest in its branches"* (Mt. 13:31&32 CJB). Here Jesus compares the mustard seed to the Kingdom, but does that change its characteristics? We can grow, and we can come closer to God, and we can learn to hear His voice.

---

1   Jn.14:20
2   Jn.3:5&6

Where is your heart? Who have you given it to? There is a warning in Revelation about those who are lukewarm.[1] Do you have something in your heart that has an equal place with Christ? Is this not what lukewarm is, an equal amount of two things? God wants us fully devoted to Him with nothing else in our hearts of equal value.[2] There are those we are to love starting from our spouse and going on out from there. But all of these have to come after God. Jesus one time said, *"If any one comes to me and does not hate [love less] his own father and mother and wife and children and brothers and sisters, yes, and even his own life, he cannot be my disciple"* (Lk. 14:26 RSV).

Here Jesus is telling us the love we have for Him needs to be so full, so completely given to Him that in comparison it would seem we hate others, even of our family. We know we are to love our spouse and our children, we are told in the scriptures this is to be. We are told to love our neighbor as our self.[3] So what is being said here is that the love we have for others is to be nowhere close to the love we have for God. Where is your heart, who have you given it to? In the Old testament the people we read of in Judges and Jeremiah have problems giving their whole heart to God. We today under the New Covenant of the gospel with Jesus now in our life should not have as much of a problem as those in old testament times. Yet I know it is a problem we have to look out for. We need to be close to God.

One good way is that we set aside some time in our day to be with God: praying, reading His word, or just sitting with Him spending some time. How often do you think of God, of His ways? Does He come at the end of the list? Do you have less thought of Him than the rest, or more thought of Him? I don't think there is any legal answer to this, but God sees our heart and He knows.[4] I take it as a warning and a caution to not let slip the place I have God in my life. This has to do with a spiritual relationship, I don't think there can be a list of this or that. Today in our reading in Matthew chapter 18 Jesus is speaking of the little child. Do you go to God as a child? This is not saying to be childish, it may have more to do with our knowledge and thought compared to His.[5]

Are you going to God with the attitude that your Daddy is great and can do anything? Little children see their fathers this way, do you see your heavenly Father this way? Jesus says this, *"What will somebody do who has a hundred sheep, and one of them wanders away? Won't he leave the ninety-nine on the hillsides and go off to find the stray?"* (Mt. 18:12 CJB). Jesus is saying that even if we stray God will come looking for us. Having this knowledge that God cares for us so much would this not cause us to come closer to Him? *"Even so it is not the will of your Father who is in heaven, that one of these little ones should perish"* (v. 14 ASV). God wants us to be as little ones. He wants us to come close to Him. He wants to watch out for us, He wants to take care of us. He wants us to live His way close to Him. Where is your heart?

---

1   Rev.3:15&16
2   Lk.10:27
3   Mk.12:31
4   Ps.44:21, Acts 15:8
5   Isa.55:8&9

Where is your journey taking you? Do you see your life as a journey? Every journey has a destination. If we get too bogged down at any point along that journey will we get to the end? Our journey is with God. It starts on the day we are saved and continues until we reach heaven. Are you keeping your spiritual eyes on the destination? It is easy to get distracted. Something along the way gets our attention and the destination of the journey fades a little.

We need to be careful because too many of these distractions will cause the destination to totally disappear from our sight. Do we look at our road map often? Sometimes we say we know where we are going and how to get there, to end up finding ourselves in a place that seems to be nowhere. We need to keep referring to the road map so we know where we are going and to be sure we don't make a wrong turn somewhere. By now you may have figured the road map is God's word, the Bible. The apostle Paul was confused in the beginning because the road map he had was outdated, it didn't include the New Covenant. Later when God set him on the right course he was lost no more. We may think the navigation system we have of the current age is great with a voice telling us how to go.

The Holy Spirit spoke to Paul guiding him on his journey. Paul kept in mind where he was going, *"I press on toward the goal for the prize of the upward call of God in Christ Jesus"* (Philp. 3:14 RSV). Paul never took his eyes off of the destination of the Journey. Paul had a lot of distractions but never allowed them to remove his eyes from that destination. There were many things in Paul's heart but two that he could not decide about, one was to be with the Lord, the other was to be the servant, *"For to me to live is Christ, and to die is gain. If I am to live in the flesh, that means fruitful labor for me. Yet which I shall choose I cannot tell"* (Philp. 1:21&22 ESV). Paul knew his destination was heaven, was to be there with Christ. Do you have your eyes set on the destination like Paul?

Today in our reading in Matthew chapter 19 the rich young ruler had too many distractions of his wealth. He needed an updated road map, the old map showed he was on the right track but when Jesus tried to get him to see the road map of the New Covenant that Jesus was bringing he looked at his wealth and could not see any further. Jesus is the destination, and this young ruler had Jesus right in front of him calling him to come follow. To be honest, how many of us do not have distractions? The thing is to forcefully keep our eyes on the destination because there will always be distractions. We need to be checking the road map often. We need to be calling home base in prayer to know if we are on track, or if we have made a wrong turn. It takes a checking the map often, a calling in to find if we still are on course, and a forcefully putting our spiritual eyes forward keeping the destination in sight.

There is a good time coming. No matter how bad things may be now we all who are in Christ can look forward to the day we will be with Him in heaven. *"Who shall separate us from the love of Christ? Shall tribulation, or distress, or persecution, or famine, or nakedness, or peril, or sword?...Yet in all these things we are more than conquerors through Him who loved us. For I am persuaded that neither death nor life, nor angels nor principalities nor powers, nor things present nor things to come, nor height nor depth, nor any other created thing, shall be able to separate us from the love of God which is in Christ Jesus our Lord"* (Rom. 8:35,37,38,39 NKJV). This is a great promise which God spoke to us through Paul. It should be a daily thought, a daily knowledge.

Jesus also gave us another promise we may not like to hear too often, *"A servant is not greater than his lord. If they persecuted me, they will also persecute you"* (Jn. 15:20 ASV). Any of the troubles in your life coming from others should not surprise you. And the closer you get to God, and the more you serve Him, the more that the persecution may be. This is also where the faith of what God has said brings us relief, *"greater is he that is in you than he that is in the world"* (1Jn. 4:4 ASV). Nothing can happen to you that is beyond God's control. There are things which may happen to you that come to you from life. Life in this world is not perfect, it has its bumps, its chuck holes, and its brick walls, and we may hit them all. God is always there to help us when these things happen.

You may ask how God can let them be there if He is a loving God? God is a loving God, He gets us out of our troubles. Back in the garden God gave mankind the ability to choose, mankind (Adam & Eve) made the wrong choice and we have been put out of the place of perfectness ever since. God being a loving God made a way for us to make it to heaven through Jesus Christ.[1] That does not change this world we live in which the infection of sin came into. The good news to us is if we have Christ in our life we will get to heaven, and nothing, but nothing, can get in the way of that.

We need to hear the encouragement Paul gave to the Ephesians, *"And now I commend you to God, and to the word of his grace, which is able to build you up, and to give you the inheritance among all them that are sanctified"* (Acts 20:32 ASV). '*the word of His grace*', this is what will get us through. Jesus tells us today in our reading of Matthew chapter 20 that no matter if we receive Him early in our life, in the middle of our life, or not even knowing our need until the last hour of our life, all will receive this grace of salvation. (v. 1-16)

This is the greatest that God has given to us in all our life, our salvation. We also read today Jesus always has time for one more. In Matthew two blind men were crying out to Him and the crowd was saying to shush and be still. Jesus stopped, having time for one more, and each received their sight. We will have troubles in this life, but maybe there could be some relief for you, have you called out to Him? Jesus always has time to hear the call of one more.

---

1   Jn.3:15, 1Jn.1:7

How is your life going today? Are you on the waters of uncertainty? Are you anchored into the Rock? Are you looking to the Holy Spirit as your guide? Do you see God working in your life as you trust Him? We all know how life is to be, at least how we want it to be. Is the way you want it to be line up with the way God wants it to be?

In this day of electronic technology, we are hot syncing to this and hot syncing to that, even wirelessly. When we connect one thing to another they have to be compatible, if anything is out of place they have difficulty connecting or don't work at all. In a way this is how it is with God, the further away we are from His ways the more difficult the connection. So, are the things you want lining up with things God wants? It is not that we do all the things that are right which gives us closeness to God. It is the things that we do which are away from His will and ways that cause interference, or even loss of connection. How is your life going today? We get so stirred up in this life almost spinning in circles losing track of God and His ways. Do you remember what Jesus said, *"Come to Me, all you who labor and are heavy laden, and I will give you rest"* (Mt. 11:28 NKJV).

Many times we see this as Jesus calling us to receive salvation. Does Jesus say that He will not give more rest afterward? We need to know, and trust, that God wants to help us in all things. Are you trusting in your life today that God will be there to help you? Nothing is too small to take to God, nothing is too big, He made it all. You are special in His eyes, He sees all that goes on in your life. He wants to bless you, are you going to Him? Or are you saying, 'I got this one Lord', do you really! How many times is it we need help but out of pride we don't ask? *"You do not have, because you do not ask"* (Jas. 4:2 RSV). God wants us to come and ask. Nothing that we might ask or say surprises God, *"your Father knows what you need before you ask him"* (Mt. 6:8 RSV).

Even though He knows He wants us to ask. Immediately after this Jesus teaches how to pray. By prayer we can get anchored to the Rock and out of those uncertain waters. Sometimes we may be in the edge of those uncertain waters but if we are anchored into the Rock nothing can happen to us that is outside of the will of God. In our reading in Acts chapter 21 today we see Paul is anchored into the Rock and knows nothing will happen to Him that his Lord Jesus does not know about. He also is being guided by the Holy Spirit which we were told yesterday. (20:22) Many times we are nearly appalled that Paul is in prison so much. Here Paul is put in prison in Caesarea where he is for about two years, and then is sent to Rome.

We may wonder how a loving God would allow him to be in prison. We remember how the angel got Peter out of prison in the middle of the night, so why not Paul? Paul was willing to go through whatever Jesus asked him to. Do you ever check how many letters Paul wrote which are in our Bible today that he wrote from prison somewhere? Some of the most valued letters Paul wrote he wrote from prison. We might not have those letters today if he was not in those prisons. Today in Matthew chapter 21 we read of Jesus' triumphant entry into Jerusalem. Have you allowed Jesus to make that triumphant entry into your life, or did you only let Him in the side door? He has to be fully King of our lives if He is to take us into a life of certainty. We want God to be in our lives, but we only have access through Jesus, [1] be sure He is on the throne of your life.

---

1   Jn.14:6

'**I am with you always.**' Do you want to know this Jesus has said is true? Jesus goes on, *"I am with you always, even to the end of the age"* (Mt. 28:20 NKJV). Jesus says He will be with us until the end of the age, when is the end of the age? This is how long He will be with us. He does not say He will be with us until we mess up. He does not say He will be with us as long as we behave. He says **always**. As long as we are willing to be with Him He is willing to be with us. Don't be confused, it is not that He will be with us only if we please Him.

It is not us who are doing the work that we may be accepted by Him. It is He who has done the work already. What we have to do (or have done) is allow the death He died on the cross for sin apply to our sins, to allow His payment for sin to apply as payment for our sins. To be clear, it takes a humble attitude to accept Jesus' payment to be applied to our sins. Pride wants to say it can do it by itself. Once we have accepted Jesus into our hearts and now belong to Him He will always be with us. There is nothing that happens to us that He does not know about. He is always with us, He is always watching over us.

At times we may wonder if He is or not, the thing is we don't know what His will is in our situation. We can go back to the course that God had Joseph on when his brothers hated him enough to sell him as a slave ending up in Egypt, getting arrested and put in prison. [1] If we were where he was we would be saying, 'God where are you, how can I be in this mess?' We all know the outcome of his family being saved from the famine. As we continue in our reading about Paul in Acts it is a similar situation, Paul is arrested and put in prison. Paul may have had some idea as the Holy Spirit had spoken to him, we just don't know since it was not recorded. For Paul it was not to save a family from a famine as it was with Joseph. But let us consider in New Testament terms of what it was that Paul was in Prison.

First of all, for Paul, he was willing to be there for Christ, *"for I am ready not to be bound only, but also to die at Jerusalem for the name of the Lord Jesus"* (Acts 21:13 ASV). Beyond this there is a famine in the land, a famine which all will die from if they do not find Christ and His salvation. Paul may never have become Governor of the land like Joseph, but he certainly became one of the governors of the word of God. From so many epistles penned by Paul as God gave guidance which came forth from those prison walls, how many over the years have been led to Christ to receive salvation, true life from death, from the famine? Is Paul's case so really different than Joseph's? Can we not see God was with them both? So we should have confidence no matter the situation we have that it is true when Jesus says He will be with us, *"And remember! I will be with you always, yes, even until the end of the age"* (Mt. 28:20 CJB). and *"I will never fail you or abandon you"* (Heb. 13:5 & Deut.31:6 CJB).

---

1   Gen.37:28, 39:20

'I am walking with you.' *"While they were talking and discussing together, Jesus himself drew near and went with them. But their eyes were kept from recognizing him"* (Lk. 24:15&16 ESV). Later after they realized it was Jesus they said, *"Did not our hearts burn within us while he talked to us"* (Lk. 24:32 ESV). How many times is Jesus with us, even talking to us, and we don't realize it? I remember how Paul has told us to pray always, rejoice always.[1] If we do this then we would be aware of spiritual things.

It is easy to be so taken up by the things of this life, and what we need to do to maintain this life, that the awareness of spiritual things slips into a back seat. Could Jesus be walking with us then but we are not noticing? Could He be speaking, and again we are not noticing? I believe most all of us have this trouble. This world is buzzing, buzzing, buzzing, and we get swept right into it. It is then that we have to make a conscious effort to always take the spiritual along with us. I don't mean walking along in a spiritual daze, I mean us have an awareness of spiritual things. Jesus wants to walk with us, do you know when He is there? He wants to reveal truth to us, are we hearing what He is saying to us? Jesus said He sent the Holy Spirit to teach us,[2] have we heard what the Spirit has said to us? Jesus said, 'follow Me', how can we do this if we are not hearing Him?

First of all we need to know what has been said to us in scripture. But the **following of Him** takes more than just this. Much of what we are told in scripture to be doing is that which the Church is to be doing. We are taught the Church is like a body with Christ as the head. We are taught that the body has many parts all working together accomplishing the work of God. How can you know which part you are and what it is you are to be doing if you are not hearing? It would not work very well if a foot was trying to be a nose and the nose was trying to be a foot. We all need this guidance. It may be difficult to hear what Jesus is saying to us, the first step is to be aware. When I say we need to hear what Jesus, or the Holy Spirit, is saying to us I don't mean when the grand voice comes from the clouds.

We are told God speaks with a still small voice. Sometimes that still small voice does not even speak with words, it is we are just impressed with something inside of us that we know did not come from us. Sometimes it is just a feeling, or desire to do something. God will move us if we are willing to be aware. If we are wanting to hear, God will cause us to know (in His timing). All this takes time of being exposed, being aware trying to hear. If we go to a foreign country not knowing their language we can be spoken to and not know it. As we spend more and more time in that country we begin to recognize more and more what is being said. It is the same recognizing spiritual things.

In our reading today in Matthew chapter 23, Jesus is saying don't get tied up in legalism. You may say you do not try to do the laws of the Old Testament. If you only take a list from the New Testament telling yourself you must try to do them, is this not legalism? We need to know the guidance of God to know how we are to attend to those things we read of.

As the head of a body, the brain, sends out commands to the different parts of the body of what to do, so Christ sends out commands to the different parts of His body (us) of what each part is to do and when. If a ball player's body does not respond to the brain and the leg is not doing what it is supposed to do, nor the arm, can the ball be delivered to its destination? We need to know Jesus is walking with us and hear Him when He speaks. The very beginning of all this may be in what Jesus said in Matthew, *"One is your Leader, that is, Christ...Whoever exalts himself shall be humbled; and whoever humble himself shall be exalted"* (23:10-12 NASB).

---

1   1Thes.5:16&17
2   Jn.14:26, 16:12-15

'I am your God. I love you and will not forsake you. You are mine and I will protect you.' Is this an assurance that you know? Is there a question in your heart? Do you have trouble believing God cares for you this much? Know that the Father put the Son on the cross to die for you to give you entitlement into the family of God.[1] None of us deserve to be accepted by anything we have done that could be considered righteous or deserving.

It is fully by Mercy and Grace[2] by which God acted sacrificing Himself in your place to make a way you can be accepted by Him. Once you know the great work that God did so you could be saved is it so hard to accept the beginning statements?

There is a grand God that loves you more than you can know. Sometimes we need to set back, take a few moments, and allow God to speak to our hearts words of love that cannot be heard. If we come to God and respond to Him He will reveal things to our hearts our brain could never know. 'I love you and will not forsake you' has been spoken of God long ago and still holds true to this very day for those who are His.[3] He wants us close, He has made a way we could be close. He ignored our behavior and found a way we could be accepted without offending His righteous requirement, *"God shows his love for us in that while we were yet sinners Christ died for us"* (Rom. 5:8 RSV).

Do you see how much God loves you? We judge ourselves more harshly than God does. God has made a way we can be saved and once we have our salvation those things which were the bad acts of our past (our sins) have now all been laid upon Christ on the cross.[4] The event of the cross has changed everything, and continues to change people's lives every day. The action and powerful work done by Christ on the cross guarantees heaven will not be empty. We all who are saved have a place in heaven which comes after our time here on this earth: *"In My Father's house are many rooms; if that were not so, I would have told you, because I am going there to prepare a place for you. And if I go and prepare a place for you, I am coming again and will take you to Myself, so that where I am, there you also will be"* (Jn. 14:2&3 NASB).

Why would Jesus tell us this if He didn't love us? We need to know His love, and know His care. As we have read in Matthew chapter 24 today Jesus tells us how it will be in the end, those days before the final judgment comes. By God's love and His care He will take us to Himself to be with Him for eternity. Think of it, how long is eternity? Would God want us with Him for eternity if He did not love us? And God wants to make sure none of us misses the coming of Christ, *"For as the lightning cometh forth from the east, and is seen even unto the west; so shall be the coming of the Son of man"* (Mt. 24:27 ASV). Can you see that God loves and cares even for you?

---

1   Mk.14:7, Isa.53.4
2   Heb.4:16, 2Jn.1:3
3   Duet.7:13, 31:6
4   2Cor.5:21, 53:6&11

Speak to the Lord, He is always listening. We get all tied up in a special approach to God. There is no special approach other than a humble heart.[1] We are told by James we have not because we ask not.[2] What is it you are not asking? Nothing is too big, nothing is too small. He is waiting, He is listening, are you asking? There is no special way to pray, it is just having a conversation with God.

I remember years ago my wife would sit down at the kitchen table with a cup of coffee and speak to Jesus as though He was right there sitting on the other side of the table. That is where she seemed to develop her closeness to the Lord that lasted her years. We can study, study, study, but nothing brings us closer to God than spending time with Him. It was Jesus' habit to go off to a secluded place to be with the Father.[3] Can we have any better example than Christ Himself? The word of God is important. I recommend people read it often. But as well as reading the word you have to have a relationship with the author. Jesus said *"I am the way, and the truth, and the life"* (Jn. 14:6 ASV) and *"Come to me, all of you who are struggling and burdened, and I will give you rest"* (Mt. 11:28 CJB).

Is this not an invitation? If you let it end at salvation only, how much are you short-changing yourself of what He offers? God says He will do far more than we can think or imagine. Our God is far greater than we ever imagine. One day each of us will arrive in heaven and when we see Jesus, the Father, and the Holy Spirit, we are going to be greatly taken back by who God is. Now we are limited in knowing, but then we will see all.[4] Closeness to God, that's what we all need. Bowing down self to God is what is needed, not just bowing of body. It is far more important that we bow our hearts to God. We can read and fill our brain with all the words of God, but what a difference if we read the words of God and fill our hearts with them. This is what develops relationship.

God's word is alive, don't lock it up in your head, let it go to your heart where it can move, and act, and bring forth fruit.[5] Prayer, His word, surrender, yielding, giving ourselves over, these are things that will bring great profit. Today our reading is in Matthew chapter 25 where Jesus is speaking of the ten virgins who come with their lamps to wait. Some it seems came determined to want on the Lord no matter how long it might be. The others not quite so determined, they did not make sure they had what they needed. These seemed to come in a bit of a flippant manner not prepared for the time it might take. The first group made sure they were prepared, they invested in extra oil. Are you investing in extra? Are you investing in spending time with the Lord? Are you investing is pouring more of His word into your heart? Do you think you have enough not needing any more until He comes? This is what the second group of virgins did. The first group invested, are you investing?

---

1   Jn.4:10
2   Jas.4:2
3   Mk.1:35, 6:46, Lk.5:16, 6:12, 9:18&29
4   1Cor.13:12
5   Heb.4:12

'Here I am to worship, here I am to bow down' This line from a popular worship song, can you say is as your own? If we come to that place of awareness of God in our lives this will be in our hearts often. The more we are aware of the good things of God in our lives the more the attitude of worship will come into our hearts. Worship is not always that of singing, singing is only one form of worship. That of stepping out of your door first thing in the morning seeing the beauty of the day and saying, 'Thank you Lord for a beautiful day' is worship. Worship is the thankful heart that becomes aware of the great actions of God from creation to the very day we are walking in.

There is a God that loves us more than we will even know here on this side of heaven. When we get to heaven then we will know, but now we are like the child who peaks through the crack in a wooden fence only seeing a sliver of what is on the other side. So little we are able to see, yet are we aware of all that we can see through that sliver? Spiritual things are not easy to see, if they were it would seem nearly all the world would be saved. Spiritual things have to be approached with faith. Abram had to have faith to be led from his secure place of home, family, and community, to a place of the unknown.

Today, or the day we were saved, somehow we heard there was a God that loved us and invited us into salvation through His Son Jesus Christ. This was an unknown, we had to enter it by faith. It still takes faith to be aware of the spiritual realm around us. I believe the spiritual realm and the physical realm co-exist, it is just that we cannot see the spiritual things that are all around us. Heaven is heaven, where the throne of God is, but that does not mean the spiritual is only there, I believe it is here where we are also. Otherwise how do you explain the unexplainable things that happen around us?

There is another evidence; where was the devil and his followers cast when they lost the battle in heaven? Where they not cast to earth where we live?[1] And are there not spiritual battles between angels and demons? So where would those battles be taking place, would it not be here on earth? Now are these not things which take place in the spiritual realm? Once we know this we begin to see how much God is involved in our every moment of our life, and it causes worship to rise in the heart.

In our reading today in Acts Paul is making his defense. He tells of the great things God had done in his life. There is a place that Paul's action speaks of how he has the awareness of this great God in his life, *"And when they had laid many stripes upon them, they cast them into prison, charging the jailor to keep them safely: who, having received such a charge, cast them into the inner prison, and made their feet fast in the stocks. But about midnight Paul and Silas were praying and singing hymns unto God"* (16:23-25 ASV). Can you say your day is worse? Paul and Silas had the awareness of the great things of God which Paul speaks of briefly in chapter 26. This awareness brings one's heart to worship in the most difficult of times.

---

[1]   Rev.12:9

Just in time. You ever think of how many times it seems God works just in time? God knows of our every situation. Nothing surprises Him. He even knows beginning to end. All things are worked out for His good purpose. We benefit from that, *"And we know that God causes all things to work together for good to those who love God, to those who are called according to His purpose"* (Rom. 8:28 NASB). We who are called, God by His purpose, works out all things for us. When we have not yet arrived at our need that we don't even know we are going to have, God has already been there and has set His purpose in place.

If God has already been there, then could He be late in what He does, or would it be right on time? There is nothing that misses His attention. He is not distracted, He sees all things at the same time and misses none of it. We think His help comes just in time, God sees it as right on time. Where is our faith in this? Faith does not mean the river will open while we are at a distance so we can cheer that it is open before we get there.

The river opens right on time, *"when those who were carrying the ark came up to the Jordan and the feet of the priests carrying the ark stepped down into the edge of the water...the waters which were flowing down from above stood and rose up in one heap, a great distance away"* (Jos. 3:15&16 NASB). If God is going to provide what we need right on time do we need to have it before that time? Here is the hard part we all struggle with, having faith that even though we don't see it ahead of time that God will provide it right on time. We really don't need it until that time comes, but we end up with anxiety worrying it won't be there. Do you think Abraham had any anxiety? *"And Abraham stretched out his hand and took the knife to slay his son. But the Angel of the LORD called to him from heaven and said, "Abraham, Abraham!" So he said, "Here I am." And He said, "Do not lay your hand on the lad, or do anything to him; for now I know that you fear God"* (Gen. 22:10-12 NKJV).

Maybe Abraham was a better man than us all, but it seems he may have had anxiety. What I do see is that there may have been anxiety mixed with faith, *"God will provide himself the lamb for a burnt-offering"* (v. 8 ASV). Abraham may have had faith that God would provide, *"Abraham lifted up his eyes, and looked, and behold, behind him a ram caught in the thicket by his horns"* (v. 13 ASV). Also there is a hit of faith that he would not have to sacrifice his son in what Abraham named that place, *"And Abraham called the name of that place Jehovah-jireh. As it is said to this day, In the mount of Jehovah it shall be provided"* (v. 14 ASV).

God was not late with a substitution for the sacrifice, it was right on time. Faith is what it takes and God will provide right on time. In our reading today about Ruth do you think as she was determined to come to Israel with Naomi she had faith that the God of Israel would provide for her somehow? Was it by chance Ruth was in his field when Boaz came around? Do you think it was by chance Boaz came around when Ruth was in his field. It could have been the day Ruth was in Boaz's field he did not come that day. It might have been the day Boaz came to his field Ruth was in another field. Do you see God's purpose here right on time? There is even more to being right on time here, *"Boaz begot Obed by Ruth, Obed begot Jesse, and Jesse begot David the king....and Matthan begot Jacob. And Jacob begot Joseph the husband of Mary, of whom was born Jesus who is called Christ"* (Mt. 1:5,6,15,16 NKJV). Do we ever know what the outcome of God being just on time will be?

'This is the day, this is the day, that the Lord has made, that the Lord has made'. How many times have you sung these words? Was it just a great melody with great words, or in your heart did you truly rejoice? You may just get to singing along with Mitch (you younger generation may have to look this one up). We can sing great tunes, but if they are not coming from our hearts to God, or about God, are they really worship. There are many who don't sing because they don't think they can sing well. Yet, any melody of praise which comes from the heart is beautiful to the ears of God. There are others who sing quite well but should keep still because they are only concerned about their great performance and none of it truly is going to God.

Praise always comes from the heart, there can even be praise in our silence. In our thoughts we praise God and He hears. (quick thought: If God speaks to us in a still small voice in our inner person, do you not also know that He will hear our quiet thoughts within as well?) There is also praise, I believe, in even being still within with no thoughts. It is the idea and thought of praise being expressed by that which we have no sufficient words to praise Him appropriately. Our stillness represents all the words that we lack which would bring His truly deserving praise. Our language is not sufficient to give all the words of praise God deserves. Sometimes we get things locked into a box and cannot get out of it. Praise comes from the heart, and can be expressed in many different ways.

There are those who say that the Church should have nothing to do with dancing. Agreed that some types of dancing we should not engage in, but this goes back to the saying, **'Don't throw the baby out with the bath water.'** If no dancing is appropriate, why does the Psalms say, *"Let them praise His name with the dance"* (149:3 NKJV).

If the person dancing is truly dancing to God as a form of praising Him, how can it be wrong? Even in our work, if we work as unto the Lord[1] for His greatness and His glory, can that not also be praise? We get locked into too much tradition, when we should have liberty. When Ruth returns to Naomi telling her the events of the day Naomi says: *"May he be blessed of the LORD who has not withdrawn His kindness from the living and from the dead...Wait, my daughter, until you know how the matter turns out; for the man will not rest until he has settled it today"* (Ruth 2:20 & 3:18 NASB).

After all the hardships Naomi experienced do you not think she was giving the high praise of her heart as she saw God's great work unfolding? In the last chapter of Matthew today we are reading of the resurrection of Christ. *"Mary Magdalene and the other Mary went to see the tomb...But the angel said to the women...He is not here, for he has risen...Jesus met them and said, "Greetings!" And they came up and took hold of his feet and worshiped him"* (Mt. 28:1,5,6,9 ESV). Here we see the women worshiping Jesus who they thought was dead. *"Now the eleven disciples went to Galilee, to the mountain to which Jesus had directed them. And when they saw him they worshiped him"* (Mt. 28:16&17 ESV).

They found that Jesus was alive and they worshiped Him. Do we not also know He is alive seated at the right of the Father in heaven? Do we not know He has made a way for us to be forgiven and receive salvation? Do we not know He has prepared a place for us in heaven and is waiting to welcome us into heaven when our time is done on this earth? Do we not surely know we also have a reason to worship and praise Him from our hearts in gladness?

---

1   Eph.6:7, Col.3:23

'**Are You there**?' Is this what you wonder sometimes about God? He is always there, even more than we are here, yet at times we are not sure. It takes a great faith and a small faith to know God is with us. How much faith on your part did it take to receive salvation? All the work was done on Jesus' side, all we had to do was believe He was real and give-in surrendering to Him asking for His salvation for us. That would have been small faith. Great faith starts with small faith. Jesus talks about the faith as a mustard seed. [1]

It takes the small faith to start out, and then it grows and grows and grows. It was not small faith that Peter had when he stepped out of the boat and walked on the water. [2] He started out with small faith when he was called by Jesus to leave his father and follow Jesus. How much Peter's faith had grown by the time he walked on water I don't know, but surely seeing all the things Jesus had done his faith did grow. There is a difficulty in knowing God is there.

God exists in the unseen world, and we, we are tied to this temporary world we live in every day. We have to come to the place in our spiritual walk we begin to believe in the unseen world more than the seen world around us. A starting point is to consider our salvation. Is there anything of this world that we can see which verifies we have eternal life? As your life has changed since that day you gave your life to Jesus, is this not an evidence of the power of that unseen world?

It is hard sometimes to put faith in something we cannot see. But are there not times when you feel the love of God in your heart which will testify to you in those times you ask, '**God, where are you**?' There are those who talk about anchor points in our life. Those are the times we seen God work mightily in our life. These things as we rehearse them in our minds, they will help us know God is there, even in the difficult times we run into. As we read of Naomi who had difficulties far beyond anything we have ever had finds herself holding a grandchild which would lead to the birth of the one to be king of Israel.

Even though many times Naomi may have asked in her heart, '**God, are You there**?', and later finding He was. Would Joseph have been asking, '**God, are You there**?' when his brothers sold him off into Egypt?[3] Yet Joseph saw later that God was there all along the way. In Romans Paul may not have been asking, '**Are You there**?', but, '**Are You going to make a way**?' *"without ceasing I mention you always in my prayers, asking that somehow by God's will I may now at last succeed in coming to you...I have often intended to come to you (but thus far have been prevented)"* (Rom. 1:9,10,13 RSV).

God does not always do things in the way we would do them. God was hearing Paul's request to go to Rome, about three years later Paul was provided his travels to Rome by the emperor - as a prisoner under arrest. We would in that situation ask, '**God, are You there**?', But Paul knew God was with Him in all his struggles and trials. Just because in our evaluation we wonder where God is does not mean He is not there, He is always there for those who have found Him through Jesus Christ.

---

1   Lk.17:6, 13:19
2   Mt.14:21
3   Gen.37:28

'To you it is given.' How about that, do you feel you have been given to by God? There is the next step higher than feeling which is faith, do you by faith believe you have been given to by God? Then there is the actual to have something which has been given by God. There are so many things God is wanting to give us. Remember, it is said that we are His children, [1] what father does not want to give to his children? The thing is for some of what He wants to give us He wants us to ask.

As a father, we can give, and give, and give. What good does this do the child? Some are even spoiled by it. For the child to ask shows it is depending on its father, and knows his love. There needs to be a relationship between father and child. If everything comes automatically from the father relationship never happens, never is needed. We need to know we need the Father. We need to know He will take care of us because of His love for us. We need to establish a relationship with Him. We are to go to the Father and ask: *"You do not have, because you do not ask"* (Jas. 4:2 RSV).

How many times do we need to hear this before we get it? We in our pride either refusing to humble ourselves to ask, or in our pride we think we can handle it. With earthly fathers do they not want us to include them even in the small things in our lives? Should our heavenly Father be any different? How many times does the Father have something He wants to give us but we think it is too small of a thing to bother God with asking Him. God wants us to be close to Him, even if we don't need anything. What God the Father wants the most from us is relationship, and the greatest thing we need from Him is relationship. That relationship started at our salvation, what has happened with it since then?

God wants us to come to Him in that secret place (prayer closet) and spend some time with Him. Are you able to develop a relationship with a person without spending some time with them? It is the same with God. The Father wants to know us, He wants to touch us, He wants to bless us. Are we so busy in our lives we don't have time for God, and then we would say, 'God, where are You' when it is that we need Him? God is a loving God, He is a longsuffering God – but how long does He have to wait!? Maybe if we took time for God we would not be quite so busy – because He would take care of some of the things we are trying to handle. In the first chapter of 1Samuel we read of Hannah.

Hannah wanted a great thing from God, *"O LORD of hosts, if You will indeed look on the affliction of Your maidservant and remember me, and not forget Your maidservant, but will give Your maidservant a male child, then I will give him to the LORD all the days of his life"* (v. 11 NKJV). Hannah was needing something from God and came to Him in the most humble manner.

God heard her and answered her prayer. What she offered to God was her child. We can give more than a child, we can give God ourselves, *"Therefore I urge you, brothers and sisters, by the mercies of God, to present your bodies as a living and holy sacrifice, acceptable to God, which is your spiritual service of worship"* (Rom. 12:1 NASB). This is not speaking of a ministry such as a missionary, pastor, evangelist, or such. This is speaking of your every day self, that no matter what you are in you have given yourself fully and completely to God in every moment of your day. God wants relationship, and if we come in that relationship asking for our need He will hear us.

---

1   1Jn.3:1

Are you so sure of where you are going? This is not about heaven or hell, it is about the assurance you have in your God. Do you question sometimes if you are really saved? What does it take for you to be sure? Very few of us will ever hear that voice from the sky, or to see it written on the clouds. It is something that has to take place in our hearts. We had a small amount of faith to be saved, did that faith continue on? It was the greatest need we had for faith, it was to get saved. It was that time we seen where we were and where we needed to be, which was with God. Can there be any greater need of faith than in our condition of sin, no matter how little that sin was, for we were short of the glory of God.[1]

In that condition in light of the righteousness of God, we were no more than heathens. In that condition how much faith did it take to believe that God loved us anyway, and that by Jesus dying for us we could be forgiven entering the family of God becoming His children to be with Him for eternity in heaven? Can there be any greater thing God will do for us the rest of our Christian life? Can there be any greater need of faith? We sometimes get so involved in our life or ministry at hand we forget the greatest thing that ever has happened to us, that is our salvation.

We need in some way to be reminded of it every day. How much easier our current Christian walk becomes when we remember the great work that has already happened to us. If we can grasp the great, great love of God which brought us salvation even though we only had a small amount of faith, can anything today decrease that love which He still has for us? And does knowing this great love that God has for us increase our faith? And that faith in His love for us will give us an assurance of our tomorrows and where we are going. Sometimes we cannot see God working when we are in the depth of something but when we look back later we see what God was doing. Memories of those times will give us more faith that God will be with us in the same way tomorrow. We read yesterday of Hannah's faith and how God gave her Samuel that she devoted to God's service.

It seems she also had faith in God having her tomorrows, *"And the LORD visited Hannah, and she conceived* [again] *and bore three sons and two daughters"* (1Sam. 2:21 RSV). Is this not the kind of tomorrows we want to have? When we ask God, do we pour out our heart to Him like Hannah, or do we hold back a little not wanting to lose face, even with ourselves? God wants us to be truthful with Him, and serious. Are you serious and truthful with God when you pray? These seem to be the elements which will bring us to that place we can say we are sure about where we are going.

---

1   Rom.3:23

'I am here for you always.' As you read the scriptures does this message come through to you? There are many, many things to learn of God. I believe the main one is of receiving our salvation, and then that He is here for us always. One day we will be in His very presence in Heaven, but until then we must live by faith. If we have faith and go to Him He does prove Himself. There are promises we need to latch onto: *"Truly, truly, I say to you, whoever hears my word and believes him who sent me has eternal life. He does not come into judgment, but has passed from death to life"* (Jn. 5:24 ESV). and *"everyone who believes in him receives forgiveness of sins through his name"* (Acts 10:43 RSV). and *"I am with you always, even to the end of the age"* (Mt. 28:20 NKJV). and *"And God is able to provide you with every blessing in abundance, so that you may always have enough of everything and may provide in abundance for every good work"* (2Cor. 9:8 RSV).

We will never know the full amount of how much God cares for us until that day we are in His presence. For now, we must know God cares for us far beyond what we could ever consider He does. He is always a much greater God than we can know. Do you know how much patience it takes to have longsuffering patience? This is what He had with us until we received salvation. I believe His longsuffering patience continues with us even after we are saved. And then there is the longsuffering patience He has had with mankind since Adam and Eve were put out of the garden. How great is our God, can we ever know this side of Heaven?

God could have abandoned us a long time ago for we did not measure up to His standards. He could allow us to be cast off into the lake of fire with the devil and those with him.[1] But He did not, He made a way we could be redeemed without lowering His standards. Amazing how God loved us so much that the requirement He made of us He provided Himself so that we would have a way we could be saved. Eternity with Jesus, how long is that, how great is that? Do we get it? Are we tied into eternity with our hearts such that it affects the way we live? That of not the measuring up, He already measured up for us. Do we have the effect of eternity on us, the greatness of what that is? When we begin to see in our hearts the reality of the eternity of heaven, the grip of this world we live in holds us less and less. Do you get this promise in our reading today, *"Pay attention to what you hear: with the measure you use, it will be measured to you, and still more will be added to you"* (Mk. 4:24 ESV).

What size measure do you use to hold what you hear? What size measure do you choose, is it large or small? Maybe it is difficult for you to know God is here for you always because you use too small a measure to hold what you hear. As you collect the words of God, what you hear increases the size of the measure and your confidence that God is here for you will also increase. With some of the scriptures I gave in the beginning do you see what Paul is telling us as we read today, *"But to him who does not work but believes on Him who justifies the ungodly, his faith is accounted for righteousness"* (Rom. 4:5 NKJV).

Is your measure large enough to hold this? Can you grasp that you are seen by God as righteous because of His doing and not your own doing? If you are always trying to measure up you will never feel worthy that God will be here for you always. But if you know that He measured up for you and the only thing you have to do is believe, that knowledge of Him being here for you will grow. Believe as Abraham believed and received the establishment of righteousness before God. Abraham believed and God was always there for him.

---

1   Rev.20:10

What do I have to say today? He who is with you is greater than he who is in the world. Who is it that is with you? What do we know about Him? First, it seems we should know who it is that is in this world. If He, Jesus, who is with us is greater, then that implies the one in this world is a threat. So who is this in this world? Is it some world leader in a nation that is a threat to all the rest of us? We won't find out in the daily list of world affairs. This one will not be listed there. We must look into the past to find who it is who today is the one in this world who is a threat to us. *"the accuser of our brothers and sisters has been thrown down, the one who accuses them before our God day and night"* (Rev. 12:10 NASB). and *"So the great dragon was cast out, that serpent of old, called the Devil and Satan, who deceives the whole world; he was cast to the earth, and his angels were cast out with him"* (Rev. 12:9 NKJV). and *"Be sober, be vigilant; because your adversary the devil walks about like a roaring lion, seeking whom he may devour"* (1Pet. 5:8 NKJV).

So now we know, and we need to be sober, and recognize the threat. The great news is He who is with us is greater than he who is in the world. The devil was cast down to the earth, he is the one who is the threat in this world but our Lord Jesus is greater. Now, what do we know about our Lord Jesus? He is from somewhere greater than this world, *"He who comes from above is above all"* (Jn. 3:31 RSV). This was John the Baptist speaking about Jesus. *"No one has ascended to heaven but He who came down from heaven, that is, the Son of Man who is in heaven"* (Jn. 3:13 NKJV). Now we know that Jesus is from heaven coming to earth and returned to heaven at the right of the Father. For all who accept Jesus He lives within us, He is the one who is in us. How much greater is Jesus than the one who is in the world? *"I by the finger of God cast out demons"* (Lk. 11:20 ASV). and *"I watched Satan fall from heaven like lightning"* (Lk. 10:18 NASB).

So it is the One who dwells in us is of heaven, the place the devil was cast out of, therefore those of heaven have the greater power. Today we read in Mark chapter 5 of the demoniac. This was one that no one messed with anymore, *"no one was able to bind him anymore, not even with a chain, because he had often been bound with shackles and chains, and the chains had been torn apart by him and the shackles broken in pieces; and no one was strong enough to subdue him"* (v. 3&4 NASB).

This guy is vicious, no one can touch him, he is uncontrollable. Yet it is not the man who is vicious, it is the demons. This is not one demon, or two, it is a Legion. A legion was in thousands. The pigs the demons went into were two thousand, so there could have been that many demons in this one man. That would certainly be a fearsome force. Yet Jesus had no trouble with authority over them. Not only did He have authority over them, they had to ask His permission to do anything different. Jesus who is in us does have greater power than the devil who is in the world.

Even a legion of the devil's forces was no match against Jesus. Go in peace knowing Jesus is greater than any force that can come against you. Here is the advice of the apostles: *"Resist the devil and he will flee from you"* (Jas. 4:7 NKJV). The devil (and his demons) will try every way they can, even to try to bluff you. But he cannot stand against Jesus who is with you. Remember, *"greater is he that is in you than he that is in the world"* (1Jn. 4:4 ASV). and *"Peace I leave with you; my peace I give unto you: not as the world giveth, give I unto you. Let not your heart be troubled, neither let it be fearful"* (Jn. 14:27 ASV).

Are you willing to wait?

Sometimes this is the course of faith. Are you willing to wait? God wants us to have faith. Faith does not come by us getting instant answers to all our prayers. The ones we have to wait on are the ones that it takes faith to receive. Of all the great characters in scripture, how many did not have to wait? Let me go backward in the scriptures with a few examples. The people came to Jeremiah asking him to go to God in prayer of a petition of theirs. Jeremiah went to God with this prayer, it was ten days before God gave him an answer.[1] This was Jeremiah! For him we would think it would be instantaneous.

How about Elijah, what do you think about him, would he have to wait? Jezebel, wife of King Ahab, threaten to kill Elijah and he ran for his life. It was over forty-one days before God began to speak to him.[2] Now there is Abraham. From the time God told Abraham he would have an heir speaking of Isaac, until Isaac was born Abraham waited more than fifteen years.[3] In our quick almost instantaneous world waiting is no common trait. With God He requires us to have faith. The only thing I know that we all get instantaneous when we ask is salvation. Faith is not the thing we have after we have received something from God, what we have then is gratitude. Faith is what we have when we are waiting for God to come through for us in our need. There are times God seems to require us to have faith right to the very moment of our need. As our faith becomes stronger does our willingness to wait increase?

As we mature our willingness to wait gets better as we gain more confidence in God. The lacking here in having confidence is not in God's court, it is in ours. As we mature the lacking in us gets less and less. The more confidence the more our faith, the more faith the more the willingness to wait. Our waiting is not much compared to eternity where God exists. There is a waiting that nearly every one of us has because it is tied to our salvation.

In our reading today in Romans chapter 6 we are told, *"For if we have become united with him in the likeness of his death, we shall be also in the likeness of his resurrection"* (v. 5 ASV). We have experienced the likeness of His death, *"Do you not know that all of us who have been baptized into Christ Jesus were baptized into his death?"*(v. 3 RSV). Because of what we are promised in our salvation, that of eternal life, we do have faith that we also will be resurrected like Christ. This waiting is a constant faith, not that many want it to come quickly, but we do all count on it. We will come to that place to enter and have life with Christ in heaven for eternity.

---

1   Jer.42:2,4,7
2   1Kg.19:2-9
3   Gen.15:4, 16:1&2, 17:16&25

How are your days going, are they well, are they blessed, are they working together as you need them? Who is it that has put them together, did you put them together, or did you offer them to God so He could put them together? You know He cares, you know He wants to do it for you, have you given them to God? God knows what will be in those days even before they come.[1] We have a tendency to get saved and then go back to being in charge of everything again. God wants our whole life, not just a little corner. If God only has that little corner then that is the only place He can bring you His blessings, they may be so small they go by and you might not even notice. Do you want to have God's blessings in all of your life, then you have to give Him all of your life. Our pride works against us, it tries to keep God out of as much of our lives as it can. Pride does not like dying.[2] We may never completely get rid of pride until we are in heaven with Christ, but we can begin starving it out more and more. God wants to help, we need to open the door and invite Him in.

We need to give Him the keys to every room in our life holding back none for our self. It is hard giving God everything, trusting Him to be in control of everything in our life, it may even seem risky. God knows we feel this way and wants to help us, but we are the ones who have to give Him a chance. He is always looking for an opportunity to bless us, but we have to open the door! What happens to the mail order you make when it is delivered waiting just outside the door and you do not open the door, do you gain a benefit from it? You have to open the door. You may even need to pray that God gives you the willingness to give all of yourself to Him. I don't believe any of us will be able to give ourselves totally over 100%.

We are like a vessel which is emptied of its contents. It is shaken out but there is still a residue on the inside surface. This residue in our flesh we will not be fully rid of until we leave this world going to heaven. This residue may give us some trouble from time to time, but nothing like the controlling contents of self that filled the vessel before. God is loving, and God is kind, He is not an invader. He has to be invited, and welcomed. You have to give Him a chance, you have to open the door. All through the book of Jeremiah there was the prophecy of the coming captivity, yet from time to time God called them to return to Him. *"the LORD persistently sent to you all his servants the prophets, saying, 'Turn now, every one of you, from his evil way and evil deeds, and dwell upon the land that the LORD has given to you and your fathers from of old and forever. Do not go after other gods to serve and worship them, or provoke me to anger with the works of your hands. Then I will do you no harm"*(Jer. 25:4-6 ESV).

God is calling them to open the door. From time to time, even while it seemed sure Israel was headed for captivity, God would call them to return to Him. God wanted to help them. God wanted to bless them. He kept calling them as though He had a great desire to bless them, but they would not hear. Is God calling to you to open the door? God greatly desires to bless us. It may even be God has a hunger to bless us. We have to open the door and invite Him in. How did you receive salvation, was it by God busting through the door of your life saying, I'M TAKING OVER HERE! No, this is not how God is, you had to invite Him that time, what about now? Will you invite Him into all of your life to take control that He might bless all of your life?

---

1   Isa.46:9&10
2   Lk.9:23

Be at peace with God. What does that mean to you? That He won't thrash you and condemn you. Or that He will give you anything and everything you want. That He will accept you into heaven. What does that mean to you? The basis of that peace is Christ Jesus. What did the angels say when Christ was born, *"Then the angel said to them, "Do not be afraid, for behold, I bring you good tidings of great joy which will be to all people. For there is born to you this day in the city of David a Savior, who is Christ the Lord...Glory to God in the highest, And on earth peace, goodwill toward men!"* (Lk. 2:10,11,14 NKJV). 'And on earth peace', that peace came by way of 'Christ the Lord'.

It was by Christ the Lord which we would receive salvation bringing peace between God and those who are saved by Christ's blood. It should have been our blood, for we were guilty. God knew there was no way for us to ever make things right between Him and us so He took it upon Himself to make a way, *"For this is the will of my Father, that every one who looks upon the Son and believes in him should have eternal life, and I will raise him up on the last day"* (Jn. 6:40 ESV).

If you have looked to the Son and believed accepting Jesus as Lord and Savior does this scripture not bring peace? How about the promise to raise us up on the last day, does that not bring peace? Sometimes we get so entangled in our current situation we forget this very sure thing that has value far beyond what it is we may be in at the moment. These words are talking about heaven and eternity. Is there anything of which we need greater than this peace? Yes, God is concerned with our current situation, but no matter how our current situation goes, in the end you know where you will be and who you will be with.

God promises He Himself will be with us for eternity, *"And I heard a loud voice from the throne saying, "Behold, the dwelling of God is with men. He will dwell with them, and they shall be his people, and God himself will be with them as their God"* (Rev. 21:3 ESV). Our eternal peace is far greater for us than our current peace. There will be ups and downs in our life on this earth, but if we believe, our eternity is settled. For what we read in 1Samuel or Jeremiah about Israel things were not settled for them. We can be glad we no longer have to meet the requirements of the Law trying to make peace with God.

In our reading in Romans today there is another law which is for us, *"For the law of the Spirit of life has set you free in Christ Jesus from the law of sin and death"* (8:2 ESV). For a greater encouragement, you might want to read through all of chapter 8 again. There is one verse I will end with that speaks of our topic today, *"To set the mind on the flesh is death, but to set the mind on the Spirit is life and peace."* (8:6 RSV).

What is on your mind? How are you processing things today? Be careful, the world will draw you off into itself quickly. The world and its attractions are strong, our flesh wants to follow. In addition, our enemy has sent out his forces to try to derail us.[1] Is your grounding into Christ strong? Are there areas that may need shoring up? Are you getting enough input of the Word? Are you checking in with the Boss first thing in the morning before you're off and running? These things are important.

We are in this world but we are not of this world.[2] Jesus who is our King said His Kingdom was not of this world. Jesus' Kingdom is not of this world yet it is in this world. This is not double talk, it is reality that we need to get this straight. Jesus' Kingdom is not operated according to the ways of this world. Yet it is in this world for we are that Kingdom, *"For indeed, the kingdom of God is within you"* (Lk. 17:21 NKJV).

Therefore the Kingdom of Jesus[3] is made up of all believers in this world, but is ruled from heaven. Since we are not of this world we need to know what we are hearing from headquarters. Our Father wants to guide us, Jesus our Lord wants to help us, but we have to check-in. We need to be in such a relationship with God that during the day we can hear the directions He is giving. Some will ask, 'how do I hear'? It is that still small voice where God speaks within you. It takes some time and faith to consider what you have heard was God.

After time it will be proven to you which voice was of God and which was not. There is a very slight difference. Even once you have found which voice is of God you have to keep your ear turned towards Him. We can get so consumed in what we are doing that God could yell and we would not hear Him. What is on your mind, are you tuned into God? Don't feel bad when you begin to listen and sometimes get it wrong.

In Mark chapter 9 where we have read today Peter, James, and John got it wrong. When they all were coming down from the Mount of Transfiguration Jesus told them, *"not to tell anyone what they had seen until after the Son of Man had risen from the dead"* (v. 9 CJB). Later as they get closer to Jerusalem and Jesus' final act of mercy, they thought He was coming into town to take the throne of King David and rule from there. They did get it wrong. 'Risen from the dead', they didn't even get it that Jesus was on his way to Jerusalem to allow Himself to be taken and killed by the authorities.

We don't always get it, but they didn't either. Something in our reading today we need to hear and stow it away in our hearts, *"he sat down and called the twelve; and he said to them, "If any one would be first, he must be last of all and servant of all." And he took a child, and put him in the midst of them; and taking him in his arms, he said to them, "Whoever receives one such child in my name receives me; and whoever receives me, receives not me but him who sent me"* (v. 35-37 RSV).

---

1   Rev.12:17
2   Jn.15:19, 17:15
3   Col.1:13

'I am your friend always.' Can you imagine Jesus saying that to you? Do you know He loves you that much that He wants you as friend. He also tells us He is our brother, do you know that? *"But as many as received him, to them gave he the right to become children of God, even to them that believe on his name"* (Jn. 1:12 ASV).   So if Jesus is the Son of God and we are the children of God that makes Jesus our brother, our Eldest Brother. Jesus did say we who believe are His friends, *"Greater love has no man than this, that a man lay down his life for his friends. You are my friends if you do what I command you"* (Jn. 15:13&14 RSV).

What do you think of that, we are Jesus' brother (sister) and friend? Jesus asked us to humble ourselves and come close to Him, [1] He wants us close. What did He say about Jerusalem who would not come to Him, *"How often I wanted to gather your children together, as a hen gathers her chicks under her wings, but you were not willing!"* (Mt. 23:37 RSV).   If we are willing to come to Jesus is it not likely then He would gather us under His wing? We are of great value to Him. Not only did he go through suffering and dying on a cross for us, He gave up His rightful position in heaven to come to earth to bring to us a way we could be saved. *"Christ Jesus, who, though he was in the form of God, did not count equality with God a thing to be grasped, but emptied himself, by taking the form of a servant, being born in the likeness of men. And being found in human form, he humbled himself by becoming obedient to the point of death, even death on a cross"* (Philp. 2:5-8 ESV). and *"For you know the grace of our Lord Jesus Christ, that though He was rich, yet for your sakes He became poor, that you through His poverty might become rich"* (2Cor. 8:9 NKJV).

Jesus is wanting to be close, are you taking time to let Him be close? Earlier we read, 'Greater love has no man than this, that a man lay down his life for his friends.' Jesus surely is our friend, doing all that He did for us. To end this let me remind you of what Jesus said in our reading in Mark today, *"Behold, we are going up to Jerusalem; and the Son of man will be delivered to the chief priests and the scribes, and they will condemn him to death, and deliver him to the Gentiles; and they will mock him, and spit upon him, and scourge him, and kill him; and after three days he will rise...For the Son of man also came not to be served but to serve, and to give his life as a ransom for many"* (10:33,34,45 RSV).

---

1   Jas.4:10

How far away are you? How far away from God's glory are you? Where is it you reside spiritually in your normal day? How close to God, how far away? God is always with you, are you always with Him? I am sure none of us could say we are always with Him in heart and mind. We still have the imperfectness of the flesh with us which always tries to draw us away.

There is always the constant struggle between Spirit and flesh, the Spirit trying to draw us closer to God and the flesh trying to draw us away.[1] We can take hope in that we know the end of the story. As long as we are trying to draw closer to God He will help us. But if we are allowing other things to come in and take our attention, and our confidence, to take us away from God we need to take caution. An equal amount of devotion given to two different things is lukewarmness (half cold, half hot).

You may not fully be there, but take caution and stay away, *"So then, because you are lukewarm, and neither cold nor hot, I will vomit you out of My mouth"* (Rev. 3:16 NKJV). Know that in your trying to move away from any lukewarmness God will help you, *"Submit yourselves therefore to God...Draw near to God and he will draw near to you"* (Jas. 4:7&8 RSV). Take courage, God is closer than you think. Come to God and receive from Him. Even the glory of God you were asked about at the beginning, know that you already have it. *"I do not pray for these only, but also for those who believe in me through their word...The glory which thou hast given me I have given to them, that they may be one even as we are one"* (Jn. 17:20&22 RSV).

If we stay close to Jesus He provides all we need. God has desired relationship since the beginning, *"And they heard the sound of the LORD God walking in the garden in the cool of the day,..Then the LORD God called to Adam and said to him, "Where are you?"* (Gen. 3:8&9 NKJV). God was seeking relationship with Adam (and Eve who was with him). God is always seeking relationship with us, the question is, are we turning toward Him, or away from Him? God wants to provide all we need. This Three-in-One God of the Father, the Son, and the Holy Spirit went to great lengths to offer salvation to us. Jesus gave up His position in heaven to come to earth and give His blood by which we could be saved.

The Father sent the Son away from His side to earth and hung Him on a cross. And the Holy Spirit has been calling, and calling, and calling us to God ever since the resurrection of Christ. God is still seeking relationship. *"and you, although a wild olive shoot, were grafted in among the others and now share in the nourishing root"* (Rom. 11:17 ESV). This is in our reading in Romans today, is nourishment from the root not speaking of a kind of relationship? *"remember that you are not supporting the root, the root is supporting you"* (v. 18 CJB). God wants to be your supply, all of your supply. But God wants you as the branch to stay tightly a-hold of Him – **relationship**.

---

1   Gal.5:17, Rom.8:6

'I am the One you listen to.' There are many voices out there, ones telling you how you can be smarter, ones telling you how to increase your finances, ones telling you how to have a healthier life to live longer, ones telling you how to get in touch with your own self and the cosmos. There are many out there speaking at you, even the commercial world wanting to get more of your money out of your pocket and into theirs. Some of these voices are very sincere believing what they are saying is true, and others are just trying to take advantage of you. You have to decide what voice you are going to listen to.

A surprise, and not a surprise, is that the devil is behind many of them, *"now shall the prince of this world be cast out"* (Jn. 12:31b ASV). and *"Your adversary the devil prowls around like a roaring lion, seeking some one to devour"* (1Pet. 5:8 RSV). and *"I am sending you, to open their eyes so that they may turn from darkness to light and from the dominion of Satan to God"* (Acts 26:17&18 NASB). Do you see any deception in the world around you? *"called the Devil and Satan, who deceives the whole world"* (Rev. 12:9 NKJV).

Many of you may ask how you can know what voice to listen to. The first step is to be familiar with God's word, reading it on a regular basis. Nothing of what God, Jesus Christ, or the Holy Spirit would say to you will disagree with God's written word. Anything that even slightly disagrees run from quickly, the devil even tried to deceive Jesus in the wilderness. You know there is one voice, and only one voice, that you should listen to. All other things said to you have to be judged by this one voice.

This voice of God you know is the only one who really cares about you, and about your well being. There are many out there telling you things that surely will make your life in this world better, but what about eternity, will they make eternity better. Some will give you a great life here, and then take you to hell! We do need to take care of what voices we listen to. The first place to start is what the voice God said which is written down for us to read in our Bible. God wants to speak to us in that still small voice, but we have to start with the written word of God. God establishes Himself and His ways in that written word.

We read today in Mark chapter 12 these words of Jesus, *"Beware of the scribes who like to walk around in long robes, and like personal greetings in the marketplaces, and seats of honor in the synagogues, and places of honor at banquets, who devour widows' houses, and for appearance's sake offer long prayers"* (v. 38-40 NASB). What we need to see is what Jesus says about the scribes in other places, *"But woe to you, scribes and Pharisees, hypocrites, because you shut the kingdom of heaven in front of people; for you do not enter it yourselves, nor do you allow those who are entering to go in...you travel around on sea and land to make one proselyte; and when he becomes one, you make him twice as much a son of hell as yourselves"* (Mt. 23:13&15 NASB).

And this is what Mark reports to us, *"And the scribes who came down from Jerusalem said, "He is possessed by Beelzebul, and by the prince of demons he casts out the demons"* (Mk. 3:22 RSV). These were reasons to beware of the scribes not listening to their voices. We have many voices today speaking to us wanting us to listen to what they have to say. Here is what Paul told us in reading Romans today, *"Do not be conformed to this world, but be transformed by the renewal of your mind, that by testing you may discern what is the will of God, what is good and acceptable and perfect"* (12:2 ESV). He is telling us to be cautious and not allow the world to conform us to its ways. It was a danger to them then, and it is a danger to us today.

Do you know where you are going? Have you settled that question, or is it still a question to You? Many of us who are saved still wrestle with that question. Have you ever tried to tune in a station on the radio but the interference was so bad you could hardly hear anything? Hearing where we are going from God to know for certain sometimes is hard to hear because of all the interference. The interference can come from a certainly confused world, and it can come from ourselves.

We need to filter out what comes from outside first. A lot of the things coming from the world that says they are certain are certainly not certain. It all has to be put along side of truth to see if it is truth. Truth comes from God but the world is confused. Pilate asked Jesus, *"Pilate said to Him, What is truth?"* (Jn. 18:38 ASV). If what is said does not line up with truth then we should not listen to it. Those things from the world creep in a little here and a little there assembling themselves in us becoming such interference that we have trouble hearing the truth. Faith is built on truth, but we have to believe before it becomes faith. Which will you believe, that which comes from God or that which comes from the world?

We have to realize all they say they know is only what they think they know. God does know, He does not have to think so. There are things that we as the human race in this world know, yet when this earth is put away and a new earth is brought out everything will change.[1] So the question is, do we as the human race really know? Better for us to line ourselves up with God's word and what He says in it. What He says may seem improbable and illogical, yet it will be. When you received salvation can you explain the change that happened to you logically? It is a mystery to us.

There are workings of God that none of us can comprehend, yet it does not change them from being truth. When we do not comprehend, cannot figure it logically, cannot reason it out, and yet are willing to believe, then we have arrived at faith. When we finally reach faith then we know where we are going, *"I AM the Resurrection and the Life! Whoever puts his trust in me will live, even if he dies; and everyone living and trusting in me will never die"* (Jn. 11:25&26 CJB). and *"so must the Son of man be lifted up, that whoever believes in him may have eternal life"* (Jn. 3:14&15 RSV).

This is how we know where we are going, God's word which is truth tells us so. What we in the world look up to and think is sure may not be. In Mark chapter 13 today the disciples are speaking to Jesus of what they think is great, the Temple. Jesus tells them it will be thrown down. About seventy years later the Romans did just that. Chapter 13 of Mark along with Mt. 24 and Lk. 21 tells us what is to come. As the world things it knows, this it does not know: *"But in those days, after that tribulation, the sun shall be darkened, and the moon shall not give her light, and the stars shall be falling from heaven, and the powers that are in the heavens shall be shaken"* (Mk. 13:24&25 ASV). We know where we are going if we are willing to believe God.

---

[1]   Ps.102:25-27, Heb.1:10-12

'This is my story, this is my song, praising my Savior all day long.' Do you start out your day this way, do you start out praising your Savior? I try to since I try to start all my days with a devotional of some type, but 365 days a year – I don't think I make it. We all find in ourselves failures we don't like, even the Apostle Paul say he finds himself doing the very thing he does not want to do.[1] Are we in serious trouble here because of it? If it were a non-fixable, we surely would be in trouble. Can we fix it, can we make up for it some way – No. Whether it is not praising our Lord as He deserves or even the deepest of sin, we cannot perform anything on our part that will correct our failure in the past. Even with the instructions that were given by Moses to the Israelites from God they failed. (Jer. 32:21-23)

There were procedures they could go through at the Temple when they had failed but were their sins forgiven? *"according to which are offered both gifts and sacrifices that cannot, as touching the conscience, make the worshipper perfect"* (Heb. 9:9 ASV). and *"for it is impossible for blood of bulls and goats to take away sins"* (Heb. 10:4 YLT).The only fix is what God has done in the sacrifice of Christ on the cross – this is where our dependency must lie. We are helpless to do anything about correcting our failures before God once they've been committed.

The only thing we can do about them is be forgiven by the grace God offers.[2] In our reading today we heard Jesus say, *"This is my blood, which ratifies the New Covenant, my blood shed on behalf of many people"* (Mk. 14:24 CJB). Our part to receive this is confession and asking for forgiveness. We are to sincerely try to live Christ-like but when we fail there is forgiveness available to us. Pride gets in the way of this great offer to us by God. Today in our reading we saw how King Saul's fear and his pride got in the way (1Sam. 15:1-11,17-19).

In our pride we want to think we can fix this thing – No we can't! If ever there had been any that could, our Lord Jesus would not have had to suffer on the cross, but there was none. Most all of what Paul speaks of in Romans chapter 14 pride will get in the way of. When we finally know that we can't fix it, it brings us to full surrender before God. We come to that place, as Jesus did in the garden of Gethsemane, and we say to God, '**Not my will Lord, but Yours be done.**' At that point we put all our trust in God knowing we live only in Christ as the Apostle Paul has told us. We have nothing to offer other than our full surrender and the use of our being, of ourselves, to God for His use in His way.[3]

King Saul did not do it God's way. Jeremiah speaks of how Israel did not do it God's way. We need to know that left to ourselves we do not do it God's way – there needs to be Christ living in us, and through us. In Rom. 14:11 Paul reminds us of what is written, *"As I live, says the Lord, every knee shall bow to me, and every tongue shall confess to God"* (ESV). Let us get a head start knowing our eternal life has come from Christ and sing His praise; 'This is my story, this is my song, praising my Savior all day long.'

---

1   Rom.7:15
2   Jn.1:16
3   Isa.55:8&9

It is the time of the year when trees are full in leaves, flowers are full with color, and the meadows are fully green. Wouldn't it be nice if our lives were so fully bright. They can be but as the seasons come and go, there are those times in our lives when things are not so bright and beautiful. There are many reasons this is so. One of the reasons may be we are away from God, whether intentionally by our behavior or by slowly drifting away not noticing the distance that has come between us and our Lord. Another reason is that we are not at a distance from our Lord but disturbance and pressure around us cause life not to seem so bright. Sometimes it is even because we have determined to come into that closer relationship that the Lord wants us to have with Him and the enemy steps up his attack against us.[1]

There is also the pruning that our God does to make our lives more productive[2] and the chastening He does to those who He loves.[3] This is not intended to be a downer for there are many seasons of brightness and beauty in our Christian lives. It is just that we need to be prepared knowing these times do come. The Christian walk is about faith and it is only accomplished through faith. We dare not be conditioned by our surroundings. There will always be pressures to push us away from our Lord and we need to recognize them when they come. Our first course of action is to pray asking God if there is something on our part that is the problem.

We may have drifted away some, we may have slipped into some sin unnoticed, or maybe noticed but not dealt with. This may be some of the causes that has to do with us. There are outside forces that can also be the cause and prayer is our first line of defense. There is power in the Name of Jesus[4] and if we are not praying in His name we should not be surprised of some of the things that are happening. Jesus said that if we follow Him aligning ourselves with Him that we would receive persecution.[5] God is also continually making us more mature followers all the time and some of that may not seem pleasant at the time but afterward we see what He was doing. The main point here is our faith determines how we experience what is happening in our lives. Our faith is how we are anchored to our Lord, our sure foundation, our Rock.[6] We let that get weak and our life becomes upset easily.

The greatest way to keep that faith strong is fellowship with the Master. Time spent each day in our prayer closet, and many times a day as we walk offering a praise of the moment as we are doing our various things, or a request for help when we get in a tight spot, or just to have an ongoing relationship and dialog with the Lord as we go through our day. He is always available, never out of touch, we can speak to Him at any time, He is always there, He said He would never leave us.[7] We see in our reading the last couple of days how King Saul goes in a direction other than what God wanted of him and his life is no longer bright and beautiful. We also see in our reading today that God is a redeeming God.(Jer. 32:36-44)

If our hearts turn rightly before Him and we truly seek Him from afar no matter how far it is, He will bring us back. In a way we all know that in our past we have been astray and far from the place God called us to be. All of Mark chapter 15 tells us of what Jesus went through to make a way that we could be brought back to God. If what Jesus did was powerful enough to pay for our sins bringing us to God it is powerful enough to bring us back if we drift away. In Romans chapter 15 Paul tells us that a very important support of our faith is communal support. We who are having a season where we are strong are to help those who are weak, having the pity in love as Christ had for us and do what we can to strengthen our brethren. We are to greet one another as Christ greeted us, with a hope that comes from God. (v. 1-7)

The whole anchor here is faith, and how we need each other at times to shore up that faith. Jesus is always close by, turn to Him often.

---

1   Rev.12:17
2   Jn.15:2b
3   Heb.12:6
4   Acts 3:6, 4:10&30, 16:18, Eph.5:20, Col.3:17, 1Thes.5:16-18
5   Mt.5:10&11, Mk.10:30, Jn.15:20
6   Lk.6:47&48, Ps.18:2&46, 31:3, 40:2, 61:2, 62:1&2, 95:1-5/Col.1:13-16
7   Heb.13:5

Here we are afraid and reluctant to move forward. We say we know but we are afraid of the unknown. How do we move forward, how can we move ahead? Our trust has to be in the right place. We have to see the other forces at work here other than ourselves. It is not unusual to find we are not alone, many fear. We are afraid to say we fear, we are afraid to even admit to ourselves sometimes that we are afraid because then we would admit to ourselves we are no longer in control of our own selves or our destiny. Fear does a terrible thing, it alienates us from others because we never really allow anyone to know us, all they know is the facade that we build.

God sees right through the facade into the depths of our lives that we continually try to hide from Him and everyone else. We are unfair to ourselves for the very interaction we try to avoid with others, especially God, is the very interaction that will bring the fullness to our life we are desiring. We don't know what we have in who we are and who our God is. We as Christians have been given something very special. We have been permitted by the blood of Christ to have a relationship with a God that is so spectacular that all the planets and stars in the universe listen to His every command.

This same God wants to have a relationship with us, even like family. We are special to Him, He went way out of His way in the work He did on the cross so we could come close to Him. He cares about our every move, our every want, our every need. The greatest need that any of us have past receiving salvation is acceptance, the being accepted by God and to be accepted by those around us. Yet we are afraid. We don't want to let our guard down, we don't want anyone to see in.

We wonder how it is we can find no help with our problem, our need, yet we only allow others to only work with and befriend our facade. Even God, although He sees the whole thing, won't invade, He only comes where He is invited. This is where we have to start, to invite God into our deepest places and in admitting how and who we are to Him we have also admitted it to ourselves. This is where it has to start.

God will begin to help us and we will arrive at a place we also can invite others into knowing who we really are. We can play the part well with a great facade but until we invite others into who we really are there will be no help and we will continue to struggle along alone. As we begin to open up we must always start with God. He is the most compassionate one we can go to. Even if our relationship with Him has been not what it should be, He is the one who will restore.

As much as Judah had messed up by the time God was sending them off to Babylon He yet says this through the prophet Jeremiah in our reading today, *"I will cleanse them from all the guilt of their sin against me, and I will forgive all the guilt of their sin and rebellion against me. And this city shall be to me a name of joy, a praise and a glory before all the nations of the earth who shall hear of all the good that I do for them"* (33:8&9 NKJV).God's nature in His love is to restore, if we will truly yield to Him and truly seek Him – He will be found. God will do good even to the rebellious if those who were rebellious will turn back to Him and truly seek Him with an open heart towards Him.

This is the **Word**. It cannot be defined. It is too advanced for total comprehension. It is too vast to contain. The **Word** of God is beyond the scope of our abilities. Our use of the **Word** is very limited but God's use goes far beyond. In the Greek it is the **logos**. For us words communicate, with God the **Word** was used to create. It was by the **Word** that things were created. It is the **Word** that saves us, we are given life by the **Word**. This is a hard thing for us to grasp. So many things of God are hard to grasp. [1]

I suppose this is why we must have faith, we are certainly not able to grasp it so we are just to simply believe it, that child like faith to believe it just because Papa says it is true. Instead of being the child too many times we want to be the Papa and say how it ought to be. We need to practice being the child and just believe. Being an adult in our busy world makes it difficult to believe like a child. We have responsibilities in this world, we have important decisions we must make, we have work that must be done – this is how the world functions and keeps going. All these things must be with life and work and living on this earth.

Yet when it comes to God He is the one in charge, we are not, we are to be like children. It is easy to let the one area of our lives drift over into the other. We are far away from what we ought to be. We have a distance to go that we must travel. As we do in the world, and are done to by the world, we want to bring the same into our relationship with God. God won't have it, and then we wonder why we have a problem in connecting with God. In the world we might have a position of responsibility but our only responsibility to God is to let Him have the responsibility. We might be assigned a task in the world to do but with God we are to align ourselves with the task He has done. [2] We might have others that we take care of but with God it is He who takes care of us. [3] We must yield to His ways if we want to go far with Him. We must not be like the people of Jerusalem who does it God's way today and then tomorrow turn around and do it their own way again (Jer. 34:8-11). God will not bless us if we do not yield to His ways. In our reading of Luke chapter one today we hear that Zachariah was caused to not speak until his son was born by having questioning faith of how it possibly could be for him to have a son at his and his wife's age.

Mary was puzzled but said *"may it be done to me according to your word"* (Lk. 1:38 NASB) - allowing God to be in charge. Back to the **Word** of God, *"I will destroy the wisdom of the wise, and the intelligence of the intelligent I will bring to nought"* (1Cor. 1:19 YLT). God brings us to a place of knowing who we are in the rest of this chapter and says in v. 29, *"so that no human being might boast in the presence of God"* (ESV). We need to know God is right. We need to come to Him, Papa, as a little child with confidence **Papa knows best**. Paul tells us what we all need to know in v. 9, ***"God is faithful,*** *by whom you were called into the fellowship of his Son, Jesus Christ our Lord"* (NKJV).Do we believe He is faithful, does our actions in our lives show it? Or are we still in charge too much of the time because we do not believe He is faithful. **We need to be the children and let Papa be Papa.**

1   Isa.55:8&9, 1Cor.1:25
2   Jn.3:16, 19:30, Lk.2:30-32
3   Lk.12:24

'I am the way, the truth, and the life.' Do you live as if this is all true? I know you believe it, but is it reflected in the way you live? I know some of us can say yes, and some of us have to ponder the question. This is something all of us should ask ourselves from time to time. I might live this week with a yes, and then next week not have such a strong yes needing to ponder the question. There is something we all need to keep in mind, we are yet imperfect and will need grace again. I am glad the scriptures tell me this, *"And from his fulness have we all received, grace upon grace"* (Jn. 1:16 RSV).

I am glad that God has stacked a high pile of grace, one upon another, for sometimes I need much. Without this grace, none of us would receive salvation. Without this grace none of us could continue walking with God, and moving more towards God. We will never reach the place we need no more grace this side of heaven. As we mature spiritually we may need less than in the beginning, but we will always need grace to walk with God. Our good is not good enough to walk with God, we will always need the grace provided by Christ to be permitted to be in the presence of God. [1]

Jesus by His grace is the way to get to God. We are all vulnerable to our own flesh. It wants to take us places we should not go. [2] It is the grace that comes by Christ that we have the Holy Spirit within us that fights the desires of our own flesh. [3] The devil is out there, and his demons are out there, but they do not have the power to cause us to sin. It is our own flesh that wants to take us down that road of destruction. [4] The only thing the devil and his demons can do is tempt us and be a coach and encourager to our flesh when it contemplates something sinful. We can be thankful for the life we have, that spiritual life leading on into eternity, the life we have received through Jesus Christ in our new birth. We always need to remember that new birth, the greatest of all miracles we will ever experience.

God reaches out in love searching for us, finding us, and drawing us to Jesus to receive salvation. [5] It is through Jesus we arrive in heaven. The thief on the cross ask, and Jesus replied, *"Truly, I say to you, today you will be with me in Paradise"* (Lk. 23:43 RSV). Is there anything we can do eternal without Christ. The only thing we can do without Christ is end up in the lake of fire with the devil and his followers. Christ is all we need and everything we need. The Father is there, and the Holy Spirit is there, but we get to nether without going through Christ. It is good to recall what Simeon said that God revealed to him, *"Lord, now you are letting your servant depart in peace, according to your word; for my eyes have seen your salvation that you have prepared in the presence of all peoples, a light for revelation to the Gentiles, and for glory to your people Israel"* (Lk. 2:29-32 ESV).

This is spoke of the Christ, the Messiah, that through Him we will receive the way, the truth, and the life. Paul was highly educated and could have swoon many high words of his wisdom, but instead he said this, *"I decided not to know any thing among you, except Jesus Christ, and him crucified"* (1Cor. 2:2 YLT). Of all Paul could have said he spoke only of that One who has all that any needs. *"I am the way, and the truth, and the life"* (Jn. 14:6 ASV).

---

1   Rev.21:23
2   Rom.7:18
3   Gal.5:17
4   Jas.1:14&15
5   Jn.6:44

'Know who I am.' God wants us to know who He is. The first thing we need to know goes outside our spectrum of understanding. Our God is one (Deut. 6:4), He is three persons. (1Jn. 5:7) Even though He is in heaven He also is everywhere else at the same time. (Jer. 23:24) The Father is God (1Chr. 29:10), Jesus is God (Isa. 9:6), the Holy Spirit is God. (Acts 5:3&4)

If we don't start out with faith we can never be saved. To know anything of God it seems it must be by faith, for nothing of God makes sense to us. The thing is, He is the Ever Being One, we and our understanding in this world are temporary. We live, we die, and then the judgment in which God decides where each person will spend eternity.[1] It is important that we know who God is before that judgment comes. None of us can do anything about how we will be judged once we end our time here on earth. So then we must settle this thing while we yet have life here. Know God, He has given us life here on earth to have time to realize He is, and to find Him.[2] For us who have found Him and are saved now it is to be in His word that we can come to know Him. Knowing God is hard, and it is easy.

We can cause it to be hard by questioning everything about Him with our understanding and our knowledge. We can make it easy by being willing to believe everything He says since He surely knows much more than we do. Knowing God comes back to faith, are we willing to believe? We cannot even be saved if we are not willing to believe Jesus died for us and can give us the new birth. How hard will you make it to know God? God is constantly calling to mankind for us to come to Him.

In Jeremiah God was time after time calling the people to repent, *"It may be that the house of Judah will hear all the disaster that I intend to do to them, so that every one may turn from his evil way, and that I may forgive their iniquity and their sin* (Jer. 36:3 ESV). God has a desire for us to come to Him so He can forgive us. God's calling for us to come, to receive forgiveness, and to be saved has been from of old as John the Baptist says in our reading of Luke today, *The voice of one crying in the wilderness: "Prepare the way of the Lord, make his paths straight. Every valley shall be filled, and every mountain and hill shall be brought low, and the crooked shall be made straight, and the rough ways shall be made smooth; and all flesh shall see the salvation of God"* (Lk. 3:4-6 & Isa. 40:3-5 RSV).

This was such a new concept to those of Israel, that sin could be forgiven without them offering a sacrifice, that God sent John the Baptist to introduce the idea that repentance could lead to forgiveness. The burden of offering a sacrifice God removed from man and put upon Himself. Now it is for us to believe what God has said, to read His word and know Him, to come close to Him and experience Him.

We are called to Him to come in Spirit as Jesus said to Nicodemus, *"Yes, indeed, I tell you that unless a person is born from water and the Spirit, he cannot enter the Kingdom of God. What is born from the flesh is flesh, and what is born from the Spirit is spirit"* (Jn. 3:5&6 CJB). In being saved we are born of the Spirit in addition to us having already been born in the flesh. In the Spirit is how we come to know God. Believing is how we come to know God. Moving from the pursuit of things by our intellect to pursuing God in the Spirit may be something new but God will meet you there if you try. Some would say it is a heart thing, that is where it begins. God calls us to know Him.

---

1   Jn.5:29
2   Acts 17:27

I am able, *"I can do all things through Christ who strengthens me"* (Philp. 4:13 NKJV). This is what Paul was able at a certain place in his life to say after listing things that he went through. Do you feel you are able to do, or go through, all things through Christ? I am not sure how many of us can answer yes to that question. The key to Paul being able to say this may lie in what he begins it with, *"I have learned in whatever situation I am to be content"* (v. 11 ESV). In this world of being driven by the pursuits of mankind we are constantly being told we need this or than to have a happy life. That pursuit to have what will make us happy causes us to end up with monthly credit card payments which surely didn't bring happiness to our life. We need to step back a few steps and ask ourselves what is the most important and valuable things in our life. God says He plants His will in us so that is where we should look first. [1]

The important values we will find there. The world will always try to take us in the other direction. We need to be careful who we listen to. Studies have been done that when we hear the same thing over and over after enough times we subconsciously accept it as truth. How many times have there been where you were told over and over you can't (not able) to do something so you don't even try? The devil is a deceiver. Others who want to take advantage of you, or to think better and higher of themselves, will tell you you can't.

The thing is we have to know who to believe. Would it not be a good thing to start out your day with some truth from God before you are exposed to all this stuff coming from the world? Even if we don't always grasp what we get from God it is still truth. Say your heart (your inner person) is growing spiritually, wouldn't it be a good thing to give it some of God's word as nutrients even if you don't know how those nutrients work. We need to examine where we are tying our life to, good anchors, or bad anchors.

We may need to begin untying from some of those things in the world and tying ourselves more into God's word, into His truth. Paul had everything, he though, until he met the risen Lord on the road to Damascus. [2] After that experience he then found Jesus Christ as Lord and he knew he had everything. As we have read in Luke today we see the devil even trying this stuff on Jesus, but Jesus knew the truth and He was having none of it. Even then the devil did not give up, he just left until he had another opportunity. (Lk. 4:13)

We need to be in the truth because the deceiver is always trying to deceive. In 1Corinthians today we hear Paul listing again those things he, and the apostles, go through, *"We are fools for Christ's sake, but you are wise in Christ. We are weak, but you are strong. You are held in honor, but we in disrepute. To the present hour we hunger and thirst, we are poorly dressed and buffeted and homeless, and we labor, working with our own hands. When reviled, we bless; when persecuted, we endure; when slandered, we entreat. We have become, and are still, like the scum of the world, the refuse of all things"* (4:10-13 ESV). Yet Paul is able to say he can do all things through Christ who strengthens him. Can you get a glimpse of what anchors Paul has the lines of his life tied to? It seems the more we begin untying our lines from untrustworthy anchors and tying them into things of God, the more and more we can say like Paul, **'I am able.'**

---

1   Philp.2:13
2   Acts 9:4-6

'For you are My planting.' Do you feel you have been planted by God? Can you look around and see that someone else certainly was involved in getting you to where you are? Can you look back at things in your past that could have turned out very bad for you, even may have lost your life, but didn't? For those of us who get saved it seems God was watching out for us even before we found Him. It is hard for us to know of the things of God, even though He tries to teach us. Can I ask you how high are the heavens above the earth, do you know? It seems to answer this question accurately the first thing we would have to know is where exactly are the heavens. Do you know exactly where so we can take a measurement? Oh, you don't exactly know–neither do I.

God gives us an unknowable measurement that we can get the impression how much greater He is than us, how much more He knows than us. It seems that the knowing of where the heavens exactly are is beyond us, so then to know how much more God knows than us is also beyond us. It is so far beyond us that it would be as though we know nothing compared to God. *"For My thoughts are not your thoughts, Nor are your ways My ways," says the LORD. For as the heavens are higher than the earth, So are My ways higher than your ways, And My thoughts than your thoughts"* (Isa. 55:8&9 NKJV).

Even as much as we may think we have our life all laid out, God may be involved and we not even know it. There may have been many things we think we got done and it was Him doing it. Did you ever have anything just seem to fall into place? Maybe it didn't fall, maybe it was planted. God plants in us His ways, His works, His will. As soon as we grasp that measurement of how much greater He is than us things in our life may get easier. We may begin to lean on Him more and ourselves less. Do you think He has your tomorrow?

Once we give our lives to God all of it belongs to Him, that of before we were saved, and all of that which is after. Are you His possession, is He your Master? If we start to contemplate these things we will begin to see that our life has been planted by Him. Of our salvation God has known about since the beginning of time, *"Come, you who are blessed by my Father, inherit the kingdom prepared for you from the foundation of the world"* (Mt. 25:34 ESV). Then there is this from Revelation: *"and all who dwell on earth will worship it, every one whose name has not been written before the foundation of the world in the book of life of the Lamb that was slain"* (Rev. 13:8 RSV).

All of us who belong to Christ are those who do not worship the beast, we are those whose names are in the Book of Life from the foundation of the world. God has known you much longer than you have thought, He is not restricted by time. Jeremiah's life was planted by God, and God knew of all that would happen to him, *"The word of the LORD came to Jeremiah while he was shut up in the court of the guard:...I will deliver you on that day, says the LORD, and you shall not be given into the hand of the men of whom you are afraid"* (Jer. 39:15&17 RSV). and *" Nebuchadrezzar king of Babylon gave command concerning Jeremiah through Nebuzaradan, the captain of the guard, saying, "Take him, look after him well and do him no harm, but deal with him as he tells you"* (Jer. 39:11&12 RSV).

Nothing will happen to us that God does not already know about. God has seen our life, He has planted it according to His own desire, and all will take place that He has ordered.

'Think of all that I have done for you.' Can you think, and consider, all that God has done for you? And the more you think, the more that there is you remember? What a marvelous Lord we have. For those of us who believe, there is so much more that God wants to do for us. Of course, the greatest yet to come is the day He takes us to heaven. What about between now and then? Are you believing and having faith, expecting God to do something more in your life? Are you seeing things God's way, or only your way? Sometimes we don't see anything of God happening in our life because we are wanting God to adjust to our way and work in it. We need to be careful because this can sneak in easily.

We should always be checking to see if our life, and wants, are lined up with God's ways, the ways He has for us. Jesus did say follow. We need to be following Him rather than to fall into a delusion of thinking He will follow us providing where we need. We all need to face it that none of us are worthy, that the only thing we deserved was the wrath of God. We have been saved from that wrath of God by salvation through the blood of Christ. Once we realize without Christ what we do deserve, everything else from there is up. We need to look for, and search, and find, the way of God so we can be aligned with Him so He can bless us. We should remember as He reigns over our lives here in this world He reigns from heaven, a spiritual place superseding this place.

Some things God says may seem strange and difficult to apply, but they are spiritual things from a realm beyond the physical world we live in. Some have said of some people that they are so heavenly-minded they are no earthly good. I stand in debate to that statement, I see one who is not heavenly mind not able to be much earthly good. We must align ourselves with God so we can follow God and know what it is He would have us do. It is when we begin tending to His Kingdom here on earth that He begins tending to our needs.

There is an interesting event in the gospels. Jesus sends out the twelve by twos to minister, see what Jesus does: *"These twelve Jesus sent out and commanded them, saying: "Do not go into the way of the Gentiles, and do not enter a city of the Samaritans. But go rather to the lost sheep of the house of Israel. And as you go, preach, saying, 'The kingdom of heaven is at hand...Now it came to pass, when Jesus finished commanding His twelve disciples, that He departed from there to teach and to preach in their cities"* (Mt. 10:5-7 & 11:1 NKJV).

Jesus sends out the twelve to tend to His Kingdom, and while they are out ministering as He sent them, Jesus Himself goes to the apostle's cities where the ones they care about are. Do you think the apostles were blessed when they heard that Jesus had gone to their own cities and ministered? There is a promise of Jesus in what we read in Luke today, *"Give, and it will be given to you. They will pour into your lap a good measure—pressed down, shaken together, and running over. For by your standard of measure it will be measured to you in return"* (6:38 NASB). Many might say this speaks of tithing or giving financially. Do you see it speak of money anywhere, or tithing? If you give of yourself to minister for God He will give back to you. As we begin to give ourselves more to Him in the place He calls us to follow, the more we will find He is doing in our lives and those we care about.

'He who is with me does not forsake me.' Are you with Jesus, is He with you? This life is difficult to walk through alone. Paul in our reading today tells us if we need a wife/husband to take one, but better because of the time to not take one. Paul, as did the other apostles, believed Jesus would return soon.[1] In that light and thought it was better to be single with no ties so the person was free to serve the Lord.

There were also difficult times in some areas as some of the Church was being persecuted which is more difficult if someone has a family. It was so much easier to not forsake Jesus without family. We all want to be considered as one who is with Jesus. At one point Jesus says if we do not hate our spouse, our children, even our parents, then we are not able to follow Him.[2] Of course, this does not mean hate in the sense we use it for we are told to love..... This is to show the depth of our love for Christ, that we are to be in relationship with Him more than any other.

Surely David was devoted to God more than any other around him, yet in our reading in 1Samuel today David takes a wife. God was always first and foremost in David's life. His devotion to God was so great that the relationship he had with any other would be as hatred in comparison. Look at what he as a youth said to Goliath: *"I am coming unto thee in the name of Jehovah of Hosts, God of the ranks of Israel, which thou hast reproached"* (1Sam. 17:45 YLT). Certainly, David would be one who was with God and would not forsake God. In Luke chapter 7 today there are two who Jesus makes a comparison of: *"A certain creditor had two debtors; one owed five hundred denarii, and the other fifty. When they could not pay, he forgave them both. Now which of them will love him more?"* Simon answered, *"The one, I suppose, to whom he forgave more"* (v. 41-43 RSV).

Do you see which of the two, the woman of sin or the Pharisees, was with Him and would not forsake Him? This is a hope for any who have a past they would rather not even think of, Jesus would say to you as He did to this woman, *"Your faith has saved you; go in peace"* (v. 50 RSV). Are you one who would say you are with Jesus and would not forsake Him? We see by the woman who came with adoration to Jesus, and no embarrassment to be seen doing such, that any of us are welcomed by Jesus so that we can be one He would say is with Him and would not forsake Him.

---

1   1Thes.4:15, 1Pet.4:7, 1Jn.2:18
2   Lk.14:26

'I am here in your presence always.' What a great thing to think of, that we are never alone. Jesus said He would always be with and in us.[1] The Holy Spirit was given to us to be with us, and even in us helping guide us and teach us.[2] We are even told God is in us.[3] How precious a promise we have been given. We need to plant it deep in our hearts that God is always with us no matter what. Jesus told us the world would not accept us easily, and because of Jesus in our lives some of us would even be persecuted.[4] In those times if we have the truth buried deep down in our hearts we will know God is with us.

Knowing God is with us gives us the strength to move forward in ministry for Him. He never sends us out ahead of Him, Jesus didn't say go out and be a trailblazer for Me establishing a great work. What did Jesus say, *"If anyone serves me, he must follow me"* (Jn. 12:26 ESV). Since Jesus said follow any work He calls us into He is already there working. We are never alone. The world will lie to us and try to convince us Jesus is not real, therefore is not with us.

The demons will lie to us and try to convince us Jesus is not there with us. Who's voice are we going to listen to? God loves us and cares about us. He will always be close. We will know this by faith, and the more our faith the more we know He is right there with us. In my life over the years many times I have mislaid my screwdriver or hammer. I would ask God, not as if He were way off in heaven, but as if He was right there, and He always showed me where they were. If we know He is with us how much easier it is to step out in what He calls us to do.

The assurance of His presence with us here in this world will give us assurance He will be with us in eternity. In our reading in 1Corinthians Paul tells us a very important thing, *"for us there is one God, the Father, from whom are all things and for whom we exist, and one Lord, Jesus Christ, through whom are all things and through whom we exist"* (8:6 RSV). If we are existing through Jesus Christ how can we not be in Him and Him in us? This is beyond our comprehension in this world, it has to be accepted by faith as being in the spiritual world, which is all around us. How close is family? In our reading today in Luke chapter 8, Jesus assures us we are His family, *"Then his mother and his brothers came to him, but they could not reach him for the crowd. And he was told, "Your mother and your brothers are standing outside, desiring to see you." But he said to them, "My mother and my brothers are those who hear the word of God and do it"* (v. 19-21 RSV).

One more thing we see in Luke today, He is with us in the storm, *"as they were sailing along He fell asleep; and a fierce gale of wind descended on the lake, and they began to be swamped and to be in danger. They came up to Jesus and woke Him, saying, "Master, Master, we are perishing!" And He got up and rebuked the wind and the surging waves, and they stopped, and it became calm"* (v. 23&24 NASB). If Jesus is always with us there will be no storm in our lives when He is not with us in it. And He has full control over the storm not allowing it to overwhelm us, or cause us to sink. Even Peter stepped out of the boat and walked on the water with Jesus not allowing him to sink when his faith failed him.[5]

---

1   1Jn.3:23&24
2   Jn14:15-17,26
3   1Jn.4:15
4   Jn.15:20
5   Mt.14:28-31

Love, Love, Love. We talk about it, but what do we know of it? The world talks about love, that we should all love one another so there will be peace in the world. We have all seen the sign, 'Imagine Peace'. That is all the farther it will ever be, it is only of the imagination. Jesus said there will be a time when even those in a family will hate each other.[1] The only time there has been perfect peace and love was in the Garden of Eden. That didn't last long, and when mankind was put out of the garden look how soon that hate came between two brothers and perfect peace and love were gone.[2] The world all around us talks about love but their idea of love is a poor substitution. Love has a depth that many do not see. The very first act of love was by God in creation. How was that love? God created mankind putting them in the garden providing all that they had need of.

He created them so He could come in the cool of the day to visit mankind and have fellowship.[3] It was a wonderful garden God created for mankind with all that mankind needed for food from every plant that grew from the ground. There was one more thing God gave in His love to mankind in creation we might not have considered. He gave mankind a free will to choose. As seen from our perspective this was a dangerous move. This meant mankind had the choice to even turn away from God.

Some would say why would God allow us to mess up so bad. If we did not have free will what would we be, and what would God have? If we had no free will we would not have the free will to love or not love, we would have no free will to follow God or not follow God. If we had no choice other than to love God because we were made that way what kind of love would that be? Could God be happy because His children loved Him if He knew that the only choice they had was to love Him. Those now who love Him He knows truly love Him by their choice to.

God chose to love us in the beginning, and when He seen that we messed up He continued to love us. Jesus was sent to show us God's love, to make a way we could be with Him and still the righteous requirements could be met. This took a level of love that none of us could do. God Himself sacrificed Himself to meet the requirements for us that we could not reach. What an act of love. One of the last things Jesus told us to do was love.[4] We do find that after we receive salvation there is a love in our hearts that was not there before, but it is still short of the love that God loved us with.[5]

It doesn't mean we should give up trying. We should continue learning and knowing more about the type of God's love and do our best we can. We have a newness within, not only of flesh, but now also of Spirit. Out of this Spirit is where real love, a God kind of love comes from. It will grow as we allow it and feed it. You might ask how do we feed it. God's word will cause it to grow, God's word will give it substance of truth and strength. In our reading today in Luke chapter 9 Jesus tells us about that love of God. Jesus asked his disciple who that they say He is.

The Father reveals to Peter who Jesus is and says, *"Peter answered and said, "The Christ of God"* (v. 20 NASB). Even the Father in showing His love to Peter, and to all of us, revealed who Jesus was and is.[6] In the New Testament when it says **Christ** that is Greek for **Messiah**.[7] One of the meanings of Messiah is redeemer or one anointed with the Holy oil. Jewish people say they had many messiahs. But only this one had the spiritual anointing.[8] Jesus also is the only One who brings to us from the love of God a spiritual redemption. Jesus tells us what He must go through to provide that love of God to us: *"The Son of man must suffer many things, and be rejected of the elders and chief priests and scribes, and be killed, and the third day be raised up...Let these words sink into your ears: for the Son of man shall be delivered up into the hands of men"* (Lk. 9:22&44 ASV).

We hear Jesus' words here and we will see it unfold in the chapters to come. This is how much God loves mankind. We are called to take up His kind of love. We can never take up the fullness of the love God loves with, but we can take up His kind of love, the love that is not deserved and expects nothing in return.

1	Lk.12:52&53
2	Gen.4:8
3	Gen.3:8
4	Jn.13:34, 15:12,17
5	Jn.3:16
6	Mt.16:17
7	Jn.1:41, 4:25
8	Jn1:32-34

'We are one in the Spirit, we are one in the Lord.' What a great song from our past. Yet it is to be of our present also. Are we one in our Lord in His love among us? Do we understand that we are one in the Spirit also? In the spirit here does not mean in temperament, in the way we act together, in our goals as Christians. It is a foundational truth, *"It is the Spirit who gives life"* (Jn. 6:63 NASB). This is the truth, every one of us who has been reborn into a new life, it is the Spirit who has given us this life and unites us. You may say that we receive that new life through Jesus Christ, that is true, we do receive it through Jesus, and we are born of the Spirit who gives it.

"What is born from the flesh is flesh, and what is born from the Spirit is spirit...The wind blows where it wants to, and you hear its sound, but you don't know where it comes from or where it's going. That's how it is with everyone who has been born from the Spirit" (Jn. 3:6&8 CJB). If we are all born of the one Spirit then we are all one by that Spirit. Sometimes we don't give enough value to the Third Person of the Trinity. All three work in us to give us life. I am not saying we are not all one in Christ, but also we should see the part of the Spirit. *"But when the kindness of God our Savior and His love for mankind appeared, He saved us, not on the basis of deeds which we have done in righteousness, but according to His mercy, by the washing of regeneration and renewing of the Holy Spirit, whom He poured out upon us richly through Jesus Christ our Savior"* (Tit. 3:4-6 NASB).

Some think of the Spirit as being a force of God working in the background. He is a person of the Trinity the same as the Father is a person of that Trinity and Jesus is a person of that Trinity. If it was not so we would serve a Duality God. Jesus seems to be the front person in providing and presenting the gospel to us. It is the Father who sent Him. (Lk.10:16) It seems to be the Holy Spirit that gives the power to the actions of Christ. *"Jesus returned in the power of the Spirit into Galilee"* (Lk. 4:14 ASV). and *"I by the Spirit of God cast out demons"* (Mt. 12:28 ASV).

We see Jesus alone in the scriptures, but He says the Father is always with Him, and we now see it was the Spirit which gave Him power. Jesus is that front person to us and we are one in the Lord. There is much going on behind what we see Jesus doing. Jesus has been sent to bring us together. Paul explains it this way in our reading today, *"The cup of blessing which we bless, is it not a participation in the blood of Christ? The bread which we break, is it not a participation in the body of Christ? Because there is one bread, we who are many are one body, for we all partake of the one bread"* (1Cor. 10:16&17 RSV). Christ to us is the bread given. We all partake through Him, therefore we all become one. A further reach is that since the Father is with Him, and the Holy Spirit is with Him, we are all one in the Triune God. **We are one in the Spirit, we are one in the Lord, we are one in the Father, all in the Triune God.**

What do you think as you travel along the road of life? I recall of two others who were traveling down the road together. They had a bit of concern because of the times they were in and what had happened. They were traveling somewhat sadly as they went from one place to another. Sometimes we are traveling somewhat sadly as we travel getting from one place to another. We are traveling only because it is something we have to do. How lonely it can be at times, even if there are two of us together.

There is a certain amount of uncertainty in this life we travel through. We can be in joy and happiness and then along comes something that takes it all away. That is what happened to the two who were traveling together, going from one place to another. There seemed to be great things happening, and then in one day's time it all collapsed. Events occurred that took away all hope, all joy, even cutting deeply into life itself. There are those days we all have, and we are not sure where things are going from there. For these two as they traveled a man came along and began a conversation with them, and the more he talked the less difficult their day seemed.

There was a gladness that began to rise in their hearts and they invited the man to stay with them. Then the identity of this man was revealed to them, and they recognized it was the risen Lord Jesus. *"And behold, on that very day two of them were going to a village named Emmaus, which was sixty stadia from Jerusalem. And they were talking with each other about all these things which had taken place. While they were talking and discussing, Jesus Himself approached and began traveling with them...And He said to them, "What are these words that you are exchanging with one another as you are walking?" And they came to a stop, looking sad...And He said to them, "What sort of things?" And they said to Him, "Those about Jesus the Nazarene, who proved to be a prophet mighty in deed and word in the sight of God and all the people, and how the chief priests and our rulers handed Him over to be sentenced to death, and crucified Him...they strongly urged Him, saying, "Stay with us...So He went in to stay with them. And it came about, when He had reclined at the table with them, that He took the bread and blessed it, and He broke it and began giving it to them. And then their eyes were opened and they recognized Him...Were our hearts not burning within us when He was speaking to us"* (Lk. 24;13-15,17,19,20,29-32 NASB).

Do you need some gladness to rise up in your heart today? Do you need some joy and happiness as you travel this life? Jesus is always traveling with us, we just at times don't recognize it is He who is with us. Even if you do not hear Him speaking to you at that moment you can recall something that He has said in the scriptures. Even if it is only one thing that can get down into your heart it will make your day brighter. The more you get accustomed to knowing Jesus is traveling with you the travel won't be so lonely, even becoming a bit joyful at times.

Today in our reading in Luke 11:1-13 Jesus teaches about prayer. Our prayers are not just for the prayer closet, it is also as we go along our way, *"Rejoice always; pray without ceasing; in everything give thanks"* (1Thes. 5:16-18 ASV). and *"I desire therefore that the men pray everywhere"* (1Tim. 2:8 NKJV). The more we begin adding prayer to our travels the more we will become aware that Jesus travels with us making our day better. Don't do all your traveling like the first part of the trip for the two travelers, begin to make it like the latter part of their trip.

Where do you do your banking? Why do you trust in a bank? Do you have a secure deposit? This is all about the business of this world, what about heaven? Can you trust your valuables there? What about your valuables; your life and your future? Do you have them deposited in Heaven? Paul tells us who have trusted in Christ: *"But God, being rich in mercy, because of His great love with which he loved us,...made us alive together with Christ..., and raised us up with Him, and seated us with Him in the heavenly places in Christ Jesus"* (Eph. 2;4-6 NASB).   Since we have accepted Christ as our savior and now live in him our life is on deposit in heaven.

As Christ speaks of Himself as the bread of life which has come down from heaven He says this: *"This is the bread which came down from heaven...he who eats this bread will live for ever"* (Jn. 6:58 RSV).   So it seems your true valuables are on deposit in heaven. Everything else here on this earth will all pass away with this earth.[1] And anything that we accumulate while here will be left behind when we leave this earth. So maybe sometimes we get uptight about some things which really don't have that much value. In our reading today Jesus said this, *"one's life does not consist in the abundance of his possessions"* (Lk. 12:15 ESV).

We are easily blinded at times by giving things of this earth more value than they should have. Our eyes may be on them and pulled a little bit away from Christ. Eternity belongs to God, our life is just a dot on the timeline. In Luke chapter 12 Jesus in trying to teach us tells this parable, *"There was a man whose land was very productive. He debated with himself, 'What should I do? I haven't enough room for all my crops.' Then he said, 'This is what I will do: I'll tear down my barns and build bigger ones, and I'll store all my wheat and other goods there. Then I'll say to myself, "You're a lucky man! You have a big supply of goods laid up that will last many years. Start taking it easy! Eat! Drink! Enjoy yourself!" ' But God said to him, 'You fool! This very night you will die! And the things you prepared—whose will they be?' That's how it is with anyone who stores up wealth for himself without being rich toward God"* (v. 16-21 CJB).

Even though we don't think of heaven every day this scripture can help you to make an adjustment to the value of things around you? We really don't want to miss out on heaven, the things on this earth only have a value for a very short time.

---

1   2Pet.3:10,12,13

Life is good. If you are saved by Jesus Christ, then life is good. We may not always feel that way, life has issues. Most of these issues that bother us are the things of life on this planet. What about spiritual issues that are of the spiritual realm? Life is good, we can say we have life. We are told in scripture that without Christ in our life, even though we are alive we are dead. This is referring to spiritual life. So much of the population of this planet is dead.

God has been trying since creation to reach mankind with truth, but we as mankind are not listening. God made it great and good for the first couple in life on this earth in the Garden of Eden, they were given everything they needed. God spoke to them of how they should live and they were not listening, they lost it all. Mankind has been struggling ever since. We, some of us, find the fix God offers, and we find life again. Considering what it is our behavior earns us, which is the wrath of God, the life we have found through Jesus Christ is good. How long did it take you to find the fix? Do you remember how you were before salvation? Compared to what you have now could you really say what you had before was really life?

God wants good things for us, He has since the beginning. Do you know that God has known you since the beginning, has known all about you, has known all of your life even though you have not lived it all yet? God has seen it all, God has known it all, and in knowing it all those of us who are saved He wrote our name in the Book of Life of the Lamb from the foundation of time![1] Can you imagine such a God as we have? That is why we have faith, because we cannot imagine or understand all that there is of our God.[2] What an assurance, what a life, to know how much our God knows us. Our names, in the Book, since the beginning of time – what a thought! Now I ask you, **Is life good?**

No matter what we are going through, no matter how hard life may be at the moment, no matter if the end seems close, if we endure hanging on to God and His promises we will see the greatest life there is, and that life is with Him for eternity in heaven. This will be far beyond our expectations, it will be far beyond what we can think, it will be beyond what we can know until we get there. There are some of you who will say that you know because you have studied the scriptures. You have studied what God has spoken to us, but God, and the spiritual realm, and heaven are such God has no words to describe it fully so we would understand. Paul tells us this, *"I have known such a man--whether in the body, whether out of the body, I have not known, God hath known, – that he was caught away to the paradise, and heard unutterable sayings, that it is not possible for man to speak"* (2Cor. 12:3&4 YLT).

We do know what God has told us about heaven but how much is there that is unutterable? And the Apostle John was in the Spirit on the Lord's day seeing such things in a vision which he tried to describe and we still don't know for sure what some of it is he speaks of. The life we have in Christ is good. Jesus says this in our reading in Luke today, *"Someone asked him, "Are only a few people being saved?" He answered, "Struggle to get in through the narrow door, because—I'm telling you!—many will be demanding to get in and won't be able to"* (13:23&24 CJB). It is us who have sought Him, entered through the narrow gate, and found Him. *"as Moses lifted up the serpent in the wilderness, so must the Son of man be lifted up, that whoever believes in him may have eternal life." For God so loved the world that he gave his only Son, that whoever believes in him should not perish but have eternal life"* (Jn. 3:14-16 RSV). Our life here on this earth may be difficult at times, but hearing these words can there be any doubt that life is good?

---

1   Rev.17:8, 21:22-27
2   Isa.55:8&9, 1Cor.1:25

Count your days and every blessing. For our character and who we are without the redemption of Christ, it would be a wonder that we would have any days left to us at all. But if that were the case more than half the population of the world would no longer be alive. God lets man live an extended period of time that they might find Him and be saved. *"He has made from one blood every nation of men to dwell on all the face of the earth, and has determined their preappointed times and the boundaries of their dwellings, so that they should seek the Lord, in the hope that they might grope for Him and find Him"* (Acts 17:26&27 NKJV). Those of us who are saved should treasure each day He gives us, and see the blessings from Him in each one of them. I believe God looks forward to that day that we all from all generations will be with Him forever. Until we leave this earth to that greater place each day is a blessing.

When we know what it is we deserve, just to have God's grace on us in our day is a blessing that is given, even though we have done nothing to deserve it. [1] We become casual with, even taking for granted, the blessings of God. We get so tied up in the things of this world, and the life around us, that we sometimes lose track of God in our everyday life. He is always there, He is always caring about us in our day, He wants to be more involved if we would invite Him in. You might say you know He is always there, but do you invite Him in? How many can tell the shower of blessings that come down from heaven each day? Do they land on you because you are inviting God, or do they totally miss you falling on others?

This world around us, as beautiful as God has made it, is sometimes as a façade. We are focused on other things not seeing that which is real that last forever. A few things we get from our reading today maybe will help us make this adjustment. In chapter 14 of Luke Jesus says, *"For every one who exalts himself will be humbled, and he who humbles himself will be exalted"* (v. 11 RSV). If we exalt ourself it is sure we will not see the blessings God is giving us, and miss many more because we (even subconscious) don't know our need. If you are in this place be careful, for you know what is coming to bring you to a humble place by what Jesus says.

As we become humble we become more aware of our need and invite God in. Jesus goes on in v. 12-14 to speak of one who gives a banquet. I can't say this is directing us how to give a dinner party, but I do believe it is addressing the attitude of our hearts and how we should be. This parable also speaks about humility, of if in our life we are exalting ourself or acting in a humble manner. As we move into this humble manner we will begin to see more blessings in our life. In our humility we will see each day as a blessing, even if it might have been difficult, you knew God was in it with you. Part of the last that Jesus is telling us in chapter 14 is we need to have things in perspective.

In v. 26&27 Jesus tells us we should hate our close relatives. I am not convinced this is what He really wants us to hear. Does He not say we should honor our father and mother. [2] Also, we men are to love our wives, even as Christ loves the Church. [3] These scriptures cannot be in conflict, if they are then we should listen to none of them. The meaning of hate here is not the meaning we would give it, it is putting things into perspective – loving them less, far less, than Him. When some came to Him saying they would follow Him, He required that they love Him more than father, mother, or wife. [4] In this chapter of Luke Jesus makes another statement, *"So therefore, any one of you who does not renounce all that he has cannot be my disciple"* (v. 33 ESV). In comparison to Him they should have little value to us.

> In **The Complete Word Study Dictionary** this is the definition it gives for renounce: *'from apo(G575), from, and tasso(G5021), to place in order. To assign to different places, allot. In the NT, only in the mid. meaning to take leave of, bid farewell; to dismiss, forsake, or renounce. Translated "forsaketh" in Luk_14:33and carries the notion of putting something aside (perhaps in its correct priority) to prevent it from being a hindrance or gaining excessive control.'*

Again, from this meaning we can see it is about perspective. If we put things of our life in the right perspective we will approach God in a humble manner and see blessings each day.

---

1   2Chr.6:36, Ecc.7:20, Rom.3:23, 1Jn.1:8
2   Mt.15:2-6
3   Eph.5:25, Col.3:19
4   Lk.9:59-61

'I am here, can you find Me?' In the beginning, it was God who came into the garden to find Adam and Eve. Since then we have had to search and seek to find God. He is there to be found and most of you reading this have found Him. He is in your life and you are in His.[1] Such a relationship we are able to have with God. In how many other religions does their god give this privilege to its subjects? We are privileged to have a relationship to our God in this way. God knows us and He wants us to know Him. Jesus Christ is our Lord, our Master. We belong to Him and He takes care of us asking us to follow Him joining in His work. Have you ever thought about how He does not require us any longer to bring Him multitudes of offerings and sacrifices? He does not ask for hundreds of sheep, or goats, or cattle.

Mankind has always sought to appease their gods with offerings of some kind. We are not required, even if we did it would do us no good. The perfect sacrifice has already been made, there is none other that will be better, or even equal. There was no spiritual man who came along like Abraham, or Moses, or Elijah who made this offering. It was God the Father that made that perfect sacrifice Himself. And the Lamb offered was no ordinary lamb, it was the very Son of God. I equate this to what God asked Abraham to do with Isaac, yet God the Father did not find a substitute at the last minute, He sacrifice His own Son.[2] The sacrifice has been made, and all of us who will allow it to stand in for what we owe will receive a benefit we did not earn.

As sorrowful as the thought of what the Father did to the Son, yet what a God to do such a thing for His subjects so we could come close to Him. Many fathers would sacrifice themselves for their child, but how many would sacrifice the oldest son for the benefit of the other children? This has to be why God tells us His ways and thoughts are high above ours,[3] we surely could not think of doing such a thing. God wants you close, do you allow Him to be close? He won't intrude, he waits for the invitation. There is a promise we have been given, *"Draw near to God and he will draw near to you"* (Jas. 4:8 RSV).

What a promise, we don't have to do great things to be close to God, all we have to do is make a move towards Him and He will move towards us. In our reading today we read of the prodigal son. Do you get what happens here: *"So he got up and came to his father. But while he was still a long way off, his father saw him and had compassion for him, and ran and embraced him and kissed him"* (Lk. 15:20 NASB).

So the son decides to return, what was the father doing all this time? What does it say happen, *'his father saw him.'* So is it that the father kept up hopes of his son's return and was always watching for him? Our heavenly Father is always looking for our turn toward Him. Let's look at something else about this verse, *'while he was still a long way off.'* How far away was the son when the father saw him? And what did the father do when he saw him, how far did the father go? This is how far the heavenly Father will come if we turn and move towards Him.

---

1   1Jn.3:24, 4:16
2   Acts 4:28
3   Isa.55:8&9

All's well that ends well. No matter what we are in today if we have Christ in our heart then we know it will end well for us. We can be sure that our end will be well because Jesus is in charge of it. *"In My Father's house are many dwelling places; if it were not so, I would have told you; for I go to prepare a place for you. If I go and prepare a place for you, I will come again and receive you to Myself, that where I am, there you may be also"* (Jn. 14:2&3 NASB). No matter what is happening around us it cannot keep us from heaven as long as we hang on to Christ. He is the one who has made a place for us, He will get us there. *"For I am sure that neither death, nor life, nor angels, nor principalities, nor things present, nor things to come, nor powers, nor height, nor depth, nor anything else in all creation, will be able to separate us from the love of God in Christ Jesus our Lord"* (Rom. 8:38&39 RSV).

His love is to have us with Him and He will not allow anything to keep us from that. God's love, can we really know what it is, know the fullness of it before we get to Heaven? I think not. Something we should rehearse often in our heart is what it took for this salvation that we now have to be given to us. It started in heaven where Jesus was willing to give up his royal place in heaven to come to earth taking on the body of a man. That was a great sacrifice. At twelve He is in the Temple speaking with others where even then He might have wanted to teach but only could ask questions, I am not sure if the question He asked was for His learning or for the learning of the one He was asking the question. Then comes His three years or so of teaching where He is disappointed many times in His disciples, and in others to where He said, *'How long do I have to be with you and put up with you?'* (Lk. 9:41 CJB).

His last 24 hours were difficult, the flesh begins to work on Him where He asks the Father for a different way, yet in the end the Spirit wins out with Him yielding all to the Father and to all He would go through. This was a great yielding because He could have got out of it at any time, but He set himself in it until the end. How much love is this, can anyone calculate it? And it was not just the love of Christ, what about the Father that for the first time the Son was not right there with Him in heaven? The Father saw everything Jesus went through, do you think it didn't touch the heart of the Father?

Here we see that depth of love again. All this to fix what we screwed up so that there was a way we could be brought to heaven without going against the righteous requirements. It is all's well that ends well, but what did it take to get us there? There are those who it will not end well for. In Luke chapter 16 today Jesus says, *"And he said to them, "You are those who justify yourselves before men, but God knows your hearts"* (v. 15 NKJV). God knows the hearts of all, for us who give Him our hearts it will end well, but for the rest it will not. Shortly after this Jesus said something that for a long time I didn't understand, *"it is easier for heaven and earth to pass away than for one stroke of a letter of the law to fail"* (v. 17 NASB). This confused me since scripture tells us this, *"In speaking of a new covenant he makes the first one obsolete. And what is becoming obsolete and growing old is ready to vanish away"* (Heb. 8:13 ESV).

In Luke it says the Law will not fail, and in Hebrews it is vanishing away. Well I found we have to put these together with all truth. Yes, the Law is vanishing away the same as the heaven and earth will vanish away, *"the heavens will vanish like smoke, the earth will wear out like a garment"* (Isa. 51:6 RSV). and *"And I saw a new heaven and a new earth: for the first heaven and the first earth are passed away"* (Rev. 21:1 ASV). The Law will vanish away when the new heaven, and new earth, and new Jerusalem come for there will be no need of the Law after the final judgment. Until then the Law has to be even though we are freed from it by Christ. That freedom that Christ gave us could have not been without the Law that gives His sacrifice value. **All's well that ends well - for those who are in Christ Jesus.**

Now is the time to rejoice. There is no day that is not a time to rejoice if we have Christ in our heart as Lord. There are bad days, there are difficult days, there are days we wish had not even come.[1] Yet in all of these we can rejoice in our salvation knowing no matter if our day gets so bad we lose our life on this earth we know where we are going. It is hard to get a grasp on heaven, and on who God is in His total fullness of His being, and to grip the thought of the never ending time of eternity. For these things to become even a little bit true in our life it takes a stopping from the great spinning of this life we are in on earth to contemplate truth. We have to stop spinning taking time to listen to God, to realize we have been born into this eternity at our rebirth, and know we are part of eternity even now.

If we have connected our self to Christ, Christ is eternal, then we also are eternal. My hope is in Christ because I know I can not accomplish. If you ask anyone who will be honest with you if there was ever a time that there was something they tried to do and they were unable to accomplish it, all would say there was. If we cannot accomplish things in this world how could we possibly accomplish spiritual things of heaven? I will not trust and have my hope in myself, I will have it in Christ which brings me to rejoice for what I have been given.

As we begin to put our thought on Christ and God we begin to grip a little of the heavenly concept. It takes a concentration of pushing back out of the way the things of this world so that we can see the spiritual things of heaven, and God, and eternity. It is a faith walk determining to believe the things God tells us about rather than all of this we see before us in this world. God has provided help for us if we take time to look toward Him. God has sent the Holy Spirit to help us learn of these things: *"But the Helper, the Holy Spirit, whom the Father will send in My name, He will teach you all things, and bring to your remembrance all things that I said to you"* (Jn. 14:26 NKJV). The Holy Spirit will work in us regenerating us: *"in accordance with His mercy, by the washing of regeneration and renewing by the Holy Spirit, whom He richly poured out upon us through Jesus Christ our Savior"* (Tit. 3:5&6 NASB).

It is the Holy Spirit who helps us to be reshaped: *"be transformed by the renewing of your mind"* (Rom. 12:2 NASB). There is hope for our gain of getting a grip on heavenly things for we are told the Holy Spirit who God sent to us is doing a renewing of our minds. God knows our shape, our form, our incapacities, He helps His children to grow in knowing Him and the heavenly place He dwells. If we are always spinning He is not able to help us much, and our spiritual growth will be very slow. There is an event that took place in what we read of Luke chapter 17 today.

Ten lepers came to Jesus asking Him to cleanse them. Leprosy is compared to sin since both destroy the body. Jesus sent them to present themselves to the priest and they were cleansed on the way. We who are saved have been cleansed from our sin and are now clean before God. Let's see what happens next, *"One of them, as soon as he noticed that he had been healed, returned shouting praises to God"* (v. 15 CJB). Do you think this one was rejoicing knowing that God had cleansed him? But he was only one out of the ten, which are you? As we turn to God seeking more of Him and the spiritual realm in our lives Paul tells us this in reading the beginning of 2 Corinthians, *"Blessed be the God and Father of our Lord Jesus Christ, the Father of mercies and God of all comfort, who comforts us in all our affliction, so that we may be able to comfort those who are in any affliction, with the comfort with which we ourselves are comforted by God"* (v. 3&4 RSV).

---

1   Philp.4:4, 1Thes.5:16-18

What is there to know of God that we can know now? We can know His word which is all about Him and what He has done. I find His word fascinating since it is something that cannot be confined. Ever since He spoke it, it has been moving about, alive and affecting in many ways.[1] We refer to our Bibles as the word of God yet they are not, they are not alive, they are not moving, they are a copy printed and recorded so we can see and know.

How can we confine within the pages of a book the living word which has been powerfully active ever since God spoke them. It is those words of God that take us to God so that we might receive salvation. Sometimes in our age today we are finding those receiving salvation by those very words which were not delivered to them by any person, it was by the Holy Spirit speaking in their heart or in a dream. God's word cannot be confined in the print on a page. God's word is working all around us.

The universe we are finding is enormous, yet each planet, each star, each sun which is a star, is kept in its place by the power of the order of the word of God. *"By the word of Jehovah were the heavens made, And all the host of them by the breath of his mouth"* (Ps. 33:6 ASV). and *"He counts the number of the stars; He calls them all by name"* (Ps. 147:4 NKJV). and *"I have made the earth, and created man upon it: I, even my hands, have stretched out the heavens; and all their host have I commanded"* (Isa. 45:12 ASV). and *"He reflects the glory of God and bears the very stamp of his nature, upholding the universe by his word of power"* (Heb. 1:3 RSV). and *"by the word of God the heavens were of old...the heavens and the earth which are now preserved by the same word"* (2 Pet. 3:5&7 NKJV).

God certainly is more than we can know in this life time on earth. Yet He reveals much of Himself in His word, sometimes even such we struggle to understand it. The important things He gets through. He gets through that we failed in the garden He so blessed man with in the beginning. We fail in the first few centuries such that He kept alive only Noah with seven of his family. After that, we as humanity fail again in allowing sin to rule us. We are before Him even today falling short of His glory and have failed.[2] Yet the important things He gets through and provides His plan of salvation for those of us who will come to Him to receive it. In our reading in Luke chapter 18 today Jesus makes it very clear how it is we must come to Him in the parable of the Pharisee and the tax collector.

It is not for us to come thinking we are a good person, never hurting anyone, always living a right way. This is not the one God accepts, it is the one who comes in humility. Jesus said, *"But the tax-collector, standing far off, would not even raise his eyes toward heaven, but beat his breast and said, 'God! Have mercy on me, sinner that I am!' I tell you, this man went down to his home right with God rather than the other"* (v. 13&14 CJB). This much God has made clear to us, that we can know how we have to come to Him, in a lowly manner not elevating ourselves thinking we are one who has conquered the maturity of Christianity. Jesus tells us how we must come or we will not receive anything, *"Truly, I say to you, whoever does not receive the kingdom of God like a child shall not enter it"* (v. 17 RSV). Better to be lowly and lifted up by God than come higher than we should and be knocked down.

---

1   Heb.4:12
2   Rom.3:23

Where is life taking you today, what leading will you follow, what leading will you trust? How many people go on in life never asking themselves this question? God has a calling on our hearts but most do not respond, or they look in other places not knowing, or not wanting to know, it is from God. God called in the garden: *"the LORD God called to the man, and said to him, "Where are you?"* (Gen. 3:9 RSV). God is still calling to all of mankind, 'Where are you?' But few are responding. Jesus says, *"For the gate is narrow and the way is hard, that leads to life, and those who find it are few"* (Mt. 7:14 RSV).

It seems the majority want to be their own god setting their own destiny. The trouble is these are not aligning their thoughts with the truth which only comes from God. Even when people are told the truth they refuse to believe it. Pilate asked, *"What is truth"* (Jn. 18:38 ASV). Pilate was not willing to accept what Jesus had just told him. Many today are not willing to accept what is true. Here is what Jesus had said to Pilate, *"You say that I am a king. For this I was born, and for this I have come into the world, to bear witness to the truth. Every one who is of the truth hears my voice"* (Jn. 18:37 RSV).

Many today do not want to hear the truth, they want their own version of truth. The devil has deceived them, not wanting them to see the truth the same way he deceived Eve in the garden convincing her to believe a false truth, a truth she was willing to accept. There are many today who think they have found truth, but it is that false truth that the devil deceives so many with. Narrow is the gate, and difficult is the way. We as Christians say receiving salvation is easy, but is it?

To accept Jesus Christ into our lives is easy, it takes no special work on our part. The difficult part is getting to that place that we are willing to accept Jesus. Our flesh fights it every step of the way. It wants to continue following its own truth, the truth it is willing to accept. Jesus came with the only truth, the devil wanted mankind to believe there is another truth. To arrive at that place we are willing to accept Jesus and His truth is a difficult battle.

It goes against our pride and self-worth. We have to face that we are sinners, that does not work with our self-worth. Our self-worth is false, it is really not going to get us anywhere. Success in this life does not take us to success in eternity. Some are so deceived, even though that call of God is in their heart, they ignore it only being willing to believe there is no eternity. They believe there is only now and then we die and rot. Where is life taking you today, what leading will you follow, what leading will you trust?

In our reading in Luke today there were those who were only willing to believe their version of the truth. *"Zacchaeus, make haste, and come down; for to-day I must abide at thy house...And when they saw it, they all murmured, saying, He is gone in to lodge with a man that is a sinner"* (19:5&7 ASV). They were not willing to believe Jesus was bringing the truth because according to the truth they were willing to believe, the false truth, a man who was holy could not eat with sinners. Again later the Pharisees show their unwillingness to believe the truth Jesus brought. *"some of the Pharisees from the multitude said unto him, Teacher, rebuke thy disciples. And he answered and said, I tell you that, if these shall hold their peace, the stones will cry out"* (19:39&40 ASV). We must decide who we will follow, who's truth we will believe.

In this world of troubles, how well do you do? We are all subject to the things of this world as long as we live in this tent.[1] Our flesh wants to take us one way and our Spirit wants to take us the other. *"For the desires of the flesh are against the Spirit, and the desires of the Spirit are against the flesh"* (Gal. 5:17 RSV). There is another thing about this, as long as we live on this earth we will have both, not able to separate one from the other. We have to decide which we will listen to. We lived solely in the flesh until we were reborn. Then the Spirit is born into us and the pushing and pulling starts. Some days the Spirit wins, and some days the flesh wins. In time as we begin to strengthen the Spirit in us as we mature more and more in Christ the flesh wins less often. With such an array around us from the world where much of the time money and wealth are the rulers,[2] and one's sin is not considered, it is not hard to be drawn off towards it.

We have to decide which way we are going to go. Many times these things will grab us, but we have to push back. Sometimes (not most times) the demonic world of the devil is involved, we have to remember what we have been told, *"resist the devil, and he will flee from you"* (Jas. 4:7 ASV). If the demonic realm is the source of the temptation, claim what you know, claim you belong to God and were saved by the blood of Jesus Christ. There have been times when I did this and the temptation vanished. As you have heard me say many times, the word of God builds up the strength of the Spirit.

The more you feed on the word of God the stronger the Spirit that is in you becomes. Infants and toddlers are not running, and jumping, and catching that fly ball. It is the same with being reborn, don't expect great accomplishments right away. But the better you feed that new birth the quicker it becomes strong. Faith is such a huge part of this, determine early in your Christian life to believe what God says regardless of how it even seems impossible. Twice in scripture we are told this is what God does, *"For with God nothing will be impossible"* (Lk. 1:37 RSV). and *"all things are possible with God"* (Mk. 10:27 RSV). Troubles around us will grip us less and less as we turn more and more towards God.

Today we read 2 Corinthians chapter 4, Paul starts out speaking of the choice he has made, *"we do not lose heart. We have renounced disgraceful, underhanded ways; we refuse to practice cunning or to tamper with God's word"* (v. 1&2 RSV). He states that he and those he speaks of as 'we' have made a choice not losing heart and turning away from the ways of the world of dishonesty to believe in and present God's word as it is. Here is a place we have to decide if we will follow the Spirit or the flesh.

The flesh would want to tamper with God's word to reshape it a bit to fit what we want to believe or to what is comfortable to us. God's word is not always comfortable, but it is always true. As we accept more and more of the truth of God's word our Spirit grows. When we received salvation there was an enlightening that happened in our hearts to begin to see the truth of God. There came an awareness of the glory of God which we see on the face of Christ that outshines the sun. *"Seeing it is God, that said, Light shall shine out of darkness, who shined in our hearts, to give the light of the knowledge of the glory of God in the face of Jesus Christ"* (2Cor. 4:6 ASV).

Paul, Peter, James, and John had all seen that light of Christ. (Mt. 17:2, Acts 26:13-15, Rev. 1:16) There is a great encouragement in this chapter to our faith, *"knowing that he that raised up the Lord Jesus shall raise up us also with Jesus"* (2Cor. 4:14 ASV). This is what we all look forward to, that God will carry us into heaven to be with Him. I will end with the end of the chapter, *"So we do not lose heart. Though our outer self is wasting away, our inner self is being renewed day by day. For this light momentary affliction is preparing for us an eternal weight of glory beyond all comparison, as we look not to the things that are seen but to the things that are unseen. For the things that are seen are transient, but the things that are unseen are eternal"* (2Cor. 4:16-18 ESV).

---

1   2Pet.1:13
2   Lk.16:13

Have faith in God and He will provide you with all you have need of. Our dependency must be on God. His way is the only way to heaven, the alternative is not a place any of us want to go. Throughout the Bible heaven is spoke of much. This is where we will be with God forever and forever and forever. None of our work is good enough to get us there. None of our righteousness or our righteous deeds are good enough to get us there. It is only by Christ, submitting to Christ, and accepting Christ into our lives that will get us there. It is through Christ and by the work that He did on the cross that we will get to the Father in heaven.[1] As we recognize this and know that we are saved by Christ we can be greatly thankful for what we have, that of eternal life with God.

The descriptions of heaven in various places in the Bible give us great expectations of heaven. Sometimes we get tied up in the needs we have while in life on this earth and forget that the greatest need we have Christ has already provided.[2] He is a loving God who has provided the greatest need we have and will provide all the rest we have as well. As we come to this awareness we are to tell others of the great God we have. God loves us so much He tells us about things to come such as being with Him in heaven.

There is much in our reading in Luke and 2Corinthians today. First thing we are to see is not to put our hopes in the wrong places, *"And as some spoke of the temple, how it was adorned with noble stones and offerings, he said, "As for these things which you see, the days will come when there shall not be left here one stone upon another that will not be thrown down"* (Lk. 21:5&6 RSV). We need to sense if the Spirit of God is in a place we go, not only that it has pretty stones. Then Jesus begins to tell of the last days and how they will be. The very first thing He says about this is, *"See to it that you are not misled"* (Lk. 21:8 NASB).

Here Jesus speaks of the imposters who will claim they are Christ, but I also believe it applies to what He goes on to say. The following could cause panic if we were not told it was coming, *"Then said he unto them, Nation shall rise against nation, and kingdom against kingdom; and there shall be great earthquakes, and in divers places famines and pestilences; and there shall be terrors and great signs from heaven"* (Lk. 21:10&11 ASV). One of these days this will be the case and we have been told of it. When those days are here Christians will be treated badly, some even put to death.

There is an interesting promise which must have to do with spiritual life, *"some of you they will put to death; you will be hated by all for my name's sake. But not a hair of your head will perish. By your endurance you will gain your lives"* (Lk. 21:16-19 RSV). Mark records this last line this way, *"But he who endures to the end will be saved"* (13:13 RSV). So those who endure not giving up their faith will be saved into eternity with God. Jesus tells us in Luke when He does return all will know, *"And then shall they see the Son of man coming in a cloud with power and great glory"* (21:27 ASV).

What Matthew records assures us even more, *"For as the lightning comes from the east and shines as far as the west, so will be the coming of the Son of man"* (24:27 RSV). Our greatest need is to be saved, Paul speaks of our acceptance, *"He died for all, so that those who live would no longer live for themselves, but for Him who died and rose on their behalf...Therefore if anyone is in Christ, this person is a new creation; the old things passed away; behold, new things have come. Now all these things are from God, who reconciled us to Himself through Christ and gave us the ministry of reconciliation, namely, that God was in Christ reconciling the world to Himself, not counting their wrongdoings against them"* (2Cor. 5:15,17-19 NASB).

God offers forgiveness, He offers salvation, and that we shall be with Him for eternity. This is our greatest need. I will end with a verse from Revelation, *"Behold, the tabernacle of God is with men, and he shall dwell with them, and they shall be his peoples, and God himself shall be with them, and be their God"* (21:3 ASV).

---

1   Col.1:20
2   Jn.14:2&3

What are we here for, who is it that is given the advantage of us being here? You ask some scientists and they would say it is for the preservation of the species – humanity. But if it is just going from one generation to the next what is the advantage? We might as well all die off and stop the process for it is going nowhere. Why do we exist?

There has to be something more than to just preserve the species. We love, or we take, or we give, but what value is it if after we die there is nothing, we go nowhere, we just rot away? Very few are even remembered past one or two generations by those who follow. Human beings do everything they can to extend their lives – why? Some will say they want to spend as much time with their grandchildren as possible, but if there is no thought after death how will they know if they did or did not? If they have no thought of what was left behind when they are dead, why are they concerned? There is something inside our being that knows bringing a fear of death. Even if people do not know what it is, they fear as though there is something coming after death that they are not ready for. We who are saved know what that is – judgment. [1]

In some way God has written within each one of us who live that we are accountable for our sins. In other religions, other than Christianity, the people are always trying to accomplish, do good enough, meeting the requirements of the god they serve to be accepted because something down inside of each of them says they got'a pay the price, got'a make it right. Then there are those who ignore it all, saying there is nothing after death, it is all over at that point so why try – have a good time, enjoy yourself, do what seems right in your own eyes, individually or jointly. God knew from the beginning of time that we could not pay for our sins and devised the plan of redemption. [2] Jesus came and paid the price we owed, our sins were forgiven, and that sense inside each of us, that we got'a pay for our sins is gone and a new life is there as each of us who are saved have been re-born. [3] The enemy, the devil, would like us to think that our sins are never fully paid for and we must keep trying to pay. He condemns us, and tempts us, always trying to cause us to think that what Jesus did on the cross was not enough. How could there be a work which God did that was not enough.

If God was not able to do the complete job should He be God? Can you say the number of stars is not complete? Can you say the trees were created the wrong color? Can you say the mountains are too short? Can you say the oceans are not deep enough? If God was able to complete all of creation then He is able to provide for the complete forgiveness of our sins. God does retain one sin that He says He will not forgive, [4] but all the rest are covered by the blood of Christ that was shed on the cross for us. [5] So now back to why are we here - we are here because God put us here, and if we seek and search we will find Him. [6]

We are here to love Him and cherish Him, to be family to Him, to be loved by Him, and to be provided for by Him. We are here, that those who would choose God, and accept God, would be in fellowship with Him for eternity. In Luke chapter 22 Jesus has His last Passover supper with His disciples. He tells them (and us) that the bread is His body that is broken for us and the wine is His blood shed for us. Jesus tells us to remember Him when we take this supper, to remember why He came, to remember what He taught, to remember where He went, and remember He is coming again to take us with Him. [7] Jesus said in v. 70, 'I AM'. There is a completeness in 'I AM'. There is nothing left out, He is complete, and what He does is complete. It is that completeness of God of why we are here. It is for His purpose and His reason that we are here. To know Him is why we are here.

---

1   Jn.5:29
2   Rom.16:25
3   1Pet.1:3
4   Lk.12:10, 1Jn.5:16
5   1Jn.1:7
6   Acts 17:27
7   Jn.14:2

'I will always, always, always be with you.' Do you know this is what Jesus Christ says to you? It is what we cannot see, but do you believe Him? We have just read what Paul tells us, *"We concentrate not on what is seen but on what is not seen, since things seen are temporary, but things not seen are eternal"* (2Cor. 4:18 CJB).

If we are saved our lives are tied up in heaven and not this earth, this world. We are here in a temporary state as in a waiting area of a grand estate waiting to be called to enter. There is an interesting aspect of God, His dwelling place is heaven and his presence emanates to all places. It emanates even to you right where you are right into the midst of what is going on in your life at this very moment. Once we are saved there is never a moment when God is not with us. [1]

Are we always aware He is there, do we sense Him or feel Him? It is as if we keep an eye on our toddler who does not know we are there right behind them watching their every move, God is always watching us. Many times we do not notice God is there in what we are going through, but later looking back we see all He was doing. Once we become aware that He is always there it raises our confidence to speak to Him of our need of the moment, even if it is only to find our hammer.

God wants to hear from His children, He wants them to know He is close. We are servants of our Lord Jesus, but we are never left alone in that serving. Remember, we are the ones following, Jesus is always there as He calls us into the work He is doing so we can be involved in it with Him. Jesus said, 'follow Me', He calls us into His work and provides all that we need, the need we have in that work and the need we have to live this life in this world. We are given the analogy that He is the Good Shepherd and we are the sheep. What good shepherd does not see that His sheep have the food they need? What good shepherd does not see that His sheep have that great place to bed down for the night? What good shepherd does not see that His sheep are protected with his eye watching over them, even as though He never sleeps? [2]

We have a Good Shepherd that watches over us. Sometimes we sheep, well you know, we don't always notice what is really going on around us. Oh, if we all could be so spiritually keen, yet we are not. The more we walk with God the more that grows. I have been walking with God over 49 years now and yet I desire to be more aware of His presence with me. That is to encourage you that we all will continue growing in this until that day we are called into our heaven place Jesus has prepared for us. [3]

Today we read in Luke all that Jesus went through to provide salvation for those of us who come to Him. We were lost sheep, certainly so, wandering around in a wilderness of sin and heard a voice calling us, a voice different than we had ever heard before, it was the voice of the Good Shepherd. It got our attention, we perked up our ears, we went in the direction it was coming from. We found Jesus, the Good Shepherd, and accepted all the good things He had for us. We are now well kept, He keeps His eye on us, He watches everything around us. He cares for us well, keeping us for that day when He will say to us as He said to the thief on the cross beside Him, *"today you will be with me in Paradise"* (Lk. 23:43 RSV).

---

1   Heb.13:5
2   Ps. 121:1-8, Rom.9:6,25
3   Jn.14:2&3

'Here I am to worship, here I am to bow down, here I am to say that You're my God.' We sing this, do we mean it? Each of us has to answer that to ourselves. Even when Jesus was on earth among the people there were those who followed until things got too difficult for them and they left. *"Upon this many of his disciples went back, and walked no more with him"* (Jn. 6:66 ASV).

Are there things that God says that are hard to deal with so you back off for a while? How easy it is to sing the words of our songs, but how hard it is sometimes to live up to what we are saying. If we bow down, are we not saying, 'You Lord are ruler of my life, I give it all to You?' How much is all, each of us is going to have to answer to ourselves. Each of us are going to have to go through things in our lives when the only thing we have to hold on to is our faith.

Have faith in God and He will get you through those hard times. The disciples were having a hard time one day not having faith, *"And a great storm of wind arose, and the waves beat into the boat, so that the boat was already filling. But he was in the stern, asleep on the cushion; and they woke him and said to him, "Teacher, do you not care if we perish?" And he awoke and rebuked the wind, and said to the sea, "Peace! Be still!" And the wind ceased, and there was a great calm. He said to them, "Why are you afraid? Have you no faith?"* (Mk. 4:37-40 RSV).

If we know who Jesus is and have faith in Him He will get us to the other side of the storm. In the storm Jesus wasn't worried. Part of having faith is making a decision. We have to decide to believe God, faith does not come by a learning process, it is the more we see our God come through for us the more our faith grows. It is not learning and learning more that brings faith, it is the deciding to believe. At one time I did a study on faith, I wanted to know everything about it so my faith could be better. That study did not help me any. It was not until one day that I realized it was so simple, yet so hard to do.

I had to decide to believe God, not myself, not the world, not the situation around me, - I had to decide to believe God. *"So faith comes from hearing, and hearing through the word of Christ"* (Rom. 10:17 ESV). What does this tell us? It is by hearing the word of God that faith comes. But if we don't believe that word of God will we acquire faith? We have to decide to believe what we read, what we hear of the word. Faith becomes much easier when we stop arguing with it, wrestling with it, and just believe. It is not building ourselves up to it, it is making up our minds we will believe whatever God says because He knows so much more than all of us put together know. How big is your God, how smart is your God, how wise is your God? These are things you will have to answer.

We have to know what God says, not what the preacher says, not what the teacher says, not what the guy down the street says, it must be what God says. Paul taught and preached, but those of Berea checked him out to see if what he said was true.[1] We need to be like those of Berea, we need to see what the Word of God says for ourselves. This is where faith grows as we decide to believe God.

As we read in Luke today how many of us does Jesus speak to as He spoke to the two men on the way to Emmaus, *"O foolish men, and slow of heart to believe in all that the prophets have spoken"* (24:25 ASV). We have to decide to believe. Don't do as the eleven did, *"returning from the tomb they told all these things to the eleven and to all the rest. Now it was Mary Magdalene and Joanna and Mary the mother of James and the other women with them who told these things to the apostles, but these words seemed to them an idle tale, and they did not believe them."* (24:9-11 ESV). Jesus call us to have faith, here is what happened when the eleven did not believe, *"Later He appeared to the eleven disciples themselves as they were reclining at the table; and He reprimanded them for their unbelief and hardness of heart"* (Mk. 16:14 NASB). What do you want Jesus to say about you? You have to decide.

---

1   Acts 17:10&11

Take hold of all that is good, there is much in this world which is not good. We must be concerned and alerted to all that is around us. We cannot allow it to press in on us. Evil from the unseen world is constantly trying to take us down, to defeat our relationship with God. The devil's whole purpose against us is to drive us away from God and what God has for us. In the very beginning, what did the devil do in getting Adam and Eve to eat the forbidden fruit? The greatest thing was not the sin, the sin was only large in having an effect on life from then on, even that of causing the flood of the whole earth. But what was the greatest thing, the greatest effect from eating the fruit? This is it:

"they heard the sound of the LORD God walking in the garden"(Gen. 3:8a ESV)
"the LORD God called to the man and said to him, "Where are you?" (Gen. 3:9 ESV)
"the man and his wife hid themselves from the presence of the LORD God" (Gen. 3:8b ESV)
"And he said, "I heard the sound of you in the garden, and I was afraid" (Gen. 3:10 ESV)

This was the greatest effect that the devil caused in the beginning, it was to separate us from our God. The devil and his demons are constantly at work all around us continuing to try to separate us from our God. [1] For a period of time until the cross, it was difficult to have that close relationship with God. Few found it, and the rest struggled with Laws and Commandments trying to get there but finding themselves short most times. The final analysis is that we all have found ourselves short, *"for all have sinned, and fall short of the glory of God"* (Rom. 3:23 ASV).

The devil hates Jesus because by Jesus being willing to die on the cross He made a way the separation could be removed by the forgiveness offered through His blood. We are accepted back into that relationship with God that was in the beginning if we accept what Jesus has done for us. If we come to God in that humble manner asking Jesus Christ to be Lord of our life and to forgive us our sins we receive salvation and the relationship is restored. We, *"being justified freely by His grace through the redemption that is in Christ Jesus, whom God set forth as a propitiation by His blood, through faith, to demonstrate His righteousness, because in His forbearance God had passed over the sins that were previously committed, to demonstrate at the present time His righteousness, that He might be just and the justifier of the one who has faith in Jesus"* (Rom. 3:24-26 NKJV).

This is what the devil hates, the devil thought that he had ruined the relationship between God and man forever and the coming of Jesus ruined what the devil had a hold on. Other than how to receive salvation this is possibly the greatest statement in all the Bible, *"And on earth peace, goodwill toward men"* (Lk. 2:14 NKJV). This was the good will of God to provide a way mankind could have peace with God and the separation be removed. Most of you reading this have that salvation, so be cautious of those things around you the enemy is trying to use to take you down. The devil wants back that power to separate you from God. With much of the world he has an affect and most will not find what is offered by God. [2]

The rest of us who have accepted God the devil will hack at not giving up. So walk in faith, you are the property of Jesus Christ and are covered in His blood of the perfect sacrifice. The devil can't touch you, only make you think he can. You may trip, and you may fall, but the devil cannot separate you from the love of God. [3] In our reading today John speaks in depth of spiritual things, *"In the beginning was the Word, and the Word was with God, and the Word was God. He was with God in the beginning"* (1:1&2 CJB).

What is the realm of the devil referred to much of the time, is it not darkness? Here is what Jesus said to Paul as part of his commission, *"to open their eyes, that they may turn from darkness to light and from the power of Satan unto God, that they may receive remission of sins and an inheritance among them that are sanctified by faith in me"* (Acts 26:18 ASV). Then we are told this by John, *"In him was life, and the life was the light of men. The light shines in the darkness, and the darkness has not overcome it"* (1:4&5 RSV). The life Jesus brings us is as a light that shines into darkness.

---

1   Rev.12:16&17
2   Mt.7:13
3   Rom.8:38&39

Keep all things in good order. How is your spiritual house, is it in good order? Our life is as a house that we have in a certain order. When we invite Jesus into our life, into that house of our heart, do we allow Him to rearrange the furniture? If you haven't then Jesus does not have full yielded control to your life. You are still holding on to some things. When we don't allow Jesus access to move a certain chair then that is what we do not allow Jesus to have full rulership over.

Jesus Christ wants to have full authority, to come into your life and rearrange all the furniture, and even to be able to say, 'I don't like that rug, it has got to go'. Have you given Jesus full control in your house? The same as Jesus does not force Himself into your life, He does not force Himself into any room of your life, you have to let Him in. Jesus will be the best interior decorator you have ever known if you give Him full reign of the house. There are many things of our heart that have to change when we invite Jesus in as savior.

When we get saved we receive a spiritual life along side of a life of flesh. (Jn.3:6) How the flesh lived before we were saved won't go anymore, rulership has to be given over to our spiritual side which Jesus is King over. As we read the word of God more and more, we begin to see how Jesus wants the furniture arranged and to give Him permission to do so. God wants to have a **hands on** work in your life, don't be like the child who thinks he can do it himself and then really messes things up.

You can help working along with God to accomplish what needs changed in your life. But there are some things which we are no help at all and have to give God permission to do the work in us, and for us. Our life is so much more beautiful when we allow the Lord to be in charge. He will change us in ways we never thought possible, He will do something in us we never thought could ever be. The work that God does has always been many mysteries. The greatest of them is this, *"the mystery of the gospel"* (Eph. 6:19 ASV).

There are things which God continues to do which are a mystery to us. There are mysteries yet to come, part of them is how He works in us changing us in ways we do not know how. This comes back to faith, open the door, allow Him in, and you will be amazed at what He can do. Part of our reading today is of Paul's writing. What we read of him today in 2 Corinthians chapter 10 is he makes his defense to the Corinthians of his ministry. If you are aware of Paul's life as Saul before being saved you will see such a change in him it had to have been that mysterious work of God. [1]

In chapter 10 he put himself forward as being humble as much as possible, this is not how he was when he chased after the church. In John chapter 2 many of the Jews, seemingly in authority, did not know about this mystery of the gospel even though it was in their scriptures, they questioned Jesus of what He was doing, *"What miraculous sign can you show us to prove you have the right to do all this"* (v. 18 CJB). They did not realize what had come to them from God. The day you got saved did it come somewhat of a surprise to you as you oddly became aware of that great mystery and invited Jesus Christ into your life. Trust God and He will bring more great changes to your life that will amaze you.

---

[1]   Acts 22:3-5

What is life if it is not Christ? *"I have been crucified with Christ; and it is no longer I that live, but Christ living in me: and that life which I now live in the flesh I live in faith, the faith which is in the Son of God, who loved me, and gave himself up for me"* (Gal. 2:20 ASV). It is hard to totally grasp what Paul is saying here. I know he speaks of himself, but can any of us be before God in any other way? We have to realize that before what we were in the spiritual sense was dead, and how we are alive now is by Christ.

Our sins caused our death, but we have been given life in Christ. As God considered our condition before salvation we were dead. Death reigned over us because of sin. Jesus allowed death to come upon Him on the cross, He allowed all the sins of the world to come upon Him as He was on the cross and died. *"But as it is, he has appeared once for all at the end of the age to put away sin by the sacrifice of himself"* (Heb. 9:26 RSV). and *"For our sake he made him to be sin who knew no sin, so that in him we might become the righteousness of God"* (2Cor. 5:21 RSV). and *"And he is the atonement for our sins: but not only for ours, but also for the whole world"* (1Jn. 2:2 AMPC).

God has given us grace through Jesus Christ that we could receive in no other way. He is the redeemer, He is the savior, He is life to each and every one of us. Without Christ we have nothing but death. We read in John 1:4&5 that Jesus came to the world bringing life which is as light shining into darkness, the life Jesus brought shines into death and brings life. We were dead, but now we have life, life which Jesus Christ provides for us. Without Christ, we have no life. Some of this stuff gets pretty thick, but we have to change, we have to ask the Holy Spirit to help us change.

We have to change the way we think of this and what we believe. We may think we're liv'n pretty good, got a good job, got a great place to live, get to go to the game every week, how could life be better? All this may be well and good in what God has provided, but we need to bore down deeper to know without Christ we would have no life at all. Thankfulness comes from realizing what we have been given, *"the free gift of God is eternal life in Christ Jesus our Lord"* (Rom. 6:23 ASV). So, even though we look in the mirror seeing life, it is no life without Christ. The great news is that it is not just life here, it is for eternity, in heaven, with God, forever.

This life is but a temporary thing, real life comes after this. Our goals should not be what we gain on this earth, it should be where we are anchored and will spend eternity. That does not say we should not enjoy the things of this earth God created, but to keep our eye on the final destination. In our reading today Jesus speaks to Nicodemus about needing to be born again. Jesus makes it most important, that none will get to heaven without this additional birth, *"Jesus answered, "Truly, truly, I say to you, unless one is born of water and the Spirit, he cannot enter the kingdom of God"* (Jn. 3:5 NKJV).

We need to remember no matter how good we have been without this birth none get to heaven. Also we need to remember no matter how bad someone has been in the past, if he has this birth he will get into heaven. It is great to read further and hear this again, *"For God so loved the world that he gave his only Son, that whoever believes in him should not perish but have eternal life"* (Jn. 3:16 RSV).

'There's a river of life flowing out through me, makes the lame to walk and the blind to see.' How many have sung this song, most all of us know it? This is certainly a spiritual action, there is no gushing waters running out of us. But this river has a greater power, more that the most raging river on any continent. The river that flows out of us is a very powerful river, and yet very gentile. It brings life to all who drink from it, a life that goes into all eternity. John tells us this river Jesus spoke of was a river of the Spirit flowing out of us. [1]

We just read recently of what Jesus had told Nicodemus of how he(and we) need to have the new birth of the Spirit into us. Jesus said that no one will get to the Father and heaven without being born of the flesh and born of the Spirit. That Spirit then resides in us, it is part of that Light of Jesus given to us in a dark world. We are told that Light that Jesus gives each of us is to shine into the world. The Spirit which is in us is also to flow out of us to a desperate world. The world does not know how desperate it is until that Light shines out of us. It illuminates their need and the river flows out of us to those who are ready to receive Jesus Christ. Do you ever consider there is a light shining out of you.

You may not be aware of it because it is always shining where you are, it is with you. But for those who are in darkness they see something. Since they are in darkness they don't know what it is, but they definitely see it. Some are drawn to it, others fight against it, or even run away. As those who are drawn to the Light get closer they begin to sense the Spirit that is flowing out of you. At this point once they decide they need Jesus and receive Him into their life, they then also have the Light shining and a river flowing. There are always those telling us we have to make our light shine. Well if we are the source of that light then we do have to work at it. But if that source is Jesus through us [2] we cannot stop it from shining, we just have to make sure that we are not hiding it. We should not cover it up by acting falsely, trying to be like the world around us. But we don't have to try to push it on them either.

I have a friend who told of once what had happened to him, and I've also had it happen to me. He said at his place of employment he never spoke to any about Christianity, or the Bible, or that they were sinners, he was just himself around them, not trying to push out the Light on them. One day a co-worker of his had a question and began by saying, "Since you're a Christian...." Both of us as this happened to us thought how did they know we were Christians since we had never said so. As long as we don't try to cover it up the Light will shine and those in the dark place will see it.

As those who are drawn near begin to give you attention that is unusually not like other times it is not because of the great words you are speaking, it is because that river flowing out of you is getting them wet. The Spirit is touching them in a place they have never been touched before. I don't mean that then they are saved, but that they are becoming aware of their need. In our reading today in John chapter 4 Jesus stops to rest at a well. A woman comes to get water and Jesus begins a conversation with the women. Remember Jesus is the Light, and the Light we get from Him shins out of us the same as it shines out of Him. This woman begins to notice there is something different about this guy.

From her own confession it seems she had been living a life of darkness and that Light was shining in. After a while she is beginning to get wet as that river flows from Jesus. She gets so wet she runs to town and tells everyone about it. Here is the result, *"Many Samaritans from that city believed in him because of the woman's testimony...And many more believed because of his word"* (Jn. 4:39&41 RSV). Jesus says these words to His disciples, *"I tell you, lift up your eyes, and see how the fields are already white for harvest"* (Jn. 4:35 RSV). Much of the grain is ripe, you don't have to make it ripe. Jesus says the Father draws men to Him, [3] the Father is who brings them to ripeness. The only thing we have to do is allow that Light we have to shine, and to let the river flow.

---

1   Jn.7:37-39
2   Jn.8:12, Mt.5:14
3   Jn.6:44

'I am here for anyone who wants to find Me, depending on Me to supply all that you need.' Something that all of us need to work on is realizing our need that is beyond the things we need in this life on this earth. Yes, God does say He will provide our food, our clothing, our dwelling, a place of employment, a place of worship, and all the other things we have need of in this life.

We need to see our needs beyond this life, those things spiritual from the need of salvation all the way into eternity. We need to work on our relationship with God. Everything, all we have has to be anchored into Him. He is where truth comes from, He is where life comes from, He is where our eternity comes from.[1] We need to pray daily that He will open our eyes to see what we have not seen. God answers our prayer if we ask this in sincerity. He may not open the grand scope of things, but little by little He will reveal things we have not seen before.[2]

Sometimes it will be things within our own lives we have not seen before which He reveals to us. Sometimes it is opening an understanding to a verse of scripture that we have read a hundred times and never seen the truth of it that He shows us. Sometimes it is an awareness of the spiritual realm around us that we have never known before. God wants to provide All we need. One part of that is to know the love He has for us that is greater than any other.

We have all fallen short of the glory of God, the holiness of God. Do you know that every time we pray the Lord's Prayer we are praying that God will continue to make His Name holy? This is what 'Hallowed be Thy Name' means. It is asking God to keep His Name holy. That which is the standard that we are all measured by. Even in that standard of holiness, in that righteous requirement, God in His great love figured out, and put into place, a way we could come to Him and still meet that righteous requirement.[3] Jesus died in our place paying for that which we owed for our sins.

That punishment was put on Him. Not only that, but according to the Law He became that sacrifice which provided the perfect blood which cleansed us from all unrighteousness. God did a work which started in heaven, then life on earth as Jesus took up the flesh of a man, then into the grave for three days, then resurrected to life among his followers for 40 days, and then back to heaven at the side of the Father. This and all its details was done for us by a God that loves us. There are many greater things to know than just what happens on this earth around us in our life.

There is the spiritual realm that started for all of us the day we were reborn by the Spirit, we are now living in that spiritual realm that is all around us that is unseen by physical eyes. Living in the Spirit is living in spiritual awareness, with spiritual eyes, and spiritual movement. To live in this life until we go to heaven takes living in the physical and living in the spiritual. The physical will last until our bodies are put off[4] and we go to God, but the spiritual will last into eternity.

God has been working, and is working because of His love, to provide that way by which we can come to Him. Most of chapter 5 of John in our reading today speaks of this. In an answer Jesus gave the Jews we can see something, *"My Father has been working until now, and I too am working"* (v. 17 CJB).

Do you notice this statement is in the past tense? This tells us God in some way has been working on this for a while. *"the Son can do nothing of his own accord, but only what he sees the Father doing. For whatever the Father does, that the Son does likewise. For the Father loves the Son and shows him all that he himself is doing"* (v. 19&20 ESV). This shows us it is a work of the Three-in-One God that loves us.[5] Here is the great love of God to us, *"Truly, truly, I say to you, the one who hears My word, and believes Him who sent Me, has eternal life, and does not come into judgment, but has passed out of death into life"* (v. 24 NASB). Jesus came to accomplish all that the Father sent Him to do. (v.36) This is God's love towards us providing what we need.

---

1   1Cor.12:6, 15:28, Eph.1:23
2   2Cor.4:18
3   Eph.1:3,7-9, 3:8&9, Rev.10:7 1Tim.3:16
4   2Pet.1:13-15, 2Cor.5:4-8
5   Jn.16:14&15

Where does your loyalty lie? Ask this question to so many people and probably you would get as many answers. Those people who are of the world have many different loyalties from their children to their favorite sports team. In some cases those loyalties become idols. What is it we live for, what is it we give our attention to? This world we live in has all kinds of distractions.

We as Christians have decided who we will give our loyalty to. Does that slip from time to time? Does something begin taking our attention, and slowly turn our loyalty? It is something we have to watch for and be careful of because it slips away so unnoticed. Does your Bible rest too many days in the same place without being touched? What is printed there is what God speaks to us, whether it be only a verse or many chapters that you read. There are many things that want our loyalty, and do compete for it. Some of the virgins with their lamps did not work at keeping their loyalties strong, their lamps began to dim and they want to lean on someone else's loyalty. [1] Is your container full, do you add to it each day?

Loyalty is something we have to work at because our flesh wants to go the other way. Then there is the enemy just around the corner wanting to coax us to go the wrong way. We need to stay focused on who our God is. We need to know He is with us all the time. Knowing He is with you all the time will keep you from going the wrong way many times because you know He knows what you're thinking and sees what you are doing. When we get close to God there is a blessing, there comes from time to time an awareness of His presence, or He speaks a word into our hearts. When we consider eternity we know what loyalty really matters. What about our tomorrow, does our loyalty matter, it might be our last day here. [2]

This is something we need to begin our day with, reminding ourselves to who it is we give our loyalty. We also need to check why we give God our loyalty. In Ezekiel we hear how Israel did not continue their loyalty to God and were sent off to Babylon. Over and over God called to them but they refused. In Galatians we see Paul is writing to them because their loyalty to Christ is beginning to turn. There were others who came to them with something a little different than what Paul had presented to them directly revealed to him by Christ. (Gal. 1:6,11,12)

Some of those who followed Jesus were not loyal to Him because He was Lord, or because of what He taught. Here is what Jesus says in our reading in John today, *"I tell you, you're not looking for me because you saw miraculous signs, but because you ate the bread and had all you wanted"* (6:26 CJB).

We need to ask ourselves why we are following Jesus. Loyalty, who are you loyal to? Sometimes we give a great effort to accomplish many good works so God will bless us. We need to be careful here, are we working to put God in debt to us so He will have to bless us? [3]

Truly Jesus tells us today in our reading what the important work is that we should do, *"Then they said to him, "What must we do, to be doing the works of God?" Jesus answered them, "This is the work of God, that you believe in him whom he has sent"* (6:28&29 RSV). This is where our loyalty should be. Here is the great promise that we read today, *"For this is the will of my Father, that every one who sees [acknowledge] the Son and believes in him should have eternal life; and I will raise him up at the last day"* (6:40 RSV). It is very clear from this verse where our loyalty should be if we want everlasting life and to be accepted into heaven. Check your loyalty, tie it down strong, make sure it won't shift when the storms come.

---

1   Mt.25:1-8
2   Lk.12:16-20
3   Lk.17:7-10

We are those who stand in the presence of our God as He is always watching over us in all that we are doing. There is not a thing that escapes his attention.[1] We cannot conclude that He does not know what goes on with us because we do not see Him acting in it. The measurement we use of if God is with us, knowing what is going on in our life, we measure it by our own ruler which may be of our own design. This was the troubles the people and the Pharisees had that we read of today, they had their own ruler and according to it Jesus could not be from God.

This is the ruler the people used, *"But others were saying, "Surely the Christ is not coming from Galilee, is He? Has the Scripture not said that the Christ comes from the descendants of David, and from Bethlehem, the village where David was?"* (Jn. 7:41&42 NASB). This is the ruler the Pharisees used, *"You are not from Galilee as well, are you? Examine the Scriptures, and see that no prophet arises out of Galilee"* (Jn. 7:52 NASB).

The reason they came to the conclusion they did is because they were not using God's ruler which measures with all truth. The ruler the Pharisees and some of the people had did not have all the truth of the ruler God was using. There also was a prejudice in the ruler they used. Even one from Galilee had a very low value for the town of Nazareth, *"And Nathanael said to him, "Can anything good come out of Nazareth?"* (Jn. 1:46 NKJV).

They were not seeing all the truth that God was seeing. Looking back with all the information we have now we know Jesus was born in Bethlehem. In that time in all that took place over those 30 years it seemed unknown that Jesus had been born of migrants, who only came to town because of the census of the Roman Emperor. And then not so many months later had to flee to Egypt because of Herod's outrage.[2] When Joseph, and Mary, and the child Jesus came back they seemed to have done it in a way which drew no attention to themselves settling back into the town they had come from those years earlier. Could it be when we measure to see if God is with us or not we use a ruler that is shaped by what we want or think should be? Do we have all the true information about it that God has?

His ruler is always the right ruler, He measures by all the information He has. It might even be that how we have our ruler shaped we may want to see something that God knows would not be good for us. Here is another thing which God has that we do not have, God knows of everything in our future. We might be wanting and praying God will help us to travel east when He knows in the near future we will have to go west. Would it be a good thing for God to bless us so we could go east when shortly after we have to go west? Our greatest thing to do is present our concerns, desires, and needs before God in prayer and have faith He will do the right thing. We all know the story of Joseph being sold into Egypt as a slave by his brothers.

There is no indication that Joseph ever lost his faith in God, but if he was taking measurements he may have not known what to think of the measurements he got. Once He looked back he could clearly see what God was doing all that time, *"God sent me before you to preserve for you a remnant in the earth, and to keep you alive by a great deliverance"* (Gen. 45:7 NASB). We need to anchor ourselves in God through Christ and have faith He knows of our every need. The greatest need we have and that which will give us faith in God is what Paul tells us today at the end of chapter 2, *"I have been crucified with Christ. It is no longer I who live, but Christ who lives in me. And the life I now live in the flesh I live by faith in the Son of God, who loved me and gave himself for me"* (Gal. 2:20 ESV).

---

1   1Jn.3:20
2   Mt.2:16

'Come and unload your load on Me.' (Mt. 11:28 my paraphrase) Jesus wants to give us relief of the load of life that is upon us. Many of you may wonder what that load is, it is that thing inside of all who have not yet accepted God into their lives which witnesses to them there is something they need to find, something that is a danger to their life. It is that moral measuring up that stirs them inside. Some people ignore it, but the weight is still there.

Some are aware of it but refuse to do anything about it except to involve themselves in things that will distract from it for a time. Those of us who have sensed it, been aware of it, and moved to God has had it lifted from us. As we heard these words of Jesus we gave it to Him, *"Come to me, all who labor and are heavy laden, and I will give you rest"* (Mt.11:28 ESV). There is a peace that comes in those days after accepting Jesus into our hearts.[1] He becomes our all in all.[2]

Our values begin to change even with no effort on our part, it is that new birth that begins to grow.[3] We can have confidence in Christ, all was created through Him, and all authority has been given to Him, *"All authority in heaven and on earth has been given to me"* (Mt.28:18 RSV). If all authority has been given to Jesus then surely He can release the load that was upon us. If you still feel that load upon you maybe you have not allowed Jesus to take it from you, yet feeling you can prove yourself in it in some way. You may have salvation but have not yet let go of the load. There is not a thing we can do to increase our salvation, Jesus said on the cross, 'It is finished'. When Jesus says it's finished what more do you think you can do?

Many keep themselves under a heavy load because they believe there is something they need to do. We need to remember Jesus' reply when one ask what they should do to do the works of God, *"This is the work of God, that you believe in Him whom He sent"* (Jn.6:29 NKJV).

This is the work that there is for us to do, to believe Jesus and allow Him to remove the heavy load we try to carry. The Jews tried it for years and years, even for centuries and were not able. The more we trust Jesus the more easier our life becomes. There may be hard times, but if we trust Jesus we will make it through those times. Jesus is wanting to help us get through. The greatest things He wants to help us with is to make it through to eternal life. No matter what happens to us here on this earth the more important thing is where do we go from here. That is the confidence we must have. Those who continue to try to carry the load doing works so they think they then are more approved do not realize they have made new laws to themselves to live by.

This is what Paul said to the Galatians in our reading today, *"It was before your eyes that Jesus Christ was publicly portrayed as crucified. Let me ask you only this: Did you receive the Spirit by works of the law or by hearing with faith? Are you so foolish? Having begun with the Spirit, are you now being perfected by the flesh?"* (3:1-3 ESV). Paul speaks of how we shall receive from God, it is faith and only faith, *"So you see that it is men of faith who are the sons of Abraham. And the scripture, foreseeing that God would justify the Gentiles by faith, preached the gospel beforehand to Abraham, saying, "In you shall all the nations be blessed"* (3:7&8 RSV). If you are still trying to carry your load lift it up to Jesus and let Him take it up from you.

---

1   Jn.14:27
2   1Cor.12:6
3   Jn.3:3

In all of the earth, there is no God like ours who cares in all things that affect our lives. He is the One who sees all, knows all, even the very future of each one of our lives.[1] If we put all scripture together to hear what it says God has known each one of us from the beginning of time.[2]

He knows all that will take place from creation to judgment, and then into the new heaven. This does not mean He orders each that comes along in our lives, if He did Adam and Eve would have never eaten from the tree they were to not. We enter into something in our lives we need to make a decision about and God is already on the other side of it and knows what decision we make. He teaches us and hopes we will choose rightly, but He does not cause us to make the decisions we do. Ever since the Garden of Eden God has been calling out to mankind to follow the good way but so many refuse to hear.

We look at the nation of Israel we have been reading about for the last several weeks seeing how many times God was calling out to them, and they went the other way. We have been given a free will to choose and it seems that some don't have either the awareness or the willingness to make the right choice. It is amazing that God continues to reach out to us, even making a way for us to come to him that by His own work that cleanses us from our evil and washes us of our sins. This is a thing about eternity, you would think all would try to get it right. There were a few of the Jews who were walking rightly before God but the many were not. Now we have it easier in receiving salvation which comes to us by God's works, and not by the works we have done. I fear I would be disqualified if I was only accepted by that of my works.

We always need to remember that of the mercy and grace of God which allows us to receive salvation which we could not earn. As we think of our salvation which we have received it should cause us to rejoice each day. Our day may be a difficult one, but deep inside of where that salvation resides we can be thankful for this amazing gift we have been give.[3] In what we read of John today there is a blind man healed who was not brought to Jesus or cried out to Him. Jesus' disciples pointed him out and Jesus took pity on him healing him. He heals this blind man who was blind from birth, but I wonder if the blind He really was aiming at to heal of blindness was the Pharisees and the Jews that were with them.

A true miracle in all fullness had happened and still the Pharisees refused to see that Jesus was the Messiah from God. Here is where God really cares, trying in many ways to get us to see truth. Jesus had been preaching much so that all might see, even the Pharisees, but the Pharisees refused even when reminded by the blind man. *"What a strange thing," the man answered, "that you don't know where he's from—considering that he opened my eyes! We know that God doesn't listen to sinners; but if anyone fears God and does his will, God does listen to him. In all history no one has ever heard of someone's opening the eyes of a man born blind"* (Jn. 9:30-32 CJB).

God cares for these Pharisees and continues to try to open their eyes. In Galatians Paul again speaks of that mystery of the ages, *"But when the fullness of the time came, God sent His Son, born of a woman, born under the Law, so that He might redeem those who were under the Law, that we might receive the adoption as sons and daughters"* (4:4&5 NASB). This is how God begins His care for us, it is to get our attention to hear and be saved. Then from that day forward He watches all that takes place in our lives providing what we have need of. *"For the eyes of the LORD roam throughout the earth, so that He may strongly support those whose heart is completely His"* (2Chr. 16:9 NASB). and *"Draw near to God and He will draw near to you"* (Jas. 4:8 NKJV).

---

1   Isa.46:9&10
2   Rom.8:29
3   1Cor.2:7-12

How are you doing today? There are many causes in the world today, which have you chosen, if any? We walk with a God who has many causes. We like to think His causes for us are important. It is because it is what wells up from the depth of who God is being brought forth by His love. If we ever feel He is inadequate to take care of our needs just go out at night and look at the stars, these are one of His causes. He keeps each one of them in its place by His Word, and knows each by its name.[1]

This is a God that even knows truly what it is that we need. Sometimes we get tied up in this world, thinking most things we need are here, if only He would provide them for us. It is a beautiful place that God has created, but it is only our launching point. We are posed here to be made ready to be taken to heaven for eternity. Yes, for most of us it is many years, let say even 100. But on the timeline of eternity it is only a speck. So everything of our life in this world becomes secondary. It does not mean it is not important, God has placed mankind on earth for the beginning part of his life.

God has told those of us who are His He will take care of us. The primary is heaven and spiritual things. We do live in the secondary, receiving our needs in this secondary place, but we must keep our eyes on the primary. It is easy to get these two priorities mixed up since the secondary is where we live every day. But the spiritual we live in every day also, we began living in it when we were re-born, when the Spirit was born in us. You may have heard of some people having dual citizenship in the world of two different countries. Even though our true citizenship is in heaven, we have a type of citizenship on earth until we leave this place. (Philp. 3:20&21)

If we have a citizenship in heaven and heaven is a spiritual realm, then we must be living in the spiritual even now. Heaven and the spiritual realm is the primary, and we must keep it in the primary place in our lives. Many things in the spiritual wiz right by us and we don't notice because we are not being aware. Maybe one of our prayers in the morning should be, 'Lord, please don't let me miss anything of the Spirit today'. Many of the spiritual things we are made aware of by the Holy Spirit. He may nudge us to speak to a certain person about Christ, one that God may have prepared to hear.

The Holy Spirit may nudge us to call a certain person who may need encouragement. The Holy Spirit knows what is going on in the spiritual realm, He is kind of like our guide there. This is where we live, here on this earth, but we are living in the spiritual realm here also, the spiritual realm is not only in heaven, it reaches all of creation. I wonder how our days could be if we were always seeking what is going on in the spiritual realm first. I don't think I have ever reached this point, but just think of it!

Oh, if we could just be a little more spiritual. The only way we can begin to be more spiritual is to try to be a little more aware of it each day. Even when you learned to walk as a young child you didn't get up and run right away, but eventually you did run. If we can begin to change this, the answer to the opening question will begin to change also. In chapter 5 of Galatians today, Paul is speaking of those who want to add works of the Law to their lives.

In a way this speaks of the things done in this world, Paul tries to point us to the spiritual, *"For through the Spirit, by faith, we wait for the hope of righteousness...But if you are led by the Spirit you are not under the law...If we live by the Spirit, let us also walk by the Spirit"* (v. 5,18,25 RSV). This is not a completely automatic thing with the Holy Spirit within us, we need to be aware, we need to be listening, we need to be sensing the Spirit inside us.

It may be hard to hear at first but that will grow as you begin to recognize the voice, which sometimes does not come with words. It is like an instant knowing of something and you have to put the words to it. The spiritual realm is all around us, let's try to connect with it.

---

1   Ps.33:6, 147:4

How can you know the way? Many attend college for four years to learn something for the rest of their life. But how well does that take them through life? Jesus says, *"I am the way, and the truth, and the life"* (Jn. 14:6 RSV). and *"the Son of Man...whoever believes in Him should not perish but have eternal life"* (Jn. 3:14&15 NKJV).

This is the way that will get us through life, and on into eternity. We depend on God to take us through life. What would life be if we didn't have God's way of salvation? Have you ever set back and thought of what your life might be like now without finding salvation in Christ? Most of us don't want to look. Yet if we don't consider it we can't realize how great things are in our life now and how God has blessed us.

Measurements are only read when there is something to measure with. Otherwise, we don't really know how large or how small something is. What we have been given in salvation is ignoramus. Sin is so horrible, whether it is 1 sin (who has only 1) or 10,000 sins, it is amazing that Christ with His blood washes us completely clean. [1] This is the way, there is no other way. The only other than this is death, eternal death. Religion tries to make Christianity more difficult than it is.

Religion always has a ritual of how to do right so the follower may be received. In Christianity Christ says, come to me, I have already been through the ritual for you. Have you ever thought of if we had to measure up to heavenly ways, the ways of God, none of us would make it. Keep this in mind, *"For My thoughts are not your thoughts, Nor are your ways My ways,"* says the LORD. *For as the heavens are higher than the earth, So are My ways higher than your ways, And My thoughts than your thoughts"* (Isa. 55:8&9 NKJV).

We would never make it if we had to meet all God's ways before being accepted. God through Jesus Christ has already done it for us. How grateful we can be just for our salvation. God has provided that we have His word and in His word we are able to find the ways God has for us to live. The world always wants to pull us their way. The devil tries to take us the wrong way. We are left to make the decision of what way we will choose. For salvation, that was a onetime decision which gives us eternal life. But what about the decision we face every day in all that comes up of which way we will go?

We read today of Lazarus dying in John chapter 11. Jesus goes to the tomb and gives this order, *"Remove the stone"* (v.39 NASB). How many times when Jesus wants us to do something His way do we think this could make a big stink. How little do we know what God intends to do. He is the one who is in charge of tomorrow, He knows what is coming. We are told, *"So do not worry about tomorrow,...Each day has enough trouble of its own"* (Mt. 6:34 NASB). What then did happen next when they took away the stone? First we have to realize that what was about to happen was to bring glory to God, and by it many believed. *"And when he had thus spoken, he cried with a loud voice, Lazarus, come forth. He that was dead came forth, bound hand and foot with grave-clothes; and his face was bound about with a napkin. Jesus saith unto them, Loose him, and let him go"* (Jn. 11:43&44 RV).

If we will follow the way God has for us to go, maybe He will bring life out of a situation we think is death. In the summation of Paul's letter to the Galatians he speaks of some of the ways of God, *"So then, as we have opportunity, let us work that which is good toward all men, and especially toward them that are of the household of the faith"* (6:10 RV). The Bible is full of God's ways for us, as we read it we will know what that ways are.

---

1   1Cor.6:11, Rev.1:5

We are not seeing things as God sees them. We are of flesh yet, even though we have been also born of the Spirit as Jesus to told Nicodemus.[1] Because we yet live in flesh it is difficult to see things that are in the spiritual realm. I am reminded of the case of the servant of Elisha who was in a panic because of the enemy he saw. Elisha prayed God would open the servant's eyes to see that of the spiritual realm all around them, *"and he saw: and, behold, the mountain was full of horses and chariots of fire round about Elisha"* (2Kg. 6:17 RV).

There is an active spiritual realm all around us, we are just not able to see it. There will not be many among us who are like Elisha, we will mostly be like his servant. This is where faith comes in, to believe what we are told in the word of God even though we don't see it. God does not see things as we do, He is not limited as we are by our flesh. One of these days when we shed this flesh then we will see those spiritual things we don't see now. I don't know what that scene will be, probably much more than any of us expect. God has His army of angels engaged all around us. (Ps.78:43-49, 91:1-11, Dan.6:22, 10:13&20, Rev.12:7-10)

Many times when we cry out to God we may not know of the battle going on around us. I don't like hard times, I don't like persecution, but Jesus told us if we follow Him we will experience these. The confidence in faith is what we must have that God will get us through it. Walking in faith is not easy, it takes a lot of dying, the dying to the self in us who wants to take over, the dying to accept God knowing best at the moment of what we need.

This is especially hard for men in our culture because we are taught by the society around us we should stand up and take charge. If Jesus Christ is Lord in our life then we have to give over charge to Him. Many will testify that they were not sure if God was going to handle things for them or not and at the last moment, God came in with all they needed. In a practical sense, we don't need God to do anything until our moment of need comes. We like to see things laid out in advance, in place, being there for when the moment comes. God does not work that way.

God knows what He is going to do, He sees what is happening in the spiritual realm, He has things lined up to take care of us. But we are like the servant of Elisha and don't see the preparations that are in place. God wants to bless us and take care of our needs, but we have to trust Him. We are told to let our supplications be known and to believe. The more we pray the deeper the relationship with God becomes and our trust in Him becomes greater.

One of the last things Jesus taught His disciples before His crucifixion was about faith. *"Now in the morning, as they passed by, they saw the fig tree dried up from the roots. And Peter, remembering, said to Him, "Rabbi, look! The fig tree which You cursed has withered away." So Jesus answered and said to them, "Have faith in God. For assuredly, I say to you, whoever says to this mountain, 'Be removed and be cast into the sea,' and does not doubt in his heart, but believes that those things he says will be done, he will have whatever he says"* (Mk. 11:20-23 NKJV).

We have to be willing to believe God is at work to accomplish for what our need is. Today we read of Jesus' Triumphal Entry into Jerusalem, *"So they took branches of palm trees and went out to meet him, crying, "Hosanna! Blessed is he who comes in the name of the Lord, even the King of Israel!"* (Jn. 12:13 RSV). These people were excited, many thought Jesus was coming to take the throne of king David to take control of their situation. They thought Jesus was going to conquer, drive out the Romans, and rule the world from Jerusalem.

Can you imagine their surprise and disbelief when Jesus was arrested and then sentenced to die on the cross. Yet this was the very thing that God could see that would conquer the enemy and bring them true liberty. What is it we don't see as we think things are going the wrong direction. We are called to pray and believe God is working it out because He sees what we don't see. The result of what Jesus accomplished by dying for us on the cross Paul speaks of in the first chapter of Ephesians. You may want to read the first 10 verses again.

---

1   Jn.3:6

'Here is what I am to say.' It is always the Holy Spirit I seek, and give myself to hear, and to write what I hear from Him. So it is He who gave the opening statement. How much He wants to give us, how much He wants to help us. Many things of scriptures as we read them are hard to relate to, we many times either don't get it at all, or we give it a errorist meaning. Spiritual things can only be known in a spiritual manner, *"These things we also speak, not in words which man's wisdom teaches but which the Holy Spirit teaches, comparing spiritual things with spiritual"* (1Cor. 2:13 NKJV).

Jesus told us it would be the Holy Spirit who would teach us all things, *"But the Helper, the Holy Spirit, whom the Father will send in My name, He will teach you all things"* (Jn. 14:26 NKJV). Sometimes we depend too much on our intellect rather than the Holy Spirit which is within us. Sometimes it takes a deep searching listening within ourselves and rejecting all that comes from other sources, even from our own intellect, our own brain which is not spiritual, it is part of the flesh.

In a country that is heavily grounded in making advancements by the intellectual pursuit it is hard to make this shift. Now I am not saying that the intellect is bad, it is just how we use it. Without the intellect we could not read the words of God printed on the pages of our Bibles. But the intellect is not what should guide us to what God is saying to us in these words.

We need to look within for the Holy Spirit to help us unpack the word we have just read. I know of people who have testified that once they began to ask the Holy Spirit do this they began to see things in scripture they had never seen before. Oh how much God has for us in His word that He wants us to know, but spiritual things have to be revealed in a spiritual way. As we read of Solomon we see he was the wisest of all in his time.

We are told how it was he had this wisdom, *"And all the earth sought the presence of Solomon, to hear his wisdom, which God had put in his heart"* (1Kg. 10:24 ASV). Do you notice where God put that wisdom? It was surely a place of the Spirit, not the intellect. God gave us the intellect, it has great value in the right order. But we need to see it in the right place, and the right order. *"For the flesh sets its desire against the Spirit, and the Spirit against the flesh; for these are in opposition to one another"* (Gal. 5:17 NASB).

If we limit ourselves in knowing what this speaks of to sexual lust, or even to the lust of the eye, we may not be seeing the greater value. What are we told here in this verse? It tells us the flesh and the Spirit are *'in opposition to one another'* both are trying to be in charge of our life, in charge of what we do. Therefore our intellect, our brain being part of our flesh, needs to be in submission to our Spirit which is working to renew us (Tit.3:5).

As we look to the Holy Spirit within us He will guide our intellect into the right knowledge God has for us. If we allow the intellect to try to guide us it sometimes gets lost taking us to a wrong place. We are told we are in this world but not of this world. [1]

Therefore we need to let go of the way the world tries to pursue truth as they turn to their intellect to guide the way. The world we are of is the spiritual world and we must allow the Holy Spirit to guide the way. Paul tells us today in our reading this, *"[God] raised us up with him and seated us with him in the heavenly places in Christ Jesus"* (Eph. 2:6 ESV).

In the first two chapters of Ephesians Paul is speaking about the Jews and the Gentiles, and in his final statement in chapter 2 he says this, *"in him you also are being built together into a dwelling place of God by the Spirit"* (Eph. 2:22 ESV). It is the Holy Spirit within us we must look to allowing it to lead our flesh, even our intellect.

---

1   Jn.17:14&18, Philp.3:20&21

'You are in my life.' Do you think this is in your heart, are you aware in the midst of the day, in all that is going on with you, that God, Jehovah God is in your life? Do you have to search inside yourself for this truth, or is there an awareness with you all the time He is with you? It takes a little effort in the beginning to come to this awareness.

It is true from the moment you accept Jesus Christ into your life. Scripture is full of reinforcing verses about the Three persons of the Trinity being in our lives. We walk with God and God walks with us. He may not always like what you are doing but He is still there. In our reading today in John in the whole chapter 14 Jesus is teaching and reassuring His disciples.

He tells us He, and the Father are with us, even in us, *"In that day you will know that I am in my Father, and you in me, and I in you"* (v. 20 ESV).   and *"If anyone loves me, he will keep my word, and my Father will love him, and we will come to him and make our home with him"* (v. 23 ESV). Jesus says also that the Holy Spirit will be in us. (v.17)

Now we have all Three persons of the Trinity in us. **We** are **Never** alone. We may not be aware of it, but the Trinity of God is with us all the time. *"All who keep his commandments abide in him, and he in them"* (1Jn. 3:24 RSV). and *"whoever may confess that Jesus is the Son of God, God in him doth remain, and he in God; and we--we have known and believed the love, that God hath in us; God is love, and he who is remaining in the love, in God he doth remain, and God in him"* (1Jn. 4:15&16 YLT).

Once we have received salvation there is not a moment that God is not with us. The Holy Spirit is teaching us, Jesus is leading us as He calls us to follow, the Father is watching over us taking care of what we need. If we are aware and expecting God to be there with us He will speak to us at times. Sometimes when we pray He responds back, sometimes when He speaks to us we are just walking through our day and He says something to us. We have to expect, we have to work at being aware He is with us.

Some may reach the point they are always aware of Him being with them and He speaks to them much. Let me conclude with a few of the verses we read in Ephesians today, *"that He would grant you, according to the riches of His glory, to be strengthened with power through His Spirit in the inner self, so that Christ may dwell in your hearts through faith; and that you, being rooted and grounded in love, may be able to comprehend with all the saints what is the width and length and height and depth, and to know the love of Christ which surpasses knowledge, that you may be filled to all the fullness of God"* (3:16-19 NASB).

It is the Spirit in the inner man, and Christ who dwells in our hearts that we are filled with the fullness of God. Can we have it any better, can we be assured any stronger? God is always with us, always working, always continuing to bring to life a new creation in us as we trust Him to do so. Give room, and awareness to God, in your life to do many good things in you.

'I am here for all to know who I am.' God wants us to find Him, receive Him, and know Him. He reaches out to a sinful world by the blood of His Son offering cleansing and salvation to all who will accept it. We messed up, all of mankind messed up, and God by a great work on His part has made a way for us to come to Him if we will only accept His way. Many of mankind try to get to eternal life by another way, but there is none.*"Jesus said to him, "I am the way, and the truth, and the life. No one comes to the Father except through me"* (Jn. 14:6 ESV).

You who are reading this have found that way finding salvation and eternal life. We realized how much we needed that cleansing and salvation. It was a great act of the love of God who reached out to us. Now that we are part of the family He wants us to know Him better. God is magnificent, He is glorious, He is beyond anything we can think, our mind cannot function well enough to know the fullness of God.

We all will be so amazed when we get to heaven and forget everything we were going to say. To consider how amazing God is consider this: As you are praying to Him, think of how many others in your city are also praying to Him at the same time. Then think of how many in your state are praying to Him also at that very moment, then go further and consider how many in your country are praying to Him at that moment, now how many in the world? In addition to this He is also managing heaven and directing the angels. Yet He gives individual attention to each, how can He do this? This is how much greater He is than us.

Many may want to totally know all about heaven. Even though we cannot find out all truth of heaven, we have a plate load piled high of what God has given us to know. God wants us to know all we can about Him. The more we discover the more He reveals. This takes a hungry heart for God, wanting to know more, and more of Him.

At some point we realize it is of the Spirit we will know the most we can know. There comes a point that to simply read the words of God is not enough, it is buy the Spirit as the Spirit allows us to see deep into the meaning of those verses we read. What was it we read yesterday, *"the Holy Spirit, whom the Father will send in My name, He will teach you all things"* (Jn. 14:26 NKJV). God wants us to know Him. The Father sent the Son to make a way we could come to Him. The Holy Spirit has revealed the truth of God so we could know Him. Yet with all of that we have to respond when He reaches out so we can get closer and closer to Him.

The closer we get to God the more we know of Him, *"Draw near to God, and he will draw near to you"* (Jas. 4:8 ESV). God created Adam and Eve and wanted them to know who He was, *"the LORD God walking in the garden in the cool of the day, and...called to Adam and said to him, "Where are you?"* (Gen. 3:8&9 NKJV). God wanted Noah to know Him, *"Noah was a righteous man, blameless in his generation; Noah walked with God"* (Gen. 6:9 RSV). God reached out calling Abram to know Him, *"After these things the word of Jehovah came unto Abram in a vision, saying, Fear not, Abram: I am thy shield, and thy exceeding great reward"* (Gen. 15:1 ASV). God wanted Moses to know Him, *"And Moses said, I will turn aside now, and see this great sight, why the bush is not burnt. And when Jehovah saw that he turned aside to see, God called unto him out of the midst of the bush, and said, Moses, Moses. And he said, Here am I...Moreover he said, I am the God of thy father, the God of Abraham, the God of Isaac, and the God of Jacob"* (Ex. 3:3,4.6 ASV).

In our reading in John today Jesus says He wants us to know Him, even abide in Him, *"Abide in me, and I in you"* (15:4 ASV). Jesus also says we are His friends, *"I have called you friends, because everything I have heard from my Father I have made known to you"* (15:15b CJB). For God is reaching far out to us, we need to reach back to Him.

Where is it we go for the great love of God? Many religions have shrines for the people to go to, to connect with their god, but does that god have love? Even in Christendom, many go to the buildings we call churches to pray to find God and His love. The heart of the love of God is in the Church, which is the assemblance of the believers in the world. Let's tie a couple of things together. We pray in The Lord's Prayer, 'Thy Kingdom come...as it is in heaven'. There certainly is a Kingdom in heaven, so there must be one here on earth which we pray will become in likeness of the one in heaven. In Colossians we are told the Kingdom here in this world is the Kingdom of Jesus, *"He has delivered us from the dominion of darkness and transferred us to the kingdom of his beloved Son"* (Col. 1:13 RSV).

We also have been told that this Kingdom has no borders as a marker line, we are told it is within, it is established in every person who has accepted Jesus as King in their lives. *"Now when He was asked by the Pharisees when the kingdom of God would come, He answered them and said, "The kingdom of God does not come with observation; nor will they say, 'See here!' or 'See there!' For indeed, the kingdom of God is within you"* (Lk. 17:20&21 NKJV). We people, us who believe, are the Church, *"and he put all things in subjection under his feet, and gave him to be head over all things to the church, which is his body"* (Eph. 1:22&23 ASV). and *"And he is the head of the body, the church: who is the beginning, the firstborn from the dead; that in all things he might have the preeminence"* (Col. 1:18 ASV).

As believers we are the body of Christ with Him as the Head, the Body of Christ is the Church. As the Kingdom here on earth is the Kingdom of Christ with Him being the Head of that Kingdom, then the Church is that Kingdom with Christ as Head. Surely the love of God fills heaven, but what about here on earth? Where do we find the love of God here on earth?

We are told, *"the love of God that is in Christ Jesus our Lord"* (Rom. 8:39 NASB). So then in Christ Jesus we find the love of God. *"For where two or three are gathered in my name, there am I among them"* (Mt. 18:20 ESV). Jesus is the one who says this, so when we are gathered in His name of at least two or three He is there. Where Jesus is is where we find the love of God. It is true that the love of God emanates from heaven out into all the universe, but the focused place we find it here on earth is among the followers of Christ when they gather together. Jesus talks of love a little in our reading of John chapter 16 today, *"for the Father himself loves you, because you have loved me and have believed that I came from God"* (v. 27 ESV).

Here we hear of the love of God which comes to us from the Father, and that love is in Christ as we read above. In the previous chapters of John we have heard what Christ repeats, and repeats, and repeats, *"A new commandment I give to you, that you love one another: just as I have loved you, you also are to love one another. By this all people will know that you are my disciples, if you have love for one another"* (13:34&35 ESV). Jesus repeats this command in 15:12, and repeats it again in 15:17.

If we are His disciples we are to love one another. If we love one another then when we are gathered together the love of God is among us. How many of you did not even know in your own life what this kind of love was until Christ came into your life as Lord when you accepted Him? This then is the evidence that it is God's love within us. In the epistles Paul speaks of loving one another in Romans, Peter speaks of it three times, John in his epistles speaks of it six times. Let me end with a verse from 1John 4:7, *"Beloved, let us love one another, for love is from God, and whoever loves has been born of God and knows God"* (ESV).

'He knows my name.' What do you think about that? Do you know there is even something deeper that may be more than what you see or think? Do you know that God knows your name now, but even in the future not only will God know your name, He will know a new name He has given you? *"The One who has the sharp two-edged sword says this:...I will give him a white stone, and a new name written on the stone which no one knows except the one who receives it"* (Rev. 2:12&17 NASB).

This is how special we are to God, that he even knows your name, both of them. Here on earth no matter what country you are in, what would you think if the leader of that country knew your name? God not only knows your name, He wants to know your name, He wants to know you. He wants to know intimate things about you, He wants to know your heart, He wants to be your friend. Jesus tells us we are His friends, *"No longer do I call you servants, for a servant does not know what his master is doing; but I have called you friends, for all things that I heard from My Father I have made known to you"* (Jn. 15:15 NKJV). and from our reading today, *"I made known to them your name, and I will continue to make it known, that the love with which you have loved me may be in them, and I in them"* (Jn. 17:26 RSV).

Here is Jesus who is God, the second person of the Godhead, who was there when all the stars were made and called by name, who has been given authority over all the world, and He wants you to be His friend. 'What a friend we have in Jesus', how many times have you heard that song? I am not sure any of us will know fully what a friend we have in Jesus until we arrive in His very presence in heaven, what a day that will be. Of all the great things we see here on this earth, if we wrap them all up together they would not amount to as much as the little toe of Jesus' foot!

Can you imagine Him - and He knows your name, wants to know your name, and to know you! Jesus' care and love for His Church (we believers) is expressed in this prayer of His in John chapter 17, *"I am praying for them... I am no longer in the world, but they are in the world, and I am coming to you. Holy Father, keep them in your name, which you have given me, that they may be one, even as we are one... But now I am coming to you, and these things I speak in the world, that they may have my joy fulfilled in themselves... I do not ask that you take them out of the world, but that you keep them from the evil one. They are not of the world, just as I am not of the world. Sanctify them in the truth; your word is truth... I do not ask for these only, but also for those who will believe in me through their word, that they may all be one, just as you, Father, are in me, and I in you, that they also may be in us, so that the world may believe that you have sent me. The glory that you have given me I have given to them, that they may be one even as we are one, I in them and you in me, that they may become perfectly one... Father, I desire that they also, whom you have given me, may be with me where I am, to see my glory that you have given me"* (v. 9,11,13,15-17,20-24 ESV).

This is Jesus Christ our Lord who knows each of our names and makes a place in heaven for us. This prayer surely is by One who is our friend, the love of a friend is what this prayer is about. Before you go off into your day maybe it would be a blessing to read above this part of Jesus' prayer again.

'I am with you always.' Jesus tells us who are His He will be with us always to the end of the age. (Mt.28:20) I know there are surely days I need this promise for I would not get through the day without Him. By Him living the life of man for thirty-some years He knows our frailty. When you read the Gospels (Mt. Mk. Lk. Jn.), do you notice where Jesus gets His strength? I have heard those as we talk about the strength of Jesus say it was because He was Jesus, He was God. Yet if that was true then the writer of Hebrews could not have said this, *"For we do not have a high priest who cannot sympathize with our weaknesses, but One who has been tempted in all things just as we are, yet without sin"* (4:15 NASB).

If Jesus had anything more than we are able to have then He was not tempted as we are, He would have had an advantage. He was man as we are with all the same problems we have. What was it we can see in the Gospels that gave Him His strength, it was prayer with the Father. It was also that He had the fullness of the Holy Spirit power[1] which we can have also, even this must be by prayer.[2] How many times do you read Jesus went to a place alone to pray to the Father. It seemed to be His course of the day, to start His day with the Father in prayer. At one place He says He only does what He sees the Father doing, this takes prayer. Since we are looking at the humanity of Jesus I will bring up a few more.

Jesus is taught like we are taught, tired from walking like we tire, hurt and cried like we hurt and cry, hungry like we get hungry.

"but as the Father taught me, I speak these things." (Jn. 8:28 ASV)
"Jesus therefore, being wearied with his journey, sat thus by the well." (Jn. 4:6 ASV)
"Now when Mary came to where Jesus was and saw him, she fell at his feet, saying to him, "Lord, if you had been here, my brother would not have died."... And he said, "Where have you laid him?" They said to him, "Lord, come and see." Jesus wept. So the Jews said, "See how he loved him!" (Jn. 11:32, 34-36 ESV)
"O my Father, if it be possible, let this cup pass away from me" (Mt. 26:39 ASV)
"And after fasting forty days and forty nights, he was hungry." (Mt. 4:2 ESV)

Jesus experienced many of the things we experience, He knows the difficulty of them, He knows our need of His help. Jesus will get all of us through to the end taking us through Himself to the Father[3] who is in heaven where we will be for eternity. There are those days we have that are difficult where we need to know Jesus is with us, *"If a man love me, he will keep my word: and my Father will love him, and we will come unto him, and make our abode with him"* (Jn. 14:23 ASV).

Some might say His coming to make His home with us means heaven. I don't think so for when Jesus talks of making a place for us He talks of going to heaven. In this verse He speaks of coming, so then He may speak of His and the Father's presence being with us. Jesus makes the way. We read in John chapter 18 today of the arrest and trial of Jesus. We can see Jesus' concern for us here for He could have got out of it at any time He wanted, they did not have power over Him. *"But Jesus said to him, "Put your sword in its place,...do you think that I cannot now pray to My Father, and He will provide Me with more than twelve legions of angels"* (Mt. 26:52&53 NKJV).

He could have been rescued. He also had power within His own speech that knock them over, *"When therefore he said unto them, I am he, they went backward, and fell to the ground"*(Jn. 18:6 ASV). Jesus went through the trial and crucifixion totally voluntarily for our behalf. *"My kingdom is not of this world. If my kingdom were of this world, my servants would have been fighting, that I might not be delivered over to the Jews. But my kingdom is not from the world... You say that I am a king. For this purpose I was born and for this purpose I have come into the world—to bear witness to the truth. Everyone who is of the truth listens to my voice"* (Jn. 18:36&37 ESV).

Jesus has become our King. We are in this world but not of this world. The world we are of Jesus is King, a good and excellent King, who knows all we are going through, every difficulty we face, and never leaves us to deal with any of them alone.

---

1   Lk.4:1&14
2   See 1Cor. Chapters 12 & 14
3   Jn.14:6

'I am in your life in ways you may not even know.' As we try to live our lives for the Lord there are times we may not even know He is working within us. There are two things here: one is we may not yet be aware of how to sense His presence in our lives, the other is almost the opposite of that – after walking with God many years becoming accustomed to His Spirit being with us that when He is working in our lives it just seems normal and we don't detect it. God wants to be involved with us, and He wants us to be involved with Him.

In our current culture today it takes an effort to be involved with God. There is the deception, the luring away by the world who goes in a totally different direction than God. Sometimes that luring is strong and it takes a push back to resist it. The great deceiver is still at work, he said to Eve, 'Did God really say', and he continues the same today trying to get us off just a little, just enough to ruin our walk with God. To confirm this is true look at what the devil said to Jesus in the wilderness.

It was off from the truth just enough to try to lure Jesus away from the Father. Even after that the devil tried again at other opportunities, *"Now when the devil had ended every temptation, he departed from Him until an opportune time"* (Lk. 4:13 NKJV). The world's affect on us is sometimes very strong pulling us in its direction. Other times it is so subtle that we may not even notice if we are not watching out for it. God wants us living His way. He has given us great things, *"For God so loved the world, that he gave his only begotten Son, that whosoever believeth on him should not perish, but have eternal life"* (Jn. 3:16 ASV).

Jesus is the beginning of that way. By Jesus we are accepted into the family of God, into the spiritual realm where is His dwelling place. The spiritual realm is all around us, it is just not visible to us. The activities go on there, the battles good against evil, the contending for the saints. Paul talks of principalities and powers, these were not of human sources he spoke of. [1]

When Paul speaks of heavenly places it is the spiritual realm he speaks of. If you look back in your life you may remember times you were in danger and wonder how you ever got out of it - God was there. I believe God knows from the beginning of time who will accept His Son Jesus and cares for them even before they are saved. I know of people which something happened before they were saved and wonder how they ever got out of that one that they should have not been able to get out of.

God is with us more than we know. We are born again at salvation, God comes into our life to begin a work, He does not leave us, but continues carrying us into eternity. Some think that we get saved, and then it is up to us to live rightly. We heard in our reading today when Jesus died on the cross He said, 'It is finished.' (Jn.19:30) It is never left up to us to finish our salvation, it is done, it is finished. Yet we are called to cooperate with God as He wants to work in us. We can fight against His work by resisting what it is He wants to do. There is a stirring that comes inside ourselves leading us towards a different way than how we have been which is that work of God. We can go along with it, or we can fight it, refusing to yield to that tug of God within us going in another way.

In our reading in Philippians today Paul said this, *"for it is God who works in you, both to will and to work for his good pleasure"* (2:13 ESV). God plants His will within us at salvation and nurtures it to grow. We can either allow it to grow or fight it. Here is another scripture telling us it is the will of God in us, *"And the God of the peace...make you perfect in every good work to do His will, doing in you that which is well-pleasing before Him, through Jesus Christ"* (Heb. 13:20&21 YLT). So God is working in your life in ways you may not sense, but He is there working bringing forth His will within you.

---

1   Eph.3:9&10, 6:12

How would you be if God was not in your life? Do you ever think of how your life would now be if you had never accepted Jesus into your life? Does it bring you to thanksgiving and praise seeing how He has worked in your life? Sometimes we get so tied up in our need of the moment we lose track of all the great things God has done in our life already. Sometimes when we are in the storm we are not seeing God in it with us until the storm has passed, then we see where He was involved. When in the storm it is good to look back at other times in our life when God brought us through safely. God is faithful and will get us through all the way to heaven when we continue to trust in Him to do it.

Sometimes it is hard to keep that trust, yet if we compare God's ability to get us through to our own ability it is obvious whose ability is greater. Taking care of us, watching over us, and getting us through God does because of His great love for us. If such a great deed He did in putting Christ on the cross because of our sins so we could be with Him in heaven, if He has already done this great thing for us, would not anything else be far less and so much more sure? The word of God is very specific at times. Could the following scripture be anything else other than what He will do? *"Draw near to God and He will draw near to you"* (Jas. 4:8 NKJV).

If you have drawn near to God then He is with you knowing every need you have and is in every storm with you. If God had not decided to provide a way of redemption then we all would be gone as are those who died in the flood at the time of Noah. Of all of the people of the earth at that time God only found one righteous man.[1] How great is God that in spite of our condition He provided a way we could be saved.[2] When we are in the depth of difficulty it is difficult to see much other. It is then that we need to put our eyes on Jesus, and the greatness of who God is, and know He will carry us through. Every time we go through one of these things our faith grows because we see the success of God in our life. The ultimate loss is when at judgment we are denied access into heaven, all other things are less no matter how important we may think they are. How many times are your children afraid and scared but you know there is no need to fear, yet your children fear until they see everything is OK?

For us with God it is the same, He sees what we cannot see, He knows what we cannot know. Sometimes we try to work out the future when God says He will work out the future for those who trust Him. *"For the Gentiles seek after all these things, and your heavenly Father knows that you need them all. But seek first the kingdom of God and his righteousness, and all these things will be added to you. Therefore do not be anxious about tomorrow, for tomorrow will be anxious for itself. Sufficient for the day is its own trouble"* (Mt. 6:32-34 ESV).

In our reading in John chapter 20 today we see how the disciples had come to a place of despair, their Lord Jesus had been killed and they didn't know what they were going to do.[3] Remember Jesus had told them He was going to rise the third day, but they didn't get it. (v. 9) *"On the evening of that day, the first day of the week, the doors being locked where the disciples were for fear of the Jews, Jesus came and stood among them and said to them, "Peace be with you." When he had said this, he showed them his hands and his side. Then the disciples were glad when they saw the Lord. Jesus said to them again, "Peace be with you. As the Father has sent me, even so I am sending you." And when he had said this, he breathed on them and said to them, "Receive the Holy Spirit"* (v. 19-22 ESV).

The disciples didn't know what to make of things and what to do. In the midst of their uncertainty, Jesus steps into the room. He gives them assurance announcing peace over them. Trust in Jesus to step into the today of your life and make a difference.

---

1   Gen.6:5,8, 7:1
2   Rom.5:8
3   Mk.16:10&11

'In the beginning.' What do you think of when you hear these words? Was there a beginning? What was it the beginning of? You may say the beginning of creation, yet I would ask creation of what? Sometimes when we think of creation our thinking is narrow. We look around us, and even in the mirror, and say this is what was created. Yes, but how much more was done by God in the beginning than we think of?

Our first thought of creation are the things we have around us, then on to all that is in the earth. The very first thing God did in creation was to create light. Did you ever consider that there was light before there was the sun, the moon, and the stars? They were not created until the fourth day, yet light was created the first day. We look into the sky at night and see multitudes of stars, the longer we look as our eyes adjust the more stars we see. We know from scientists and their telescopes that the universe is huge.

God created all this, *"By the word of the LORD the heavens were made, and all their host by the breath of his mouth"* (Ps. 33:6 RSV). and *"He determines the number of the stars, he gives to all of them their names"* (Ps. 147:4 RSV). and *"I made the earth, and created man upon it; it was my hands that stretched out the heavens, and I commanded all their host"* (Isa. 45:12 RSV). and *"by the word of God the heavens were of old...the heavens and the earth which are now preserved by the same word"* (2Pet. 3:5&7 NKJV). and *"He reflects the glory of God and bears the very stamp of his nature, upholding the universe by his word of power"* (Heb. 1:3 RSV).

Stars have their nature and planets theirs, the scientist can tell you all about them and how they are held together, this is the work of God. He created them in their place and gave them their path. In this God created gravity and centrifugal force as the stars and planets spin in place. God created geometric forces which hold an object in place by its spinning motion. And the list goes on, and on, and on. **'In the beginning' - what a thought.** Then we could go on to the atom which is what forms all things. With us being aware of even this smaller part of creation, how great is this God that loves us?

Even with all this going on He wants to know about the smallest detail of your life, your specific life. When we see His greatness it is easy to see how He can take care of all our needs, it is as a very small task to Him. What an amazing God that loves us, cares for us, walks with us, carries us when we are unable to walk, provides our every need – then makes a way by His work to forgive us so we are accepted into heaven to be with Him forever. Our big troubles are so small to Him, and how He wants to take care of every one of them.

Here is what Paul tells us in what we read today in Philippians, *"And my God will supply all your needs according to His riches in glory in Christ Jesus"* (4:19 NASB). Your faith depends on what you think of your God. The more time we spend with Him, the more our relationship with Him grows, and the greater our faith becomes as we find more and more who He is. In the beginning He saw you and put your name in the Lamb's Book of Life. *"And those who live on the earth, whose names have not been written in the book of life from the foundation of the world"* (Rev. 17:8 NASB).

This is about those who follow the beast, and we are the ones who were written in the Book at the foundation of the world. In the beginning all was considered that Jesus would do on earth, even the very details of what we read in the last chapter of John today. Jesus loved His disciples to the very last moment He could be here on earth, and continues to love us. I spoke of how great the creation of the universe is. Here John says if all was written about what Jesus did then the world would not be large enough to contain all the books. How big is our Jesus, and how little do we know of Him?

In the beginning, God knew all things. God knew the character of man. God knew He must give man free will for man to do of his own choosing. God knew man would choose wrongly. God knew He would have to develop a plan to bring man back to Himself once man had sinned. God knew man did not have it within himself to gain forgiveness for sin. God knew man would try to gain that forgiveness, but that God Himself would have to provide it for their redemption. God has seen our troubles from afar, and has known us from afar. **'I am searching for you and seeking you to do good for you'**, says the Holy Spirit of God. God loves us in spite of our behavior, God loves us and wants us close, God loves us and cares to redeem us to Himself.[1]

It is hard to fathom that this God would love us this much. For some of us, we would say that there are things about ourselves we know that make it difficult to believe God could love us. We need to remember with God there is only black or white, and if you are not white like Him then you are black and God provides the same cleansing for all who come to Him to make them white. It is the blood of Christ that makes us white, no matter if we were just a little dark or in the depth of darkness, it is all sin. Sin is what separates us from God. God is holy, He is pure, and anything less than pure cannot enter eternity where He is.

Through Christ we are sanctified,[2] we are made holy, we are cleansed to be pure, we are made clean like snow.[3] When we hesitate to go to God for forgiveness because we are not wanting Him to know what we did He already knows and has forgiveness waiting for us if we will come to Him and ask for it. In all of scripture in all sin, there is only one that cannot be forgiven.[4] Other than this one, all sin no matter how great you think it is He will forgive if you ask. God is a loving God, He has loved us since the beginning. Man has tried to make another way with many other religions, and many methods to please God, but there is only one way, and that is through the forgiveness offered in Jesus Christ.[5]

This has been offered since the beginning of time held in mystery. We are told about this in our reading in the first chapter of Colossians today, *"he has now reconciled in his body of flesh by his death, in order to present you holy and blameless and irreproachable before him,...the hope of the gospel which you heard,...of which I became a minister according to the divine office which was given to me for you, to make the word of God fully known, the mystery hidden for ages and generations but now made manifest to his saints"* (v. 22,23,25,26 RSV).

God has loved us since the beginning, God has had a plan since the beginning. He is willing and able to forgive all who come to His holiness for forgiveness. We are now beginning to read the gospel of Matthew where we will see this mystery unfold. The whole thing starts with Jesus leaving heaven to be born as a man through a woman in a supernatural pregnancy with the Holy Spirit being the father. We are told of this action of Christ in Philip. 2:5-7, *"Christ Jesus, who, though he was in the form of God, did not count equality with God a thing to be grasped, but emptied himself, taking the form of a servant, being born in the likeness of men"* (RSV).

He came to be the offered sacrifice by the Law that we could be accepted by God. When Joseph planned to divorce Mary an angel spoke to him in a dream, part of that instruction was to name the child Jesus. (Mt.1:21) God has known us from the beginning, He worked out a plan of redemption, He sent us help that we needed to come from Him. Mary and Joseph, each separately, were instructed to name the child Jesus. The meaning of the name Jesus is: 'help of Jehovah'. From the beginning this was God's plan, from the beginning He was sending Jesus.

---

1 1Tim.2:3-6
2 Heb.10:10
3 Ps.51:7, Isa.1:18
4 Mk.3:28&29
5 Heb.9:26, 10:12

God will always be by your side. God gives us assurance with His many promises to be with us, even in us. This is an assurance we need as we live in this world waiting our time to go to the next. This earth and all that is in it is God's creation. Yet how beautiful it would be if sin had never entered. When sin entered the world by the disobedience of mankind there was an infection that came into the world affecting all that there is.[1] We also were infected by it, unable to be perfect.

We have received by salvation He who is perfect giving us eternal life. Christ is in us and we are in Him, He brings to us who are imperfect the perfectness of Himself making us perfect before God. With God being with us it enables us to live in an imperfect world. We are told we are different than the world, *"I have given them thy word; and the world hated them, because they are not of the world, even as I am not of the world...They are not of the world even as I am not of the world"* (Jn. 17:14&16 ASV). We are now children of God, *"But as many as received him, to them gave he the right to become children of God, even to them that believe on his name"* (Jn. 1:12 ASV).

We are in this world but we are of heaven, *"For our citizenship is in heaven, from which we also eagerly wait for the Savior, the Lord Jesus Christ, who will transform our lowly body that it may be conformed to His glorious body, according to the working by which He is able even to subdue all things to Himself"* (Philip. 3:20&21 NKJV). Those who are with God have a covering which separates them from the world. This covering is the blood of Christ and His righteousness, *"according to the foreknowledge of God the Father, in sanctification of the Spirit, unto obedience and sprinkling of the blood of Jesus Christ"* (1Pet. 1:2 ASV). and *"Unto him that loved us, and washed us from our sins in his own blood"* (Rev. 1:5 KJV). and *"the righteousness of God is through the faith of Jesus Christ to all, and upon all those believing"* (Rom. 3:22 YLT).

God is always closer than we think, *"Whoever confesses that Jesus is the Son of God, God abides in him, and he in God"* (1Jn. 4:15 RSV). God is surely with us and by our side in all we do. There are times we seem strange to the world because we are following a nature of life, that nature of the Spirit, as He guides and directs us and it is different than the world. They do not understand for they do not have the Spirit of God, what we do seems strange and unusual to them.

In God we always have a help close by. In our reading today in Colossians Paul establishes how strong our connection to God is. *"you have come to fulness of life in him, who is the head of all rule and authority...you were buried with him in baptism, in which you were also raised with him through faith in the working of God, who raised him from the dead. And you, who were dead in trespasses and the uncircumcision of your flesh, God made alive together with him, having **forgiven us all our trespasses**, having canceled the bond which stood against us with its legal demands; this he set aside, nailing it to the cross"* (2:10,12,13,14 RSV).

There is nothing in the way that will prevent God from being with us. It is through Christ and His blood that we have been brought to God. It is not by our behavior, but by the work of Christ on the cross that God is with us. He will be there because the work has been done by Himself and we have accepted, and received it.

---

1   Rom.8:21

Let us pray. What kind of prayer do you use? I'm not so much speaking about a type, but when and where. It is important to be in God's word, but just as important to pray. We read God's word to know about God, know what he tells us about ourselves, and what He has done for us. Prayer is not so much about asking for this, or that, or another.

Prayer is being in a conversation with God talking about all kinds of things, what we did today (or are going to do), or about the beautiful walk we took through His beautiful creation, or how much a blessing your children are to you, or just how you are feeling today. Prayer is not just a request line, it is a friendship line and friends talk about all kinds of things. Sometimes these prayers are done at various times of the day as you are in these things. Sometimes prayer is done at the moment of need. I have ask God many times, 'Lord help me find my screwdriver' and He has always helped at that moment. Prayer is like talking to a friend, it creates fellowship, and relationship. This is how God wants us to come to Him. He doesn't want us to think He is a scowling giant that we better approach in the proper form. He calls us to Him, He wants us close.

We are to come humbly having a fearing reverence, but not a fearing terror to get close to Him. Prayer is that spiritual pushing out to touch God. He is never too busy, He is never too far away, He is always ready to hear from us. We, here in this life, cannot know the fullness of who God is, but He knows the fullness of who we are. He is never astonished at anything we tell Him, but He might be astonished that we would hesitate to come to Him with our prayer.

If God so loved the world to give us His only Son certainly He would give time to us to hear our prayer. Relationship, is that not what you want with your children, or children want with their parents? Why should God be different? Do you not realize that our desire for relationship in our family has been given us as a design feature of the relationship within the Trinity, the family of God? Yes, God wants relationship, He has given it to you so you can have a relationship with Him.

After being confronted by the Lord in a blinding light on the road to Damascus Saul went through a transformation arriving at a spiritual place where Jesus Christ taught him by direct revelation.[1] Saul knew his Lord, spent time with the Lord, developed that close relationship with the Lord. Paul (earlier called Saul) taught much about prayer telling us this, *"pray without ceasing, give thanks in all circumstances; for this is the will of God in Christ Jesus for you"* (1Thes. 5:17&18 ESV). *'pray without ceasing'* cannot mean in our prayer closet on our knees. We read today in Colossians to do our work even as unto the Lord.*"Whatever you do, work heartily, as for the Lord and not men"* (Col. 3:23 ESV). *'pray without ceasing'* therefore must mean an attitude or awareness, always in a conscious state of knowing God is with us. When I lose my hammer I know God is right there with me so I ask for help. As we begin Colossians chapter 3, Paul says this, *"Therefore, if you have been raised with Christ, keep seeking the things that are above, where Christ is, seated at the right hand of God. Set your minds on the things that are above, not on the things that are on earth"* (v. 1&2 NASB).

What Paul speaks of here is an attitude and awareness of the things above, prayer is part of that attitude. We read today in Matthew about John the Baptist. I wonder what a prayer life he had. What it would have been to listen in when he was alone with God in prayer, if I could have even only a tenth of what he must have had, Oh what a blessing that would be.

We know God spoke to John because of what he said in the gospel of John, *"I saw the Spirit descend from heaven like a dove, and it remained on him. I myself did not know him, but he who sent me to baptize with water said to me, 'He on whom you see the Spirit descend and remain, this is he who baptizes with the Holy Spirit"* (1:32&33 ESV). We need to keep moving closer to God in prayer and believe what God has said to us, *"Draw near to God, and he will draw near to you"* (Jas. 4:8 ESV).

---

1   Gal.1:1&12, Eph.3:2,3,16,17

"Come to me, all of you who are struggling and burdened" (Mt. 11:28 CJB). Sometimes this is limited by many as referring to salvation. Salvation is the first step, but it goes on into our Christian lives with Christ. Salvation is instantaneous, it is at the moment we accept Christ into our lives. It is not a process, otherwise we could claim some credit for our salvation. Christ did it all on the cross, **it is finished**, there is nothing left for us to do to gain salvation. *"Take my yoke upon you and learn from me"* (Mt. 11;29 CJB).

We receive our salvation from Jesus and then we are to learn from Him. Learning takes time, we will be learning more and more the rest of our lives here on earth. So by what Jesus says in v. 29 it would make v. 28 also true for the rest of our lives. So then when we have those difficult days what is it we are suppose to do? Christ is always there, He says to us, 'come to Me, I will help you'. There will always be some difficult days in our life. Perfection comes in heaven, but until we reach heaven we live in the imperfect. Paul lived in this imperfect world having many struggles, but he looked forward and set his mind on the place he had in Christ, *"did raise us up together, and did seat us together in the heavenly places in Christ Jesus"* (Eph. 2:6 YLT).

We have our troubles in this world, but being in Christ the eternal life will be of perfection, happiness, and joy. Our days now we must depend on Christ to carry the heavy part of the yoke while we walk along with Him learning as we go. Since the fall in the garden when mankind sinned there has been a defect in mankind called pride. Even though Christ calls us to come to Him for help, in our pride we hesitate, or refuse, or think we can handle it ourselves.

As is said, 'Sometimes we are our own worst enemy'. We should not wait until we are crushed all the way down crawling on the ground before we ask for His help, it should be as soon as we feel a bit weak. Jesus wants our life to be better, that is why He died on the cross. His death on the cross was not just for our day of salvation, it was for all of our life, our day of salvation, and all the days after. Jesus died to patch up a divide that was between God and us, sin was a barrier wall we could not get past. Now because of the cross of Christ, all of our life is connected with God. Now that Christ has taken care of the hard part providing salvation for you, is there anything else He would not do? We need to trust Him, we need to call on Him, we need to ask Him to go with us into our day. He is always there but He wants to be invited to be involved.

We all need help, we should not hesitate to ask the Lord. Sometimes it is the Lord directly that helps us, and sometimes it is brethren that He sends. We might have a tendency to think the Son of man never needed any help. Being as a man He went through all we go through, there were times He needed help. First of all, He was daily, or even more often, in prayer to the Father. He had a couple of hard days He needed some help and the Father sent those to help Him. We read of one of those times in our reading in Matthew today, *"and behold, angels came and ministered to him"* (4:11 RSV).

The other hard day Jesus had was when He deeply struggled to give in to the will of the Father to die on the cross for us. *"Father, if You are willing, remove this cup from Me; yet not My will, but Yours be done." Now an angel from heaven appeared to Him, strengthening Him"* (Lk. 22:42&43 NASB). Jesus no longer struggles the struggle of man, He is at the right of the Father in heaven. But we, we still have the struggles of mankind, we still need help at times. So when Jesus was here in the weakness of man (Heb.4:15) He had some bad days and needed help. Certainly, we in our bad days do need help. Jesus is waiting and ready to help. *"Come to me, all of you who are struggling and burdened"* (CJB).

'I am at your right hand, and I am at your left.' Have you arrived at the place in your spiritual walk that you believe God is at your right and your left? He is if you have salvation. He is even in you working His works if you have invited Him to do so.[1] There is not a way you can be outside His presence. There is not a thought you have that He does not know about, there is not an emotion of your heart He does not sense. Now as you go along your day with God within you, at your right, and at your lift, do you think anything can happen to you He does not know about? This is a faith-building thought.

If God's presence is in all the universe can you imagine it is not with you? God is said to be omnipresent.[2] I think of it this way, God's dwelling place is in heaven, but His greatness is such that it emanates out into all of creation. It emanates even to you, and into you. God is said to be omniscient, there is nothing about you He doesn't know.[3] With me I believe God knows much more about me that even I know. There is much concern about if we are living in the right way for God. We wonder if we are walking with God or not. Have you invited Him to walk with you? If you have He is a faithful God and has come and is walking with you, how then can you not be walking with Him? He works inside you, He stirs you to do His good works, those that He has chosen for you.

How often do you get a notion or a feeling to do something that is an unnormal thing for you? That is God stirring you. Move into it, He is taking you there and will give you success in it. God takes us out of our comfort zone so that we will know He was who did it. This is what God did with Gideon and spoke to him this, *"The people with you are too many for me to give the Midianites into their hand, lest Israel boast over me, saying, 'My own hand has saved me"* (Jdg. 7:2 ESV).

When it is that which you are not normally able to do it is when God gets the glory. God is with us all the time, He is teaching us all the time, He is leading us all the time. 'I am at your right hand, and I am at your left.' This is an awareness we have to set into our soul. This is not something you set in your brain to remember, it has to go into the inner man changing you from there outward. Anything that goes into the brain for us to remember is very similar to a law, it is a way for us to act. What goes into our inner man (soul, spirit, heart) changes who we are, causing it to be in our natural nature of who we are.

God wants to do so many great things for us, He wants to do it for each individual person. If you have been listening to some of the previous daily comments, then you may already be starting to draw close to God. Have you begun to sense Him drawing closer to you? It is that relationship you are beginning to develop with Him which will gain you many great things. There are many great things in this world, but nothing is greater than the spiritual awareness that God is with you, the spiritual knowledge of heavenly things, the spiritual power that works things in our world. I won't say arriving there is easy, it takes a seeking, are we not to seek God and all He has? God will respond to those who respond to Him.

God is invisible but not inactive. He wants to speak to us, He wants to work in us, He wants to work through us. In reading of what Paul wrote today it seems these people were seeking God so much it became evident to others. *"For we know, brethren beloved by God, that he has chosen you; for our gospel came to you not only in word, but also in power and in the Holy Spirit and with full conviction...And you became imitators of us and of the Lord, for you received the word in much affliction, with joy inspired by the Holy Spirit; so that you became an example to all the believers in Macedonia and in Achaia...your faith in God has gone forth everywhere"* (1Thes. 1:4,5,6,8 RSV). It seems that these had a hunger and a searching for God. This is what I want for myself, is it what you want for yourself?

---

1   Philp.2:13
2   Jer.23:24
3   Ps.139:1-10

There is a storm coming. You may look around thinking there is a lot of evil in the world. Well yes, the devil is seeking whom he may devour.[1] He rules over all the unsaved.[2] Yes, there is evil in the world around us, we see it everywhere. But there is a storm coming, it is the end of the age called the great tribulation. Evil will come upon the world in such force as never seen before. It will be in such force it will even overtake some of the saints.[3] Even those who are overcome by the beast will in the end find their home in heaven with God, that is His promise if we believe in the Son Jesus Christ.

I say this not to cause anyone to fear, I say it so we can live in the awareness of the age we live in. The apostles probably did not have the book of Revelation since John was the young one and he wrote it while he was a prisoner on a prison island. Yet all the apostles had the books of the prophets. They lived in an expectance of the final judgment, and the taking of the saints to heaven. *"Therefore, brethren, be even more diligent to make your call and election sure, for if you do these things you will never stumble; for so an entrance will be supplied to you abundantly into the everlasting kingdom of our Lord and Savior Jesus Christ"* (2Pet. 1:10&11 NKJV).

In our blessings we receive from God in our lives we can become complacent to evil in the spiritual world around us and not notice the interference they cause. We are free of them because we are covered by the blood of Christ. Yet the demon forces will try to browbeat us into thinking the blood does not protect us, convincing us to panic. We are free, we are liberated, from the doom of the world who rejects Christ and His offer of salvation. Jesus said He goes to prepare a place for us,[4] why would He do that if we are not going to get there? We need in a spiritual sense to see past the physical substance of this world and know from what we are told in scripture of what goes on around us.

We need to stop sometime, taking our eyes off of what we see in the world around us and ask God to help us be aware of that which is unseen. After all, is that not what faith is about, believing in what we don't see? And we are to walk in faith so is that not walking in the awareness of the unseen, even of that which is also unseen all around us? We have been given a great privilege to be given life, spiritual life, a life that will go into eternity. That life exists in the spiritual realm, yes we are on this earth with physical features as a body and physical substance of the earth all around us. But the part that lives forever is our Spirit, the inner man, that within the body, within our tent.

We read of the Lord's Prayer in our reading in Matthew chapter 6 today, *"Our Father who art in heaven, Hallowed be thy name. Thy kingdom come. Thy will be done, On earth as it is in heaven"* (v. 9&10 RSV). Now the coming of God's Kingdom could be speaking of the Kingdom spoken of in Revelation 21:1&2, but I think not. I think it speaks of what we read in Colossians, *"He has delivered us from the dominion of darkness and transferred us to the kingdom of his beloved Son"* (1:13 RSV). Here we are told of the Kingdom of Jesus, even Jesus speaks about this Kingdom, *"for lo, the kingdom of God is within you"* (Lk. 17:21 ASV).

We the saved are the Kingdom of Jesus, and we are here on this earth. So the Kingdom is here all around us, it is what Jesus died on the cross to establish. If it is the Kingdom of Jesus then it is a spiritual Kingdom in a physical world. We do see the trees, and beautiful flowers, and the great mountains of God's creation all around us. But there is also a spiritual Kingdom all around us also. It won't be us waiting until we arrive in heaven to be of the spiritual world, in our rebirth we were born into a spiritual world, *"That which is born of the flesh is flesh; and that which is born of the Spirit is spirit"* (Jn. 3:6 ASV).

Even of the living in the spiritual, as well as the physical, it was spoken to you today in reading 1 Thessalonians, *"charged you to walk in a manner worthy of God, who calls you into his own kingdom"* (2:12 ESV). We are not called into a physical kingdom, we are called into a spiritual kingdom.

---

1   1Pet.5:8
2   Acts 26:18
3   Rev.13:7
4   Jn.14:2&3

The cry goes out among the people. There is a call of God that goes out amongst all mankind. God is calling all of us back to Him, but how many do respond? There is a scripture that may speak of how many, it fits with the wide gate and narrow gate. I don't claim it speaks of how many will be lost and how many saved, but it is interesting, *"Strike the shepherd, that the sheep may be scattered; I will turn my hand against the little ones. In the whole land, says the LORD, two thirds shall be cut off and perish, and one third shall be left alive"* (Zech. 13:7&8 RSV).

This is certainly speaking of Jesus as the shepherd. God calls, but many ignore, or refuse to listen. All of mankind have cold hearts towards God, but some of us have faced our evil, repented of our sins, and accepted Jesus to be Lord and Master of our lives. Now we have come, God no longer calls us in this, He calls us now to follow, *"If anyone would come after me, let him deny himself and take up his cross and follow me"* (Mt. 16:24 ESV).

Jesus showed us the example of how we should live, *"I am among you as the one who serves"* (Lk. 22:27 NASB). and *"For I have given you an example, that ye also should do as I have done to you"* (Jn. 13:15 ASV). Jesus calls us to service, but how many listen? We want someone to bless us, but what about us being a blessing to someone else, to serve them. Pride is a very big rock in the road preventing us from getting to those who need our service. We need to blast that rock and blow it to bits, we need to remove it from our lives. As long as pride is within us weighing us down we will never be able to truly serve others like Christ served us. Christ gave all.

As long as we have pride fighting this in us we will not be able to give of ourselves very much. We are called to follow, to follow in the works Jesus is doing, calling us into that work with Him. The calling is what we need to listen for, the calling is what we need to hear. To some He calls to be fishers of men, to others He calls to wait on tables, and to others He calls to pray for the sick. These are not all of the things He calls those who follow to do, but they show that each of us are not called to do it all, each is called to do a part. This is why it is so important to hear what Jesus calls each to do, the hand cannot be a foot and the ear should not be in the place where the nose is. [1]

It is important for us to hear what Jesus is calling to each one of us. A church full of only evangelists would be a large church but never very physically healthy. A church full of only those who pray for the sick would be very healthy but would never grow in size. All the parts of the body need to be there, and we each need to pray to find out which part we are. It is important to follow, but it is more important to hear, otherwise how will we know where to follow? It takes spiritual growth to be able to hear. It takes time for most of us to learn which voice is that of God and which is not.

I have been listening for over 40 years, and once in a while don't know for sure who is speaking and have to pray more. If we don't take time to listen then we will never hear that still small voice God speaks with. *"And there he went into a cave, and spent the night in that place; and behold, the word of the LORD came to him, and He said to him, "What are you doing here, Elijah?"...Then He said, "Go out, and stand on the mountain before the LORD." And behold, the LORD passed by, and a great and strong wind tore into the mountains and broke the rocks in pieces before the LORD, but the LORD was not in the wind; and after the wind an earthquake, but the LORD was not in the earthquake; and after the earthquake a fire, but the LORD was not in the fire; and after the fire a still small voice"* (1Kg. 19:9,11,12 NKJV).

Spending time with God, being close to God, praying to God, being quiet with God, these are the things that will help you to begin to hear that still small voice. After some time you will learn to recognize that voice, even in the noisiest of places.

---

1   1Cor.12:14-21

Have trust in God. Who is God to you? A super-being in the sky? A lovely Jesus who sprinkles you with blessing bits? A Triune authority of three who glares down at all creation? Well, none of these is what God tells us of Himself in His word. He is a great magnificent God beyond anything we here on earth can ever know. There are certain aspects of God that we can know, in a way. All that we are, are some of what He is, we are made in His image. He has emotions as He has made us with emotions. The greatest of all His emotions is love. Everything good He has worked towards us is from His love. *"For God so loved the world"* (Jn. 3:16 ASV).

We know the rest of the verse, but God's love towards us didn't end with giving His Son, it only was the beginning. The giving of the Son was the most important and it could have ended there because that was what we needed to get into heaven, but it did not end there, it started. The thing we need to remember about God though is He has His own thoughts and ways, He is not like our thoughts and ways. We have our ways, and we have our thoughts, but God tries to draw us to His ways, and to His thoughts. For those of us who received salvation as adults, we had our ways and our thoughts pretty well set, it was difficult to let go, or to twist them around so they begin to be like God's.

There are things about God that are so far beyond us we can't even connect to them now, that will have to wait until we arrive in heaven with Him. His power and authority is extreme, He orders the stars in their place. [1] He has authority over all times, [2] and acts, [3] and even over our powerful enemy which God will judge and put him in his eternal place. [4]

God has such a right to be harsh with us, yet He does not, He even does what we cannot so we can have eternity with Him. *"For God so loved the world, that he gave his only Son, that whoever believes in him should not perish but have eternal life. For God did not send his Son into the world to condemn the world, but in order that the world might be saved through him. Whoever believes in him is not condemned...whoever does what is true comes to the light, so that it may be clearly seen that his works have been carried out in God"* (Jn. 3:16,17,18,21 ESV).

Once we give ourselves to God He even works in us to change things we cannot. *"for it is God who works in you, both to will and to work for his good pleasure"* (Philp. 2:13 ESV). How little we know of God, and how great He is. Once we have given ourselves to God, certainly we can trust Him.

Once we learn of His greatness, we can trust Him. How could we come to know all we know about God, and then not have trust in Him? If we don't have trust in God, then who would we trust in? Would we trust in ourselves, we couldn't even get saved without Him, we are not much able to do anything without Him. *"for all have sinned, and fall short of the glory of God"* (Rom. 3:23 ASV). God it is who reaches out to us, He gives us time in this life to find Him. *"And He has made from one blood every nation of men to dwell on all the face of the earth, and has determined their preappointed times and the boundaries of their dwellings, so that they should seek the Lord, in the hope that they might grope for Him and find Him, though He is not far from each one of us"* (Acts 17:26&27 NKJV).

In our reading today in Matthew chapter 8 the centurion trusted, so we should trust, Peter's mother-in-law was healed, so we should trust. The disciples thought they were going to perish in the sea but Jesus calmed the storm, so we should trust. Paul speaks of what we will receive from trusting God, *"For the Lord himself shall descend from heaven, with a shout, with the voice of the archangel, and with the trump of God: and the dead in Christ shall rise first; then we that are alive, that are left, shall together with them be caught up in the clouds, to meet the Lord in the air: and so shall we ever be with the Lord"* (1Thes. 4:16&17 ASV).

---

1   Ps.8:3, 147:4, Isa.45:12, Heb.1:3
2   Acts 1:7
3   Mk.13:32
4   Rev.20:10

Be kind to one another for none of you knows about tomorrow. When tomorrow comes, today is gone and will never return. There are life-changing events that come with tomorrow and then we walk with regrets of what we did not do yesterday. It seems to be a human nature to take some things for granted and then when they are gone we have our regrets. Jesus pushed the issue, 'love one another'. Jesus and His disciples told us this more than 20 times. This surely is for the benefit of the other, but what about it helping us not end up with regret we would rather not have. Our flesh wants to be all about self. God wants us to be all about others.

This is not something we can do on our own, we need that new birth of the Spirit in us to help us do this. Before I got saved there was not much concern in me about the other person. After I got saved and the regenerating work of the Holy Spirit began, I found a strangeness of carrying about other people. Now we can shirk this off not doing it even though it is stirred in our heart, this is why we are told to love. It is easy to hold it in for whatever reason, even though it is something new stirring within us. There are many gifts which God gives us but if we keep them in they never come to the surface to do anyone any good. It is one of those things that once we begin to do it it is much easier than we thought. Love is one of those things, it is a nature of God, which we have in His image once we are born again.

The greatest at hatred sometimes after salvation becomes the greatest at love. God takes what is broken and makes it whole again. We have heard it over and over and over, 'God so loved the world'. He has planted that kind of love in us but we must let it out. One thing that has to happen is we have to see the full spectrum of love, some of us have a very narrow view. 'Love your neighbor as yourself', what kind of love is that? It may be a new consideration for some of us. Love is a main theme in all of scripture. God was trying to reach out to a broken world to help it, and continues to do so. Can you imagine, if God did not help you and me, we would not make it to heaven.

Now God wants us to help others as He helps us. He calls this love, even the depth of love. Be kind to one another, love one another today, don't wait for tomorrow, tomorrow might not be there. In Matthew chapter 9 at the beginning we see love in action. Four men brought to Jesus a man who needed a healing, love had to be a motivation that they brought him. Jesus goes to eat at the house of a tax collector, eating there with other tax collectors and sinners. There were objections to Him being there and His answer to them was, *"Those who are well have no need of a physician, but those who are sick. Go and learn what this means, 'I desire mercy, and not sacrifice.' For I came not to call the righteous, but sinners"* (v. 13&14 RSV).

We can see Jesus' love all through this statement. Further in the chapter we see Jesus' love as He comforts a frightened woman who touched His garment, *"Take heart, daughter; your faith has made you well"* (v. 22 RSV). The last thing Jesus says (to us) in this chapter to do is that which our motivation to do should be love, *"The harvest is plentiful, but the laborers are few; pray therefore the Lord of the harvest to send out laborers into his harvest"* (Mt. 9:37&38 RSV).Love is what the motivation would be for us to pray for the harvest. We also read Paul's writing today in 1 Thessalonians chapter 5. He says an interesting thing here, *"put on the breastplate of faith and love"* (v. 8 RSV).

Paul put faith and love together, this is what the four who brought the paralytic to Jesus to be healed had, faith and love. Paul tells us later in the chapter what part of love is, *"admonish the idlers, encourage the fainthearted, help the weak, be patient with them all. See that none of you repays evil for evil, but always seek to do good to one another and to all"* (v. 14&15 RSV). Paul also speaks of how God so loved the world, *"For God has not destined us for wrath, but to obtain salvation through our Lord Jesus Christ"* (v. 9 RSV). This is how God loves us, this is how we are to try to love others.

Holy is the Lord. Can God be anything other than Holy? He is the standard of what holy is. He was holy before creation was brought about. He is holy now. He will be holy in all the time after the end of what we know of creation. God is always holy. There is no hope of us accomplishing holiness as God is holy. We are told in scripture that we are short of His glory.[1] When we get saved we receive an inheritance from Him, spiritually we have become His offspring. We become holy because He is holy and we inherit it from Him. Jesus cleanses us and we become holy. We are called to maintain and continue in that holiness. We are not to make ourselves holy, but we are responsible to continue in what we have been given. *"You shall be* [continue] *holy, for I am holy"* (2Pet. 1:16 ESV).

We also have to be maintaining what God tells us is holy. We have to be careful to do what God says is holy, not what other men may say, some will make it short and others will take it too far. We are made holy by what Christ did on the cross, *"But you were washed, you were sanctified, you were justified in the name of the Lord Jesus Christ and in the Spirit of our God"* (1Cor. 6:11 RSV).

This is how we become holy, it is by the work of God. It is a mystery to me how anyone could refuse such a great gift. God is holy, and all of us who become holy are from His holiness. I fear that I am way far short of measuring up so I depend totally on what God has done for me confessing my sins and trusting Him to cleanse me. My eternity is all wrapped up in God, without Him I will not make it. Each of us can be thankful God does not require us to become holy on our own.

A long time ago God created man and woman, He created them holy as He was holy. There was one requirement for them to stay that way. They were told not to eat of only **one** tree in the garden, all the rest was for them to enjoy, even the tree of life. They were told if they ate of the tree of the knowledge of good and evil they (their holiness, their spiritual being) would die, and it did. Not only that, but all the provisions God had made for them they lost as they were driven out of the garden.

Mankind has been in this condition ever since. We struggle, and struggle, and struggle, to get back what Adam and Eve had in the beginning, with no success. It is God we must go to in a humble manner to receive the gift of salvation in order to be considered by God as being holy again. 'Hallowed be Thy Name', this in the Greek is a broad statement, 'Father continue to make Your Name Holy before us, displaying before us Your Name's great Holiness, so we will see it Holy, and honor it as Holy, and worship You'. Holy is the Lord, and holy have we become because of His holy work that brings that holiness to us.

One day there will be no more of the maintaining work of our holiness because our flesh, which opposes holiness,[2] it will die and then be resurrected in perfection arriving in heaven where all always is holy. Until then we continue to depend on God, continue to follow Jesus, continue to maintain what we have been given. God gives an image of how we who were dead in our sins came to life.

In Ezekiel chapter 37 dry bones come to life and lived again. We were the dry bones very dead until Christ came into our lives, giving us salvation, making us holy. It tells us these dry bones became a great army. We, the redeemed, are now an army of the Lord being sent out into the world to declare the Kingdom of God. We read today in Matthew chapter 10 of the first ones Jesus sent out, *"These twelve Jesus sent out... And preach as you go, saying, 'The kingdom of heaven is at hand"* (v. 5&7 RSV). We have a holy Lord, and today we are still going out as His holy people to tell the world, *'The kingdom of heaven is at hand.'*

---

1   Rom.3:23
2   Rom.7:17&18

Be certain of your goal and destination. Success in this world does not relate to success in the next. I know most all who are reading this are saved followers of Christ. Yet it is so easy to get sucked off our path by the things of the world. It comes at us from all directions. Even our own flesh tries to get us to go in directions we should not. We need to make our Spirit as strong as possible so the flesh does not win. *"the flesh doth desire contrary to the Spirit, and the Spirit contrary to the flesh"* (Gal. 5:17 YLT).

The battle goes on and we need to keep strengthening the good side. Becoming aware of this pushes us into the Word of God and to be close to His side. If we only could see what is going on in the spiritual realm around us, first we would be in a bit of fright, then we would realize why it is important to stay spiritually strong. We have a great hope and a great help, that of God in Jesus Christ. It does not all depend on us, it all depends on Him. Our assurance is in Christ, our walk is what we learn from Him. We will make mistakes, we are human only made perfect by the blood of Christ. [1]

We should not fear of not being strong enough spiritually. I have learned to try my best, do what I can, and allow God to supplement my efforts where I am short. The more I learn and develop the less God has to supplement, although I will always need some of that help of God until I am there with Him. Paul assures us of God's love, *"we are more than conquerors through Him who loved us. For I am persuaded that neither death nor life, nor angels nor principalities nor powers, nor things present nor things to come, nor height nor depth, nor any other created thing, shall be able to separate us from the love of God which is in Christ Jesus our Lord"* (Rom. 8:37-39 NKJV).

With this assurance we know God's love will always be with us so we can never be overpowered, yet that same love yearns moving us forward more and more into the spiritual life. It is so easy to get distracted from spiritual things, from the right into the wrong. Our enemy the devil has been trying to distract us since the Garden of Eden. It takes an effort on our part to live the spiritual life.

Just because we are born again receiving salvation doesn't make this spiritual walk automatic. If it was automatic why would we need so much of the word of God? God wants us to know His nature, He wants us to know the life He has for us and the way to live it. I don't write with the intent to teach you all things, I write with the intent to help you move closer to God. Jesus Christ is said to be the teacher, and the Holy Spirit was sent to us to also teach us all things, [2] they are the ones who will help you become more spiritual. I try to point you to God and to His word. The more spiritual you become, the less you will have need of those like me to direct you.

Remember, as the Spirit gets stronger in us the flesh becomes weaker. The stronger the Spirit the less we are distracted. The world will not change, it will not get better, it will only get worse as it approaches the end. Those things around us will not get better, it is us who must change. One of these days we will be with God for ever, now is the time to begin moving closer to Him. There are two small things to see in our reading today. We need to have our goal and destination set because deception is coming. Paul tells us, *"Let no one deceive you in any way"* (1Thes. 2:3 RSV). If this day comes in our life or not, I do not know. The thing is, then and now, in our intellect we will not always recognize the deception, it is our spiritual maturity that we will be aware of it.

We need to grow in God, taking on more and more of the Spirit. Part of that growth is coming to know more about God, more about the Father. Jesus says this in Matthew today, *"no one knows the Father except the Son and any one to whom the Son chooses to reveal him"* (11:27 RSV). Get close to Jesus and He will help you to know the Father, and they will help you to grow spiritually. Know what your goal is and the destination you intend to arrive at.

---

1 Rev.1:5
2 Jn.14:26, 16:13&14

'I am always on your side.' Do you believe this is what the Holy Spirit says to you? You know He is always there. The Father sent Him to be right there with you, *"I will ask the Father, and He will give you another Helper, so that He may be with you forever...But the Helper, the Holy Spirit whom the Father will send in My name, He will teach you all things, and remind you of all that I said to you"* (Jn. 14:16&26 NASB).

The word Helper does not bring the full view of what we receive when the Holy Spirit is sent to us. When Christ went to heaven He and the Father sent one of the same stature as Christ, one to be all the things Christ was when He was with mankind. The Holy Spirit has been sent to us, and is in us, guiding us and directing us – if we will listen. In our reading yesterday Jesus said this, *"he who is having ears to hear--let him hear"* (Mt. 11:15 YLT). This means we need to pay attention, to listen carefully. The Holy Spirit may be speaking, we just are not listening. We can pray that God will help us to develop an ear that we can hear the Holy Spirit. The Holy Spirit is within us, *"do you not know that your body is a temple of the Holy Spirit within you, whom you have from God"* (1Cor. 6:19 NASB).

If the Holy Spirit is in you is that not as close to being on your side as any could be? He is even our advocate before God, *"the Spirit helps us in our weakness. For we do not know what to pray for as we ought, but the Spirit himself intercedes for us"* (Rom. 8:26 ESV). We know our prayer needs help, here is our help. We know we should act differently than we do, here is our guide to go a better way. It is that ear that we need to develop to hear what the Spirit inside us is saying. He helps us to know right from wrong. Many times demonic forces will try, and even our own flesh will try, to convince us something is right when it is actually wrong.

This is where the Holy Spirit within us is a help. If one goes through the scripture to see what all the Holy Spirit is to us He has a massive work in us. He is a great benefit to us. The more we trust Him, the more we listen to Him, the better our life becomes. Have you ever wondered what the Father or the Lord Jesus is wanting to say to you? We are told this in scripture, *"He will glorify me, because he will receive from what is mine and announce it to you. Everything the Father has is mine; this is why I said that he receives from what is mine and will announce it to you"* (Jn. 16:14&15 CJB). From v.13 you will see 'He' Jesus speaks of is the Spirit. The Holy Spirit is our comforter, our helper, our counselor, our advocate. What a great help we have on our side. In our reading today in Matthew chapter 12, the prophet Isaiah 42:1-4 is quoted, *"Here is my servant, whom I have chosen, my beloved, with whom I am well pleased; I will put my Spirit on him, and he will announce justice to the Gentiles"* (v. 18 CJB). We are told, *"And John bore witness: "I saw the Spirit descend from heaven like a dove, and it remained on him"* (Jn. 1:32 ESV). We are told, *"And Jesus returned in the power of the Spirit"* (Lk. 4:14 ESV).

The Spirit, the Holy Spirit, which we are told we receive at salvation, the Spirit which is sent by Jesus and the Father to be with us and in us, is this Spirit we receive in any way deficient of the Spirit which came to be in Jesus? If it is the Holy Spirit that comes from heaven, then does it not have to be the same Spirit that came to Jesus? I believe the only difference is Jesus had no trouble hearing and being guided by the Spirit, where we have our difficulties hearing Him.

We will never hear and sense the Holy Spirit like Jesus did, but it is the same Holy Spirit who was sent to be our comforter, our helper, our counselor, and our advocate. Now we need to ask God to help us gain an ear that we can hear with. **"He who has an ear, let him hear what the Spirit says."** This was said many times in Revelation: 2:7,11,17,29, 3:6,13,22. This speaks of the end times, but do we not need to hear the Spirit even in these times we are in right now?

All's well that ends well. How many times have you heard this said? What does it mean, that things just bounce along with some bouncing to what is well and some bouncing to what is bad? It seems it is leaving all things to chance and the things that end well are what we have well. This life is not about chance, it is about choice.

We, as humanity, have a God that loves us offering a way that will end well.[1] All of you reading this I assume have made that choice. Finding a God that loves you, and saves you, and blesses you, regardless of your past, it has to bring a gratitude to your heart for what He has done. The apostle Paul voices this in our reading today, *"formerly I was a blasphemer and persecutor and insolent opponent. But I received mercy...Christ Jesus came into the world to save sinners, of whom I am the foremost. But I received mercy...To the King of ages, immortal, invisible, the only God, be honor and glory forever and ever. Amen"* (1Tim. 1:13, 15-17 ESV).

The apostle Paul knew his past, and knew the mercy given to him, it brought him to praise and worship. Our lives seem so complicated at times, yet that is only the complications of this world we live in. There should not be complications in our life with God, He has taken care of all the complications, all we have to do is humbly give ourselves over to Him. If we find complications in our life with God it is because we don't fully know His mercy and grace. Paul knew his past, when he was called Saul persecuting the church, approving of the killing of followers of Christ, of raiding houses hauling Christians off to Jerusalem to be judged. He knew his past, and he knew the mercy of God, and he laid all those things of his past at the feet of Jesus. Is your life with God complicated because you have not yet laid all the things of your past at the feet of Jesus accepting forgiveness?

It is easy to feel guilt for those things, but once we have asked for forgiveness we have to know the power of God's grace that covers all that we think cannot be forgiven. Paul discovers this power of forgiveness and says, *"the grace of our Lord abounded exceedingly"* (1Tim. 1:14 ASV). and *"God is able to make all grace abound to you"*(2Cor. 9:8 NASB). And the apostle John says this, *"the only Son from the Father...And from his fulness have we all received, grace upon grace"* (Jn. 1:14&16 RSV). Do you know how much grace upon grace is? It is always enough, it is never lacking. What is the greatest of mercy, is it not this, *"For God so loved the world that He gave His only begotten Son, that whoever believes in Him should not perish but have everlasting life"* (Jn. 3:16 NKJV).

This is the greatest of God's mercy and grace towards us which comes from His love. And about His love Paul tells us this, *"For I am persuaded, that neither death, nor life, nor angels, nor principalities, nor things present, nor things to come, nor powers, nor height, nor depth, nor any other creature, shall be able to separate us from the love of God, which is in Christ Jesus our Lord"* (Rom. 8:38&39 ASV).

If nothing can separate us from the love of God where His mercy, and grace, and forgiveness is found, can anything prevent you from being forgiven? All ends well that you choose to end well. It will end well for all who choose Christ with the forgiveness which is offered by the Father. Choose well, and choose All the forgiveness that is offered to you through Christ Jesus.

---

1   1Tim.2:4, Rom.6:23

King of kings and Lord of lords - that is who Jesus is. It is difficult for a country who has no king to quite grasp this relationship. A king is absolute in power and authority. A country without a king may have a president who does not have absolute power and authority. For us who have no king as head of the country, it is not easy to understand the loyalty given to one person. Jesus Christ is absolute in power and authority over all of creation, even demons bow to Him.[1]

Many of us get the love part of Jesus, but do we get the King with authority part? We may think, Oh that is for someone else, sinners, and evil people, etc. No, that is for us also, in accepting Him as Lord of our lives He is also King with a Kingdom, we are that Kingdom.[2] What makes Jesus different than other kings is that all that He does comes from love.

That does not mean we don't have to listen to what He says because He will forgive us, it means He is fully King in our lives loving us, being concerned for us, telling us what is better for our lives. After salvation, forgiveness is for the times we slip, or can't quite make it as we ought. There is a reverence that is owed to any king, that reverence towards Jesus should be even higher since He is Lord, and God, and our Savior. Reverence truly given is when we do things because it is what He wants of us, not because He tells us we have to. John tell us, *"We love Him because He first loved us"* (1Jn. 4:19 NKJV).

John understood this, in the book of 1John he uses the word love 42 times in 5 chapters. Once we experience His love to us we want to return something to him. Some of us get this mixed up in the beginning wanting to do some great work for him. It is not work from us He wants, it is love involving reverence, relationship, fellowship, loyalty, and a desire to live the way He says is right. I think that making Him fully, completely King in our lives takes a lifetime to do.

This does not release us from attempting to do so. If we find this true love of Christ it will spurn us on to do all we can do to attain it. If we truly treat Him as King in our life we will find it moves us on to the place He calls us friend. A true friend will not let us get away with things we shouldn't do, he will help us to find a way to quit doing them. Paul in our reading today in 1Timothy reminds us of God's actions of love, *"For there is one God, and there is one mediator between God and men, the man Christ Jesus, who gave himself as a ransom for all"* (2:5&6 ESV).

Jesus was a ransom, it was put on Him what should have been put on us.[3] This is the depth of love, the way Jesus and the Father loves us. There were many crowds that came to hear Jesus teach. He was concerned for the people, He could have sent them away to find food, but as in our reading in Matthew He told His disciples, *"you give them something to eat"* (14:16 ESV).

When Jesus feeds the four thousand He voices that He has compassion for them, *"I feel compassion for the people, because they have remained with Me now for three days and have nothing to eat; and I do not want to send them away hungry, for they might faint on the way"* (Mt. 15:32 NASB). This is the kind of King that we have who has compassion on us to help us. He is a good King, and because of this we should treat Him with great reverence in love as King.

---

1   Mt.28:18, 8:31
2   Col.1:13
3   1Cor.15:3

'I am your love.' This is what Jesus Christ says to us constantly. He and the Father even loved us before we were saved, *"For God so loved the world that He gave"* (Jn. 3:16 RSV). and *"God shows his love for us in that while we were yet sinners Christ died for us"* (Rom. 5:8 RSV).

If God the Father and God the Son loved us before we found them and accepted Jesus into our lives as Lord, how much more do they love us now? Jesus is our Master, He is our Lord, He is constantly with us, He is closer than any other can be, and He is constantly loving us. How could it be that the love Jesus had for us before we were saved, going through all the suffering He did to save us, then after that not love us that much anymore? God's love for you is great, greater than anything else you will ever know.

God's love for you will go on into the endlessness of eternity. 'God so loved the world', can you let that sink into your being? Once we know that love of God it brings us an assurance, it brings us a peace. Jesus said, *"Peace I leave with you; my peace I give to you. Not as the world gives do I give to you. Let not your hearts be troubled, neither let them be afraid"* (Jn. 14:27 ESV). Are these not actions of love towards us? And He loves us in so many other ways as well. 'I am your love' is a statement about a two-way love, *"We love, because he first loved us"* (1Jn. 4:19 ASV). Because He loved us it causes us to love Him. Our hearts become changed at salvation, the Spirit is born into our lives, we are a new creation. *"if any man is in Christ, he is a new creature: the old things are passed away; behold, they are become new"* (2Cor. 5:17 ASV).

Here is another great act of love. When we accept Christ and are saved we are not only forgiven of our sins, He makes us a new person, a new creation no longer to be stuck in the stuff we were in before. Jesus' love continues on with us in everything, it is with us all the time. This is spoken by the writer of Hebrews to the Church which you are part of, *"for he has said, "I will never leave you nor forsake you." So we can confidently say, "The Lord is my helper; I will not fear; what can man do to me?"* (Heb. 13:5&6 ESV).

This is the greatness of love, He will be always with us. The level of love which God has for us is at a higher level of love than we have ever known, it is a higher level of love that we can ever know while we remain on this earth. The full level of this love will only be known to us when we arrive in heaven where all is in its full perfectness. How great is that love that God has for us. There is nothing in this world to compare it to, it is always greater than what we can know. Only God can encompass the fullness of this love and He offers it out to us who come to Him. God so loved the world - even before we loved Him, can you imagine what kind of love that is?

Reading today in Matthew chapter 15 a Syrophoenician woman comes to Jesus asking help for her daughter. Jesus basically says, I have come to the sheep of Israel, not for foreigners. She tells Jesus even the leftovers, the bits and bare crumbs are enough for her. Jesus tells her, *"O woman, great is your faith! Be it done for you as you desire"* (v. 28 ESV). In that statement can you see the great love of Jesus for this woman, she was willing to believe what even most of His own countrymen were not willing to believe. We who are Gentiles have been accepted into the sheepfold of God, *"just as the Father knows me and I know the Father; and I lay down my life for the sheep. And I have other sheep that are not of this fold. I must bring them also, and they will listen to my voice. So there will be one flock, one shepherd"* (Jn. 10:15&16 ESV).

All of us who are willing to believe have been accepted by God, and loved by God, giving us the gift of salvation and the lifetime of God's love on into the endlessness of eternity. Jesus' love is never ending and is always flowing out to you.

'There is always a place in My heart for you.' This is true of God who desires that all people would accept salvation, *"God our Savior, who desires all people to be saved and to come to the knowledge of the truth... Christ Jesus, who gave himself as a ransom for all"* (1Tim. 2:3-6 ESV).

This is true of God reaching out to any who would come to Him. For us who have a relationship with Him, even being children of God it is much more true. *"Come to me... and I will give you rest...I am gentle and lowly in heart, and you will find rest for your souls"* (Mt. 11:28&29 ESV). What a great promise of the Lord to us. It seems to be a natural thing for people to worry, but we must confront our worry with the truth which God speaks to us applying it in faith. Our faith is found in the inner person, that which has been given life by the Spirit of God. We must lean toward that Spirit who is also called the Spirit of Truth, *"the Spirit of truth, whom the world cannot receive, because it neither sees Him nor knows Him; but you know Him, for He dwells with you and will be in you"* (Jn. 14:17 NKJV).

If we listen to the Spirit of Truth rather than all the other voices around us it will help us have faith not giving in to worry so much. There is always a voice which wants to take you to worry. We hear our own voice within in that place of uncertainty, we hear voices from the world around us who want us to fear - many times because it gives them an advantage. And sometimes it is of the enemy of God who wants to ruin God's children.[1] We are told this about the devil, *"resist the devil, and he will flee from you"* (Jas. 4:7 ASV).

It may be that resisting in the other areas may work as well, telling ourselves what is truth to confront the lie. If we allow these worries to come upon us it is hard to believe we have a Lord who constantly is carrying for us. As we know more of what is truth the more we will know of His heart that is for us always. Faith is being willing to believe what we cannot believe, to believe it because it is what God says. The more we refuse the so-called knowledge of man and accept the knowledge of God the more peace we will have. Even though our life on this earth is very short compared to eternity it seems long to us.

Each day another day, one coming after another, yet in every one of them God is with us. Jesus in His teaching tries to help us with worry saying this, *"So do not worry about tomorrow; for tomorrow will worry about itself. Each day has enough trouble of its own"* (Mt. 6:34 NASB). Even in Jesus trying to help us in saying this we can see His heart is for us. We read today again more of the heart of Jesus as He prepared to give Himself as a ransom for many. *"From that time Jesus began to show his disciples that he must go to Jerusalem and suffer many things from the elders and chief priests and scribes, and be killed, and on the third day be raised"* (Mt. 16:21 ESV).

This was what Jesus allowed to happen to Himself for our sake. In the greatness of His heart He tells us this, *"Greater love has no one than this, that one lay down his life for his friends."* (Jn.15:13 NASB) As we begin to know of more and more of His heart towards us the more of His peace enters in.

---

1   Rev.12:17

Is there something missing in your life? Are you fully content in how you are? If we don't ask these questions we will not be searching for more of God in our lives. The Lord wants to be in our lives more and more. God is the standard, we are the strivers. Our lives will be a constant striving to become more like Christ. The interesting thing is this does not mean more work, it means less work, it means more dying to self and self desires. Christ is our example, what did He do to come to earth becoming a man?, *"Christ Jesus, who, though he was in the form of God, did not count equality with God a thing to be grasped, but emptied himself, taking the form of a servant, being born in the likeness of men"* (Philp. 2:5-7 RSV).

If we are to become more and more like Christ we have to empty ourselves more and more. [1] We will never accomplish the great emptying of what He did. He had a right to be in Heaven as part of the Godhead and gave it up to come to earth to serve as a sacrifice to redeem mankind, to redeem me and you. Even though we can't accomplish the greatness of dying to self that He did in coming to earth we should continue to empty ourselves as much as we can. It seems we cannot truly begin the giving for others and to others until we die some wanting less and less for ourselves. This is one of those places where if we want more we must become less. Who did God reveal the mystery of the gospel to? It was not the ones who thought they had all the answers, *"I praise You, Father, Lord of heaven and earth, that You have hidden these things from the wise and intelligent and have revealed them to infants"* (Lk. 10:21 NASB).

It was not those who had more, it was those who had less. When we want more with God, we have to come in a humble manner, giving up more of our self for His goodness and His purpose. If we come to Him in this manner He will bless us, *"whoever exalts himself will be humbled, and whoever humbles himself will be exalted"* (Mt. 23:12 RSV). Being exalted by the Lord is greater than anything else we could do to exalt ourselves for Him. It seems crazy to us, but dying to self more, trying less on our own part, is what gains us more with God. Jesus came as our example, showing how to give of our self selflessly. [2]

In our reading in Matthew chapter 17 today we see a little of the splendor of who Jesus was as He was with men, *"As they watched, he began to change form—his face shone like the sun, and his clothing became as white as light. Then they looked and saw Moshe [Moses] and Eliyahu [Elijah] speaking with him...a bright cloud enveloped them; and a voice from the cloud said, "This is my Son, whom I love, with whom I am well pleased. Listen to him!"* (v. 2,3,5 CJB).

Here is a little of who Jesus is, spectacular, overwhelming, glorious in His appearance. Yet in leaving there He speaks of His emptying of Himself to be a servant to mankind as he speaks of what is coming, *"Don't tell anyone what you have seen until the Son of Man has been raised from the dead"* (v. 9 CJB). Jesus speaks of the very end of the work He was giving Himself in service to others, to all of us who are saved by the blood He gave up on that day of the cross. Jesus humbled Himself giving Himself over for the serving to redeem mankind with His rising from the dead as the last act, that we also would be able to rise as did He.

As great as Jesus was He put himself down to be less so that we could be redeemed. This is what we must do, we must become less. This is how we gain with God and find that something that is missing in our lives.

---

1   Jn.3:30
2   Mk.10:45

Where is the love of Christ? This could be asking different questions. As we look around the world with all its complex problems we could wonder where the evidence of the love of Christ is. We could be in a situation in our own life that is difficult and we wonder where is the love of Christ in our difficulty. Then it could be the Church is not as it should be and those outside could be asking were the love of Christ is among these people who are to represent Him. Many are the questions but for the very heart of it we must look to Christ. There is nothing that Christ did or said that does not come from His love. [1] We have to remember God's love is not always our thought of love.

To help us and bring us to a better place in our spiritual walk God is willing to hurt us to get us to that better place. How many of you have been broken by God to bring you to a better place? I have, which took a few years, and it hurt. Did I come into a better spiritual place than I was before, Yes! And I would not go back to where I was before for anything in the world. We want to help people but we would never think of hurting them to get them there, and truly we don't know how, but God in His love does. When we look at all Jesus did and said it came out of a love which was desperately trying to bring us to a better place. The whole sermon on the mound is not so much a new law of how to live, but to show us how much we need His mercy, grace, and forgiveness.

The gospel is not about following all those things He spoke of on the mound, even though they do point us in a right direction of how to live, the gospel is about the free gift of salvation that we can receive because of what Christ did in His love for us on the cross. I do not hear many teachings about this, yet it is right there in scripture for us to see; The very first act of love of Christ to offer redemption to us was to willingly give up His rightful place in heaven in order to come to earth. *"Christ Jesus, who, though he was in the form of God, did not count equality with God a thing to be grasped, but emptied himself, taking the form of a servant, being born in the likeness of men"* (Philp. 2:5-7 RSV).

He had a rightful place as part of the Godhead to be in heaven, He gave it up, and even emptying Himself to come take the likeness of Man, coming into this world as we all do, being born of a woman. How much love for us do you see in this very first act He did to bring us salvation? It started there, surely was in His heart even before, and continues on even to this very day. You may sometimes wonder where His love is, but even if you don't know it or see it, it is there. We don't always see love as He sees it. He was always confronting the Pharisees seemingly hoping they could see the truth, and some of them did. In Matthew chapter 18 today we read of the parable of the unforgiving servant.

Every parable Jesus spoke was for the hope that some would see truth. Here in verses 23-35 Jesus lays out a situation of a man being brought before the king who owed multitudes of money to the king. He claimed he could pay it back but the king knew better. The King seeing this man's situation, even better than what the man himself could see it, decided to completely forgive the whole debt. The man left the presence of the king owing absolutely nothing, Then finding another man who owed him a trifle began to choke him saying pay me what you owe me.

The king found out about it and took back the forgiveness he had given the man and had him thrown into prison. This was about a man who had been given a great forgiveness and then was not willing to forgive his fellow man. This parable was told by Jesus because of His love for mankind, yet this is a very hard one to take. Here is what v. 35 says, *"So My heavenly Father also will do to you if each of you, from his heart, does not forgive his brother his trespasses"* (NKJV). Not many want to hear this, it tells us that if we hold back forgiveness from even one person God will take back His forgiveness given to us and we will be put out with the unbelievers. Jesus in His love is desperately trying to get us to see we need to forgive all, and to love as He loves.

---

1   Jn.17:23-26

Kindness and love are the ways of God. God has had, and continues to have, great kindness towards mankind, towards us. **'In the beginning God'** – Do you ever think about that, that in the beginning there was only God, the God who is eternal? Because of the way time works in the world we live in we only go forward thinking of eternity going on forward with no end. Do you ever realize if it is eternity it also goes the other direction with no end?

In that eternity is where God dwells. At some point in that eternity God created the universe. Then He created the Earth, the Sun, the Moon, the Stars, all the vegetation on the Earth, all the animals on the Earth, and lastly us of humanity. All was perfect, and for mankind to be perfect was given the freedom to choose. Then the trouble came because mankind chose wrongly and all that was perfect was not perfect any more, and all of this world was infected with sin.[1] At that point we, humanity, had no right to any of what was perfect.

God is perfect and there cannot be anything imperfect in the presence of God. We as mankind were excluded, never able to come near again, never acceptable any more. God is kind and full of love, and He seen our troubles, He had pity for us, and He took it upon Himself to make a way we could come to Him, and be near Him, and be in eternity with Him. This is what the gospel is, the kindness of God, of the free gift of salvation to us, a difficult and hard work done by God to make us acceptable.

We all know the story, we all know of the scourgings, we all know of the nails, the crown, we all know of the drops of blood that ran down that cross to the ground were all blood of the sacrifice is to be poured.[2] Jesus gave His all, so that all could be given to us. This is a kind and loving God that cares about us.

Many times I have said that if God only gave me salvation with no other blessings to follow I would still have enough to give thanks to God for the rest of eternity. His love and His kindness are unending as His eternity is. I don't think anyone who has salvation can justifiably say God does not love them. We deserve nothing, and we are given everything. Who can say God is not kind? His love reaches to all the earth, none can say that they don't know, only that they do not want to know.[3] God's love is offered to all.[4]

It is only when we know the fullness of what we deserve because of our sin that we can know the fullness of the love that was given to free us from it. My God is great and there is none like Him. In our reading of 2Timothy today did you catch Paul's introduction, *"Paul, an apostle of Christ Jesus by the will of God, **according to the promise of the life which is in Christ Jesus**"* (RSV) What a statement! What a promise! Further on we read, *"share in suffering for **the gospel in the power of God, who saved us** and called us with a holy calling, not in virtue of our works but **in virtue of his own purpose and the grace which he gave us in Christ Jesus ages ago**"* (v. 8&9 RSV).

What great love and what great kindness has given such things to us. This is a great God we serve as we draw near to Him and He promises to draw near to us, *"Draw near to God and he will draw near to you"* (Jas. 4:8 RSV). Sometimes in this crazy world we live in we don't notice God's love and kindness towards us. We have to stop, take a moment, find a prayer closet – a quiet place to get alone with Him, and allow Him to love us a little.

---

1   Rom.8:21
2   Lev.9:9
3   Jn.1:9
4   1Tim.2:4

'I am your way, follow Me.' Do you hear Jesus, do you hear Him say this to you? There are times we say we don't know which way to go. Jesus is always trying to let us know. I wonder how many times when Jesus and the disciples got ready to leave a place they had been the disciples asked, 'Which way Lord?' It is not wrong to not know which way to go, but it is wrong not to ask assuming we know or can figure it out. We serve Jesus and He is the director, He said, 'Follow Me'.

When the disciples were with Jesus and they wanted to know which way to go He was there to tell them. What about us today, Jesus has gone to heaven, how are we to know? Well now there is One here with us where we are told by Jesus that will be the same as He was. Jesus tells us, *"Nevertheless, I tell you the truth: it is to your advantage that I go away, for if I do not go away, the Helper will not come to you. But if I go, I will send him to you... When the Spirit of truth comes, he will guide you into all the truth, for he will not speak on his own authority, but whatever he hears he will speak, and he will declare to you the things that are to come. He will glorify me, for he will take what is mine and declare it to you"* (Jn. 16:7,13,14 ESV).

Here the word 'Helper', in other translations 'Counselor' or 'Comforter', in the Greek is 'parakletos'. **The Complete Word Study Dictionary** gives as part of its meaning; *'one who comes forward in behalf of and as the representative of another.'* In John 14:16 Jesus uses these words, *"I will ask the Father, and he will give you another Helper"* (ESV). Here the word 'another' is the Greek word 'allos', which one of the meanings given by the same dictionary is: *'which means another of equal quality'.* So we do have one to ask the same as the disciples had Jesus.

We might want to question this but it is Jesus saying it so we know it is true. It is we need to search for the Holy Spirit who is in our life and learn to hear Him.[1] In the scriptures above we also were told by Jesus the Holy Spirit would receive from Jesus and then tell us.[2] That still small voice of God, which will also be the voice of the Holy Spirit, is so small that we need to search for it inside us to find it. Sometimes it takes quietness, sometimes it takes stillness, sometimes it takes us yielding all we are over to God to hear His direction. God wants to do so many great things here on this earth, but are we listening as He sometimes wants to use us?

God has chosen sometimes to work through us, but if we are not listening, if we are not hearing, how can we know what He is saying, and how will His work be done? He wants us to know His will, His specific will for each of us, as He leads us into the work He has for us. There is much to learn of God as we live our Christian lives, some from the teachers who teach us, and some by being still in quietness with God. In our reading in 2Timothy chapter 2 today Paul tells Timothy (and us) both of these ways to learn in the first seven verses. To learn from teachers Paul says, *"what you have heard from me in the presence of many witnesses entrust to faithful men, who will be able to teach others also"* (v. 2 ESV).

We know Paul learned from Christ, and he tells Timothy to learn from him, and to teach others so they can also teach. Then Paul tells Timothy to depend on the Lord to help him to know, *"for the Lord will give you understanding in everything"* (v. 7 ESV).

There is a spiritual way God wants to teach us along with what we learn from the teachers sent to us. The Holy Spirit wants to help us know what Jesus is saying as He repeats to us what He has heard. Know for sure that the Holy Spirit will never tell you a thing that is contrary to the Word of God. The Holy Spirit takes what is of Jesus and speaks it to us, always agreeing with what Jesus and the Father have already spoken in the scriptures. Take a break from this world, give an ear to God, hear what He is saying to you today.

---

1   Tit.3:5
2   Jn.16:13&14

'Be down'. We normally think of ourselves as needed to be up. Being in good spirit, and being up, may be two different things. Being in good spirit before God knowing of His great blessing towards us and the things He has done in our life is surely a good thing. What do we mean in saying we are up? Being up may have more to do with the condition we bring ourselves into, talk ourselves into.

It may be stirring ourselves up into a confidence for the day. There are many books on the market sold as self help books. What are these books about? They are that which leads us to bring ourselves up by our own strength and thinking. All this about helping you to be up may be in opposition to God's way. What does God say to us, *"Humble yourselves before the Lord, and he will lift you up"* (Jas. 4:10 CJB). and *"humble yourselves under the mighty hand of God, so that at the right time he may lift you up. Throw all your anxieties upon him, because he cares about you"* (1Pet. 5:6 CJB).

We have been reading through Paul's epistles and he is constantly battling against those who lift themselves up saying they are somebody. This is not what Paul did even though he was highly trained in the Jewish ways, *"when I came to you, brothers and sisters, I did not come as someone superior in speaking ability or wisdom, as I proclaimed to you the testimony of God...my message and my preaching were not in persuasive words of wisdom, but in demonstration of the Spirit and of power"* (1Cor. 2:1&4 NASB).

So did Paul go to them to pumped up or did he go to them with himself down? He could have came to them declaring his high training, *"I am a Jew, born in Tarsus of Cilicia, but brought up in this city, at the feet of Gamaliel, instructed according to the strict manner of the law"* (Acts 22:3 ASV). and *"I advanced in the Jews' religion beyond many of mine own age among my countrymen, being more exceedingly zealous for the traditions of my fathers"* (Gal. 1:14 ASV). Surely Paul could have came on strong in all his education being educated by one of the highest in Jerusalem, *"Gamaliel, a teacher of law honoured by all the people"* (Acts 5:34 YLT).

We are to be in life in a humble manner presenting ourselves in a lowly attitude before God allowing Him to place us in that higher place He has for us. This is where we find ourselves in good spirit, it is God who has lifted us up, *"he who humbles himself will be exalted"* (Lk. 14:11 RSV). Many things with God seem inside out. If you want to be up you must get down, *"Be of the same mind toward one another. Do not set your mind on high things, but associate with the humble. Do not be wise in your own opinion"* (Rom. 12:16 NKJV). Jesus is the conquering King, yet how does the scriptures say He came into Jerusalem? We read this in our reading of Matthew chapter 21 today, *"Behold, your king is coming to you, humble, and mounted on a donkey, on a colt, the foal of a beast of burden"* (v. 5 ESV).

At the end times Jesus will come with none able to confront Him, but before us He came putting Himself down to the Father's will, *"My Father, if it be possible, let this cup pass from me; nevertheless, not as I will, but as you will"* (Mt. 26:39 ESV). Pride is what the world rides on, but it is not the way we are to be. In this chapter we read of the Pharisees who positioned themselves up by their own strength and thinking. Jesus tells them they need to be humble like those who know they are sinners, *"Truly I say to you that the tax collectors and prostitutes will get into the kingdom of God before you"* (Mt. 21:31 NASB). Jesus tells us, *"If anyone wants to come after Me, he must deny himself, take up his cross, and follow Me"* (Mt. 16:24 NASB).

Denying self is about putting ourselves in a low position considering others first. I will leave you with what Jesus said about one who came thinking himself up, and one who came as down, *"The Pharisee stood and began praying this in regard to himself: 'God, I thank You that I am not like other people: swindlers, crooked, adulterers, or even like this tax collector. I fast twice a week; I pay tithes of all that I get.' "But the tax collector, standing some distance away, was even unwilling to raise his eyes toward heaven, but was beating his chest, saying, 'God, be merciful to me, the sinner!' "I tell you, this man went to his house justified rather than the other one; for everyone who exalts himself will be humbled, but the one who humbles himself will be exalted"* (Lk. 18:11-14 NASB).

King of kings and Lord of lords, that is who our Jesus is. He is full of authority, He rules over all things, nothing happens outside of His control. Dominion and righteousness are His. He cleanses all who come to Him. He is majestic in all He does. He brings to completeness everything before God. When He completes all He will hand them back over to God the Father, *"Then comes the end, when He delivers the kingdom to God the Father, when He puts an end to all rule and all authority and power"* (1Cor. 15:24 NKJV).

What kind of a God do we serve, what kind of Savior is this who has given us the light of hope in the salvation He gives? Do you ever wonder about how much you don't know about this divine being who came from heaven and has done so much for each of us? He is called JESUS, and rightly so, *"And behold, thou shalt conceive in thy womb, and bring forth a son, and shalt call his name JESUS."* (Lk. 1:31 ASV). and *"And she shall bring forth a son; and thou shalt call his name JESUS; for it is he that shall save his people from their sins"* (Mt. 1:21 ASV).

His name means: **Help of Jehovah.** We need to see as much as we can about the name **Jehovah**, although the fullness of it will be far from us in this world. In our reading today in Matthew chapter 22 verses 37 Jesus quotes from the old testament, *"thou shalt love Jehovah thy God with all thy heart, and with all thy soul, and with all thy might"* (Duet. 6:5 ASV). This is the name of the God that apostle John speaks of, *"because three are who are testifying in the heaven, the Father, the Word, and the Holy Spirit, and these--the three--are one"* (1Jn. 5:7 YLT). There is God that can be speaking of the Father, [1] there is God that can be speaking of the Son, [2] there is God that can be speaking of the Spirit. [3]

But when it is **Jehovah** that is spoke of it is the assemblance of all three together as the Triune God. **Jesus** was sent to us as **help from Jehovah,** from the Triune God, the presence of the Highest in all the universe. This is who was sent for our help. Further in Matthew chapter 22 Jesus quotes king David in verse 44, *"The Lord said unto my Lord"* (ASV). This is taken from Psalm, *"Jehovah saith unto my Lord"* (110:1 ASV). Here again we can see the high position the name **Jehovah** holds. This is the One who sent Jesus to us. When we begin to consider it, it is almost overwhelming. Jesus as one of the three, sent to us to die on a cross, to take upon Himself all our sins, to pay for them with His death, and then to rise from the dead. Who is this we call Jesus? Certainly, He is King of kings and Lord of lords.

We thank Him, we worship Him, we praise Him, but now with this knowledge He is even higher. Such a high God, the One who said to Moses, **"I Am That I Am,"** that this God would send **Jesus** who is even part of that God, to help us, to be concerned about us, even each one of us. **We are loved by a God who's description goes far beyond our understanding.** How does this make you feel about yourself, that this God, Jehovah God, sent Jesus to be help to you? What a value this gives each of us, this God did all this to help us. Apostle Paul had a grip on some of this beyond us. He was taught by direct revelation from Jesus Christ his Lord. [4] He, speaking of himself as another man, had been to the third heaven and heard things he could not repeat. [5]

We read today of Paul being aware that his end was soon. This is the end of his second letter to Timothy where having a knowledge given him by God he says this, *"in the future there is laid up for me the crown of righteousness, which the Lord, the righteous Judge, will award to me on that day; and not only to me, **but also to all who have loved His appearing**"* (4:8 NASB). Can you imagine that, such a thing from such a great God? Now you can go off into your day wondering of all this.

---

1   1Pet.1:2
2   Isa.9:6
3   Acts 5:3&4
4   Gal. 1:12, Eph. 3:3, 1Cor. 11:23
5   2Cor. 12:2-4

There are many fish in the sea. How many times have you heard this? I'm not so sure it is about fishing. Can you imagine the kind of life of the people in Jesus' day over 2,000 years ago? There were fishermen, those near these seas. There would have been farmers, vinedressers, and shepherds, and those who took care of the animals. I would suppose it seemed a normal life to them all, although we would see it as a hard life. Jesus came into this life to bring good news to mankind, Jews first, and all the rest after. [1]

Jesus, being trained by Joseph, was a carpenter, a skilled craftsman at that time. Can you imagine what Mama would say today if her son who had a great business going which he inherited from his father said I am leaving, giving it all up to become a teacher of religion? But we all know Mary knew something like this way would happen someday, she had many things hidden in her heart about him. [2] But Jesus didn't go out to fit in with the rest, He taught a radical, rebellious religion.

Those who were in charge at the Temple didn't agree with Him. Many of the Jewish people didn't agree with Him. Yet there were those who were listening. And then when He began to heal people, things heated up to where the religious leaders said this, *"If we let Him go on like this, all the people will believe in Him, and the Romans will come and take over both our place and our nation"* (Jn. 11:47&48 NASB). Many fish in the sea, the sea was Israel, and the people were the fish. What was it Jesus told Peter and Andrew, and James and John, *"Follow Me, and I will make you fishers of people"* (Mt. 4:19 NASB).

Jesus who is in the very image of the Father was speaking truth, but few recognized it. He taught in parables which some understood some of what He said, and some didn't get it at all. Even the disciple many times ask what they meant. When we don't get it today we are not in such bad company. For most, the gospel was radical, since all they knew was the Law, the hardness of the Law. And the Pharisees had twisted it to fit their comfort, even adding to it for their advantage. This thing that Jesus was bringing, which was the truth of God, unsettled all they were doing. There is something interesting Jesus does at the beginning of His ministry and at the end. Shortly after His first miracle at Cana He went up to Jerusalem and to the Temple where He found it as a market place and said this, *"Get these things out of here! How dare you turn my Father's house into a market"* (Jn. 2:16 CJB).

Then about three years later Jesus is returning to Jerusalem for the last time before His death, He enters riding on a donkey in triumphal entry and goes to the temple again finding it a market place and says this, *"It has been written, 'My house will be called a house of prayer.' But you are making it into a den of robbers!"* (Mt. 21:13 CJB). These seem to be as parenthesis on each end of His ministry.

The Jewish leaders did not like this Jesus. They later ask what right He had, and what authority. In our reading today in Matthew chapter 23 Jesus speaking to the people gives a sharp rebuke to the scribes and the Pharisees. He says, *"The scribes and the Pharisees have seated themselves in the chair of Moses. Therefore, whatever they tell you, do and comply with it all, but do not do as they do; for they say things and do not do them. "And they tie up heavy burdens and lay them on people's shoulders, but they themselves are unwilling to move them with so much as their finger"* (v. 2-4 NASB).

Jesus is in His last week of teaching holding nothing back, He pours it on. He says in the ways of God, *"The greatest among you must be your servant, for whoever promotes himself will be humbled, and whoever humbles himself will be promoted"* (v. 11&12 CJB). This was not the scribes and Pharisees way, to be frank it is not our way either, this is part of denying self and growing into Christ. Jesus goes on in the rest of the chapter and tells them how wrong they are. Jesus tells them they are like whitewashed tombs, beautiful on the outside, but full of dead man's bones. Be careful where your beauty is, give God access to your heart so He can dress it as he sees beauty.

---

1   Rom.1:16
2   Lk.2:19,35,51

'Find Me and you will see.' In a way, God says this to us. Our whole existence on earth of each one of our lives is the opportunity to find there is a God and be saved. The scriptures tell us this, *"so that they should seek the Lord, in the hope that they might grope for Him and find Him, though He is not far from each one of us"* (Acts 17:27 NKJV).

God invites us to find Him. There are those we hear of in the world today who receive the salvation of God with no human being ever speaking to them about God. All of creation declares His greatness. Jesus tells us the Holy Spirit testifies of Him. The way Jesus says it, it may be that we have it backward. Most that encourage the people of the Church to witness tell them it is their responsibility, and that they should pray for God (the Holy Spirit) to help them. Here is the way Jesus says it, *"But when the Helper comes, whom I shall send to you from the Father, the Spirit of truth who proceeds from the Father, He will testify of Me. And you also will bear witness, because you have been with Me from the beginning"* (Jn. 15:26&27 NKJV).

So because of the word '**also**' who is helping who? It is the Holy Spirit who is the primary witness, and then we are to help. We should not be surprised that there are those who are saved without ever being witnessed to by a Christian. This does not let us off the hook, the word '**also**' means we are also to be witnessing. But it is true God has created an awareness within each person that God is there, *"because that which is known about God is evident within them; for God made it evident to them"* (Rom. 1:19 NASB). Every age of the Church has had its difficulties, and every country its troubles. Yet we are to continue to testify, Jesus said to go forth, *"Go ye into all the world, and preach the gospel to the whole creation"* (Mk. 16:15 ASV).

Therefore we should seek the Holy Spirit as guide for He is the only one who can tell us who the Father is drawing to Jesus for salvation. Only those who the Father draws will be saved, *"No man can come to me, except the Father that sent me draw him: and I will raise him up in the last day"* (Jn. 6:44 ASV). Don't get downhearted when many you testify to do not accept Jesus, but you will run across those who the Father is drawing. Ask the Holy Spirit to reveal to you when you are walking past one that the Father is drawing so that you might testify.

I was very confused for many years because the day I got saved the pastor said at the end of his sermon in a few moments he would give the opportunity for those who want to receive salvation to raise their hand. I found my hand wanting to go up before time, I had to forcefully hold it down. I know now it was the Father strongly drawing me to Jesus.

We do have a choice, I could have refused, but I am so glad I didn't. One of the great things we need to learn in this avenue of things is this, *"Not by might, nor by power, but by my Spirit, saith Jehovah of hosts"* (Zech. 4:6 ASV). and *"But we received, not the spirit of the world, but the spirit which is from God; that we might know the things that were freely given to us of God"* (1Cor. 2:12 ASV).

We need to testify, we need to listen, and we need to be guided by the Holy Spirit. '**Find Me and you will see.**' In our reading a few days ago Paul tells us He found, and saw, and believed, *"For this reason I also suffer these things; but I am not ashamed, for I know whom I have believed, and I am convinced that He is able to protect what I have entrusted to Him until that day. Hold on to the example of sound words which you have heard from me, in the faith and love which are in Christ Jesus"* (2Tim. 1:12&13 NASB).

We who have found God do see and it is the Holy Spirit in us that will guide us. Paul speaks in our reading today in Titus of the finding and seeing, *"For the grace of God has appeared, bringing salvation for all people...waiting for our blessed hope, the appearing of the glory of our great God and Savior Jesus Christ"* (2:11&13 ESV).

'I am sending you love.' Do you know that is what God has been saying to us since the beginning of time? Even in allowing Adam and Eve to have the opportunity to sin was an act of love. He gave us choice, He didn't create us in the prison of dominance of force causing us to be able to do nothing other than what He dictated into us in our creation. God's love even allows us to make mistakes!

This creates a problem, a huge problem, only what is holy can be close to God. That would mean we would not be able to be with God in any way because sin removes us from being holy. To get to God, to be close to God, to enter heaven where He is we have to be holy – big problem. In the ages, and ages, and ages, this problem has been with mankind. Yet God knew it even when He was making Adam from the dust and Eve from Adam's rib, God knew. Interesting statements throughout scripture that we don't always catch tells us some about God's doing. We read of such a verse in Titus, *"in hope of eternal life, which God, who never lies, promised before the ages began"* (1:2 ESV).

This gets all tied up in Paul's opening of his greeting to Titus where sometimes we don't see it. If you put this with the other verses around it, it is clear that God from the beginning has had a plan of redemption, since He already knew what we would do. It was the hope of eternal life we needed which God has had in mind and had working since the beginning of time. Imagine that, even before we got ourselves in trouble God already had a fix in place to be revealed at the proper time.

This is God's love for us, He gave us the ability to choose, then had a fix in place for when we chose wrong. How many times do we do the same thing with our children? He gives us the fix and then asks us to live His way, always ready to help us live that way. Redemption, salvation, sanctification, justification, even the righteousness we have are all gifts from God if we come to Him to receive them. This surely is love. How quick we all could be disqualified and cast into outer darkness. How many times in some difficult day we may wonder if God loves us?

God has been loving us right from the start. If we have went to God, received the salvation He offers, continuing the desire to be close to Him, His love will continue with us all the way into the distance of the depth of eternity. When we accept Christ the Holy Spirit comes into our lives and begins to shape us to the ways of God. There is a lot of assurance in the book of Titus. It begins with the statement about the preparation of eternal life from before time began. Then we are told, *"but in his own seasons manifested his word in the message"* (1;3 ASV).

This was the gospel message of the offered redemption through Jesus Christ which had been prepared since the beginning of time. Paul in many places speaks about the mystery of God revealed. Here in Titus he tells us of that mystery, *"For the grace of God has appeared, bringing salvation for all men, training us to renounce ungodliness and worldly passions, and to live self-controlled, upright, and godly lives in the present age, waiting our blessed hope, the appearing of the glory of our great God and Savior Jesus Christ, who gave himself for us to redeem us from all lawlessness and to purify for himself a people for his own possession who are zealous for good works"* (2:11-14 ESV).

Paul in chapter 3 of Titus gives us a good picture of God's love towards us, *"But when the kindness of God our Saviour, and his love toward man, appeared, not by works done in righteousness, which we did ourselves, but according to his mercy he saved us, through the washing of regeneration and renewing of the Holy Spirit, which he poured out upon us richly, through Jesus Christ our Saviour; that, being justified by his grace, we might be made heirs according to the hope of eternal life"* (v. 4-7 ASV). This is God's love to us which has been there since the beginning of all time.

Always delight in the Lord for He loves you. This is a very important thing to know, the devil will try to beat you down telling you, 'you are not worthy'. It is true we are not worthy because of anything we do, but we are worthy because of what God has done for us in His love. We all have heard the scripture, *"For God so loved the world, that he gave his only begotten Son"* (Jn. 3:16 ASV).

In the fact that God did give His only Son Jesus Christ shows He determined we are worthy in His eyes. The devil will always try to tell us we are unworthy. When he does this we need to also remember John 3:17, *"For God did not send His Son into the world to condemn the world, but that the world through Him might be saved"* (NKJV). If we were unworthy as the devil tries to convince us then God would condemn us, but this verse tells us He did not. All that are not of God will try to put us down, *"If you were of the world, the world would love its own; but because you are not of the world, but I chose you out of the world, therefore the world hates you"* (Jn. 15:19 RSV).

Sometimes we Christians get the idea the world would love us because we are good people since God has saved us. The truth is the opposite according to the verse we just read. Here is the problem, *"to open their eyes, that they may turn from darkness to light and from the power of Satan unto God"* (Acts 26:18 ASV). It is that the devil hates God and the world is under his authority so they hate us because we belong to Christ. Don't let what they say drive you down. Don't listen to the lies the devil and his workers the demons, and the world around you, say about you. Jesus tells us the devil is a liar, *"the devil... He was a murderer from the beginning, and does not stand in the truth because there is no truth in him. Whenever he tells a lie, he speaks from his own nature, because he is a liar and the father of lies. When he speaks a lie, he speaks from his own resources, for he is a liar and the father of it"* (Jn. 8:44 NASB).

We are to know what God says about us. All truth comes from God. God loves us, and because He loves us we know we are worthy in His eyes, no matter who says otherwise, even ourselves. God tells us He loves us, *"Therefore be imitators of God, as beloved children. And walk in love, as Christ loved us and gave himself up for us"* (Eph. 5:1&2 RSV). and *"We love, because he first loved us"* (1Jn. 4:19 RSV). Before we knew God He counted us worthy reaching out to us in His love to give us salvation. As we come to know God's love more and more it gives us reason to rejoice and be glad.

In our reading in Matthew chapter 26 we hear the words of Jesus which show His and the Father's love for us, *"My soul is very sorrowful, even to death; remain here, and watch with me." And going a little farther he fell on his face and prayed, saying, "My Father, if it be possible, let this cup pass from me; nevertheless, not as I will, but as you will"* (v. 38&39 ESV). Here the Father is preparing to put Jesus on the cross as a sacrifice. He sacrificed Jesus because of His love for us to provide a way we could come to Him. Jesus shows His love for us in this, *"And he took bread, and when he had given thanks, he broke it and gave it to them, saying, "This is my body"* (Lk. 22:19 ESV).

We know from Luke 22:19 Jesus was giving His body for our sake. He allowed Himself to be broken for us, that we could receive the salvation God was giving us because of His love for us. Jesus goes on and says, *"Then He took the cup, and gave thanks, and gave it to them, saying, "Drink of it, all of you; for this is my blood of the covenant, which is poured out for many for the forgiveness of sins"* (MT. 26:27&28 RSV). His blood was cast upon a new altar of the sacrifice where the blood was always poured out, it was poured out at the base of the cross. Every time we look at the cross it should declare to us the love of God and all that He did to bring us redemption.

'I want to be in your heart, am I there?' Is this a question Jesus would ask you? Do you have Him in your heart as Lord and Master? Or do you only have Him as Savior on the exterior of your heart since you are still running your life? Jesus came to help you, but He needs to be Lord of your life seated in the throne of your heart. We don't make good decisions, that's what got us into the fix that Jesus needed to save us from. We need Jesus in everything we do and in every decision we make. We need to yield to Jesus - give over all of our life to Him.

By rights, He could order us,[1] but He does not, He wants us to invite Him fully into our hearts. We invited Him into our lives for salvation, why not all the way, even into the fullness of our hearts? Jesus wants to help us with our lives, but if we still keep making the mistakes in our decisions He can't help us unless we give Him full control. Half yielded is only half value, wouldn't you like to have full value? Even though it sounds weird, a surrendered life is a full life. This is how it works with God, *"For whoever would save his life will lose it, and whoever loses his life for my sake will find it"* (Mt. 16:25 RSV).

Have you found all of your life yet, Jesus wants to open it up. He is not a tyrant, He is not a bully, He is there to help you, not defy you. For how many years do we all struggle until we reach this point where we give it all over to God, even every nook and cranny? God can only bless what is yielded to Him. God intends to bless our lives to the full, but God has to have our lives to the full. This may not be what you want to hear today, but you do want more of God's blessings. God's way is not always easy, and we sure do not understand. God tells us about His ways, *"For My thoughts are not your thoughts, Nor are your ways My ways," says the LORD. For as the heavens are higher than the earth, So are My ways higher than your ways, And My thoughts than your thoughts"* (Isa. 55:8&9 NKJV).

This is where we must have faith. We must believe He knows what He is talking about and just follow it. God speaks much to us in His word but do we listen? In our reading today is the trial of Jesus before Pontius Pilate the governor. In Matthew chapter 27 God speaks but Pilate doesn't listen, *"And while he was sitting on the judgment seat, his wife sent him a message, saying, "See that you have nothing to do with that righteous Man; for last night I suffered greatly in a dream because of Him"* (v. 19 NASB).

God sent a message to Pilate through his wife but he did not stop the trail. We don't know if anything according to scripture happened to Pilate, but it seems at least his wife suffered in some way in a dream. I wonder how many times we suffer because we did not listen. Pilate tried to slide out from under what his wife said by offering to release Jesus by the custom but that backfired as the priest and the people they stirred up asked for Barabbas. Do you ever try to slide out from under something God has said to you?

Pilate began listening because after trying to release Jesus He washed his hands of the whole affair. Even in Jesus' death Jesus knows our ways and says, *"forgive them; for they know not what they do"* (Lk. 23:34 ASV). Then a little later He says, *"My God, my God, why have you forsaken me"* (Mt. 27:46 ESV). Jesus gave everything up for us, should we not give everything to Him? If you have not yet, just go to Jesus in prayer, it does not take any great work, only humility. Tell Jesus you give Him all of your life, even every nook and cranny.

---

1   Acts 20:28, 1Cor.6:20, 7:23

If you are leaning a little toward the way of the world, find a spiritual prop that will push you back the other way. We all have troubles, we are all tempted, we all have sinned. Who is our great support, is it not Jesus? *"I am laying in Zion a stone that will make men stumble, a rock that will make them fall; and he who believes in him will not be put to shame"* (Rom. 9:33 RSV). and *"Every one who comes to me and hears my words and does them, I will show you what he is like: he is like a man building a house, who dug deep, and laid the foundation upon rock"* (Lk. 6:47&48 RSV).

Jesus is the rock of our salvation, it is Him we get strength from. Anything of Jesus, or God, can become that prop which will push us back the other way, back towards Him. It might be a song, it might be a prayer, it might be a poem, it might be just one verse of scripture, it might be to remember something someone said about God, It may be something of many things spiritual. It is that which we need to take a hold of it in times we begin to lean a little towards the ways of the world. Our flesh will always try to take us that way, we need to strengthen our Spirit to push back the flesh. There is a constant battle with these two, *"For the desires of the flesh are against the Spirit, and the desires of the Spirit are against the flesh; for these are opposed to each other"* (Gal. 5:17 RSV).

Which one will you allow to be the strong one? We always need to be putting into our lives things that strengthen our Spirit. The spiritual life is not easy, the world is always pushing back at us, even our own flesh is pushing back. This is where we need to build our faith. This is not done by lifting spiritual weights until we are strong, it is a deciding to believe God, believe what He says, and decide to live His way. Faith is not so much about building strength as it is about making a decision. It is amazing as we begin to align ourselves with God He begins to align Himself with us. It is then we begin to build that strong wall in relationship with Him that will keep us from leaning towards the world where we will seldom need those props to push us back in the right direction.

I will remind you God is always reaching out to you in His love. The very act of sending Jesus to die for us on that cruel cross is the greatest act of God to us. As long as we keep trying to move to where He is He will meet us where we are. The absolute refusal of God brings to us His wrath, but turn to Him just a little, accept what Christ has already done for us, and we're in, all God has is for us. We begin to grow spiritually, and the more we grow the more we see of God's love for us.

Oh, - God has reached out to us from so long ago with so much love we really won't see it all until we reach heaven. God has so much love for us we don't have the capacity to see all of it now. The more we know of God's love the less we lean towards the world.

All those things I mention to use as a prop to push you back the other way, don't put them aside when you don't need them for a prop any more, those are what will keep you moving in the direction of God, use them wisely. In our reading today you may have read of king Josiah who growing up had a father who reigned fifty five years doing nothing but evil. As things were at that time Josiah became king as a boy. When he was twenty six years old they found the book of the Law in the temple. Josiah decided to believe God, of what was written, and to repent seeking God. God responded with kindness toward Josiah, *"because your heart was tender, and you humbled yourself before the LORD...I will gather you to your fathers, and you shall be gathered to your grave in peace"* (2Kg. 22:19&20 NKJV).

Today you might have read of Daniel who had that great relationship with God because he stayed close to God and prayed three times a day.(6:10) It came about that the government of the time made a law that no one could pray to any other than the king himself for thirty days.(6:7) Daniel did not turn away from God by stopping his prayers, by not turning away from God because of the threat it was in a way of Daniel turning **more** towards his God. Because Daniel continued to pray to God he was thrown into the lion's den. God kept the lion's mouths closed and Daniel was removed the next day unharmed.(6:16-22) When we move towards God He moves towards us.

'I am the One who knows you.' Do you believe God knows all there is to know about you? If He didn't, would He have a right to be declared as God over all creation, including you? Now there is a thought that He knows even more about you than you know yourself. God knows the heart, He knows the inner man, *"You are the ones who justify yourselves in the sight of people, but God knows your hearts"* (Lk. 16:15 NASB).

So then there is no reason to not open up all our life to God. Do you want to be a better person, do you want to find that place where you have come to a better person than you were before? God will do it, and He has a way, *"Humble yourselves in the sight of the Lord, and He will lift you up"* (Jas. 4:10 NKJV). An interesting thing with God, the way to get up higher is to get down lower. This sure goes against our pride, it seems pride needs to be sacrificed on the altar to God. I say it needs to go on God's altar because ultimately He is the only one who can fully do the job in us.

We can grab that pride in us ripping it out but we will never get it all. We will get rid of part of it, but we need then to put the rest on the altar giving permission to God to take out the rest. Pride is the very reason the devil was cast out of heaven, it was the reason Eve ate the forbidden fruit, it was the reason Cain killed Abel. Pride is a vicious thing, the sooner we are rid of it the better for us. God wants to bless but pride gets in the way. Are you seeking God's blessings, is pride in the way?

Each of us has much change to do within ourselves. We all are short before God, short in many areas and we are always changing inside ourselves to come closer to what God has for us to be. God has a holiness waiting for us when we reach heaven, until then we will continue to grow spiritually, but when that moment comes for us to go it will all rest on what Christ has already done for each of us. We are to continue to change at coming into the image of Christ, but in the end it is all about what He has done for us. Humbleness at first is not a very comfortable place to be but later it becomes like a soft cushy pillow.

Being in God's arms in humility is the greatest place to be, He can do for you in a moment what you thought never could be. Once we reach this place worship will be easy, and thanksgiving will be always. God's way is always better, but it seems for most of us it takes a while to get there. How great it will be when we get to heaven where nothing will be opposing trying to keep us from getting close to God, He will be our every moment and our every care.

In 2Kings chapter 23 Josiah does all he can to make things God's way in all the land of Judah, and even into the remaining land that was the land of Israel. You might say Josiah had an encounter with God, they found the word of God that had been ignored by several kings before him.[1] When he heard the words of God it cut him to the core, to know what the other kings before him had done in turning from God.[2] He determined to change, to change everything.

We read today the first chapter of Mark about John the Baptist. Is there something or someone as him in your life now, something or someone that is preparing the way turning your attention more towards God? Is it time to make some changes, is it time to move in another way? Here is what Jesus said to his first disciples, *"Follow Me, and I will have you become fishers of people"* (Mk. 1:17 NASB). Is Jesus saying this to you to become more involved in the Kingdom? Is He even calling some of you to enter into His ministry to serve Him?

---

1   2Kg.22:6&13
2   2Kg.22:11

'I have lived so that you might live.' Is this something you could hear Jesus saying to you? Jesus came to this earth putting on the cloak of human mankind for one reason, so that we could find eternal life. Without Him none have a hope, we are all guilty of sin, and the judgment laid upon it.[1]

There may have been those who came close, but it would have to had been one who lived their whole life without ever having one sin, none has been able. Jesus came and lived among men that we could find life. In God's economy even though we have been born and exist we are dead by spiritual value until we receive Christ into our life, then it is we begin to live. Christ's life here on earth has come down as a dot on the timeline of eternity. His appearance affects everything on that timeline from one end to the other. We are locked into time seeing the effect of an event from its point onward. In eternity all is now. As seen in light of eternity when Jesus came to earth it was at every point on that time line, for all was the same moment. It is hard for us to wrap our heads around this, that is why we must have faith willing to believe what God says is true. All are guilty of sin deserving the wrath of God, but Jesus lived that we can also live accepting His offering of Himself as the sacrifice for our sins.[2]

We have a great and loving God that did not leave us abandoned in our own mess. Jesus came and lived. Even without bringing in all His teaching, this is a great thing in and by itself. We have been saved, we try to learn and live the way He wants us to, but where would we be if Jesus never lived as mankind on this earth. Jesus lived so that we can live. Death is when in reality we have nothing, so when we have life through Christ then it is we have everything, everything that is truly important. Our life on this earth does seem long at times, but it also is only a dot on that timeline of eternity. Jesus tells us not to be concerned (with focus) about tomorrow, *"Therefore do not be anxious about tomorrow, for tomorrow will be anxious for itself. Let the day's own trouble be sufficient for the day"* (Mt. 6:34 RSV).

Jesus came to bring life, life to those of us who did not have life. Each day is a blessing, each day God has something new for us; whether it is a beautiful sunrise, an inspiration from a verse we read, a beautiful flower He has created showing His creativity, or the white snow on the mountain peak. There is much each day if we take time to notice it. Life is a blessing and without Jesus coming we would not have it to live. How grateful we can be to God for the great work He did to bring us His salvation that can give us eternal life without offending His righteous requirements. God is a God of love reaching out to us to bring us redemption that we can have life.

Do we really know Jesus, the more we know about Him the more we realize how much it is we don't know about Him. One of these days we all will be with Him knowing so much more than we ever knew before. God is our keeper if we have turned over our life to Him, each of our days are kept by Him, He has our eternity, each of us, set in His hand. There is a great encouragement in our reading in Hebrews today, *"Since then we have a great high priest who has passed through the heavens, Jesus, the Son of God, let us hold fast our confession. For we have not a high priest who is unable to sympathize with our weaknesses, but one who in every respect has been tempted as we are, yet without sin. Let us then with confidence draw near to the throne of grace, that we may receive mercy and find grace to help in time of need"* (4:14-16 RSV). We can have confidence since Jesus came and lived amongst mankind so that now we also would have life.

---

1   Jn.3:36, Rom.1:18
2   Rom.5:8&9

Calmness in the midst of the storm. Who of us fully has it? Can anyone say they are never afraid? The disciples on the sea were afraid calling on Jesus because they feared the storm would overtake them. It is easy to become fearful in a storm that rages around us, it is a visual thing, and faith is a thing unseen. The disciples went to Jesus in desperation, 'Jesus don't You care that we are going to sink?'

This is what we must do when we are in a storm, we must go to Jesus crying out to Him. We don't see much faith in the disciples in the boat yet, but if there was no faith in what Jesus could do why did they go to Him? We in our faith many times go to God asking, which in itself is an act of faith.

Jesus did not turn down the request of the disciple – He took authority over the situation ordering the storm to be still. He will always hear us when we come to Him in prayer, He will always consider our situation, He will always act in authority, He will do what is right for us at the time. Jesus knows our need, sometimes it is immediate rescue, sometimes it is to learn patience and trust in Him over a period of time.

Many have struggled with faith, no matter how much one has it will always seem we need more because we will always see our lack no matter how much it is we have. The only exception to this may be the one who is given the spiritual gift of faith by the Holy Spirit which has heavenly power to believe. Yet our faith will grow as we seek more and more of God in our lives. He wants to bless us so we have to trust Him and keep coming back to him again and again.

In Daniel chapter 9 today, we see that Daniel in response to what God had said in the books, reading that they would be captive in Babylon for 70 years, he then began to pray for their delivery. There is an interesting thing that God has revealed to me in recent months, that is He will tell us what He is going to do (by His decision) and then He will call us to pray to Him that He will do it. It makes no sense to us that if God has already decided He would do something that we would then need to pray for Him to do it, yet what is faith other than believing (and sometimes doing) what makes no sense to us.

Here we see Daniel's faith as he confesses Israel's sins and asks God to do what God has already said He would do. Faith builds upon Faith. In Mark chapter 3 today we see crowds of people come to Jesus to be healed, so many so that He was nearly being crushed. In the beginning of Jesus' ministry He heals a few people. The more He heals the more it is that comes. As we see with the crowds, it is in our own life, the more we see Jesus act in response to our prayer of faith the more faith we gain, faith builds upon faith.

The last thing in our reading today is in Hebrews chapter 5 where it is declared that Jesus is the perfect and final High Priest who is in the perfect temple of heaven. Our High Priest Jesus has offered the perfect and final sacrifice for sin. Since Jesus is sinless He does not need to leave the Holy of Holies and is continually there to present his prayer to the Father for us. [1]

In this we can take faith, we can go to Him in the storms of our lives when it seems all is sinking, we can pray asking Him to be in authority of our situation taking victory over it for us. Sometimes we don't see the results right away, but when they come it increases our faith. Faith builds upon faith.

---

[1]   Heb.7:25

He who is close to God is cared for by God. Sometimes we get things backwards as far as the way God operates. We think we have to get ourselves in a right spiritual attire and behavior before we can get close to God. We don't have the ability to dress ourselves properly to appear before God and we cannot condition our behavior sufficiently to appear before His presence.

These are the very reasons we need to be close to God, that He in His caring for us can help us in this area. We forget how our salvation came, it was not by our accomplishment, it was by God's accomplishment for us. He is always helping us to come into a better condition before Him. The hardest thing for most Christians to do is give up, that is what coming to God in humility is.

Humility says I can't, I need help, can You help me? Our society says, 'Work hard, accomplish, then you will be accepted.' God says to us just the opposite, 'Give up trying, confess you are a sinner, know you will never measure up by your own works.' Does this mean as Christians we never need do good works, No, it means God is the One running the show and by putting His will in our hearts He will direct each of us to what work He has for each of us to do.

It will be work of the Kingdom with the King in charge. We can't know about what comes tomorrow so how can we know what work we ought to be doing. He sees everything, knows everything, so He knows what needs to be done and who it is that He decides should do it. We remove a lot of weight off our shoulders when we allow Him to run the Kingdom.

Of course the kingdom I speak of is the Kingdom of the Son,[1] which is the Church with Jesus as head.[2] Oh why do we get ourselves so tangled up, we try to lead instead of following the One who has it all figured out already. Jesus said He is the way, not just the way to heaven, to the Father, but He is the way in everything. We just need to remember we are the followers. I am glad He is the leader for He is much more wiser than I am. We try so hard, we struggle so much, God says, 'Here, let me carry that for you, let's do it this way, it will work out better.'

Oh how hard we try needlessly. When I got saved many, many, years ago I was so amazed with what God did for me I told Him I would serve Him in some way to pay Him back. After years I realized this is impossible. How do you pay someone for pulling you out of a pit you couldn't get out of yourself? There is no work we can do that equates it. He put each star in place, can we go get Him another one? He is the giver, we are the receiver, we have to let it go at that.

The best we can do is come to Him with nothing and ask, 'What is it You have of me to do?' God is always loving, God is always reaching out, we need to open ourselves as a receiver, and condition ourselves to connect in following with what He is doing. We will never be able to be in charge and to accomplish or we would have already done it and would not need Jesus to do it for us. What is it Jesus first calls us to do, *"repent, and believe in the gospel"* (Mk. 1:15 RSV).

Repent meaning turn from your own ways to God's ways. Believe meaning to accept, embrace, give credit to the one you believe in doing as He directs. This then means turning from what we think we ought to do, credit Him of knowing what should be done, and then listen for us to know what He has for us to do. In the beginning of Hebrew chapter 6 today we see this, *"Therefore let us leave the elementary doctrine of Christ and go on to maturity, not laying again a foundation of repentance from dead works and of faith toward God"* (v. 1 RSV). It is for us who have been walking with God to now move forward in our relationship with Him. He tells us He has planted in our hearts the will He has for us, *"for God is at work in you, both to will and to work for his good pleasure"* (Philp. 2:13 RSV).

This is a spiritual planting in us, so it is in our heart that God puts His will. So it is not from our brain we will know what God is wanting us to do. It is in our hearts we will know what God is wanting us to do, add faith to what our heart is leading us to do and we may be amazed at what is accomplished. We are told God will notice when we have responded to His will, *"For God is not unjust so as to forget your work and the love which you have shown toward His name"* (Heb. 6:10 NASB).

---

1   Col.1:13
2   Col.1:18

"This is my commandment, that ye love one another" (Jn.15:12 ASV). These were the words Jesus left with His disciple on that last week on His way to the cross. He wanted us to be like Him for He loved us, even in His struggle in the garden of Gethsemane He loved us and the victory of that struggle was what brought us salvation. Love seems to be the foundation that all else is built on. Some would say the foundation of our Christian lives is obedience. We have to see farther than ourselves before God, we have to look all the way back to the beginning.

The very core of who God is, is love. In creation of man, God could have created us to always do His will, but giving us no freedom would not truly be love. The greatest honor God gave us was to have the freedom to choose, even though He knew we would choose wrongly. This is love at the very core, to consider that of the other which in this case was us. We can see more of God's love that was even before time began.[1] It was then that the plan of salvation, that which would repair the damage we did to ourselves when we chose wrongly, was all worked out even though it did not take place until centuries later.

Love, we don't even really know much about what it is, not God's kind of love that He loves us with and calls us to love others with. Jesus starts out very early in His ministry at the sermon on the mound speaking about love.[2] He later sums up the whole law into two laws which both speak of love, our love of God and our love of our fellow man. And then again Jesus, even though He had spoke of love many times during His three-year ministry with His disciples, reminds them again to love one another. Paul who was taught of the ways of God directly, not through other men, knows that love is so important that right in the middle of teaching about the heavenly powers (the empowering from on high) that we are supplied by God to conduct His ministry on earth stops, and makes the case that love is most important, more than all the rest.[3]

Those who may have said that the foundation of Christian life is obedience have missed the point that obedience can be done without the motivation of love. Paul wanted to make it very clear that all the obedience, and all the heavenly power to get the work of the Kingdom of God done, is useless if it is not because we love. Heavy stuff – God's kind of love, who can know what it is, let alone it needing to be the motivation by which we do all that we do. This love can only be ours by constantly asking God to be filling us with His kind of love every day.

In Mark chapter 5 today, we read of Jesus' love. It was because of His love that He freed the demoniac of the legion of demons so that the man was clothed and in his right mind. It was because of love that Jesus was willing to go to Jairus' house and heal his daughter who had died. It was because of love that Jesus sought out the woman who touched his garment and was healed. Jesus could have only thought to Himself as he felt the power go out which healed her, 'Another one, may My Father bless her', but He did not.

The woman could have slid away through the crowd possibly even thinking she had stolen a healing from Jesus. No, in Jesus' love he did not allow her to leave this way, He called her to Him and told her of her faith, and then said to her to go in peace. What a great love towards this woman Jesus had. She left with something far richer than physical healing, she left with the honor which Jesus gave her in confirming to her her faith and sent her away with the words of peace from His own mouth which surely would have stayed with her the rest of her life, with no wondering question in her heart of if she had stole a healing from Jesus.

This is the kind of love Jesus wants all of us who follow Him to take up and be the motivation for all we do. It is impossible for us to take up this kind of love on our own, we need God to plant it within us. We are told in scripture that if any of us lacks wisdom to ask God and He will give it, this is the first of wisdom – to know that His kind of love working in us can only be there by asking Him daily to plant it there and cause it to grow. I need to go to God and ask Him today to put His kind of love in me, how about you?

---

1   Rom.16:25, Eph.3:8&9,
2   Mt. chapters 5,6,7
3   1Cor. Chapter 13 – take note of first 3 verses

God is here to stay, He is eternal. How glad are you that God is eternal? First of all He is eternal in both directions, it is a thought hard for us to grasp, He has always been, and He will always be. Can you think of anyone else that would be more knowledgeable? Could we have any better council? Faith should be easy if we are willing to believe this. If faith is not easy then we are not believing. We have to come to the place that in our heart, and our brain, that where we live now and what we know is temporal. It will all be swept away. This earth as we know it will be gone, the heavens will be gone, and there will be new ones.[1]

Even us, we will not be the same. In Revelation we read this, *"Behold, I make all things new"* (21:5 ASV). Do you realize we are part of '*all things*' which are made new? We will be better than we ever have been before, there will no longer be the taint of sin in our flesh for it will be a resurrected body holy as God is holy. We will know more than we have ever known, *"For now we see in a mirror dimly, but then face to face. Now I know in part; then I shall know fully, even as I have been fully known"* (1Cor. 13:12 ESV).

Oh, how great it will be to be in a condition greater than we ever have been before! The high life with God will be so great, the temporal we have now is just that, temporal. I thank God that I am in His hands, I could not get there any other way. Faith is believing all that God says is true, and, what is around us, what we attach ourselves to more than we ought, is temporary. Temporary housing is not something to get attached to because it is temporary. On the other hand if it is temporary because later we will be receiving a house much greater it is an exciting place to be because of what we know is coming.

We are in temporary housing on earth. Knowing the greater is coming later should give us a bit of excitement. All the years stretched out as they are in our life seems long, but they are only an instant on the timeline of eternity where we will be in our future. How great God is to make that way for us by which we can come to Him and know we will be in that eternity. We have some days on this earth that we think are so great and so grand, yet they are dull compared to what we will have later with God forever.

God is good all the time, and oh how good it is of Him to make such a place and a way for us to get there. How often have you planned a vacation in a far place and then read everything you could find on it before you went? Are you reading about God, and about heaven, and about your future? We have not left yet so we are still in the preparation mode. How are you preparing?

We can know about God, we don't have to wait until we get to heaven. We can know about eternity, we don't have to wait until we get there. We won't know all until we get there but we can get a head start. God allows us to know Him, even before we are there right in His very presence. As far as eternity goes, if you are born again you are in eternity right now. God has great things for us, and we should believe by faith beginning to enjoy some of that right now, here, today.

You should get a little excited when you read the beginning of our reading in Hebrews today, *"We have such a high priest, who sat down on the right hand of the throne of the Majesty in the heavens, a minister of the sanctuary, and of the true tabernacle, which the Lord pitched, not man"* (8:1&2 RSV). Jesus is waiting for us, and He told us as He told His disciples, *"In My Father's house are many dwelling places; if it were not so, I would have told you; for I go to prepare a place for you"* (Jn. 14:2 NASB).

Jesus is waiting for us, He is expecting us, He will greet us when we arrive. In Mark chapter 6 we read today, those of Jesus' hometown didn't realize who stood before them. At the end of the chapter Jesus walks on the water, this is the Jesus we know about. He will be waiting for us when we arrive in heaven. As you go into your day seeing all that there is around, remember, there is something far greater yet to come.

---

1   Rev.21:1

Life is good all the time. It is good all the time if you are one who has asked Christ into it. Most of you reading this have done this. Know that your life is good all the time, for you have put it into the hand of God, and all that He does is good. So on those days you have difficulty or things are coming against you know that your day is still good no matter how bad it may seem. We all struggle at times; struggle with attacks of the enemy, struggle with opposition of those who have no use for God nor even believe He exists, struggling with the difficulties in life, even struggling with those unholy thoughts within our self. The struggles are part of life, the imperfect life we all live with.

Ever since sin entered the world through the sin of Adam and Eve all of the perfect world God had created became infected with sin, and its effect.[1] We are part of that imperfection. We have been saved and cleansed by the blood of Christ and to God we are seen as perfect, yet we are still in our imperfection. Paul talks about his struggle to be holy in his character and he is unable. He sees and realizes that the imperfection of sin is in the flesh, and in our Spirit we will war against the flesh[2] until our body dies and we in our Spirit are relieved to go to God. Paul tells us the things he wants to do and be, but he is unable, and the very thing he does not want to do or be is what he does.[3]

It is the sinful nature that dwells in the flesh that tries to take us to sin, we have to bring our Spirit to the strength in us that it can control the flesh. The longer we walk with God the stronger our Spirit becomes and the less we allow the flesh to have control. This is part of the good of God, as we give ourselves more and more over to Him and His way the less sin has a hold on us. It is also true that the longer we walk with God the more spiritual we become and the less those things outside of us have affect on us.

There is a time we come to in knowing more about our enemy, and then he does not get away with as much as he did before. There also comes a time when we are not affected any longer as before by the things said by the opposers of God and of us His followers. God is good in the final outcome, no matter what has happened to us in life. We are permitted to enter into heaven being with God for eternity, can anything else be better than that? It is something we do not deserve, yet it is what we receive, this certainly is the good God that does this for us. *"The LORD is high above all nations, and his glory above the heavens! Who is like the LORD our God, who is seated on high, who looks far down upon the heavens and the earth? He raises the poor from the dust, and lifts the needy from the ash heap"* (Ps. 113:4-7 RSV).

Who is like our God who saves the lost and lifts up those who are His? Even in the deepest of our trouble, He has lifted us up in promising salvation to those who come to Him. How many of us, if we truly consider it, can see the condition of life we would be in if we did not have God's salvation? That condition would be much worse than what we have now no matter how difficult now it may be.

We get stuck in the moment sometimes not remembering the great things God has done for us in our past, and the great things He promises yet to do. Let me remind you of what we read in Hebrews today, *"But when Christ appeared as a high priest...he entered once for all into the Holy Places...by means of his own blood, securing an eternal redemption...so Christ, having been offered once to bear the sins of many, will appear a second time, not to deal with sin but to save those who are eagerly waiting for him"* (9:11,12, 28 ESV).

This is what has been done for us, can we ask for anything better? No matter who we are, or how disqualified we may think we are, to receive good from God think of the Syro-Phoenician woman in Mark we read of today. At that time she was considered as outside of those Christ was ministering to, yet because she was willing to believe Jesus would help her, He gave her what she requested. It is not a matter of who we are, or what we have done, it is a matter of do we believe Jesus will hear us and respond to us in what we ask.

---

1   Rom.8:19-21
2   Gal.5:17
3   Rom.7:15

Is there love in the sky? Almost sounds like a 70s folk song. Yet for us who are Christians, we know that God is love and His dwelling is up and out in the sky somewhere. His dwelling is in a place unseen, from our perspective, we could say there is love in the sky. The great thing is God's love is not just in heaven, it is not just in the sky, it is all around us. We are able to reach out at any time and God is there. There is no barrier of distance between God and us, God is omnipresent, no matter where we are He is there.

David the Psalmist said, *"O LORD, you have searched me and known me! You know when I sit down and when I rise up; you discern my thoughts from afar. You search out my path and my lying down and are acquainted with all my ways. Even before a word is on my tongue, behold, O LORD, you know it altogether...If I take the wings of the morning and dwell in the uttermost parts of the sea, even there your hand shall lead me, and your right hand shall hold me. If I say, "Surely the darkness shall cover me, and the light about me be night," even the darkness is not dark to you; the night is bright as the day, for darkness is as light with you. For you formed my inward parts; you knitted me together in my mother's womb. I praise you, for I am fearfully and wonderfully made. Wonderful are your works; my soul knows it very well. My frame was not hidden from you, when I was being made in secret, intricately woven in the depths of the earth. Your eyes saw my unformed substance; in your book were written, every one of them, the days that were formed for me, when as yet there was none of them"* (Ps. 139:1-4 & 9-16 ESV).

This is more scripture than I usually include, but we need to hear this from time to time. This is the great God we belong to, this is the great God who has given us life, this is the great God who expects our arrival in heaven when we go from here. Yes there is love in the sky, and many days we need to know this love is there, there for each one of us no matter what is going on in our day. There is a God that cares, He has cared for us even from the beginning of time. He has cared for each of us individually, He has known each of us from the beginning. There is nothing about us He does not know.

If you ever think to yourself that if God knew a certain thing about you He would not care for you – He already knows, He still cares. How do we know He cares about each one of us? He has known you since the beginning, He knew you in your mother's womb, He knew you before you even had substance, yet He sent Jesus to redeem you. *"the works that the Father has given me to accomplish, the very works that I am doing, bear witness about me that the Father has sent me"* (Jn. 5:36 ESV).

The Father has sent Jesus to do the works that would provide redemption to those who would come to Him to receive it. Are you one who has accepted Jesus? Then these works have been done for you, Jesus was sent for you, you were seen from afar, God cared for you from the beginning, even knowing you before you had form. David says, *"Such knowledge is too wonderful for me; it is high, I cannot attain unto it"* (Ps. 139:6 KJV).

God loves us in a way we cannot understand or know the depth of it. Jesus tried and tried and tried to teach and reveal truth to His disciples and yet in our reading today He says, *"Do you not yet understand"* (Mk. 8:21 RSV). It is difficult for mankind to understand the greatness of God and the greatness of His love for us. Here is some of what we are told from our reading in Hebrews today, *"For since the law has but a shadow of the good things to come...when Christ had offered for all time a single sacrifice for sins, he sat down at the right hand of God,...For by a single offering he has perfected for all time those who are sanctified"* (10:1,12,14 RSV). We are those sanctified. Yes, there is love in the sky.

Is your heart moved today? Have you sensed that God is with you? Does He touch you in a way you know He is there? Some days we don't feel His presence, it is those days we need to recall those times in the past that you knew He was there. It does us good to remember the day of our salvation, and the days that closely followed. These are what confirm that God is in our lives.

There are other days with even more to come, but none will be like those first days when our whole life was changed. Any of the things we experience now are just add-ons. One of these days, for each one of us, the work will be final, we will be completed, and we will be in the fullness of spiritual life in the very presence of God in heaven. That will be the day! For now, it is for us to continue in the relationship we have with Him while we continue here. God is always wanting us to come closer and closer and closer. Scripture tells us this, *"Draw near to God and he will draw near to you"* (Jas. 4:8 RSV).

There are great things for those who would come close to God. Moses had a curiosity with a hunger of heart as he made his long track up the mountain to see this curious thing of the bush afire and yet did not burn.[1] We need to have that spiritual curiosity to draw us close and that hunger of heart to have more of God in our lives. God invites us to come close, He gives blessings to those who come. There are many blessings of God we receive in this earth, yet the greatest blessings are those times we know we are in His presence, and we sense Him in our being. God promises to reward those who come. In our reading today in Hebrews we hear this, *"For whoever would draw near to God must believe that he exists and that he rewards those who seek him"* (11:6 RSV).

As we seek Him He rewards us. Who is there that is like our God, who can be compared to Him? What a privilege we have received, we have been called the children of God.[2] We are not just forgiven, we are not just saved, we are accepted into the very family of God. This is an eternal family that will go on and on and on. It will be nothing like we can imagine, nothing like we have ever experienced before. In Revelation we are told this, *"Behold, the tabernacle of God is with men, and he shall dwell with them, and they shall be his peoples, and God himself shall be with them, and be their God"* (21:3 ASV).

What a deal, what a great blessing, God will be there with us forever, and we will be with Him. No imagination can ever show us what this will be like, it is beyond imagination. As we draw closer and closer to God we begin to experience Him in ways we have not before. There is always more and more of God for us to experience as we come close to Him.

It seems that now I am experiencing more of God in my latter years than I ever did before, there is always more of God than we can think. He is a God that loves us. He is a God that searches for us. He is a God that reaches out to us. He is a God that has seen us from afar. He is a God who has known us since the beginning of time. He is a God who laid out a plan of redemption. He is a God who sent Jesus to die for us paying for our sins. Oh, what a God we have! Can you think of anything greater to have in your life? Even no matter how impoverished you may be, this God is all to you.

No matter how wealthy you may be, this God is all to you. If we have this God, truly we have what we need. This life is momentary, but the next is eternal. In our reading in Mark chapter 9 today it opens with these words of Jesus, *"Truly, I say to you, there are some standing here who will not taste death before they see that the kingdom of God has come with power"* (v. 1 RSV).

This is the Kingdom we now belong to, a Kingdom of power, power to save, power to redeem, power to carry us right into heaven when our time is done here. Further in this chapter Jesus tells us how all this is going to come about, *"The Son of man will be delivered into the hands of men, and they will kill him; and when he is killed, after three days he will rise"* (v. 31 RSV). This we cannot hear too many times, it is by how we have been saved and given eternity in heaven. Seek God and He will draw near to you, being near, you will experience Him move in your heart.

---

1   Ex.3:1&2
2   1Jn.3:1

There is a God that is involved in all our lives. There is an interesting thing about God, it is that we don't have to go along our way in living, gradually working our way to a level where we can come before Him, that we have to prove ourselves in some way. God is there at any time, in any of our conditions, willing and wanting for us to turn to Him.

It is said He takes care of our greatest needs. HE IS our greatest need. How little we know what our need is until we see ourselves truly as we are. How great it is that we have a God that is always there, always involved in our lives, even before we knew Him. He is in our everyday life, there to help with our every need. The more we trust Him the more we receive from Him. Our lack of trust does not restrict God's ability to give, it restricts our ability to receive.

Even then God sometimes overrides this giving even when we are not fully trusting. A couple of days ago we read of the father with the son who had a dumb spirit not being able to speak which would throw him into the fire and the water. Here is this father desperate as the Syro-Phoenician mother who had a daughter with an unclean spirit. As parents, we are desperate to find anything that will help our child. This Father would go to great lengths for his son. Jesus said, *"All things are possible to him who believes"* (Mk. 9:23 RSV). When the father heard this he was willing to totally expose himself, that he did trust, but did not fully trust, *"Lord, I believe; help my unbelief!"* (9:24 NKJV).

The father knew his trust in God was short and was willing in front of all the rest to confess it. Even though his trust was not what it should have been, Jesus overrode his lack of faith and cast out the demon, restoring the boy to health. God is there any time we need, He wants to be involved in our life with us. God's greatest involvement in our lives is to get us to heaven, *"God our Savior, who desires all men to be saved and to come to the knowledge of the truth"* (1Tim. 2:3&4 RSV).

This is the ultimate desire of God, but He also is concerned about our life even now in this world. In our reading in Mark today after the rich man left and Jesus said how hard it is for the wealthy to get to heaven, the disciples ask how can any then be saved. Astonished, Peter followed saying they had left everything to follow Him (the unspoken question is, 'what about us?'). Here is what Jesus said to them, *"Truly, I say to you, there is no one who has left house or brothers or sisters or mother or father or children or lands, for my sake and for the gospel, who will not receive a hundredfold now in this time, houses and brothers and sisters and mothers and children and lands, with persecutions, and in the age to come eternal life"* (10:29&30 RSV).

God wants to see we have everything we need for life here in this world, along with that in our heart which will get us to heaven when we finish here. God is involved in our lives even though we don't see Him many times. Ever wondered about that time you had trouble getting out of the house to leave for work, then on the news that evening you saw there had been an accident on the road you take to work about the time you normally pass there. God was involved in keeping you safe but at the time all you thought of was 'I'm late for work'. How many times is God involved but there is no news that tells us what happened?

How many times God sees something coming ahead for us and turns us another direction or maneuvers us in some way so we are protected from it? How little we know His involvement, how much we need it. It is joyful to God, joyful to Jesus, to provide what we need. Here is what we heard in Hebrews today, *"looking to Jesus, the founder and perfecter of our faith, who for the joy that was set before him endured the cross, despising the shame, and is seated at the right hand of the throne of God"* (12:2 ESV). It was joy to Jesus to bring to us salvation and everything else that goes with it for our lives here is this world. There is a God that is involved in all our lives.

The glory of the Lord is final. There is no glory that is greater. There is no glory that goes beyond the glory of the Lord. His glory is the great glory. His glory is the eternal glory. His glory is that which encompasses all of the universe. Jesus spoke of His own glory, and the glory of the Father, *"Father, glorify Me together with Yourself, with the glory which I had with You before the world existed"* (Jn. 17:5 NASB).

This was a glory which the Father and Jesus had before we existed, before man was created, before any of the universe was even here. We give God glory for what He has done, yet God had a glory that was totally His before we gave any. The same as God's love was part of His makeup, so His glory was part also. God is great in all that He is. Are we not blessed to have such a God that cares about us!?

Walking with God can be a pleasant stroll through this life. If we come to Him in a humble manner He takes us with His arm and walks close beside us. And as we walk along His glory emanates engulfing us. We are blessed by receiving great things from God. When we see God as greater, then His blessing becomes greater in our eyes as we see greater the One who has given them. How could such a God care about us, yet He does. There is such a vast difference between God and ourselves, *"For My thoughts are not your thoughts, Nor are your ways My ways," says the LORD. For as the heavens are higher than the earth, So are My ways higher than your ways, And My thoughts than your thoughts"* (Isa. 55:8&9 NKJV).

How great a difference, yet He cares about us. Even this, that He cares about us makes Him greater in our eyes. Paul didn't have much regard for Jesus Christ before he ran into Him on the way to Damascus.[1] But afterward, after being faced with the glory of Jesus, such that Paul could hardly describe it, Jesus was in Paul's every word, and maybe in his every thought.

In Paul's epistles he uses Christ's name 392 times. After experiencing Christ's glory Paul could not speak of Him enough. Have you ever had a chance to be in the presence of someone you greatly admired, remember the affect it had on you? Now multiply that by at least a hundred and add a great light to that presence. The glory of God is even beyond what we can think, except for those few who have experienced it to some level. Charles Finney, one of the great evangelists speaks of a time when the glory of God's light shone around him, he was struck with the awareness of the greatness of God and that mankind still rejected God.

The only thing Finney could do was weep, and weep. God's glory, so revealing, it exposes everything hidden. It exposes the greatness of God, it exposes the sinfulness of mankind, it exposes the grace in Christ. There is not a way to describe the glory of God for it is so bright that we while in this world are not capable of seeing the fullness of it. If we have received Christ into our life the glory of God shines upon us.

There is a little short verse in our reading of Hebrews today that gets swallowed up in the whole of what is being said about Jesus, *"For here we do not have a lasting city, but we are seeking the city which is to come"* (13:14 NASB). The writer of Hebrews says we seek the one to come. Check yourself to see if this is your desire. Let's take a look at that City, *"Then came one of the seven angels... and spoke to me, saying, "Come, I will show you the Bride, the wife of the Lamb." And in the Spirit he carried me away to a great, high mountain, and showed me the holy city Jerusalem coming down out of heaven from God, having the glory of God, its radiance like a most rare jewel, like a jasper, clear as crystal"* (Rev. 21:9-11 RSV).

This is the City we long for where the glory of God is to come. Further in the chapter it tells us this, *"the city has no need of sun or moon to shine upon it, for the glory of God is its light, and its lamp is the Lamb"* (v. 23 RSV). For most of us it is by faith we know of the glory of God, but one day it will be what illuminates all of our life.

---

1   Acts 9:3-6

All who are worthy may enter. That is the righteous requirement of God for all who will enter heaven and eternal life. Are you worthy? The first thing that may enter your mind is your sin and your unworthiness. What should come to mind is knowing what Jesus has done for us and that by what He has done we are credited with worthiness.

None of us enter heaven by anything we have done or by any righteousness we may have. All depends on Christ, all righteousness comes from Him. [1] We are righteous because Christ has made us righteous. We walk in righteousness which is His righteousness He has given us, *"If, because of one man's trespass, death reigned through that one man, much more will those who receive the abundance of grace and the free gift of righteousness reign in life through the one man Jesus Christ"* (Rom. 5:17 RSV).

It is Jesus who has made the way for any of us to enter heaven. What was before Christ came was blocked because none could measure up to the righteousness needed to enter. There can be nothing in the presence of God that is not righteous and worthy. We have a great privilege to be permitted to be in the very presence of God for all of eternity, by the blood of Christ, the perfect sacrifice made on the cross that was made by God Himself. We can lay no claim to accomplishing any of our righteousness or worthiness, it is all a gift. Such a great thing God would do. We are told in our reading in James this today, *"Every good endowment and every perfect gift is from above, coming down from the Father of lights with whom there is no variation or shadow due to change"* (1:17 RSV).

It is a gift given that will not change, what a thing it is God has done. We all know it was because of His love for us, but let's back away from that for a moment. You know yourself like I know myself, as I look for a reason that the Father and the Son Jesus should do what they did for me I can find none. This goes beyond any reason man can come up with, even to say it is love, it is a love man does not own, a love not in his being. This is a love far beyond us, as far as the heavens from us, as far as the reaches of the universe. When we begin to grapple with knowing of this kind of love of God, can we do anything other than worship? Such love, such sacrifice, such given.

We can be struck with nothing but awe of a God that would do so much. I believe our gratitude and worship will continue to increase right up to the day we depart from this earth. The more we walk with God the more we know of God, and the more we know of God the more we worship Him. Sometimes it seems we must stop in our lives and allow the weight of what God has done for us bringing salvation to settle down into us to allow the full level of gratitude to rise up out of our being and be given to God. Our gratitude is insufficient, but it is all we have. We need to give what we have and hold on to Him tightly trusting Him with every ounce of our being.

God has reached out to us to give us salvation, there can be no one other able to do more than He has done for us. He deserves our very being, and all that we are. Our life must be given over to Him, every intent, every thought, every action. This does not mean all intents, thoughts, and actions will be none of our own, it means we allow God to lead us and to alter or change any of them whenever He chooses. With knowing all He has done for us can we give Him anything less than all we are?

In our reading today in Mark Jesus is asked what is the greatest commandment and Jesus answers, *"Hear, O Israel: The Lord our God, the Lord is one; and you shall love the Lord your God with all your heart, and with all your soul, and with all your mind, and with all your strength"* (12:29&30 RSV). This is the commandment, but with what we now know of God do we need it to be a commandment? Our love should flow forth like an ever flowing fountain giving thanks to God for what He has done for each of us.

---

1   Jer.23:6, Rom.5:19, 1Cor.5:21, 1Jn.2:29, Rom.3:22&24, Philp.3:9

Life is good all the time. We have to see life within the term of eternity. You have come into being, you have life. We have a choice of eternal death or eternal life. In Godly terms, we are considered dead until we accept Christ, *"he who hears my word and believes him who sent me, has eternal life; he does not come into judgment, but has passed from death to life"* (Jn. 5:24 RSV).

No matter how things go for us here on earth, good or bad we have life. We have been given life by God, and however our course here on earth goes, when we are done here we have life in heaven with God. It will be an eternal life with this life on earth seeming as a speck in comparison. Life is good because we have it, it has been given to us by God, we are living, spiritually living. Through Jesus Christ we came alive, we were re-born. Our life will never seem that good until we can separate the life we had before salvation (which scripture shows us was death) and the life we have after salvation. We need to see the difference, that before we didn't even have life. Now we know we have life and will go to heaven.

A Christian brother of mine says he will be happy even if his job in heaven is polishing rocks, at least he is in heaven. This is what will give life to our life, knowing we will be accepted into heaven to be with God for eternity. Troubles in this life will come, Jesus says, *"Sufficient for the day is its own trouble"* (Mt. 6:34 ESV).

This does not mean every day of our life we are going to have troubles, He is saying whatever is going on today is enough to be concerned with, you don't need to be so concerned about tomorrow. This just tells us we will have days with troubles, but the troubles are temporary, they will not last into eternity. When we get to heaven God is going to have it all worked out for us, He will be in charge, there will be no more troubles. Life is good, even if we have to wait a bit for the really good life to come. Knowing what we have coming should cause us to be willing to go through here whatever may come. There have been many of our fellow brethren who have went through persecution, and even some martyred for the joy of knowing what God had for them when this life is over here on earth. It is a good reality check to read even a few chapters of the book 'Foxe's Book of Martyrs'.

The very, very, basis is that all mankind is disqualified from entering heaven, none are good enough, we have been given a free gift of life which we do not qualify for – life is good. As we begin to see that the life we have been given is good, in each of our days we will see something we can be thankful for. Even in the midst of all our troubles we know God still has control of the situation. The disciples thought the boat was going to sink and they would drown.[1]

After Jesus calmed the storm He asked where was their faith. No matter how bad the storm, God has the control. Sometimes God is testing our faith, sometimes He is building character. When we get our eyes off Jesus, that is when we start to sink. Peter walked on the water making it all the way to within reach of Jesus and then began to sink because he gave too much attention to the storm.[2]

Storms are difficult, we may have to bail water, but Jesus will make sure we get to the other side. In our reading of Mark today we read of things of the end. Jesus tells us of all the troubles that will come at that time, but in the midst of all this He is talking about He says this, *"But he who endures to the end will be saved"* (13:13 RSV).

There is hope, we will make it through the storm. For those of that day whenever it comes, God makes sure they will make it, *And if the Lord had not shortened the days, no human being would be saved; but for the sake of the elect, whom he chose, he shortened the days"* (13:20 RSV). Have faith in God, He will get you through - even if He has to shorten the storm. With a God that takes care of us, even in the worst of storms, we have life, eternal life. Life is good all the time – because God is in charge of it all.

---

1   Lk.8:24
2   Mt.14:28-30

Be on guard at all times. The enemy roams around the world seeking whom he might devour. Be aware but not afraid. James tells us, *"Resist the devil and he will flee from you"* (4:7 RSV). Paul speaks, *"For our wrestling is not against flesh and blood, but against the principalities, against the powers, against the world-rulers of this darkness, against the spiritual hosts of wickedness in the heavenly places"* (Eph. 6:12 ASV). Then Paul goes on to tell us how to cover ourselves. In another epistle Paul gives warning, *"let us therefore cast off the works of darkness, and let us put on the armor of light"* (Rom. 13:12 ASV). When the seventy returned from their ministering to the people Jesus says this, *Behold, I have given you authority to tread upon serpents and scorpions, and over all the power of the enemy: and nothing shall in any wise hurt you"* (Lk. 10:19 ASV).

Some of these verses may give you a little fear but let's look at why we should not be afraid. James in the first part of 4:7 tells us this, *"Submit yourselves therefore to God"* (RSV). Peter also speaks of the same, *"Humble yourselves therefore under the mighty hand of God, that in due time he may exalt you. Cast all your anxieties on him, for he cares about you. Be sober, be watchful. Your adversary the devil prowls around like a roaring lion, seeking some one to devour"* (1Pet. 5:6-8 RSV). Paul goes even further in giving a long discourse on how we should be with God in the first nine verses of Ephesian chapter 6 following with this, *"Finally, my brethren, be strong in the Lord and in the power of His might"* (v. 10 NKJV).

We need to be on our guard, we need to resist, and we need to know of God's protection with the power He has given us. We cannot be nonchalant about this, we need to pay attention. In His word God has shown us how to not be afraid, we need to be following His way.

In His way we are covered by Him. God watches all things at all times, He don't miss noth'n! We may need to fight a few battles, but we know Who it is that helps us win, we do have the **Victory**. In our Old Testament readings we see the nation of Israel fighting many battles, when they are doing things God's way God fights on their side and they are victorious. The same is for us. An interesting book in the Bible is the book of Job. We see a lot of things there. And we see how the devil gave Job much trouble.

The thing I see that encourages me is that the devil, even as furious as he tries to make himself, had to ask permission. The devil cannot do anything to us without the permission of God. God is always watching, He is always caring. But He wants His children to be mature knowing the power He has given them. He has not left us helpless, He has given us great power in the Name of Jesus and by His blood.

We need to remember we are Jesus' property, and we are covered in His blood. That covering is powerful, and Jesus don't let nobody mess around with His property. In the book of Job did you notice God said, **"My servant Job."** That is how we resist without being afraid, knowing we belong to God. **Who has the victory? If you know it, stand on it.** Take note: the more you give yourself as a servant of God the more the devil hates you. Yet that is the very place that you are the most protected. The devil was cast to the earth as he tried to overthrow God in rebellion. Now the devil is restricted to the earth, we are told we are not of this world, so we are not subjected to the control of the devil. He tries to come at us but we have the power to repel him. We don't need to be afraid, we need to remember what God has told us.

Reading in James today he speaks of one of the largest problems we have in doing things God's way. James speaks about our unruly tongue and the things we say. This is what James says about our tongue, *"So the tongue is a little member and boasts of great things. How great a forest is set ablaze by a small fire!"* (3:5 RSV). This is where we need to kick out pride and take on humbleness. James goes on telling us how to combat this, telling us what true wisdom from God is. Today in Mark we read of the arrest and trial of Jesus. Here we see true humbleness to the fullest. Jesus could have thrown that arrest and cross off at any time, but He went through it to provide what we needed, He didn't need it, we were the ones. We are His, and we need to become more like Him. We need to be on guard and know the victory we've been given.

We receive a love that none of us can fully know until we reach heaven. Even though we cannot fully know does not mean it will not have the full effect that God has purposed it to have in our lives. Once we give our lives to God He is at work all the time to make us into a new creature more and more every day. His love is having an effect on us that we don't even recognize, but others see it not knowing how it is happening.

Even God's love is what keeps this world going, He rightfully could have done away with it, and us, long ago. God gives mankind chance after chance after chance, *"do you despise the riches of His goodness, forbearance, and longsuffering, not knowing that the goodness of God leads you to repentance?"* (Rom. 2:4 NKJV).

There is a love which is of God that none of us can now know. Its scope is too broad and too high for us to be able to even touch. It is part of who He is which He Himself has said His ways are higher above our ways as the heavens are above the earth. There is no way we can touch this, the only thing we have left for us to do is to believe it by faith knowing it is true. Jesus so many times tries to get us to realize God wants us to be like Him in this area:

"A new commandment I give to you, that you love one another; even as I have loved you, that you also love one another" (Jn. 13:34 RSV).

"This is my commandment, that you love one another as I have loved you" (Jn. 15:12 RSV).

"These things I command you, so that you will love one another" (Jn. 15:17 ESV).

"love one another with brotherly affection" (Rom. 12:10 RSV).

"through love be servants of one another" (Gal. 5:13 RSV).

"bearing with one another in love" (Eph. 4:2 ESV).

"and may the Lord cause you to increase and overflow in love for one another"
(1Thes. 3:12 NASB).

"you yourselves have been taught by God to love one another" (1Thes. 4:9 RSV).

"love one another from the heart fervently" (1Pet. 1:22 ASV).

"Above all, keep fervent in your love for one another" (1Pet. 4:8 NASB).

"For this is the message which you have heard from the beginning, that we should love one another" (1Jn. 3:11 RSV).

"And this is his commandment, that we should believe in the name of his Son Jesus Christ and love one another, just as he has commanded us" (1Jn. 3:23 RSV).

"Beloved, let us love one another; for love is of God, and he who loves is born of God and knows God" (1Jn. 4:7 RSV).

"Beloved, if God so loved us, we also ought to love one another" (1Jn. 4:11 RSV).

"if we love one another, God abides in us and his love is perfected in us" (1Jn. 4:12 RSV).

"And now I beg you, lady, not as though I were writing you a new commandment, but the one we have had from the beginning, that we love one another" (2Jn. 1:5 RSV).

This is how much God wants us to be like Him, to love like Him. We will never know how much He totally loves us until we are in His presence. We receive the benefits of all that love even now, yet we are unable to know the fullness of it. Our God is good to us, far more than what we realize or know. Today we continue to read in Mark of Jesus' arrest, trial, and execution on the cross.

He went through much maltreatment and disrespect being executed on a Roman cross of death. This He gave Himself to, to acquire the righteousness by which He could offer to us salvation by the price He paid. Jesus has said this, *"Greater love has no man than this, that a man lay down his life for his friends"* (Jn. 15:13 RSV). This is the kind of love God has for us, the Father sacrificed the Son so we could be saved. This is where we begin to know of God's love.

King of kings and Lord of lords. I may have said this before, but is not Jesus Christ worthy of all praise given Him? Can we proclaim this too much? Maybe it is we proclaim it too little. I wonder, if all the people of the world were praising all at the same time if it would be sufficient, maybe He is even greater than this. The angels bow down, the twenty-four elders bow down, the four living creatures bow down,[1] and when we are in heaven we all will bow down.

God is worthy of this much praise, and maybe more. We here on earth are able to touch only such a small portion of who God is. There is no way to know His greatness. We look around us on this earth and see such beauty. The human being and all the animals are His work, and we are not able to totally figure out how we all function.

We are amazed as we look at all that is in this earth, even the core of this earth, do we really understand? Then the earth spins just at the right speed not to cast us off into space, nor to drive us into the ground by the force of gravity. So many more amazing things, so many more questions. We are not even done with thinking of all that is of the earth, then we look up and see the stars, Oh, how many, there are more and more.

Now with great telescopes we see even more and more of the universe that is magnificent, how much more can there be? And then scripture says this, *"For I see Thy heavens, a work of Thy fingers, Moon and stars that Thou didst establish"* (Ps. 8:3 YLT). and *"He counts the number of the stars; He calls them all by name"* (Ps. 147:4 NKJV).

How great is this God of ours? And yet how kind to us He is. Do we think that there could ever be sufficient praise we could give Him? He is so far beyond our consideration, so far beyond what we could know. King of kings and Lord of lords, Yes, Yes, and so much more. Can you really consider God, the fullness of who He is, His great ability of all He can do, and the great power by which He moves all things. Does it not cause us to step back in awe when we truly consider Him? WOW, what a God, and He still loves each one of us. Who is this God who has given life to us?

All that He is, and all that He does, and He still wants a personal relationship with each one of us. Knowing all of this, does it not take you back a little in awe? Such an amazing God, and yet He cares about each one of us. Oh, the word of God, He piles knowledge on top of knowledge on top of knowledge and reveals it to us piece by piece. If we are seeking Him, and truly want to know more of Him, every time we are in His word there is something new. A new emphasis, a new meaning, or a new understanding. There are times we read the same verse as many times before, no new emphasis, no new meaning, no new understanding, but this time we are touched in our heart by it as we never have been before.

Does God deserve our worship, does He deserve our praise? Everything about God brings us to thanksgiving, to worship, to praise. For the last two days we have read in Mark about Jesus' arrest, His trial, and His crucifixion, how He died for us for the forgiveness of our sins.

Today we read of His resurrection, *"And entering the tomb, they saw a young man sitting on the right side, dressed in a white robe; and they were amazed. And he said to them, "Do not be amazed; you seek Jesus of Nazareth, who was crucified. He has risen, he is not here; see the place where they laid him"* (16:5&6 RSV). This is what gives us hope, at the end of time our bodies will also rise and we will be with God forever, for eternity. For this we praise, for this we worship, for this we give thanksgivings. King of kings and Lord of lords, **GLORY!**

---

1   Rev.4:8-11, 5:8-14, 7:9-12, 19:1-7

You are loved by God beyond your knowledge. He interacts with you in the Spirit. It is difficult for us to know of that communication which takes place in the Spirit. God causes us to change when we are born anew, and we know not how. Our life, likes, manners change such that sometimes others notice before we do. Our inner man which now is brought to life by the Spirit of God coming into our lives is something new to us, possibly such we don't have an awareness of that activity within ourselves. Over time we know a little more, and a little more, yet not knowing the full activity of what all goes on within us by the Spirit. [1]

It is quite a special work of God to put His Spirit into us when we receive salvation. This itself is a great act of love that we may never fully have a grasp of this side of heaven. Do you realize God started on His love for you at the foundation of time? God has a great investment of love in you. What we knew of love before God revealed His type of love to us was no more than a shadow that is from the great light of love. How little we know of the great things of God, love seems to be the major part of who He is.

It is even His love that moves Him to discipline us to bring about that character that He knows will be good for us. His love has been with us since the beginning of time, and at salvation it comes into us in a full manner to bring about growth into the mature Christian character God is creating in us. He never leaves us to develop our Christian character on our own, it would be deeply flawed and ill-shaped. He works in us in ways we do not know. We think of all the scriptures which indicate to us the image of who God is. We wonder how much He is like us since we are made in His likeness. Have you ever realized one of the main forms of God is His love? What kind of shape is love?

It is not really about shape, it is about being. God's being is largely made up of love, a genuine love, a perfect love. How many times have we heard, 'God so loved'? Do you see, it is God's love that moves Him. It is God's love that has been moving toward us, each one of us, from the foundation of time. His eye has been on us even though we had not yet even been formed in the womb, *"Your eyes saw my substance, being yet unformed. And in Your book they all were written, The days fashioned for me, When as yet there were none of them"* (Ps. 139:16 NKJV). How much love is that?

How much is it He loves you? We are loved so much more than we will ever know. God loves us with an eternal love, not the type of love that is found in this world. He is always looking, always guiding, always moving, always laying out a path before us. There is nowhere we are going that He does not know about. As we go forward He knows, as we enter the wilderness going astray He knows, as we enter the storm He knows. There is nowhere we go that He does not know, and He goes with us. [2] God loves us with a love that is beyond our knowledge.

One day we will know it, the moment we enter heaven we will hold it within us. Until then we will continue to receive it and it will be forming in us as we become more and more like Christ our savior. That great love which God held for us since the beginning, of making a way by which we could be saved, Peter speaks of in our reading today, *"knowing that you were not redeemed with perishable things... but with precious blood, as of a lamb unblemished and spotless, the blood of Christ. For He was foreknown before the foundation of the world, but has appeared in these last times for the sake of you who through Him are believers in God, who raised Him from the dead and gave Him glory, so that your faith and hope are in God"* (1Pet. 1:18-21 NASB).

All this is given to us by the love of a great God. In Luke today it tells us of what we were being given even before Christ our Savior was born. The father of John the Baptist spoke these words by the Holy Spirit, *"And you, child, will be called the prophet of the Most High; for you will go before the Lord to prepare his ways, to give knowledge of salvation to his people in the forgiveness of their sins, through the tender mercy of our God"* (1:76-78 RSV). How much is it that God loves you?

---

1   Tit.3:5
2   Ps.139:1-16

God is in all your ways. You may wonder this at times. Is God in you, did He not promise to be with you? So if He is with us then would He not be in all our ways? Sometimes we are so busy in trying to order our situation that there is no place for God to enter into it with us. We may pray for His help and then go off to try to force through it without ever asking Him into it. We may ask Him to make us strong, to give us wisdom, to help us have faith, but all that is about us in it. We need to ask God into it, even to go ahead of us in it.

All those things asked before are not wrong, but it has to be more than just about us. How many times do we read of King David asking of God before he went out to battle? The first thing David asked was 'should I go up, should I enter this?' Do we ask these questions, or are we in our mess where we should have not even entered into it at all? Then David trusted in God to strengthen him, and his army, but he always depended on God for the outcome.

God is in all our ways, for He is within us, but is He invited in to be involved and to guide us. In our own thinking we would not do like Moses leading the people right up against the sea with no escape when the enemy was in pursuit? But God was the One guiding Moses. With God involved He can give us better guidance than we can come up with on our own.

There is no need to ask ourselves if God is with us if we keep Him involved in what goes on in our life. It is so easy to get so focused on that which is around us trying our best to move forward in life, we forget about the unseen that can be involved if we invite all that God has to go with us. Even Jesus in His life on earth needs the help of angels twice that we are told about, *"Then the devil left him, and behold, angels came and ministered to him"* (Mt. 4:11 RSV). and *"Father, if you are willing, remove this cup from me. Nevertheless, not my will, but yours, be done." And there appeared to him an angel from heaven, strengthening him"* (Lk. 22:42&43 ESV).

If Jesus needed angels to help Him surely we need help too. If we ask the Father for help, and for Him to be involved in what is happening in our lives, maybe the Father will send angels to help us, just because we don't see them doesn't mean they are not there involved in our situation. There is an unseen spiritual world all around us, why should we not seek help from there where God is. The kindness of God is always flowing towards us, should we not ask the Father that some of it flow into our fix we're in to help us? Oh, the battles in the spiritual realm that go on all around us and we don't even know. Michael came to relieve Gabriel so he could go speak to Daniel. [1]

The warriors of heaven with their horses and chariots were ready all around Elijah, but his servant could not see them and was in panic. [2] An angel came and escorted Peter out of prison and Peter didn't even realize it was real until he found himself in the streets outside the prison. [3] And the apostles arrested and put in prison were brought out by an angel and sent to the temple to speak. [4] Are there more we need to speak of to realize the angels of God are at work? God is with us, and even in us, the scriptures tell us this. [5] So our faith has to come to the place that we know of the spiritual realm around us so we don't have to go it alone.

The thing we should do is make a high place in our heart for God knowing He is in control of all things. If we invite Him into our situations of life He will be in control there on our behalf. As we make God of more importance in our life, in our heart, we will find things not so difficult. We have seen King David make a high place in his heart for God and say this, *"There is none like you, O LORD, and there is no God besides you, according to all that we have heard with our ears"* (1Chr. 17:20 ESV).

This is the kind of thing that should be in our hearts continually, and the same sort spoken from our lips. Remember God's promise, *"Draw near to God and he will draw near to you"* (Jas. 4:8 ESV).

---

1   Dan.10:12-14
2   2Kg.6:17
3   Acts 12:10
4   Acts 5:17-20
5   1Jn.3:24, 4:15&16

You are standing at the threshold of success. I'm not talking about you becoming rich. I'm not talking about you becoming the leader of a great movement. I'm not talking about you even getting a great job. I am talking about your soon-to-be entry into heaven forever being with God where He is your God and you are His people. Many of you young people may be say'n, 'Wait here a minute, I've got a lot of liv'n to do before I'm leav'n this earth'. Yes, that is true in terms of earth time, but according to heaven time, it is tomorrow or sooner.

The point is that anyone who has accepted Jesus Christ as Lord and Savior has a place in heaven and a guarantee of success, because that success does not depend on them, it depends on Jesus. There is nothing that Jesus Christ does that is not a success. We are part of what He is doing. He died on the cross paying for our sins – a success. He leads the way showing we will rise from the dead – a success. He has went to heaven and prepared a place for us – a success. Are you on the threshold of success? Are you saved with the next big great move in your life is to enter eternity in heaven?

Every one of us should be living with this expectation no matter how many years we may have left in our lives on this earth. Once we are saved there will not be an event in our lives on this earth that will be greater than our arrival in heaven. If we live with this expectation then even our days may change because we have put the focus where it should be. Everything we do in our lives should be governed by the knowledge of heaven and how important it is to us. We never know when that day for us to leave this earth will come, it might be just around the corner or just over the next hill.

We have no idea of how many years we will have on this earth. I don't mean you should be worried about getting into heaven, I'm speaking of the excitement of arriving in heaven being in the very presence of the resurrected, living forever, authority over all things, savior of all, Lord Jesus Christ. This is our success, to be in His presence accepted for eternity, never having to ever leave again, forever and ever with our Lord. It will be an existence beyond our imagination, a life greater and happier than we have ever had or thought of.

No more pain, no more sorrow, no more tears, no more death – who could not get excited? There is no one who has had pain that would not be glad for it to go away. There is no one who has had sorrow that would not be glad to have it go away. There is no one who has had tears that would not be glad for them to go away. This will be a great upward change for us when it is time. I'm not saying it should be rushed in any way, but it should be looked forward to with excitement. And that excitement would change how we see each day we live here on this earth giving us a joy that the unsaved do not have. In 1Peter today we read this, *"but in your hearts honor Christ the Lord as holy, always being prepared to make a defense to any one who ask you for a reason for the hope that is in you; yet do it with gentleness and respect"* (3:15 ESV).

When others see the joy we have Peter tells us we should be ready to tell them why we are happy. If we were going to a great event here on earth; a ballgame, a great theatrical event, a big dance, whatever it was, if others ask why we were so happy as we looked forward to it, would we not tell them? This is the type of excitement we need to begin to grow in our hearts about heaven. We sometimes get borrowed down in our difficulties and lose sight of what is coming for us.

It seems that those in the past that were weighed down the most looked up the most. Do you need to go through be weighed down so you will look up, why can't you start looking up today? Keeping in mind the greatest success you will ever experience in life by what another has done for you is the thing that will keep you looking up. Jesus is always looking down keeping an eye on you, don't think He doesn't know what is going on with you. In our reading in Luke chapter 3 today we hear the words of Isaiah quoted, *"And all flesh shall see the salvation of God"* (v. 6 ASV). Receiving salvation, is this not success for all who receive it?

Kindness is always available from God. Our relationship with God is not something to take for granted. What person in relationship with you would not want you to spend time with them? And if that person supplied things that you need surely they would like you to come and ask knowing they would give it. Do we do this with God? Do we wonder sometimes where His kindness for us is at? Do we take time to go to Him and ask?

If we are going to be spiritual people then we have to give place in our lives to spiritual things. Jesus was the greatest spiritual man who ever lived, yet He took time to be in prayer with the Father. Is Jesus not our example of being a spiritual person? How much the Father wants to bless us, He desires to have fellowship with us. The deeper the relationship with God the deeper the awareness that He will take care of us. Let me throw a new angle on a verse heard many times. *"faith comes by hearing"* (Rom. 10:17 NKJV).

I know where Paul uses this he refers to salvation, but would that limit its effects? **Faith comes by hearing**, would this not also be true of us spending time with God in prayer and at times hearing His voice, that still small voice, speaking to us? Would this not cause our faith to grow putting more and more trust in God? God does not always speak the first time we come in prayer, nor even the second, *"I will pray unto Jehovah your God according to your words... And it came to pass after ten days, that the word of Jehovah came unto Jeremiah"* (Jer. 42:4&7 ASV).

God wants to know if you are consistent, and how serious you are. The interesting thing I have found is that I may spend a good amount of time in prayer and hear nothing, and then later as I am walking along or at my work, out of seemingly nowhere God speaks to me. There may have been a pause between when I prayed and when God spoke, but it is connected to my time in prayer. Jesus got up early, or stayed up late, to spend time with the Father in prayer. Many of our days are full and crowded, so we must carve out a time to spend the most important moments of our day.

There even may have to be something sacrificed so we have time to spend with God. Our God is worth it, He gave the Son Jesus Christ to die on a cross so we could receive salvation and entrance into heaven when our life here is over. God wants fellowship. In the garden He called out, **'Adam where are you?'**. God is calling out today saying; Tom where are you, Jim where are you, Roy where are you, Nancy where are you, Alice where are you, Nichole where are you? He wants fellowship. What about you, do you want fellowship with Him? This is what it comes down to, do we want fellowship with God?

We can't very well expect His blessing on our lives if we are not taking time to be in a relationship with Him. Our entrance to heaven was marked sure on the day we accepted Jesus as Lord, but our blessing from God until that time comes is in relationship. Surely Jesus knew the Father better than any of us could, but He still spent time in prayer, time in relationship.

We know from the Psalms King David spent time with God, and we read in the scriptures of the blessings God gave him. In our reading in Luke today Jesus goes out early before it is light to spend time in prayer with the Father, *"And when it was day, he departed and went into a desolate place"* (4:42 ESV). A parallel to this is found in Mark, *"And rising very early in the morning, while it was still dark, he departed and went out to a desolate place, and there he prayed"* (1:35 ESV).

Here is our example, here Jesus takes time early, other times it is at night, He takes time out of a schedule more important and busier than yours to pray to the Father. Time to pray has to be carved out, otherwise there will never be time for it.

Life is good and God is blessing every day. There are always more blessings to come. We may think not, we may fear not, but God never runs out, and He never stops giving. It might be that He is not giving what you want, but that does not mean He is not giving. We are given a hint to why sometimes God is not giving by James, *"You ask and do not receive, because you ask wrongly, to spend it on your passions"* (Jas. 4:3 RSV).

God wants us to grow spiritually, He wants His Church to grow, He wants His Kingdom on earth to grow, these are what He gives for. This doesn't mean that He won't help you with your livelihood, a place to live, a good job, your need for transportation, etc. But that boat, or motorcycle, or a whole house full of new furniture, those things for your pleasure you may have to get on your own. God gives us things that are so much greater, many of which have eternal value.

Remember something Jesus said in His prayer to the Father, *"they do not belong to the world—just as I myself do not belong to the world. I don't ask you to take them out of the world, but to protect them from the Evil One. They do not belong to the world, just as I do not belong to the world"* (Jn. 17:14-16 CJB).

Our focus in life is not to be on this world and what it has, it is to be on God, on our future with Him, and what He has for us here now, today. God wants us all to be living for His Kingdom, the Kingdom of His Son[1] that is here on earth now.[2] God wants His Church strong, God wants the world to see His goodness, part of that is seen by the world as they see us. As we give ourselves to these things He will give us what we need for them and what we need for our life.

The greatest God gives is spiritual, not something we can put our hand on, but so much more valuable than anything we can touch. God is always giving to us so we can grow spiritually. When we read the word God gives us, the Holy Spirit is to help us understand.[3] Do you ask the Holy Spirit to help you know the word when you read? The word of God is not something cold and dry on the page, it is alive and active.[4] It is not for us to take the cold dry words off the page putting them into our brain, they are alive and moving, they are to be taken hold of and planted in our hearts.

God has so many spiritual things He is doing in our lives and we don't even know it. We are constantly growing, sometimes we have a part in it, and sometimes we don't, we just notice something in our spiritual life is different. Jesus came that we could have a new birth. That birth is the birth of the Spirit in us, it is a brand new part of us that starts to grow. Jesus told Nicodemus, *"That which is born of the flesh is flesh; and that which is born of the Spirit is spirit"* (Jn. 3:6 ASV).

That which is the Spirit is what causes us to grow, it is found in the inner man, that which is not part of the flesh. Take a moment and think of all the things that have changed in your life since you received salvation, those things material and those things spiritual. How many are there, can you count them? Is life good and is God blessing every day? Sometimes we get stuck in our moment of need and forget all that God has already done. Remembering the things God has done in our past is what builds our faith for the moment we are in. We can't always see past the corner, or over the hill, or to the end of the storm, but that does not mean God is not there, that He is not giving in some way.

In 1 Peter today we read one of the keys of receiving from God, *"Therefore, humble yourselves under the mighty hand of God, so that at the right time he may lift you up. Throw all your anxieties upon him, because he cares about you"* (5:6&7 CJB). If we come to God in a humble manner, trusting Him, He will take care of our needs. The only thing you need to do to know this new life God has given you is good is to think of what it would now be like without Him in it.

God is constantly giving, He is constantly blessing, He is constantly helping us through every moment. What Father does not help his child when they are in need?

---

1   Col.1:13
2   Lk.17:20&21
3   Jn.14:26
4   Heb.4:12

There is life all the way through to the end. The end being judgment day and the end of life as we know it. Many people talk about eating at the banquet table in the Kingdom of God, or set'n by the river, or eating the fruit from the trees. All those things relate to things we experience here on earth. Just to experience life as the way God experiences life, to be a fully spiritual person as angels are, [1] this is a drastic change from what we know.

Let me ask you a question, and let the answer you give cause you to consider how extremely different heaven will be. In Revelation, we are told that the New Jerusalem measures in width, same as the length, same as its height of twelve thousand furlongs. [2] This distance has been estimated at 1200 – 1500 miles. It is going to be a big place, my question is what is the need for it to be so high? So already we see heaven is not going to be anything like here on earth, after all it is heaven, The New Jerusalem. All are interesting thoughts of what it will be like in heaven.

Now Jesus said He was going to prepare a place for us for when we arrive. [3] If He goes to so much trouble to do that then certainly He will be with us in this life until we get there. Jesus has given us life, we have been born again. As long as we continue to reach out to Him as Lord He will be with us in this life making the journey with us to the day of our departure from earth and entrance into heaven. We need to remember of when the Lord and His disciple were in the boat going across the lake. The disciples thought they were not going to make it, but they did. [4] He always makes sure we get through the storm, any storm, all the storms, depending on Him as Lord in our lives He will get us all the way to heaven. Nothing will stop that, nothing will prevent it, He will get us through. [5]

Because of Jesus Christ we will have life all the way to the end – and past that end, when we enter heaven. We will find such a life so much greater than we have ever had we will then know there is no comparison. We will live and have a life just like the angels have. You can't imagine that! We have given our lives to Jesus, we are His property, He paid a high price for us. [6] Can you imagine a king who owns property that he paid a high price for leaving it behind, would He not make sure doing all that was needed to take it with him. So we are the property of Jesus, we are the children of God, [7] we are part of the spiritual family, how could we be left behind.

God, the Three in One God, the Father, the Son Jesus, the Holy Spirit, can you imagine they would not be attentive to us to be sure we have life all the way to the end of this life we have here, and then into the new life in heaven? We are so unaware of the great things they do in our lives every day. What a lovely loving God we have. In our reading in 2Peter today his opening statement is the very thing we need to hear:

- *"His divine power has granted to us all things that pertain to life and godliness*
- *through the knowledge of him who called us to his own glory and excellence*
- *by which he has granted to us his precious and very great promises*
- *that through them you may become partakers of the divine nature*
- *having escape from the corruption that is in the world because of sinful desire"*

(1:3&4 ESV).

Do these words sound like God is going to give you life to the end, to the end of life on this earth and then into an even greater life in heaven with Him? Let all these words sink in, let them get into your heart. Take these with you for your day, use them like water in watering a tree, let them sink in deep nourishing and strengthening the depth of your heart.

---

1   Mk.12:25
2   Rev.21:16
3   Jn.14:2
4   Mk.4:37-39
5   Rom.8:38&39
6   1Cor.6:20
7   1Jn.3:1

There is a God in the world who knows everything that goes on and everything that happens. This comes out clearly in the book of Job. God knew all about Job, He knew his place in life, He knew of his standing in the community, He knew of his standing in his family, He knew of his heart towards God. Ever have anyone brag about you?

God bragged about Job, He said, 'You see Job who there is none like him in all the land, who is blameless and upright, who fears God and shuns evil'. God knew all about Job, and He knows all about you, and He knows all about me. If we have something in our life we don't want God to know about, this then is not good news. On the other hand if you are looking to God to help you in your life with the things you go through this is good news. In my wife's early years she would go way out into the field and yell at God about her complaint. Many would say this is disrespectful of God, but she would say He already knew what was in her heart, why should it not also be on her lips.

Of course you know who always won those arguments. There is nothing that God does not know, can you imagine He created us and then doesn't know about us? God knows us from the foundation of time, He knew us before we were formed in the womb, He knew us even before our parents were alive. *"Thy eyes beheld my unformed substance; in thy book were written, every one of them, the days that were formed for me, when as yet there was none of them"* (Ps. 139:16 RSV).

He knows what you went through yesterday, He knows how your day is going today, and He knows what your tomorrow will be. This is a God who gave a way that we could be saved, He knew all about us, and He knows what the rest of our life will be.

He is at the beginning, yet He is at the end, and knows everything that will ever be. God is not restricted to time like we are, to Him everything is now. Does He know about our every concern, does He know about our every joy, does He know about every step we will take. The answer is yes! The more we know about God the greater He gets in our eyes, I wonder what it will be to be in heaven and know all that He is. Could we possibly do anything other than worship and sing His praise? The bigger God gets to us the more sure we are that He can take care of our needs.

At times life is difficult, partly because of the effect of sin in this world that came about by Adam and Eve's disobedience in the Garden of Eden. The other thing that makes life difficult is that we now belong to God. You might wonder what I am talking about since I have been saying God will take care of us, this is still true. Jesus said this, *"Remember the word that I said unto you, A servant is not greater than his lord. If they persecuted me, they will also persecute you"* (Jn. 15:20 ASV). Some of our difficulties will come because we belong to Jesus. None of this will overwhelm us since God is always there with us in it, *"Whoever confesses that Jesus is the Son of God, God abides in him, and he in God. So we know and believe the love God has for us. God is love, and he who abides in love abides in God, and God abides in him"* (1Jn. 4:15&16 RSV).

God is always going to be with us (even when we are not being what we should – He is still there), He will always be with us in all we go through. And He will get us to heaven at the end to be with Him forever. If you are one who question how God will treat you because of your past behavior see what Jesus said in our reading today to the sinful woman who washed His feet with her tears, *"Therefore I tell you, her sins, which are many, are forgiven, for she loved much"* (Lk. 7:47 RSV).

Do you love Him much, then take comfort from what Jesus said of this woman, and also says of you. Jesus came to call us, you and me for we are sinners, *"I have not come to call the righteous, but sinners to repentance"* (Lk. 5:32 RSV). None qualify by their performance, those such as the Pharisees who thought their standing was good will not be lifted up because they did not repent. The woman repented and loved. Which are you?

'**They that wait upon the LORD.**' Do you wait, do you seek Him, do you invite Him into all of your life, do you wait allowing Him to give you guidance? Do you want to be strong? Do you want to be able to hover over your troubles instead of weighed down in them? Do you want to go forward without weakness? Do you want to walk with God in faith? Then hear the rest of the verse, *"they who wait for the LORD shall renew their strength, they shall mount up with wings like eagles, they shall run and not be weary, they shall walk and not faint"* (Isa. 40:31 RSV).

This verse is spoken to us who have Christ in our lives. The chapter starts out in verse 3 speaking of John the Baptist and then goes on to speak of Christ. The very first verse is this, *"Comfort, comfort my people, says your God"* (RSV). How many names have been given to our Savior? A couple are Emmanuel, Jesus, Wonderful Counselor, and Price of Peace. The last two are self-defined, Emmanuel means '**God with us**', Jesus, which Mary and Joseph individually were instructed to name the child, means '**help of Jehovah**'. Do these all sound as though they fit the first verse of Isaiah chapter 40 that speaks of comfort? God is concerned about us, even from the beginning of time He has been concerned. His concern about each one of us has been since the foundation of the world. In Revelation 13:8 & 17:8 it is speaking about the unsaved whose names are not written in the Lamb's Book of Life. Therefore it is our names that have been written in the Lamb's Book of Life since the foundation of the world.

This God is a caring God, this God is a loving God, this God is a longsuffering God. Can you think of anyone else better to wait on, to trust, to have faith in? Our God will take care of us. Sometimes we think He doesn't care, doesn't know our condition or situation. Let me ask you a question, do you know what is going to happen tomorrow, do you know what is sure to happen even a minute from now?

God knows. God is way out there, in that place of heaven, beyond anything we can know. He is so far beyond anything we can be. He said, '**let there be light**' and there was light. He created the stars, all the stars, more than we can count (because we have not seen them all yet). He has given names to all of them. I think He is fully able to take care of us, we need to trust Him, to wait on Him, to be guided by Him, even within ourselves to be strengthened by Him.

It is not a matter of trying to measure up before Him, we were short in the beginning needing the blood of Christ, so why try to measure up now? It is our giving in that He wants of us, humbling ourselves, saying we can't - asking Him to work in us so we can by His doing within us. When we put our full dependence on God it is amazing what He can do through us who are given over to Him fully and totally. Waiting and trusting is what He wants from us. Today in our reading in Luke chapter 8 we read of those who were not trusting and were taught to trust. The disciples were in the boat, the storm was ragging, and they cried out to Jesus, *"Master, Master, we are perishing!"* (v. 24 RSV). Were they perishing, did they perish? What did Jesus do? He took control of the storm that was ragging around them and settled it.

Then they said, *"Who then is this, that he commands even wind and water, and they obey him"* (v. 25 RSV). This is He who also was involved when God said, '**let there be light**'. Are you trusting Him? At that time there were those who waited and were trusting. Jairus was waiting for Jesus and trusted that He could bring life back to his daughter.[1] There was a woman who needed a healing who was also waiting and trusted, that even in the midst of the commotion as Jesus was starting out to go to Jairus' house, that if she could only get a chance to touch even the outer edge of His clothing it would be enough.[2]

We all know what the results for these two were that waited His arrival and trusted He could help them. '**They that wait upon the LORD.**' Are you one of those who are waiting with trust that God can take care of your need, or to get you through the storm that rages around you? He cares, He has since the foundation of the world.

---

1   Lk.8:41&42
2   Lk.8:43-48

'I am where you are at, it is not for you to understand, it is for you to follow.' Do you think God ever says this to you? How many times do we think God is not with us because what is happening makes no sense to us, we don't understand it. Can we think the things God thinks, can we work the things God works. God said to Job, *"Where were you when I laid the foundation of the earth? Tell me, if you have understanding"* (38:4 RSV).

We have to keep in mind we are the created, and this world we live in is the created. How great and marvelous we are, the scientists still have not figured out fully all the functions of our body. And this world, how marvelous and beautiful it is, do we dare question the loving God that has made us and put us in such a marvelous world? When we cannot see how God can be with us and working in our life we must put on our faith. Faith does grow, but there is a putting it on, it is deciding to believe God, even when it seems unbelievable to us, we have to put it on. God is always with us working in our lives.

You may not see what He is doing and how, but were you there seeing what God was doing and how He did it when He said, 'let there be light'? Do you even understand it now? We must allow God to work as He does by believing He is doing it even when we don't see.

Do you remember the servant of Elijah who could not see what was going on, what it was God was doing? *"Will you not show me who of us is for the king of Israel?" And one of his servants said, "None, my lord, O king; but Elisha, the prophet who is in Israel, tells the king of Israel the words that you speak in your bedchamber." And he said, "Go and see where he is, that I may send and seize him." It was told him, "Behold, he is in Dothan." So he sent there horses and chariots and a great army; and they came by night, and surrounded the city. When the servant of the man of God rose early in the morning and went out, behold, an army with horses and chariots was round about the city. And the servant said, "Alas, my master! What shall we do?" He said, "Fear not, for those who are with us are more than those who are with them"* (2Kg. 6:11-16 RSV).

This is a lot of times where we are, we feel surrounded or something has come against us. As Elijah tells his servant, 'do not fear, we're covered' how many times is God telling us the same. We must have faith that God's got it - His way. When Elijah finally prayed that God would open the eyes of the servant what did he see? *"and behold, the mountain was full of horses and chariots of fire round about Elisha"* (2Kg. 6:17 RSV).

Whether God opened the eyes of the servant or not, did it change anything God was doing, anything that God was working? How many times does God have our backs covered and we just can't see it? Faith is about trusting God even when we cannot see what is going on, knowing He's got us covered. Sometimes it takes faith to step out where we cannot see where we are going. Abraham did this, he did not know where his steps were taking him, he only knew God called him to come, that God knew where he was going. Abraham is one of those of great faith, and before him was Noah.

They trusted God in their faith, even though they could not see what God was doing. We must trust God, only in our hindsight can we sometimes see what God was doing. Just think about the Israelites looking back of how God brought them through the sea and used the sea to destroy their enemy, [1] their hindsight was good then. Today in our reading in Luke chapter 9 Jesus sends the twelve out without staff, bag, food, money, or extra tunic. This is surely not the way we would go.

Sometimes God knows more about it than we do. Again we see Jesus knows what He is doing, but the twelve said, *"Send the crowd away to go into the surrounding villages and countryside to find lodging and get provisions, for we are here in a desolate place"* (v. 12 ESV). Listen to what Jesus tells them, *"You give them something to eat"* (v. 13 RSV). What!, the disciples had just told Jesus what must be done for all to have something to eat, and now He says this! We don't know what God will do, we just need to trust and follow.

---

[1]   Ex.14:28

Be ready at all times for you do not know when God will use you. It is good for us to remember we are not in charge of the timing of this, it is the Father who has in His own authority the times.[1] We may never know when He wants to use us until the very moment. Paul tells Timothy, *"be ready in season and out of season"* (2Tim. 4:2 ESV).

This is for us as well, we never know when the Father has someone right in front of us who He is drawing to Jesus intending to use us.[2] There also is the opportunity to be of service to someone the Father wants to bless. We should be in the condition in our hearts that we can know God's moving us to minister. Giving ourselves over to the guidance of the Spirit is not easy. We live in a world that drives us to be in control at all times. We do have to move in our lives in a manner which lays our life in order in this world which takes a certain amount of control, the key is being tuned into God's move and pliable enough to let Him change our course at any time.

He has a far better wisdom than we do, and He knows the future and what is next. Oh, we could make great plans if we knew exactly what was going to happen tomorrow or the day after that. God does know and wants to help us along the way. He also knows where He wants to use us that may require a change in our course a day or two before. We may wonder what is going on, we thought that God led us a certain way and we see nothing happening. What we don't realize is it is God lining certain things up to bring about an event He has scheduled to happen.

What the really amazing thing is that this God who created everything in six days by saying, 'let there be...' and it was, would include us in anything He is doing. Do you realize what a privilege He gives us? He could do these things by Himself, but He brings us into it to be involved with Him. In my opinion knowing who I am I would leave me out of it but the Father wants His child included in what He is doing. We have to remember the largest makeup of God is love.

Nothing that we see around us would probably be if it were not for God's love. It was His love to want to create us and all we see. It was His love that was longsuffering waiting for us to turn around going in His direction. It was His love to decide not to ever flood the whole world again because of the behavior of mankind. It was because of His love that a plan of redemption was laid out so we could be cleansed enabling us to be with Him eternally.

We could go on and on as we consider the things God does because of His love. We should be very grateful that God has so much love, because rightfully we should be doomed because of our sin, yet Jesus was willing to die paying for our sins so we could be accepted, accepted by God, and accepted into heaven. Amazingly this God wants to work through us to minister to the world. He wants health in His body, the body of Christ. He wants us ministering within the church to each other so we are strong, and He wants us ministering to the world so that they will know who He is.

It is not about us being in control, even if within that control we think we are doing good works for God. God is the only one who knows what good works He is wanting from each of us, we have to be listening and sensing His move within us to be doing the works He has in mind for us. In our reading in Luke chapter 10 we read what Jesus said, *"The harvest truly is great, but the laborers are few; therefore pray the Lord of the harvest to send out laborers into His harvest"* (v. 2 NKJV).

Are you praying for the harvest, are you ready to be sent, or even used on the spot, if God calls you? If we are rigidly controlling our lives we are not available to be a harvester, or any other ministry God wants to use us in. We have to live in a humble manner, always being ready to be used in any way at any moment God calls us. We can be a blessing to others if we are available for the use of God.

---

1   Acts 1:7
2   Jn.6:44

From here where do we go? First, we have to recognize where here is. We do tend to get hung up on here, the life we live on this earth for so many years. For a child or young person, it looks like forever. When we are older, we say, "Where did the years go?" Even then there is an illusion.

We subconsciously attach the greatness of life here as we are on this earth. We want to live good long years as though that was the thing. Even though we believe that all of us who are saved will go to heaven there is a disconnection of our subconscious that one's end on this earth is not a good thing. Somehow we see the end of someone's life here on this earth as a loss to the one who is gone. There needs to be a readjustment of our subconscious to adding that which we believe in our hearts.

We know God's word about eternal life, we decide we will believe it in our hearts, but somehow it doesn't always get to our subconscious. We have to drive ourselves into the truth so we see the life on this earth for what it is. God has given a purpose to all things in His creation. Our time God gives us on this earth before our end here is to have a chance to realize He is true and to find Him for salvation. God is not in a rush and is gracious so He gives us many years to find Him.

Paul in speaking about God says this, *"He has made from one blood every nation of men to dwell on all the face of the earth, and has determined their preappointed times and the boundaries of their dwellings, so that they should seek the Lord, in the hope that they might grope for Him and find Him"* (Acts 17:26&27 NKJV).

In those years we get so attached to this life we live on earth we let slip away the truth that the greatest life is yet to come. The value of the life we have on this earth that we will leave behind will have the lesser value, it will be like when a flashlight is overpowered by a beacon. All that each of us may think is so great here may not even be thought of any more by us when we are in the very presence of God Himself, and all His heaven, and that place that is prepared for us by Jesus.

Once we get to heaven and look around, what use to be so great to us on earth we won't even notice any long, and that which we will be is for eternity. We tend to think when someone is gone and no longer on this earth they will miss this or miss that – they a'nt miss'n noth'n. The things of this earth we give value to, such as water falls, majestic mountains, beautiful flowers, sunsets and sunrises, etc., these were all created by the God who dwells in heaven.

If the earth looks like this what must the place it was created from be like. We have to give ourselves a head and heart adjustment. Every day we should be thinking of God, and maybe we should add of thinking of where He dwells, where we shall dwell. I'm sure we won't get it right, for who can imagine, but we should consider the greatness that has to be that place where God dwells.

It may be that as we begin to think this way we will find this place we live, even as great as it is, begin to become less and less important to us compared to where God is. Then will develop the yearning within us looking forward to the day the Father has set for us to come to Him. Paul speaks of this, *"For to me to live is Christ, and to die is gain. If it is to be life in the flesh, that means fruitful labor for me. Yet which I shall choose I cannot tell. I am hard pressed between the two. My desire is to depart and be with Christ, for that is far better. But to remain in the flesh is more necessary on your account"* (Philp. 1:21-24 RSV).

Paul had this desire, he look forward to that day, yet desiring more to be here serving the Lord in help to us. In our reading in 1 John today He tells us we are God's children. If we are children then our homeplace is where God is. Now that we are saved in a sense we are foreigners here on earth. John goes on, *"Beloved, now are we children of God, and it is not yet made manifest what we shall be. We know that, if he shall be manifested, we shall be like him; for we shall see him even as he is"* (3:2 ASV). In a way there is a longing in John's words to get to that place where he will be like his Lord. Do you look forward to this?

'How long am I going to have to be with you?' Jesus said this to the crowd, and maybe even to his disciples.[1] Sometimes the disciples didn't get it. Other times He said to them, 'Do you not yet understand?'[2] Of the state they were in, not having the salvation that would later be given by Christ's death, it was difficult for them to know or understand. Yet we would think, 'they walked with Jesus'.

They walked with Jesus, saw His great miracles, heard His great truths that He taught. After centuries of tradition with all the Jews, it was probably hard for them to grasp who Jesus was, and what He was telling them. Yet they walked with Jesus, ate with Jesus, touched Him, and traveled with Him, so they should have got something. Gradually they did. Part of the problem was they had a different outcome in mind than did Jesus. Thinking we got it figured out is sometimes what keeps us from seeing also.

The Disciples at some point figured out Jesus was the son of David, they were sure that by the power of God He was going to take back the throne, conquer the Romans, and rule the world from Jerusalem. Not quite what Jesus had in mind. How many times do we, because we have a thought in our mind beforehand miss what the Lord is saying? Sometimes it is what we have been taught in error, or we listened and concluded in error coming up with that which is not what the scripture is really speaking of and we miss it altogether.

After being a Christian for a few years we develop preconceived ideas and thoughts. We read through a scripture thinking, 'I know what this is about', and we don't even hear the words even though we are reading them. It helps to switch translations every so often so we are not hearing exactly the same words over and over. We should not get down on ourselves if we don't get it, sometimes the disciple didn't either.

We need to enter the word of God asking Him what new understanding does He have for us today. No matter how much you learn about the Bible and about God He always has more for us. There is another world out there God is trying to tell us about.

Interesting thing is Paul kinda turns it around saying this is a foreign place we are in, that we are citizens of somewhere else, *"For our citizenship is in heaven, from which we also eagerly wait for a Savior, the Lord Jesus Christ; who will transform the body of our lowly condition into conformity with His glorious body, by the exertion of the power that He has even to subject all things to Himself"* (Philp. 3:20&21 NASB).

Even though Paul was still here on earth in a way he saw himself as belonging to heaven.[3] There is so much in the word of God we will spend the rest of our life here on earth learning even so much more. Then when we get to heaven we will find out about the large great amount we didn't know.

God is beyond our understanding, His knowledge is unending, His character is unknowable while we are still here in this world. What a surprise we will have when we enter heaven. Yes, sometimes we think we will never get it, never understand. Jesus knew we would have trouble, He set us a helper, *"But the Helper, the Holy Spirit, whom the Father will send in my name, he will teach you all things and bring to your remembrance all that I have said to you"* (Jn. 14:26 ESV).

The Holy Spirit is who I look to and listen for when I write. He guides me and shows me what to say. This is the help we all need as we read scripture. The Holy Spirit helps us to know God, and know the Son. Jesus says the Holy Spirit will testify of Him, *"But when the Helper comes, whom I will send to you from the Father, the Spirit of truth, who proceeds from the Father, he will bear witness about me"* (Jn. 15:26 ESV).

We approach the Christmas season when the angels said 'Peace on Earth'. So many want to say this speaks that we could all get along together and be happy. Again we have a preconceived thought about what peace the angel was speaking of and are in error.

In our reading in Luke today we see that this peace was not that which would be between people, Jesus says this, *"Do you think that I have come to give peace on earth? No, I tell you, but rather division; for henceforth in one house there will be five divided, three against two and two against three"* (12:51&52 RSV). The Holy Spirit will help you with what you don't get and that which you do not understand, ask Him to help you.

---

1   Mt.17:17
2   Mt.15:17, 16:9
3   Eph.6:20

All in all is what our God is. Many countries or societies have many gods, one in control of this, another in control of that, and still another in control of other things. Our God is in control of all things. Some might say not, that evil is controlled by the devil. Guess who is in control of the devil, the devil is out on bail right now, but his sentencing is coming up soon.

God is in control of All. What we need to remember is what sin did to the world when Adam and Eve willingly sinned. You might say that was Adam and Eve, tell me truly if you have not done your part to keep sin continuing on in this world. Even nature has been affected by sin entering this world.[1] God is good to us, He gave us a way to receive redemption rather than His wrath as we should receive.

The blood of Christ redeems us. Talk about all in all, the forgiveness we have received is not just all, it is everything. Even our farthest existence of life in eternity is taken care of by God. A lot of times in our thinking of God taking care of us, taking care of our all, we only think of the things of this world we live in now. Our all is taken care of all the way into our eternity. We must be careful of how we judge of if our all is being taken care of by God. Here is what we are told in scripture, *"You ask and do not receive, because you ask with the wrong motives, so that you may spend what you request on your pleasures"* (Jas. 4:3 NASB).

God is in charge of all, in the beginning He said 'let there be', and there was. In the end at the final judgment He will be in charge, and when His gavel comes down all will know where they are going. In this world all messed up by sin, the sin that started in the garden and continues on in our streets today. God interferes when He decides to, our salvation is an interference into this world full of sin. Nothing any would receive because of their sin would be unjust. It is the unjust that is saved by what was done unjustly to the innocent who took what we had coming because of our character.

Our only hope is found in what was done unjustly to the innocent who allowed it to be done to Him. You have heard scripture where it tells us that God swore by Himself because there was none higher to swear by.[2] Well, God Himself within Himself did what mankind could not do making a way we, the sinner, the unjust, could be forgiven, even totally cleansed.[3] How much of an all do you want from a God who owes you nothing? When it comes down to it, forgetting about our stuff of our life in this world, to receive a gift of life saved, in this world and then eternity of life that God is taking care of – how much of an all do you want??

God is all in all providing all that we need now, and all we will need in our future. We have to be careful that what we have the devil doesn't get to sneak into our life to interfere in. The devil thought he should have all, that he should be in charge of all, and if he didn't get it, then his all was not taken care of. When we think of our all the first thing we need to know is we deserve nothing – nothing! All are short, none deserve anything. You ever think about the rainbow, that was God's promise to never destroy the whole earth again because of what mankind deserved.[4] We have a good God, He gives us more than we could ever hope for.

In our reading in 1 John today we read these verses;

"Every one who believes that Jesus is the Christ is a child of God" (5:1 RSV).
"this is the testimony, that God gave us eternal life, and this life is in his Son" (5:11 RSV).
"These things I have written to you who believe in the name of the Son of God, so that you may know that you have eternal life" (5:13 NASB).
"we know that the Son of God has come and has given us understanding, to know him who is true; and we are in him who is true, in his Son Jesus Christ. This is the true God and eternal life" (5:20 RSV).

John makes it very clear, that the greatest thing of all things as a gift has been given to us in and through Jesus Christ, the Son of God. This gift, our salvation, is the greatest of all things and everything else is just perks.

---

1   Rom.8:21
2   Heb.6:13
3   Acts 15:8&9, Rev.1:5, Eph.5:26 (here 'her' is the Church, you are part of the Church)
4   Gen.9:14-16

'You are my pride and joy, the gem that is beautiful to My eye.' Do you think God would ever speak to you this way? And why wouldn't He? He has used up all of His life on the cross to buy you, you must be highly valuable to Him. There is none in this world among us who would give such a high price for any gem, no matter how great. Sometimes we can feel down on ourselves because we are disappointed in our behavior and think God thinks as we do. Is God disappointed in His children sometimes? Yes. But we are His children, He treasures us higher than we could ever know.

He wants us with Him for eternity. Why else would He create us being loving enough to allow us to have free will knowing we would not do right, and then do the work of the cross so we could come back to Him even though we had messed up bigtime? How much do you think He treasures you? He has done everything needed for us to return to Him, it is complete needing no work or performance on our part, the only thing we have to do is surrender to Him accepting what He has done for us.

Look to God, and He will always love you. When you feel you are under His hand of correction remember what He says, *"My son, do not regard lightly the discipline of the Lord, nor lose courage when you are punished by him. For the Lord disciplines him whom he loves, and chastises every son whom he receives"* (Heb. 12:5&6 RSV).

God works in our lives to make us a better person, He guides us and shapes us in various ways. God is preparing us for that day we come to Him to be there forever. Can you imagine forever, and forever, and forever? How much does God love you, are you beginning to get the picture?

You are precious to Him, He has done a lot of work to obtain you, He wants you close to Him. There is even scripture that tells us God is in us and we are in Him. In the spirit realm there is some sort of merging that has taken place and we are part of Him and He is part of us. *"Whoever confesses that Jesus is the Son of God, God abides in him, and he in God. So we know and believe the love God has for us. God is love, and he who abides in love abides in God, and God abides in him"* (1Jn. 4:15&16 RSV).

With someone who loves you so much do you think He would not say, 'You are my pride and joy, the gem that is beautiful to My eye'? We really don't know the fullness of God's love for us, we will experience it when we arrive in heaven. There is no example of love on this earth that will relate the love that God has for each of us. How much love do you think God had when He was taking some dust beginning to shape Adam?

As He added more and more giving the first man that perfect shape that He was envisioning, His love for man was already growing. And then God was finally ready, ready to breathe life into what He created, His love peaked at that moment and He gave man life. You; man, woman, child, God loves you this way as you are part of what He created that day. Not so much depends on what we do for us to have God's love as it is how much He will do. All we have to do is come to Him believing He wants to give it.

There is only one thing in us that gets in the way, our pride. It either keeps us away from what God wants to give us, or it tells God He is wrong to give it to us because we know who we are and should not receive it. God has known who you are from the beginning of time.

In 2Chronicles chapter 6 King Solomon is dedicating the Temple. He asks God not to forget them, and when they mess up and repent that He would forgive. We know Israel messed up, messed up really bad being sent off to Babylon away from the land God had given them. So because Israel messed up so bad are they completely gone today surviving no more?

No, God has brought them back to their land. God's love continues on, it continues on for you also. Today we read the second letter of John to the church. Hear again how He starts the letter, *"because of the truth which abides in us and will be with us for ever: Grace, mercy, and peace will be with us, from God the Father and from Jesus Christ the Father's Son, in truth and love"* (v. 2&3 RSV).

God is always there, always watching, always close by. Did you ever try to imagine what it would have been like to have walked with Jesus as one of the apostles? They knew, but didn't know, this one who they were with. If they knew He was God they would not of thought He was a ghost walking on the water, they would have known it was their Lord. Yet they touched Him, ate with Him, traveled from town to town with Him. As far as human to human they knew Him.

When they were frightened they were going to sink in the storm on the sea He got up and ordered the sea to be claim and it obeyed. They said amongst themselves, 'Who is this?'[1] Well we might not be able to touch Him but we know who He is. He knows everything that goes on, He has always been, He is in all places at the same time, He is enthroned in heaven, He is our savior who has given us life. I don't know if any of His apostles knew any of this, maybe after His resurrection.

In Acts we read this, *"as they were looking, he was taken up; and a cloud received him out of their sight"* (1:9 ASV). By this time they knew He was someone special. To just say they knew He was God would have not included all they knew about Him then. Jesus was someone special, even in the Godhead. The Father gave Him all authority, everything was put under His feet.[2]

By now they had walked, and talked, and ate with the risen Lord. Do you know who He is, has He touched your life and made you a new person? Paul tells us, *"Therefore, if any one is in Christ, he is a new creation; the old has passed away, behold, the new has come"* (2Cor. 5:17 RSV).

God is always close by, He wants to work in our newness making us better and better and better. Have you died to self? If not you may be in the way of what He wants to do in your life. Yesterday we read this, *"Whoever does not carry his own cross and come after Me cannot be My disciple"* (Lk. 14:27 NASB). Do you realize what bearing your cross is? It is yielding ourself to serve others – even when it cost us something. Dying to self is laying no claim to ourselves coming to God with all we are and giving it over to Him, for anything He cares to do with us.

Have you spent your time in your garden of Gethsemane yet? That is where Jesus struggled with Himself giving up all to the Father for what the Father wanted.[3] Have you struggled with yourself yet giving all over to the Father?

When you do you will be surprised of what God is able to do with your life and through your life to others. He is always there, He is wanting to work good things in your life, He is wanting to bring you closer to Him. I believe all of us who are saved want God to be close by us, but we have to get out of the way so He can.

It is not we who approach Him, it is He who comes to us. The Father drew us to Christ so we could be saved. Jesus Christ came from heaven to give us life. It is not our work that gets us close to God, it is the work Jesus did on the cross that allows us to be close to God. He is the One who has made the way. I will come to God in a humble way so that He will take me up. I will start at His feet, and He will take me on from there. Our God is a loving God. He cares about each one of us. He is getting the wedding banquet ready, soon we will be dressed as the bride.[4] What great things God wants to do for us.

In our reading in Luke chapter 15 today we hear Jesus say, *"What man of you, having a hundred sheep, if he has lost one of them, does not leave the ninety-nine in the wilderness, and go after the one which is lost, until he finds it"* (v. 4 RSV). This is what God does to find us, and then hear what He does once we are found, *"And when he comes home, he calls together his friends and his neighbors, saying to them, 'Rejoice with me, for I have found my sheep which was lost"* (v. 6 RSV).

Do you think that if God is so happy when He finds you that He is not going to continue to bless you? How does Jesus depict God the Father in the next parable, *"But while he was still a long way off, his father saw him and felt compassion, and ran and embraced him and kissed him...the father said to his servants, 'Bring quickly the best robe and put it on him, and put a ring on his hand and shoes on his feet. 'And bring the fattened calf and kill it, and let us eat and celebrate"* (v. 20, 22, 23 ESV). Do you think God loves you, do you think God cares?

---

1   Mk.4:41
2   Mt.28:18, 1Cor.15:27
3   Mt.26:42
4   Jn,3:29, Rev.19:7, 21:9

Lord, You are the light of all the world. Can you agree with me in this, that the Lord is the light of all the world? When we think about it in the way He created us, that with these eyes we see all the creation around us. It is interesting when scientists talk about the light spectrum and how it works for us to see colors. It is interesting that something green absorbs all of the colors of the spectrum other than the ones it takes for us to see green and reflects back those colors to us.

It does not generate green, it reflects back to us those colors which come from the source of the light. This process was created by God when He created them all. So a red rose is not red, it absorbs all the colors except red reflecting that back to us, marvelous what God has done. Light is an interesting thing, when it is intense it can bring about fire by its heat, concentrated it can cut through metal, yet broadly it allows us to see to walk this earth. Could we ever list all the effects that took place when God said, 'Let there be light'? We probably could spend a lifetime discovering more and more of what was connected to those words of God. And that was only the first day! There is also our term of finding an understanding to a subject by gaining light into it. There is scripture speaking of this about our spiritual life and growth, *"He was the true Light, which doth enlighten every man, coming to the world"* (Jn. 1:9 YLT).

Jesus was the One who enabled us to know of God, and the great salvation that was offered to us. It was as though He turned a light on in our soul so we could see. Will we ever reach the end of seeing spiritually as we grow and mature? We are constantly being enlighten more and more. [1] It is great the light that lights up the world, such as the sun, the moon, the stars, and the lights that man has discovered and created. Yet the light that shines within us is the greater, and the more illuminating light. Jesus said He is the light which came into the world. [2]

The more we look around us, and within us the more we see. Jesus is even said to be the light of heaven, He would then be the eternal light. This is said about the New Jerusalem, *"And I saw the holy city, new Jerusalem, coming down out of heaven from God, made ready as a bride adorned for her husband... And the city hath no need of the sun, neither of the moon, to shine upon it: for the glory of God did lighten it, and the lamp thereof is the Lamb"* (Rev. 21:2&23 ASV). Paul in speaking to Timothy about Jesus says, *"the King of kings and Lord of lords, who alone possesses immortality and dwells in unapproachable light"* (1Tim. 6:15&16 NASB).

So much light of God. We as mankind have applied a characteristic of UV light that sanitizes making everything in its light pure. We know that God is a holy God, a pure God – interesting thought. The light of God, how much is His light in all applications involved in the world we live in. It seems we cannot even find Him without the light. Lord Jesus, You are the light of all the world. As we begin to look, examine, and see, how immense we find His light to be in this world. Jesus is the One who has brought the light of God into the world. The greatest of the punishment of hell is to be separated from that light, the Lord Jesus the Savior, *"These will pay the penalty of eternal destruction, away from the presence of the Lord"* (1Thes. 1:9 NASB).

Without the Lord they have no light. This is what we read in Jude today, *"These are spots in your love feasts, while they feast with you without fear, serving only themselves. They are clouds without water, carried about by the winds; late autumn trees without fruit, twice dead, pulled up by the roots; raging waves of the sea, foaming up their own shame; wandering stars for whom is reserved the blackness of darkness forever"* (v. 12&13 NKJV).

By the light of God that Jesus has brought to us we won't be in this blackness of darkness. There are many references in the scriptures about stumbling, and that we do not because we have the light. [3] With that in mind let's read Jude's closing, *"Now to him who is able to keep you from stumbling and to present you blameless before the presence of his glory"* (v. 24 ESV). Lord, You are the light of all the world.

---

1   Eph.3:9
2   Jn.12:46
3   1Jn.20:10

There will come a day we all will find there is no truth except from God. As the world approaches the time of the end we are told there will be less and less truth in the world. It will be a world that most people turn away from God, they will be cold-hearted toward each other.[1] Their sole purpose of life will be for self, none other will matter other than their own use of others for self. Scripture is full of these declarations, even Jesus speaks of some of them. I don't know when this will arrive, will it arrive in my generation, the next generation, or yet many generations from now. The thing is it will come, the end will come, just before the end things will be strange – and then steps in the antichrist who seems to fix everything.[2]

The thing for us as believers is to stay close to God, to be the five virgins with plenty of oil in our lamps,[3] the watchman keeping an eye on the horizon,[4] the servant busy at his work,[5] the shepherd taking care of the flock.[6] We are to live one day at a time keeping our eyes open and our spiritual ears tuned into God. It is not our job to predict the future of the day of Christ's return, God does that (He does speak through prophets of some things to come).

We are to be about the work God assigns to each one of us individually,[7] and to the Gospel. If we spend time trying to figure Christ's return of when, how many months, how many years, or even if it will be next month, what time have we used up that we were supposed to be doing that work God had told us personally we were to be doing and of the spreading of the Gospel? We have to be careful where and how we spend our time, or when we get to heaven God will be asking why we did not do what He assigned to us to do.

Tomorrow is out of our hands, we may make tentative plans but God makes the final decision about the tomorrow for each of us. Look at what the man was told who built bigger barns for his bumper crop, **'tomorrow someone else will have them because you won't be here.'**[8] God has overriding control of everything, and knows all that will be – we need to stay tuned into Him. God's word, which we all have a copy, is truth, and we need to be in it often. There He tells us how tomorrow will be, how we should be today, and what He has to say to us. The one thing Jesus told us to be very busy at is to love one another.

This will even help us to spread the Gospel, we will be wanting to tell others, not the what they got'a do for God, but how much God loves them and what He wants to do for them. God does not have a quota that He wants us to meet, He has a list of who He is calling.[9] We are to help them find Him. One of these days there will be very little truth left in the world.

We need to be very grateful that we have found the truth. Our life with the Lord is very important, it is what will get us through the day if we find we are in the generation when the truth of God vanishes away. The believers in that generation will have to depend on the truth they have because they will not be hearing any in the world. It may come to where every conversation will be based on a lie, a lie that will help self only, not caring about any others.

This is not the kind of world we want to live in but God has told us it is coming, the thing we don't know is when. The cultivated life with God is what will get us through it if we find ourselves in it. We began our reading in Revelation today. God wants us to know, it opens this way, *"The revelation of Jesus Christ, which God gave him to show to his servants"* (ESV).

God establishes who He is, *"I am the Alpha and the Omega, the Beginning and the End,"* says the Lord, *"who is and who was and who is to come, the Almighty"* (1:8 NKJV). There is a sure sense of authority there, our God is in charge. At the very end, when all is done, we will be with Him in the New Heaven, the New Jerusalem, on the New Earth. There is an assurance in God, and an assurance for us who will be with Him.

In Luke today we read what Jesus said about His return, none would miss it, all would know it, *"For just like the lightning, when it flashes out of one part of the sky, shines to the other part of the sky, so will the Son of Man be in His day"* (Lk. 17:24 NASB). But in that day it will be as in the days of Noah when only eight followed. Stay close to God for He is our only sure hope.

---

1   Mt.24:12
2   2Thes. 2:3,4,9,10,12
3   Mt.25:4&10
4   Eze.33:2&3 in a New Testament sense.
5   1Cor.15:58, 2Cor.9:8, Col.1:10, Heb.6:10-12
6   Mt.24:45&46
7   Mk.13:34 'to each his work', Eph.4:12&16
8   Lk.12:18
9   Rev.3:5

Why? Here is a God who is master of the universe, holder of all time, creator of all we know, declarer of holiness, displayer of the only true righteousness, why, why would He want to know me? Do you feel that way sometimes? I think we all ask ourselves that question at one time or another in our life. It does not make sense in our mind, but we have to remember we are the created, He is the creator.

There are things He is going to do, things He is going to think, ways He is going to move that make no sense to us. It is because that is the part of Him that goes beyond what He put in us. In His image does not mean exact copy, it means some things of Himself He put in us, and some things He did not. A watchmaker can make all the intricate parts needed, put them together just right, and in a sense make it come alive as he starts the mechanism and it starts to tic, tic-tock, tic-tock, it is almost like a heart beating. Does the watch know what the maker knows, can it move like the maker moves, can it think of the things the watchmaker thinks? We are the watch, lots of moving parts, we tic to the beat He gave us, but we are not the maker. Now once we've settled that let us take our eyes off of ourselves as we have judged ourselves and put our eyes on our maker, that is where we will find our answer of why.

First of all He was when nothing else yet was. We are His imagination, we are His dream, we are what He thought up in His mind and desired to make. There are massive amounts of information in action in the first two chapters of Genesis, we just don't know how to decipher them. We just see on the surface of what was going on. When we ourselves start to think figuring something out or how to make something we say we got the wheels in our heads turning.

With God it was way more than wheels turning, think about it for a moment. What all was going on that things came into being possibly just because God was thinking it, or that He had such authority that when God said to be, there was no way to not be, that it must come into existence. That is only a couple things we can think, what about all the things that went on that we have no capacity to think? Oh the amount of things going on in those first two chapters, how could we possibly know? A God like this, and He decides to love us, and know us, and to bless us.

Even if He was to explain it all to us we probably wouldn't understand any. We are told many things throughout the Bible as God tries to communicate a little to us, and some of that at times is difficult to grasp. At least we are told this about when we get to heaven, *"For now we see obscurely in a mirror, but then it will be face to face. Now I know partly; then I will know fully, just as God has fully known me"* (1Cor. 13:12 CJB).

That is a great thing to look forward to, but for now we are here. This is where our faith is necessary, we have to believe what God says is true. If He says He loves us, He loves us. If He says He is going to give to us, then He gives to us. If He says He wants to know us, then we need to know that He really wants to know us. He doesn't what to know all about us, He knew us even before we were born,[1] He wants to know us in relationship, a relationship takes at least two. Believe it when He says He loves you, be willing to get close, allow Him to touch your heart.[2] Don't be so protective of God in judging yourself keeping yourself away from God because you are such that He should not associate with you.

In the very beginning of Jesus' ministry in Luke we hear someone else feeling that way, *"But Simon Peter, when he saw it, fell down at Jesus' knees, saying, Depart from me; for I am a sinful man, O Lord"* (5:8 ASV). Yet we all know Jesus said to Peter, '**Come**'.

We must be willing to believe God wants to know us, wants to get close, we are not so messed up He wants us to stay away. The only thing He wants from us is that we repent. Here is what we read in Luke today, *"But the tax-collector, standing far off, would not even raise his eyes toward heaven, but beat his breast and said, 'God! Have mercy on me, sinner that I am!' I tell you, this man went down to his home right with God rather than the other. For everyone who exalts himself will be humbled, but everyone who humbles himself will be exalted"* (18:13&14 CJB). Take a chance, let God love you.

---

1   Ps.139:16
2   Jas.4:8

'**Thy Kingdom come Thy will be done.**' How many times do we say this, how many times do we really mean it? If we truly mean it there are many of our ways that have to change. I don't know about you, but I know I don't always live as the will of God would be for me.

I am very grateful for the measuring up I need Jesus has done for me on the cross. There is no way I would get to heaven if it was not for what Jesus, and the Father, and the Holy Spirit, have done for me. One thing, that is all it takes, one sin that disqualifies any of us from getting into heaven on our own merit. Nothing is permitted into the dwelling place of God, to be in the presence of God, that is not completely holy. I am only holy because of what Christ Jesus has done for me, and being cleansed in His blood.

He gave me forgiveness of my sins and washed me in His blood, *"But you were washed, you were sanctified, you were justified in the name of the Lord Jesus Christ and in the Spirit of our God"* (1Cor. 6:11 RSV). and *"Purify me with hyssop, and I shall be clean: Wash me, and I shall be whiter than snow"* (Ps. 51:7 ASV). and *"though your sins be as scarlet, they shall be as white as snow"* (Isa. 1:18 ASV). and *"To Him who loved us and washed us from our sins in His own blood"* (Rev. 1:5 NKJV).

In the verse from Corinthians above it does not say 'we will be (as we work at it) sanctified', it says 'you were sanctified'. All of those things said about us in that verse are in the past tense, they have already been done by someone else. Jesus declared, *"It is finished: and he bowed his head, and gave up his spirit"* (Jn. 19:30 ASV). From time to time we need to visit this place, knowing how unworthy we are, and knowing how we have been made holy to be accepted by God. When we truly visit it the thanksgivings will come forth, and spawning from it comes Praise and Worship.

Our flesh doesn't always want to worship, but in our hearts, we know why we should, don't let your flesh win the battle. God is an awesome God, and He would still be awesome even if He had not provided a way for us to be saved, He would still be an awesome God. When we see the true picture of Him, and the true picture of us, we realize when we go to Him for salvation and He purchases us by His blood there is nothing left of us that is ours. We don't like the word 'slave' because we connect it with brutality and cruelness, that is not what it means, that was the character of the slave owner.

The basic meaning of 'slave' is fully owned by another. We are slaves belonging to Christ Jesus who paid a high price[1] of His own blood for us, how can we push back from that trying to say we are not exactly slaves? I belong to someone else, He has the full right to say what is to go on in my life. We have a very forgiving Lord who does not force us into every way He wants. The more we see the truth the more affection we find in our hearts for the Lord.

We were in a heap of trouble, and we needed help to get out of it. The heart of God is revealed in what He says about Israel in Micah 2:13. In the verses before God was talking about their evil and then says this, *"He who opens the breach goes up before them; they will break through and pass the gate, going out by it. Their king will pass on before them, the LORD at their head"* (ESV).

In our reading in Luke today the tax collector Zacchaeus, which the Jews seen as evil, was accepted by Jesus. In an action of repentance Zacchaeus gave half of his goods to the poor and offered to repay anyone he cheated fourfold. I don't think any of those Pharisees who were condemning him would have done such. When Jesus saw Zacchaeus' heart He said, *"To-day salvation did come to this house"* (19:9 YLT). Jesus is looking for a heart of repentance, not an accomplishment of works.

In Revelation today we read about the Laodicea Christian types. Jesus said they had become lukewarm. Jesus did not condemn them, but called trying to get their attention and said this, *"Those whom I love, I reprove and discipline, so be zealous and repent. Behold, I stand at the door and knock. If any one hears my voice and opens the door, I will come in to him and eat with him, and he with me"* (3:19&20 ESV). Jesus is always welcoming, always waiting for a repentant heart.

---

1   1Cor.6:20, 7:23

All things will come to an end. We are in a temporary world and life. For us who are saved there is eternal life, but it won't be in this world. This one will be put away like an old garment[1] and then there will be a new one which will be forever[2]. All things as we know it will come to an end, except our relationship with the Lord. Who we are will even change, we will have a new makeup in a resurrected purely holy body living in a totally different form of life. When all this comes about we don't know. The disciples ask Jesus when, He said times are left up to the Father's authority.[3]

The only thing we know is Jesus told us about what the signs of the end were going to be.[4] There are many things to take place yet so we need to be doing the work of the Kingdom. In the end, there may be few of us who believe, Jesus said, in the end, it would be as in the days of Noah, people will be busy about their lives with little or no thought of God. There is a verse in the Bible that Jesus says that has always bothered me a bit, *"when the Son of man comes, will he find faith on earth?"* (Lk. 18:8 RSV).

It sorrows me to think this is the condition the world will come to before the Lord returns. All will come to an end, everything as we know it will be gone. What this leaves to us now is that we live in each day as the Lord taught us to be living. We won't be looking into the sky every day and searching around us for the signs, we will be doing the Lord's work. When He comes He won't miss us, He knows right where we are. We are to be letting others know He is coming, and to be building up His Church. I want to be looking every day for God with my heart, reaching out to Him as He reaches out toward me.

I want the best relationship I can have with Him now. If I have that He will take care of the later. I will arrive in heaven just as He has planned. Instead of keeping your eyes to the sky how about keeping your eyes to Jesus? One of these days we will be in a New Jerusalem on a New Earth in the presence of our God forever[5]. For now we are to live the life Jesus taught us, living in this world to the fullest we can for Him. We have a life to live in this world, and it needs to be shaped and guided by the ways of God for us. There are many around us who are not living God's way.

We are to tell them about Him, but we cannot force them to live God's way, the only thing we can do is live it before them to see. There were those in the Old Testament that were not part of Israel but believed in God because they saw He was with them. Could it be that those you cannot convince by your words will be convinced by the way you live your life.

God is not the only one watching how we live. Even the most vial person acting in vial ways towards you is watching what you do. Sometimes our greatest witnessing is done without words. There is one other thing here, we are not the only one witnessing about Jesus, *"But when the Helper comes, whom I shall send to you from the Father, the Spirit of truth who proceeds from the Father, He will testify of Me"* (Jn. 15:26 NKJV).

When the Holy Spirit convinces someone they need Jesus in their life, sometimes the Holy Spirit needs someone with boots on the ground to help that person into the Kingdom, are you available? Not anything of this world will last forever, but until the end does come we know what it is we must be about. How many can we help before the end is here?

As we think about the end we read Jesus say this in Luke today, *"those who are accounted worthy to attain to that age and to the resurrection from the dead"* (20:35&36 RSV). We are counted worthy by what Christ has done for us on the cross dying in our place. We will be accepted because of what He has done. And in Revelation we read some of what we will see, *"and behold, there was a throne set in heaven, and one sitting upon the throne; and he that sat was to look upon like a jasper stone and a sardius: and there was a rainbow round about the throne, like an emerald to look upon..and before the throne, as it were a sea of glass like a crystal"* (4:2,3,6 ASV). All of chapter 4 tells us much. All things of this world will come to an end, and then our life in eternity starts.

---

1   Isa.51:6, Heb.1:10-12
2   Isa.66:22, Rev.21:1
3   Acts 1:7
4   Mt. chapter 24, Mk. chapter 13, Lk. chapter 21
5   2Pet.3:10,12,13, Rev.21:1, Ps.102:25-27

Why praise at all? If we only praise on church day why praise at all? Is not God worthy all the days of the week? Even in the offering made by the son of those kicked out of the garden of Eden, there was praise to God. [1] Down through the ages, there has been praise by many we read of in the Bible. David and the other Psalm writers speak much about praise to God.

The apostle Paul said to rejoice in the Lord always – rejoicing brings praise for what God has done. If God had only given us salvation and nothing more in our remaining life on this earth it would be enough to praise Him. Do you take time to review the past days to see where God has given more gifts of blessings in your life? If we look and we see we will praise, we will rejoice, we will worship – have you looked?

Our minds and thoughts sometimes are like the evening news broadcast – only the bad news gets our attention. We are quick to complain about the bad, are we as quick to praise about the good? Some of this is about conditioning. We may need to start with a reminder, a note to ourselves: a set alarm in our smartphone or our computer to ask ourselves, 'Did I see anything good today that God has done?' After a while we won't need the reminder anymore, we will be excited about what God is doing every day and will look with expectation to see what God is doing now.

We have a great God, He is doing great things. If we begin to look and see what God is doing it will strengthen our faith in Him. We who are saved are children of God, [2] He cares for His kids. Have you ever seen the kid who though their parent was the greatest, their parent could do anything. Are you that way about your heavenly Father?

For all who see their heavenly Father like that little child have the expectation that all He does is good, and we are excited with anticipation about what He is going to do next. Jesus said we have to come like little children to God, maybe this expectation is part of that. When we see all the great things God is doing in lives of others and our own it causes praise to well up in us from our deepest places within. Sometimes it is hard to see what God is doing in us so maybe we should search to see what He is doing in others.

Get a report from a missionary in Africa, or another country where God is touching them, and see what God is doing there. It is amazing what God is doing in some of the most unexpected places in the world. Jesus said; *"I praise You, Father, Lord of heaven and earth, that You have hidden these things from the wise and intelligent and have revealed them to infants. Yes, Father, for doing so was well pleasing in Your sight"* (Lk. 10:21 NASB). [A thought: maybe we in America – even us who are Christians – have become more like the 'sophisticated and cunning' that Jesus speaks about, and those God is working through in unexpected places have that childlike walk with God.]

Praise, it comes from knowing who God is and what He is doing. Even when things in our lives don't seem to be going so well, look to the promises Jesus spoke to us in our reading today about what is coming for those who follow Him, *"But not a hair of your head will perish. By your steadfastness and patient endurance you shall win the true life of your souls"* (Lk. 21:18&19 AMPC). If we are in Christ having salvation by His blood there is nothing the world, or even satan, can do to keep us from going to heaven, the true life for eternity.

In our reading now in Revelation we get a peak of what heaven will be and what will go on there. In our reading in chapter 5 today we see the praise God is receiving in v. 9-14. Hear again what v. 13 says; *"And I heard every created thing which is in heaven, or on the earth, or under the earth, or on the sea, and all the things in them, saying, "To Him who sits on the throne and to the Lamb be the blessing, the honor, the glory, and the dominion forever and ever"* (NASB). The question at the beginning today is, **'why praise at all'.** Can you answer that question now to yourself and any other person who would ask it?

---

1   Gen.4:3&4
2   1Jn.3:1

Glory to God in all things. Surely all glory goes to God. Jesus came from God to earth to help us who were poor, poor in Spirit that is. For most of us we were messed up and didn't even know it. The devil had us so blinded we didn't even know there was sin, we didn't know there was life after death. For many of the rest they thought there was life after death and that they were in. They were so blinded they did not know how holy they had to be to get into heaven.

I am very glad we found the truth about our sins and the power of the blood of Christ that washed us clean. Can glory truly be given to anyone else for what we have received? It is right to glorify the Lord God. A couple of days ago we read about Jesus' Triumphal Entry.

There is something to see here; Jesus was the Son of God, He came from heaven to help mankind, in His whole ministry He never sinned, He was the Holy One. He deserved glory and told the Pharisees if the people did not praise Him then the stone would break out in praise because He deserved glory. It is not God that demands glory, it is His character that creation recognizes must have glory given to Him.

In Isaiah God says that because the word from His mouth is going to accomplish and bring such joy that the mountain shall sing and the trees will clap. *"so shall my word be that goes out from my mouth; it shall not return to me empty, but it shall accomplish that which I purpose, and shall succeed in the thing for which I sent it. "For you shall go out in joy and be led forth in peace; the mountains and the hills before you shall break forth into singing, and all the trees of the field shall clap their hands"* (55:11&12 ESV).

We could say that poetically the writer wants to show the great joy that it will be. But truly how do we know how the mountains and trees act before God? If Jesus says the stones would cry out, then maybe the mountains would sing, and the trees would clap. Do you know in the universe of creation how much Glory God deserves?

'**To God be the glory, great things He has done.**' We sing it, is it not true, such great things that God has done? The greater we see God the greater glory we realizes He deserves. Sometimes it takes those personal acts of God in our lives to open our eyes that we can see. Until we each reach heaven we will not know the fullness of the glory God should be given, but we can begin giving some even as we are here now.

Can you begin to think of each good thing God has done for you in your life making a list? Is there two, three, four? How many are there as you take time to remember, is the amount of glory God deserves growing with the list? We will never finish giving God enough glory for what He has done in our lives, let alone in the whole universe.

My life, it would be in hell for eternity if it was not for the redemptive work God done so I could be forgiven, and made holy. You may not feel holy, I don't feel holy, but I know what we have been told, that we have been washed in the blood of Christ, we have been cleansed by His blood,[1] that makes us pure, that makes us holy. Because we have been made holy we will be permitted into heaven.

In our reading today in Luke it begins the last day of Jesus before His death on the cross. At the Passover meal He tells the disciples this, *"And he took bread, and when he had given thanks he broke it and gave it to them, saying, "This is my body which is given for you. Do this in remembrance of me"* (22:19&20 RSV). Knowing that to give this to us Jesus went through such a struggle within Himself to do the Father's will that *"His sweat became like great drops of blood falling down to the ground"* (v. 44 NKJV). As we begin to know what He did, and focusing on it we even begin a little bit to feel what Jesus went through, our glory to Him rises more and more. **Yes, Glory to God in all things!**

---

1   Rev.1:5

'I have no fear.' This should be the statement we all could make. We serve a God who has made the way clear to get to Him. He is compassionate and kind. He reaches out to us in love. In knowing our character and sin we tend to shy away at times. He was willing to save us even while we were yet in sin so why should we shy away now.[1] The other thing is in our shying away we may think we are hiding something from Him.

God sees all, knows all, even the very private thoughts of our heart.[2] He has sent Christ to pay for our sins, once the blood of Christ is applied to our sins we are clean, completely clean. *"and from Jesus Christ, the faithful witness, the firstborn from the dead, and the ruler over the kings of the earth. To Him who loved us and washed us from our sins in His own blood"* (Rev. 1:5 NKJV).

Is there anything that Jesus does that is incomplete? If He has washed us are we not completely clean? If after salvation, in which we were made completely clean, we sin again asking forgiveness, are we not made completely clean again? *"but if we walk in the light, as he is in the light, we have fellowship with one another, and the blood of Jesus his Son cleanses us from all sin...I am writing this to you so that you may not sin; but if any one does sin, we have an advocate with the Father, Jesus Christ the righteous...You know that he appeared to take away sins, and in him there is no sin"* (1Jn. 1:7, 2:1, 3:5 RSV).

We are forgiven, we are cleansed, we are washed in the blood of Christ. It was the blood of the sacrifice of the heavenly Lamb which has made us clean. In the Old Testament it was the blood of another, the animal which was given in sacrificed, which covered the sins of the people. This seems to be the Law of God. It may even have been given to the Israelites as a preparation for us to know what the blood of Christ does for us all. If we were just going along in life without this awareness of the sacrifice, and God said to us, 'I have killed Him for your benefit' would we not think that barbaric?

The Law of the sacrifice was given to the Jews, who had God's word given through Moses, so we would know what the sacrifice accomplishes. Jesus has been given as that perfect sacrifice, His blood cleanses those who come to Him. We are no longer under the Law of the Old Covenant, we are under the Law of the New Covenant, yet even though the old Law does not apply to us it still stands, it still has power. Jesus said, *"For truly, I say to you, till heaven and earth pass away, not an iota, not a dot, will pass from the law until all is accomplished"* (Mt. 5:18 RSV).

The sacrifice of Jesus giving His blood would have no value if the Law of the sacrifice did not still have force. By His blood through the Law we are released from the Law to receive salvation through the gospel, through the New Covenant based on the work of Christ. If we have repented asking forgiveness at our salvation, and repent when we slipped afterward, we are cleansed. So then we have no reason to shy away from God. We may have been guilty, but we have been cleansed, therefore we should have no fear before God.

All of Luke chapter 23 is about all that Jesus went through for us, for our redemption. There are three we should take note of: first there is Pilate who could find no wrong in Jesus, second there is Herod who only wanted to see Jesus work some magic, third we see the thief on the cross who repented of heart knowing his own guilt and confessing he knew Jesus was innocent.

Even though we do not hear the thief say the words, Jesus reads the heart, and told the thief he would be with Him in paradise. Which are you? Like Pilate who found no wrong in Jesus but seemingly went no further? Like Herod who only wants to see some miracles worked by Jesus? Or are you like the thief who repented of heart asking Jesus that he might be with Him? If you are as the third all is forgiven with no reason to fear.

---

1   Rom.5:8
2   1Chr.28:9, Job 42:2

"I am with you always, even unto the end of the world" (Mt. 28:20 ASV). This is a comforting thought, it goes along with, 'I will never leave you nor forsake you.' For all of us who are saved Jesus is always there. You might think, 'was He there when I.......?' Yes, He was there, nothing is hidden from God. Even with all He knows about us He is always with us, there is nothing we do that surprises Him. He forgives, and loves, and takes care. It is hard for us to consider this for it is surely not in our human nature.

This is where the Holy Spirit is renewing us more and more and more.[1] We become less and less and less as we used to be, God is constantly growing us further into the image of Christ. He is always with us, He is always working in us. There is never a moment He is not with us, never a moment He is not working in our life. Just because we do not feel it or see it does not mean He is not there.

As humankind we have developed great technologies. We can start a tunnel from the two different ends with each end moving forward and then they meet in the middle. Those digging in one tunnel cannot see those in the other tunnel, yet they know where they are, and each doing their work completes it such as it is right where it needs to be to meet the other. If man can do this, how much better God? He continues the work in us and when we reach heaven we will be spiritually right where we are supposed to be. We have our part to play, but mostly it is yielding to Him in humility.[2]

For us now it is a matter of presenting ourselves to Him for the work. I see some Christians so hard at work trying to accomplish the long list of good works, they are so busy God can't get a hand in sideways to do much in their lives. It takes a denying of self, a presenting of our self in a humble manner, and an offering of our self for whatever He may want of us. You may not want to be a missionary, but if that is what God wants are you willing to offer yourself? Are you willing to offer yourself to any ministry He may want you in? When we are fully willing is when God is fully able to work in us. God is always with you, and He is always working in you, how much do you want to be fully what He wants? It is all about surrender, the more we surrender the more He works, and the more we feel His presences.

It comes down to this, God is always there, how much will you allow Him to be there? From the time we ask Jesus into our life as Lord and Savior God is there and we begin to grow. How fast and full do you want to grow? God wants to be more and more in your life working in you and through you to others, how much do you want this? There is much we can do to further the Kingdom of Jesus here in this world. Are you willing to move the direction He wants you to move?

It is easy to go along raking in the benefits, are you willing to be part of what builds the Kingdom? Are you willing to be sent by Jesus? It might be to the other side of the world or it might be to your knees to be an intercessor in prayer. Jesus is always with you, are you willing to be more with Him listening to what He has for you to do? In our reading of Luke today Jesus is concluding His time on earth with His disciples. He says this to them, *"Thus it is written, that the Christ should suffer, and rise again from the dead the third day; and that repentance and remission of sins should be preached in his name unto all the nations, beginning from Jerusalem"* (24:46&47 ASV).

This is what Jesus called us His followers to do. Some may go to far off lands, some may pray, some may support, some may teach, and some may preach. The thing is we are all to be for this cause, that mankind would hear the gospel and some be saved. We are all to play a part, but we have to check with Jesus to know what the assignment is He has for each of us.

---

1   Tit.3:5
2   Jas.4:10

Life is good. Three words, do you believe them? A short phrase, but if we have Jesus in our lives, because of Him it is good. There may be some difficult times in our life here in this world, Jesus said if they persecuted Him they would persecute us because we belong to Him. Yet because we belong to Him life is good.

Besides salvation, how many other things has God brought to your life that are good? We should look at some of those people we read of in the Bible. We know of Noah, and then Abraham and Sarah, then comes along Moses, all these because of God in their lives, they surely felt life for them was good. How about Naomi, she had a very hard life? Let's talk about Ruth - lost a husband early, struggles in life with Naomi who she refused to leave all alone. With Ruth being a Moabite who knows how she was treated in Israel at first, Naomi was welcomed back but nothing is said about her daughter-in-law.

For these two life had been hard for each. But God gave a turn of events for them and Ruth becomes the wife of well-to-do Boaz becoming the great grandmother of King David. At that point in Ruth's life do you believe she thought life is good. Now back to Naomi, here is what the word tells us, *"Then the women said to Naomi, "Blessed is the LORD who has not left you without a redeemer today, and may his name become famous in Israel. "May he also be to you one who restores life and sustains your old age; for your daughter-in-law, who loves you and is better to you than seven sons, has given birth to him." Then Naomi took the child and laid him in her lap, and became his nurse"*(Ruth 4:14-16 NASB).

With that child on her lap do you think Naomi would have said life is good? We see countless ones in the New Testament, many healed of leprosy, the widow given back her son who had died, the Samaritan woman that talked with Jesus at the well – and then all the people from her village.

All of these with the effect in their lives from having a close encounter with Jesus would have surely said life is good. Then there were those in the book of Acts who had their lives blessed because of the risen Lord, they I believe would say life is good. The risen Lord continues to work in our lives bringing about good things. Just the fact that those of us who are saved will be permitted to enter heaven should be enough for all of us to say life is good. Think about it a moment, if you made a line representing eternity (the line would have to keep going in both direction with no end), on that line would be marked your life in this world as a small, small, dot. All the rest of it is your eternity – is life good? Our 70, 80, or even 100 years of life here seems long because we live it one day at a time, but looking back from heaven we may not even notice it.

As we see more and more what God has done for us we begin to see the things that are important in our life, not those other things that had us distracted for a while. I won't say that getting through some of those days are not hard, there are hard days. But we all can look back in our past and know we do get through those hard days.

The Apostle Paul had hard days in his ministry, even stoned and left for dead once. Here was Paul's attitude, *"More than that, I count all things to be loss in view of the surpassing value of knowing Christ Jesus my Lord, for whom I have suffered the loss of all things, and count them mere rubbish, so that I may gain Christ"* (Philp. 3:8 NASB). Just before this Paul says, *"But whatever things were gain to me, these things I have counted as loss because of Christ."* (v. 7 NASB)

Do you think Paul would say life is good? In our beginning of reading in the book of John today he tells us why life is good, *"In him was life, and the life was the light of men. The light shines in the darkness...all who received him, who believed in his name, he gave power to become children of God...And from his fulness have we all received, grace upon grace"* (1:4,5,12,16 RSV). **Life is good.**

Take your time to find the true word of God. It will not be hidden from you if you search for it. You will be rewarded with much joy once you find it. It will comfort you, it will uphold you, it will strengthen you, and it will carry you through. There is nothing on earth greater than the word of God. We are told this about the word of God, *"For the word of God is living and active, sharper than any two-edged sword, piercing to the division of soul and spirit, of joints and marrow, and discerning the thoughts and intentions of the heart"* (Heb. 4:12 RSV).

We mistakenly speak of the word of God as that printed and in our hand. What we have in our hand is only ink on the page showing us what the word of God is for us to read what it is. But the word of God is living, and powerful, and moving, and active all around us. God's word moves things to and fro. It is by the action and authority of the word of God which hold in place the universe, *"For this they willfully forget: that by the word of God the heavens were of old,...the heavens and the earth which are now preserved by the same word"* (2Pet. 3:5&7 NKJV). and *"He [the Son] reflects the glory of God and bears the very stamp of his nature, upholding the universe by his word of power"* (Heb. 1:3 RSV).

It is this word of God that holds and moves all things. The word of God is what was spoken from His mouth and has authority over all things. It was this word of God by which things were created. God said 'let there be' and it existed. We live today because of what God has said. *"Now to Him who is able to establish you according to my gospel and the preaching of Jesus Christ, according to the revelation of the mystery kept secret since the world began but now has been made manifest, and by the prophetic Scriptures[word of God] has been made known to all nations, according to the commandment of the everlasting God"* (Rom. 16:25&26 NKJV).

We have read of this today in Revelation, *"but in the days of the sounding of the seventh angel, when he is about to sound, the mystery of God would be finished, as He declared to His servants the prophets"* (10:7 NKJV). All that God has said will come about, it will be fulfilled.

All of this creation of the universe, and of the earth, and of us will be completed. Then the sun, and moon, and stars, and earth, will all be put away and God will make a new earth with the New Jerusalem coming down out of heaven upon it. *"However, the Day of the Lord will come "like a thief." On that Day the heavens will disappear with a roar, the elements will melt and disintegrate, and the earth and everything in it will be burned up"* (2Pet. 3:10 CJB). and *"And I saw a new heaven and a new earth: for the first heaven and the first earth are passed away; and the sea is no more. And I saw the holy city, new Jerusalem, coming down out of heaven from God, made ready as a bride adorned for her husband. And I heard a great voice out of the throne saying, Behold, the tabernacle of God is with men, and he shall dwell with them, and they shall be his peoples, and God himself shall be with them, and be their God"* (Rev. 21:1-3 ASV).

The words of God will never fail, all will come about just as He has said. *"So will My word be which goes out of My mouth; It will not return to Me empty, Without accomplishing what I desire, And without succeeding in the purpose for which I sent it"* (Isa. 55:11 NASB). We need to be in the word daily to know of God, and all that He has said, and all that He is doing from the creation until the judgment. He will accomplish the end and we who have trusted Him accepting Jesus Christ into our lives trusting the work He did for us on the cross will enter that New Jerusalem and live with God for eternity.

It is time to know we are. We are the child of the King, the Lord of all. He, Jesus Christ, is the sustainer of all who come to Him. We have life in Him, and Him only. No matter how many good things we do, or bad things we do, no one gets to God except by Jesus Christ. Much of the world serves other gods who are false, who are only demons deceiving them. [1] There is only one true God, Yahweh, the three-in-one God. Even with being aware of this there are many in the world who believe in God but will not get to the Father in Heaven because they don't find their way to God through Jesus Christ.

Jesus said, *"I am the way, the truth, and the life. No one comes to the Father except through Me"* (Jn. 14:6 NKJV). So many people try to find a way into the next life but does not want to find it God's way. There seems to be a yearning within most people to find something that is more than themselves. It seems there is an awareness we have that we are not fully complete, that there is something more, or something missing.

In our reading today this seemed to be stirring within Nicodemus when he came to Jesus with his need. Jesus sees right through Nicodemus as He also sees right through each of us. Nicodemus may not have even known this was his need. He may have had another thing bothering him that he came about. No matter what we think our need is, Jesus knows what our true need is. We can't truly see what stirs us sometimes, but Jesus always knows the cure.

Are we willing to lay ourselves open before God for Him to see all we are. We really cannot hide anything from God, but there needs to be an awareness on our part that we have a need of Him, of something that is in our life which we know is amiss. God will help to find what is amiss if we will yield to Him giving Him permission to address it. Nicodemus had a need, Jesus knew what his need was but did not go running him down, Jesus waited until Nicodemus came to Him. We must go to Jesus before He can help us even though He knows what the trouble is.

He will not run us down, He will wait until we come to Him. Even after receiving salvation there are still many troubles in this world that affect us. We will not escape these things completely until we arrive in Paradise and Heaven. Then all tears, and death, and sorrow, and crying, and pain, will be gone [2] but now they are amongst us in this life. As long as we are in this flesh we will have needs, none of us will mature to the place we no longer have needs.

The interesting thing is that as we mature the greater awareness of our needs do we find. Jesus is always waiting for us to come to Him with our needs. He didn't say to Nicodemus, 'Why have you come, what do you want?' Jesus will not turn us away when we come to Him with our needs. It may be we think we know what our need is, but Jesus will know truly what it is, and He will address it. It is up to us to know something is amiss and be willing to go to Jesus seeking His help and truth.

---

1   Duet.32:16&17
2   Rev.21:4

It is a pleasure to know, to know that there is a God that loves us. It seems that all other so-called gods of the world make demands on those who follow them. It is only Yahweh God who sent Jesus from Himself to us in His love to die for us making a way we could not find that we would have an opportunity to enter heaven. Other gods require people to serve and then receive if their work measures up.

Our God measures up for us if we are willing to accept what He has done by Jesus dying on the cross in our place. In His love, God reaches out to us with the gift of salvation that we would receive from Him even before we start to follow. Even then it is not a level in our following that we have to reach in order to continue in salvation. If we give our hearts fully to Jesus Christ who died on the cross for us, in our following this is what God asks from us. You may judge yourself more harshly thinking you have to measure up to a certain mark you have set for yourself, but it is not God's mark He has set.

The greatest thing He asks us to do is die to self, to deny self in our lives, allowing Jesus who we have in our hearts to guide and direct our lives. He will set the goals for us. We are to follow, not to go out forging ahead in a new territory for Him, we are only simply to follow.

Today in our reading we have read of Jesus speaking to the Samaritan woman. She speaks of the controversy of where one ought to worship. Jesus replies that it is neither on the mountain or in Jerusalem, it is worship in Spirit and truth that the Father wants. Yesterday we read of the conversation between Jesus and Nicodemus. Jesus made no high demands on Nicodemus, only that he needed to be born again, born of the Spirit.

Nicodemus, as we all, have been born in the flesh, but Jesus said we must also be born in the Spirit if we are to enter the Kingdom of God. Here again as Jesus speaks to the Samaritan woman He speaks of that of the Spirit. The Spirit is the focus, we must be born in Spirit and we are to worship in Spirit as well as in truth. Many of us may worship in truth, it is truth that God is who has saved us. But do we worship in Spirit? Jesus tells the woman at the well, *"If you knew the gift of God, and who it is that is saying to you, 'Give me a drink,' you would have asked him, and he would have given you living water"* (Jn. 4:10 RSV).

This is speaking of the gift of God, that gift of salvation. Here Jesus calls it **'living water'**. Where else does Jesus relate this gift to water? *"If any one thirst, let him come to me and drink. He who believes in me, as the scripture has said, 'Out of his heart shall flow rivers of living water"* (Jn. 7:37&38 RSV). So here again we hear Jesus speaking of **'living water'**. What is this living water? We are told as we read on in John, *"Now this he said about the Spirit, which those who believed in him were to receive"* (Jn. 7:40 RSV).

So here we are back to the Spirit. It is the Spirit that flows in us, and it is the Spirit which flows out from us to others. Are you letting the Spirit flow? Are you allowing your head to control your heart, controlling what you allow to flow or not flow out of you? It is the heart that must control the head if the Spirit is to follow out of us as living water to a thirsty world. It is the Spirit which speaks in our heart urging us to love others and share of what we have, that they also may receive this gift, this **living water**, this gift of God of salvation.

"I am the light of the world" (Jn. 8:12 ASV). Do we really get this? Jesus came into a dark world where mankind could not really see. Before Jesus came what man saw was only darkness so he thought this was life. Darkness is not life, it is the absence of being able to know. Jesus brought light into the world that we could begin to see truth. For those who are willing to follow Him He gives light so we can see the truth of life.

The greatest truth for us is to realize we are sinners, and, that God loves us and gave a way by which we could be saved even while we were still in our sin. [1] He is good and knows our weakness, providing for us what we could not provide for ourselves. I have said this truth is the greatest truth of all we receive in our lives, the greatest thing of all for us who are in Christ, is that we have received salvation. It is true that it is a great thing that God is in our lives and that Jesus is always with us never to forsake us. [2]

What we need to see here is that even though it is a great thing that God is with us in our lives He would not be there if it were not for this great salvation He has provided for us. I have said many times that if God had only given me salvation and then no other blessing afterward I would have enough to thank and worship Him for the rest of eternity. We must not allow the awareness of the salvation given us to slip into the shadows of our mind. We know of His love, we know of His gift of salvation, because Jesus brought light into the darkness that we could see and receive.

Today in our reading in John chapter 5 Jesus says that for a while John the Baptist was a shining light. (v.35) Then Jesus says, *"But the witness which I have is greater than that of John; for the works which the Father hath given me to accomplish, the very works that I do, bear witness of me, that the Father hath sent me"* (v. 36 ASV). Jesus came as a light greater than that of John. In the second half of John chapter 5 Jesus is revealing truth to us, He is shining light on what we could not see before. There is an interesting thought here, when we are in darkness and a bright light is turned on we are nearly blinded and we are able to see very little. John was sent to be a smaller light than Jesus.

When a smaller light is turned on first in that darkness it prepares us to see the things of the great light when it comes. John was that smaller light so we could see when Jesus came as the great light from heaven. John was sent to prepare the way for Christ. [3] Salvation, what a great thing has been brought to us. We read in John chapter 5 that the Father sent Jesus to accomplish works, and to bring to a finish those works.

Teaching us, bringing the truths of heaven to us, and teaching us how we should live was those works Jesus did for three years in His ministry. But that which finished the works, which made it all possible for us, was His going to the cross to die for us, and then rising from the dead which He has promised to all who follow Him. [4] Jesus is the Light showing us things we could not see. Do you have your eyes open? Are you seeing the things He is showing you?

---

1   Rom.5:8
2   Jn.14:17-19
3   Lk.3:4
4   Jn.11:25, Rom.6:5, 1Cor.15:42-44

Have faith in God. Is this something we need to hear each day? Are we anchored in it and not need to hear it? Is our faith to the fullest not needing any further growth? We all need encouraged now, but one day we won't for we will be with Jesus. Until that day we need all the encouragement we can get. There is encouragement we get from others, but the greatest encouragement is from God's own words. We need to meditate on God's word, carry it in our heart, know it in our mind. God gives if we seek and search, He is the supply of all we need to know. We have people on this earth who have great knowledge, but God knows what they know and so much more. He created man, He created this earth, He spoke and the stars of the universe came into being.

All of the great knowledge we need He has. Does it not seem right we should go to Him for the knowledge we need? His knowledge for us He has put in His word. We have His word given to us so we have it to find knowledge. Do we seek it as one seeks water when they have a great thirst? Are we hungry for it as one who searches for food? Real life is what life? Is it not that eternal life? If eternal life is the goal, and not this temporary life here on earth, then where should we look for the knowledge of it?

We find it in God's word. His word is the revealer of truth, truth about this life on earth, and our lives in heaven that comes after this life. All of truth which we need to know God has put in His word. God's word is living and active stirring within us if we invite it in.[1] It will deliver us to God, it will guide us to Jesus through whom we must go to get to the Father in heaven. Our good deeds will not get us there. Our great study, even the study of God's word, if we don't go to Jesus to receive life, it will not help us. God is the eternal One, and if we are to be in eternity with Him we must have Jesus within us.

We must invite Him into our lives as Lord and King. Jesus will get us to heaven if we yield our lives over to Him. The three-in-one God is the One who is eternal, and if we are to be in eternity with Him the only way is by Jesus. *"I am the way, the truth, and the life. No one comes to the Father except through Me"* (Jn. 14:6 NKJV).

Jesus today in our reading is trying to get this truth across to those He is speaking to. They're all hung up on Moses and manna. Those things were the truth for that time, but Jesus is trying to tell them about the eternal truth. Jesus is saying He is the eternal bread, He is the eternal Passover Lamb, and He will be the great sacrifice given for all mankind. He even says, *"I am the living bread that has come down from heaven; if anyone eats this bread, he will live forever. Furthermore, the bread that I will give is my own flesh; and I will give it for the life of the world...Whoever eats my flesh and drinks my blood lives in me, and I live in him. Just as the living Father sent me, and I live through the Father, so also whoever eats me will live through me"* (Jn. 6:51, 56, 57 CJB).

Since we don't have the thoughts of God then when He speaks truth to us sometimes it is hard to accept.[2] There were those there who were following Jesus until He said these things, and then left Him. We must have the substance of Jesus in our lives. Our nourishment of eternal life comes from Him. Jesus puts it here in terms we understand of how we get nourishment for our lives here on earth. It is Jesus we must spiritually consume, taking Him into our lives so that we live, so that we have eternal life. No matter how difficult it is to accept some of the things God tells us in His word we must say as Peter, *"Lord, to whom shall we go? You have the words of eternal life"* (Jn. 6:68 RSV).

---

1   Heb.4:2
2   Isa.55:8&9

There is a way we all know to go. The struggle is this: what of ourselves do we allow to lead us? There are many forces pulling on us and in us. There are forces outside of us that pull on us, our society that we live in is not prone to follow after God, so they are a force trying to pull us away from God. If we are in the universities or colleges, most pull us away from God, even challenging if there is a God. Many times it is the workplace which does not have Godly ethics, so they pull us away from God. Certain social events and sports many times can pull us away from God.

Then underlying it all is the very enemy of God, the devil who tries to ruin us all.[1] Those of us who are saved know the way to go, but it is difficult to walk the right path at times. This is where we need to be turning to Jesus who is always with us ready to help.[2] You remember the disciples and the storm on the lake, they thought they were going to die. They did not die, when they went to Jesus for help He was ready to help, not only did He save their lives, He made the storm go away.[3] He doesn't always make the storm go away, but He does get us through the storm alive and safe. We should not always conclude He is not helping us because of the difficulties we are in. He did say we would be persecuted, *"A servant is not greater than his lord. If they persecuted me, they will also persecute you"* (Jn. 15:20 ASV).

This does not mean the storm will overtake you, Jesus will get you through. There may be the ultimate persecution that will take someone's life, yet they have the greater victory for they are then with their Lord in heaven. Paul wrestled with the idea, He said if he was to die it would be gain for him, but if he lived on that would be more for Christ and His Kingdom.[4]

Regardless of what we are in, or tempted by, or strongly pulled in the wrong direction, Jesus is always there to help. Jesus is the One who will help us follow the way we know to go. No matter how determined we are to live rightly there will be those times our strength is not enough. So if ultimately we are going to have to ask Jesus for help, why not just invite Him along in all our doings? He is a big guy, we won't be depriving someone else His help they need, Jesus is able to help us all at the same time any time. When Jesus said, 'come to Me you who are heavy laden' He didn't say, 'get in line'.

The only way we are able to go the way we know we should is in relationship with Jesus as He goes along with us to guide and help us. Paul tells us we have a war going on even inside of us, it is the flesh against the Spirit, and the Spirit against the flesh.[5] The thing is which one do we allow to be in charge, which one is leading the way? If we choose the Spirit that helps us to have that relationship with Jesus. If the flesh is allowed to be in charge we will have trouble having very little relationship and needing someone to help get us out of the storm. Our flesh has never wanted to go God's way, and never will. We must strengthen our Spirit which will strengthen our relationship with Jesus.

You may ask, how do I do that? Well if you have a plant which you want to grow well what do you do? It needs the rain and it needs nutrients, the rains come from God, so pray God will rain His blessing on your Spirit. The nutrients are the word of God, make sure your Spirit gets a good dose of the nutrients of the word every day. Jesus gives us the example, in our reading today in John chapter 7 Jesus says this, *"My teaching is not mine, but his that sent me"* (v. 16 ASV). Jesus trusted in the word He received from the Father.

It is easy to assume Jesus had it all, that is how He knew what the Father had for Him to teach. Well yes, and well no. No doubt Jesus had something special that helped Him know, but He still followed the course we need to. *"Jesus advanced in wisdom and stature, and in favor with God and men"* (Lk. 2:52 ASV). In Hebrews it tells us Jesus was as we are, yet did not sin. So how would He increase in wisdom? The other thing Jesus did which we need also is prayer: *"But Jesus Himself would often slip away to the wilderness and pray"* (Lk. 5:16 NASB) [Also see: Mk. 1:35, 6:46, Lk. 6:12, 9:18, 9:29]. We think Jesus had it all together, part of His having it together was His praying to the Father often.

---

1   Rev.12:17
2   Jn.14:23
3   Lk.8:24
4   2Cor.5:8, Philp.1:21-25
5   Gal.5:17

There is love in the world. It is not the love of the of the hippie generation, that was really not love because there was no commitment that went with it. So much of mankind does not have real love for the same reason, that of commitment. We as Christians look to God to learn what real love is. We know Jesus' words that He said, *"Greater love has no one than this, than to lay down one's life for his friends"* (Jn. 15:13 NKJV). Jesus demonstrated His great love for us, the lost, in being willing to go to the cross taking our sins upon Himself and dying for our sins.

Jesus said He loved us and this was His commitment to us, and He also said this, *"the one who believes in Me will live, even if he dies, and everyone who lives and believes in Me will never die"* (Jn. 11:25&26 NASB). This is a depth of love that none of us can accomplish, yet we are to move in that direction of love, and to proceed as far as we can get. This is what the second greatest commandment is about, *"You shall love your neighbor as yourself"* (Mt. 22:39 RSV).

This is the great love in life that God calls us to. This is the love that Jesus demonstrated, but there is also the love of the Father, *"For God so loved the world that He gave His only begotten Son"* (Jn. 3:16 NKJV). This is the very thing God asked of Abraham, *"Take your son, your only son Isaac, whom you love, and go to the land of Moriah, and offer him there as a burnt offering upon one of the mountains of which I shall tell you"* (Gen. 22:2 RSV). Any of us who are fathers cannot even imagine the deep cutting into our hearts this would be, to think of giving our son as a sacrifice. We all know the outcome, that at the last minute the angel of the Lord said, 'STOP, don't lay your hand on him or do anything to him'.

It was that God could 'NOT' say 'STOP' to Himself when He sacrificed Jesus on the cross since it was the way for us to be redeemed. This was the Father's love to us with deep and great sacrificing commitment to us. Jesus never did anything wrong. He, willing out of love, gave His first sacrifice to us by being willing to give up His rightful place in heaven to come to earth taking on the body of a man, *"Christ Jesus, who, though he was in the form of God, did not count equality with God a thing to be grasped, but emptied himself, taking the form of a servant, being born in the likeness of men"* (Philp. 2:6&7 RSV).

This is how we know what love is, it is always about the other, whoever they are. In the same way as Christ, our love to others goes as far as a sacrificing love.[1] A friend of mine many years ago said that if his wife wanted him to go with her window shopping and he wanted to go play golf, that true love for her would be for him to sacrifice his wanting to play golf and to go with her window shopping, which he hated to do. Many times true love is about giving something up, this was not the hippie type of love. Is there love in the world, yes, because God is in the world. And this is how love is in us, *"Beloved, let's love one another; for love is from God, and everyone who loves has been born of God and knows God"* (1Jn. 4:7 NASB).

There are things that change in us in ways we don't know how when we get saved and are re-born. I remember in the week or two after I got saved I had a concern for other people that I didn't have before. That was a love that was born in me at my new birth. It is born in us as a new-born and begins to grow as a new-born child grows. A new-born child grows to a place it begins to walk.

Now it can determine to walk and do things, or it can decide to just sit there even though it knows how to walk. It is the same with us with love born in us, we can decide, as we are instructed, to love others, or we can just sit not using what was born in us. Jesus said, *"A new commandment I give to you, that you love one another; even as I have loved you, that you also love one another"* (Jn. 13:34 RSV). In our reading today in John chapter 8 we read of the woman who the scribes and Pharisees brought to Jesus accusing Her. Jesus in His love did not accuse, but it seems He forgave saying to her, *"Neither do I condemn you; go, and from now on sin no more"* (v. 11 ESV). She also did receive the forgiveness that was offered by His love to all by His dying on the cross for our sins. Jesus says this a few verses later, *"So if the Son makes you free, you will be free indeed"* (v. 36 RSV). There is love in the world.

---

1   1Jn.3:16

'I am God, Do you hear me?' 'I am God who speaks to you.' Do you hear Me?

I wonder how many times God is saying this to us. Do we take time for Him to speak to us? Do we take a moment out of our busy life to listen if God is trying to speak to us? He wants to guide us and help us in our life, are we listening? At this point what is your thought? Not always does God speak to us when we want, He chooses the time and we have to be attentive to hear. There are times He speaks to us in our prayer closet. There are times He speaks to us in the oddest place, even while we are doing the oddest things where we have no thought of Him speaking then.

God is always with us, so then it seems He could speak to us at any time. He chooses the moment, do we know His voice when it comes? It is that still small voice that if we are not listening it will pass on by without any notice by us. Thoughts are going through our minds all the time, it is that thought which seems to have no origination in our mind that may be God speaking. Whatever or however He speaks to us it will never go against His word the Bible. Sometimes it is not even as a thought but more like as instant awareness of something that has no words, only meaning which we give words to. Sometimes it is a bit of scripture we read or hear from another that strikes us in an unusual way where God is wanting us to take note.

Years ago when I was in my first year of Bible College three of us were hired temporarily by the college to do some work. When we took our break we felt led to pray together. During that prayer one of the others was impressed we should read Isa. 55:8&9. He read it and each turned to the other and asked if this spoke to anything in our lives, none of us thought of anything. Yet that scripture has stuck with me ever since. At the moment it didn't seem to be anything unusual, but it did not leave me fading into the mist as other things did. Sometimes what God speaks does not relate to anything at the moment, yet it is still God speaking to us. His voice is a very unusual voice and very easy to miss.

Sometimes I even ask, "Lord was that You speaking?" Sometimes God acts in some way in our presence to guide us. We have to be sensitive in our Spirit to recognize these things when He does them. Those around Jesus had this trouble all through His ministry. In our reading today Jesus heals a blind man who had been blind since birth. The people marveled at the things Jesus did, but the religious leaders wanted to condemn Him for what He did.

The healing and miracles Jesus did was not done according to the leaders acceptable way so they condemned Him for it. One thing Isa. 55:8&9 has taught me is that because of God's ways and thoughts being so high above ours what he does does not always line up with our thoughts. God wants to do good things in our lives but we need to be sure we don't get preconceived ideas that will blind us from hearing what He is saying.

This is what was happening with the religious leaders at the time Jesus was speaking. God was moving, the Father had sent the Son, He was teaching the Jewish people and the rest of the world about His way and His thought. God's way and thought was not to put a New David on the throne to rule the world, it was to put the man Jesus on the cross to die. This made no sense to them, and it would probably make no sense to us if we did not have God's word to tell us why. Jesus was trying to tell them but their ears were closed. God can be speaking to us and we are not hearing.

I hope you remove the obstacles that might be in the way and turn a spiritual ear upward so you can hear what God is saying.

He is the One all must go to. In one way or another, all will go to God. All of us who are saved have gone to Him voluntarily, the rest will be forced to Him for judgment. In the days that Jesus ministered amongst the Jews, there were many who did not accept Him as the Messiah, as the Son of God. We as mankind have a lifetime to find we need to go to Him. We are given an opportunity to know Him. He calls all men to come to Him, but there will be those who refuse, they will refuse over their whole lifetime going by the wide road never entering in the narrow way.

There will be an answering up for all mankind.[1] For those of us who are saved Jesus said this, *"Truly, truly, I say to you, the one who hears My word, and believes Him who sent Me, has eternal life, and does not come into judgment, but has passed out of death into life"* (Jn. 5:24 NASB).

We have listened, and we have heard His word, and we have believed. In this world that narrow way is not approached by many.[2] In the end, they will be forced to where they do not want to go. We hear in Revelation that in the tribulation there will be those who even want the rocks to fall on them to hide them from God. The world does not want to hear that there is an all authoritarian God. That same authoritarian God who forces all the unsaved into judgment, also is that gracious loving God who offers forgiveness and salvation to all who will come and receive it. Who is to say God is not a loving God? We all know because of our sins we deserve the wrath of God, but by His mercy and grace we have been saved freely without cost to us other than surrendering our life to Jesus Christ.

Now that we belong to Christ the King we are taken in with Him when He goes in. We have been reading through many chapters of Revelation and it won't be a good time for the unsaved. During this time now God woos all mankind to Himself without making demands, but at the judgment He will demand to know of their citizenship.[3] Jesus tells a parable of a wedding feast, of how one is rejected, *"when the king came in to look at the guests, he saw there a man who had no wedding garment...Then the king said to the attendants, 'Bind him hand and foot, and cast him into the outer darkness; there men will weep and gnash their teeth"* (Mt. 22:11&13 RSV).

We can be glad we have found the narrow way and we forced ourselves into it. There is a God who has always been, and will always be, who created the whole universe solely by His commands, who cares enough for us to send His Son to die on a cross for our sins and give us salvation. Who other, what other, could compare with Him? There is none, yet He had mercy on us. This is a God that is even difficult to know, not because He does not want to be known, but because of who He in Himself is, how can we know of such a God? We are told that when we arrive in heaven we will then know, *"For now we see obscurely in a mirror, but then it will be face to face. Now I know partly; then I will know fully, just as God has fully known me"* (1Cor. 13:12 CJB).

Until we get to heaven it is our place to get as close to God as we can, hear the things in His word He says about Himself, and believe what He has said. In the end He is the One all must go to. We have received His mercy and grace being given salvation by the Son Jesus who died for us. Can we ever contemplate the full value of our salvation? Just to think of it should carry us to thanksgiving and praise. All other things in our Christian lives are secondary to this. Today in our reading in John chapter 10 Jesus tells us this about Himself, *"I came that they may have life, and have it abundantly. I am the good shepherd. The good shepherd lays down his life for the sheep"* (Jn. 10:10&11 RSV).

As we enter into the Christmas season we should remember the words, **'I came that they may have life'** and know it is about so much more than just the baby Jesus in a manger. This was the great love of a huge God reaching out to us with salvation so that we can spend eternity with Him in heaven. Because Jesus came, when all go to God for judgment, we will be able to enter heaven by the blood of that Perfect Lamb.

---

1   Jn.5:29
2   Mt.7:13&14
3   Eph.2:19, Philp.3:20&21

All things are in the control of God. There would be many who would debate with this. They see so much evil in the world and ask how could God be in control with all this. We have to first see where all this comes from. God created a perfect world, and perfect people in it. The people were so perfect they even had the choice to choose their own future. As we all know they did not choose wisely. The desire to know as God knows was too great and they ate the forbidden fruit. Because of this they were put out of the perfect garden and everything has been imperfect since. [1]

God gives humanity the right to choose, so if He was to override their choice He would be taking away the right He gives to humanity. So the evil in the world is from humanity and in God's control He allows them to have it. This evil which is in the world causes all kinds of trouble, even the sicknesses we have comes from this. When mankind in the garden sinned an infection of sin entered the world affecting everything in the world. God is in the world but does not go against our free will He gave us. In a sense, you could say we set in our own soup. The mess we are in is of our own doing, Adam and Eve sinned, and we have continued it.

We have a gracious God, that even though it is our own doing, He has provided a way we can be forgiven. Sin does not have to take a full toll, anyone who repents taking Christ into their life as Lord and Savior can make it to heaven escaping hell where we all were headed. Even though God does not twist our arm or force us into anything, He says 'Come'.[2]

In this God does take control, He takes control to provide a way we can get to heaven. All things are in control of God, and if He took that control without mercy you and I both know where we would be headed. We as the createe too often only see things from our own vantage point rather than that of the creator. Oh if we could see to trouble our sin causes we would want to run from it as fast as we could. But we can't because we are in this flesh that always wants to take us that direction. Our flesh has been this way ever since the perfect flesh of Adam and Eve was ruined by sin. The best thing we can do is give ourselves over to God receiving His salvation for us and turn away from our own understanding seeking His.

Once we begin to align ourselves with God's truth after a while we begin to see how wrong our way is. This is part of the renewing of our minds. This is a joint effort. The Holy Spirit is the One who does it, but we have to yield ourselves to it, accepting it not pushing back against it when the Holy Spirit begins to change us inside.[3] As long as we think we know something there will not be any room for us to receive the knowing God wants us to have.

As we yield to this there will be a time coming when we do know something, a spiritual something that we get from God. God is wise in all His ways, even in how to help us. God is in full control, the final stage is set. When it comes all will not have a choice, all will be forced to appear before God and the judgment will be His. The very opening of our reading in Revelation today says this, *"Hallelujah! Salvation and glory and power belong to our God, for his judgments are true and just; he has judged the great harlot who corrupted the earth with her fornication, and he has avenged on her the blood of his servants"* (19:1&2 RSV).

Does this sound like a God in control? Until the judgment God does not intervene in the trouble in the world except for those who belong to Him. One occasion in great control we read Jesus did this, *"And a great storm of wind arose...he awoke and...said to the sea, "Peace! Be still!" And the wind ceased, and there was a great calm"* (Mk. 4:37&39 NKJV). God was definitely in control. Again another time in our reading in John today, *"Jesus said, "Take away the stone"...he cried with a loud voice, "Lazarus, come out." The dead man came out"* (11:39,43,44 NKJV). God was defiantly in control.

At times when I think of Jesus I like to think of the Victorious Warrior, **'He comes on a white horse judging and making war, His eyes are like fire and on His head many diadems, clothed with a robe dipped in blood, and from His mouth comes a sharp sword and He rules with a rod of iron.'** (From Rev. 19:11,12,13,15) In the end God **WILL HAVE CONTROL** over all things.

---

1   Rom.8:19-22
2   Mt.11:28, Rev.18:4, 22:17
3   Tit.3:5

There are many who are not willing to give up their life. Even after we have accepted Christ into our lives receiving salvation there is a struggle in giving all over to Him. The ol' flesh does not want to give up easily. We have given over to God as far as needing Him for our salvation, but we still like to feel we can handle most other things in our lives. Sometimes giving up totally causes us to feel like we are a failure. But that feeling of failure only comes from the judgment that is made by ourselves and the others in this world.

In the truth of God, we already are a failure not being able to be truly holy on our own. Yet when we accept Christ we are considered by God to be a success because Jesus has washed us clean and we are considered holy. Amazing, we can be considered holy by what Jesus did for us. Once we are saved Jesus calls us to give everything of our life over to Him, allowing Him to make the decisions, allowing Him to call the shots. *"If anyone would come after me, let him deny himself and take up his cross and follow me"* (Mt. 16:24 ESV).

We all want to follow Jesus, yet before we can follow Jesus we have to pick up our cross, and before that we must deny self. The very first thing we must do is the hardest of all three. It means letting go of the control of our lives. This is scary, it seems uncertain, yet it is the most certain thing we can do because Jesus always knows better than we do. Still, it is hard to turn our lives over to someone else. We have to fully trust Jesus having faith in all that He will do in our lives.

This does not mean to get up in the morning and not move until you hear a command of the Lord. It means trusting in Him to work out our future, it means making tentative plans for our day allowing Him to change it at any moment. It means trusting Him to get you through when the storm comes, and to get you across the chasm of uncertainty when it comes. It is turning your life over to Him to use us in any way He decides, whether it is to go to the mission field where He wants you to serve, or to stop and pray for the person you are walking past when He directs you to pray for them.

We think we know what is best for us, but God **does** know what is best for us. It is a matter of letting go totally, giving all we are over to Him. The rich young rule was ready to follow the Law, but not ready to give himself totally over to Jesus, *"a man ran up and knelt before him, and asked him, "Good Teacher, what must I do to inherit eternal life?...You know the commandments...And he said to him, "Teacher, all these I have observed from my youth." And Jesus looking upon him loved him, and said to him, "You lack one thing; go, sell what you have, and give to the poor, and you will have treasure in heaven; and come, follow me"* (Mk. 10:17,19-21 RSV).

It is not easy to be willing to give up everything to follow Jesus. Unless Jesus specifically tells you to sell everything like He did this young man it is not the selling of everything He wants, it is the being willing to give it up any at any time. This is a deeper thing of the heart, are you going to trust in your possessions, or are you going to trust your whole life to Jesus? Once the heart fully belongs to Jesus everything else does also. This is probably one of the hardest parts to maturing in Christ, being willing to give all up.

Jesus was willing to give all up when He left His place in heaven to come to earth. He had a right to stay in heaven but He gave it up. [1] Jesus was willing to give Himself over to the plan of salvation by giving Himself up to man to be mistreated, flogged with Roman whips, and nail to a cross – when all along He had the power to escape at any time. [2] We are called to follow Jesus, here is part of His example, He gave Himself over to the Father as we are to give ourselves over to Him. We are to **'deny our self, and take up our cross, and follow Him'**. In our reading in John today Jesus makes it very clear of how we are to consider ourselves, *"The one who loves his life loses it, and the one who hates his life in this world will keep it to eternal life"* (12:25 NASB). Jesus came to serve, and was willing to die to do it. We are to serve and be willing to die 'to self' to do it.

---

1   Philp.2:5-7, 2Cor.8:9, Jn.1:29
2   Mt.26:53

'I Have Decided to Follow Jesus' How many of you know this song? I remember it from my early days as a Christian. It is a conscious decision we have to make. We can get saved without ever deciding we need to follow Jesus. I don't know what kind of spiritual condition a person this way is going to be in, but I would think it is not a good place to be. Jesus calls us to follow, we have to make that decision. There are four types of soil, so which one would this type of person be? I want to be that fourth type of soil. As I think of that song the words come later 'no turning back'.

The apostle Paul speaks of this, *"Brethren, I do not regard myself as having laid hold of it yet; but one thing I do, forgetting what lies behind and reaching forward to what lies ahead, I press on toward the goal for the prize of the upward call of God in Christ Jesus"* (Philp. 3:13&14 NASB). Paul had great reasons for disqualifying himself, and he decide to not disqualify himself, but to follow Jesus even knowing his past.

Knowing the call of Jesus Paul left all behind, not giving it any value in either way, only looking forward to His Lord making a decision to follow no matter what his past had been. Is your past keeping you away from making that decision, disqualifying yourself without giving Jesus a chance? Paul said the past is in the past, I'm going forward with Christ. When we make that decision we have to be willing to give up all. Jesus very seldom asks someone to give up all, but we have to lay more value on Him and following Him than any other thing in our lives.

There were a couple of guys who wanted to follow Jesus but were not willing to give up something.*"Another of the disciples said to him, "Lord, let me first go and bury my father. "But Jesus said to him, "Follow me, and leave the dead to bury their own dead"* (Mt. 8:21&22 RSV). and *"Another also said, "I will follow You, Lord; but first permit me to say goodbye to those at my home." But Jesus said to him, "No one, after putting his hand to the plow and looking back, is fit for the kingdom of God"* (Lk. 9:61&62 NASB).

Jesus wants us to be willing to give up all even though He doesn't always ask for all. Following Jesus in our day does take a commitment, we don't fit into the things of the world anymore. If we have accepted Jesus we are now different. Paul says, *"Who gave himself for us, that he might redeem us from all iniquity, and purify unto himself a peculiar people, zealous of good works"* (Tim. 2:14 KJV). And Peter says, *"But ye are a chosen generation, a royal priesthood, an holy nation, a peculiar people; that ye should shew forth the praises of him who hath called you out of darkness into his marvellous light"* (1Pet. 2:9 KJV).

Once we have chose to accept Jesus we become 'a peculiar people' so we might as well decide to follow. We won't fit into the world any more because our heart is not the same as theirs any more. If this is not so, you need to check your heart and talk to Jesus about it. 'I Have Decided to Follow Jesus', what a great song of commitment, we can sing it with sincerity confirming our dedication to the Lord Jesus. Christmas is coming soon and then shortly after the end of the year, what a good time to take account of what really matters to us in life.

The first four verses of our reading in Revelation today are these, *"And I saw a new heaven and a new earth: for the first heaven and the first earth are passed away; and the sea is no more. And I saw the holy city, new Jerusalem, coming down out of heaven from God, made ready as a bride adorned for her husband. And I heard a great voice out of the throne saying, Behold, the tabernacle of God is with men, and he shall dwell with them, and they shall be his peoples, and God himself shall be with them, and be their God: and he shall wipe away every tear from their eyes; and death shall be no more; neither shall there be mourning, nor crying, nor pain, any more: the first things are passed away"* (21:1-4 ASV).

I would not want to miss out on that for anything. Jesus in John chapter 13 today calls us to be a servant following His example. As we celebrate this Christmas, the plan of redemption being sent to us from God in a little baby who becomes our Savior, we need to consider how we will live our life in the new year to come.

'I Have Decided to Follow Jesus' - 'no turning back, no turning back '

'You are my lovely one.' If we are the bride of Christ is not this how we would see Him? Seems a little too romantic of an address to the Lord Jesus, yet is it. He sees us as His bride. There are places around the world where the custom is a man and woman get engaged and then the man begins to build and prepare a home to bring his wife to when they are married. We have just read this in our reading today, *"In My Father's house are many dwelling places; if it were not so, I would have told you. I go to prepare a place for you"* (Jn. 14:2 NASB). And also this a few days ago, *"Let us rejoice and be glad and give the glory to Him, for the marriage of the Lamb has come and His bride has made herself ready"* (Rev. 19:7 NASB).

We the Church are that bride, we will be married to Christ, and He has prepared a place for us to dwell with Him. A romantic statement seems a little odd to us, but it is the relationship we will have in heaven with Christ. We are to come close to Christ. The word of God puts us in a place much closer than just Lord, King, Master. The word of God marries us to Christ in marriage. This will be a heavenly marriage which will be way beyond anything we think of here in this world.

Are you ready to be a heavenly bride, do you realize you are already engaged to Christ? We think of Christ as being a Master who is to be obeyed, yet as an engaged Bridegroom to us He is so much more. He is our protector, He is our covering, He is our provider, He is the one who leads the way. We follow, we listen for His call, we trust Him to guide and direct us. He cares for us tenderly and lovingly.

We husbands are told by Paul to love our wives like Christ loves the Church. So would the example work the other way around? We are told how our marriage on earth will be, would be also as our marriage with Christ in heaven will be? Here is what we are told: *"a man...shall cleave* [be glued] *to his wife; and the two shall become one flesh"* (Eph. 5:31 ASV).

We have been told in scripture we are in Christ and He is in us. But this even goes deeper, it is not just us being in Him or Him in us, it is we are us, we are one with Him. When we were engaged to that person here on earth that was to become our spouse we always had time for them, made time if we needed to. Maybe this is how we should think of Christ, always having time for Him and thinking of Him much. We should call out, 'Lord Jesus come close to me, be close to me, walk close to me'. He is a lover towards us, are we a lover towards Him? He is our constant companion whether we are aware of it or not, *"do you not recognize this about yourselves, that Jesus Christ is in you"* (2Cor. 13:5 NASB). and *"Whoever keeps his commandments abides in God, and God in him"* (1Jn. 3:24 ESV).

In some marvelous way we are more than engaged to Christ, we are entwined with Him somehow. He is in us and we are in Him, do you get that? It takes faith to believe it because it is unbelievable. We love Him because He first loved us. The love He gives us we reflect back as we love Him with the love He gave us. We could not even love Him if we did not receive the love that comes from Him. Without knowing God we could not know what true love is. We are the bride, the Church is the bride, and the Bridegroom is madly in love with us, He was even willing to die for us.

'Rejoice!' We are to have such a confidence in God that we do rejoice. Not every season is a happy one, but knowing we have salvation that will go into eternity should give us confidence in the future that will give us lasting peace even in the midst of turmoil. We read today Jesus did say there would be hard days, *"If they persecuted me, they will also persecute you"* (Jn. 15:20 ASV).

There will be those days of difficulty, but it is because we belong to Him. And if we belong to Him, He will take us to Himself at the end of the age and we shall be with Him forever. This awareness gives us a reason to rejoice. I am reminded of what Paul and Silas did at midnight as they were in the depths of prison with their feet in the stocks, *"about midnight Paul and Silas were praying and singing hymns unto God, and the prisoners were listening to them"* (Acts 16:25 ASV).

Could I possibly be that cheerful as they in that situation, I don't know. There was something working in their hearts that we have to get into ours. It seems part of this change has to be of what we see as important in our lives. It is easy to get all tied down to what goes on in this world we live in. It is what we touch, it is what we move in, it is what we have of success or failure in. Yet this is the temporary place for us, it is as a passing blur in the life of eternity. Sometimes we allow this world to get us tied down to its troubles, Paul and Silas did not do this.

There is reason to rejoice if we can tear our eyes off of the troubles of this world. The majority of the people of Israel could seemingly only see the things of this world. The Prophets were always trying to turn their attention to God and the good things He had for them in the future. The man who was accounted righteous because He was willing to believe by faith did not see in his lifetime the great promise God had made to him. God promised Abraham the land he walked on, yet he did not receive the space of a foot in it. Here is a man, a man of faith, who dickered with God about the intended destruction of Sodom. [1]

God did listen to Abraham and said if there were ten righteous men there He would not destroy it, ten were not found. Abraham's eyes were not on the things of this earth that belonged to him, they were on God and intercession for men of this world. We need to change our focus from the things of this world to what is truly important. When we do this we will find we can rejoice as Paul and Silas at midnight. The same as God wanted the people of Israel to see and think of the things of the future He wants us to do the same. We can be thankful and rejoice knowing that we are of the few, *"For the gate is narrow and the way is hard, that leads to life, and those who find it are few"* (Mt. 7:14 RSV).

We can be thankful that with God's help we have found the way, so many will not. Knowing our situation, we should be as Abraham keeping our eyes on God and giving prayers of intercession for the lost that they might find the way before the end of their days on earth. We must remember that we should treat others as we would want to be treated. [2] And God tells us to ask so that we can receive what He has for us. We need to walk close to God, we need to be close to God, that we can know His ways.

We need to remember what Jesus taught about the two men who built their house. [3] One did not build his house on a foundation and it fell. The other built his house on a sure foundation with which when the storms came, the storms of life, his house was not swept away, it held firm to its foundation and survived. If we find that solid foundation, if we tie ourselves to the Rock Jesus, we will find reasons to **'Rejoice!'**

1   Gen.18:32
2   Mt.7:12
3   Lk.6:48&49

'This is My way for you that you will know My way to go.' Jesus is always trying to help us to find His way, it is His way that gets us to the Father, and His way that gets us to heaven. Once re-born we are to be spiritual people. We learn by the Spirit, and we learn from the printed word of God. The printed word of God tells us about who He is, and about His ways. It helps us to know of how to begin to be spiritual people to walk by the Spirit, and be active in the Spirit. These are the ways Jesus uses to teach us His way. His way is very different than ours, or should I say different than the world's way. The world's way is all we know until we get saved, then we go through a re-birth and are in new ways which are different, ways that will change who we are. We learn from Jesus who is the great Master.

Even what we learn from the apostles and epistle writers are from Jesus. Did you ever consider how the early church grew so rapidly not having the New Testament as we have today? Those of the early church are the ones who wrote the New Testament. The apostles taught many, other leaders in the early church also taught, Paul came along years later being commissioned by Christ Himself. But even these being few compared to the growth of the Church, how could such growth take place?

The activity of the Holy Spirit within the body of Christ, the Church, is much more than many want to give credit to. As He was active then He is active now. We today don't take that time to listen to the Holy Spirit because we have the New Testament to turn to looking for our guidance there. The early church did not have what we have now to turn to, they learned from what the apostles and leaders taught them, in addition turning to the Holy Spirit as they had been taught to do. Many of us today do not have this additional help because we are not taught to turn there.

These are the ways Jesus teaches us: His printed word, the word which is alive and active, and by the Holy Spirit who brings to us what Jesus gives to Him. This is what we read in our reading of John chapter 16 today, *"However, when He, the Spirit of truth, has come, He will guide you into all truth; for He will not speak on His own authority, but whatever He hears He will speak; and He will tell you things to come. He will glorify Me, for He will take of what is Mine and declare it to you"* (v. 13&14 NKJV).

What a great source of spiritual growth many of us are missing. As you go through your day you don't always have time to pull out the scriptures, but the Holy Spirit, He who is with you, even in you giving you this new life, He is always there to help us to grow. We need to learn to hear his voice amongst all the noises of this world, we need to hear what the Holy Spirit is saying to us. He will never speak anything that disagrees with the word of God. In our translations Jesus speaks in John 16:7 of the Holy Spirit as: helper, councilor, comforter, advocate. All these describe the One who is in aid to us. He is waiting and ready to help us, we need to turn to Him more to know the way God is taking us.

'I am in your life' Do you know Jesus is saying this to you? Sometimes we are not sure if He is with us our not. Sometimes we have done something that might offend Him and we wonder if He is still with us. If we are saved by the blood of Jesus which was give at the cross then He is with us, *"this is his commandment, that we believe in the name of his Son Jesus Christ and love one another, just as he has commanded us. Whoever keeps his commandments abides in God, and God in him."* (1Jn. 3:23&24 ESV).

Jesus is with us all the time and hears our every word. If we pray under the tree, in the garden, on the road, at home, or at work he hears us. Prayer does not only need to be in the church. The other thing about prayer is it is not a formality, it is a familiarity with your Lord who you are having a conversation with. Jesus did not provide you with salvation and then say, 'I'll see you at the end of time'. Jesus is with us all the time. We don't need to make an appointment with Him for a time of prayer. I wonder if we saw all the things Jesus does for us during the day that we would be astonished.

We speak of God in general a lot without dividing the Godhead to three persons. Yes, Jesus is in the Father and the Father is in Jesus. To know this we have to step into a reality that is outside of ours. God's reality is that God is One with three individual persons who always act like one. In the person of the Father we find Jesus. In the person of Jesus we find the Father.

The Father saves us through the blood of Jesus. If Jesus and the Father were the same person Jesus could not say, *"No one comes to the Father except through Me"* (Jn. 14:6 NKJV). The Father is the person we are coming to, Jesus is the person we are going through. The Father has given all things into the hands of Jesus, that includes us, *"the Father of glory...put all things in subjection under his feet, and gave him to be head over all things to the church"* (Eph. 1:17&22 ASV).

In our reading today we read Jesus' priestly prayer in John chapter 17. In this prayer as Jesus prays we see that He receives from another who is the Father, *"Holy Father, keep through Your name those whom You have given Me"* (Jn. 17:11 NKJV). Jesus will be with us because it is to Him we belong, He owns us, *"the one who was called as free, is Christ's slave. You were bought for a price"* (1Cor. 7:22&23 NASB). Within the Godhead is the third person the Holy Spirit. Part of what He does is testify about Jesus the savior, *"When the Helper comes, whom I will send to you from the Father, namely, the Spirit of truth who comes from the Father, He will testify about Me"* (Jn.15:26 NASB).

Part of what the Holy Spirit does is tell us of things which Jesus and the Father have for us to hear, *"I still have many things to say to you, but you cannot bear them now. When the Spirit of truth comes...he will take what is mine and declare it to you"* (Jn. 16:12-14 ESV). The Holy Spirit also helps us to know and to remember, *"he shall guide you into all the truth"* (Jn. 16:13 ASV). and *"But the Helper, the Holy Spirit whom the Father will send in My name, He will teach you all things, and remind you of all that I said to you"* (Jn. 14:26 NASB)

The Holy Spirit is the representative to us from God, the Holy Spirit is in every person who is saved. *"the love of God has been poured out within our hearts through the Holy Spirit who was given to us"* (Rom. 5:5 NASB). We serve a three-in-one God. And this three-in-one God has said in many ways in scripture, 'I am in your life.'

Life! What a gift, that of a gift of eternal life to be with God forever and ever and ever. Can you imagine eternity, that with no end, a forever and ever with God? Many of us not so long ago would have thought of something so great and wonderful as a pipe dream. Yet it is true. God the Father sent the Son who made the way that we all could enter and have eternity. Oh, as we begin to contemplate it our mind goes to places as out-of-this-world thoughts.

It is a totally foreign thought to most in the world who are still in the captivity of sin. Some of them have trouble going from today to tomorrow, let alone thinking of a life in eternity. Some of them don't care about tomorrow, or any eternity. Some are so busy with life they don't stop long enough to think about any of it. Some of us may have been some of those before, but now we have Christ in our lives and look forward to eternity, even though we may not now totally understand all there is to eternity.

The apostles talk about the hope we have, what a great hope it is. Some days it is the only thing we have that gets us to tomorrow. Other days we have such a grasp on this hope we want to celebrate. Many of the unsaved think they have life, but Jesus says they are dead,[1] and they don't even know it. If they do not find Christ, they will go from being dead in this world to dead in the next world. We have hope, we have life, we have the very Spirit of God living inside of us.

We have a life that those unsaved cannot even connect with when they hear us talk about it. It would be like trying to explain to a person who all of their life had lived in the desert with only enough water to drink, to explain of what it is like to swim in the ocean. Once in a while we need to stop and tally up what a great thing we have in the salvation that God has given us. Eternity, in heaven with God, no more death, no more sorrow, no more pain, no more tears, for eternity with God – can you imagine it? People talk about the good life, we are in it no matter how difficult things might be for us in this world, we have the good life that will be spent with God for eternity.

We live waiting the day we leave this earth and go to join God in His dwelling place. Remember how the apostle Paul talked about this, *"For to me to live is Christ, and to die is gain. If I am to live in the flesh, that means fruitful labor for me. Yet which I shall choose I cannot tell. I am hard pressed between the two. My desire is to depart and be with Christ, for that is far better. But to remain in the flesh is more necessary on your account"* (Philp. 1:21-24 ESV).

The thought of going to be with Christ was a grand and joyous thought to Paul, but the thought of being here still longer to serve His Lord and to be a blessing to us was far greater. This must be our mindset, that we will intend to serve every day we are given here, until that day that the Father has marked out for us to come to Him. Service to the Church, who are God's people, and to the world who does not know Him, should be our daily goal. The day we depart is God's business and we should not be concerned with it, we should be concerned with the business of the day and what He has for us to do. Our life, our hope, our eternity, are all sobering thoughts, but how we are to serve today should be an even more sobering thought.

Christ has called us to serve others just as He has served us. Today in our reading in John chapter 18 we hear Jesus say this to Pilate, *"My kingdom is not of this world...You say correctly that I am a king. For this purpose I have been born, and for this I have come into the world: to testify to the truth"* (v. 36&37 NASB).

Jesus was born for this cause, to bring to us the truth, that through Him and only through Him we could receive life, eternal life. This was His service to us, what service is He calling you to to help others in the Church or outside the Church? God has blessed you, can you be a blessing to others? This Christmas season may be a good time to ask that question, that if you find that place to serve it will carry on into the new year.

---

1   Jn.5:24&25

Time, all have time to find God and be saved. [1] There will be those who refuse, but all have time. We have a great God who has found us in our difficulty of sin and provided a way we can be forgiven. God is a lovely God, more than we will know until we arrive in heaven. If Christ is the bridegroom then we are the bride engaged to be married to Him. As a woman who is engaged to a most wonderful man in her eyes, this is how we should be seeing Jesus, as that most wonderful person in our lives.

We are receiving great things now, but wait until we are married to Him, what a life will be after that. The thought of this is what keeps us focused on the life we live for Him here now, service to our King, our betrothed. Think of life forever with Jesus as our Husband taking care of all our needs and wants. [2]

We know what Paul teaches us as Christian husbands, of how we are to love our wives, this is what Jesus will do for us, and do it perfectly. Time, it can take forever, or it can be gone before we know it. If there are things to get ready for the bridegroom don't let them go, time will pass quickly and He will be here. Five of the ten virgins did this and were left out, *"Those who were foolish took their lamps and took no oil with them...And at midnight a cry was heard: 'Behold, the bridegroom is coming; go out to meet him!'...And the foolish said to the wise, 'Give us some of your oil, for our lamps are going out...No, lest there should not be enough for us and you...the bridegroom came, and those who were ready went in with him to the wedding; and the door was shut. Afterward the other virgins came also, saying, 'Lord, Lord, open to us!' But he answered and said, 'Assuredly, I say to you, I do not know you"* (Mt. 25:3,6,8-12 NKJV).

Is your lamp burning, and your container full? Our life gets so busy sometimes we forget to check our container. For us who are saved, spiritual assessment is needed from time to time. We can't leave it all to the pastor and the leaders of the church, we need to make it a personal responsibility. If the bridegroom comes and we are not permitted in, we cannot point at them saying it is their fault. Time, we wait on it forever, and then we blink our eyes and it is gone. Don't let time consume you.

Jesus talked about today and tomorrow, *"Therefore do not be anxious about tomorrow, for tomorrow will be anxious for itself. Let the day's own trouble be sufficient for the day"* (Mt. 6:34 RSV). This may not be a way you have thought of this verse before. Part of our trouble for today, and for every day, is to see that our container is full, not letting it go until tomorrow. Time, how easily we become a victim of it, don't let it slip away without checking on your spiritual condition. Get close to God and time won't get you. It is not difficult, I remind you of the scripture, *"Draw near to God and he will draw near to you"* (Jas. 4:8 RSV).

Something to think about, when we get to heaven time won't be there. There is a benefit in going through the effort to get close to God, once you have reached a certain point, your desire will rise to be closer and closer. Once we find that place it will not be difficult to keep our container full. Hunger can be a painful thing or a joyful thing, when it is God we hunger for it is joyful, and the closer we get the more joyful it is. You may have read Malachi today and read this in the beginning of chapter 3, *"Behold, I send my messenger, and he shall prepare the way before me: and the Lord, whom ye seek, will suddenly come to his temple; and the messenger of the covenant, whom ye desire, behold, he cometh, saith Jehovah of hosts"* (ASV).

The word **suddenly** here may apply both to Christ's first coming and His second coming. He surely came when Israel did not expect Him, so in His second it may be the same, *"Therefore you too must always be ready, for the Son of Man will come when you are not expecting him"* (Mt. 24:44 CJB). In our reading in John today, Jesus says this, *"It is finished"* (19:30 ASV). **We all know what comes next, Time, don't let it get you.**

---

1   Acts 17:27
2   Lk. 12:37

Now is the time of great celebration, to recall the redeeming act of God that came in such a beautifully small package. The baby Jesus who would grow to be a man who would die on a cruel cross so that we could be forgiven. This is a theme we need to remember, it will give us great reason to rejoice throughout this whole season. That baby in a manger so long ago came whose entry was unnoticed by so much of the world around.

The shepherds were the first to worship the One of whom they had been told by the angels who appeared in the sky above them. We who are saved by that loving grace that did appear in a babe sent by God do still worship Him. How quaint is this, that we are given, an innocent baby coming from God to take upon Himself the sins of the whole world. We have just finished reading in John of the trial and crucifixion of Jesus, all that He went through to bring to us salvation cleansing us from our sins.

This may bring a tear to the eye as we clearly think of this tender beautiful babe going through such a horrific end. This He did out of love, first His love of the Father as He yielded to the will of the Father in the Garden of Gethsemane, and second His love to us who He died to pay for our sins. How do you wrap that up in a package, will it fit under the tree, is it far greater than anything any could give? Many Christmas gifts yet unwrapped, but this one is fully unwrapped, and we all have received from it. In a way there is of our giving gifts at Christmas a speaking of the gospel.

For many days, maybe even weeks, we wait for the day to come when we could unwrap the mystery of the Christmas package under the tree to know what is inside. The apostle Paul talks about the mystery of God that mankind waited and waited to unwrap to know what was in it. *"Now to Him who is able to establish you according to my gospel and the preaching of Jesus Christ, according to the revelation of the mystery which has been kept secret for long ages past, but now has been disclosed, and through the Scriptures of the prophets, in accordance with the commandment of the eternal God, has been made known to all the nations, leading to obedience of faith"* (Rom. 16:25&26 NASB).

Such a gift, such a mystery, such a blessing! This gift not only brought us forgiveness of sins, not only gave us salvation, it gave us the right to be in heaven with the Father, with the Son, and with the Holy Spirit throughout all of eternity. Can you find any other gift so valuable? We may look at the gifts under the tree wondering what they are, but the greatest gift we have already received. What if every time you look at one of those gifts under the tree you would think of Jesus? Would this bring rejoicing and thanksgiving to your heart? Christmas, it is a time to remember.

Today we read the last two chapters of John, it is the unwrapping of the gift from the Father. It is the proof of life after death. It is the power of the promise to us all. In the end our graves will be empty, our bodies rising from the dead. Here is the first time that the gift of salvation could be given, this was the first time after Jesus died on the cross paying for our sins. Here Jesus appears to the disciples saying to them, *"Peace be with you. As the Father has sent me, even so I send you." And when he had said this, he breathed on them, and said to them, "Receive the Holy Spirit"* (20:21&22 RSV). Jesus breathed on them, what a marvelous thing that He did. You may wonder why, this is why, *"And the LORD God formed man of the dust of the ground, and breathed into his nostrils the breath of life; and man became a living being"* (Gen. 2:7 NKJV).

Jesus said before we are saved that even though we live we are dead, not much more than dust. God breathed into Adam and he became alive. Jesus breathed onto His disciples and they became spiritually alive as in the re-birth. He also said, 'receive the Holy Spirit'. Paul tells us this, *"you have received a spirit of adoption as sons and daughters by which we cry out, "Abba! Father!" The Spirit Himself testifies with our spirit that we are children of God"* (Rom. 8:15&16 NASB). Enjoy the greatest gift that any Father could have ever given to His children.

Today in our reading schedule we begin reading about Christ coming to earth to bring salvation to mankind from God. I want you to be reminded from these scriptures about what this Christmas season is all about. In many countries, we are reminded by the commercial industry in advertisements, slogans, even songs, that we have got to buy the best for those we love – no matter what the cost.

The motive of love, even though it is mentioned, is removed and the idea or the just right performance in what we buy for another is set in love's place. The idea that just the right gift to give, no matter what the cost is what we are presented with, the idea of love is replaced with performance. But God has no confusion here, He gave the best He had, no matter what the cost, to a people undeserving, motivated totally by His force of love.

As we Christians enter this season of celebration of what God has done for us we must guard and protect the force of love which God has given to each of us, to love like He loves. This season is not about receiving or giving just the right gift, it is about love and giving that love in all that we give this season. We are to maintain it no matter how much the world buffets us in opposition to push us into the wrong reason to give.

This season is to celebrate love that was given to us in the Savior Jesus Christ, and to give it to one another as Jesus said, *"I am giving you a new command: that you keep on loving each other. In the same way that I have loved you, you are also to keep on loving each other"* (Jn. 13:34 CJB). In these four days until Christmas I will be focusing my comments on what the scriptures tell us about our Savior who came to us. As you enter these next few days let that Love of God sink down into you so you are a blessing to others, and by it you find you are blessed yourself. Let's remember by what has been phrased by others, 'Jesus is the reason for the season'.

There has been a knowledge in the spiritual realm from the beginning of time that a savior would be sent from God to a lost people.[1] We are the beneficiaries of that plan of salvation and that Savior. When He came His own did not know Him.[2] For ages and ages the prophets spoke of His coming but the people did not understand.

It was prophesied with much accuracy but mankind did not see it. The simpleness of how God brought that Savior to the world was not recognized. Yes, it was miraculous since it was a virgin birth, but who of those at that time knew other than a very few? To outsiders it was a sinful birth. What could possibly be holy about that? Even though Joseph did marry her, anyone with a little math knew Mary was pregnant before they were married. The evidence of truth was certainly not in that current situation.

The evidence was in the scriptures of prophecies. There were many beliefs and many thoughts, many believed the Christ would come from David's city Bethlehem, but Jesus was from Nazareth. There were also those who thought that no one would know where He comes from.[3] There seems to have been a belief that Christ would have no known beginning or end as the Hebrews writer uses this argument because they spoke about Christ who would be in the order of Melchizedek,[4] *"For this Melchizedek... without father, without mother, without genealogy, having neither beginning of days nor end of life"* (7:1&3 NKJV).

Isaiah 9:6 prophesies the savior would be a child born, but it seems these did not know about this prophecy or apply it to the Christ. There were many different theories about how the Christ would come. Isaiah 61:1&2 is what Jesus reads declaring it being fulfilled in their hearing but they were not willing to accept that it spoke of Him. The majority of the Jews were not ready to accept that Jesus was the Savior sent from God. There were a few though as Simeon which we read of today in Luke chapter 2 who was in the Temple and by the Spirit recognizes this infant brought by His mother and supposed father, that He was the Savior sent by God.

Even though the word from God has spoken of the Christ coming being Savior of the world from the very beginning there are still those today who will not believe. We can be thankful that we have found Him, and been saved by Him, and promised a place in heaven by Him. This Christmas season let's remember who He is and what He has brought to us.

---

1 Rom.16:25
2 Jn.1:11, 1Jn.3:1
3 Jn.7:25-27
4 Ps.110:4

In all the kingdoms of all the earth, there is none like Jesus. His appearance on earth as prophesied long before was unnoticed by most. His coming had been from long ago. He came in a power that none other had. No person in all of creation had ever lived a life without sin. Yet the world had no reason to not know.

There are dozens and dozens of times in the Old Testament scriptures that The Christ is being spoke of, but without that name. We are told in one places His name is called: Wonderful, Counselor, Mighty God, Everlasting Father, Prince of Peace. In another it is Immanuel which means **God-with-us**. The specific name of **Jesus** which was told to both Mary and Joseph to name the child means **Help of Jehovah**. Moses spoke of Him, King David spoke of Him.

Isaiah, Jeremiah, Ezekiel, Daniel, Zechariah, Malachi, all speak of the **One** coming. Malachi was the last prophet in Israel at about the time of the return of the Jews from Babylon. It was more than 400 years from Malachi until the coming of Christ, in which there was time to know. Jesus had been coming since the beginning of time, it was the mystery of God, none knew when the time would be. They were told, *"For unto us a child is born, unto us a son is given; and the government shall be upon his shoulder"* (Isa. 9:6 ASV). and *"the Lord himself will give you a sign: behold, a virgin shall conceive, and bear a son"* (Isa. 7:14 ASV).

This Savior, this Christ, has been coming from the ages, being sent to a lost people, those who had no way out of their sin, forbidden to be near God because of that sin. A Savior indeed, what all mankind needed, a redeemer who could save the people by His own work and what He would do. He came to mend up the brokenhearted, to free the prisoners from their captivity, to get liberty to those who were in bondage. Yes, the world needed this Savior, He came for all, He came for you, He came for me, He came for any who would accept Him as Lord.

It is this time of year that we celebrate that coming of Christ as that Savior. Let your celebration be full, recount from scripture all that we have been told of His coming and the great things He would do. Each of us who once where dead now have life because of His coming. **Let us celebrate!!**

We have been blessed, we have received, we have been taken into the family of God. None of us deserve it, none of us has earned it, it truly is the great gift from God. This is the great day we celebrate such a great thing God has given mankind. It has been spoken of in the ages, prophesied to come into the world, the remedy for what ailed all peoples. *The people who walked in darkness Have seen a great light; Those who dwelt in the land of the shadow of death, Upon them a light has shined.*" (Isa. 9:2 NKJV).

We have received greatly from God, the Savior has been coming for a great long time. In our reading today we have seen some of what the prophet Isaiah wrote during the time of the latter kings before the deportation of Judah to Babylon. That is how long ago Jesus the Messiah (The Christ) has been spoken of. There were even those before Isaiah who spoke of the coming king who would reign forever. Moses even said *"a prophet like me"* (Duet. 18:15 RSV).

There was a redeemer who was on His way with the great blessing of God from the beginning. Isaiah tells us He would come, but few would notice. Even though He would be the Son of God He would be treated badly by mankind. Then we are told that all the defects of all mankind would be laid on Him, our sins He would carry to the cross where He would pay for them all. He was removed from the life on this earth for the transgressions of the people, for the transgressions of each of us. He said nothing even though He could have been delivered out of that course of the cross at any time.

Many have said it was the guilt of the Romans and the Jews who put Jesus on the cross, yet Isaiah makes it very clear that it was God who crushed Him to make an offering for our guilt. It is by what Jesus did that we are accounted as righteous. Last verse of Isaiah chapter 53 says this, *"he bore the sin of many, and made intercession for the transgressors"* (RSV). He bore my sins, and He prays for me a transgressor. He bore your sins, and prays for you a transgressor. This is the hope we have, it had been coming for many years, by this hope we now have received everlasting life. This is the day we celebrate the arrival of that hope that had been coming for many years which brought us the eternity of life. Yes, for this we must celebrate, and be thankful.

The life we live, it is before God. There is nothing that He does not see, nothing He does not know about each of us. We can try to hide parts of our life, or we can give it all to Him giving Him permission to enter into all that we are. He has known each of us since the beginning of time. Remember the words of King David who was a prophet and a man after God's own heart, *"My frame was not hidden from thee, When I was made in secret, And curiously wrought in the lowest parts of the earth. Thine eyes did see mine unformed substance; And in thy book they were all written, Even the days that were ordained for me, When as yet there was none of them"* (Ps. 139:15&16 ASV).

The apostle Paul tells us this, *"Blessed be the God and Father of our Lord Jesus Christ, who has blessed us in Christ with every spiritual blessing in the heavenly places, even as he chose us in him before the foundation of the world"* (Eph. 1:3&4 RSV). We don't realize how much each of us is in the eye of God, therefore in the heart of God. Those of us who turn to Him for salvation become part of Him in a way. Don't ask me to explain it, I can't. That is what faith is, believing something we cannot explain. The scriptures tell us this, *"Whoever confesses that Jesus is the Son of God, God abides in him, and he in God"* (1Jn. 4:15 NKJV).

We are also told this, *"and raised us up with Him, and seated us with Him in the heavenly places in Christ Jesus"* (Eph. 2:6 NASB). God knows us more than we know our self. There is nothing He does not see, no knowing He does not know. Our greatest accomplishment would be to pour ourselves fully into God. In our reading today we read in Psalm 8 how great God is. There are also verses speaking of the Christ, but some verses also speak of mankind, *"When I look at your heavens, the work of your fingers, the moon and the stars which you have set in place, what is man that you are mindful of him"* (v. 3&4 ESV).

When I look at some of the pictures of the universe as seen through our telescopes, I think, 'How could God even notice that I am here?' He notices, He even knows each of us who have come to Him, even to notice each one of our hairs on our head. Psalm 23 which we read is all about trusting God. Even as we each ask as David in Psalm 8, 'how can you be mindful of me' we are assured He is in our reading today in Matthew chapter 6, *"But you, when you pray, go into your room, and when you have shut your door, pray to your Father who is in the secret place; and your Father who sees in secret will reward you openly...For your Father knows the things you have need of before you ask Him"* (v. 6&8 NKJV).

We are to ask, but He knows even before we ask. Amazing! Yes, He is mindful of us and His eye is on each of us. As we will soon enter a new year, know that God knows you, and will take care of you, that He will hear your prayer, and take care of your needs.

This is the day we have come to. Yesterday we had no full knowledge of today, and today we have no full knowledge about tomorrow. There is only One who knows about tomorrow, and the day after that, and the day after that, etc. All of time is now to Him, a concept we can't even consider.

This is all the more reason we need God in our life. How lost we are without Him, how misguided we were before we knew Him. Even some of what we thought of as good was bad, and part of what we thought was bad was actually good. How little did we know. Even now as God has opened our eyes to truth there is still so much more to know. God tries to speak to us, He sends His word through the prophets, some of it we get, and some of it we are still scratching our heads.

King David was considered a prophet. His Psalms are full of prophecies and God's knowledge. God tries to reach out, God tries to tell us of things, and yet sometimes we don't get it. This is God trying to tell us about heavenly things, about eternal things. I believe that Three are One, that One is of Three, but don't ask me to explain it, or how there is no before, or today, or future – it is all 'now' to God. This is where I have to come back to say we must have faith, because we cannot know of any of this any other way. God does try to tell us, and some of it we do get.

We have understood enough, and with the Holy Spirit speaking to our hearts, we have found salvation. Everything is up from there, and even one day up all the way to heaven to be with our Lord. God loves us and reaches out to us and tries to help us understand. As we come to know more of what God is trying to reveal to us we end up rejoicing about what we have found. David starts out this way in Psalm 33 with praise, *"Praise the LORD with the harp; Make melody to Him with an instrument of ten strings. Sing to Him a new song; Play skillfully with a shout of joy"* (v. 2&3 NKJV).

In verses 4&5 we are told why David is praising, it is about the character of God and what He does. There is an interesting verse here, it shows how all three persons of the Trinity were involved in creation, *"By the word of Jehovah were the heavens made, And all the host of them by the breath of his mouth"* (v. 6 ASV). Here it begins speaking of the '*word of Jehovah*' who we know about from the beginning of the book of John, it is Christ. It also speaks of the '*breath of His mouth*'. The Hebrew word here for breath means; spirit, breath, wind. [Note: It is similar with the Greek of the New Testament.] So looking at the verse this way it is the Father who speaks, it is the Spirit as His breath which is the force, which moves out the Word Jesus who creates.[1]

It was the combined action of the Godhead who created all things, *"For he spoke, and it came to be; he commanded, and it stood forth"* (v. 9 RSV). As with David, the more we know about God, the more we praise. In Psalm 34 David continues to speak about God and praises Him for all He does and all He is. Psalm 145 is a psalm of praise. Is your heart a heart after God's own heart? Is there praise coming forth from your heart and your mouth? Now is a good time to look back over the year to see how many great things God has done in your life.

---

1   Col.1:16

The way of the Lord is good. That can go in many different ways. For us it is to follow in His ways as He leads us which we know is good. No matter what happens in this life we know in the end we will be in heaven and that will be very good. For now we continue on in this world in the ways of Jesus which sometimes, as He said, bring us into persecution.

The thing that is good, even in this, is that we know we will not be overcome by an enemy, whether people in this world who hate us because we name the Name of Christ in our lives or those enemies in the demonic forces of the devil. Without the Lord in our life even if it seemed good in this world we would end up in disaster in what comes after this life. The way of the Lord is good. He takes us down no bad paths, only those which take us to a better place in life.

Sin has taken over life, it has infected this world we live in. But Jesus has provided a way of escape for those who will take it. We, those who have accepted Christ, have been given a way to be forgiven of our sins removing sin's grip on us. We most all can remember what our life was like before our salvation, and now in our new life we can see that it is good.

Today in Luke chapter 15 we read of the prodigal son. Some of you may think that you have not been a prodigal son (daughter) because you have never left God to come back to God. We all have strayed away from God. In the beginning God gave out His call to those who were in the Garden, *"And they heard the sound of the LORD God walking in the garden in the cool of the day,...Then the LORD God called to Adam and said to him, "Where are you?"* (Gen. 3:8&9 NKJV).

God has been wanting mankind with Him since the beginning. Mankind was in closeness to God in the beginning until sin entered in, since then we have all been a prodigal until we return. The other great thing to see in Luke is that if we stray He will come searching for us as a lost sheep until He finds us. When He finds us, we all can refuse and say 'Don't touch me', but would we not rather He pick us up, caressing us saying how much He missed us, and then put us on His shoulders and carry us back into the flock? God is always calling, from the beginning, saying 'Where are you', even to today when one of us who are His steps off the path a bit. He is always wanting us with Him. Maybe it is time for us to go lay down for a while close to the Good Shepherd.

'How could I go on without Christ?' Have you ever asked yourself that question? Has it ever been a thought in your heart? Do you consider the value of having Christ in your life? All these are questions we ought to ask ourselves. If we ask them it will help us to know that foundation we have in Him. He leads our way, He causes solidness to be under every step we take in faith. I am glad for all the words of king David, many times we see he has been in the same place we are at times. He also tells us many things about God that help us.

Today we read some of his words, David said to God, *"You know when I sit down and when I rise up; You understand my thought from afar. You scrutinize my path and my lying down, And are intimately acquainted with all my ways...You have enclosed me behind and before, And laid Your hand upon me...Where can I go from Your Spirit? Or where can I flee from Your presence? If I ascend to heaven, You are there; If I make my bed in Sheol, behold, You are there. If I take the wings of the dawn, If I dwell in the remotest part of the sea, Even there Your hand will lead me, And Your right hand will lay hold of me"* (Ps. 139:2,3,5,7-10 NASB).

This is the protection we have from God. How many of us could put it in such words as David? We must know in person, and in knowledge, the foundation we have in Christ. He is the love that carries us through, and He is the solid rock that never moves.

Jesus taught about this, *"He is like a man building a house, who dug deep and laid the foundation on the rock. And when the flood arose, the stream beat vehemently against that house, and could not shake it, for it was founded on the rock"* (Lk. 6:48 NKJV).

With all the things in the world we could attach ourselves to for security, Christ is the one solid thing that will not move, *"Jesus Christ is the same yesterday and to-day, yea and for ever"* (Heb. 13:8 ASV). and *"I am the Alpha and the Omega," says the Lord God, who is and who was and who is to come, the Almighty"* (Rev. 1:8 RSV).

How can we go wrong putting our trust in Christ? He is the solid foundation, He is the One we must have. Life without Him would not be life. We have just read in John today what Jesus said about Himself, *"I am the way, and the truth, and the life"* (14:6 ASV). If we don't have Him, certainly we don't have life. Life is found in Him and only Him. Now what do you think, could you go on without Christ?

'You are the love of my life.' Do you know this is what Jesus says to you? First, we will look at it in its broad address. What is it we all know will take place at the end of time after the judgment is done, is it not the marriage of the Lamb? Who is it He marries? It is the Church who we all together are. So then the Church is His fiancée, and how does a man feel about his fiancée? Is he not terribly in love with her? God puts things of Himself in terms we can understand. From this can you know how much Jesus loves the Church?

Now let's narrow this down to each person, down to you, down to me. How much does Jesus love you, you as an individual, *"What man among you, if he has a hundred sheep and has lost one of them, does not leave the other ninety-nine in the open pasture and go after the one that is lost, until he finds it? "And when he has found it, he puts it on his shoulders, rejoicing"* (Lk. 15:4&5 NASB).

This is spoken about our salvation, but what is there to indicate He will love us any less after we are saved? Kings do not have a personal relationship with each person in their kingdom, surely king David did not have a personal relationship with each person in his kingdom. Jesus does have, He has a personal salvation He gives to each one of us. We are not saved in a lump of people, it is individually that we are saved. And Jesus desires a personal relationship with each one of us. Are we to go into our prayer closet with a large group of people to spend time with the Lord?

There are times that we do pray as a large group. But as an individual we are told this, *"But you, when you pray, go into your inner room, close your door and pray to your Father who is in secret, and your Father who sees what is done in secret will reward you"* (Mt. 6:6 NASB).

Can you imagine it would be any different when you spend time with Jesus in prayer? This indicates a very personal relationship. In our reading today we read the prayer of Jesus, He says this, *"even as thou gavest him authority over all flesh, that whatsoever thou hast given him, to them he should give eternal life"* (17:2 RV). 'Whatsoever' is an interesting word, most translations use the word 'all' or 'everyone'.

This word is similar to 'whosoever' in this verse, *"And whosoever will, let him take the water of life freely"* (Rev. 22:17 KJV). The word 'whatsoever' in Jn. 17:2 seems to have the meaning of: each and everyone of all. **The Complete Word Study Dictionary** gives this meaning: *"everyone who, whatsoever, meaning everyone who or whosoever."* By the word so many of the translations use we miss that Jesus is praying about each and every person that the Father had given Him.

Many here would say this prayer is only for the apostles, but we read this, *"I do not pray for these alone, but also for those who will believe in Me through their word"* (v. 20 NKJV). Do you believe because of the apostles' words that have come down through the ages in God's word to you? Then if yes, Jesus is praying for you also. Jesus does see us as a whole which is His Church, but He also sees each and every one as an individual in relationship. So Jesus is thinking of **His fiancée**, each and every one of them.